BETWEEN THE SPECIES: READINGS IN HUMAN-ANIMAL RELATIONS

Arnold Arluke

Northeastern University

Clinton Sanders

University of Connecticut

PEARSON

Boston • New York • San Francisco
Mexico City • Montreal • Toronto • London • Madrid • Munich
Paris • Hong Kong • Singapore • Tokyo • Cape Town • Sydney

Executive Editor: Jeff Lasser
Series Editorial Assistant: Lauren Macey
Marketing Manager: Kelly May
Production Editor: Patrick Cash-Peterson
Editorial Production Service: Progressive Publishing Alternatives
Manufacturing Buyer: Debbie Rossi
Electronic Composition: Progressive Publishing Alternatives
Cover Administrator: Joel Gendron
Cover Designer: Joel Gendron

For related titles and support materials, visit our online catalog at www.pearsoned.com.

Between the time website information is gathered and then published, it is not unusual for some sites to have closed. Also, the transcription of URLs can result in typographical errors. The publisher would appreciate notification where these errors occur so that they may be corrected in subsequent editions.

Library of Congress Cataloging-in-Publication Data

Arluke, Arnold
   Between the species : readings in human-animal relations / Arnold Arluke.—1st ed.
      p.   cm.
   Includes bibliographical references.
   ISBN-13: 978-0-205-59493-1
   ISBN-10: 0-205-59493-X
   1. Human-animal relationships.   2. Animals—Social aspects.   I. Title.
QL85.A748 2009
304.2—dc22

                                                                    2008043011

Printed in the United States of America

10   9   8   7   6   5   4   3   2   1   HPC   12   11   10   09   08

CONTENTS

ACKNOWLEDGMENTS

We want to thank the following colleagues for their comments and suggestions in the development of our manuscript:

Leslie Irvine, University of Colorado
Philip S. Arkow, Camden County College
Cheryl Ann Joseph, Notre Dame de Namur University
Kathleen M. O'Neil, Denison University

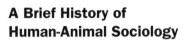

INTRODUCTION

A Brief History of Human-Animal Sociology

Since "the social sciences tend to present themselves pre-eminently as the sciences of discontinuity between humans and animals," (Noske 1990,66) animals have, until fairly recently, been virtually ignored within sociology. The basic foundation for this lack of attention to human-animal issues was established in the seventeenth century by the philosopher René Descartes (1976) who regarded animals as machines that did not think and, more importantly, as unable to feel pain. This last presumption provided a ready excuse for treating nonhuman animals with thoughtless cruelty. The Cartesian orthodoxy that has, until only recently, excluded animals from social scientific analysis is based on the linguacentric assumption that because animals lack the ability to employ spoken language, they consequently lack the ability to think.

Nonetheless, though they tended to offer relatively unsystematic, highly emotionalized, and unempirical discussions, a handful of nineteenth-century sociologists did focus on animal abilities and human-animal relationships. For example, Harriet Martineau ([1865] 2003), an early pioneer in observational methods, wrote about the problems caused by feral dogs in urban areas; and in the *Quarterly Review*, Frances Power Cobbe ([1872] 2003) speculated about the relationship of dogs' physical characteristics to their mental abilities.

Despite this limited attention, early twentieth-century sociology continued to largely disregard nonhuman animals as social actors. Although he frequently discussed nonhuman animals in his writing, George Herbert Mead (1962, 1964) employed descriptions of the *behavior* of animals as the backdrop against which he juxtaposed his model of human *action*. In laying the intellectual groundwork for what would later become symbolic interactionism, Mead maintained that, although animals were social beings, their interactions involved only a primitive and instinctual "conversation of gestures" (the dog's growl or the cat's hiss, for example). From Mead's perspective, animals lacked the ability to employ significant symbols and were therefore unable to negotiate meaning and take the role of cointeractants. Their behavior was directed toward achieving simple goals such as acquiring food or defending territory but, unable to use language, their behavior was devoid of meaning. As Mead (1964) put it:

> Gestures may be either conscious (significant) or unconscious (non-significant). The conversation of gestures is not significant below the human level, because it is not conscious, that is, not self-conscious (though it is conscious in the sense of involving feelings or sensations). An animal as opposed to a human form, in indicating something to, or bringing out a meaning for, another form, is not at the same time indicating or bringing out the same thing or meaning to or for himself; for the animal has no mind, no thought, and hence there is no meaning here in the significant or self-conscious sense. A gesture is not significant when the response of another organism to it does not indicate to the first organism what the second organism is responding to. (168)

For Mead, languageless animals were mindless, selfless, and emotionless, and the view that nonhuman animals have more sophisticated mental, emotional, and social lives was based merely on anthropomorphic projection.

Interestingly however, Max Weber, writing before Mead, had acknowledged the possibility of including nonhuman animals in sociological analysis because their behavior did not merely stem from instinct. "In so far [as the behavior of animals is subjectively understandable] it would be theoretically possible to formulate a sociology of the relations of men to animals, both domestic and wild. Thus, many animals 'understand' commands, anger, love, hostility, and react to them in ways which are evidently often by no means purely instinctive and mechanical and in some sense both consciously meaningful and affected by experience" (Weber 1947, 104).

Despite Weber's apparent willingness to include animals, Mead's anthropocentric orientation largely laid the groundwork for the conventional discounting of animals and lack of attention to their interactions with humans that dominated sociological thought until the latter quarter of the twentieth century. The sole dissent to Mead's myopia was offered by Read Bain, an early positivist and Mead's colleague at the University of Chicago. In a little-known but significant paper entitled "The Culture of Canines," Bain (1929) criticized the anthropocentrism of sociology and advocated the development of an "animal sociology." In his article, Bain maintained, "Just as animal intelligent and emotional behavior, anatomical and physiological structure and function, and group life, have their correlates in human behavior, so the dividing line between animal and human culture is likewise vague and arbitrary" (555). Notwithstanding Bain's dissent, sociology continued to exclude animals until Clifton Bryant (1979), in a seminal article, issued a call for sociologists to focus serious attention on what he referred to as the "zoological connection." In this paper, Bryant bemoaned the fact that "Sociologists . . . have been singularly derelict in their failure to address the zoological component in human interactions and attendant social systems. We have tended not to recognize, to overlook, to ignore, or to neglect . . . the influence of animals, or their import for, our social behavior, our relationships with other humans, and the directions which our social enterprise often takes" (339).

Central Areas of Interest in Human-Animal Sociology

Sociologists working in human-animal studies typically employ conventional substantive areas to contextualize their studies and discussions. One of the most popular substantive contexts is work and occupations. Many of the major discussions examine the experience of workers involved in animal-related occupational settings. For example, since the late 1980s, Arnold Arluke has emerged as the major figure in this topical area beginning with his 1988 article based on the ethnographic research he conducted in biomedical laboratories (Arluke 1988). Arluke's paper laid the groundwork for a theme that has become central to the substantive field—the dichotomy between defining animals as "pets" or functional objects and the impact of this determination on how animals are treated. Arluke expanded on this theme in his later writings emphasizing the job-related ambivalence experienced by animal shelter workers (Arluke 1991), veterinary students (Arluke and Hafferty 1996), researchers in primate labs (Arluke and Sanders 1996), and humane law enforcement officers working for animal welfare organizations (Arluke 2004). The number of studies focused on animal-related occupations has grown significantly as Carole Case (1991) has studied racetrack workers, Clinton Sanders has written about veterinarians (Sanders 1994, 1995) and guide dog trainers (Sanders 1999, 89–110), Leslie Irvine (2004) has explored the occupational experiences of workers in an animal shelter, and Mary Phillips (in this volume) has discussed laboratory workers' perceptions of animal pain and emphasized the importance of whether or not laboratory animals were assigned names by those who had the job of caring for them (Phillips 1994).

Public interactions and the impact of being with an animal upon a person's interactional experience and identity have also become important issues in the sociology of human-animal relationships. The groundwork for this focal issue was laid by Peter Messent (1983) who observed people walking in a London park. Those accompanied by dogs were significantly more likely to speak with strangers they encountered than were those who were alone. Later work by Robins and his associates (1991) explored the ways in which dogs facilitated interactions and the development of longer-term relationships in a dog park; and Sanders (2000) examined both positive and negative public encounters of people with visual disabilities precipitated by their use of guide dogs.

In an earlier article, Sanders (1990) focused on the connection between everyday dog caretakers' association with a dog and the impact of canine misbehavior on people's public identity. Basing his analysis on the sociological literature on "vocabularies of motive" and "aligning actions" (e.g., Mills 1940, Stokes and Hewitt 1976), Sanders identified eight "excusing tactics" used by caretakers to realign normal interaction and reestablish their identities when their dogs misbehaved. Comparing his work to that of Cahill (1987) and others who had explored the child-adult "with" in public, Sanders stressed the central importance of people's public association with animals in shaping public identity, and emphasized the potential of investigations of the human-animal relationship for advancing a general understanding of social interaction. In a key statement, Sanders connected the human-animal relationship and the self-concept. He ended by observing the importance of the sociological study of human associations with animals for the expansion of an understanding of social life (a point that is of central concern in this collection).

> It is here in the public behavior of acting units composed of one (or more) socially competent actor(s) and an, at best, marginally socialized member (companion animal, child, retarded person, and so on) that we encounter a major element in the linkage between other-objects and the self. The associated "possession" is attached to the competent actor as an extension of self and "its" misbehavior may degrade the actor's self identity. Self-control includes and necessitates control of the associated other. In turn,

> failure to adequately exercise this form of self-control attacks the "owner's" sense of self as demonstrated by his or her common experience of public embarrassment. . . . [T]his discussion represents an attempt to further incorporate animal-human interaction into sociological discourse. Interactions and relationships are major foci of sociological interest and the narrow emphasis upon interhuman exchanges unnecessarily limits our understanding of both human and animal behavior. It is through the systematic examination of unexplored areas of social activity and the comparison of this information to that collected in more conventional settings that the process of building a general understanding of social life can proceed. (87–88)

Another popular substantive area in which sociologists interested in animal issues have been working is social movements. Here the focus is on the animal rights movement and, for the most part, this literature employs sociological approaches that have been used to examine and explain other types of social movements (Groves 1997, Jasper and Nelkin 1992, Sperling 1988, Tester 1992). This body of work, together with ecofeminist discussions (e.g., Adams 1994, Gaard 1993, Noske 1997) and the currently popular (and somewhat controversial) work focused on the presumed relationship between the abuse of animals and human-on-human violence (e.g., Arluke *et al.* this volume, Flynn 1999, Kruse 1999), has firmly situated human-animal sociology in the arena of political analysis and advocacy.

Yet another topic of interest in human-animal sociological studies is the symbolic role of animals. Fine and Christoforides (in this volume), for example, discuss the "metaphorical linkage" between the English sparrow and immigrants in nineteenth-century America. More recently, Reuben May (2004) discussed the symbolic significance of rodents in the "ideoculture" of young, African-American males. Based on data drawn from ethnographic research with a high-school basketball team, May stresses that the participants used mice, and aggressive talk about them, to symbolically define their masculinity.

One of the richest issues given systematic attention within sociological human-animal studies has been the everyday interactions between people and their companion animals. As indicated above, this work has been done primarily by scholars working within the perspective of symbolic interactionism and centers on a direct critique of Mead's anthropocentric discounting of animal abilities. Key recent examples are Clinton Sanders' (1999, 2003) research with dog owners, Gene Myers' (1998) study of the interactions between children and animals in a preschool program, and Janet and Steven Alger's (2003) book on a cat shelter. These writers examine the intersubjectivity that emerges when people routinely interact with animals; the process by which people construct an understanding of the individuality, emotionality, and identity of animal others; and, in turn, how association with animals shapes the identities of human actors.

The sociological work on everyday interactions between people and animals has already had considerable impact on social psychological conceptions of mind. Sociologists who take a symbolic interactionist approach have sought to establish an orientation toward mind that de-emphasizes this view of mindedness as a linguistic phenomenon and returns to an understanding of mind as the outcome of social interaction and social experience. Basing their discussions on the prior work of researchers who have examined the interactional worlds of people with Alzheimer's disease (Gubrium 1986), those with severe physical and mental disabilities (Bogdan and Taylor 1989, Goode 1994), and infants (Stern 1985), sociologists involved in human-animal studies have called into question the centrality of language use to mindedness and have emphasized the interactional process of "doing mind." As Dutton and Williams (2004) observe:

> The attribution of meaning or intention to behavior hinges crucially on the extent to which such behavior is considered meaningful *within the context of the social relationship*. Social relationships actually provide rather clear conditions and parameters for what constitutes "mindful" behavior in contrast to those behaviors that do not seem to merit an intentional explanation because they seem inappropriate within the context of relationship. . . . To see (doing mind) as simply folk psychology or a useful social heuristic, would be to ignore the importance of the social relationship in structuring and scaffolding intersubjective understanding. (215–216, emphasis in original)

Mind, therefore, seen in this way as arising from mutual, consistent, and emotionally connected experience, is cast as an element of the meaning structure that those who interact with alingual others, like those who engage in conventional exchanges with language-users, devise in understanding and constructing their interactions (see the selections in Part 9).

The Future of Human-Animal Sociology

As a relatively new substantive area within sociology, the study of human-animal interaction offers a wide variety of alternatives for future research. Since much of the extant research literature is focused on people's everyday relationships with cats and dogs—the animals most commonly incorporated into households—studies of relationships with "exotic" animals such as ferrets, potbelly pigs, reptiles, insects, and rabbits would be new and instructive. Consequently, there is considerable opportunity for researchers to explore interactions with other types of animals. Thus far, there has only been limited sociological attention to wild animals (Dizard 1994, Kalof and Fitzgerald 2003, Scarce 2000); farm animals and livestock (Wilkie 2005, Wipper 2000); animals in zoos, circuses, and other leisure settings (Case 1991, Lawrence 1984, Malamud 1998); and animals involved in blood sports (Darden and Worden 1996, Marvin 1988). In this volume, we have attempted to include some of the few major discussions of these relatively unexplored topics. There are also a number of animal-related occupations (for example, the work of veterinary technicians, wildlife rehabilitators, zookeepers, professional dog handlers, animal behavior consultants, circus personnel, and K-9 police) available for fruitful investigation. Finally, as Arnold Arluke (2003) has observed, sociologists now have amassed sufficient basic understanding of human-animal interaction to begin to *apply* this knowledge in an attempt to effectively deal with problems in urban human-animal relations, veterinary medicine, animal control activities, and other settings and exchanges that constitute the "dark side" of this key form of social interaction (see Part 3 in this volume).

Despite continuing resistence, the study of nonhuman animals and people's relationships with them is a growing and exciting field within contemporary sociology. In attending to the zoological connection, academic sociology is encouraged to acknowledge that we live in mixed species societies in which human-animal relationships play a central role. The topical area has already expanded, and will continue to extend, sociology's substantive and theoretical understanding of social processes, interactions, and relationships impelled by the understanding that other animals are always cultural constructions. By continuing to move nonhuman animals into the realm of "sociological visibility" (Oakley 1974, 5),we can learn about the shared interactional life of people and animals, enrich the sociological enterprise, and gain a better understanding of what it is to be human.

Meaning and Metaphor

Although animals have a physical being, once in contact with humans they are given a cultural identity as people try to make sense of them, understand them, use them, or communicate with them. They are brought into civilization and transformed accordingly, as their meaning is socially constructed. To say that animals are *social* constructions means that we have to look beyond what is regarded as innate in animals—beyond their physical appearance, observable behavior, and cognitive abilities—in order to understand how humans will think about and interact with them. "Being" an animal in modern societies

may be less a matter of biology than it is an issue of human culture and consciousness.

Indeed, how academics and the laity refer to "animals" and the humans who take responsibility for them is further evidence of this constructionism. We recognize that the terms *pet* and *owner* are seen, by some, as indicating possession and oppression of the nonhuman animals with whom we have the closest relationships. The labels *companion animal* and *caretaker* or *guardian* have been devised as more politically acceptable alternatives (though some reject these terms and their implied relationships as well). In this volume you will find all these designations used both in the introductions and the included selections. While both of the editors have strong feelings and commitments with regard to our relationships with animals, we have chosen to employ the relational terms used by the original authors and, in so doing, do not intend to make any particular political or ethical point.

The language we use to talk about animals, and the meanings we give them, are cultural phenomena—part of the normative order of the society in which they occur. Much like other cultural phenomena—love of country, motherhood, or the success ethic—animal meanings are passed from generation to generation. They seem fixed and enduring, at any one time and place. Yet their meaning is hardly so clear or certain, changing as culture changes. In different places and times, people will assign animals different meanings.

For example, in contemporary American homes it is taken for granted that dogs will be regarded in a certain way. A puppy is transformed into a make-believe or pretend family member that is named, fed, groomed, dressed, photographed, talked to, mourned, slept with, given birthday parties, and taken to "therapists" for behavior problems. According to Lucy Hickrod and Raymond Schmitt (1982), this process begins when a dog is taken into a home. Naming the new pet begins its transformation from a generic puppy to a specific member of the family. The name affords the dog an identity and makes it easier to talk about and direct activities toward it as though it were part of the family. Acquiring a status in the family is contingent on family members' willingness to meet the pet's needs. Pets that do not obey house rules or that are considered too difficult may be given away or euthanized. If pets survive this probationary period, many family members develop intense feelings about them. During this "engrossment stage," personal qualities such as loyalty or humor are often attributed to pets, who are seen as being more consistent in displaying these attributes than are most humans.

Soon they begin to communicate their feelings for their pets to people outside the family so they too can participate in this definition of the animal as family member. This may entail introducing pets to newcomers by mentioning their names and discussing their personal histories, as well as nonverbally communicating this status through fondling, special dressing, or the like. These "tie signs" minimize the social boundaries between pets and humans, thereby demonstrating their special position to strangers.

After becoming engrossed in their dogs, most owners come to the realization that they are treating their pets as genuine family members or very good friends (Gosse and Barnes 1994, Katcher 1989). Stallones *et al.* (1988) found that 95 percent of companion animal owners regarded their pets as friends. Cain (1983) found that 87 percent of the respondents considered their companion animals to be members of the family, while in Voith's (1985) study, 99 percent did so. Sixty-five percent of owners report buying a Christmas gift for their dog, 21 percent report celebrating their dog's birthday, 41 percent report displaying a picture of their pet in their home, and the most popular place for a dog to sleep is on the owner's bed (American Pet Association 1998). Indeed, some researchers claim that a person's attachment to a companion animal can be even closer than that had with a human companion (Carmack 1985). In America, 33 percent of dog owners report they are closer to their dogs than they are to any family member (Barker and

Barker 1988). Pets can become so important to some owners that there can be circumstances in which they would give a scarce drug to their pet in preference to a person outside the family (Cohen 2002).

There are other indications that pets are increasingly seen as family members in America. Some owners remain in touch with their dogs while separated, just as they would with other family members when apart. Phones or answering machines are used by 33 percent of dog-owning Americans to talk to their dogs when away from home (Consumer Reports 1998). Live web cams are increasingly becoming a standard part of "doggy day care" so remote owners can verify that their dogs are happy and well cared for. Some owners also send their dogs to pet spas, pet camp, doggy daycare, pet school, and pet retreats. Other owners refuse to leave their pet "undressed," especially in inclement weather; upscale clothing retailers (e.g., Ralph Lauren, Coach, Macy's, Lord & Taylor, and Swarovski) increasingly anthropomorphize dogs by offering quality canine clothing. And many pet owners have shown increasing interest in and willingness to pay for advanced veterinary services, including expensive and complicated procedures (e.g., kidney transplants) provided by veterinary specialists (e.g., cardiologists) in state-of-the-art facilities (e.g., cancer treatment centers) that often rival those provided to humans.

This bond can be so strong, pet owners may not evacuate from a disaster area if they cannot take their pets with them (DeLorenzo and Augustine 1996, Nelson *et al.* 1988). According to one study, 20 percent of household evacuation failures after natural disasters are attributed to pet ownership (Heath *et al.* 2001). Another report claims that one quarter of the nation's 58.3 percent of households that own at least one pet will not evacuate due to pets (AVMA 2003).

Given this degree of attachment, it is not surprising that the death of a companion animal can be just as devastating as the loss of a human significant other (Hart *et al.* 1990). Gerwolls and

Labott (1994) found that the mourning for deceased animals can be as intense as it is for humans; subjects at 26 weeks following the death of a companion animal did not score significantly lower (indicating less grief) on the Grief Experience Inventory than did those who had suffered a human loss. Quackenbush (1985) found specific grief reactions among those mourning deceased animals that rivaled those among human mourners; 97 percent of his subjects experienced disruption in their daily routine and social activities and suffered from eating and sleeping disorders, excessive crying, and inability to concentrate. Carmack (1985) found that the kinds of losses experienced by animal mourners were similar to those experienced by human mourners. His subjects experienced a loss of a family member, loss of special qualities inherent in the companion animal, loss of intimacy, and loss of being needed. In addition, the companion animal's death caused disorganization in the family's usual way of functioning. As with grief over human loss, companion animal owners have extended grief reactions, though not quite as long on average. Carmack's (1985) anecdotal study claimed that grief over the loss of a pet lasted from 6 months to a year with an acute phase of 1 or 2 months.

After pets die, their intimate connection to families may be remembered when stories are shared about the animals' exploits or when later pets are given the same names. Since human emotional response to the death of a pet can be as intense as those precipitated by the loss of any family member, it is not surprising that there is a modest but growing interest in burying pets in animal cemeteries in order to maintain this connection. That dead animals are typically treated as kin can be seen in the intense public disapproval generated by media reports that Roy Rogers stuffed his faithful steed Trigger so that it could be displayed in Rogers' living room. This negative reaction, no doubt, arose because the public regarded the horse as a pet or member of the Rogers family. Presumably, for these people, the stuffing of a pet, rather than a hunting trophy,

seemed to deny an emotional tie by turning Trigger into an object.

However, a pet is still something less than a full-fledged family member because of ever present "frame breaks." Bystanders, media presentations, and certain situations constantly call into question this definition of the pet as a family member and reinforce its definition as an animal or a toy. Signs reading "No Pets Allowed" or "Beware of Guard Dog," as well as instances when pets nonchalantly vomit in living rooms, eat their own excrement, or mate in public are reminders that they are, at best, make-believe members of families.

Yet dogs in another setting might be anything but adjunct members of the family. In the context of a dog track, for instance, they are racing machines. This utilitarian construction requires impersonal identities, and the dogs are assigned special names and numbers. Their official names appear in the programs but are almost never used, except when announced with their position numbers at the checkpoint. These official names, like the names of race horses, exist outside everyday human usage, and their meanings are clear only to those deeply involved in the race world. These names are not even anthropomorphized, but usually refer to abstract images or emotional states—such as Peaceful Darkness, Fine Style, or Surprise Launch. When names are humanized, they are almost always in the possessive form, such as Tara's Dream or Bobby's Showtime, suggesting that the names apply to the owners and not the dogs. Transforming the dogs into machines reduces their identities to numbers that appear on racing blankets, starting gates, programs, handlers' armbands, and monitors displaying betting odds. The numbers are also used by track announcers when dogs pass through the checkpoint and during the race to indicate their position as well as by betters who shout numbers, not names, as they cheer on their choices.

Standard handling practices also help to construct a numbered machine, suppressing the dogs' personalities. For example, when the dogs are presented to interested betters in the paddock, steel bars keep onlookers about 5 feet from the thick glass behind which dogs, handlers, and judges do their work. The distance and glass muffle all sounds, although one can still hear the barking of unmuzzled dogs in cages turned away from the public's view. When in view, they are muzzled and tightly controlled. Muzzling partially covers their faces, restricts their barking, and gives them a badge of human dominance. Handlers rarely look at, talk to, or touch their dogs, and the exceptions only point to the more pervasive construction of these animals as machines. Occasionally, when handlers talk to each other, they might quickly pet or scratch a dog's head or neck. This touching looks more like a reflex or afterthought, because they neither look nor talk to the dog as they do it, nor do they try to solicit any response from the dog. For the most part, the dogs themselves have little response. No dog, for instance, responds by licking a handler's hand or jumping up on the handler. Indeed, the greyhounds rarely initiate any interaction with each other; they are trained not to do so, and the handlers stop any attempt. At the rare times when people try to interact with the greyhounds, the handlers immediately restrain the dogs and ignore the people, almost as though nothing had happened. Even when the dogs and the handlers are not busy, such interactions are prevented.

That dogs can be seen as pets or machines shows the flexibility of animal symbols. Indeed, beyond their objectification as machines, dogs can sometimes be seen as enemies or victims to target for abuse (Arluke 2002, 2006). These varied definitions are significant because of their consequences; at one extreme, they facilitate the pampering of animals, while at the other, they facilitate their torturing. To better understand this confusion over the nature and significance of animals in human society, we need to better understand ourselves.

Anthropocentrism and Anthropomorphism

Historically, the dominant perspective in the natural and social sciences has been that humans and nonhuman animals are qualitatively different beings. This assumption has, for centuries, led to the view that humans and their interests are ethically, mentally, and materially superior. Consequently, anthropocentrism directs primary attention to the advancement of human welfare over that of animals, since humans are deemed more valuable than are nonhuman animals. Three general forms of anthropocentrism are commonly identified. The first variety is *dominionism*. This perspective is based on the biblically based belief that God gave "man" dominion "over the fish of the sea, and over the fowl of the air, and over every living thing that moveth upon the earth" (Genesis 1:28). Animals and other elements of nature, from this point of view, are resources meant to be exploited by humans. It is important to note that this form of *strong anthropocentrism* was denied within a variety of cultures and philosophical schools of thought. For example, Plato and his followers regarded animals as carrying reincarnated human souls and the Cynics held that animals were superior to humans (Sorabji 1993, 9–12, 158–161).

Another foundation for anthropocentrism is that God has given humans *stewardship* over animals. This perspective, sometimes referred to as *weak anthropocentrism*, is found in both Judeo-Christian and Islamic ideologies and in the belief systems of numerous indigenous peoples. While the stewardship view casts humans as superior to animals, it emphasizes the importance of intelligent management and conservation of nature. Humans are superior but nonhuman animals have value and are worthy of special consideration.

The third conceptual foundation of anthropocentrism is *evolutionary*. From this perspective, survival and reproduction are evolutionary requirements. These natural demands inevitably generate conflict and competition among species. Out of this competition, the human species has emerged as dominant and, by extension, the advancement and the welfare of humans inevitably leads to the good of the beings and resources that constitute nature.

As is routinely emphasized in the growing literature on human-animal relationships, ambivalence and ambiguity are central to how people view, feel about, and act toward animals. The definition and treatment of animals as objects to be eaten, used in scientific experiments, confined in zoos, and exhibited in circuses are premised on anthropocentrism—and is often so routine and commonsensical that it is rarely acknowledged or examined by most people. The view of animals that stands in opposition to anthropocentrism presents them as thoughtful, planning, at some level self-aware, and emotional. This perspective emphasizing that nonhuman animals have human qualities and abilities is generally referred to as *anthropomorphism.*

Until recently, the charge of anthropomorphism has been leveled at discussions within ethology and other "natural" sciences that are seen as romanticizing animals and as employing sentimental rather than rational bases for interpreting their behavior. As a consequence, when ethologists employed terms such as *think* or *feel,* they were either condemned by their conventional colleagues as being "sentimental" (Strum 1987,153–156), or were careful to tack on disclaimers such as: "Note that the words 'decision' and 'choice' are not intended to imply anything about conscious thought, they are a shorthand way of saying that an animal is designed to follow certain rules" (Krebs, quoted in Mitchell and Thompson 1986, 361). As seen in this quote, in order to avoid the charge of anthropomorphism, ethologists, comparative psychologists, and other scientists routinely used "scare quotes" to set off descriptive words that could imply conscious intention or other human abilities on the part of the animals they were discussing.

As people interact with companion animals in their daily lives, they commonly employ an anthropomorphic model to understand and talk about their animals' behaviors. Caretakers tend to cast their animal companions as humanlike in that they appear to feel happiness, fear, excitement, sadness, or have other emotional experiences and to behave in ways similar to how humans behave when they feel these things. This kind of "sentimental" anthropomorphism (Irvine 2004) often leads to animals being dressed in human clothes, provided with human food, and otherwise treated as small, hairy, and not terribly intelligent humans. Understandably, many scientists and philosophers see this kind of everyday anthropomorphism as a naive example of the "folk psychology" people commonly employ to make sense of their own mental and behavioral experiences and to understand those of others. In a way, anthropomorphism is inevitable since our own experience is the most basic foundation for understanding the experience of others and, consequently, their behavior. As the ethologist Marc Bekoff (2000) emphasizes, anthropomorphism derives necessarily from the fact that language is used to describe the inner life and behavior of animals or any other actors. While inevitable, when used uncritically, anthropomorphism may result in misunderstandings and mistreatments as harmful as those premised on anthropocentrism. In seeing nonhuman animals as more "clever than they really are" (Dawkins 1993, 178), we risk not gaining a clear understanding of nonhuman perspectives and not coming to fully appreciate animal abilities.

The alternative to everyday, emotionalized anthropomorphism is what some sociologists (e.g., Irvine 2004, Sanders 1999), ethologists (e.g., Bekoff 2006), and others (e.g., Burghardt 1991, Fisher 1991) have referred to (and advocated) as *critical* or *interpretive* anthropomorphism. This perspective acknowledges Darwin's (1965 [1872]) position that humans and animals advance and change as they move together along the path of "evolutionary continuity." Consequently, it is reasonable to employ human experience and explanations as a heuristic basis for making judgments about the experiences, feelings, and actions of nonhuman animals. To a major degree, interpretive anthropomorphism is grounded in the routine, immediate, and intimate experience people have with animals. While it helps us to ask questions about animals and develop models for empathetically judging their experiences and interpreting their behavior, critical anthropomorphism requires that analysts respect the physiological, cognitive, and other differences between humans and other animals. As an analytic tool, critical anthropomorphism can provide a useful guideline for understanding how animals think and feel in the same way that empathy allows us to gain insight into the subjective experience of our fellow humans.

Ambiguity and Ambivalence

Ambivalence is a key emotional experience people encounter in their everyday lives. This emotional experience is generated by ambiguity—the conflict or confusion of meanings, ideas, and situational definitions (Weigert 1991, 16–32). One form of ambivalence, what Merton (1976) refers to as *sociological ambivalence*, derives from the complexity of contemporary culture and the contradictory demands built into the structure of social statuses, roles, and situational definitions. For many, these cultural contradictions generate *psychological ambivalence*—"conflicting emotions, contradictory attitudes, conflicting definitions of self or other, and contradictory relationships" (Weigert 1991, 43). What is especially interesting is that people seem quite adept at holding contradictory ideas, perceptions, and definitions. In part, this is due to an ability to psychologically compartmentalize conflicting ideas. However, cultural messages also play a key role since culture both generates and helps resolve ambiguity (Weigert 1991, xiv).

Ambiguous perceptions and ambivalent emotions are central to the forms of relationships between humans and nonhuman animals. To a major extent, this confusion and these mixed emotions are grounded in what Andrew Rowan (in Herzog 1993, 349) refers to as the "constant paradox"—the definition and treatment of animals as functional objects, on the one hand, and sentient individuals, on the other.

In the typically ambivalent way animals are regarded in our culture, pets can be seen as both social objects and as subjects. As *objects*, they are possessions that display and help enhance their owners' status and function as assistants and physical extensions. But the social place of companion animals as *subjects* is far more significant and sociologically interesting. As parts of our everyday lives, nonhuman companions with whom we associate are cast in the role of persons. Like human persons, they listen, offer affection, and in a variety of other important ways, provide us with those social things we need in order to feel that we are valuable, individual, and have a place in a world that is often experienced as alienating and chaotic.

This ambivalence about the status of animals is understood and played out in a variety of ways. For the most part, animals are legally defined as pieces of property that people own; though, by defining animals as sentient beings, most believe they should be protected from acts of overt cruelty. The definition of companion animals as property—and the ambivalence surrounding this definition—is illustrated by two court decisions. In a Florida divorce case in which the parties were contesting custody of their pet Rottweiler, the judge awarded the dog to the husband and ruled that, because the animal was legally an item of personal property, the wife was not allowed the visitation rights she requested (*The Hartford Courant*, January 26, 1995, p. A2). However, in another case heard at about the same time, a New York judge ruled that the plaintiff's dog was "somewhere between a person and personal property" and that he was eligible to receive more than the "fair market value" from the owners of the veterinary clinic in which the dog had died as the result of surgery (*Erwin v. The Animal Medical Center, New York Law Journal*, Aug. 29, 1996 at 24, col. 4 [(N.Y. Civ. Ct. 1996)].

In his well-known analysis of the ambivalence that typifies human relationships with animals, the philosopher Yi-Fu Tuan (1984) focuses on this issue of unequal power. Interactions with nonhuman creatures (and other elements of nature), he maintains, are characterized by the linked, but conflicting, feelings of dominance and affection. Humans dominate animals through breeding and castration, training, functional use (herding, hunting, and so forth), confining them in zoos, and subjecting them to the indignities of circuses and other performance situations. By transforming animals into objects to be controlled, humans symbolically display and act out the dominance of culture over nature. At the same time, however, the impersonality and affective impoverishment of modern life prompt people to focus consistently on animals as objects of affection.

Of course, feeling ambivalence is better than feeling the guilt and remorse that would arise were we not to have the safe category of animal-as-thing and be forced to regard all animals as thinking, feeling, self-aware subjects. As Joy Williams (1997) put it: "Humans don't want to enter into a pact with animals. They don't want animals to reason. It would be an unnerving experience. It would bring about all manner of awkwardness and guilt. It would make our treatment of them seem, well, unreasonable. The fact that animals are voiceless is a relief to us, it frees us from feeling much empathy or sorrow" (60).

The contradictory and conflicting definitions people have of animals are especially apparent when one examines human interactions with and use of service animals. Guide dogs and other service animals are regarded both as "objects" that serve, protect, and assist, and as individual companions with whom one interacts and develops a shared emotional bond. In this latter role as companion, the relationship with the service dog develops an especially strong emotional component given the mutual functional dependence of the association (Sanders 1999, 39–58). This dichotomous definition of service dogs—as both assistance equipment and companions—has clear implications for approaches to their training as well as the human-animal relationship in general. As objects, dogs are subjected to behavioristically modeled training processes intended to *mold* their *behavior* so that they will *behave* in acceptable and predictable ways. As sentient individuals, on the other hand, dogs are primarily *taught* in the context of a developing relationship in which the animals *learn* expectations and roles so that they *act*

in appropriate ways (see Sanders' [2006] discussion of patrol dog training).

Animals, therefore, play both utilitarian and affectional roles in many peoples' lives. For example, a person might consider one animal to be a pet and another of the same species to be an object as when farmers name, pamper, and feel affection for one particular calf while seeing the others simply as future meat or as producers of dairy products (Wilkie 2005). Sometimes one may regard the same animal as both a companion and an object. In the rural south, for example, hunters commonly see their dogs as useful partners for hunting and guarding and value them for their abilities and faithfulness. At the same time, these hunters frequently treat their dogs so callously as to indicate they consider them to be of little real value (Jordon 1975). Finally, people may see the same animal as either a functional object or a companion who is seen as an individual and regarded with affection. For example, some children taking riding lessons may view the horse as a form of vehicle while others relate to it as a large pet (Lawrence 1988).

It is relatively seductive to draw basic dichotomies when developing analyses of central elements of culture and social life. To regard nonhuman animals either as individuals or things, as friends or possessions, as objects to be dominated or pets to be regarded with affection is easy, commonplace, and somewhat obvious. On the other hand, social life and the interactions that compose it are changeable, complex, and multifaceted. It makes sense, therefore, to move beyond simple dichotomies and to see the place of animals in human society as arrayed along a continuum. This continuum reveals our most essential conceptions of the social order and unmasks our most authentic attitudes toward people. The meanings we attribute to animals have wide implication because with them we create a "natural order" that creates distance—or reduces it—not only between humans and animals, but among humans themselves, as we see next.

The Sociozoologic Scale

Societies rank everything on a ladder of worth, including people and animals, and systems of social control perpetuate these rankings. Such vertical social orders make inequality of privilege seem natural, as not everyone or everything will be regarded equally. Those who land at the bottom, because they are in some inferior category, can justifiably be exploited and oppressed. Our ability to rank-order animals—and the inconsistencies that follow—may, for systems of social control, be a useful form of thinking to justify the inconsistent treatment of humans. Once in culture's hands, animals may offer one such social control device, becoming useful vehicles by which humans express their image of society's ladder or serve as a means of enforcing these expectations. That animal symbols can work this way presumes that members of contemporary societies classify animals not only on biological grounds, but on moral and social ones as well. While phylogenetic systems of classification rank animals on the basis of biological distinctions, sociozoologic systems rank them according to how well they seem to "fit in" and play the roles they are expected to play in society. How well animals seem to know their place and stay in it will determine worth and position on the social ladder.

At the top of the sociozoologic scale are humans, although, as we describe below, different groups of humans appear at every rung of the social ladder. Following humans are the best animals—so tame they are almost like humans. Pets seem to love their place in the social order, appearing almost genetically predisposed to be part of the civilized world and eager to learn and follow its ways. Much like animals that submit to authority, some groups of people have been regarded as domesticated, quiet, and tame. Accepting (or seeming to accept) their given place in society, they foster a sense of orderliness, subject to the will and social restraints of those in power. According to the dominant group, they need to be taken care of paternalistically like pets, farm animals, or children—so long as they stay in their

place. According to Berta Perez (1986, 19), such "petification" entails confining, domesticating, or diminishing humans in order to make them small. "Making small," in turn, involves controlling others so they become "creatures of submission," displaying dependency and needing guidance.

Minority group members who accept their subordinate place in society are often petified, reducing their status to that of children. Depicted as "irresponsible," "impulsive," "fun-loving," and "immature," minorities are seen as dependent on the "more mature" dominant group for their survival or for guidance to accomplish the tasks they are assigned. Historically, the "little black Sambo" image was used extensively to establish the ideology of a "white man's burden," by which enslaved people would perish without the paternalistic "protection" of whites. To this day, the epithet "boy" recalls the infantilization of slavery (Blassingame 1972). Similarly, women before the liberation movement of the 1960s were often called "baby," "girl," "honey," and "sweetie." The elderly in America also are petified by the media, health-care personnel, or relatives who consider them unable to manage their own lives due to the incapacities of "second childhood." In its most extreme form, infantilization can be found in mass media images of the toothless, hairless, wrinkled, bent, and drooling elder as a "newborn" who is increasingly dependent as he or she approaches death (Arluke and Levin 1990).

Bad animals, however, have a problem with their place in the social order. In response, society may ignore, marginalize, segregate, or destroy them. As is true with good animals, the morally laden symbols of bad animals can serve as useful instruments of human social control—that they are highly flexible symbols makes them all the more useful.

Some bad animals are "freaks"—they do not have a clear place in the social order. Their status is confused and ambiguous because they mix categories that are considered by many people to be pure and sacred. Although there is no urgency to destroy them, their questionable moral status puts them on the margins of society. They are, at best, objects of curiosity, but more likely they are ignored, pitied, scorned, or found repulsive. For example, in the nineteenth and early twentieth centuries, "freaks" that appeared to mix human and animal features were immensely popular in circuses and carnivals. Today, most people commonly respond to such anomalies with fright, disgust, contempt, or uneasiness, because they seem to violate a sense of physical or perhaps even spiritual sacredness or purity. No doubt this discomfort accounts for some of the public horror precipitated by the 1984 Baby Fae case, in which an infant received a transplanted baboon's heart at California's Loma Linda Hospital. Similarly, one aspect of the growing public outcry over genetic manipulation is a moral concern over what is seen as the unnatural mixing of different animal species, with a potential for producing freaks and monsters.

As an instrument of social control, the construct of "freak" can be applied to groups of people whose biology is entirely human. According to Robert Bogdan (1988) and Susan Sontag (1977), "freak" has become a metaphor for the dark, or not understood, side of human experience and the marginality that is associated with it. Homeless people, recent immigrants, and other marginal or deviant groups of humans are seen as anomalous creatures—not fully human or "like the rest of us" to many Americans. For example, homeless people living in the subway tunnels of New York City are called "mole people," a pejorative term among homeless advocates and an insulting one to some tunnel dwellers, because one pictures wretched and disgusting subhumans whose abodes might easily be taken for those of burrowing animals (Toth 1993). Though Toth humanizes the homeless and dismisses the fantasy that they are animal-like cave dwellers, the freakish and horrible images conjured up by the term "mole people" are exactly the sort of morally laden images that are essential for animal constructs to serve as effective instruments of social control.

"Vermin" are below freaks in the sociozoologic scale, because they are seen as greater dangers to the social order. They are pests or nuisances that not only stray from their place but also threaten to contaminate individuals or the environment. Although vermin are not usually a physical threat, people often have feelings of disgust or hatred toward them because they are thought to be literally or symbolically "dirty." They are believed to pollute what is regarded as pure and create disorder out of order. Segregation, avoidance, or destruction are frequent responses to them.

Groups of humans may be seen and treated as vermin when they cross human-drawn boundaries. The history of the Jews abounds with examples of their animalization as unwanted pests who come too close for the comfort of other people. During the mass migration of Jews to the United States in the late nineteenth century, anti-Semitism gained momentum. Jews were depicted as subhuman, genetically inferior to Anglo-Saxons, evil, and parasitic. Michael Selzer (1972, 42–43) cites an 1881 publication entitled "The Wolves of New York," which described Jews as animal-like in their greed. Depicted as "eager for prey and plunder," Jewish businessmen were compared to "ferretlike" creatures with "long clawlike fingers" grasping their money, to "jackals" waiting for the remains of the lion's prey, or to "vultures" waiting for their meal of carrion. Other publications from this period often characterized Jews as weasels, hedgehogs, vampires, bats, or rats.

Below vermin on the sociozoologic scale are the worst animals—commonly portrayed in popular culture as fiends, predators, or maneaters—that contest the established social order itself. "Demons" mount a serious and evil challenge to the way things "ought to be" by trying to reverse the fundamental master-servant relationship present in the traditional phylogenetic order. These animals do not fear humans, humans fear them; they hunt humans, humans do not hunt them; they have power over humans, humans do not have power over them. The typical response to demons is to kill them before they disempower or kill humans.

Groups of humans may be demonized through animal images if they are seen as a threat to majority-group domination, such as minority group members who challenge the status quo. For example, black Americans were demonized during the Reconstruction, as white groups felt their social and economic status directly threatened by the newly emancipated slaves. In 1867, during the controversy over blacks' voting rights, a pamphlet argued that blacks were not descendants of Adam and Eve but had entered Noah's ark with the beasts (Craige 1992). And by the turn of the century, racist literature of the day argued that blacks were a subhuman species whose members should be forced out of the United States (Frazier 1949; Woodward 1966). Typical representations of blacks pictured them as gorillas dressed up like men (Frazier 1962).

While it may be years before it becomes clear in retrospect who our contemporary bad animals are, events involving pit bulls in the later part of the twentieth century strongly suggest that certain groups of people associated with these dogs are even now being pictured this way. And once again, animals may be useful symbols to accomplish this labeling. Recent reports of pit bull attacks, and subsequent bans, are not new. From the middle to late 1980s, several American cities reported an epidemic of pit bull bites, many of which were allegedly fatal. Serious attacks by these dogs seemed to increase sharply, for no discernible reason. Any episode involving a pit bull became cause for widespread alarm, being seen as part of a larger pattern, both new and exclusive to this one breed of dog. Suddenly, the American media had its latest number-one enemy. The headline of a 1987 article in *U.S. News and World Report* proclaimed that pit bulls were "The Most Dangerous Dog in America." "America's baddest dog," claimed the author, was in a separate league from shepherds, Dobermans, and rottweilers, because these breeds cannot "chomp through a chain-link fence" like pit bulls. Cities passed ordinances that restricted or

banned pit bulls, and the media kept the hysteria going by reporting every pit bull attack while ignoring those of other breeds. One pit bull, as evidence of the uproar, was firebombed while it was playing in its own enclosure. Some of this public hysteria was also directed at pit bull owners. In response, some owners have gone out of their way to present their pit bull pets as anything but aggressive and dangerous dogs (Twining *et al.* 2000).

Although some pit bulls can become extremely dangerous, claim veterinary experts, statistical data do not show that these dogs are over-represented among biting animals (Rowan 1986). The evidence suggests that pit bull bites were just as common long before the rash of newspaper stories; so were biting incidents involving lots of Saint Bernards, huskies, Malamutes, and Great Danes. And, according to Hearne (1991), the statistics themselves were extremely unreliable—many were collected secondhand, the definition of a dog bite was ambiguous, and the breed of the attacking dog was itself often not reported.

Hearne (1991) argues that pit bulls became a metaphor for something larger and scarier to many people who displaced their fear onto these dogs. Reports of attacks by these dogs were invariably accompanied by value-laden descriptions of their owners that were guaranteed to threaten mainstream America. Criticisms of these owners noted, with anecdotal evidence only, that ownership of pit bulls was macho; presumably, the meaner the dog, the meaner the human (Rowan 1986). Capitalizing on class fears, pit bull reports by the media and even some humane organizations were peppered with references to poor urban blacks and Hispanics who kept their dogs in dope dens and fed them raw meat to make them as mean as possible, or less often, to heavily tattooed white thugs with shaved heads who starved their heavily chained dogs to increase their ferociousness. "Decent citizens" were not the root of the pit bull problem, because they were responsible owners, according to the press.

People's fear was certainly stirred up, but it may have been as much or more their fear of a perceived dangerous class of evil humans than of a breed of dogs. Was it dogs or humans whose behavior needed to become "more appropriate and docile"? Why else did sensational media stories about pit bulls suddenly vanish by the late 1980s? Certainly, efforts to curtail their attacks or change their breeding could not have had such an immediate effect. Having a short half-life in the media, the pit bull crisis faded as quickly as it had started. These dogs were a convenient hook on which to hang our growing sense of vulnerability to crime and our fear for personal safety—not from dogs, but from other humans. Interestingly, crime rates in recent years have started to climb again in various American cities, and so too have reports of pit bull attacks.

Members of the underclass, then, may be our modern demons—at least to mainstream America. Feeling threatened by them on the streets and imprisoned at home, many Americans fear for their personal safety and experience angst over losing control over the social fabric. They describe these humans as demonic, antisocial creatures who live in a culture of sociopathy—outside the pale of the civilized world. Of course, this view of the underclass is distorted, but that is irrelevant. It is the construction of its members as a growing and encroaching "menace" to America that is sociologically important. Indeed, some sociologists argue that this fear and hatred has become so common and intense among America's white middle class that it rates a special term—*afrophobia*—when it is targeted at members of the black underclass who are seen as dangerous thugs, murderers, and rapists.

Whether pet or demon, tool or vermin, the sociozoologic scale is a type of story that humans—with the help of animals—tell themselves and each other about the meaning of "place" in modern societies. As stories often do, they explain and rationalize certain relationships that are expected of people—where they belong in or out of society and how they are expected to behave. Those who believe and even share a particular story probably do not see the inconsistency of their own behavior toward other groups. Quite the contrary, they may feel that their actions—even if seen by others as hypocritical—are morally justified. That social constructions of animals are highly flexible and rich symbols—as pointed out years ago by anthropologists who knew that animals are "good to think"—is no doubt why animals are such useful instruments through which humans can express their conflicted feelings toward fellow humans.

Organization of the Book

We have chosen to organize this reader around three central questions influencing the nature and place of animals in contemporary western societies. More specifically, how do we construct different meanings of animals and what implications do these meanings have for animals and humans? How do our social institutions deal with animals and what implications does this treatment have for animals and humans? And finally, how are our perceptions of animals changing and what implications do these changes have for animals and humans?

Unit One of this book explores the connections among the complex structure of interactions and relationships conventionally (and conveniently) referred to as "society." We situate both animals and people within this social web. Specifically we are concerned with the place of animals as they play key symbolic roles in society. We also focus on the relationships people have with nonhuman animals—both those that are positive and rewarding and those that are filled with considerable suffering for the parties involved. Finally, we focus on discussions of people's understandings of and encounters with those animals that are outside the conventional boundaries of the home and the farm.

Unit Two focuses on animals within the context of the webs of functional relationships that sociologists refer to as "institutions." Here we first pay particular attention to the place of animals as objects and actors in the world of science. We then turn to examine the controversial transformation of animals into "meat" and the perspectives of those committed to rejecting this construction and the use of animals as food. Finally, we focus on the use of animals for human entertainment with particular attention to animal competitions, zoos, and the way animals are presented within the mass media.

Unit Three examines some of the new understandings and significant discussions of human-animal relationships that have emerged in the recent literature. The articles in this section focus on the role of animals in human physical and social health and the importance of human-animal studies in expanding our understanding of key social psychological concerns. The unit concludes by focusing on the collective efforts directed at improving the lot of animals as their place and treatment in the larger society comes to be seen as inhumane, immoral, and worthy of ameliorative social action.

References

Adams, C. 1994. *Neither Man nor Beast: Feminism and the Defence of Animals*. New York: Continuum.

Alger, J., and S. Alger. 2003. *Cat Culture: The Social World of a Cat Shelter*. Philadelphia: Temple University Press.

American Pet Association. 1998. Fun Pet Statistics. www.apapets.com/petstats2html.

American Veterinary Medical Association (AVMA). 2003. "AVMA Urges Americans to Include Pets in Home Security Plan." Press release, February 28.

Arluke, A. 1988. "Sacrificial Symbolism in Animal Experimentation: Object or Pet?" *Anthrozoös* 2:98–117.

Arluke, A. 1991. "Coping with Euthanasia: A Case Study of Shelter Culture." *Journal of the American Veterinary Medical Association* 198:1176–1180.

Arluke, A. 2002. "Animal Abuse as Dirty Play." *Symbolic Interaction* 25:405–430.

Arluke, A. 2003. "Ethnozoology and the Future of Sociology." *International Journal of Sociology and Social Policy* 23:26–45.

Arluke, A. 2004. *Brute Force: Animal Police and the Challenge of Cruelty*. West Lafayette, IN: Purdue University Press.

Arluke, A. 2006. *Just a Dog: Understanding Animal Cruelty and Ourselves*. Philadelphia, PA: Temple University Press.

Arluke, A., and F. Hafferty. 1996. "From Apprehension to Fascination with 'Dog Lab': The Use of Absolutions by Medical Students." *Journal of Contemporary Ethnography* 25:191–209.

Arluke, A., and J. Levin. 1990. "Second Childhood: Old Age in Popular Culture." In W. Feigelman, ed., *Readings on Social Problems*, 261–265. New York: Holt.

Arluke, A., and C. Sanders. 1996. *Regarding Animals*. Philadelphia: Temple University Press.

Bain, R. 1929. "The Culture of Canines." *Sociology and Social Research* 13:545–556.

Barker, S., and R. Barker. 1988. "The Human-Canine Bond: Closer than Family Ties?" *Journal of Mental Health Counseling* 10:46–56.

Bekoff, M. 2000. *Strolling with Our Kin: Speaking for and Respecting Voiceless Animals*. New York: Lantern/Booklight.

Bekoff, M. 2006. *Animal Passions and Beastly Virtues*. Philadelphia: Temple University Press.

Blassingame, J. 1972. *The Slave Community*. New York: Oxford University Press.

Bogdan, R. 1988. *Freak Show*. Chicago: University of Chicago Press.

Bogdan, R., and S. Taylor. 1989. "Relationships with Severely Disabled People: The Social Construction of Humanness." *Social Problems* 36: 135–148.

Bryant, C. 1979. "The Zoological Connection: Animal Related Human Behavior." *Social Forces* 58(2): 399–421.

Burghardt, G. 1991. "Cognitive Ethology and Critical Anthropomorphism: A Snake with Two Heads and Hog-Nosed Snakes that Play Dead." In C. Ristau, ed., *Cognitive Ethology: The Minds of Other Animals*, 53–90. Hillsdale, NJ: Lawrence Erlbaum.

Cahill, S. 1987. "Children and Civility: Ceremonial Deviance and the Acquisition of Ritual Competence." *Social Psychology Quarterly* 50:312–321.

Cain, A. 1983. "A Study of Pets in the Family System." In A. Katcher and A. Beck, eds., *New Perspectives on Our Lives with Companion Animals*, 72–81. Philadelphia: University of Pennsylvania Press.

Carmack, B. 1985. "The Effect on Family Members and Functioning After the Death of a Pet." *Marriage and Family Review* 8:149–161.

Case, C. 1991. *Down the Backstretch: Racing and the American Dream.* Philadelphia: Temple University Press.

Cobbe, F. 2003 (1872). "The Consciousness of Dogs." *Sociological Origins* 3:19–26.

Cohen, S. 2002. "Can Pets Function as Family Members?" *Western Journal of Nursing Research* 24:621–638.

Consumer Reports. 1998. "Feeding Fido (and Fifi, Fluffy, Max . . .)." *Consumer Reports* 63(2):12.

Craige, B. 1992. *Laying Down the Ladder.* Amherst: University of Massachusetts Press.

Darden, D., and S. Worden. 1996. "Marketing Deviance: The Selling of Cockfighting." *Society & Animals* 4(2):211–231.

Darwin, C. 1965 (1872). *The Expression of Emotions in Man and Animals.* Chicago: University of Chicago Press.

Dawkins, M. 1993. *Through Our Eyes Only? The Search for Animal Consciousness.* New York: W. H. Freeman.

Descartes, R. 1976. "Animals Are Machines." In T. Regan and P. Singer, eds., Animal Rights and Human Obligations, 60–66. Englewood Cliffs, NJ: Prentice Hall.

DeLorenzo R., and J. Augustine. 1996. "Lesson in Emergency Evacuation from the Miamisburg Train Derailment." *Prehospital Disaster Medicine* 11:270–275.

Dizard, J. 1994. *Going Wild: Hunting, Animal Rights and the Contested Meaning of Nature.* Amherst: University of Massachusetts Press.

Dutton, D., and C. Williams. 2004. "A View from the Bridge: Subjectivity, Embodiment and Animal Minds." *Anthrozoös* 17(3):210–224.

Fisher, J. 1991. "Disambiguating Anthropomorphism: An Interdisciplinary Review." In P. P. G. Bateson and P. Klopfer, eds., *Perspectives in Ethology (Vol. 9): Human Understanding and Animal Awareness,* 49–85. New York: Plenum.

Flynn, C. 1999. "Animal Abuse in Childhood and the Role of Companion Animals in the Lives of Battered Women." *Society & Animals* 8:99–127.

Frazier, E. 1949. *The Negro in the United States.* New York: Macmillan.

———. 1962. *Black Bourgeoisie.* New York: Macmillan.

Gaard, G. 1993. *Ecofeminism: Women, Animals, and Nature.* Philadelphia: Temple University Press.

Gerwolls, M., and S. Labott. 1994. "Adjustment to the Death of a Companion Animal." *Anthrozoös* 7:103–112.

Goode, D. 1994. *A World Without Words: The Social Construction of Children Born Deaf and Blind.* Philadelphia: Temple University Press.

Gosse, G., and M. Barnes. 1994. "Human Grief Resulting from the Death of a Pet." *Anthrozoös* 7:103–112.

Groves, J. 1997. *Hearts and Minds: The Controversy over Laboratory Animals.* Philadelphia: Temple University Press.

Gubrium, J. 1986. "The Social Preservation of Mind: The Alzheimer's Disease Experience." *Symbolic Interaction* 9:37–51.

Hart, L., Hart, B., and B. Marder. 1990. "Humane Euthanasia and Companion Animal Death: Caring for the Animal, the Client, and the Veterinarian." *Journal of the American Veterinary Medical Association* 197:1292–1299.

Hearne, V. 1991. *Bandit.* New York: Harper Collins.

Heath, S., Kass, P., Beck, A., and L. Glickman. 2001. "Human and Pet-Related Risk Factors for Household Evacuation Failure During a Natural Disaster." *American Journal of Epidemiology* 153:659–665.

Herzog, H. 1993. "Human Morality and Animal Research." *American Scholar* 62:337–349.

Hickrod, L., and R. Schmitt. 1982. "A Naturalistic Study of Interaction and Frame: The Pet as 'Family Member'." *Urban Life* 11:55–77.

Irvine, L. 2004. *If You Tame Me: Understanding Our Connection with Animals.* Philadelphia: Temple University Press.

Jasper, J., and D. Nelkin. 1992. *The Animal Rights Crusade.* New York: Free Press.

Jordon, J. 1975. "An Ambivalent Relationship: Dog and Human in the Folk Culture of the Rural South." *Appalachian Journal* 2:68–77.

Kalof, L., and A. Fitzgerald. 2003. "Reading the Trophy: Exploring the Display of Dead Animals in Hunting Magazines." *Visual Studies* 18:112–122.

Katcher, A. 1989. "How Companion Animals Make Us Feel." In R. Hoage, ed., *Perceptions of Animals in American Culture,* 113–127. Washington, DC: Smithsonian Institution Press.

Kruse, C. 1999. "Gender, Views of Nature, and Support for Animal Rights." *Society & Animals* 7:179–198.

Lawrence, E. 1984. *Rodeo: An Anthropologist Looks at the Wild and the Tame.* Chicago: University of Chicago Press.

———. 1988. "Those Who Dislike Pets." *Anthrozoös* 1:147–148.

Malamud, R. 1998. *Reading Zoos*. New York: New York University Press.

Martineau, H. 2003 (1865). "Dogs: Unauthorized, Unclaimed, and Vagabond." *Sociological Origins* 3:7–9.

Marvin, G. 1988. *Bullfight*. Oxford: Basil Blackwell.

May, R. 2004. "Of Mice, Rats, and Men: Exploring the Role of Rodents in Constructing Masculinity Within a Group of Young African American Males." *Qualitative Sociology* 27:159–178.

Mead, G. H. 1962. *Mind, Self, and Society*. Chicago: University of Chicago Press.

Mead, G. H. 1964. *George Herbert Mead on Social Psychology*. Ed. Anselm Strauss. Chicago: University of Chicago Press.

Merton, R. 1976. *Sociological Ambivalence and Other Essays*. New York: Free Press.

Messent, P. 1983. "Social Facilitation of Contact with Other People by Pet Dogs." In A. Katcher and A. Beck, eds., *New Perspectives on Our Lives with Companion Animals*. Philadelphia: University of Pennsylvania Press.

Mills, C. W. 1940. "Situated Actions and Vocabularies of Motive." *American Sociological Review* 5:904–913.

Mitchell, R., and N. Thompson, eds. 1986. *Deception: Perspectives on Human and Nonhuman Deceit*. Albany: State University of New York Press.

Myers, E. 1998. *Children and Animals*. Boulder, CO: Westview Press.

Nelson, C., Kurtz, A., and G. Hacker. 1988. "Hurricane Evacuation Behavior: Lessons from Elena." *Public Affairs Reporter* 2:1–3.

Noske, B. 1990. "The Question of Anthropocentrism in Anthropology." *Focaal* 13:66–84.

Noske, B. 1997. *Beyond Boundaries: Humans and Animals*. Montreal: Black Rose Books.

Oakley, A. 1974. *The Sociology of Housework*. New York: Pantheon.

Perez, B. 1986. "Midwesterners' Perceptions of and Attitudes Towards Pets." *Central Issues in Anthropology* 6:13–24.

Phillips, M. 1993. "Savages, Drunks, and Lab Animals: The Researcher's Perception of Pain." *Society & Animals* 1(1):61–82.

Phillips, M. 1994. "Proper Names and the Social Construction of Biography: The Negative Case of Laboratory Animals." *Qualitative Sociology* 17:119–142.

Quackenbusch, J. 1985. "The Death of a Pet: How It Can Affect Owners." *Veterinary Clinics of North America: Small Animal Practice* 15:395–402.

Robins, D., Sanders, C., and S. Cahill. 1991. "Dogs and Their People: Pet-Facilitated Interaction in a Public Setting." *Journal of Contemporary Ethnography* 20:3–25.

Rowan, A. 1986. *Dog Aggression and the Pit Bull Terrier*. North Grafton, MA: Tufts School of Veterinary Medicine, Workshop Proceedings, July.

Sanders, C. 1990. "Excusing Tactics: Social Responses to the Public Misbehavior of Companion Animals." *Anthrozoös* 4:82–90.

Sanders, C. 1994. "Annoying Owners: Routine Interactions with Problematic Clients in a General Veterinary Practice." *Qualitative Sociology* 17:159–170.

Sanders, C. 1995. "Killing with Kindness: Veterinary Euthanasia and the Social Construction of Personhood." *Sociological Forum* 10:195–214.

Sanders, C. 1999. *Understanding Dogs: Living and Working with Canine Companions*. Philadelphia: Temple University Press.

Sanders, C. 2000. "The Impact of Guide Dogs on the Identity of People with Visual Impairments." *Anthrozoös* 13:131–139.

Sanders, C. 2003. "Actions Speak Louder than Words: Close Relationships between Humans and Nonhuman Animals." *Symbolic Interaction* 26:405–426.

Sanders, C. 2006. "'The Dog You Deserve': Ambivalence in the K-9 Officer/Patrol Dog Relationship." *Journal of Contemporary Ethnography* 35:1–25.

Scarce, R. 2000. *Fishy Business: Salmon, Biology, and the Social Construction of Nature*. Philadelphia: Temple University Press.

Selzer, M. 1972. *"Kike!" A Documentary History of Anti-Semitism in America*. New York: World Publishers.

Sontag, S. 1977. *On Photography*. New York: Farrar, Straus & Giroux.

Sorabji, R. 1993. *Animal Minds and Human Morals*. Ithaca, NY: Cornell University Press.

Sperling, S. 1988. *Animal Liberators*. Berkeley: University of California Press.

Stallones, L., Marx, M., Garrity, T., and T. Johnson. 1988. "Attachment to Companion Animals Among Older Pet Owners." *Anthrozoös* 2:118–124.

Stern, D. 1985. *The Interpersonal World of the Infant*. New York: Basic Books.

Stokes, R., and J. Hewitt. 1976. "Aligning Actions." *American Sociological Review* 41:838–849.

Strum, S. 1987. *Almost Human*. London: Elm Tree.

Tester, K. 1992. *Animals and Society*. New York: Routledge.

Toth, J. 1993. *The Mole People*. Chicago: Chicago Review Press.

Tuan, Y. F. 1984. *Dominance and Affection*. New Haven, CT: Yale University Press.

Twining, H., Arluke, A., and G. Patronek. 2000. "Managing the Stigma of Outlaw Breeds: The Case of Pit Bull Owners." *Society & Animals* 8:1–27.

Voith, V. 1985. "Attachment of People to Companion Animals." *The Veterinary Clinics of North America: Small Animal Practice* 15:289–296.

Weber, M. 1947. *The Theory of Social and Economic Organization*. New York: Free Press.

Weigert, A. 1991. *Mixed Emotions*. Albany: State University of New York Press.

Wilkie, R. 2005. "Sentient Commodities and Productive Paradoxes: The Ambiguous Nature of Human-Livestock Relations in Northeast Scotland." *Journal of Rural Studies* 21:213–230.

Williams, J. 1997. "The Inhumanity of the Animal People." *Harper's*, August, 60–67.

Wipper, A. 2000. "The Partnership: The Horse-Rider Relationship in Eventing." *Symbolic Interaction* 23:47–70.

Woodward, C. V. 1966. *The Strange Career of Jim Crow*. New York: Oxford University Press.

PART ONE

Thinking with Animals

Introduction

In an oft-quoted passage, the anthropologist Claude Levi-Strauss (1963, 89) observed that "animals are good to think." By this, Levi-Strauss meant that animals act as metaphors, as powerful cultural labels well-socialized members of a society use to understand, and share an understanding of, culturally significant ideas and experiences. Nonhuman animals, as central elements of Western language and lore, "stand-in" for, or clarify a way of thinking about, elements of human character (e.g., "dogged," "slippery as a snake"), appearance (e.g., "leonine," "foxy"), and behavior (e.g., "he wolfed down his dinner," "she watched him like a hawk").

In a very basic way, the use of the term animal in reference to humans and their behavior demonstrates the ambivalence that characterizes the contemporary Western orientation toward nonhuman animals. The label can be used as both a positive and negative designation. For example, in sport cultures, especially those like football or boxing in which controlled violence plays a central role, referring to an individual as "an animal" is laudatory. In this context, being a "real animal" means that the person demonstrates the aggressiveness that is valued as a means of achieving competitive success. Conversely, in other contexts being labeled an "animal" has a very different impact on one's social identity. In the occupational world of law enforcement, for example, those labeled as "animals" are dangerous and uncontrolled. Keeping "animals" (a designation typically connected to a person's racial or class characteristics) "in line" (that is, within the bounds of conventional norms) is the primary role of social control agents and institutions. In short, the basic term animal is used to think about people, their characters, their place in the society, their potential for valued or disvalued behavior, and other key elements of social definition.

Specific animals have been, and continue to be, used to represent groups of people, and the character and behavior they are defined as possessing and displaying (see the selection by Fine and Christoforides in this part). Often, this connection of specific animals (and their presumed "natural" characteristics) with human groups is a move in socially defining the group as a threat and mounting a "crusade" designed to eliminate or, at least, control this problematic group.

Here we need to understand the two basic ways in which sociologists think about social problems. Traditionally, sociologists have seen social problems as having objectively describable features, as presenting specific forms of social harm, and as having identifiable solutions (presuming, of course, that the character and cause[s] of the problem have been ascertained). This objectivist perspective is a somewhat more complicated version of the way most people tend to think about problems in society—there are things that are wrong, these things are harmful to individuals and the society at large, and people pretty much agree what these problems are and how to solve them.

More recently, sociologists have come to see social problems in a rather different way. This constructionist perspective rejects the idea that social problems have objectively identifiable "problematic" characteristics. Instead, constructionists stress that social problems are issues that come to be seen as threatening within the society and therefore come to be the focus of social concern and ameliorative action. The people who attempt to convince others about the social problem that concerns them are referred to as claims-makers. These central actors use the resources and contacts available to them to define the problem, describe its causes and social consequences, and identify a viable solution. Understandably, individuals with social power and status tend to be the most active and successful claims-makers and focus their claims on issues, groups, and activities they dislike or that threaten their interests. Obviously, the mass media is central to social problem construction. The dominant media are controlled by those in authority, and the linguistic and visual messages "media managers" put on the TV screen, in newspapers and magazines, and disseminate through other outlets define problems for the media audience (see Best 1989, Ibarra and Kitsuse 1993, Spector and Kitsuse 1987).

Defining the problem and marshaling resources to confront it proceed most rapidly—the claims-makers are most successful—when the process generates a strongly emotional public response. Constructionist analysts of social problems call this emotional response a moral panic and see the most effective mechanism for generating this reaction as involving the use of status politics. This rhetorical device involves symbolically connecting the defined social problem to a group that already is widely regarded as dangerous, immoral, dirty, or otherwise undesirable. While disvalued human groups have historically been connected to supposed problems, animal species have as well. The article by Fine and Christoforides in this part offers a striking example of how a group of animals have been used metaphorically to encourage the public to think about a particular social problem (see also Jerolmack 2007, May 2004, Scarce 2005).

Animals and animal-related activities also stand in for cultural and national groups and provide a way for both members of the culture and those outside it to focus their thinking about the group. The symbolic significance of the bullfight for Spanish and other Latin cultures, the fox hunt for members of the British upper classes (see Marvin's selection in this part), and the sacred cow in India are clear examples of the way that animals and animal practices represent social groups and the presumed characteristics of group members.

Yet another way in which members of human society "think with" animals is evident in the concern with how animals think and what they think about found within both academic and everyday social worlds. Renowned philosophers such as R. G. Frey (1980) and Jacques Derrida (2002) have speculated about whether the animal mind exists, what animal thought might consist of, and the ethical implications of mindedness in nonhuman animals. In "What Is It Like to Be a Bat?" one of the best-known philosophical discussions of animal subjectivity, Thomas Nagel (1981), after considerable meandering, comes to the conclusion that one would have to *be* a bat to know what it is like to be, and think like, a bat.

Academic interest in thinking with animals has even generated a subfield within the discipline of ethology (the study of animal social groups and interactions). Impelled significantly by the thinking and writing of Donald Griffin (e.g., 1984, 1992), cognitive ethology holds that neither instinct nor behaviorist assumptions provide adequate explanations for animal behavior. Instead, cognitive ethologists see animals as consciously aware of themselves and their material and social surroundings. Conscious thought and intentionality are most apparent when animals encounter prob-

lematic situations and respond with novel and adaptive behavior (see Allen and Bekoff 1997, Ristau 1991).

Thinking with animals is also of concern to people who share their everyday lives with nonhuman companions. Being able to achieve some degree of empathy with animals is an important foundation for effective and mutually satisfying human-animal interaction. Numerous popular dog training manuals (e.g., Fennell 2004, Fogle 1990, Ross and McKinney 1992) offer insight into how one may learn to think with a canine companion and thereby construct a cooperative relationship. One indication of the central significance of thinking with animal companions is seen in the routine situations in which caretakers both speak *to* and speak *for* their animals. In speaking *to* their animals (often employing the speech styles adults use when talking to young children), caretakers presume that animals have some understanding of the intended meaning—that the animal is able to think with his or her human associate. In speaking *for* animals, caretakers act on the assumption that their familiarity with their animals has provided them with the ability to understand and verbally interpret their animals' subjective (and uniquely individual) experiences (Arluke and Sanders 1996, 61–81).

In summary, thinking with animals refers to the ways in which animals are used as metaphorical resources to think about and communicate key elements of human social life. Animals are also used as reference points to position an understanding of other humans as both individuals and collectives. Finally, thinking with animals involves acknowledging and accessing their subjective experiences and, as one does in any viable social relationship, using that understanding to shape human-animal exchanges.

The first selection by Daston and Mitman provides an excellent introduction to the various ways in which nonhuman animals provide a metaphorical focus for human thinking. They focus much of this discussion by using the concept of anthropomorphism—the view that nonhuman animals think, feel, and respond as do humans. While this view is common and is used, as the authors point out, to sell products and communicate moral principles, in contemporary "rational" society, anthropomorphism is problematic. If animals are so like us, then eating their flesh, keeping them captive, making them perform, and—especially—using them in scientific experiments represent a grave injustice. Thinking *with* and *about* animals in this way is scientifically disreputable, a modern heresy. Further, thinking with animals leads to seeing them as individuals. Animals are understood as unique individuals with their own tastes, interests, personalities, and histories (see the selections by Irvine and Sanders in this volume). In sum, Daston and Mitman present animals as a special screen upon which we project our human thoughts, fantasies, desires, and fears.

The selection "Dirty Birds, Filthy Immigrants, and the English Sparrow War" was touched on in the preceding comments about the place of animals in the construction of social problems. Fine and Christoforides stress the metaphorical connection between the English sparrow and immigration that emerged in the United States following the Civil War. In the face of increased immigration from Europe and Asia, nativist interest groups used the sparrow to condemn that which was foreign, competed with natives, and of an immoral character. According to this politico-cultural construction, these avian invaders, like the human immigrants they represented, should be eliminated from the native (i.e., earlier immigrant) American community.

The next selection offers another discussion of the symbolic connecting of animals to disvalued human beings. Certain racial groups are thought of and referred to as "animals," and their animal-related practices are seen as demonstrating their marginality and disrepute. Elder, Wolch, and Emel stress that this "animalizing" of certain ethnic and racial groups acts to maintain the power and status interests of those groups involved in the activity. The human-animal divide is used to establish and solidify social hierarchy (cf., Arluke and Sanders, 1996, 167–186).

The final selection in this part deals with the foxhound and fox hunting as potent cultural symbols in Britain. The foxhound, like other domesticated animals, is seen as an object to be used by humans to achieve their own ends. The dog is culturally constructed in part to set the boundary between that which is "wild" and that which is "domestic." In Britain, according to Marvin, the foxhound is central to a cultural ritual through which individuals define themselves and appropriate social relationships are demonstrated.

References

Allen, C., and M. Bekoff. 1997. *Species of Mind*. Cambridge, MA: MIT Press.

Arluke, A., and C. Sanders. 1996. *Regarding Animals*. Philadelphia: Temple University Press.

Best, J. 1989. "Introduction: Typification and Social Problem Construction." In J. Best, ed., *Images of Issues,* xv–xxii. Hawthorne, NY: Aldine de Gruyter.

Derrida, J. 2002. "The Animal That Therefore I Am (More to Follow)." *Critical Inquiry* 28:369–418.

Fennell, J. 2004. *The Dog Listener*. New York: Harper Collins.

Fogle, B. 1990. *The Dog's Mind: Understanding Your Dog's Behavior*. New York: Howell.

Frey, R. G. 1980. *Interests and Rights: The Case Against Animals*. Oxford, UK: Oxford University Press.

Griffin, D. 1984. *Animal Thinking*. Cambridge, MA: Harvard University Press.

Griffin, D. 1992. *Animal Minds*. Chicago: University of Chicago Press.

Ibarra, P., and J. Kitsuse. 1993. "Vernacular Constituents of Moral Discourse: An Interactionist Proposal for the Study of Social Problems." In G. Miller and J. Holstein, eds., *Constructionist Controversies,* 21–54. Hawthorne, NY: Aldine de Gruyter.

Jerolmack, C. 2007. "Animal Practices, Ethnicity, and Community: The Turkish Pigeon Handlers of Berlin." *American Sociological Review* 72:874–894.

Levi-Strauss, C. 1963. *Totemism*. Boston: Beacon Press.

May, R. 2004. "Of Mice, Rats, and Men: Exploring the Role of Rodents in Constructing Masculinity Within a Group of Young African American Males." *Qualitative Sociology* 27(2):159–178.

Nagel, Thomas. 1981. "What Is It Like to Be a Bat?" In D. Hofstadter and D. Dennett, eds., *The Mind's Eye,* 392–403. New York: Bantam Books.

Ristau, C., ed. 1991. *Cognitive Ethology: The Minds of Other Animals*. Hillsdale, NJ: Lawrence Erlbaum.

Ross, J., and B. McKinney. 1992. *Dog Talk: Training Your Dog through a Canine Point of View*. New York: St. Martin's.

Scarce, R. 2005. "More than Mere Wolves at the Door: Reconstructing Community Amidst a Wildlife Controversy." In A. Herda-Rapp and T. Goedeke, eds. *Mad about Wildlife,* 123–146, Boston: Brill.

Spector, M., and J. Kitsuse. 1987. *Constructing Social Problems*. Hawthorne, NY: Aldine de Gruyter.

Lorraine Daston and Gregg Mitman

The How and Why of Thinking with Animals

The Irresistible Taboo

We are animals; we think with animals. What could be more natural? The children's section of every bookstore overflows with stories about animal heroes and villains; cartoons and animated feature films show the adventures of Bambi, Mickey Mouse, and the Road Runner to rapt audiences; countless pet owners are convinced that their dogs and cats understand them better than their spouses and children; television wildlife documentaries cast the lives of elephants and chimpanzees, parrots and lions, in terms of emotions and personalities that appeal to human viewers around the world. The reflexive assumption that animals are like us, despite obvious differences of form, food, and habitat, is not confined to popular culture. From Aristotle to Darwin down to the present, naturalists have credited bees with monarchies, ants with honesty, and dogs with tender consciences, all on the basis of firsthand observation. In many cultures, the fundamental moral and prudential lessons of human life are taught via myths about animals, such as Aesop's fables, which have been told and retold for millennia. Literature from many epochs and societies explores the psyche of animals, and humans never seem so indelibly human as in fiction that turns them into animals, as in the case of George Orwell's allegorical novel *Animal Farm*. The weirdest aliens dreamed up by sci-fi filmmakers resemble humans more than most animals, and yet it is animals, not aliens, who evoke an immediate, almost irresistible pulse of empathy: humans past and present, hither and yon, think they know how animals think, and they habitually use animals to help them do their own thinking about themselves.

This is the double meaning of the title of this book, *Thinking with Animals*: humans assume a community of thought and feeling between themselves and a surprisingly wide array of animals; they also recruit animals to symbolize, dramatize, and illuminate aspects of their own experience and fantasies. This book is about the how and why of thinking with animals in both of these senses and how both humans and animals are transformed by these relationships.

Until recently, the how and why of thinking with animals were rarely posed as questions; far more attention has been paid to whether it is good or bad to do so. Anthropomorphism is the word used to describe the belief that animals are essentially like humans, and it is usually applied as a term of reproach, both intellectual and moral. Originally, the word referred to the attribution of human form to gods, forbidden by several religions as blasphemous. Something of the religious taboo still clings to secular, modern instances of anthropomorphism, even if it is animals rather than divinities that are being humanized.

If thinking with animals has become a focus for reflection and debate, it is in part because there has been so much thinking (and rethinking) *about* animals in the past decade. Among scholars and scientists, the biology, ethics, sociology, economics, anthropology, geography, and hermeneutics of animals furnish the stuff of a growing number of studies and surveys. Among political activists, endangered species, laboratory animals, livestock, hunters' prey, and pets are the objects of vocal and occasionally violent protective campaigns. Among citizens at large, deliberations about what to wear and eat, the rights of pets and the responsibilities of their owners, and

5

the legitimacy of zoos, aquariums, wildlife parks, and other sites of animal captivity open up a new area of practical morality with potentially vast economic, social, and political consequences. Cultural critic Akira Mizuta Lippit suggests that animals are more present than ever in thought because they have never been less present in daily experience: "Modernity can be defined by the disappearance of wildlife from humanity's habitat and by the reappearance of the same in humanity's reflections on itself: in philosophy, psychoanalysis, and technological media such as the telephone, film, and radio."[1] Jennifer Ham and Matthew Senior take the more optimistic view that thinking with animals signals moments of historic cultural creativity: "To invent new languages and civilizations it was necessary to give animal voices to political, philosophical, and moral actors."[2] Yet anthropomorphism (and its converse, zoomorphism) remain matters of intellectual and ethical ambivalence: Why?

In the sciences, to impute human thoughts or emotions to electrons, genes, ants, or even other primates is to invite suspicions of sloppy thinking. Although a metaphor like the "selfish gene" might be tolerated in popularizations, to use the term literally is to be accused of making a category mistake. Genes (or radios or planets) are not the kind of things that can think or feel; to believe otherwise is considered a mark of childishness or feeble-mindedness. Since the early nineteenth century, historians, philosophers, and anthropologists have repeatedly linked the rise of modern science with the waning of anthropomorphic attitudes toward the natural world. For example, the beliefs that the planets and stars were celestial intelligences or that heavy objects fell because they were seeking their natural place—beliefs held by many European natural philosophers before the Scientific Revolution of the seventeenth century—were regarded as signs of a "primitive" mentality. Despite the fact that the alleged analogy between the psychological development of children and the intellectual development of whole cultures has been largely discredited, the view that anthropomorphism of any kind is incompatible with modern science lingers.

The theory of evolution makes it more difficult to draw a hard-and-fast line between humans and animals, since common descent and the gradual process of natural selection on random variation make it plausible to assume some continuity of traits, including psychological traits, among closely related species. But ethologists who study animal behavior, including that of primates with close phylogenetic links to humans, have long made it a principle not to infer humanlike mental states from humanlike behavior. Indeed, until the recent emergence of the field of cognitive ethology, many scientists in this field frowned upon any discussion of animal mental states. Their reasons were in part methodological (how can we know what animals are thinking, since they cannot talk to us?) and in part historical, a reaction against the sentimental animal stories cited so enthusiastically by earlier comparative psychologists. Few of these tales could be substantiated under laboratory conditions; moreover, the default assumption that other species thought and felt as humans did seemed lazy, a failure of scientific ingenuity to formulate and test alternative hypotheses. Hence not only in astronomy and physics but even in zoology, post-Darwin anthropomorphism became almost synonymous with anecdote and sloth and opposed to scientific rigor and care.

There is a moral as well an intellectual element to critiques of anthropomorphism. On this view, to imagine that animals think like humans or to cast animals in human roles is a form of self-centered narcissism: one looks outward to the world and sees only one's own reflection mirrored therein. Considered from a moral standpoint, anthropomorphism sometimes seems dangerously allied to anthropocentrism: humans project their own thoughts and feelings onto other animal species because they egotistically believe themselves to be the center of the universe. But anthropomorphism and anthropocentrism can just as easily tug in opposite directions: for example, the Judeo-Christian tradition that humans were the pinnacle of Creation also encouraged claims that humans, being endowed by

God with reason and immortal souls, were superior to and qualitatively different from animals. In this theological context, it made no sense to try to think with soulless animals. Even if anthropomorphism is decoupled from anthropocentrism, the former can still be criticized as arrogant and unimaginative. To assimilate the behavior of a herd of elephants to, say, that of a large, middle-class American family or to dress up a pet terrier in a tutu strikes these critics as a kind of species provincialism, an almost pathological failure to register the wondrous variety of the natural world—a provincialism comparable to that of those blinkered tourists who assume that the natives of the foreign countries they visit will have the same customs and speak the same language as at home.

In recent years, another moral dimension of anthropomorphism has been opened up by the debate over animal rights. Should animals be treated as moral persons, with rights like those accorded to human beings? If so, would animal rights imply that humans ought to embrace vegetarianism, stop wearing fur and leather clothing, and abandon experiments on animals that do not serve the animals' own interests, for the same reasons that cannibalism and instrumental experiments on humans should be rejected as ethically repugnant? Since many (though not all) of the arguments pro and contra in this debate hinge upon the degree of analogy between humans and other animal species, and more particularly on the analogy between thoughts and feelings, the ancient and almost universal practice of thinking with animals has taken on new significance. If this practice is invalid—a childish illusion or a self-centered projection, as critics of anthropomorphism have claimed—then the position of those who support animal rights—at least for species that allegedly suffer pain, remember the past and plan for the future, and/or register kindred feelings—is weakened. And if the practice is valid—if further research were to confirm key commonalities among human and animal psychologies—then the acceptance of animal rights on this basis might well drive a wedge between the two senses of

thinking with animals. That is, if humans were correct in their anthropomorphic assumption that, *grosso modo*, animals thought and felt as humans did, for that very reason humans would no longer be justified in using animals as stage props to act out certain ways of being human—no more than other humans may be used as a means to serve the ends of others.

The moral is not only central to debates over anthropomorphism, it is also at the core of epistemological and methodological debates in scholarship on animals and society. Can we ever really think *with* animals? The question raises important issues of representation and agency. Thinking with animals is not the same as thinking about them. Anthropological, historical, and literary analyses of animals in human culture have revealed much about changing human attitudes toward animals and the changing economic, political, and social relationships of human societies. But in what sense is the animal a participant, an actor in our analyses? Has the animal become, like that of the taxidermist's craft, little more than a human-sculpted object in which the animal's glass eye merely reflects our own projections? In thinking with animals, how might we capture the agency of another being that cannot speak to reveal the transformative effects its actions have, both literally and figuratively, upon humans? Emphasis on the "textual, metaphor animal," Jonathan Burt observes, risks reducing "the animal to a mere icon," placing "the animal outside history." The difficulty becomes how to "achieve a more integrated view of the effects of the presence of the animal and the power of its imagery in human history."[3]

This is the highly electrified field in which current discussions about thinking with animals take place. The stakes are high and are being played for openly in science, art, politics, and global commerce. More subliminally but no less powerfully, ways of thinking with animals affect collective forms of feeling and seeing. The widening of the circle of human empathy and sympathy to include seals and elephants, whales and wolves, has altered both the subjective experience of identification with others and also its objective expression, as measured by contributions to organizations like the World Wildlife Fund. The proliferation of animal images, accessible to viewers across boundaries of language and culture in global image banks and advertising campaigns, has recalibrated vision and attention: the anthropomorphized expressions of animals may now be viewed as more humanly intelligible than those of other humans. Throughout the world, pitched battles are being waged over wildlife management, livestock farming, scientific and medical experimentation on animals, the rights and responsibilities of pet owners, hunting, and forms of animal entertainment ranging from animated films to dolphin shows at aquariums. The outcome of all of them depends crucially not only on how we think *about* animals but whether, and above all how, we think *with* them.

Why Think with Animals?

Thinking with animals is useful. Animal images sell products and create moods; pets enhance the health and happiness of their owners; animal personalities move the public and politicians more effectively than wildlife statistics; editorial pressure is put on makers of wildlife films to "hook" audiences with a story of heroes and hope. Apparently people nowadays often find it easier to think with animals than to think with other people. Pet owners (especially dog owners) regularly profess themselves to be emotionally closer to their animal familiars than to friends and family and are further convinced that they and their pets understand one another's most intimate thoughts. Striking images of animals are in great demand by global advertisers because—in contrast to equally striking images of humans—age, race, class, and culture do not interfere with identification and the desire to acquire. In films, even films sold as documentaries, broadcasters like National Geographic International look for a "hero character" among the animals with whom viewers can identify. Environmental and conservation legislation sometimes pits the interests of humans against

those of animals: the trappers whose livelihood is at risk when seals can no longer be hunted or the families who stand to starve when antipoaching laws deny them access to animals in newly created wildlife preserves. Yet the spectacle of suffering animals increasingly sways voters more strongly than that of suffering humans. No wonder that anthropomorphism has been assiduously cultivated: money, love, and power are all to be had by thinking with animals.

There are other, harder-to-name yearnings that are also expressed by thinking with animals. Ancient Indian myth uses a parallel cast of animals to try out alternative plots and personalities. The monkeys who echo but also alter the human configurations of lovers, rivals, allies, and enemies in the *Ramayana* epic act as a kind of narrative thought experiment: What would happen to the story if this detail of character or action were changed? This rearrangement of the pieces of the story can be likened to dream work, according to Freud's account: the world of the monkeys turns into a projection of the human hero's unconscious, allowing him to act more freely there than in the conscious sphere of human society. The animal shadow plot opens up possibilities that no mere doubling by means of another human subplot could. The differences between the monkeys and the humans are as important as the similarities; otherwise, the animals could not serve as a kind of furry subjunctive case for the story, a "what would happen if" that ends up acting back on the indicative plot of the humans.

Thinking with animals can take the form of an intense yearning to transcend the confines of self and species, to understand from the inside or even to become an animal. This is a desire with a long history and that it was once directed as ardently to angels as it now is to animals. In certain historical and cultural contexts, the longing to think with animals becomes the opposite of the arrogant egotism decried by critics of anthropomorphism. Instead of projection of one's own way of thinking and feeling onto other minds, submersion of self in the genuinely other is fervently attempted—but never achieved. It is a virtuoso but doomed act of complete empathy. Ethologists who have devoted their lives to the study (and often the preservation) of elephants, gorillas, and other at-risk animal species develop deep identifications with their chosen subjects. Among scientists who investigate animal behavior, such feelings are not uncommon, and even those who disapprove of anthropomorphism in ethology in principle admit that in practice the arduous life of the observer in the wild would hardly be tolerable without some such emotional bond. It is a commonly remarked phenomenon among ethologists that the tendency to anthropomorphize the animals under study increases rather than decreases with more experience in the field. The yearning to understand what it would be like to be, say, an elephant or a cheetah scrambles the opposition between anthropomorphism and zoomorphism, that is, between humanizing animals and animalizing humans. This extreme form of thinking with animals is the impossible but irresistible desire to jump out of one's own skin, exchange one's brain, plunge into another way of being.

These longings for transcendence by taking thinking with animals to the limit often emerge in the context of field sciences like ethology, in which the researcher "goes native" in order to investigate animals in the wild. Laboratory studies of animals have usually stood opposed to anthropomorphizing tendencies: the proper scientific attitude is defined as cool, distanced, objective. The situation in the nineteenth-century laboratory sciences of physiology and biology was considerably more nuanced. Much depended on which species was on the vivisecting table. Frogs were turned into scientific instruments and generally excited as little empathy or sympathy as other lab machines did. In contrast, experiments on dogs and other domestic animals not only triggered protests by anticruelty leagues, but also forced experimenters to steel themselves manfully against their own outbursts of sympathy in the service of science. Opponents of animal experimentation worried about the brutalization of the scientists caused by such emotional repression as well as the treatment of the beasts at their

hands. Moreover, many if not most of the experiments were undertaken with the aim of understanding human biology and psychology better, so the analogy between humans and animals was a precondition for their validity. Hence, despite the official ban on anthropomorphism in science, thinking with animals permeated practice in the field and the lab. Both animal and human were transformed in the process. If nineteenth-century graphic methods morphed frogs into laboratory technologies, the participation of animals in experimental systems also altered the material, economic, and moral relationships of science. Similarly, while ethological studies have transformed elephants and orangutans into celebrities, the performative roles animals play in science has impacted the identity, careers, and practices of field biologists.

The advent of evolutionary theory, which posits phylogenetic continuities between humans and other animals, has made the ban on anthropomorphism difficult to sustain in principle as well as in practice in the life sciences. A more symmetric program of scientific inquiry into what animal and human cognitive capacities have in common would worry as much about committing the error of "anthropodenial" (underestimating commonalities) as "anthropomorphism" (overestimating them). Ingenious recent experiments test whether humans and chimpanzees think alike, and while the jury is still out, the matter can be decided empirically, albeit only on a case-by-case and species-by-species basis. Whether or not the scientific respectability of thinking with animals would survive comprehensive investigation is an open question, but the heuristic utility of anthropomorphism in generating hypotheses to test in the study of animal behavior is beyond question. The science of animal thinking makes constant, one is tempted to say necessary, use of thinking with animals.

How to Think with Animals

Thinking with animals is eminently useful, and that is no doubt partly why it is so pervasive. But to say the habit is pervasive is not the same thing as saying that it is permanent. There is good evidence of multiple and changing ways to go about thinking with animals, with new ones being invented to exploit the possibilities of new forms of experience and new media. Animals are not "morphed" into humans in an Aesopian fable or a medieval bestiary in the same way they are in the latest nature film released for television. What it means to think with animals varies with time, place, and medium.

In fables animals are humanized, one might even say hyperhumanized, by caricature: the fox is cunning, the lion is brave, the dog is loyal. Whereas the same stories told about humans might lose the moral in a clutter of individuating detail of the sort we are usually keen to know about other people, substituting animals as actors strips the characterizations down to prototypes. Animals simplify the narrative to a point that would be found flat or at least allegorical if the same tales were recounted about humans. We are still avid for animal stories, but photography, film, and a distinctly modern preoccupation with the individual have transformed the way they are told. Pet owners do not have a warm and trusting relationship with just any old dog or cat, no more than parents love a generic child: the mutual understanding is one between named individuals, and it presupposes idiosyncrasies (endearing or not) on both human and animal sides. Naturalists trying to protect elephant herds from hunting and culling have shifted from statistics and aerial photographs of animal aggregates to "pachyderm personalities": individual elephants, named rather than numbered, with biographies and photographs done in the style of high-fashion celebrity portraits. The latter way of presenting the elephants to legislators and citizens' groups was strategically more effective in winning converts to the conservation cause. But it was also the way in which the naturalists themselves had come to think about the animals they studied, despite the fact that their training had emphasized populations rather than personalities. Sarita Siegel makes a similar point about her film *The Disenchanted Forest*: National Geographic International may have had its own marketing reasons for wanting her to endow the orangutans with individual personalities, but Siegel acknowledges that this was also the way the naturalists who knew most about and cared most for the animals discussed them. In both scientific and popular contexts, thinking with animals is increasingly thinking with individual animals. That historical shift in the "morphos" of anthropomorphism, which can be readily traced to the late nineteenth century, has not only structured how we think with animals but how we act in relationship to them as well, fueling debates about the agency and moral standing of animals in human society.

It is also thinking about what it would be like to *be* that animal, as opposed to thinking about the structures and processes of animal cognition and emotion. The contrast roughly parallels that between an introspective approach to human thought, in which the psychologist turns inward and examines the contents of his or her own consciousness as data for understanding the workings of human consciousness, and the methods of the cognitive sciences, which attempt to model the mind with programs that could be executed by computers. The best-known example of the latter approach is artificial intelligence, which attempts to replicate what human intelligence can do (though not necessarily in the way that humans do it) with algorithms that can be executed by machines. In this case, it would make little sense to ask, What is it like to be a machine?—even if the robot or computer in question accurately mimicked human accomplishments. Only in certain fanciful science-fiction settings do we credit machines with a subjectivity that would warrant the question, What is it like to be one? There is no need, however, to have recourse to computer models in order to find examples of anthropomorphism practiced without appeal to subjectivities. Medieval angelologists tried to understand angelic thought and emotion anthropomorphically but not subjectively. Only in the nineteenth century did the problem of understanding other minds, including those of animals, come to be formulated as seeing the world from the perspective of another, experiencing its experiences. Although this is, historically and logically, only one way of thinking with animals (or with aliens), it has become the dominant mode.

Before either animal individuality or subjectivity can be imagined, an animal must be singled out as a promising prospect for anthropomorphism. We do not choose to think with any and all animals. There seems to be no simple explanation as to why some species are singled out as good to think with and others not. Phylogeny may be part of the answer, and domestication, another: chimps and dogs are prime candidates, amoebas and eels are not. Evolutionary biologists, such as Stephen Jay Gould, have also suggested that we identify with certain species or animal characters like Mickey Mouse that display neotenic features similar to those of humans. Disney animators knew well that the large eyes of Bambi would elicit an emotional response from audiences more akin to the affection displayed toward a human child than if they had drawn the deer's eyes to scale. Baby fur seals display similar neotenic features, but what about elephants? Why should they, or dolphins for that matter, become favored species? Doniger observes that although the attribution of language to animals in Indian myth humanizes them (and, conversely, the denial of language to humans animalizes them), there are very few anthropomorphic stories featuring parrots. There are strong evolutionary grounds for using chimpanzees for studies in comparative human-animal psychology, but a great deal of the research in this field has been conducted on dogs, starting with Darwin himself.

Once again, medium can make the message. Just as the studio-like portraits of individual elephants created a different relationship between them and humans than aerial photos had, the right photographic angle can spotlight a species in human imaginaries. Frogs became the "Job of physiology" because they inspired so little creature-ly spirit among Victorians, yet photographer Tim Flach's brilliant staging of a frog peering out from a leaf—or bats wrapped in their wings like opera cloaks—can unleash a floodtide of identification in viewers. The animals to be found in the Getty Images archives inhabit a technological environment of temperature-controlled rooms, enormous light fixtures, and digital image banks as complex as any scientific laboratory or slaughterhouse. Thinking with animals also entails thinking about technology. If the technologies of factories and farms and laboratories and zoos were the predominant modes through which animal-human relationships were mediated in the nineteenth century, the explosion of new scientific, communication, and manufacturing technologies in the twentieth and twenty-first centuries has created new avenues of relationships. Technology, Akira Lippit writes, "and more precisely the technological instruments and media of the [late nineteenth and early twentieth centuries] began to serve as virtual shelters for displaced animals."[4] How these technological environments have transformed the habitats and ecologies of animals and animal-human relationships remains relatively unexplored.

Performing Animals

Thinking with animals casts animals in performances. By this we do not just mean bears riding bicycles at the circus or thoroughbred horses showing off dressage or even cartoon dalmatians. But we do mean outward spectacle, a way of making something abstract, hidden, or conjectural visible and concrete. The frog "demonstrated" in the laboratory, the talking monkeys in myth, the orphaned orangutans on film, the poster elephant for a conservation campaign, even the chimpanzee following the gaze of a human around a barrier—each of these animals serves to reveal something that would have remained unconscious, unknown, or unarticulated. In each case, it is possible to imagine a nonperformative version of the revelation: a textbook explanation of reflex action, a literary gloss on the unconscious motives of the human actors, an impassioned plea for the preservation of orangutans and their habitats, a magazine article reporting observations on elephant behavior, an analysis of the cognitive and perceptual competences required to possess a theory of mind. These versions would be at least as informative and almost always more detailed and explicit than the performances. But something would be missing, the something that makes animals good to think with, in the sense that fingers are good to count with.

Animals are not just one symbol system out of many, one of the innumerable possibilities to externalize and dramatize what humans think. They are privileged, and they are performative. They do not just stand for something, as a word stands for a thing or a rhetorical trope figures something else; they do something. Even in cases of complete ventriloquism, in which thinking with animals is reduced to a blatant projection of human thoughts, feelings, and fantasies, there is some added value in the fact that the blank screen for these projections is an animal. To take an egregious example, dog breeders who pander to human tastes in cuteness by selecting pugs with faces so flattened that breathing is impeded are guilty of anthropomorphism and anthropocentrism bordering on cruelty; ditto the doting pug owners who encourage these breeding practices. Why do they do it? Why can the craving for flat-faced cuteness not be satisfied by dolls or cartoons? Why make live animals perform these fantasies? The answer seems to lie in the active reality of animals. Plants are beautiful, endlessly varied, and marvels of organic adaptation. Yet they radiate none of the magnetism animals do for humans. Even the most enthusiastic fancier of orchids or ferns rarely tries to think with them, in either sense of the phrase. As Aristotle observed, the distinctive mark of the animal is self-locomotion; they move themselves, with all of the roaming autonomy movement implies. Unlike dolls or robots or any other product of human skill, however ingenious, animals are not our marionettes, our automata (which originally meant "puppet" in Greek). They are symbols with a life of their own. We use them to perform our thoughts, feelings, and fantasies because, alone of all our myriad symbols, they can perform; they can do what is to be done. We may orchestrate their performance, but complete mastery is illusion. Eyes peer through the human mask to reveal another life, mysterious—like us or unlike us? Their animated gaze moves us to think.

Notes

1. Akira Mizuta Lippit, *Electric Animal: Toward a Rhetoric of Wildlife* (Minneapolis: University of Minnesota Press, 2000), 2–3.

2. Jenifer Ham and Matthew Senior, *Animal Acts: Configuring the Human in Western History* (New York: Routledge, 1997), 5.

3. Jonathan Burt, "The Illumination of the Animal Kingdom: The Role of Light and Electricity in Animal Representation," *Society & Animals* 9 (2001): 205.

4. Akira Mizuta Lippit, "… From Wild Technology to Electric Animal," in *Representing Animals,* ed. Nigel Rothfels (Bloomington: Indiana University Press, 2002), 125.

A R T I C L E 2

Gary Alan Fine and Lazaros Christoforides

Dirty Birds, Filthy Immigrants, and the English Sparrow War

The viewpoint of the Sparrow
Is arrogant and narrow,
He knows that he excels.
He is selfishly obsessed;
He would not give an ostrich best.
His children leave their shells
Puffed to their very marrows
With pride at being sparrows.

"The Sparrow" by Marie de la Welch
(1929, quoted by Summers-Smith 1963: 1)

Social problems appear in diverse sizes and shapes. Readers of popular journalism often express surprise at the topics that have passed as concerns in other eras and other places. People define all manner of frustrations as social problems, which in retrospect become curiosities. From a social constructionist perspective, the analysis of such problems exhibit strategic advantages over problems that we "know"—in our gut—to be real and pressing. Past problems permit us to examine the development and usage of asocial concern without passion, if occasionally with a smug and ironic detachment. Further, such problems, in not being "eternal," remind us of the historical grounding of troubles.

As the examination of social problems from a constructionist stance has uncovered, social problems are constructed rhetorically (Schneider 1985; Spector and Kitsuse 1977; Best 1989). Diverse techniques of problem construction have been emphasized, including the use of experts (credibility), problem magnification (salience),

and the depiction of dramatic victims (personification). In this analysis, we wish to examine another technique of framing a public concern: *metaphorical linkage.* By linkage we refer to the use of metaphor to connect an emerging social problem with another well-recognized problem. While on occasion the two problems are structurally quite similar (e.g., cocaine use and heroin use), linkage can occur when the problems are ostensibly very dissimilar. For example, the metaphor of addiction has expanded from a focus on hard drug use to "addiction" to soft drugs or cigarettes ("psychological addiction") or even "addiction" to sex or food—what used to be considered a personal lack of willpower. Tethering a novel or trivial problem to one with a longer lineage or greater gravitas is one means by which the more recent or less serious problem can gain status, allowing it to survive the competition of public discourse. In addition, the metaphorical connection can be used by proponents of the other problem to provide a dramatic image for their own concerns.

Sociologists have begun to examine their own writings as sources of metaphor, but all writing has a metaphorical element. A metaphor is a frame of vision, a perspective, by which objects or events are placed within a comprehensible meaning system. The core of metaphor is the analogy that A is like B in certain critical respects, and this makes the implicit claim that A should be treated as B.

To indicate the power of metaphor to shape the perception of social problems we rely on a curious, yet compelling, ornithological dispute from the late nineteenth century—what has come to be known as the "Great English Sparrow War." This moniker refers to the diffusion of English sparrows on the North American continent during the period 1850–1890, and to whether anything should be done to control this species. We argue that the framing of the "sparrow issue" is, in part, a function of the metaphorical way in which this ornithological dispute was linked to the problems that commentators perceived with the incorporation of immigrants from the Far East, and then Southern and Eastern Europe (the "New Immigration") in the period after the Civil War, while the nation was attempting to heal the wounds inflicted to the idea of the American community and reestablish a moral order. The nativism evident in the reaction to immigrant laborers, so dramatically expressed in the passage of the 1882 Exclusion Act and the responses to the 1886 Haymarket Riot, was equally evident in a biological nativism which turned its hostility to these birds who found American soil so much to their liking. The accepted nativist ideology of the period of the Sparrow War proved easily adaptable to the ornithological realm. Our claim is not that the proponents of attacks on sparrows cynically manipulated nativist rhetoric in order to inflame passions, but rather this set of nativist beliefs made sense in explaining the dangers of a foreign interloper to the community of American birds.

The Sparrow as Problem

All birds are not created equal—at least in the eyes of bird watchers. The house sparrow, formerly known as the English sparrow (*Passer domesticus*), is one such stigmatized bird. The English sparrow is technically neither English, nor a sparrow, but a European house finch or Weaver-bird. While outsiders may believe that ornithologists admire and respect all birds, this is not so. It would not be far off to describe the sparrow as "despised."

Henry Mayhew in his classic analysis of London poverty, *London Labour and the London Poor* (1861: 11) quotes one rat-catcher, who describes sparrows as "the rats of bird." It is alleged that in ancient Sumerian cuneiform writing, the sparrow was the symbol for "enemy." Contemporary scholarly authors describe sparrows as "pests"—a term that is nicely ambiguous in being simultaneously technical and moral. This view is shared by bird-watchers, whose "hatred of the English sparrow exceeded even [their] dislike of cats and squirrels." The sparrow is one of the few songbirds not protected by federal conservation legislation. Although, as we shall describe, the pinnacle of abuse toward the sparrow in the United States occurred in the late 1870s and 1880s, even today this Rodney Dangerfield of birds gets no respect. While the sparrow is defined as ugly, unpleasant to listen to, and contends with more privileged birds, its harm beyond that of being a nuisance has never been demonstrated in the writings of those who condemn it. The sparrow's role as a nuisance is for some a matter of debate, but at the very least the sparrow certainly did annoy many of the human beings who chose to write about its presence.

The English Sparrow in America

William Leon Dawson (1873–1928), a respected American birder, claimed, with hyperbole, that "without question the most deplorable event in the history of ornithology was the introduction of the English sparrow" (quoted in Kastner 1986: 45). Certainly it was among the most successful avian transplantations in history, as the house sparrow is found throughout the North American continent, and is one of the most numerous birds found in North America today.

It was not always so. The house sparrow was first brought to this country in the fall of 1850, when the Brooklyn Institute imported eight pairs from England. However, when they were released from their cages in the following spring, they didn't thrive. In 1852 and 1853, more sparrows were freed in Brooklyn, and these were fruitful and multiplied. It was believed that sparrows would be useful in controlling insect pests, especially the dropworm, the larva of the snow-white linden moth (*Ennomos subsignarius*). Originally they were imported with the intent to solve one problem and in the process were defined as causing another—a classic instance of the *chaining of social problems.*

However, as with so many seemingly successful answers, the latent "danger" embedded in the solution was not recognized for some time. Throughout the 1850s and 1860s, and into the 1870s, communities throughout the Eastern United States imported these birds to help stem the tide of caterpillars. City councils purchased the sparrows as pest killers, and their investment seemed justified because they multiplied so rapidly and did consume some caterpillars. During the period 1855–1870, the majority sentiment was that the importation of these birds benefitted the community.

In an 1874 article in the *American Naturalist*, Elliott Coues, a distinguished ornithologist and author of *Key to North American Birds*, openly attacked the English sparrow. This article began a bitter debate between the attackers of the birds (led by Coues) and their defenders (led by another prominent ornithologist, Thomas Mayo Brewer). Even before Brewer's death in 1880, the sparrow-haters had won the argument, perhaps in part because of their success in linking the sparrow to the "blight" of immigration. Ostensibly the objection to the sparrow was economic in that critics believed they ate more grain than insects, but apparently the effects of their destruction of human foodstuffs was marginal at best. As we shall describe, the attackers spent equal time and certainly more vigor attacking the sparrows' moral character and their threat to "native birds." It is significant that for over twenty years after the original introduction of the bird there was no substantial dispute about its value.

In the late 1870s, there were a stream of accounts attacking the house sparrow and several spirited defenses. By the early 1880s, the controversy was largely resolved as those hostile to the sparrow dominated the public arena, and

the sparrow was consensually recognized as an ornithological problem. The attention to the sparrow was capped with the publication in 1889 of a lengthy report from the U.S. Department of Agriculture on the economic effects of the sparrow on American agriculture, which was based on an extensive survey of five thousand people. This document concluded, "The English Sparrow is a curse of such virulence that it ought to be systematically attacked and destroyed" (Barrows 1889: 164). During the 1880s, at the same time as the debates about the new immigration and the problem of "foreigners" were common, state legislatures removed protections for the sparrows, instituted bounties for killing them, and even made it a misdemeanor to protect the birds. While anti-sparrow feelings certainly continued beyond the 1880s, the fury of the debate subsided, just as the degree of racial and ethnic conflict was not as high in the 1890s as in the previous decade. With the conflict over Chinese immigration and the "problem" of "foreign radicals," the late 1870s and 1880s represented one of the most active periods of the American nativist movement.

The Sparrow and the Immigrant

For an outsider, it is an odd experience to read articles and books written by birding enthusiasts, exhorting their compatriots to kill birds—in this case, sparrows—ruthlessly. The accounts from Barrows' official report details the numerous ingenious, if ultimately ineffective, ways that concerned citizens devised to kill sparrows. As clergyman Henry Van Dyke noted at the time: "The kingdom of ornithology is divided into two departments—real birds and English sparrows. English sparrows are not real birds, they are little beasts" (Van Dyke 1899: 57). Why were they so despised?

While sparrows certainly did eat fruit and grain, no evidence demonstrated that this consumption had any significant economic impact. Rather the hatred seems to stem from moral qualities attributed to the birds: (1) they were foreign "immigrants," (2) they attacked native ("American") birds, (3) their character (cleanliness, noise, sexual habits) was seen as disreputable, and (4) they needed to be controlled as a foreign enemy. These four basic themes, found again and again in the literature on the sparrow, bear remarkable similarity to the metaphors used in the debate over immigration from Europe and Asia. The two problems were framed in nearly identical ways. From these data it is evident that those who defined the sparrows as a social problem explicitly drew upon the images involved in attempts to close America's shores to immigration during this period. Further, both problems drew upon the same underlying issue—the nature and boundaries of the American community. Defending the boundaries of the American community "made sense" to both nativists and birding enthusiasts.

Sparrows as Immigrants

American ornithologists distinguish between native species and those that have been introduced or imported. The latter are known as "exotics" or "foreign" birds. The checklist of American birds, maintained by the American Ornithological Union (AOU), and the debates over which species should be included in this list, pay heed to the significance of nationalism in the birding world. For example, in discussions over whether to add English sparrows to the AOU's American bird checklist in 1884, the issue was framed in terms of whether the sparrow was a "naturalized resident in this country." At the time, it was decided that it was not.

In this light, it is not surprising that the most common designator of the house sparrow was that they were "foreign." Yet, the designation of the sparrow went beyond this rather neutral label. Again and again, they are referred to as "immigrants," and the fact that they are labelled "English" sparrows, rather than "house" sparrows (a different metaphorical designation, now more widely used) is a case in point. These birds were seen as alien and "un-American"—as "foreign vulgarians" (Coues, cited in Brodhead 1971:

429). While it might have been more apt metaphorically in terms of the debate on immigration to label them "Chinese Sparrows" or "Italian Sparrows," such a designation ran up against the reality that they were imported from England. Even the construction of social problems has obdurate boundaries set by reality of the situation.

However, the persecutors of the sparrows attempted to use all human immigrants as the point of comparison to measure—and denigrate—the sparrow. Their homes were referred to as "avian ghettoes." (Kastner 1986: 42). Ernest Thompson Seton, the early leader of the American Scouting movement, noting the habits of the sparrow, remarked that these birds behaved like Cockneys (Seton 1901:109). The *New York Nation* described them as "an imported nuisance beside which the hand-organ appears a benefaction" (1878: 84).

The sparrows were foreigners, their importation was largely the doing of foreigners, and they could only be loved by foreigners, who were nostalgic for their homes. Sparrows were out-of-place, un-American, and, as we shall see, anti-American. Significantly the metaphor went in both directions as human immigrants were referred to, using animal metaphors, as "swarms of foreigners" (e.g., *Public Opinion* 1887: 50) or as a "motley herd" (Panunzio 1927: 50). The metaphor that immigrants were "subhuman"— physically, morally, and in intelligence—was an important part of the public debate in this period.

Sparrows and Native Birds

Sparrows do more than come to live on our shores and in our cities, they harm decent Americans—American birds. Barrows after his exhaustive survey came to the conclusion that "no candid reader will ever again deny that the Sparrow molests our native birds, and in many cases drives them away from our gardens and parks . . . there seems, then, no possible escape from the conclusion that the Sparrow exercises an important and most harmful influence on our native birds" (Barrows 1889: 78–79, 95). He provides numerous anecdotes of the attacks of sparrows on birds as diverse as woodpeckers, pigeons, crows, hummingbirds, robins, and chickens. Of the 767 detailed reports received, only 42 were favorable to the sparrow; 725 spoke of attacks by the sparrow on native birds.

Some critics of the sparrow go further, and make it clear that their opposition is grounded in nativist political metaphors.

Gentry notes that native birds show, in contrast, "a friendly and neighborly feeling, which tolerates others within their territory. . . . The same good and kindly feeling would be shown towards the sparrow, were there a disposition to reciprocate it" (1878: 39). Elliott Coues makes the political issue more explicit:

> The introduction of these exotics clutters up ornithology in a way that a student of geographical distribution may deplore, and interferes decidedly with the "balance of power" among the native species. Whatever may be said to the contrary notwithstanding, these sparrows *do* molest, harass, drive off, and otherwise maltreat and forcibly eject and attempt to destroy various kinds of native birds, which are thereby deprived of certain inalienable rights to life, liberty and the pursuit of happiness. (Coues and Prentiss, 1877: 192–193)

This rhetoric parallels similar arguments in the late 19th century that *human* immigrants were taking jobs and housing from American workers, and, thus, depriving *them* of their political rights. When discussing the "peon problem" of Mexican immigrants settling in America border communities, C. M. Goethe, an associate of the nativist, Madison Grant, could use the English sparrow problem as an explicit analogy.

> The peon problem, biologically, is akin to the English sparrow problem. America's native birds are largely songsters, insect destroyers, weed-seed eaters. There was brought in a songless immigrant, the English sparrow, to destroy the so-called "measuring-worms" in New York City. . . . In a new favorable environment, it multiplied, like the peon, with startling

rapidity. . . . As they advance, they displace native songsters, weed-seed eaters. In our border cities, the old Type American similarly is being displaced with Mexican slum inhabitants. (Goethe 1930: 128)

Immigrants of all species are linked in the harm they do to society.

The Immoral Immigrant

The viciousness of the verbal (and too often physical) attacks on European and Asian immigrants is a well-known and sorrowful chapter of late nineteenth century social history, and needs no further discussion here. More relevant is the realization that these traits—filthiness, sexual immorality, dishonesty, laziness, mob violence, impudence, noisiness—that were said to characterize immigrants were also alleged to describe their avian cousins. Brodhead (1971: 432) notes in passing the similarity of nativist rhetoric to attacks on the sparrow, a fact he considers "merely coincidental" to the attempts at limiting immigration.

> [Sparrows] crowded the cities; they were filthy, homely, noisy, and lascivious. Only the worst elements of the indigenous population, the cowbirds, consorted with them, even the native "blacks" ("the crows") were superior to the "foreigners." The sparrows lived in jerry-built dewllings; their diet (which included horse manure and garbage) was disgusting. They were ungrateful to America, and they did not fulfill their obligations as "contract laborers" [i.e., to eat the caterpillars they were imported to devour]. They were either "too clannish" or "too gregarious." (Brodhead 1971: 432)

These were urban birds—"rowdy little *gamins*" (Coues and Prentiss 1877: 192). Sparrows were birds of the street, with all the connotations of such a label in Victorian society. With the impact of Darwinian evolutionary theory during this period, long-term consequences of these moral traits had even greater significance for the future of the community of birds than they might otherwise have had. The sparrows were defined as representing precisely what American society of that period feared, while the decorous, native birds stood for wholesome American citizens, who otherwise could live in harmony.

The personification of the sparrow perhaps reaches its pinnacle in a children's book, co-authored by Elliott Coues, aptly entitled *Citizen Bird*. In this volume, the authors speak of an avian community, with each species representing a type of public persona. Children are taught that sparrows are the archetypal bad citizens.

> They increased very fast and spread everywhere, quarrelling with and driving out the good citizens who belong to the regular Birdland guilds, taking their homes and making themselves nuisances. The Wise Men protested against bringing these Sparrows, but no one heeded their warning until it was too late. Now it is decided that these Sparrows are bad Citizens and criminals; so they are condemned by every one. . . . This disreputable tramp not only does no work for his taxes—he hates honest work, like all vagrants—but destroys the buds of trees and plants, devours our grain crops, and drives away the industrious native birds who are good Citizens; so the Wise Men, who have tried the Sparrow's case, say that he is a very bad bird, who ought to suffer the extreme penalty of the law. (Wright and Coues 1897: 204, 182)

While the preponderance of the rhetoric speaks to the sparrows' disreputable character, a few writers defend the bird's moral character and claim they have a rightful place in the American community, for instance the abolitionist minister, Henry Ward Beecher:

> Among themselves they have little spats, just enough to settle questions of precedence and give a relish of activity to life—but no more than occur in all well-regulated neighborhoods among human beings. (Beecher 1877: 103)

For Beecher, it is Coues who is the enemy of peaceful order, causing a "riot" against these domesticated birds, now threatened with "extermination." These birds should be praised, in the words of one respondent to Barrows' survey, "for their bravery in standing up to an unkind world where people hate them, boys stone them and

cats eat them" (Kastner 1986: 44). The social position of these birds is isomorphic with that the more despised immigrant population, and their claims for sympathy—for their involuntary importation and the labor that was their lot—are similar as well.

Dealing with the Menace

Human immigrants should have been grateful that they were not birds. Despite the violence targeted at them, they were never threatened with mass extermination in nineteenth century America. While occasionally a naive observer suggested shipping all sparrows home again, the more common reaction was to attempt to destroy large portions of the population—through poisoned grain, the destruction of sparrow eggs, gunfire, a bounty for dead sparrows, sales of sparrows for food, and the like.

By the 1880s, states were adopting legislation to deal with the sparrow problem. New York made it a misdemeanor to feed or shelter the sparrow, and Michigan paid a bounty of one cent per dead bird. The Barrows report suggested that all legislation protecting the sparrow be repealed; that the killing of the sparrow at all seasons of the year be made legal, including the destruction of its nests, eggs, and young; that it be made a misdemeanor to give the sparrow food or shelter, or to interfere with its destruction; that birds, such as the Great Northern Shrike, that preyed on sparrows be protected; that each town appoint an officer whose official role it is to destroy sparrows; and that it be made illegal to import the sparrow into new areas. Importation of sparrows had, in practice, already been closed off by the 1870s, and the goal now was to control the sparrow population still present. For the sparrows, there could be no melting pot, only a stew pot.

That these attempts at biological control were done to protect American birds is clear. However, the connection to racialist philosophy is made explicit in an article by the prominent architect Philip Johnson, allegedly a fascist sympathizer in the 1930s. Michael Sorkin, in detailing the anti-semitic and fascist beliefs of Johnson, notes that Johnson in calling for active eugenics and warning about the dangers of racial suicide, uses the example of the sparrow to justify the need for action.

> Human will is a part of the biological process. . . . Our will . . . interferes constantly in the world of the lower animals. When English sparrows threaten to drive out our songbirds, we shoot the sparrows, rather than letting nature and Darwin take their course. Thus the songbirds, thanks to our will, become the 'fittest' and survive. (Johnson, quoted in Sorkin 1988: 140)

While it would be extreme to claim that the antagonists of the sparrows were proto-fascists or crypto-racists, it is evident that their calls for action are grounded on a desire to purify the American environment, a desire that met the spirit of the age. They asserted that America was for Americans, and all Americans should be able to live at peace with each other. In the aftermath of the Civil War, many social problems were defined as originating outside the polity.

Social Problems and Metaphors

The way in which a social situation will be defined and responded to is, as has been well-noted, not inevitable. In order to understand what is happening, people must tame their world cognitively. Symbols are presented that help to frame the issue. To cope with a new trouble people must come to believe that what they must deal with is comparable to something they have faced in the past or something that they are currently facing. Social movements may use framing techniques to convince actors that they should respond to a trouble in an appropriate way (Gamson *et al.* 1982). The goal is to create a bundle of related meanings that place the circumstance in a preexisting category. In other words, the public debate is an attempt to persuade others of the validity of a proposed metaphor.

Perhaps because of the distance between sociology and poetry, the socio-political significance of metaphor has not been emphasized as much as it deserves in social problems theory. Connecting social problems metaphorically is particularly effective, as in the linkage between immigrants and sparrows, when a novel social problem is linked to a better recognized, more consensually validated problem. In a sense, the sparrow issue "piggy-backed" on the larger issue of how to protect the American community from the presence of outsiders.

While the Sparrow War never gained the social importance of the debate over immigration, within the world of gardeners, naturalists, and ornithologists it was a topic of great controversy. Sparrows became so controversial because it was so easy to borrow the "hot" metaphor of natives vs. foreigners to model the debate. Further, this was a metaphor that appeared to participants to "work," to explain the information about the sparrow with which they were confronted. In this debate the critics of the sparrow had the advantage of drawing from a richer, more metaphorically dense, and better accepted set of images. Yet, even the sparrows' supporters chose to accept the same metaphors in defending the sparrow.

While our focus has been on the way in which the sparrow controversy mirrored debates over immigration, it is clear that to a more modest extent, immigration foes could and did use the sparrow controversy and ecological niche arguments more generally to define why immigrants did not belong in the American polity. Both the birds and the immigrants were "out of place," and, thus, were dirty, bad, and morally suspect (Douglas 1966).

In general terms, being able to build public support for the interpretation of one problem by placing it on the shoulders of another helps gain a hearing in the competitive arena of public discourse. To the extent that this arena is a competitive one, some means of highlighting the importance of a claim is essential. While the importation of the sparrow was not the first instance of an ecological interloper, it was the first to receive significant public attention—as evidenced by reports in such elite organs as the *New York Times* and the *Atlantic*. The time was ripe to extend the idea of national character to non-human Americans: to see that America had a self-contained environment.

Ultimately, this suggests that the constructionist view of social problems should not only examine the creation of issues in isolation, but as part of a nexus of images, symbols, beliefs, and metaphors: a master problem. Each age has its central themes, and these themes transcend the way that they apply to a particular set of "facts." There is a symbolic construction of current events, not only in terms of narrow problems, but in terms of a more universal Weltanschauung—the same process that permits us to understand years or decades as having particular themes.

In the late 1870s–1880s the boundaries of the American community were under stress and being redrawn, through a radical transformation of the industrial economy, the influx of immigrants, the expansion of the frontier, and the effects of reconstruction (and its termination) in the southern states. In the 1980s we had become fearful of morally disreputable strangers who were already hidden in our midst, as our ideology of tolerance conflicted with our anxieties about heterogeneity. Those social circumstances that tapped these themes were the ones that emerged as challenges with which the society and its agents had to deal. Each age has these themes, and it challenges sociologists to think like literary critics to understand what these themes tell us about the age.

References

Barrows, Walter B. 1889. *The English Sparrow (Passer Domesticus) in North America*. Washington: Government Printing Office.

Beecher, Henry Ward. 1877. "Sparrows to the Rescue." *Christian Union*. August 8, p. 103.

Best, Joel, ed. 1989. *Images of Issues: Typifying Contemporary Social Problems*. New York: Aldine.

Brodhead, Michael J. 1971. "Elliott Coues and the Sparrow War." *New England Quarterly* 44 420–432.

Coues, Elliott. 1874. "English Sparrows. *"American Naturalist"* 8: 436.

Coues, Elliott, and D. Webster Prentiss. 1877. "Remarks on Birds of the District of Columbia." *Field and Forest* 2: 191–193.

Douglas, Mary. 1966. *Purity and Danger*. London: Penguin.

Gamson, William, Fireman, Bruce, and Steven Rytina. 1982. *Encounters with Unjust Authority*. Homewood, IL: Dorsey.

Gentry, Thomas G. 1878. *The House Sparrow at Home and Abroad*. Philadelphia: Claxton, Bemsen, and Haffelfinger.

Goethe, C. M. 1930. "Immigration from Mexico." pp. 122–130 in *The Alien in Our Midst*, edited by Madison Grant and Chas. Stewart Davison. New York: Galton.

Kastner, Joseph. 1986. *A World of Watchers*. San Francisco: Sierra Club Books.

Mayhew, Henry. 1861. *London Labour and the London Poor*. London: Griffin, Bohn, and Company.

Panunzio, Constantine. 1927. *Immigrants Crossroads*. New York: Macmillan.

Schneider, Joseph. 1985. "Social Problems: The Constructionist View." *Annual Review of Sociology* 11: 209–229.

Seton, Ernest Thompson. 1901. *Lives of the Hunted*. New York: Scribners.

Sorkin, Michael. 1988. "Where Was Philip?" *Spy* (October): 138–140.

Spector, Malcolm, and John Kitsuse. 1977. *Constructing Social Problems*. Menlo Park, CA: Cummings.

Van Dyke, Henry. 1899. *Fisherman's Luck*. New York: Scribners.

Wright, Mabel Osgood, and Elliott Coues. 1897. *Citizen Bird*. New York: Macmillan.

No author. 1878. No title. *The Nation* 24 (August 8), 84–85.

No author. 1887. "The Tide of Immigration." *Public Opinion*. May 14, p. 97–99.

Glen Elder, Jennifer Wolch, and Jody Emel

Race, Place, and the Human-Animal Divide

Introduction

Former Hollywood sex goddess and French animal rights activist Brigitte Bardot was reported to be considering self-imposed exile from her French homeland. Her reasons: the invasion of France by late-twentieth-century Moslem infidels with their ritualistic animal slaughter practices. Bardot stated that "from year to year we see mosques flourish across France, while our church bells fall silent." To further polarize her anti-immigrant stance, Bardot invoked the image of "tens of thousands of poor beasts whose throats are slit . . . with blades that are more or less sharpened by clumsy sacrificers who have to repeat their gesture several times, while kids splashed with blood bathe in this magma of terror, of blood spurting from badly-slit jugulars."[1] Despite its provocative images of idolatrous heathens, messy blood-letting, and animal terror, Bardot's high-camp performance was in fact unoriginal. Her role and lines were snatched from a long string of previous performers, including explorers, colonialists, slave holders, modern-day racists and xenophobes, and right-wing politicians. All of these characters have constructed racial difference by casting the Other as "savage" or uncivilized on the basis of their interactions with animals.

Visceral arguments about animals and race have in fact become increasingly common, particularly in Europe and the United States. Animals and their bodies appear to be one site of struggle over the protection of national identity and the production of cultural difference. Why are animals used (and so useful) in such sociopolitical

conflicts? In this chapter we attempt to address this question. Following a series of illustrative case studies about conflicts which involve animals and race in the United States, we argue that practices that bring harm to animals are being used to racialize immigrant groups. On the basis of post-colonial theories of racialization and the impacts of postmodern time-space compression in a globalizing economy, we suggest that this process of animal-linked racialization works to sustain power relations between dominant groups and subordinate immigrants, deny their legitimacy as citizen-subjects, and restrict the material benefits that derive from such status.

Animal practices are extraordinarily powerful as a basis for creating difference and hence racialization. This is because they serve as defining moments in the social construction of the human-animal divide. While universally understood in literal terms, the divide is a shifting metaphorical line built up on the basis of human-animal interaction patterns, ideas about hierarchies of living things (both human and nonhuman), and the symbolic roles played by specific animals in society. Certain sorts of animals (such as apes, pets, or revered species) become positioned on the human side of this metaphorical line, rendering some practices unacceptable. But other harmful practices are normalized, to reduce the guilt (or at least the ambivalence) associated with inflicting pain or death, and to justify them as defensible behaviors differentiated from the seemingly wanton violence observed in nonhuman nature.

Norms of legitimate animal practice are neither consistent nor universal. Instead, codes for harmful animal practices are heavily dependent on the immediate context of an event. Here, the critical dimensions of context include the animal species, human actor(s), rationale for and methods of harm, and site of action involved in the practice. And because animal practices emerge over long periods of time as part of highly variable cultural landscapes, place is also implicated in constructing the human-animal divide. When distinct, place-based animal practices are suddenly inserted into new locales by immigrants and are thus decontextualized, conflict erupts. Those newcomers who violate or transgress the many-layered cultural boundary between people and animals become branded as "savage," "primitive," or "uncivilized" and risk dehumanization, that is, being symbolically allocated to the far side of the human-animal divide.

Driven by anxiety over declining global hegemony, economic and social polarization, and growing population diversity that threatens the country's image as "white," dominant groups in the United States are waging an intense battle to maintain their positions of material and political power. Moreover, they seek to protect a socially constructed national identity built upon some particular (and typically reified) categories of people and places in part defined in contradistinction to others.[2] In this situation, racialization of those immigrants whose darker skin color feeds into entrenched racial ideologies, stereotypes, and discursive practices serves to demarcate the boundaries of national culture and belonging to place, and to exclude those who do not "fit." Conflicts over animal practices, rooted in deep-seated cultural beliefs and social norms, fuel ongoing efforts to racialize and devalue certain groups of immigrants. Animal practices have thus become tools of a cultural imperialism designed to delegitimize subjectivity and citizenship of immigrants under time-space conditions of postmodernity and social relations of postcoloniality.

Our readings of the links between race, place, and animals imply that violence done to animals and the pain inflicted on them are inevitably interpreted in culturally- and place-

specific ways. It is therefore both difficult and inappropriate to characterize one type of harm or death as more painful or humane than another. This categorically does not imply, however, that animal suffering, agony, and death are mere social constructs; *they are only too real.* Indeed, our ultimate purpose is to stimulate a profound rethinking of *all* "savage practices" toward animals as well as toward "othered" people. As our title suggests, we promote a "wild practice" (or *pratique sauvage*) in which heterogeneous others use their marginality as a position from which to pursue a radically open, anarchic, and inclusive politics.[3] We conclude by raising the possibility that a truly inclusive *pratique sauvage* could encompass animals, the ultimate other.

Postcolonial Animal Stories

We launch our arguments by telling a series of stories drawn from recent events in the United States. Unlike colonial animal stories such as *Babar,* in which the animals are representations of colonists and "natives," these postcolonial stories focus on the treatment of animals by subaltern groups and the ways these practices are used to devalue them. Their practices, interpreted as "out of place" by dominant groups, serve to position them at the very edge of humanity—to racialize and dehumanize them through a complicated set of associations that measure their distance from modernity and civilization and the ideals of white America.

The Rescue Dog

Late in 1995, a three-month-old German shepherd puppy was beaten to death in a residential neighborhood of Fresno, one of the fastest growing urban regions in California's vast Central Valley.[4] The puppy death created a public furor. Neighbors complained to local authorities, and the man responsible for the dog's death was taken into custody on felony charges of animal cruelty. Later these charges were reduced to misdemeanor cruelty, to which the defendant pleaded guilty. The man charged in the case was Chia Thai

Moua, a Hmong immigrant from Laos who had come to the United States in the 1970s. Moua was also what the press reports termed a "shaman." Curiously, his shaman's logic in turning to the puppy was precisely that of so many others who use dogs to serve people: he was trying to rescue another human (in this case, his wife). He explained that he had killed the dog in order to "appease an evil spirit" that had come to plague her in the form of diabetes. The sacrifice could drive out the spirit and effect a cure. According to Hmong beliefs, "a dog's night vision and keen sense of smell can track down more elusive evil spirits and barter for a sick person's lost soul." Other animals, such as chickens and pigs, are sacrificed first, but if the killing of such animals does not solve the problem, then, according to Moua, "If it is a serious case . . . I have no other choice" but to "resort" to a dog. Moua stated that each year he performs a special ceremony to release the souls of all the animals who have helped him, so that they can be reborn. Thus, according to Moua, Hmong people from the highlands of Laos "are not cruel to animals. . . . We love them. . . . Everything I kill will be reborn again."

Moua's reliance on the Hmong conception of the human-animal border and the appropriate uses for certain animals puts him at odds with mainstream American ideas on the subject. He killed a dog. His reasons for doing so had no resonance or legitimacy for members of the dominant culture, who only sanction a limited number of contexts for dog killing. Dogs can be "laboratory workers" and "give" their lives to science, or they can be "entertainment workers" and be legitimately killed when no longer "employable"—witness the large numbers of "surplus" racing greyhound dogs that are killed each year. (Note that some forms of entertainment such as dog fighting, in which the *purpose* of the event, rather than the *result*, is dog injury and death, are strictly illegal.) But neither canine "lab workers" nor "entertainment workers" can be pets: dogs are usually purpose-bred for both the laboratory and the track.

Because Moua killed the puppy in his home, the dog was automatically a pet (and a pet of a revered breed at that). People are expected to dote on pet puppies in their homes, lavishing on them toys, tidbits, and attention. Barring unfortunate accidents, humans are not supposed to kill pets, except for veterinarians or euthanasia technicians in an animal shelter. Moua was neither. Worse, instead of using medicalized instruments such as the scalpel or syringe, to be wielded in the name of science or "kindness," Moua used a method (bludgeoning) widely seen as "inhuman"— a gross act of physical force that suggests a deeply disturbing animality.

An insightful head investigator for Fresno's Humane Society claimed that he could "count on my hand the actual cases [of Hmong dog sacrifices] I know about. . . . A lot of the false complaining is racism, pure and simple." Nonetheless, the publicity around Moua's deed and arrest did nothing to resolve ethnic tensions between the Anglo population of Fresno and the sizable Hmong population, which continue to fester.

The Bowser Bag

Two Long Beach men were charged with cruelty to animals for allegedly killing a German shepherd puppy and eating the dog for dinner on a March evening in 1989. A Los Angeles area judge ruled that there was no law against eating dogs, and that the animal had not been killed in an inhumane fashion. The charges were therefore dropped.

The case did not die, however. Rather, it spurred the introduction of a law, signed by then-Governor George Deukmejian, making pet-eating a criminal misdemeanor, punishable by a six-month jail term and a $1000 fine. Pets are defined in this statute as any animal commonly kept as a pet. Killing and eating wildlife, poultry, livestock, fish, or shellfish remain legal since these sorts of creatures fall beyond accepted definitions of "pet."[5]

But all this is beside the point, which is that Americans eat hot dogs, not dogs. In fact, given the status of most pet dogs and cats as quasi-human members of the family, eating a dog or cat is much too close to cannibalism for comfort. Indeed, the puppy involved was killed in an apartment complex, at home, it was all in the family. But the two men above were not "American," they were refugees from Cambodia. Trying to minimize the backlash against his community, the head of the Cambodia Association of America claimed that "Cambodians don't eat dogs," but it is widely known that many people from various parts of Asia do. (Isn't this how chow-dogs got their name?) And some Asians eat cats as well; civet cats, for example, are eaten in many parts of China and Southeast Asia. But in the Asian context, dogs and cats are "speciality" meats, considered "delicacy" foods. While most people see nothing wrong with eating many animals for food (including baby animals) and even taboo animals under conditions of duress, killing a cute helpless puppy for a luxury meal is another story—an act guided by self-indulgence, not the hand of necessity.

As initially drafted, the pet-protection bill only covered cats and dogs. Protests by Asian civic organizations led to an extension of the killing ban to all animals "commonly kept as pets." Curiously, however, the law still disregards pet turtles, rabbits, and pigeons, which are commonly eaten by Anglos. As Vietnamese-born editorial writer Andrew Lam claimed, the legislation implied that "[t]he yellow horde is at it again, that the eating habits of South East Asians, specifically the Vietnamese, are out of control" while "[i]t remains chic in a French restaurant to eat squab, as it is an accepted ritual for American fraternity boys to swallow live goldfish. And rabbit is nice in red wine."[6]

The Blood of the Lamb

In April 1987, a church practicing Santeria announced plans to open a house of worship in Hialeah, Florida. This announcement, along with a spate of angry calls from residents reacting to "whole piles of animals, stinking and with flies" that had been left behind following a sacrifice, prompted the Hialeah City Council to hold an emergency meeting in June. At that time, the council adopted a resolution noting that the Santeria religious group was potentially threatening public morals, peace, and safety, and passed an ordinance extending Florida's animal cruelty laws to cover ritual sacrifice, thus imposing criminal sanctions on the activity. The attorney general of Florida also expressed an opinion that religious animal sacrifice was not a "necessary" killing and so it was prohibited by state law. A few months later, the council adopted an ordinance that went further, prohibiting the possession, sacrifice, or slaughter of an animal with the intent to use such animal for food purposes. The prohibition applied, however, only if the animal was killed in any type of *ritual* regardless of whether the animal was in fact consumed for food. This left as legal the killing of animals in properly zoned and licensed establishments.[7]

The Hialeah ordinance was followed by bans in other cities. Los Angeles, for example, became the first city in the nation to outlaw ritual sacrifice (termed "torture-killings" in one headline) under any circumstances; and San Francisco followed with a ban of its own, amid news reports about an estimated one thousand cases of ritual slaughter, "disemboweled chickens" and "decapitated native songbirds" left as evidence. In San Francisco, where Santeria "high priest" Pete Rivera claimed that only high priests extensively trained in ritual sacrifice techniques were allowed to kill four-legged animals and that "[t]he gringo doesn't understand our religion," the ban created a furor and prompted the city council to allow sacrifices if the resulting meat was to be used primarily for purposes of consumption.

Ernesto Pichardo, founder and priest of Hialeah's Santeria church, located on a former used-car lot, took the city to court. In the face of protests by animal rights and humane society groups (as well as local Catholic and Baptist clergy), Pichardo argued that the city had violated the church's rights under the free exercise of religion clause of the Constitution's First Amendment. Santeria sacrifices were integral to key Santeria religious ceremonies (birth, death, marriage events) and were used to intervene with *orishas* or minor gods that are believed to have powers to help people with certain kinds of problems. An action for declaratory, injunctive, and monetary relief was filed in the U.S. District Court, which ruled for the city on the grounds that the jurisdiction had a right to prevent health risks and emotional injury to children, protect animals from cruel and unnecessary killing, and restrict the slaughter of animals to areas zoned for slaughterhouses. The U.S. Supreme Court, however, thought otherwise and on 11 June 1993 ruled that the city had not demonstrated a "compelling interest" in implementing the ban and had unfairly targeted a religious practice, sacrifice, used only by Santeros. The Court thus declared the ordinance void under the First Amendment.

This ruling was hardly surprising. To do otherwise could easily have opened up a Pandora's box for the Court and indeed the nation, since a finding of cruelty, for example, would have threatened such long-standing religious practices as Kosher slaughter, and could even have raised serious questions about the "humaneness" of conventional killing techniques practiced on the slaughterhouse floor. The visceral reaction at the local level thus necessarily faded away in the weighing of such national interests. The question remains, however, why the local response was so swift and so vehement.

The animals killed in Santeria practice include a wide range of domestic animals, including lambs, goats, and chickens, but also turtles, snakes, and (according to some reports) dogs. Most of these animals are eaten, but it is also traditional to leave remains at a major crossroads, leading one observer to note that it is "not uncommon to find decapitated chickens at the intersection of 98th Street and Broadway [in New York City]." Such practices thus violate the human-animal border in the dominant culture

(where the killing of animals occurs on a vast scale but is almost completely hidden from view, and offal is "processed" rather than left on the roadway to stink in the sun). But more critical is the perception that the people doing the killing and their reasons for killing are deeply suspect, associated with some of the most threatening populations and illegitimate purposes.

These suspicions come through in most media and even scholarly accounts, in which the Santeria religion is described as a fusion of traditional African religious elements (mostly Yoruba) with parts of Roman Catholicism (the *orishas* are named after the Catholic saints or *santos*). Such descriptions imply that Santeria was "imported" from Africa, and more recently the Caribbean, and thus is not indigenous to the United States. But both the history and the geography of these accounts are misleading. Emerging during America's slave-trade past, Santeria is in fact as "American" as Mormonism and less of an "import" than Catholicism or Presbyterianism, neither of which have adapted as much as Santeria to the cultural context within which they are practiced. The religion is also typically referred to as a "sect" or "cult" rather than a religion, despite an estimated 75–100 million practicing Santeros worldwide; Santeria is the majority religion in Brazil, Haiti, and Cuba. In the United States, Santeria has spread rapidly among Latinos from Central and South America and among African Americans. Although the religion is not a form of *voodun*, it has certain common historical origins, thus conjuring up images of Satanism, demonism, and (literally) black magic. The frequent addition of the adjective "ritualistic" to descriptions also implies that Santeria is somehow primitive and simultaneously that "modern" religions, such as Catholicism, are *not* ritualistic. In addition, the African roots of Santeria link the religion in many minds to adjectives such as barbaric, backward, primitive, and irrational. All of these aspects of Santeria practice, as described or exaggerated in media accounts, deny it the legitimacy of a "world religion," thus throwing its rituals into question and also reducing the status of Santeria priests in comparison with other clergy.

To celebrate the Supreme Court victory, Hialeah-based Santeria priest Rigoberto Zamora held a public sacrifice. The local newspaper described the event, at which Zamora "poked a steak knife" into the throats of goats and rams, then "sawed through vocal cords and arteries until blood spurted," and finally took small birds and "twisted off their heads." How uncivilized, especially compared to battery-caged chickens, crated veal, factory-farmed hogs, and BST-laced milk from downer cows.

Postcolonial Racialization and the Human-Animal Divide

Our cases illustrate how, in the contemporary United States, racialization of others is fostered by postcolonial interpretations of the human-animal boundary or divide, under time-space conditions of postmodernity. Many forms of racialization have, in fact, long relied upon a discourse about human-animal boundaries, namely the dichotomous division of sentient beings into categories of "human" and "animal." The most basic and durable criteria used to fix the boundary have involved differences in *kind*. But although humans and animals do manifestly differ (a point that is universally recognized), the interspecific divide is not solely a behavioral or biologically determined distinction. Rather, like so many other common categorizations (such as race or ethnicity), it is also a place-specific social construction subject to renegotiation over time. Moreover, the reasons for assigning one human group to one side of the boundary or another may also change between times and places.

From its earliest beginnings, Christian theology identified the soul as the defining feature of humanity. Even with the advent of Enlightenment ideas about animals, such as Descartes' identification of animals with machines, the boundary rested on the presence/absence of souls. With the rise of a more secular Western science, the key differences in kind became biological and behavioral characteristics; criteria such as language or intentionality were employed

to maintain the borders.[8] But Darwin's theory of evolution cast a fundamentally new light on the issue. The boundary distinguishing humans and animals was reinterpreted in the West to involve not only differences in kind but also differences *in progress* along an evolutionary path. This path began with "lower" life forms, proceeded through intermediate stages inhabited by "higher" animals, and reached its pinnacle with (white) "man."

This scientific, evolutionary recasting fit squarely within an interconnected set of understandings about the human geography of the colonial world, in which the "discovery" of "races" raised complex questions of human taxonomy. Categorizing exotic-looking peoples from distant lands as lower on the evolutionary scale and thus closer to animals echoed and relied upon a myriad of similar divisions used to separate some humans from others: primitive versus modern, civilized versus savage, heathen versus Christian, cannibal versus noncannibal. In turn, the human-animal division construed as a continuum of *both* bodily form/function and temporal stage in evolutionary progress was used to reinforce these intrahuman categorizations and interpret them in temporal, evolutionary terms rather than in solely social or geographic ways.

In postcolonial, Western capitalist space, the idea of a human-animal divide as reflective of both differences in kind and in evolutionary progress has retained its power to produce and maintain racial and other forms of cultural difference. The dominant uses of human-animal distinctions during the colonial epoch relied upon representations of similarity to animals to dehumanize and thus racialize particular cultural groups. Contemporary arguments, in contrast, are primarily characterized by a focus on animal practices employed by subdominant cultural groups as cruel, savage, criminal, and *inhuman*: the literal blood-letting of animals, the slicing up of their bodies. But although the precise terms of reference have shifted over time, the postcolonial moment is one that continues to use putative human-animal boundaries to inscribe totems of difference (savage, barbaric, heathen, or archaic versus civilized, Christian, or modern).

We will say more about each of these uses of the human-animal boundary in the racialization process in the sections of the article that follow. Here, we want to understand why, in postcolonial times, animal practices have become a key aspect of the human-animal boundary used to racialize and produce difference. We locate our explanation in radically changing time-space relations that epitomize postmodernity. Just as in the colonial period, when the dimensionality of the world as perceived through Western eyes suddenly expanded in the wake of European exploration and "discovery," time-space relationships have altered dramatically during the course of the twentieth century, particularly over the last two decades. Indeed, a compression of time-space, or shrinking of the world's time-space fabric, is a hallmark of postmodernity. This compression creates what Fredric Jameson terms *"postmodern hyperspace,"*[9] which brings visible difference "home" instead of restricting it to a distant, exotic colonial space. Those seeking to produce racial difference are no longer separated by vast continents and long journeys from groups they wish to dehumanize. Instead, the targets live next door (figuratively and, not uncommonly, literally), inviting an inspection of their unsettling otherness. This implies that fanciful representations of people-as-beasts are less potent than images of people-acting-beastly toward animals. Since older evolutionary interpretations of racial difference persist within postmodern culture, not only immigrants but native-born people of color are sometimes constructed by their animal practices.

Animals and the Body Politic

Racialization is far from a monolithic or static process but instead is situational and shaped by racial ideologies and stereotypes.[10] Exactly how and why does this postcolonial, postmodern form of racialization around animals occur? We argue that in the present instance, animal bodies have become one site of political struggle over the construction of cultural difference and maintenance of American white supremacy. By scrutinizing and interpreting subaltern practices on animal bodies (or simply "animal practices") through their own lenses, dominant groups in the United States simultaneously construct immigrant others as uncivilized, irrational, or beastly, and their own actions as civilized, rational, and humane.

In general, animal bodies can be used to racialize, dehumanize, and maintain power relations in three key ways. First, animals serve as absent referents or models for human behavior.[11] Being treated "like an animal" is typically interpreted as a degrading and dehumanizing experience, and such treatment is therefore a powerful tool for subjugation of others. The specific "treatments" in mind here are not the many loving forms of human-animal interaction, but rather involve abuse or violation, physical and/or emotional. The key aspect of such violent treatment that makes it dehumanizing, however, is not just the abuse or violation: it is the fact that victims are *objectified* and used like animals, who are commonly objectified and used without second thought.[12] Abusive treatment of slaves by masters, for example, was modeled on how people use animals without consideration of their subjectivity.[13]

Second, people are dehumanized by virtue of imputed similarities in behavior or bodily features and/or associations with the animal world in general or certain animals in particular. (Human identities also derive meaning and an enormous range of positive values from imputed similarities, of course, such as bravery, speed, and cunning.) Imputations are often made on the basis of associational representations of both humans and the animals to which they are being linked: colonial images of Africans as "ape-people" come readily to mind. Similarities can also be drawn on the basis of theories of human-animal continuity. For example, in Western thought, women's bodies have been deemed "like" animals due to their biological role, seemingly uncontrolled passions, and perceived irrationality.

Using this logic turned on its head, queer bodies are deemed transgressive because they engage in "unnatural" behavior; animals are (supposedly) all heterosexual, thus queerness constitutes a perversion of nature. Turning to race, as we have argued, people of color (especially Africans) were historically situated by Westerners as lower on the "chain of being" and thus in closer evolutionary and behavioral proximity to nonhuman animals (especially the great apes). Colored bodies were thus both more primitive and uncivilized, and closer to animals and their unbridled biological urges and passions. Such associations persist and are often made explicit; in contemporary pornography, for example, it is most often people of color depicted in sex scenes involving intercourse with animals.

The third and least explored manner in which animals play a role in the social construction of racial difference, and the one which we argue characterizes the postcolonial, postmodern moment, involves specific human practices on animal bodies. Such practices have been used to construct other groups as well: in Medieval Europe, for instance, women who harbored feline "familiars" were often regarded as witches. And taboos about which animal bodies to eat (and which body parts) are common amongst contemporary peoples, with the result that outsider groups not observing such taboos may be viewed with disgust and disdain. The many other sorts of practices on animal bodies—such as those described in our animal stories—that can constitute powerful weapons for the devaluation and dehumanization of people of color have been less remarked. We turn now to an analysis of why certain animal bodies and body practices are taken up in this fashion.

Animal Practices and Dehumanization

What makes one animal practice acceptable and another a potent symbol of savagery that can be used to dehumanize those who engage in it? We have argued that every human group defines the boundary between humans and other animals in part on the basis of their treatment of animal bodies or animal practices. Specific forms of human-animal interactions, legitimized and rationalized over time, are part and parcel of the repertoire of "civilized" behavior that defines the human-animal divide. Those who do not stay within this field fall over the human-animal boundary or at least into the netherworld of "savagery"; if the practices are too far over the line, they can be interpreted as cannibalism, the ultimate act of inhumanity. Policing the human-animal boundary through the regulation of animal practices is necessary to maintain identity as humans and, not coincidentally, to sustain the legitimacy of animal practices of dominant groups.

It is widely recognized that in most societies certain types of animal practices are taboo. Taboo practices involve sexual relations with animals (bestiality is rarely sanctioned, although sometimes tolerated). Beyond bestiality, the killing and eating of the "wrong" species or categories of animals (especially totemic species or those seen as too similar to humans) can also be forbidden. For example, the consumption of apes is widely interpreted as tantamount to cannibalism, since simians occupy an ambiguous position along the human-animal boundary. They are not fully inside the human camp: one would not marry King Kong or have sex with Bonzo (even at bedtime!). But apes are seen almost literally as "inferior" humans because of their physiological similarity to humans. Eating them is thus strictly taboo. Similarly, in societies where pets are perceived to be members of the family and household, they can also come to occupy ambiguous or intermediate positions. Eating them, like the Cambodian men in our story did, becomes out of the question for civilized people.

Despite the importance of animal species or category in determining which animal practices fall beyond the bounds of humanity in any given society, practices are rarely considered (un)acceptable on the basis of species alone. Species is only one part of the immediate context through which animal practices are interpreted. Often, it is only this immediate context that separates "civilized" from "savage," thus revealing both the presence of unspoken criteria for judging animal practices and the extreme cultural relativity of these judgments.

Specifically (as our animal stories illustrated), there are at least four other key elements of context which define the human-animal borderline. One is reason or rationale for harm. Was a specific harmful practice necessary for survival or to minimize human or animal pain/death? Few humans raise objections to killing and eating taboo animals if the alternative is starvation; the most commonly stated reason for killing laboratory animals (even "pet" species such as dogs and cats) is to prevent suffering or death; and "euthanasia" of companion animals is justified as a way to reduce animal suffering. When the rationale for harm is seen as unnecessary or irrational, or the results are defined as damaging, however, practices may be condemned.

Another important aspect of context is the social location of the perpetrator: was the person(s) involved in the harmful practice "appropriate"? For example, if an animal was killed for purposes of human consumption, did a butcher or slaughterhouse worker perform the act? Or if a companion animal was killed, was a veterinarian presiding? As our cases illustrate, problems arise when the human actor does not have the role and/or training deemed necessary by the dominant group to legitimize the act. Religious functionaries, for example, are no longer normally linked with animal sacrifices: Christian clergy are trained to deal in immortal souls, not corporeal affairs; and rabbis only serve to ensure that kosher methods of killing are used. Thus, as religious specialists, neither Hmong shamans or Santeria priests are seen to have the credentials to sacrifice food animals, much less companion animals. Similarly, where the actual killing of animals has become industrialized, professionalized, and removed from the course of everyday life, lay people (such as the Cambodian men charged with pet eating at home) have no legitimacy as animal killers.

A further contextual element revolves around the means or methods of harm: how was the harm inflicted? What techniques or tools were utilized, and did they fall within the range of local convention? Or were methods seen as archaic, barbaric, or brutally employed? A puppy can legitimately lose her head in a laboratory decapitator, but bludgeoning her to death is deemed too brutal. Similarly, bolt-guns are acceptable for dispatching a lamb led to (professional) slaughter, but the kitchen knife is no longer seen as civilized or humane. Certainly "twisting off the heads" of small birds is completely beyond the pale.

Lastly, the site of harm is perhaps the most crucial aspect of context in determining the legitimacy of an animal practice. Was an animal killed in a slaughterhouse or in the backyard barbeque pit next to the pool? Were rats killed in the lab or were they disemboweled in the living room? The issue of site has two dimensions. One is whether the harmful action is carried out in purpose-built quarters or reserved places (slaughterhouses, labs, shelters, forests during hunting season) or "out of site" in unspecialized spaces more typically used for other purposes or banned for the animal practice in question (residential areas, posted lands). A second site-related issue is whether the action occurs "out of sight" in abattoirs or factory farms banished from the city or in labs behind locked doors, or in highly visible places of everyday life such as homes, street corners, or church. Although in traditional societies the killing and death of individual animals was (and in many places remains) a quotidian experience, keeping mass, mechanized, and industrialized violence toward animals "out of sight" is necessary to legitimize suffering on the vast scale required by the mass market's demand for meat and medicine.

Place and the Borders of Humanity

Human-animal borders and human practices on animals vary according to place. In representational politics that seek to dehumanize people by associating them with certain animals, place is often used to reinforce such associations.[14] Places are imbued with negative characteristics because they harbor (or are thought to harbor) certain feared or disliked animals, and then these places are linked to people who take on the dirty, polluted, or dangerous aspects of the place (and its animals). For example, "jungles" are dangerous places in the Western popular imagination, conjuring up images of dense foliage beneath which poisonous snakes slither and vicious beasts wait to pounce on unsuspecting humans. More concretely, marginalized groups such as gypsies are often relegated to residual places in urban areas (such as dumps), often inhabited by "dirty" and "disease-ridden" animals, for example, rats. Thus a "dirty—unsafe—rats—gypsies" association arises, linking a so-called pest-species to a particular subaltern group. This associational process has long been used to connect poor people, "dirty" animals, and dirt more generally.

In the case of animal practices, however, place plays both more straightforward and more nuanced roles. At a basic level, specific repertoires of animal practices evolve and become normalized *in place*. Such repertoires are in part environmentally determined, since the diversity of animal species available to kill, eat, or otherwise use is shaped by environmental factors, as are particular modes of subsistence linked to specific animals (for example, pastoralism). In addition, however, cultural ideas about animals (like other aspects of culture) evolve in place over time due to social or technological change generated within a society, or by externally driven events such as migrations or invasions. Thus values and practices concerning cosmological, totemic, or companionate relations between people and animals, and the material uses of animals as food or clothing, medicines or aphrodisiacs, shift as a result of social dynamics, technological change, or culture contact. The result is a shifting but place-specific ensemblage of animals, valued and used according to particular, legitimized codes. Transgressions of such place-specific codes or boundaries of practice *by definition* situate an

individual or group as "outsider," "savage," or "subhuman."

What happens when the coding of animal bodies and the codes of animal practice shared by people dominant in one place are broken or challenged by people from another place, who do not share these codes but share the same space? When people are uprooted and brought to new places, they encounter different human-animal boundary constructions and if they persist in their indigenous practices are much more likely to transgress the border than locals. During much of (pre)history, the pace of such culture contact was relatively slow, allowing both host and newcomer groups to adjust; in earlier international migration waves to the United States, origins of immigrants were sufficiently similar to host populations that conflict on the basis of animal practices does not appear to have been rife. With the economic globalization, escalating geopolitical instabilities and conflicts, and vast international population flows that characterize the postmodern condition, the "empire" has come home. Newcomers from a wide variety of radically different environments and cultural landscapes are suddenly living cheek by jowl. Typically, immigrants must move into the territories of a more powerful host community. Adjustment possibilities are foreshortened; for the largest immigrant groups, the need to adjust may be obviated by the emergence of relatively self-contained immigrant districts, such as "ethno-burbs."[15] Thus in the contemporary United States, immigrants whose indigenous animal practices clash with the codes of dominant society are at the greatest risk of racialization and dehumanization.

Nevertheless, non-immigrant people of darker (versus lighter) color can also be at risk on the basis of their animal practices. Here, place plays a more nuanced role, by exoticizing the imaginary places of origin of such groups. Risk in this case arises not only because dominant norms of animal practice are contravened, but also because of the deeply engrained evolutionary connotations of the primitive, exotic, racialized "homelands" lurking in the Western imagination just below the surface of contemporary race relations. Thus cock fighting among Native Americans or Chicanos, the adoption of Santeria on the part of many Chicanos and African Americans, or the keeping of aggressive, vicious dogs (or, worse, dog-fighting) among youth in inner-city communities of color can place such subaltern groups on the far side of the human-animal boundary. When problematic practices occur in racialized and marginalized places, such as "ghetto" areas that are already indirectly and sometimes even explicitly linked to Africa (by virtue of names like "The Jungle"), prospects of racialization on the basis of animal practices may rise still higher.

Lastly, there may be time-space displacement of one group's animal practices onto another group located in a different place. With globalization of environmental degradation and the rise of international efforts to prevent species extinction, local groups may risk racialization by virtue of animal practices occurring in their ancestral or natal-origin countries or regions rather than their *own* behavior toward animals. By a quick twist in the logic of postmodern hyperspace, they can in effect be held suspect while being thousands of miles away from the action.

Toward *Le Pratique Sauvage*

Our purpose in attempting to explicate the links between race, place, and animal practices has been to show how deeply engrained ideas about people and animals have been used to produce cultural difference and devalue subaltern groups. In the United States, such differences play into a multifaceted and dynamic process of racialization in which immigrants who appear to threaten dominant cultural identities are powerfully marked as outside the project of becoming American, and thus excluded from its associated benefits. This exploration reveals the extreme relativity of legitimate animal body codes and practices with respect to time, place, and culture. Ironically, however, our consideration also exposes the universality of human violence toward

animals. We are left with a dual challenge: how to break the links between animals and racialization, and stop the violence done to people racialized on the basis of their animal practices; and how to make the links between animals and people, and stop the violence directed at animals on the basis of their nonhuman status.

We maintain that making the links between animals and people requires a rejection of "dehumanization" as a basis for cultural critique. For the connotations of the very term are deeply insidious. They imply human superiority and thus sanction mastery over animals and nature, and also suggest that violent or otherwise harmful treatment is acceptable as long as the targets are nonhuman beings. Thus dehumanization not only stimulates violence toward people, it implicitly legitimizes violence toward animals.

This does not mean that the human-animal boundary should simply be banished for good. For, as Val Plumwood argues, the denial of difference can be as harmful as its production.[16] Instead, difference—whether amongst humans or between humans and animals—must be respected and valorized. Stopping the violence means neither dismissing difference nor using it to legitimize harm or domination. Rather, in our view, stopping the violence requires adopting recipes for "wild practice" and extending them to embrace animals as well as people.

What changes in human thought and practice does *le pratique sauvage* imply? We see three basic shifts as necessary. One is that humans, especially dominant groups, accept rather than deny some of the vulnerability that animals have always known and reject the illusion that a devaluation of others (human or animal) either empowers or offers protection from harm. Another is that all humans need to abandon the drive for overarching control and instead choose a position of humility or marginality with respect to the Earth that balances needs for safety and security with consideration for the needs of other lifeforms. Such marginality must be internally imposed (as opposed to the marginality that humans impose on each other to oppress or gain power) and its costs must be fairly borne. Finally, this sort of *pratique sauvage* implies that people must actively engage in a radically inclusive politics which considers the interests and positionality of the enormous array of animal life and lives, as well as the lives of diverse peoples. Neither human nor animal lives can ever be fully known, of course. We are obliged, however, to discern them as best we are able, through both the practices of interaction and exchange, and the exercise of all our powers of empathy and imagination.

Notes

1. Brigitte Bardot, as quoted in Reuters Ltd., 26 April 1996.

2. See Jan Penrose, "Reification in the Name of Change: The Impact of Nationalism on Social Constructions of Nation, People and Place in Scotland and the United Kingdom," in Peter Jackson and Jan Penrose, eds., *Constructions of Race, Place and Nation,* Minneapolis, Minn: University of Minnesota Press, 1994, pp. 27–49.

3. We draw this phrase (originally introduced by Althusser) from Gayatri Chakravorty Spivak, *The Post-Colonial Critique: Interviews, Strategies, Dialogues,* New York: Routledge, 1990, p. 54. For a useful discussion of her ideas, see Edward Soja and Barbara Hooper, "The Spaces that Difference Makes," in Michael Keith and Seve Pile, eds., *Place and the Politics of Identity,* London and New York: Routledge, 1993, pp. 183–205.

4. See Max Arax, "Hmong's Sacrifice of Puppy Reopens Cultural Wounds," *Los Angeles Times,* 16 December 1994, pp. A1,5; and Anonymous, "Sacrifice of Dog Highlights Clash of Cultures in Central Valley," *San Francisco Chronicle,* 19 December 1994, p. A22.

5. See David Haldane, "Culture Clash or Animal Cruelty?" *Los Angeles Times,* 13 March 1989, sect. II, p. 1; David Haldane, "Judge Clears Cambodians Who Killed Dog for Food," *Los Angeles Times,* 15 March 1989, sect. II, p. 1; Clay Evans, "Bill Outlawing Eating of Pets Clears Senate," *Los Angeles Times,* 29 August 1989, sect. I, p. 20; Paul Jacobs,

"Governor Signs Pet Protection Bill but Opposes Penalties," *Los Angeles Times,* 19 September 1989, p. B3; Greg Lucas, "Governor Signs Bill Outlawing Dining on Pets," *San Francisco Chronicle,* 19 September 1989, p. A8; Katherine Bishop, "U.S.A.'s Culinary Rule: Hot Dogs Yes, Dogs No," *New York Times,* 5 October 1989, sect. A, p. 22.

6. Andrew Lam, "Cuisine of a Pragmatic People," *San Francisco Chronicle,* 9 August 1989, p. A17.

7. The Santeria case is United States of America, *U.S. Supreme Court Reports,* 1993. Church of die Lukumi Babalu Aye, Inc., and Ernesto Pichardo v. City of Hialeah, 124 L Ed 472. Media reports include Paul M. Barrett, "Court to Test Religion Rights in Sacrifice Case," *Wall Street Journal,* 18 October 1992, sect. B, pp. 1, 7; Joan Biskupic, "Animal Sacrifices Ban Tests Religion Rights," *Washington Post,* 1 November 1992, sect. A, pp. 1, 8, 9; Anonymous, "Santeria Priest Performs Sacrifices," *Sunday Telegram,* 27 June 1993, sect. A, p. 5. Earlier reports described Santeria in general (for example, Rick Mitchell, "Out of Africa: An Ancient Nigerian Religion Comes through Caribbean to the United States," *San Francisco Chronicle,* 1 May 1988, magazine 15, p. Z25); and the bans in Los Angeles and San Francisco are described in Anonymous, "L.A. Animal Torture-Killings Blamed on Sect," *San Francisco Chronicle,* 22 July 1988, sect. A, p. 14; Anonymous, "Ritualistic Animal Sacrifice Is Outlawed by L.A. Council," *San Francisco Chronicle,* 3 October 1990, sect. A, p. 17; Suzanne Espinosa, "Resistance to S. F. Ban on Animal Sacrifice," *San Francisco Chronicle,* 24 July 1992, sect. A, p. 24; Elaine Herscher, "Panel Compromises on Animal Sacrifice," *San Francisco Chronicle,* 19 August 1992, sect. A, p. 20.

8. In a fascinating departure from such evolutionary taxonomies, the surrealists Breton and Aragon denounced the natural sciences for classification mania and argued against reductive typologies privileging exterior detail—anatomic or ethologic in the narrow and individualized sense of the term. Breton and his associates adopted, instead, the idea of analogic thought—a means of viewing the relations of an entire biotype with its milieu (for example, all Mexican animals were named specifically). In addition, mimicry or mimetism was one of Breton's requirements in biological classification: the nuptial dance among birds was like passion among humans. The result was a sort of surrealist totem. See Claude Maillard-Chary,

"Le Sentiment de la nature chez les surréalistes," *L Homme et la société,* nos. 91–2, pp. 157–72.

9. Fredric Jameson, *Postmodernism, or the Cultural Logic of Late Capitalism,* Durham, N.C.: Duke University Press, 1991.

10. Laura Pulido, "A Critical Review of the Methodology of Environmental Racism Research," *Antipode* 28, 1996, pp. 142–59.

11. See Carol J. Adams, *The Sexual Politics of Meat: A Feminist-Vegetarian Critical Theory,* New York: Continuum, 1990.

12. A long line of ethical reasoning, perhaps epitomized by Kantian theory, argues that humans have only indirect moral duties to animals because they lack subjectivity and thus can be treated like inanimate objects.

13. Marjorie Spiegel, *The Dreaded Comparison: Human and Animal Slavery,* Denmark: Heretic Books, 1988.

14. David Sibley, *Geographies of Exclusion,* London: Routledge, 1995.

15. See Wei Li, *Chinese Ethnoburbs of Southern California,* Ph.D. diss., Department of Geography, University of Southern California, 1997.

16. Val Plumwood, *Feminism and the Mastery of Nature,* London: Routledge, 1993.

Garry Marvin

Creating and Representing Foxhounds

Foxhounds are unusual nonhuman animals in terms of their relationships with both humans and other animals and in terms of the location and purposes of animals in English rural spaces. Hunting hounds have a unique existence poised between the worlds of humans and wild animals. Although a docile and domesticated dog, foxhounds are not companion animals ("pets")—animals created for close emotional relationships with individual humans. Nor, despite living in large groups in purpose-built animal shelters in rural space, are they livestock—animals created for the exploitation of their bodies or bodily products. The Huntsman and his assistants have close, emotional, and enduring relationships with the hounds, but such relationships are not personalized into an individual pet relationship. In a sense, the relationship of care is close to that of the husbandry associated with the care and management of livestock: They must be housed, fed, watered, and exercised, their living quarters cleaned, and the sick attended to. In terms of the specific culture of dog-keeping in England, they are also curious animals. Foxhounds are, as it were, single-purpose dogs. Individuals of other breeds of dogs might find themselves related to the human world in many different ways. Labradors, for example, might become pets, guard dogs, or seeing-eye dogs. They might work with the police, the military, the rescue services, or alongside a gamebird shooter. This never happens with foxhounds; they never transfer out of the context of hunting world into which they are born; they are only ever hunting hounds. These are working animals. Their task is to hunt foxes, not a simple utilitarian task—it is one that is construed by humans as a performance. No other

dogs are kept in such large groups in England: Hounds are domesticated dogs, but they are expected to interact as a pack and, to some extent, exhibit behavior similar to that of a pack of wild dogs. They constitute a culturally created *pack*, a pack created for performance; each hound is specially bred for its role in this performance.

Hunting the Fox

Although this article will not be concerned in any detail with hunting per se, it is necessary to give some context for understanding the role of the foxhound. There are some 200 officially recognized and registered Hunts in Great Britain, and they hunt, usually twice a week, in a season that lasts from autumn until early spring. The main participants consist of horse-mounted riders, a pack of hounds, and a group of people who follow on foot or in vehicles. Although there are several officials in any Hunt, the most important in terms of the practice of hunting is the Huntsman. He is the person concerned with much of the breeding and care of the hounds and with sole responsibility for how they actually hunt the fox. In terms of the interpretation of foxhunting developed through this anthropological research, it is argued that humans are not themselves directly hunting—they have no immediate relationship with their prey. They do not attempt to find, track, pursue, and kill foxes—these are the tasks of the hounds. The human participants are actually only following hounds, described by the hunting expression as "riding to hounds."

On a hunting day, the mounted riders, the officials, the foot followers, and the Huntsman with his hounds (he will usually have 20 or so hounds with him) will meet, by the invitation of the owner, at a farm, countryhouse, or pub and will be served drinks and snacks by the person hosting the "Meet." This is a short, convivial social event in which all the participants mix. When the day's hunting begins, there is a separation of these participants. The Huntsman will lead the hounds away from the Meet to the place it has been decided to begin hunting, and the riders follow some distance behind. The Huntsman will encourage the hounds to begin exploring a hedgerow, wood, or field for the scent of a fox. It is important to emphasize that foxhounds work mainly through their sense of smell—they are scent hounds and do not *look* for foxes. If some find the scent of a fox, they will begin to cry excitedly, sounds that draw other members of the pack to them. They should then all set off in pursuit of the scent. The Huntsman will follow them, and, allowing him some distance, the mounted riders will follow. If the hounds are able to follow the scent successfully, they will begin to close the distance between themselves and the fox, who may have crossed the countryside some time before realizing that he or she was the object of attention. Becoming aware of the hounds, the fox will actively flee—with the hounds now in direct pursuit. A moment will come when they are able to see their prey. They will increase their pace, surge forward, and the leading hounds will seize and kill the animal. The Huntsman and the mounted field, if they have been able to successfully negotiate the obstacles of the countryside—fences, hedges, walls, and impassable fields—will arrive at the spot where the hounds are tearing at the carcass of the fox. After a short pause, the Huntsman will call the hounds to him, and they will set off to repeat the process.

Distinction, Creation, and Pedigree

In the hunting world today, the hound continues to have an elite image, compared with other dogs. Hunting hounds are always referred to as *hounds* and never *dogs*—unless one is referring to male hounds. It is a mark of ignorance, outsider-

ship, or a direct insult to ask a hunting person about *the dogs*, and any such use will bring a swift comment of disapproval and correction. The use of the term *dog* in this way reveals, in terms of those who hunt, a failure to understand the special nature and status of the animals and their place in the event. This distinction is also clearly marked in the use of the contrasting terms *hound* and *cur*. A *cur* is any dog—even one who has an illustrious pedigree—who is not a *foxhound*. Although this is a term for marking and distinguishing hounds, the use of *cur* does not have the normal disparaging sense of a despicable or vile dog in this context. Indeed, most of those who hunt and often make such a distinction are owners of pet dogs who are not in any sense regarded as vile or despicable. The most common use of the distinction is heard when hunting and a group of people is listening for the sounds of a distant group of hounds. If one hears canine sounds far away, he or she might ask, "Are those hounds?" To which a more knowledgeable person might reply, "No, those are curs barking."

The modern foxhound is the product of some 250 years of careful selection and breeding: Individual Hunt records from the eighteenth century and the Foxhound Kennel Stud Book from the mid-nineteenth century chart the history of the breed and celebrate notable exemplars of it. The aim here is not to explore the history of the breeding of this animal, but it is important to stress the perhaps obvious point that the creation of the foxhound is, as with the creation of any domesticated animal, the result of cultural ideas in combination with a natural form.

Those responsible for the breeding of hounds are involved in a continual play, in a series of playback mechanisms, between representation and presentation, between an ideal and the actual embodied presence—a continual becoming. Hounds are unable to have a first-order being in the world without human intervention. They are not permitted to embody, reproduce, and re-embody themselves of their own volition. Each hound is a representative of an image, perhaps only a part image, which each breeder has in his mind.

The reproduction of and for the particular form is also intimately connected with the knowledge or experience of past and present representations of embodied hounds. It requires vision, imagination, knowledge, and skill to attempt to mold the processes of biological reproduction to bring about the forms they would like to produce. All hounds produced are not only themselves but are situated in a continuum from the past and become the basis for other potential hounds; or not. Breeders can control the nature of the present animals by refusing their presence—the breeders will kill them if they do not conform to their idea or ideal—and the breeders can reject their potential for the future by refusing to breed from them.

Of first concern to the breeder is the production of the body of the hound. As an athletic, working animal who will have to run maybe 50 miles twice a week on hunting days, the body of the hound should be fit for the purpose. Here, great attention is paid to the relationships between length of leg, the chest, feet, tail, size of body, and the proportions of the head—this is the physical conformation of the animal, the basis of the hound's athletic quality of speed, drive, and stamina. Each breeder will have a clear idea, based on some generally shared cultural notions, held within the world of hunting, of what this physical conformation ought, ideally, to be. Each will have views about how the physical attributes relate to the hunting quality of the hound and will strive to bring them into a harmonious relationship of form. Close attention will also be paid to the color of the coat of the animal—different Hunts favor different color combinations and markings—a physical attribute, but one related more to aesthetics than to hunting ability.

In this creation of a canine form, foxhound breeding shares something with the breeding of any pedigree dog—the continual approximation to an ideal. Where it differs significantly, though, is in who controls the image of the ideal and the acceptability of any individual representation of the ideal. Unlike the setting of standards for other pedigree dogs that are generally set and controlled by specific Breed Clubs in association with national associations (such as The Kennel Club in the United Kingdom and American Kennel Club and the United Kennel Club in the United States), there is no such attempt at breed standardization for working foxhounds. Although there is a Foxhound Kennel Stud Book (for the registration of hounds) controlled by the Masters of Foxhounds Association, there is no authoritative organization that defines the appropriate or any acceptable standard of the physicality of the foxhound. The physical appearance of the hounds of any pack will depend on decisions made by those responsible for their selective breeding to express the ideas they have of what and how a foxhound should be. The breeders of each Hunt work toward forming or maintaining a "type" for their pack, which means that each hound included in the pack is a representative of that type—a point that will be further explored below. Breeders will have clear ideas about their ideal of the foxhound and will express this in terms of the size, shape, density, and overall conformation of the animal. This ideal is not only related to aesthetic concerns but also will be closely related to the practicalities of how the body of the hound ought to relate to the physical demands of the terrain over which the hound will hunt. Breeders also seek to breed for a uniformity of "look" within the pack. This is not an idea that all the hounds should be as nearly as possible exact replicas of each other but rather that the diversity of individuals should come together in an aesthetic of unity—something that is expressed as a "level pack"—which then becomes the distinguishing expression of the identity of the pack belonging to a particular Hunt.

Nose, Voice, and Fox Sense

Apart from the concern with the physical body of the hound, breeders are also seeking important, but less tangible, qualities—qualities that they hope to develop in all members of the pack but which cannot be selected for in terms of any ideas of the scientific breeding for inherited characteristics. There is an attempt to link the physical body of the hound to that of the hound's purpose and performance as a hunting hound. Such qualities include "nose," "voice," and "fox sense." "Nose" is basically the scenting ability of a hound and is fundamental for this style of hunting.

Hounds must have the ability to find and, as it were, fix on the scent of a fox and keep it in their nostrils as they move at speed across the countryside. All hounds should be able to do this, but particularly admired are those who demonstrate that they can find a very weak scent, who can follow it in adverse conditions (when the scent dissipates in rain, wind, or the warmth of sunshine, or on difficult and confusing scenting surfaces such as asphalt roads), or who can follow it despite the evasive tactics of the fox. Huntsmen will also speak with pleasure and admiration of individual hounds who can do this when the majority of the pack are experiencing difficulties.

A hound who finds the scent of a fox begins to make a "yipping" or "squeaking" sound that becomes a fuller "baying" as the animal becomes more convinced by what the sense of smell communicates. These sounds excite the other hounds and draw them to the hounds who are "proclaiming" the scent. Once they, too, pick up the scent, they join in the general chorus. Hounds should never act as individual, silent hunters and set off after a fox on their own—this is a collective venture, and hounds should communicate with each other. There is, thus, an intimate connection between "nose" and "voice"—the former should stimulate the latter. The notion of "voice" is highly elaborated in the discourse of foxhunting. Not only are hounds spoken about as having "voices" but they also "speak," and as soon as the pack begins a definite baying chorus, the human participants will excitedly comment, "Listen, hounds are speaking" and will be fairly certain that the hounds are in pursuit of a fox. The qualities of "voice" and "speaking" are also features that distinguish hounds from *curs* who merely "bark"—such dogs are never referred to as "speaking," and the quality of their barking is never attended to by hunt participants.

The interpretation, understanding, and appreciation of "voice" is wonderfully complex in hunting. As this author has pointed out elsewhere: '("Voice") . . . is not something that is interpreted anthropomorphically—although they "speak," this does not suggest that they have anything to say. What the Huntsman must be certain of, though, is that they are "speaking truly"—that they really do have the scent. As one Huntsman commented, "It must be 'meaningful,'" and "they should speak authoritatively." The Huntsman must know that the first voices he hears are true so that he can encourage other hounds, who are perhaps some distance away and cannot possibly have the scent, to go to those who are speaking. Some hounds, however, will use their voices without really having the scent—often they are merely imitating others who might have caught the scent of a fox. As the same Huntsman commented, "You don't want those who are too liberal with their tongues—babblers." Just as being "mute," refusing to use the voice, is undesirable, so is a hound who "speaks" for no good reason.

There is another, purely aesthetic elaboration of the sound made by foxhounds. Hounds are regarded as having soprano, tenor, or bass voices, and these are highly appreciated by Huntsmen. They speak of attempting to develop a range of such voices in their pack to create a pleasing and melodious chorus, and all aficionados of foxhunting will refer, explicitly, to "the music of hounds." Here the basic vocalizations of an animal are responded to in a cultural register.

The final quality of interest to the breeder and to the participants in the hunt is that of "fox sense." This refers to the ability of a hound to establish, through scent alone, a relationship with the absent fox. This becomes especially important when, after following the scent for some time, it seems to disappear or perhaps becomes confused by other scents and smells. At this point, the hounds stop running, they mill around the point where they lost the scent, and often they become confused. A hound with good fox sense will begin to move away from this area and begin to search once again for the scent of the same fox. A hound who begins to do this very deliberately and who appears to be thinking of where the fox might have gone, given the type of terrain and the micro-climatic conditions (such as wind direction), is referred to as exhibiting good fox sense. Such behavior is interpreted by humans as though the hound was engaging in an animal version of anthropomorphism—thinking like a fox. It is as if the hound, attempting to follow a difficult scent line, was saying, "From what I know of foxes and given these conditions and the nature of this place, what is this one likely to have done?" Fox sense is always tied to the presence or absence of scent. It is not a quality associated with any apparent tactical ability—hounds should never, as it were, attempt to second-guess the fox, to plan, and attempt to outwit the fox. Hounds should only follow a scent; the fox should determine the passage across the countryside. The fox sets the agenda for the hunt, and the hounds should follow this as closely and directly as possible. They should never, for example, try to circle ahead of the animal and appear from a direction the fox is not expecting, nor should they lie in wait or attempt to ambush the fox. There is no space here to explore the structures of hunting as a cultural practice in terms of rules of engagement, appropriate relations between the animal and human participants, and notions of fair play. It is worth suggesting, however, that the notions of appropriate and inappropriate fox sense indicate that the event is predicated on ideas of "natural" rather than "cultural" abilities. The hound is culturally created to participate in the event, but it is expected that such participation will be directed by the hound's immediate senses rather than by intellectual processes.

The Pack: Natural Instincts, Cultural Performance

The hound breeder not only creates individual animals, but he must bring these together in a series of close relationships that form a harmonious ensemble. Each hound is known individually and

each will have individual skills, but this individuality must be merged into the collective. The Huntsman creates the pack, its purpose and its performance. Although people in the hunting world often comment on the pack sharing similarities with a naturally occurring pack of wild canids, it has a very different social construction and set of behavioral practices from such a pack. As has been shown above, such a pack does not come about through natural selection. Members of a pack of foxhounds are often closely related, but there are no family or other social groupings; neither are any hierarchies allowed to develop as they would in a wild pack. Most Huntsmen comment that it is they who are, and must be, "top dog."

Although foxhounds hunt using their natural senses, their purpose in hunting is cultural rather than natural. It is humans who seek an engagement with wild foxes through hunting; it is *they* who both create the hound for this purpose and *they* who decide on which other animals the hounds should or should not pay attention to in their world. Unlike a wild pack, they are not hunting a prey that is a potential source of food for them (nor for their human masters), for the fox is not eaten—they are hunting a particular prey that has been decided for them by the Huntsman. Hounds must hunt purposefully, but this purpose has been established for them. Huntsmen comment that hounds should be willingly and enthusiastically engaged in hunting, but a careful balance must be maintained—they are both hunting for themselves and as agents of someone else. "Natural instincts" are shaped, controlled, and given meaning by human desires. The relationships between presentation and representation become complex at this point. Those interested in the hunting performances of hounds will talk about them as behaving in certain ways *because* they are foxhounds. This, however, is not spoken of as though the hound is merely unconsciously revealing natural qualities but rather in terms of the hound's *knowing* what is expected because this animal is a foxhound—who has, as it were, an awareness of foxhoundness—a human construct. The hounds, then, actively present themselves in terms of their representation, a process generated by some form of understanding of that representation.

Such performances, both individual and ensemble, are shaped and maintained through complex mechanisms and relationships of discipline and control between the Huntsman and the hounds. On the hunting field, he must maintain a delicate balance in his relationships with the hounds between control and freedom, between direction and improvisation. Ideally, hounds should be able to find and follow a scent without commands from the Huntsman, and if they lose it, they should not immediately look to him for help in redirecting themselves. The Huntsman should understand and sense his animals so well that he should know when they need to be encouraged to move along because there is no scent or when they need more time to work carefully and uninterrupted at a faint scent. Although he directs the hunt, it is felt by most Huntsmen that they must demonstrate trust in their hounds; as

one Huntsman commented to the author, "The dimmest hound usually knows more than the best Huntsman."

It is the expression and enactment of these relationships that many who follow the Hunt come to observe, experience, and comment on. Throughout the day, there is a multi-voiced commentary on how the hounds are performing, how the Huntsman is relating to them, and how both are relating to the challenges presented by the countryside and by the absent or present fox. Hunting people refer to the "invisible thread" that unites hounds and Huntsman—a thread that slackens and tightens and sometimes breaks. This metaphorical thread does not simply attach hounds to the man and the man to hounds in a linear fashion, but it turns and twists, it crosses and re-crosses to bind them into a web of mutually reinforcing and meaningful representations. Neither makes sense without the other; both have presence only in terms of the other; each represents the other.

PART TWO

Close Relationships

Introduction

Most social scientists adamantly hold to the view that people's relationships with their animal companions are similar to those one might have with a car, computer, or other material object and, until fairly recently, the legal system regarded companion animals as owned property. Those who share their lives and homes with animals see things very differently. The most common way that caretakers describe the animals with whom they live is as "members of the family" or "close friends" (Cain 1983, Nieberg and Fischer 1982). Seen in this way, companion animals are defined as unique individuals, the focus of love and seen as giving love in return, incorporated into the rituals of the home, and mourned when they die.

Close relationships, like those between friends, lovers, or family members, involve the participants having long-term experience with each other, knowing what each likes or dislikes, and having a clear sense of how each party thinks and behaves in certain situations. Close relationships are what sociologists refer to as *primary relationships*. They are intrinsically rewarding for those involved and not mainly "instrumental"—that is, useful because they can provide participants with something apart from the direct emotional rewards of the relationships themselves. In short, friends and family members know each other well and enjoy being in each other's company. They remember a mutual past and anticipate a future together. They are committed to the shared relationship. Close relationships involve sharing. Members touch each other, exchange gifts, spend time together, and interact regularly (see Fehr 1993; Simmel 1950, 122–133; Suttles 1970).

These features of intimacy are present in our close relationships with nonhuman animals as well as those we have with other humans. We come to know our animal companions as individuals with unique likes and dislikes, with identifiable emotional responses, and as behaving predictably in certain situations. We come to know how our animal companions think and feel and use this knowledge to shape how we act toward them. In turn, we make the (reasonable) assumption that the animals in our lives have some sense of who we are as individuals, what

we like and dislike, feel some form of love for us, enjoy being with us, and have some knowledge of the emotions we are experiencing at any particular time.

Like relationships with human friends and family members, those between caretakers and their animal companions involve a variety of shared experiences and patterns of interaction. Typically, people and animals share certain rituals that have evolved through routine interactions and help define the time spent together. For example, Sanders (2007) describes a routine with one of his dogs that emerged over time, came to be anticipated by both caretaker and animal, and helped define their relationship.

> I always feed my own dogs between 7 and 8 in the morning. As in the case of going for walks . . . , when this time approaches the dogs begin to watch me carefully and to follow me from place to place. If I am late, they will begin to make "impatient" noises and look longingly at the metal food bowls kept on the kitchen counter. When I take the bowls into the basement where their food is stored, they wait expectantly at the top of the stairs and then mill about and bark with anticipation as I prepare their meals. Over time, Cynder, the older of my Newfoundlands, has devised a unique postprandial routine. After I put the other dog out to take care of elimination, Cynder takes her bowl over to a place by the couch and waits expectantly. I go to her, rub her ears, and say a few kind words. After this special attention she lies down and chews on her bowl for a few minutes until she falls asleep. I then return her bowl to the counter and let the other dog back into the house. It is clear from her demeanor that this is an enjoyable and expected routine. If I am distracted or busy and do not follow the established pattern, she will continue to sit with the bowl in her mouth and watch me until I realize my failure to meet her expectations. This routine, together with a number of others, is a component of our shared history. We all remember how routines have played out in the past and structure present interactions on the basis of these memories, we anticipate the exchanges in the future, and Cynder's personal shaping of the routine is part of my knowledge of her unique selfhood. (326–327)

When people and animals share time and experience, as in humans with human friendships, they increasingly come to understand each other better. So-ciologists refer to the key social ability to see things from another's perspective as *taking the role of the other*. As close associates mutually develop this abil-ity, their understanding of each other increases and, consequently, their ability to coordinate their mutual behavior increases. In the case of close human-animal relationships, regularly interacting and trying to under-stand the animal-associate's mind lead to regarding the animal as a unique individual. Psychologist Ken-neth Shapiro (1989) describes the importance of his shared experience with his dog Sabaka in shaping his view of the dog's unique identity.

> History informs the experience of a particular an-imal whether or not it can tell that history. Events in the life of an animal shape and even constitute him or her. . . . Sabaka is an individ-ual in that he is not constituted through and I do not live toward him as a species-specific behav-ioral repertoire or developmental sequence. More positively, he is an individual in that he is both subject to and subject of "true historical particulars.". . . I cannot replace him, nor, ethi-cally, can I "sacrifice" him for he is a unique in-dividual being. (187)

Actually *knowing* one's animal companion, then, is a consequence of the human-animal relationship and the interactional experience the parties share. Shared experience leads to shared feelings. The person and his or her animal companion feel comfortable together, ex-perience similar emotions in certain situations, and can read and respond appropriately to each other's feel-ings. For example, Sanders (1999) quotes a husband and wife movingly describing the calming and cohesive emotional role their dog plays in the family.

> *Wife*—He pulls us together as a family. He just melts you down. If there is ever any stress or conflict or something Bones will come up—right when we are having an argument. I mean, how can you be mad when this sweet little dog is here? It is almost like a lesson. He reminds me just how simple things really are and not to get all overworked about things in life.
>
> *Husband*—He's very constant. He's very sen-sitive to everyone's moods, but he never really basically changes. He's always the same, you can always depend on him. I will seek him out

if I am a little down about something. Or, if I realize I am uptight and I want to calm down, Bones is the source of that. I will want to sit with him and just have him nuzzle up. It just brings things into perspective. I think it is be-cause he is constant. (31)

The readings in this part of *Between the Species* focus on these intimate, emotionally rich, and mutu-ally rewarding relationships that people have with an-imals. In the first selection, Clinton Sanders emphasizes the similarities outlined above. Following a discussion of some key pieces of literature dealing with human-animal relationships, he focuses on three important ways in which close human-animal rela-tionships are demonstrated and maintained. People and animals play together, pay close attention to each other, and the human party in the relationship commonly "speaks for" the animal as he or she ver-balizes what the other is understood to be thinking and feeling. He stresses the importance of play as a demonstration that animals and people can share a particular "definition of the situation" and use this un-derstanding of what is going on to shape an exchange that is bounded, ritualized, pleasurable, and set apart from that which is "serious" or "ordinary." Mutual gaze is central because it is by looking at each other and focusing on particular objects that the person and his or her animal companion gain a sense of what each is thinking and regards as important. Fi-nally, it is through the act of speaking for the animal that the close relationship is most clearly demon-strated. As the party with linguistic abilities, the human member of the human-animal dyad verbalizes what he or she understands to be the animal's thoughts and feelings. Sanders then moves to dis-cussing what this kind of close relationship has to say about what it is to be a "person," what it is to have a "mind," and what we mean by "culture." He sees people as regarding and acting toward their an-imal companions as socially defined persons; as ac-knowledging how the animals think and what they think about (an internal process that is independent of the ability to use language); and as sharing the rit-uals, habits, experiences, and understandings of ob-jects and places that compose the basic mutual culture that binds close friends together. He concludes by advocating an expanded sociological understanding of the phenomena of mind and personhood and emphasizes the importance of including nonhuman animals in our analyses of social life.

In the second reading, Michael Ramirez focuses on how gender shapes the human-animal relationship. Using information drawn from interviews with dog owners, Ramirez examines the role a person's gender plays in the process of choosing a dog. Not surprisingly, he finds that women tend to acquire dogs that reinforce and demonstrate their femininity (or they choose cats, an animal traditionally associated with women), while men choose breeds and individual dogs that display masculine characteristics. Another way that a person's gender shapes the human-animal relationship is that caretakers use conventional gender understandings and expectations as a "lens" through which they view their dogs' behaviors. While women tend to interpret certain behavior as nurturant or motherly, for example, men see the same behavior as simply demonstrating friendliness. Men value activeness and strength in their dogs while women value "sweetness" and emotionality. Finally, Ramirez discusses the way people use their canine companions as "props" as they present and confirm their own gender identities. In this light, dogs are key features in the process of "doing gender" (West and Zimmerman 1987), as both men and women demonstrate their manliness or femininity through the dogs with whom they associate and by talking about the personality characteristics they most value in their animal companions. Echoing Sanders' discussion, Ramirez emphasizes that women and men interpret and value their close relationships with animals in different ways. While both men and women routinely describe the relationship as friendship, men more typically present their dogs as partners in physical activities. Women, on the other hand, stress the childlike personality characteristics of their animal companions. The author stresses that gender stereotypes significantly shape what people look for in their relationships with animals and how they understand these relationships and present them to others.

The third selection continues Ramirez's focus on gender and adds the important social element of ethnicity. In "She Was Family," Christina Risley-Curtiss and her colleagues examine human-animal relationships within "communities of color." The authors maintain (correctly) that little attention has been paid to how social connections and interactions with companion animals are organized in minority households. Using data collected through the use of semi-structured interviews, the authors reiterate the central theme in the previous articles in this part. Like others who share their daily lives with animal companions, women from racial and ethnic minority backgrounds typically see their animals as friends and confidants and incorporate them as members of the family. Of considerable interest is the authors' finding that the attitudes regarding relationships with animals of the minority women they interviewed were shaped significantly by their involvement with mainstream American culture.

References

Cain, A. 1983. "A Study of Pets in the Family System." In A. Katcher and A. Beck, eds., *New Perspectives on Our Lives with Companion Animals,* 71–81. Philadelphia: University of Pennsylvania Press.

Fehr, B. 1993. "How Do I Love Thee? Let Me Consult My Prototype." In S. Duck, ed., *Individuals in Relationships,* 87–120. Newbury Park, CA: Sage.

Nieburg, H., and A. Fischer. 1982. *Pet Loss.* New York: Harper and Row.

Sanders, C. 1999. *Understanding Dogs: Living and Working with Canine Companions.* Philadelphia: Temple University Press.

Sanders, C. 2007. "Mind, Self, and Human-Animal Joint Action." *Sociological Focus* 40:320–336.

Shapiro, K. 1989. "The Death of the Animal: Ontological Vulnerability." *Between the Species* 5:183–193.

Simmel, G. 1950. *The Sociology of Georg Simmel.* Trans. Kurt Wolff. New York: Free Press.

Suttles, G. 1970. "Friendship as a Social Institution." In G. McCall, M. McCall, N. Denzin, G. Suttles, and S. Kurth, eds., *Social Relationships,* 95–135. Chicago: Aldine.

West C., and D. Zimmerman. 1987. "Doing Gender." *Gender and Society* 1:125–151.

Clinton R. Sanders

Close Relationships between Humans and Nonhuman Animals

Relationships, which are composed of routine and patterned interactions, are central to the symbolic interactionist view of social life. Relationships range from those that are instrumental, emotionally uninvolving, and typically of short duration to those that are intrinsically rewarding and long-term and in which participants have considerable emotional stake. Conventionally, interactionists and other analysts of social life have seen the interdependence, commitment, and emotionality of close relationships as existing within, and sustained by, the symbolic exchanges of humans. I maintain that this characterization of close relationships is overly restrictive. It excludes from consideration a class of affiliations that are commonplace, imbued with emotion, and central to the shaping of the identities and selves of those involved. Traditionally, conventional sociologists have ignored or denigrated relationships between people and their companion animals. However, the intense, involving, and routine interactions forming these relations are worthy of serious attention and have the potential of adding significantly to the sociology of intimate exchanges.

Until fairly recently, sociologists have disregarded human-animal relationships. Constrained by what Rollin (1997) calls the "commonsense of science," sociology routinely has portrayed nonhuman animals as mindless, emotionless, selfless, reacting rather than acting, apprehending rather than comprehending, and existing only in the immediate situation. It has defined people's associations with them as "fictive" or the consequence of anthropomorphic "folk delusions."

In the following discussion, I reexamine close relationships to move beyond the limiting anthropocentric orthodoxy that presents the bonds and interactions between humans and nonhuman animals as qualitatively different from—and, by implication, inferior to—those between humans. Following a brief overview of the key discussions of human-animal relationships that exist, I examine the close relationship with a companion animal as a form of friendship. Like human-to-human friendships, those between people and companion animals assume intersubjectivity. Play, as I argue, requires participants to evaluate the situation, define the perspective of the other, and—in the context of mutually understood rules—make decisions about how to act in concert. In addition, I discuss gaze and mutual direction of attention as central elements of the intersubjectivity that supports interspecies friendship. This section on human-animal friendship concludes with a brief presentation of a typical feature of the relationship. Caretakers commonly give voice to what they understand to be the thoughts and feelings of their animal companions. This process of "speaking for" demonstrates the practical definition of the (animal) other that arises out of routine relational experience.

After discussing central components of human friendships with animals and showing how these relationships are established and sustained, I suggest three issues of basic interest that we may conceptualize more broadly and fruitfully explore by directing systematic attention to interspecies relationships. First, I maintain that a sociology of human-animal relationships provides a rich context in which to explore how we construct and assign the designation "person." Next, I present the issue of "mindedness" and argue that the conventional, linguicentric perspective on mind-as-internal-conversation is inadequate and confining. In contrast, I propose an expanded view of mind that, like personhood, we can best understand as arising out of social interaction. In essence, I maintain that people "do mind" as a cooperative interpretive process that does not depend on the ability of all parties to express their thoughts linguistically. Finally, I discuss culture as a collection of shared understandings that arises out of face-to-face interaction. Culture provides the basis for evaluating immediate situations, interpreting the perspective of others, and devising means for achieving goals, and, as such, it establishes the foundation for effective collective action. As caretakers pursue the everyday routines that express and solidify their relationships with their animal companions, they cooperatively create a private, interspecies culture that is simple and immediate and acts as an effective practical basis for interaction.

Identity, personhood, empathy, love, mindedness, culture, and other key issues are of considerable interest to interactionists and are of central relevance for the sociology of close relationships. The central point of this article is that these key issues may be fruitfully explored if we turn serious and appreciative attention to the human-animal bond and the social exchanges that both define and result from this unique form of sociation. This task requires that we move beyond the analytic restraints imposed by the presumption that shared symbols are the sole foundation for "real" intimate relationships and "authentic" interactions.

The Literature on Human-Animal Relationships

Since Bryant (1979) advocated that increased attention should be paid to the "zoological connection," analysts of social behavior from a variety of disciplines have been heeding his call. Due to early interest in the therapeutic utility of interactions with animals, a significant proportion of the extant literature has focused on the positive impact of relationships with animals on the physical and psychological well-being of their human partners. A related body of work has examined the uniquely intense relationships between people with disabilities and their assistance animals. These works highlight the impact of the human-animal relationship on people's identities and self-definitions, emotional health, and public encounters.

Since people's interactions with companion animals typically occur in the family context, the place of animals in familial relationships has received considerable attention. This literature regards household pets as full-fledged participants in the family system and as playing a significant role in shaping relationships among human family members.

Arguably, the richest body of literature dealing with human-animal relationships focuses on how people come to define their animal companions as unique individuals, comprehend their mental experience, and organize everyday exchanges based on these understandings. Fidler, Light, and Costall (1996), for example, interviewed students about their evaluations of dogs' thought processes after showing them a series of videotaped sequences. They found that experienced pet caretakers were significantly more likely to define the filmed behavior as having resulted from the dog's understanding of the situations and responding with deliberate actions. In a similar vein, Rasmussen, Rajecki, and Craft (1993) surveyed students to ascertain their perceptions of animal mentality and, in a later study, used the same research approach to examine the defined differences between the thoughts and feelings of dogs and humans (Rasmussen and Rajecki 1995). In general, the authors found, although the students acknowledge that dogs and humans have different cognitive abilities, they hold that the mental processes of dogs and humans are qualitatively similar.

Studies employing ethnography, semistructured interviews, and introspective analysis of personal experience with companion animals have added depth to the portrayal of people's understanding of the mentality and emotions of animals and how they use this understanding to shape interactions and relationships. For example, Sanders (1993) discussed how dog owners come to regard their nonhuman companions as unique, thoughtful, and emotional participants in social exchanges. In a parallel article, Alger and Alger (1997) examined the similar perceptions and experiences of cat owners. Focusing on human relationships with dogs and horses, respectively, Shapiro (1990) and Wipper (2000) have emphasized the central role played by touch in establishing the human-animal relationship and communicating feelings and intentions in the course of interaction.

Although this is not an exhaustive list of the growing literature on human-animal relationships produced by analysts of social relationships and behavior, it provides ample testimony to the increased interest in the topic. As I maintain, this area of interest provides an excellent foundation for examining not only the substantive issues listed above but also matters of central relevance to the interactionist study of intimate relationships. Since companion animals typically are regarded as friends and act as partners in everyday interaction, attention to people's associations with them can offer a unique view of how close relationships shape the construction and communication of identity, give rise to routine interactions that express and sustain friendship, and may be effectively grounded in empathetic understandings without the limits imposed by language.

The Human-Animal Friendship

If you want a friend for life, get a dog.
—Harry Truman (quoted in Rubin 1985:15)

As a general form of association, close relationships are those in which participants mutually shape and connect their behavior, emotions, and thoughts. This interdependence consists of shar-

ing strong and enduring commitments with frequent interactions. In friendship, a special type of close relationship, mutual understanding of the perspectives and routine responses of the parties involved is of key importance. This understanding allows friends to construct a stable and durable relationship and provides the foundation for anticipating a mutual future. In turn, friendships are emotionally rich because friends share companionship, provide mutual support, act as confidants, and enjoy shared activities. Emotional connectedness assumes that friends like each other, see each other as warm and supportive, and recognize each other's unique and appealing personal characteristics. People symbolize and reinforce their friendship relationship by close proximity, physical contact, and mutual gaze.

People commonly understand their connections to companion animals through defining them as "members of the family" (Cain 1983; Voith 1983). Alternatively, or in conjunction with this familial incorporation, caretakers most commonly define their pets as "special" or "close" friends (Nieburg and Fischer 1982). They understand and sustain their friendships with animal companions in much the same way as they do human-to-human friendships. The partners in the relationship spend time together and share routine activities. People feed, groom, touch, speak to, and incorporate their pets into holidays and other ritual events.

Play is a social activity in which players direct their actions toward a mutually defined goal, but shared understandings about "appropriate" moves and counter-moves constrain the means of achieving this goal. Play participants recognize that the interaction is supposed to be frivolous or pleasurable. Mutual play is a central mode of interaction between people and their nonhuman friends. In contrast to human-with-human play, in which competition is a central factor, human-animal play does not have winners or losers since keeping the play interaction going is the primary shared goal. In addition, because human and animal players have different levels of mental and physical ability (humans are more deceitful and animals more agile, for example), participants must learn to adjust their efforts in order to sustain the play interaction. In other words, both person and companion animal must, in a rudimentary way, take the role of the other and adjust their actions on the basis of this orientation.

Human-animal play requires that the players communicate the definition of the situation and the "rules" and goals of the game through their actions. Mechling emphasizes the communicative nature of play in describing interaction with his Labrador, Sunshine:

> The game of fetch was truly interactive. I was not always in control of the game. Sometimes Sunshine would fetch the ball but stop on the way back to me some ten feet away. He would begin a slow retriever stalk, then drop the ball in front of him and assume the familiar canine "play bow"—forepaws extended flat on the ground, the body sloping upward toward his erect hind-quarters, tail wagging. This is the canine invitation to play. In this case, however, we were already engaged in a game, so his message to me was that he, too, could exert some power and control in the game. (1989:313; see also Shapiro 1990:186)

As a routine form of friendly interaction, then, human-animal play involves communicating a mutual definition of the situation and designating certain physical objects as "game pieces." Playing necessitates that the players recognize and anticipate each other's orientations and expectations. Although ostensibly frivolous, play is a key example of human-animal communication. Within its mutually understood boundaries the players honestly or deviously signal their intentions, adjust and shape their own and the other's actions, and reinforce the communicative connection at the heart of effective collective action.

Shared focus of attention and mutual eye contact are central to all forms of face-to-face interaction, but they are of special significance in interactions between friends. Sharing attention demonstrates a measure of shared subjectivity. Sanders, using observations made while interacting with his companion dogs, discusses the importance of mutual gaze and its implications for taking the role of the other:

> When [the dogs] look at me they usually pay attention to my eyes. I have noticed on walks how important looking is to them. A common way that one will communicate to the other that she wants to play is by staring. During play they have a variety of ways of signaling "time out." In addition to stopping and avidly sniffing someplace, a player can effectively suspend the game by staring fixedly off into the middle distance. The other dog typically responds to this move by looking to see if there is actually anything important to look at. They do the same with me. If on the walk I stop and look in a particular direction, they will stop, glance at me, and gaze off in the direction I am looking. This seems a fairly clear indication of their elemental ability to put themselves into my perspective. In a literal sense they attempt to assume my "point of view." If I look at something they conclude that it is probably something important. (1999:144)

Sustained eye contact signals the close character of the relationship to coactors and to those in their presence. The research on people's interactions with their companion animals shows that mutual "face gazing" is an extremely common form of nonverbal interaction. As in close human relationships, sustained eye contact is an element of intimacy that symbolizes and reinforces the human-animal connection, and attention to facial expression provides interactants—both human and animal—with information about the subjective experience of the other. In their observations of the interactions between veterinary clients and their animals in a waiting room, Beck and Katcher (1996:43, 85–89) noted that a person would frequently hold the animal's head and stare into his or her eyes in much the same way parents make eye contact with their children.

The ability to give voice to what another is thinking is a key indicator of intersubjectivity and an important element of the mutual knowledge of the other shared by intimates. This activity is commonly seen when parents speak for their infant children and is an important factor in defining the nonlinguistic other as a person. This display of intersubjectivity is also a common feature of people's relationships with their companion animals. Myers (1998:12), for example, notes how the nursery school children he observed tended to "put words in the mouth" of the animals with whom they interacted. Similarly, Arluke and Sanders (1996:61–81), using observations of human-animal interactions in a veterinary clinic, describe a number of examples of people giving voice to what was "on the [animal's] mind." Frequently, speaking for the animal is "primed" when the caretaker asks the animal a question and then voices his or her response. In the veterinary clinic clients would commonly speak for the patient when describing the symptoms that precipitated the visit. In speaking for his or her animal in this way, the person demonstrates special knowledge of the other and cooperatively constructs the mind of the nonhuman friend.

All of these friendly routines are sustained within a highly emotionalized relationship. Caretakers regularly speak of the ability of their animals to feel emotion and empathically understand the emotions of their human friends. This understanding of the other's emotional experience orients the human actor's behavior toward the animal and acts as a practical basis for successful and satisfying collective action. Further, the animal's defined ability to read and respond appropriately to the caretaker's emotional experience enhances the friendship. An individual interviewed by Sanders touchingly described his golden retriever's empathetic abilities:

> He just seems to sense [your mood] somehow. You can be in a different room and be down. Recently when [my daughter] was in her room he just seemed to know where to go . . . he sensed that somewhere in this house—his doghouse— there was something that was not quite right. He sought [her] out and was just there. One day I was sitting on the front porch kind of blue about some things and he just snuggled in there— totally noninvasive. Just "If you want to pet me, pet me. I'm here if you need me." (1999:21–22)

Close relationships, which involve emotional bonds and shared intimate knowledge, have negative as well as positive elements. Intense conflicts, fear of loss, concern with overinvolvement, and other painful experiences are part of the "dark side" of friendships. Consequently, friends commonly experience some degree of ambivalence about the quality, consequences, and course of their shared close relationship.

In that people perceive them as both objects to be possessed and used and individual beings to be understood and loved, companion animals have a liminal status that results in a distinctly ambivalent general cultural orientation to them. This cultural ambivalence, together with the subordinate status of companion animals within the human-animal association, all too frequently leads to abuse, thoughtless disregard, and, ultimately, termination of the relationship.

More commonly, however, the emotional connection that binds the typical close relationships between people and their companion animals means that committed owners anticipate and react to the termination of these relationships—through illness, accident, straying, or voluntary euthanasia precipitated by the animals' age or infirmity—with intense sorrow. For example, a dog owner interviewed by Sanders offered an "acquisition story" in which she described special feelings she had for her dog and her sorrowful anticipation of eventual loss:

> I just told my parents I wanted a dog. I was living with my parents then. A lady down the street had a litter. I went in and immediately he came right over to me. It was love at first sight—he chose me. I remember it was really snowing that night and we couldn't get to the grocery store. My mother made him chicken soup. To this day he goes wild when he smells chicken soup. Every time I make it he gets half. Sometimes this annoys my roommate "Hey, I wanted some of that." But he is more important. He's not a dog to me. He's my best friend. He loves me and I love him. When I come home from work he's happy to see me and I am happy to see him. I try to spend quality time with him every day. . . . He gives me love. He can't live without me and

I can't live without him. It's so hard to see him getting old. I just don't know what I would do without him. (1999:23)

Like other close relationships, then, those between people and companion animals are characterized by commitment and ambivalence, rewards and problems, connectedness and loss. As seen above, these sociologically "neglected" relationships share many of the characteristics found in friendships between humans. However, unique differences between the participants in these common and emotionally involving relationships—specifically, that the interactants are members of different species and the animal partner lacks the ability to use human language—provide a foundation for exploring issues of key interest and expanding the scope of symbolic interactionism. In short, through examining the everyday exchanges between people and animals we can gain an enriched understanding of the social processes by which the designation "person" is constructed and applied, the phenomenon of "mind" arises within social relationships, and culture is interactionally created as a framework for effective collective action.

Persons, Minds, and Culture

The designation "person" is the most elemental social identity. It provides the foundation for, and is constructed in the context of, relationships. As a basic categorical identity, personhood may be acquired or lost, given or taken away, solidified or adjusted within the flow of interaction that comprises relationships. Everyday, face-to-face social exchanges provide the materials used in the "collaborative manufacture" (Cahill 1998:136) of the person as interactants define the immediate situation, act in particular ways, and attend to each other's responses. To the extent that responses are "appropriate" to the situation and coactors' understanding of each other, person-identities are enacted and reinforced.

Based on a shared history and knowledge of the other's unique personality, tastes, emotions, and routine responses, caretakers come to regard the companion animals with whom they have relationships as persons and treat them as such. The animal's personhood is an interactive accomplishment based on his or her definition as it arises in the context of the relationship. In applying a "person schema" (Howard 1995:93) to shape and understand his or her interaction with the animal, the caretaker commonly makes a distinction between "person" and "human." The animal is a person in the sense that his or her perspective and feelings are knowable; interaction is predictable; and the shared relationship provides an experience of closeness, warmth, and pleasure. In an important way, the distinction between relationships with humans and with animal-persons is central to the special character of the human-animal bond. Because they are not human relationships, those with companion animals are constant rather than contingent. The animal's response to his or her companion does not depend on the latter's appearance, age, economic fortunes, abilities, or the other vagaries that, for good or ill, constrain human-to-human relationships.

Similarly, mind is an interactional accomplishment. Mead (1962:73) regarded mind as an internal linguistic activity, and, therefore, denied its existence in nonhuman animals. This Meadian conception of mind-as-self-conversation is, I maintain, unnecessarily restrictive. As we interact with others, we premise our actions and responses on the presumption that the content of our minds has some basic relationship to what and how our coactors are thinking. However, the elemental evidence for this presumption is drawn from our interpretations of others' behavior and the predictive utility of these interpretations. As people interact with infants, alingual humans, and nonhuman animals, they regard the ability to focus attention, manipulate objects, seek or avoid certain experiences, and engage in action directed at achieving particular ends as persuasive evidence of mind. The greater familiarity with the other—the closer our relationship with him or her—the more confidence we have in our understanding of the content of his or her mind and our ability to gauge his or her intentions. Casting off the linguicentric and anthropomorphic restraints of conventional views of mind frees us to appreciate an expanded world of social relationships and understand the interactions from which they are constructed.

Culture, like personhood and mindedness, is constructed and shared through interaction. As Becker (1986) observes, the "most minimal definition" of culture is that it is composed of mutual understandings ("conventions") that interactants use to coordinate their activities ("collective action"). Culture arises as a response to situations and lends predictability to interaction.

In the relational context of friendship, interactants commonly create what Fine (1981:267) refers to as a "private culture." Friends use these "dyadic traditions" to "test whether they are sensitive to the same aspects of the immediate experience and whether they share a common orientation toward this experience, to symbolize their intimacy, and to activate a sense of a shared past" (Mechling 1989:312–13). As is the case in human-with-human friendships, close relationships between people and companion animals give rise to a dyadic culture that encompasses established routines, mutual knowledge of and feeling for the other, and expectations about the predictable course of interaction. What is unique about the culture shared by humans and animals, and of special significance in advancing an interactionist understanding of human-animal relationships, is that these conventions arise and are effectively communicated despite the fact that the parties in the relationship do not share the ability to employ a common system of linguistic symbols. As with the definition of personhood and the social construction of mind, the creation, communication, and competent use of culture is not dependent on language.

Conclusion

I have offered a brief, and admittedly somewhat rhetorical, discussion of a type of close relationship that until fairly recently has been largely unexamined in conventional sociology. My primary goal has been to advocate the movement of inter-

species interactions and relationships into the repertoire of issues on which interactionists focus. This movement requires that we reject (or at least bracket) conventional social scientific and cultural beliefs about the qualitative differences between humans and nonhuman animals. Serious attention to human-animal relationships requires that the anthropocentric "commonsense of science" be replaced with the "ordinary commonsense" of everyday social actors derived from their routine experiences with their animal companions.

The primary goal of symbolic interactionism is to make social life intelligible. The central orienting principle guiding the achievement of this goal is that humans act toward things based on the meanings that emerge through social interaction. It may be that the "reality" of those who foster close relationships with companion animals, see them as thoughtful and reciprocating, construct their unique identities, and regard them as full-fledged partners in collective action is an anthropomorphic "delusion."

But, to remain true to the interactionist view of human beings as actively involved in evaluating situations, defining others, having goals, devising reasonable plans of action, and coordinating their interactions with others, I submit that we must see those who foster close relationships with animals as more than the delusional victims of "folk psychology." As active and practical creators of meaning, caretakers base understandings of their animal companions and construct effective relationships with them on routine experience with their "behavior in context" (Mitchell and Hamm 1997).

Theories—be they folk or sociological—are best judged by how useful they are rather than by whether they are right or wrong. Because of linguicentric constraints, we have emphasized the differences that exist between humans and nonhuman animals and have "lost sight of all that we share with them" (Murphy 1995:692). In failing to recognize the fact that we live in an interactional community composed of both human and nonhuman members, we have ignored an area of social life that is commonplace, emotionally rich, and of significant analytic interest. Moving nonhuman animals and people's relationships with them into the realm of "sociological visibility" (Oakley 1974:5) promises to shed light on commonplace worlds of social interaction to which conventional interactionism has, until recently, turned a blind eye.

References

Alger, Janet, and Steven Alger. 1997. "Beyond Mead: Symbolic Interaction between Humans and Felines." *Society & Animals* 5:65–81.

Arluke, Arnold, and Clinton Sanders. 1996. *Regarding Animals.* Philadelphia: Temple University Press.

Beck, Alan. and Aaron Katcher. 1996. *Between Pets and People: The Importance of Animal Companionship.* Lafayette, IN: Purdue University Press.

Becker, Howard. 1986. "Culture: A Sociological View." pp. 11–24 in *Doing Things Together.* Evanston, IL: Northwestern University Press.

Bryant, Clifton. 1979. "The Zoological Connection: Animal-Related Human Behavior." *Social Forces* 58:399–421.

Cahill, Spencer. 1998. "Toward a Sociology of the Person." *Sociological Theory* 16:131–48.

Cain, Ann. 1983. "A Study of Pets in the Family System." pp. 71–81 in *New Perspectives on Our Lives with Companion Animals,* edited by A. Katcher and A. Beck. Philadelphia: University of Pennsylvania Press.

Fidler, Margaret, Paul Light, and Alan Costall. 1996. "Describing Dog Behavior Psychologically: Pet Owners versus Non-Owners." *Anthrozoös* 9:196–200.

Fine, Gary Alan. 1981. "Friends, Impression Management, and Preadolescent Behavior." pp. 257–72 in *Social Psychology through Symbolic Interaction,* 2d ed., edited by G. Stone and H. Farberman. New York: John Wiley.

Howard, Judith. 1995. "Social Cognition." pp. 90–117 in *Sociological Perspectives on Social Psychology,* edited by K. Cook, G. A. Fine, and J. House. Boston: Allyn & Bacon.

Mead, George Herbert. 1962. *Mind, Self, and Society.* Chicago: University of Chicago.

Mechling, Jay. 1989. "'Banana Cannon' and Other Folk Traditions between Human and Nonhuman Animals." *Western Folklore* 48:312–23.

Mitchell, Robert, and Mark Hamm. 1997. "The Interpretation of Animal Psychology: Anthropomorphism or Behavior Reading?" *Behavior* 134:173–204.

Murphy, Raymond. 1995. "Sociology as if Nature Did Not Matter: An Ecological Critique." *British Journal of Sociology* 46:688–707.

Myers, Gene. 1998. *Children and Animals.* Boulder, CO: Westview Press.

Nieburg, Harold, and A. Fischer. 1982. *Pet Loss.* New York: Harper and Row.

Oakley, Ann. 1974. *The Sociology of Housework.* New York: Pantheon.

Rasmussen, Jeffrey, and D.W. Rajecki. 1995. "Differences and Similarities in Humans' Perceptions of Thinking and Feeling of a Dog and Boy." *Society & Animals* 3:117–37.

Rasmussen, Jeffrey, Rajecki D. W., and Heather D. Craft, 1993. "Human Perceptions of Animal Mentality: Ascriptions of Thinking." *Journal of Comparative Psychology* 107:283–90.

Rollin, Bernard. 1997. "Anecdote, Anthropomorphism, and Animal Behavior." pp. 125–33 in *Anthropomorphism, Anecdotes, and Animals,* edited by R. W. Mitchell, N. Thompson, and H. L. Miles. Albany: State University of New York Press.

Rubin, Lillian. 1985. *Just Friends: The Role of Friendship in Our Lives.* New York: Harper and Row.

Sanders, Clinton. 1993. "Understanding Dogs: Caretakers' Attributions of Mindedness in Canine-Human Relationships." *Journal of Contemporary Ethnography* 22:205–26.

Sanders, Clinton. 1999. *Understanding Dogs: Living and Working with Canine Companions.* Philadelphia: Temple University Press.

Shapiro, Kenneth. 1990. "Understanding Dogs through Kinesthetic Empathy, Social Construction, and History." *Anthrozoös* 3:184–95.

Voith, Victoria. 1983. "Animal Behavior Problems: An Overview." pp. 181–86 in *New Perspectives on Our Lives with Companion Animals,* edited by A. Katcher and A. Beck. Philadelphia: University of Pennsylvania Press.

Wipper, Audrey. 2000. "The Partnership: The Horse-Rider Relationship in Eventing." *Symbolic Interaction* 23:47–70.

Michael Ramirez

Dog Ownership as a Gender Display

While scholars have investigated how cultural constructions of gender appear in everyday life, they have generally overlooked these constructions in people's relationships with their pets. Pet ownership in the United States is booming. Researchers have explored how defining pets as near persons justifies relationships with them as authentic, as well as how relationships with pets shape individuals' identities and well-being. Sanders (2003:420) recently underscored the sociological imperative of including "interspecies interactions and relationships in the repertoire" of interactionist research agendas. Likewise, Irvine (2004a:15) suggests that "animals contribute something to the experience of human selfhood." I build on these advances in symbolic interactionism by examining how human beings construct gendered meanings for their pets, as well as the ways animals contribute to one particular aspect of owners' selfhoods—their gender identities.

In this article, I explore pet ownership as a relationship individuals construct in accordance with gender norms that characterize relationships among human beings. I explore the gendered nature of people's relationships with their dogs in three specific areas: (1) how owners use gender norms to select appropriate dogs, (2) how owners reveal their gender ideologies in their constructions of their dogs' behaviors and personalities, and (3) how owners use pets as props to display gender.

Gender Norms and Choice of Pets

Gender norms influenced both the types of pets that owners chose to acquire and, among those who decided to get a dog, its breed, size, and sex. Of course, only some dog owners made such con-scious choices when selecting dogs, as half of my sample acquired dogs in other ways, such as by adopting strays. All the dog owners with whom I spoke had a history of owning pets, a finding consistent with other research indicating that most current pet owners had pets during their childhood. Most adult pet owners remain "loyal to the species" they owned as children. Among my respondents, all ten men and all but one of the sixteen women had owned or had grown up with dogs. However, two women were self-confessed former "cat-people" whose current dog was their first. Discussing her past views of dogs, Kristen explained, "I used to have something against dogs. They were drooling and too heavy. I always associated cats as more of a 'female' animal and dogs as more of a happy-go-lucky 'male' kind of animal." Bruce provided a contrasting comment about cats. He mentioned that he grew up with both dogs and cats, but did not now plan to get a cat. Asked if his decision was motivated by any foreseeable complications that could arise between the cat and his dachshund, Dylan, he responded, "No, not that. I just don't want one—they're too feminine, you know?"

People have historically identified dogs as masculine and cats as feminine (Serpell 1988b), and my respondents confirmed this pattern. Fogle (1985:27) contends that cat ownership is associated with sexual orientation, as cats are the "favored species of pet" among gay men, although he provides no empirical data to substantiate this claim. While my participants did not explicitly equate men's cat ownership with homosexuality, they did seem to agree that a man who owns a cat constitutes a greater violation of gender norms than a woman who owns a dog.

Explaining Dogs' Behaviors: Through a Gendered Lens

Regardless of how they acquired their dogs, owners described them in gendered terms and used the gendered norms that characterize human relationships. For example, as I took my place on Aimee's couch to begin the interview, Jade, her Yorkshire terrier, jumped up to lie beside me. After several failed attempts to get Jade to sit with her, Aimee remarked, "She's not gonna listen. She likes men." Aimee then proceeded to speak for Jade, saying, "I'm a flirt. I can't help it." Other women described similar behaviors in their dogs as stereotypically feminine signs of being "emotionally needy." In comparison, men owners were more likely to depict behaviors similar to Jade's as mere friendliness.

Women generally described their dogs, whether male or female, in more feminine terms. Eight of the sixteen women described their dogs as either nurturing or needing to be nurtured. Only one man interpreted his dog's personality in this way. Discussing Nima's personality, Anna said, "If a dog can be nurturing, she's nurturing. She's very nurturing and very reserved and passive." Contrasting Nima with the other pets in her household, Anna claimed that Nima "wanted to be everybody's mother." Similarly, describing the interaction between her female dog, Shep, and her other pets, Louise remarked,

> She gets along really well with the other animals [in my house]. And I think that's the sweetest part of her nature, that she senses that's my cat and she would never mess with that cat. And she doesn't really like him. They're definitely not friends, but . . . I think that she just knows that cat is important to me and I love it, so she just makes do. . . . She just knows what's important to me and what's okay and what's not okay without really being told and I think that's so sweet of her.

In essence, Louise described Shep as having high self-control and as being compliant. While self-control has usually been interpreted as a masculine trait, Louise categorized it as a more feminine, "sweet" trait.

Owners evoked gender norms not only when describing their dogs' physical appearances but also in more general discussions about their pets. For instance, men owners almost always described their dogs in terms of activity and strength. Anthony's description of Bettencourt made the dog sound like a heavyweight boxer: "It's just that, pound for pound, they're the most physical. They are the strongest dogs." Although his description was a bit more extreme than that of other owners, most men described their dogs as being physical. Women rarely used these descriptors when talking about their dogs, male or female.

In those instances when the dog's behavior failed to meet stereotypical expectations, owners still tried to sustain gender stereotypes. Explaining Jake's failure to meet her expectations of "male dog behavior," Juliana said,

> Jake is more nurturing and maternal. He does a lot of things that I would expect the female dog to do, a lot of the care taking. You know, if [another dog is] doing something that Jake knows is wrong, he'll guide him the right way.

Juliana's explanations exhibited two important aspects of gender stereotypes. First, she interpreted Jake's behavior as "wrong" for a male. Rather than questioning her gender stereotypes, Juliana instead used the example of Jake's behavior to further reinscribe ideologies about sex differences. Second, she defined nurturing and helpful behavior as generally feminine characteristics. A male who was nurturing, maternal, and displaying caretaking responsibilities not only was rare but was also transgressing assumed gender dispositions.

One might expect owners of larger, more traditionally aggressive dogs to categorize them in more "masculine" terms. However, such gendered characterizations rested more on the owner's gender, regardless of the dog's breed. Men did not own large dogs exclusively, nor did all women own toy breeds. However, men who owned fairly small dogs described them in similar terms as men who owned larger ones. Bruce described his dachshund Dylan as tough, despite his small size:

> He thinks he's the shit, pretty much. He has small-dog syndrome. When I take him back to my parents' house in Atlanta—they have a lab-collie mix, a big, about eighty-five-pound dog, and a big alley cat, about twenty-five pounds. They both tower over Dylan, but Dylan will antagonize them and try to kick their ass.

Dylan may have been a small breed, but his assumed masculine personality trumped his small stature. Overall, owners consistently used gender to interpret their dogs' personalities. At times, they even went as far as to reframe unconventional gender behaviors into traditional ones, thereby maintaining stereotypical characterizations of gender.

Dogs as Gender Props

Later in our conversations, the topics shifted to the owners' favorite aspects of ownership and the routines they shared with their dogs. Owners often remarked that they used their dogs as displays or props to confirm their own gender identities. One of the most obvious differences between men and women dog owners emerged when I asked participants what they valued most about their dogs. Evan mentioned how his relationship with Rusty and Luke compared with his wife's relationship with them: "They play with me more. Like I'll take them to exercise more than she will. But she's more of the lovey-affection with them. It's like they both mesh with both of us." Although I did not have the opportunity to confirm these distinctions, comments from other women owners corroborated Evan's explanation. Relationships with dogs emulated human relationships, particularly in terms of gender stereotypes and expectations. Reproducing traditional roles of father and mother, Evan was more involved in playing with the dogs, while his wife was more concerned with nurturing them.

Daniel, the owner of Lola and Cruise, perhaps best expresses the key difference between men and women owners. What he liked most about owning dogs was the opportunity to participate in outdoor activities with them. In contrast, Monica, his wife, who co-owns both dogs, replied with the following:

> [I like] the joy that they bring to our lives, to my life. They're just somebody to talk to also and interact with other than another human being. And it's just fun. I don't know, sometimes I wish they could talk so they could tell me what's going on in their heads.

Almost all the women stated that they valued companionship. Among them, those who lived alone particularly felt that their dogs prevented the loneliness they would otherwise experience.

When asked what they valued most about dog companionship, fourteen of the women mentioned their dogs' abilities to act as a source of comfort. This response is consistent with historical changes in attitudes toward pet ownership (Serpell 1988a). In the past, pet ownership was considered a luxury, but today it is considered as the "outcome of normal human social behavior and needs" (Serpell 1988a:49). People commonly see their pets as capable of both understanding their owners' emotions and feeling emotions themselves. Although men occasionally mentioned valuing this perceived quality as well, women often cited it as one of the most meaningful aspects of owning a dog. Anna said that she valued

> the constant companionship and unconditional love. Especially with Bailey, I'd come home and all I'd have to do was talk to him in a completely normal voice and he just wags his tail and gets completely excited and [thinks] I am just like the best thing in the world. Especially after a crappy day, you come home and there's nobody there and this dog just thinks you walk on water. It's pretty cool.

More specifically, women were more likely to recognize and *verbally* value the support they received from their dogs. While men did not mention this particular aspect of support when asked directly about it, they did, however, suggest it while discussing other topics.

Although there were a few exceptions among women, men were more likely to cite joint activities with their dogs as valuable. Of course, women did go to parks with their dogs or take walks with them, but they did not indicate that they valued these aspects of the relationship more than others. Men spoke at length about outdoor activities (such as jogging, biking, and backpacking) in which they took part with their dogs. David stated that his relationship with his dogs turned out better than he had initially anticipated, thanks in large part to the activities in which they were involved:

> I'm spending a lot more time doing things with them and playing with them and enjoying things with them. We've taken them hiking up in the Appalachian Trail and other things. And I'd like to take them camping with us [and] try to do other things too.

Though they participated in similar activities with their dogs, both women and men emphasized those activities that typified traditional gendered behaviors and attitudes.

Configuring Dog-Human Relationships

While sharing details of their day-to-day lives with their dogs, the owners discussed their interactive relationships with their dogs at length. Men saw themselves as master, friend, or playmate to their dogs. Women saw their relationships similarly, but added roles such as "mother" or "parent."

Art, the owner of a service dog named Max, described their relationship as having two alternating dimensions: a means of assistance to him in public, but a companion at home. Asked if he saw Max as a service dog or as a pet, Art responded without hesitation, "More as a friend," signaling a third category. This view was typical of those of other men owners, although Art's case was atypical in that Max was a service dog

as well as a pet. Echoing Sanders's (2003) observation that owners interact with pets as they do with human friends, the men in my sample typically described their dogs as they would their human friends. Eight of the ten men mentioned the role of their dog as either a "workout partner" or a companion with whom they engaged in physical activity. David, who brought his basenji-boxer mix named Monk along on mountain bike outings, stressed the benefit of now having "someone" with whom to exercise. Anthony, a college athlete himself, held similar sentiments about Bettencourt, who "goes through [training] seasons" just like he does. Anthony's athletic training averaged six months of the year, and he concentrated on Bettencourt's training for the remainder of the year. Whereas other men saw their dogs as workout partners, Anthony went one step further by casting himself as Bettencourt's personal fitness trainer.

Like men, women often identified their dogs as a "best friend." Fourteen of the women, but only three men, characterized relationships with their dogs as similar to—or exactly like—those between a parent and a child. Women owners, more so than men, tended to see their dogs as "eternal children" (Kete 1994:82; Serpell 1986). Shirley, the owner of a poodle named Daisy, said,

> She's my baby. I carry her like a baby. I guess, in my mind, it's like having a baby. I talk to her, I kiss her, she minds me. . . . To me, I see her in my mind as a little girl. I don't see her like a dog.

Similarly, when asked about her expectations after first getting Mason, her golden retriever, Ginger confessed that she did not expect her attachment to Mason to be nearly as intense as it was. She then described herself as "motherly" and admitted that Mason was her "prebaby" baby. But childless women were not the only ones to describe dogs as children. Both the women owners who had children described their dogs as a "second set of kids."

Lastly, many of my participants shared ownership of their dogs with their romantic partners. In two couples, I was able to interview the partners separately and compare their individual descriptions of the dogs. For example, Christina and David, a couple who owns three dogs, characterized each of their dogs quite differently. Christina described Layla as "incredibly smart and sweet"; David characterized her as "outgoing" and "tough." Christina distinguished Monk as "intense"; David saw him as "standoffish and nervous" because it takes him longer to get comfortable with other dogs. Christina described their third dog, Missy, as "just cute"; David depicted her as "a ball of energy." Asked which of the three dogs they believed most resembled themselves and which resembled their partner, Christina and David offered different answers. Christina said she was most like Missy in that she "tries to be cute all the time." David, in contrast, saw Christina as similar to Layla in that she was the "more outgoing" partner in the couple. He saw himself, however, as quite similar to Monk: "He's more reserved. He's slower to come to, to a good relationship with somebody. He's much more cautious and slow to approach things rather than just jumping into things." In other words, confirming stereotypes of masculinity in heterosexual relationships, he saw both Monk and himself as more rational in their relationships. On the whole, owners assigned their dogs multiple roles, most of which were gendered. Both men and women regarded their dogs as more than "just" pets, but as genuine friends. While most of the men saw their dogs as some variation of a workout partner, women more often depicted their dogs as children.

Conclusion

This analysis of the relationships men and women establish with their dogs suggests that people "do gender" with their pets (West and Zimmerman 1987) and thereby illustrates the power of gender stereotypes to shape expectations and interpretations of *all* relationships, not simply those with other human beings. Likewise, owners define what are more likely generational differences ("I'm not like how my dad was with dogs") or cultural ones ("My boyfriend wanted a hunting dog, and I wanted one as a pet") as exclusively gender differences.

Owners' discussions of their relationships with their dogs highlight two gendered patterns. First, there were considerable differences between what men owners value and emphasize in their relationships with their dogs in comparison to women owners. While women emphasize the caretaker role more than any other one, men see themselves as friends, exercise partners, and "coaches" for their dogs, but rarely as a "parent." Even when they are parents, men have the freedom to center their identity on other roles related to occupation or leisure. In contrast, women with children may find it harder to define themselves in a role that takes precedence over that of "mother." Furthermore, the same-sex tendencies among my respondents resemble human relationships in that people actively select friends of the same sex. Also, men's and women's descriptions of their dogs mirror qualities that each gender values in romantic relationships. While men most often mention appearance, women discuss personality. Women's accounts of what they value in their relationships with their dogs may also be linked to their traditional responsibilities as nurturers. When deciding whom to nurture, they do not rely on trivial factors such as appearance.

The second gendered pattern is the finding that owners use their dogs as props for their gender identities. Much like clothing or other material possessions, owners use dogs to display gender qualities. The mere company of a dog displays manhood, as evidenced by the owners' uniform agreement that a dog is *man's* best friend. While owning a dog maintains a man's sense of masculinity, a woman dog owner can use her dog to reinforce her sense of femininity and to potentially exceed traditional conceptions of femininity. Women expand the construct of femininity by owning an animal culturally labeled as "man's best friend." However, they articulate the ways their "versions" of ownership differ from men's. Women often ground their relationships with their pets on intimacy rather than the more traditional (masculine) criterion of physical activities. As such, women's discussions of their dog-owning practices reproduce the image of women as docile, family oriented, and nurturant. In *If You Tame Me*, Leslie Irvine (2004b:7) argues that the appeal of searching for animals at shelters is that it allows for the "'trying on' of possible selves." To extend her theory, my data indicate that upon acquiring a dog, owners not only imagine—but actively attempt to secure—these "possible" selves in gendered ways. While I do not presume that the owners select their dogs with the conscious intention of hoping to achieve particular gender identities, I do argue, however, that an additional benefit of acquiring a dog is that it enables the owners to manipulate the relationships in ways that support their constructions of appealing gender identities.

The routines owners develop with their dogs also reinforce the gendered activities the owners themselves enjoy. Because of the obvious communication barrier between owners and their dogs, the latter cannot verbally confirm that their "favorite" activity is indeed what their owners contend. Although recent research suggests that animals do indeed have emotions, personalities, and preferences (Irvine 2004b), animals communicate their preferences much less clearly than human beings do. But since the owners know their dogs better than anyone else, they can convincingly interpret or redefine their dogs' preferences to fit normative gender ideologies.

While many owners describe their dogs through traditional gender stereotypes, others violate them to characterize their dogs. These transgressions primarily occur when the owner's sex is different from the dog's, such as instances when women own male dogs. Despite this dissimilarity, however, these owners do not necessarily view the sexes as more alike than different, because their descriptions of their dogs are essen-

tially descriptions of themselves. In constructing their dogs' personalities, owners project their gender identities onto them, regardless of their dogs' sex. Owners with dogs of the other sex thus have the potential for creating contradictory roles for their dogs. These "gender problematic" descriptions (such as of men's female dogs behaving in "masculine" ways) illustrate that dogs serve as gender displays *for the owners*, reinforcing stereotypical gender identities even if not "correctly" matched to the dog's sex. In such cases, the nontraditional description of the sexes maintains, rather than disrupts, gender stereotypes.

This study illustrates the extent to which pet owners' powerful status allows them to ascribe gendered meaning while enacting impression management strategies. Fronts, which individuals use to define the situation for onlookers by intentionally showcasing a particular image of one's (often gendered) self, are traditionally conceptualized as inanimate (Schlenker 1980). Dogs, however, can be the "exceptional circumstances" of personal fronts in that they accompany owners across settings. But if dogs are advantageous props because they are animate, does this characteristic make them more difficult to manipulate? On the one hand, it may be more difficult for people to control their dogs' behaviors in every situation. On the other hand, owners may have an easier time manipulating the *meaning* of the dogs' behavior, which is, after all, illustrative of the power differential between owners and their dogs.

Second, as allies in "staging" routines in public, dogs are partners in the "performance teams" (Goffman 1959:79). As Goffman insists, successful teams require selecting members who cooperate in the staging of a situation, are unanimous in their positions, and can be trusted to perform properly. Dog owners choose teammates whose behaviors they can wholly interpret (and even control) without incurring the risk of being contradicted. Thus the human partner in the owner-dog team is more advantaged than are those who participate in two-person teams. Others contend that because dogs are not "in" on the performance in the same ways as their owners, they tend to be "notoriously unreliable members of performance teams" (Robin, Sanders, and Cahill 1991:23). This analysis, however, suggests that while the dogs' actions may be unreliable, the owners ultimately still have the discretion to interpret the meaning of their actions. In so doing, owners impose their own meanings that construct their dogs as quite "reliable" team members.

While the dog owners I interviewed are similar in their attachments and commitments to their dogs, there were substantial gender differences in their descriptions of the dogs' personalities and behaviors, which I explain in two ways. First, owners' descriptions of their relationships with their dogs are undoubtedly colored by selective perception. Both women and men appear to be "keyed in" to behavior that they could construe as feminine or masculine, respectively. For instance, despite rarely discussing these aspects of their relationships with their dogs, men "cuddle" with their pets as much as women do, and women engage in outdoor physical activities with their dogs. Owners highlight behaviors that corroborate their gender identities while downplaying—if not completely overlooking—conduct inconsistent with those identities. When owners observe pet behavior that is gender inappropriate, they completely reframe it to minimize gender nonconformity, much like men renaming their jobs when they do "women's" work. These strategies are possible only because the owners themselves hold the power to selectively see or interpret their dogs' behaviors.

Power is central to these identity-management strategies. In relationships between owners and their dogs, the owners have almost complete power, as dogs obviously cannot verbally contradict (much less know) how the owners interpret their behaviors and generally present their relationships. Developing a definition of the situation in any social relationship requires cooperation by all participants, but pet owners have far more power to define situations than their pets do. Owners can define situations in ways

that enhance their identity, so long as the pet's behavior confirms the interpretation. The power imbalance inherent in owner-dog relationships allows the owner to interpret the pet's behavior in gendered terms. More broadly, this analysis illustrates how people involved in any relationship characterized by a power imbalance may be able to present particular gender displays in ways that they desire.

The interaction of men owners with their pets seems more tightly linked to normative gender roles than that of women owners. The similarity in men's characterizations of their pets, and the meanings they assign pet ownership, suggest that attaining a proper gender identity may be more important for men than for women. Men describe their relationships with their dogs in narrower terms that are largely consistent with hegemonic forms of masculinity valued in Western culture. Women report a somewhat broader set of images of their dogs' personalities as well as a broader set of values they derive from their relationships with their pets.

My research suggests that among adult women and men, gender displays go far beyond simply fashioning the body with material adornment. Relationships with others, including relationships with pets, help validate one's gender identity. Dogs become participants in symbolic exchanges, offering animated affirmations of interpretations put forth by their human owners, but only rarely contradicting them. Owners interpret the behaviors of their dogs in ways consistent with their definitions of reality and actively engage their dogs in enactments of their gender identities. Human and animal interactions can help maintain linkages between institutionalized patterns of gendered relationships in society and individuals' consciousness, thereby helping reaffirm the "naturalness" of a gender order in nearly all aspects of human (and animal) life. This analysis has illustrated the salience of gender in people's perceptions and expectations of others—even when these others are non-human. More precisely, this research has extended symbolic interactionist understandings of animals in society, demonstrating that while the human-animal divide may be blurry, gender boundaries, on the other hand, are quite fixed in our perceptions.

References

Fogle, Bruce. 1985. *Pets and Their People*. New York: Penguin Books.

Goffman, Erving. 1959. *The Presentation of Self in Everyday Life*. New York: Doubleday Anchor Books.

_____. 1979. *Gender Advertisements*. Cambridge, MA: Harvard University Press.

Irvine, Leslie. 2004a. "A Model of Animal Selfhood: Expanding Interactionist Possibilities." *Symbolic Interaction* 27:3–21.

_____. 2004b. *If You Tame Me: Understanding Our Connection with Animals*. Philadelphia: Temple University Press.

Kete, Kathleen. 1994. *The Beast in the Boudoir: Petkeeping in Nineteenth-Century Paris*. Berkeley: University of California Press.

Robin, Douglas M., Clinton R. Sanders, and Spencer E. Cahill. 1991. "Dogs and Their People: Pet-Facilitated Interaction in a Public Setting." *Journal of Contemporary Ethnography* 20:3–25.

Sanders, Clinton R. 2003. "Actions Speak Louder than Words: Close Relationships between Humans and Nonhuman Animals." *Symbolic Interaction* 26:405–26.

Schlenker, Barry R. 1980. *Impression Management: The Self-Concept, Social Identity, and Interpersonal Relations*. Monterey, CA: Brooks/Cole.

Serpell, James. 1986. *In the Company of Animals: A Study of Human-Animal Relationships*. Oxford: Blackwell.

_____. 1988a. "Pet-Keeping in Non-Western Societies: Some Popular Misconceptions." pp. 34–52 in *Animals and People Sharing the World*, edited by A. N. Rowan. Hanover, NH: University Press of New England.

_____. 1988b. "The Domestication and History of the Cat." pp. 151–58 in *The Domestic Cat: The Biology of Its Behavior*, edited by D. C. Turner and P. Bateson. New York: Cambridge University Press.

West, Candace, and Don H. Zimmerman. 1987. "Doing Gender." *Gender & Society* 1:125–51.

ARTICLE 7

Christina Risley-Curtiss

Lynn C. Holley

Tracy Cruickshank

Jill Porcelli

Clare Rhoads

Denise N. A. Bacchus

Soma Nyakoe

Sharon B. Murphy

Women of Color and Animal-Human Connections

The health and well-being of companion animals and humans have long been intertwined, but only recently have they been the subject of empirical study. Knowledge of this relationship is growing, and there is evidence of the powerful connections between people and their animals. For example, among the elderly, reduced blood pressure (Katcher *et al.*, 1983) and relief from depression (Garrity *et al.*, 1989) have been found to be associated with having companion animals. Research has also suggested that these relationships are complex and vary, depending on a number of factors, including ethnicity (Risley-Curtiss, Holley, and Wolf, 2006; Wilson and Netting, 1987). This topic is pertinent for social work because companion animals are increasingly being included in work with a range of vulnerable persons (e.g., Fine, 2000).

Unfortunately, relatively little attention has been paid in the broad professional literature to factors that influence people's relationships with animals, particularly those related to ethnic cultural views, and essentially none has been paid in the social work literature even though social workers are increasingly including animals as adjuncts to treatment. The purpose of the qualitative study that is presented here was to begin to address these gaps by exploring the experiences of women of color with companion animals. We studied women of color because (1) almost all research in this area has focused on whites or, at least, has implied a monolithic perspective; (2) our multicultural feminist perspective led us to center on the perspectives of often-marginalized women; and (3) many social work and animal welfare staff, as well as social work clients, are women. The interviews were conducted by 15 social work students, 14 of whom are women, which allowed for gender matching in all but one interview.

Sixty-two percent of U.S. households have reported having companion animals (American Pet Products Manufacturers Association, 2003), and 68 percent of Americans consider companion animals to be family (Brookman, 1999). Thus, social workers are likely to work with families for whom companion animals are part of their ecology. Furthermore, given an ecological practice perspective, the inclusion of companion animals in our practice and research should be a natural extension of our work with humans, their challenges, coping mechanisms, and resilience factors. Understanding the potential impact of companion animals on people's lives may significantly affect social workers' ability to help their clients. With appropriate knowledge and training, social workers are in a position to do much to enhance the lives of both people and their companion animals.

Method

This exploratory qualitative study was designed to allow women to describe their experiences and views about their companion animals from their own perspectives. Multicultural feminist frameworks that emphasize centering the experiences of women of color informed all aspects of the study.

Interviews

The literature on animal-human relationships and approaches to ethnographic interviewing informed the development of a semistructured interview guide. The students pilot-tested the guide during and after the training, and some changes were made on the basis of their feedback. Open-ended questions allowed the participants to talk about experiences and perspectives that were important to them. Examples of these questions included, "Think about one companion animal or pet that meant a lot to you for some reason. Can you tell me about her or him?" The topics covered such areas as whether companion animals were "family members" and, if so, what being a family member meant; whether their views on pets had changed from childhood to the present; and the ways in which other women of their ethnic or racial community might think or feel about the animals that the participants talked about. Data that were collected using closed-ended items included ethnic identification; age; education; urban, rural, or suburban residence; social-class identification; and current occupation.

Audiotaped face-to-face interviews were conducted in Spring 2004 at locations that were selected by the participants. The participants were invited to select pseudonyms; these pseudonyms, as well as pseudonyms for their pets, are used in this article to protect their confidentiality.

Sample

The convenience sample of 15 women was composed of women who (1) were identified as women of color, (2) were aged 18 or older, and (3) lived in the state in which the university is situated. The sample was stratified by ethnic/racial group to ensure that women from a range of ethnic groups were interviewed. This theoretical sampling technique allowed for the inclusion of women who likely would hold a range of perspectives about animals. Each student in the course was instructed to recruit one woman who fit the sample's parameters for participation in the study.

Of the 15 women, 9 were Latina, including 1 each from El Salvador, Puerto Rico, Guatemala, and Mexico; 2 were from Asia (1 from Japan and 1 from Korea); 2 were Indigenous (1 Navajo and 1 Hopi/Pima); and 2 were African American. Eleven women were in the social work field. The women shared stories about dogs (13 women), cats (7 women), birds (3 women), hamsters (3 women), fish (2 women), and a rabbit (1 woman).

Findings

Reciprocity in Women's Relationships with Pets

An overarching theme in the majority ($n = 13$) of the women's stories was the concept of reciprocity, or mutuality, in their relationships with their pets. Illustrating this theme was Patty, who said, "Whenever [my dog] likes to be smothered [with love or attention] or I need to be smothered, he comes up to me or I go up to him. . . . We're just able to give each other that love or something." Roz echoed this attitude when she said, "Your everyday need is to make sure they have all that they need, [and] their need is to make sure that you have all that you need. . . . It's a sharing process."

Thirteen women described their contributions to this reciprocal relationship as meeting their pets' needs for food and veterinary care, providing love and attention, and/or playing with their animals. All 15 women said that animals brought something to them and/or their families in childhood, adulthood, or both. The women's childhood and current social-group memberships (e.g., social class; urban, suburban, or rural residence; age; ethnicity; and national origin) did not appear to be related to the types of contributions that they mentioned.

Friendship was the most commonly mentioned contribution of pets. Seven women described their pets with such words as *friend*, *buddy*, or *companion*. Two women described the importance of these friendships when they were living in difficult circumstances. For example, Marie talked about her relationship with a cat when she was 5 years old: "It was kind of like my only little friend that I could talk to. . . . I didn't have good communication in the family . . . so it was kind of like my friend—my cat was my buddy that I talked to and stuff."

In addition to friendship, pets were perceived to provide fun and entertainment ($n = 5$), relief of stress or comfort ($n = 4$), love ($n = 4$), constancy ($n = 4$), a sense of protection ($n = 4$), and loyalty ($n = 2$). Mary Jo described a childhood dog as both fun and loving: "We had a dog named Major that I think was more comic relief than anything else. . . . And he was funny, and he was adorable. And he loved us." Lily perceived animals as a source of loyalty and love: "[They are] so loyal, and they like you regardless, and they see you as gods even though you're not at your best. You know, you could be a murderer, and your dog still loves you." Margaret A. told of receiving comfort and constancy from her cat: "When I was by myself, he always knew when to come and sit on my lap—just sit there while I was watching TV. . . . When I was [feeling sad], he always knew just when to jump up and be by me. . . . When things were good he was there, too." Four women said that their animals provided a sense of protection. Felicia, for instance, described a childhood dog as "always at our side; [he] went everywhere with us. He was real protective over us."

It is interesting that when they talked about animals with whom they had close relationships,

the women did not always refer to long-term "family pets." The relationship that Marie described, for example, referred to a stray cat that was around her house for less than a year, and Mary Jo described being close to a bird that died after living with her family for only three days.

The Meaning of "Family Member"

When asked whether they considered their pets to be family members, 13 women said that they did. When explaining the "family" nature of these relationships, they talked about their devotion to their pets, their pets' devotion to them, or both. No patterns related to social-group memberships emerged in the women's responses to this question.

Many women who explained the family nature of the relationship used such terms as *child*, *our boys*, *brother*, *baby*, or *grandchild* when talking about their pets. For example, Patty said, "I like to spoil my dog, and I don't treat my dog [like] he's just an animal. I treat him like part of our family. He's my baby, you know. . . . I treat him as a part of me." Roz, on the other hand, explained the family nature of the relationship in terms of her pet's devotion to people: "She was . . . very much so a member of the family, and it was so wonderful. Like when you came home from being tired and so stressed out from work, and there would be Sparkles greeting you at the door, smiling and so happy to see you."

Although 10 of the 13 women who said that their pets were family members used terms that commonly are used to describe humans (e.g., *child*), 3 women did not see their pets as family members in the same way. For example, after saying that her pet was a family member, Stacia stated, "She was my dog . . . so there was never like this, like a relative. . . . [pause] She was like a part of our family. . . . [longer pause] But it wasn't like a relative."

Family Contexts

The majority of women appeared to have attitudes toward pets that were similar to those of their families. A large minority ($n = 7$), however, shared childhood experiences that indicated that they had different attitudes toward animals than did other family members. Six of these women described an early attachment to animals that their families did not share. For example, Margaret A. and Stacia each told a story about allowing a cat or a dog on their beds even though, as Stacia said, "My mom would freak out." Danna told of an experience in which she learned that her family did not condone her attitude toward the family's sheep:

> I remember getting into a lot of trouble because I wasn't supposed to name them. But no one had ever . . . sat me down and said, "You don't name these . . . animals because we're going to eat them or because we're going to sell them." I just thought, you know, these are baby animals and they had no names, so I named it. I remember the first few times, um, when they butchered sheep, being traumatized.

In contrast, Latisha's family saw their cat as "family," while she saw the cat as "just a cat."

Changes in Animal-Human Relationships over Time

Most women ($n = 12$) mentioned changes in their views about pets over time. Common changes were taking more responsibility for them, spending more time with them, handling them more carefully, and deciding to allow pets into the house all or part of the time.

Although the majority of the women grew more attached to pets as adults, one woman did not. Latisha said that she is less attached to animals as an adult, although she gave no reason for this change.

Several women's comments indicated that they perceived that simply becoming adults led to their changes in attitudes. Other women described reasons that fell into the following three categories:

Attachment/Exposure to Specific Animals

Three women said that they changed their attitudes after they became attached or exposed to particular animals. Marta, who grew up on a farm, said, "Before, I always thought that animals should be outdoors and that they've a job to do. . . . But now that I'm older and I've gotten attached to these little ones, my views have changed. They are . . . more like our little boys." On the other hand, Maria was not allowed to have pets as a child and consequently had little exposure to dogs. Her attitude toward dogs changed after being around them.

Influence of U.S. Culture

Two immigrant women said that exposure to U.S. culture influenced how they treat pets. Sung Hee said, "We look at our animals here like pets, so we are more concerned about their health and things like that than you'd be in Korea." Patty explained:

> "I don't want to sound racist or anything, but I think American or white people—like you see it on the TV. . . . You see the happy family and the family dog. . . . I just saw the difference between how Americans were raised and . . . how I was raised with my [Salvadoran] culture. . . . Like the dog [as a] companion. . . . We don't have that thing about . . . "Let's give the dog a hug or let's play with the dog." [pause] I don't know if I'm making sense, but [pause] I feel that I [am able] to express [my feelings] now. . . .

Deaths of Pets

The deaths of treasured animals caused two women to change their attitudes toward whether to have pets. For example, Margaret A. said that after the death of her 19-year-old cat, she did not want other pets "because then they will die."

Perceptions of Ethnic Communities' Views of Animals

Four women said that their views about animals are not related to their ethnic-group membership. As Lily said, "I think that in . . . every community there are people who love animals, and there are people who neglect them. . . . I mean, there is a whole spectrum of . . . feelings in our community." Women who perceived that their ethnic communities held certain views related to animals often talked about views about the purposes of animals and whether animals were considered to be family members. As is evident in the following discussion, the women often talked about the intersections of ethnicity; social class; rural, urban, or suburban residence; and national origin in describing their communities' views.

Purposes of Animals Eight women perceived that some or most members of their ethnic communities considered some animals to be useful for protection ($n = 6$), work ($n = 4$), and/or food ($n = 2$). Patty noted that her family kept dogs for protection: "We . . . had two dogs. . . . We weren't allowed to play with them or make 'em friendly because those dogs were there to protect us . . . from the neighbors because we lived in a very dangerous neighborhood." Danna, who grew up on a farm, described her family's view that dogs were useful for work: "Dogs were considered work animals. They would herd the sheep and take care of the house, so the dogs were . . . always supposed to be working; they were not supposed to be companions." Danna explained that her family's view that animals are mainly for work arose from her ethnic group's beliefs: "Most of the stories are related to . . . animals having to have a purpose." She said that she still would avoid having certain animals as pets because of the influence of cultural beliefs that, for example, rabbits are in communication with "skin walkers."

Animals as Members of the Family Eight women said that some or most members of their ethnic communities consider pets to be family members. They told about their parents grieving when pets died, a parent cooking a meal for a dog, hiding a dog from a landlord, and getting immunizations or other treatment for their pets— often at a great sacrifice owing to the families' low incomes. Two of these women emphasized that animals who were "family members" could be kept outside as well as inside. As Marta explained, "I think that many [people in my ethnic group] have our dogs outside, but many of us have indoor dogs . . . but I don't know if that

makes any difference." Felicia reported that her father's, but not her mother's, ethnic community considers pets to be family members. As she explained, "My father's family always had animals. They had horses, and the dogs were always like part of the family because they helped with the rounding up of cattle and horses."

On the other hand, 3 of the 12 women who said that their pets are family members said that their parents and/or their larger ethnic or national communities did not hold such views. For example, when asked whether she perceived that most members of her ethnic group would share her perspective about dogs, Irene B. said, "No. Definitely not. . . . [Dogs] were there just to protect us." Sung Hee said, "In Korea, we don't think about the dog . . . as part of the family."

Influence of the Social Context Several women said that their nations of origin, social classes, or geographic contexts influenced their communities' views about animals. Sung Hee, who grew up in Korea, said, "[In] my opinion, [in] developing countries they treat animals or pets [a] little bit cruelly. . . . But [in] America or developed countries, they [think about a dog as a] family member or pet. Actually, we don't call [dogs] pet[s]. . . . 'Pet' and 'dog' are a little different." Another immigrant, Stacia, related the treatment of animals to both social class and living in a rural area in her home country of Mexico:

> For those [in] lower socioeconomic [situations], you don't spend money . . . doing any of those extra things. When you are done eating, you just put [leftover food] out there for the dogs. And then there is the other side, where you just buy the premium dog food . . . and they are part of the family. . . . But I do see some trends in that [for] the more rural people. The animals are just "there"; you don't bring them in the house.

Two women who grew up in the United States also spoke about the effect of social class on their communities' care of animals. For example, Felicia told about her mother's reaction when her father sought veterinary treatment for an injured dog: "We took him to the vet, and it cost us over $70 to get him fixed up, I remember. But she thought it was way too much for us to spend on him because . . . my parents were working poor."

Discussion and Implications

Several important findings emerged from this exploratory study. First, a majority of women said that they had reciprocal relationships with their pets. Although other researchers have indicated that humans may have powerful connections with pets, the mutuality of these relationships is not often recognized. Rather, the social work literature generally focuses solely on how animals benefit people (e.g., animal-assisted therapy). This reciprocity was recognized by the women themselves and may be likened to the reciprocity found in human parent-child and friend-friend relationships. For example, in what is referred to as "reciprocal socialization," infants and mothers develop a mutual relationship, with each responding to the other's needs and closely coordinating their actions; it is a process by which children socialize their parents just as parents socialize their children ("Reciprocal Socialization," n.d.). It appears that many of the women in this study had similar relationships with their animals.

Second, and consistent with previous research (Brookman, 1999; Johnson & Meadows, 2002; Risley-Curtiss *et al.,* 2006), most of the women in this sample (13 of the 15) considered their pets to be family members, and 8 of the 15 said that members of their ethnic communities commonly share this view. Our findings go beyond these previous studies by shedding light on what women may *mean* when they say that a pet is a family member. The use of terms such as *baby* and *child* may suggest that some women considered these animals to be equal to humans. All the women described their pets as providing friendship, fun, love, comfort, and/or constancy for themselves or their children or both. Each quality may be considered an important contribution of a human in a healthy family relationship. Our

findings also suggest that some people who consider their pets to be family members may be referring to other—perhaps more concrete—contributions that an animal makes to the family, such as engaging in work or providing protection from harm. These attributes may be another way in which some human members contribute to their families.

Third, as was suggested by other researchers (Brown, 2002; Wilson and Netting, 1987), the findings revealed that the intersections of family contexts, ethnicity, national origin, geographic setting, and social class influence human-animal relationships. These influences are complex and far from deterministic, however. Whereas most women had views about animals that were similar to those of their families, almost half did not. Two women who held different views attributed this difference to the influences of white U.S. culture, but many women appeared to have developed strong attachments early in childhood simply by connecting with specific animals, even when their families did not model such connections. Conversely, another woman appears never to have been as attached to animals as her family had been. In addition, whereas many women described the ways in which ethnicity, national origin, setting (urban, suburban, or rural), and social class shaped their or their families' views about animals, many women described personal attitudes toward animals that differed from their perceptions about the views of others in these social-groups. Indeed, almost a third of the women reported that their views about animals were not related to their ethnic-group memberships, and their stories never referred to any social-group memberships. It is possible, of course, that membership in these social groups did influence the women's attitudes, but that the women were not aware of these influences.

Model of Influences on Views about Animals

On the basis of the findings from this exploratory study and building on the work of Wilson and

Individual Perceptions and Experiences
- Opportunities to interact with animals (e.g., family pets, work animals, stray animals)
- Initial feelings of attachment to animals (e.g., [no] sense of connection)
- Perceptions of what animals and humans bring to the relationship (e.g., comfort, friendship)
- Perceptions of the views of family and social groups about human-animal relationships (e.g., is [not] a family member, is [not] a companion)
- Personal experiences that may draw one to seek relationship with animals (e.g., no human confidants)

Family Perceptions and Experiences
- Same as individual perceptions and experiences, above

U.S. (White, Middle-Class) Culture
Perceptions about appropriate purposes/positions of various animals (e.g., as resources for companionship, work, protection, food) and about how various animals are to be treated (e.g., how "pets" should be cared for) as depicted in:

- Laws
- Media
- People's daily care of animals
- Economic practices

Perceptions and Experiences of Peers at Intersection of Ethnicity, National Origin, Social Class, and Urban/Suburban/Rural Setting in which the Family and/or Individual Lives
- Same as individual and family perceptions and experiences, above
- Housing type, resources available to care for animals, beliefs about animals related to intersection of groups

FIGURE 7.1   **Model of Multiple Influences on Women's Relationship with Animals**

Netting (1987), we offer the following model as a way of understanding various influences on women's views about companion animals (see Figure 7.1). Reflecting our findings, the model demonstrates that *perceptions* and *experiences* that are related to the Individual, Family, intersections of social-group memberships (Intersections), and the U.S. white middle-class culture (U.S. Culture) spheres may all influence a girl's or woman's views about, and relationships with, animals. The model indicates that specific views about animals are generally not innate, but, rather, are created by girls and women as they interact with animals and live their lives within the Family, Intersection, and U.S. Culture spheres

that have socially constructed views about appropriate ways of viewing and interacting with animals.

We assume that there are competing views about animals within each sphere, although certain views may be more prevalent and thus have more influence than may others. In viewing the model, it also is important to note that although the *Family sphere is depicted as the closest to the individual*, a girl or woman may be equally or more strongly affected by the Intersections or the U.S. Culture sphere than by her family. The exploratory nature of this study precludes hypothesizing about the relative weight of these influences. Furthermore, we assume that smaller spheres may affect larger spheres: Girls may influence the views of families, girls and families may influence the views of others at the Intersection sphere, and so forth.

This model also recognizes that views about and relationships with animals may change over time. As a girl or woman ages, she has more experiences with potential influences at all four levels. These life experiences may lead her to change or solidify her existing views about animals. In addition, a girl or woman may either voluntarily or involuntarily change her relationships with her family or other spheres of influence (e.g., strengthen her ethnic identity, migrate to a different geographic or national setting, or move into a different social class); any of these changes may affect her views about human-animal relationships. Just as individuals' views often change over time, so do prevailing views within other spheres.

This model does not include one-on-one or group-level interpersonal interactions beyond those that are related to the Family, Intersections, and U.S. Culture spheres. The model also excludes international influences on U.S. culture. We omitted these potential influences because no women in our sample described them; further studies will likely reveal the importance of such influences.

Implications for Research

Further research is needed to clarify the findings of this exploratory study. That many women described animals as providing friendship or comfort in times of stress suggests the need for research on the roles of animal-human relationships as sources of resilience or as protective factors during childhood and adulthood. The women also described their animal-human relationships as reciprocal and their pets as family members. Limited research suggests that women have delayed leaving abusive situations because of their fear for their animals' welfare (Ascione, 1998). More research needs to be done in this area, including research on effective strategies for seeing that animals are cared for in such situations. In addition, many women

shared intrafamily differences in perspectives about animals. What is the extent of conflict that such differences cause? How can these conflicts be resolved? We presented a model depicting multiple influences on women's views about and relationships with animals. Further research is needed to identify other influences and to examine the relative weight of each sphere of influence.

Our findings also suggest that if pet-attachment instruments, such as the PAQ, reflect the U.S. white middle-class culture's construct of "pet," they may include questions that fail to reflect the levels of attachment that some women have with their animals. For example, some participants who indicated that they were strongly attached to their animals kept them outside. How would they respond to a question asking whether pets have the same privileges as human family members? Instruments that are grounded in the experience and perspectives of communities that differ in ethnicity, social class, national origin, and geographic setting are needed if we are to understand the nature of attachment within these communities.

In addition, research is needed to address the limitations of this study. We interviewed a small convenience sample: Do other members of women's ethnic, social-class, national-origin, and geographic social groups share similar perspectives and experiences? What are the views of women of color who are not predominantly middle class, highly educated, and in the social work field? Are the views of boys, men, whites, and women from social groups that were not included in this sample similar to those of the women in this sample? Further research also needs to explore the ways in which religion and spirituality influence animal-human relationships.

References

American Pet Products Manufacturers Association. (2003, April 14). New survey reports 77.7 million pet cats, 65 million pet dogs owned in U.S. Retrieved from www.appma.org/press_releases/detail.asp?v=ALL&id=36.

Ascione, F. R. (1998). Battered women's report of their partner's and their children's cruelty to animals. *Journal of Emotional Abuse*, *1*, 119–123.

Brookman, F. (1999, October 25). The things people do for pets. *Discount Store News*. Retrieved from www.findarticles.com/p/articles/mi_m3092/is_20_38/ai_57443535.

Brown, S. E. (2002). Ethnic variations in pet attachment among students at an American school of veterinary medicine. *Society & Animals*, *10*, 455–456.

Faver, C. A., and E. B. Strand (2003). Domestic violence and animal cruelty: Untangling the web of abuse. *Journal of Social Work Education*, *39*, 237–253.

Fine, A. (2000). *Handbook on animal-assisted therapy*. San Diego, CA: Academic Press.

Garrity, T. F., Stallones, L., Marx, M. B., and T. P. Johnson, (1989). Pet ownership and attachment as supportive factors in the health of the elderly. *Anthrozoös*, *3*, 35–44.

Johnson, R. A., and R. L. Meadows (2002). Older Latinos, pets and health. *Western Journal of Nursing Research*, *24*, 609–620.

Katcher, A., Friedmann, E., Beck, A., and J. Lynch, (1983). Looking, talking, and blood pressure: Physiological consequences of interaction with the living environment. In A. H. Katcher and A. M. Beck (eds.), *New perspectives on our lives with companion animals* (pp. 351–359). Philadelphia: University of Pennsylvania Press.

Reciprocal socialization (n.d.). *Wikipedia*. Retrieved from http://en.wikipedia.org/wiki/Reciprocal_socialization.

Risley-Curtiss, C., Holley, L. C. and S. Wolf, (2006). The animal-human bond and ethnic diversity. *Social Work*, *51*, 257–268.

Wilson, C. C., and F. E. Netting (1987). New directions: Challenges for human-animal bond research and the elderly. *Journal of Applied Gerontology*, *6*, 189–200.

PART THREE

The Dark Side

Introduction

In the past, academics have been somewhat reluctant to study the mistreatment of animals—or what Andrew Rowan (1992) calls the "dark side" of human-animal relationships—due to the topic's unsavory nature. In fact, as late as the 1980s, one national humane organization—itself committed to protecting animals—regarded this topic as taboo, avoiding discussion of it at its annual meeting and in its scholarly journal at the time. However, a comprehensive and complex understanding of human-animal interaction requires attention to what Carl Jung called the shadow—our vices, jealousies, and vanities, or the side of ourselves we would rather deny. By studying shadowy encounters with animals—and cruelty is one such encounter—along with those that are positive, heart warming, and caring, we can see human-animal interaction for what it is rather than how some feel it ought to be.

A number of different approaches have been taken to defining animal cruelty. Since the late 1800s, state legislators in America have approached cruelty by defining it in abstract if not ambiguous ways. Statutory law typically defines cruelty as the infliction of unnecessary suffering, but there is widespread disagreement over what this means or how to determine it in particular cases. Focusing on these cases, epidemiologists have approached animal cruelty by inductively defining it on the basis of the act itself. Exhaustive lists are compiled of cruel acts that are reported to humane societies, such as burning, stomping, stabbing, and crushing, rather than relying on abstract legal definitions. But such list-making, by only focusing on the act's outcome, tells us nothing about what the abuser was intending to do when committing these acts. Addressing this omission, psychologists have approached animal cruelty by focusing on individual motivation—intent to harm animals—as the basis for defining it. While this focus gets closer to the perspective of animal abusers, cruelty's meaning is limited to the thoughts and actions of individuals, ignoring how its definition depends on social context. Remedying this limitation, sociologists have focused on how groups determine the meaning of certain acts toward animals in particular situations. Taking this relativistic approach means that some groups will not define certain acts as cruel, even though under law or by societal norm they would be, while other groups will see certain acts as cruel, when they are not illegal or even contrary to public opinion.

Confusion over how to best approach and define animal cruelty has not stopped the trend to prevent and punish it. Humane law enforcement departments were created in Boston and New York in the late 1800s, primarily to monitor the treatment of horses. Today, there are numerous humane societies and animal control departments throughout America that police cruelty toward all animals and prosecute these cases in court (Arluke 2004). Some of the work of "animal cops" has even been showcased on the nationally syndicated Animal Planet cable station. These humane agents conduct investigations, obtain and execute search warrants, make arrests, and sign and prosecute complaints, when the crime involves animal cruelty. The bulk of their cases involve "everyday" animals—strays, pets, vermin, and small-farm livestock—that are neglected or sometimes deliberately mistreated by individuals. Agents also visit and inspect stockyards, slaughterhouses, racetracks, pet shops, guard-dog businesses, service-dog businesses, horse stables that rent or board horses, kennels, and animal dealers licensed by the United States Department of Agriculture. During a typical year, for example, one humane law enforcement department in Massachusetts conducts approximately 5,000 investigations and 1,000 inspections, involving more than 150,000 animals (Arluke and Luke 1997). Since such complaints are also lodged with other organizations in the state, estimates of abuse complaints easily surpass 10,000 annually in Massachusetts and show evidence of steadily mounting over time. Of course, this increase may be due to growing public sensitivity to animal welfare, greater visibility of humane law enforcement departments, or simply improved record keeping. Although most alleged abusers do not end up in court, those that do now face increased fines and jail time because many states have redefined animal cruelty as a felony crime instead of a misdemeanor.

Alongside this growing criminal justice trend to deal seriously with animal cruelty, researchers, policy makers, animal advocates, and mental health practitioners have sought to understand the causes of cruelty. Such knowledge will hopefully provide clues for preventing abuse and treating abusers. Some explanations are biologically oriented. As with violence in general, animal cruelty is predominantly a male enterprise (Herzog and Arluke 2006). Men are overwhelmingly convicted for extreme forms of cruelty, such as beating, shooting, mutilation, and burning. And men are also more likely to be involved in lesser forms of cruelty. Other explanations are more psychologically oriented, explaining cruelty at the level of individual personality and pathology. From this perspective, people harm animals because there is something internally wrong with their thinking and feeling. Antisocial personality syndrome is typically cited as the culprit. Surely, personality plays some role in how we sometimes treat animals; but by focusing on individual pathology, this level of explanation fails to consider the role played by the social and cultural context surrounding the abusive situation. The latter is more the charge of sociologists who often take a macro-level approach to understanding the roots of animal cruelty. Leaving behind the individual, they look at how large-scale features of society—its economic, political, entertainment, or scientific institutions—produce and perpetuate the oppression of animals (see Articles 17 and 31).

Social psychological explanations lie between those that are individual-pathological and macro-societal. We know that many behaviors in general— both constructive and destructive—arise from demands placed on individuals from their interactions with others, encounters with various situations, and participation in different groups. No doubt, these forces also influence how people see and act toward animals. For example, studies of college students report that a large percentage (from 35 to 55 percent) recall harming animals. Many of these students speak of their former abuse as "just" another form of idle play—an "entertaining" distraction that reduces "boredom" (Arluke 2002). They remember their abuse as idle play for several reasons. In their minds, it was like playing Nintendo games or burning toy soldiers,in part because they did not lose control of their emotions and become explosively violent when harming animals. Had they lost control of their emotions, they claimed that it would have been harder to define their acts as mere play, suggesting something more

serious and disturbing to them. Students also felt that their former abuse was idle play because they restricted its nature and scope, whether this meant psychologically tormenting animals rather than physically harming them, or physically harming them short of causing excessive suffering.

Yet students regarded their animal abuse as more than ordinary play—it had a serious edge that made it "cool" or "thrilling," unlike memories of everyday play. This feeling stemmed, in part, from the challenge of carrying out abuse because it could be hard to find a suitable target, succeed in harming it, and avoid detection by adult authorities; and from the unpredictable and sometimes human-like response of the victims, if harmed. These recollections of abuse as serious and "cool" resonate with Thorne's (1993) description of cross-gender borderwork among children. Although such play is episodic, like animal abuse, its dramatic, ritualistic, and highly emotional qualities make it particularly memorable. It is not just "play" or "fun" because more is going on at an unarticulated and volatile level as ambiguous meanings and culturally expected identities are explored and experienced. Play, according to Thorne, is a fragile definition despite efforts by participants to maintain boundaries between play and not-play; more serious meanings lurk close to the surface as children use cross-gender play to try on, enact, and perpetuate cultural constructions of masculinity and femininity. Similarly, the thrill of "everyday" animal abuse is due to the opportunity it affords adolescents to contemplate, sample, and appropriate adult identities. By defining certain animals as suitable victims for abuse, these adolescents can feel empowered, however briefly and superficially, because their cruelty allows them to behave in ways that the adult world keeps off limits. They are interloping behavior from which they feel excluded and about which they are curious.

Although it is important to understand the causes of cruelty, social scientists have been more preoccupied with examining its consequences. Perhaps the most controversial issue in the field concerns the putative relationship between animal abuse and human-directed violence. The graduation or escalation model claims that those who deliberately mistreat animals in culturally unsanctioned ways will subsequently become aggressive and violent toward people. In this model, animal abuse is a nodal, developmental event that can predict future antisocial behavior. The animal abuser is thought to become desensitized to violence, get rehearsal for doing it, and perhaps have their thirst increased for more.

That harming animals affects people—but only in negative ways—is an old idea. As early as the seventeenth century, the philosopher John Locke suggested that harming animals had a destructive impact on those who inflict it. In later centuries, the psychologist Anna Freud and the anthropologist Margaret Mead followed suit, arguing that cruelty could be a symptom of character disorder. Children or adolescents who harmed animals were thought to be on a pathway to future violence because these acts desensitized them or tripped an underlying predisposition to aggression. By releasing destructive impulses and turning them on animals, the floodgates restricting violence opened and future targets were likely to be human—or so it was argued.

Researchers have tried to verify what is now known as the link. In 1963, John Macdonald proposed that assaulting small animals was one of three precursors—along with fire-setting and enuresis—of extreme cruelty toward humans. But in a controlled study of personal histories, Macdonald himself failed to establish that violent psychiatric patients were significantly more likely than nonviolent psychiatric patients to abuse animals. However, more recent research does support the idea that there is some connection between animal abuse and human violence. In 1985, Kellert and Felthous uncovered significantly more animal cruelty in the childhoods of "aggressive criminals" than in the childhoods of "non-aggressive criminals" or "noncriminals." Estimates of the percentage of extremely violent individuals who have engaged in animal cruelty tend to be substantially higher than in the general population. In their study of serial killers, Wright and Hensley (2003) found that 21 percent had a known history of childhood animal cruelty—although the authors failed to report either the nature or the extent of that animal cruelty. Ressler, Burgess, and Douglas (1988) similarly determined that a large number of convicted sexual murderers admitted having engaged in animal cruelty. Despite these more recent

findings, the causal nature of the relationship between animal abuse and future violence directed toward humans has not been established (Piper 2003).

Some researchers and advocates have focused on a different kind of link—the relationship between animal cruelty and domestic violence toward spouses or children. For example, studies of families in which child abuse occurred have found that family members also frequently abuse pets (e.g., DeViney, Dickert, and Lockwood 1983). And studies of battered women and their companion animals have found high rates of animal abuse. Quinlisk (1999), for example, found that among women seeking shelter from domestic violence, 67 percent of them saw their partners abuse their pets, while their children were present 43 percent of the time. Knowledge of this link has led to calls for cross reporting between animal control agents and social workers, since discovery of either animal abuse or domestic violence may serve as a red flag for the other problem.

The results of these studies have enabled activists to argue that cruelty should be prevented because it is either predictive of further violence in general or associated with domestic violence in particular. By the end of the twentieth century, the link became the dominant focus of organizational campaigns against cruelty, such as the First Strike program of the Humane Society of the United States (HSUS). Even those who do not care about animal welfare might now be concerned about preventing cruelty, given the urgency felt by many to identify adolescent red flags that signal a future violent adult and to more effectively intervene in cases of domestic violence, for the sake of both people and animals.

The selections in this part of *Between the Species* explore the roots and consequences of animal cruelty. First, Robert Agnew develops a social psychological model to explain abuse when it is broadly defined to include the sanctioned institutional use of animals in settings such as biomedical labs or shelters. One direct cause of such abuse is the ignorance of people who are unaware that they contribute to the environmental harm of animals, use products that were tested on animals, or participate in activities that abuse animals. Another direct cause is the ability to justify or excuse abuse by claiming that animals have low moral worth, serve human needs, deserve to be harmed, or would suffer more if not harmed, and by criticizing those who condemn abuse or deny responsibility for it. A third direct cause is that the financial value of abusing animals is great, while guilt is easy to neutralize and formal sanctions are weak and rarely implemented. However, these direct influences are moderated by individual characteristics such as empathy, socialization, level of stress, level of control, social position, and the nature of the animal that is targeted, explaining why abuse varies from person to person and situation to situation.

The second selection, by Arnold Arluke and his co-researchers, examines the consequences of animal abuse for later violent behavior. To test whether abusers "graduated" from harming animals to harming people, they compared the criminal records of prosecuted animal abusers and matched nonabusing controls. Criminal records tracking noted violent offenses as well as other forms of antisocial behavior, such as property crimes or drug offenses. As expected, the animal abusers were much more likely to have been arrested for a variety of offenses than were the controls. They did not, however, commit a disproportionate number of violent offenses as opposed to property or drug offenses. In addition, animal abuse was no more likely to precede than to follow either violent or nonviolent offenses. Rejecting the graduation model of abuse, this study's results support the deviance generalization theory, which says that those who commit one form of deviance are likely to commit other forms as well, and in no particular time order.

Although animal cruelty may not have a causal relationship with later violence, the two may be associated. Clifton Flynn, in the final article, explores the relationship between battered women and their animal companions. Interviews with clients at a shelter for battered women found that their violent partners used companion animals to control, hurt, and intimidate the women. These women treated their companion animals as surrogates for human-human interaction, thinking of them as children, friends, and confidants. For the batterers, these animals often served as enemies—either as scapegoats or as targets of abuse directed at their partners. In addition, the animals responded to the women's victimization by initiating interaction with them, attempting to protect women during an assault or sensing that they were needed after a violent episode. The animals also appeared to be emotionally stressed after the women were abused. Some of the women delayed going to the shelter because they were afraid to leave their animal companions at home, fearing their harm. A few found caretakers to take the animals, but most were left worrying about their animals' fate because they had to be left in the hands of their abusive partners.

References

Arluke, A. 2002. "Animal Abuse as Dirty Play." *Symbolic Interaction* 25:405–430.

Arluke, A. 2004. *Brute Force: Animal Police and the Challenge of Cruelty*. Purdue University Press.

Arluke, A., and C. Luke. 1997. "Physical Cruelty toward Animals in Massachusetts, 1975–1996." *Society & Animals* 5:195–204.

DeViney, E., Dickert, J., and R. Lockwood. 1983. "The Care of Pets within Abusing Families." *International Journal of the Study of Animal Problems* 4:321–329.

Herzog, H., and A. Arluke. 2006. "Human-Animal Connections: Recent Findings on the Anthrozoology of Cruelty." *Brain and Behavioral Science* 29(3): 230–231.

Kellert, S., and A. Felthous. 1985. "Childhood Cruelty toward Animals among Criminals and Noncriminals." *Human Relations* 38:1113–1129.

Macdonald, J. 1963. "The Threat to Kill." *American Journal of Psychiatry* 120:125–130.

Piper, H. 2003. "The Linkage of Animal Abuse with Interpersonal Violence: A Sheep in Wolf's Clothing?" *Journal of Social Work* 3:161–177.

Quinlisk, J. 1999. "Animal Abuse and Family Violence." In F. Ascione and P. Arkow, eds., *Child Abuse, Animal Abuse, and Domestic Violence*, 168–175. West Lafayette, IN: Purdue University Press.

Ressler, R., Burgess, A., and J. Douglas. 1988. *Sexual Homicide: Patterns and Motives*. New York: The Free Press.

Rowan, A. 1992. "The Dark Side of the Force." *Anthrozoös* 5:4–5.

Thorne, B. 1993. *Gender Play: Girls and Boys in School*. New Brunswick, NJ: Rutgers University Press.

Wright, J., and C. Hensley. 2003. "From Animal Cruelty to Serial Murder: Applying the Graduation Hypothesis." *International Journal of Offender Therapy and Comparative Criminology* 47: 71–88.

Robert Agnew

The Causes of Animal Abuse

This article develops a comprehensive theory of the causes of animal abuse: a theory designed to integrate previous research and direct future research by criminologists and others. In particular, this theory draws on social learning, strain, control, and certain other theories of crime in order to explain *why individuals abuse animals* (the term animal will be used to refer to nonhuman animals).

Definition of Abuse

Most of the harm inflicted on animals is legal. In fact, it is debatable whether most harmful activities would qualify as "abuse." Definitions of abuse typically state that the harm inflicted on animals should be (1) socially unacceptable, (2) intentional or deliberate, and/or (3) unnecessary. Many of the activities which contribute to the suffering of animals, like the consumption of meat, are condoned by most people, are not performed with the intention of harming animals, and are perceived as necessary for health, economic, or other reasons. As a consequence, many studies of animal abuse ignore such pervasive forms of abuse as "factory farming" and animal experimentation. Likewise, most animal *welfare* (as opposed to animal *rights*) organizations ignore such abuse. Rather, such studies and organizations focus on harmful acts that are clearly deliberate, unnecessary, and socially unacceptable—most often the serious abuse of companion animals by private individuals.

This article employs a different approach. Drawing on Vermeulen and Odendaal (1993), abuse is broadly defined as any act that con-tributes to the pain or death of an animal or that otherwise threatens the welfare of an animal. Such abuse may be physical (including sexual) or mental, may involve active maltreatment or passive neglect, may be direct or indirect, intentional or unintentional, socially approved or condemned, and/or necessary or unnecessary (however defined). The focus of this article is on sentient animals: those who have the capacity to suffer or enjoy (see Rollin, 1990). The theory advanced in this article, however, is also capable of explaining the harm inflicted on *all* animals. It is recognized that this broad definition includes many acts that would not be defined as abusive by most people, but I believe that such a definition has several advantages.

First, it encompasses those activities that account for the vast portion of animal harm including factory farming, animal experimentation, hunting and trapping, and the use of animals for entertainment purposes. The number of animals killed and harmed by such activities staggers the imagination. It is estimated that approximately nine and a half *billion* animals are killed each year in the United States. Nine billion are killed for food, approximately 200 million by hunters and 15 to 20 million by trappers (Plous, 1993), 20 to 100 million in animal experiments (Plous, 1993: 12), and 5 million by animal "shelters" (Waggoner, 1997). In addition, well over 100 million animals are used for entertainment and recreational purposes (Plous, 1993: 12). Further, the vast majority of the animals killed live their lives in what can only be described as torturous conditions. For example, almost all chickens and most pigs in the United States are now raised on "factory farms." They are confined in pens and cages, where they are "crowded, restricted, stressed, frustrated, held in barren environments and maintained on additive-laced, unnatural diets" (see also Mason, 1985: 92).

Second, this broad definition of abuse is not tied to prevailing beliefs about animals, including beliefs about the acceptability or necessity of activities that are harmful to animals. Such beliefs vary by time and place, and are largely if not entirely social products. Currently, animal rights groups are in a heated battle with the "animal industry" and its allies to shape such beliefs. If we accept current beliefs, we let those political and social actors with the greatest power determine our definition of animal abuse. By employing the broadest possible definition of abuse, we can treat such beliefs as variables that influence our behavior toward animals and we can study the determinants of such beliefs. This increases the applicability of the theory which follows. Regardless of the particular definition of abuse that one may employ, be it narrow or broad, the theory will be of some relevance. The theory, in particular, is relevant to individuals who deliberately beat their companion animals for socially unacceptable

reasons as well as to individuals who unknowingly harm animals through their purchase of products that contain animal ingredients, like photographic film or house paint. Further, the theory will remain relevant as beliefs regarding animals and definitions of abuse change. The theory, in fact, may help explain such changes.

Employing such a broad definition of abuse does have a problem: the causes of different types of abuse may differ. For example, strain or stress may play an important role in the serious abuse of companion animals but little role in those socially acceptable activities that indirectly (and often unknowingly) harm animals—like the purchase of products with animal ingredients. The theory, then, must specify whether certain variables are more relevant to some types of abuse than to others.

The theory is presented in two parts. First, I describe those individual factors that directly increase the propensity for animal abuse. Second, I describe an additional set of factors that have both direct effects on animal abuse and indirect effects. This model of animal abuse is shown in Figure 8.1 and is described in the remainder of the article.

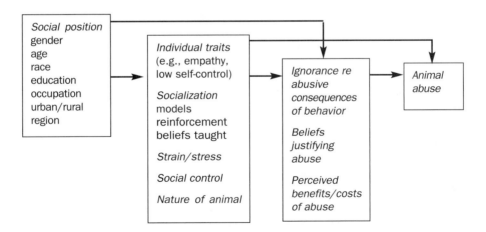

FIGURE 8.1   A Social Psychological Model of Animal Abuse

Factors Directly Increasing the Likelihood of Animal Abuse

Ignorance Regarding the Abusive Consequences of Our Behavior for Animals

Our actions often directly and indirectly affect the treatment of animals; among other things, our actions may result in the death or physical injury of animals or limit their ability to satisfy basic needs (see Fox, 1990: 39). Data, however, suggest that people are often ignorant of these abusive consequences. This is not to say that knowledge of such harm would end all abuse, but such ignorance likely accounts for some of the abuse inflicted on animals.

Ignorance of How Our Behavior Affects the Treatment of Animals   Three major categories of behavior fall in this area:

1. Participation in a wide range of behaviors that contribute to environmental pollution and the destruction of natural habitats, perhaps the two greatest threats to animal welfare. Many individuals are unaware of the fact that certain of their behaviors contribute to these problems and—even if aware—they do not realize the serious threat that these problems pose to animals (see Kellert, 1980).

2. The purchase of products that contain animal ingredients or that were tested on animals. Data indicate that individuals are often unaware of the fact that many of the products they purchase contain animal ingredients or were tested on animals (Plous, 1993). And if they are aware, they typically lack knowledge of the abusive ways in which the involved animals have been treated.

3. Participation in activities that use animals for entertainment/educational purposes, such as rodeos, circuses, zoos, and aquaria. Once again, many such individuals are unaware of the abusive ways in which such animals are often treated.

Ignorance of the Pain/Suffering That Animals Experience as a Result of Our Behavior   Many individuals are aware of how their behavior affects the treatment of animals, but they are ignorant of the pain/suffering that results from such treatment. Many individuals believe that animals do not experience pain or, in less extreme forms, that animals have a higher threshold of pain or do not experience pain in response to the same stimuli as humans. Such beliefs are rooted in western religion and philosophy, although they have been the subject of serious challenge in recent years. Nevertheless, individuals involved in animal abuse still sometimes claim that the animals feel no pain or do not suffer greatly. Survey data, for example, suggest that many respondents believe that fish do not feel pain—despite evidence to the contrary (Fox, 1990). And data indicate that people involved in different forms of animal abuse often deny or minimize the pain felt by the animals they abuse. Some cockfighters, for example, claim that chickens are too dumb to feel pain or that the pain they feel is different from that felt by humans (McCaghy and Neal, 1974).

Sources of Such Ignorance   Ignorance of the above types is partly fostered by the fact that we are physically and symbolically isolated from the negative consequences of our actions. We are physically isolated from factory farms, slaughterhouses, animal laboratories, and the backstage areas of rodeos, circuses, zoos, and similar institutions. Many of these institutions are located in remote areas, and most are off limits to the general public. Our physical isolation is reinforced by the media and educational institutions, which do not report on the conditions that exist in these institutions. The media tend to limit their reports on animals to wildlife and companion animals (Kellert and Westervelt, 1981).

At a deeper level, we are isolated from the negative consequences of our actions through our language and the packaging of animal products: both of which de-emphasize the fact that we are involved in the abuse of living, sentient creatures.

For example, hunters and trappers do not "kill" animals, but rather "harvest" them. We do not eat "cows" or "pigs," but rather "hamburgers" or "pork chops." Such euphemistic labeling is commonly used to mask objectionable activities or make such activities appear respectable. Such labeling is employed in all aspects of the animal industry, and individuals are often deliberately instructed in its use. Likewise, when we purchase meat, we purchase it "as a commodity, processed, cut up, packaged and renamed in ways which set us as consumers at a safe distance from any recognition of our purchase as the carcass of a once-sentient being" (Benton, 1993: 72). As Plous (1993) points out, special care is taken to remove those parts of the animal associated with life or personality—such as the eyes or head.

This physical and symbolic isolation extends to those who are directly involved in animal abuse, such as slaughterhouse workers and animal experimenters. Such workers, in particular, are able at least partially to distance themselves from the ways in which they treat animals and the pain that these animals experience. This is done in a variety of ways, most of which involve limiting contact with individual animals, routinizing the contact which does occur, and relabeling the animals as something other than sentient beings with unique identities.

In addition to such physical and symbolic isolation, the above types of ignorance are also partly a function of the assurances we receive from others regarding the well-being of the animals we abuse. In particular, both the media and educational institutions present a misleading image of the conditions under which many animals live. For example, the impression is given that most farm animals live contented lives in idyllic settings. These distortions are partly supported by the animal industry, which supplies educational materials to schools and sponsors advertising/public relations campaigns in the media. Representatives of the fur industry, for example, assure us that the animals raised on their ranches are well treated, even "happy" (Olson and Goodnight, 1994). Animal researchers claim that safeguards are in place to ensure the humane treatment of animals used in experiments (e.g., Baldwin, 1993).

While our ignorance is to some extent deliberately fostered by the animal industry, it is important to note that many people are willing participants in the process. Survey data indicate that most people in the United States are concerned about animal welfare. At the same time, these people contribute to activities that cause serious harm to animals (see Braithwaite and Braithwaite, 1982). One way that people cope with this potential conflict is by distancing themselves from the consequences of their behavior. They may avoid or discount information regarding the consequences of their actions. And they may more readily accept information suggesting that their actions do not have harmful consequences. This is especially easy to do since such information is often provided by trusted individuals and organizations, like the American Medical Association and the federal government. As Singer (1975: 228) points out, many individuals tell themselves that the government would intervene if animal abuse was as bad as some people claim.

Belief That Abusive Treatment Is Justified

Many individuals knowingly act in ways that cause animal suffering and they make no attempt to deny or minimize this suffering. In many such cases, it is claimed that the animals involved are not worthy of moral consideration or are worthy of only limited consideration. The moral consideration accorded to animals ranges along a continuum. At one pole, individuals claim that animals are not worthy of any moral consideration. Drawing on the western religious/philosophical tradition, they may claim that we are very distinct from and superior to animals, that we have been granted divine dominion over animals, and that animals are here for our use.

This extreme position is less common today than in the recent past, but survey data suggest that a significant minority of people hold a predominantly utilitarian or dominionistic orientation toward animals. That is, they focus on the material and practical value of animals for humans or on the satisfaction to be obtained from the mastery and control of animals (Kellert, 1980). At the other pole, individuals feel that animals are worthy of the same moral consideration as people and that few circumstances justify abusive treatment. This position has been advanced by certain philosophers and feminist theorists in recent years. It is quite common among people in the animal rights movement—although impressionistic data suggest that it has its roots less in a careful consideration of philosophical and social theory and more in what has been called an "ethic of caring."

Survey data suggest that most people in the United States fall between these poles; they believe that animals have a general moral right to be free from suffering, but that animal abuse is justified in situations where there is a compelling human interest (Kellert, 1980). For example, Gallup and Beckstead (1988) found that most respondents in their sample said that they were very concerned about the pain and suffering of animals, but that they would support research on animals if it would help save human lives. Likewise, most respondents approve of the consumption of meat and they approve of other abusive activities *under certain conditions*; for example, they approve of hunting if it is done for meat rather than sport (Plous, 1993).

Data suggest that one's moral orientation toward animals is associated with animal abuse. First, people in the animal rights movement have a very different moral orientation than those directly involved in animal abuse. While animal rights activists tend to accord animals the same moral status as humans, animal abusers have a more utilitarian and/or dominionistic orientation toward animals. Such abusers include livestock producers, hunters of certain types, trappers, fishers, slaughterhouse workers, and cockfighters. Second, these differing moral orientations are related to one's willingness to help abused animals and to one's views on issues like the protection of endangered species. Finally, individuals who self-report animal cruelty often list the desire to dominate or control animals as a motive.

Animals Deserve Abuse First, individuals may claim that animal abuse is deserved in certain cases. Most commonly, we believe abuse is deserved because the animal does something we do not like or possesses traits that we do not like. Our abuse of animals is facilitated through their definition as savage, filthy, ruthless, evil, dumb, pests, vermin, etc. (Serpell, 1986: 160). In this area, Kellert and Felthous (1985) found that self-reported animal abusers often said they engaged in abuse to retaliate against an animal they thought had wronged them, to eliminate undesirable traits in an animal, or to satisfy a prejudice against a particular species or breed—like cats.

Although less common, people may also feel that abuse is deserved in situations where there is no dislike or hatred of the animal. For example, cockfighters and some hunters have the greatest respect for the animals they abuse (McCaghy and Neal, 1974). Cockfighters admire the courage and tenacity exhibited by their birds, while hunters often express admiration for the cunning, strength, "fighting spirit," and beauty of the animals they kill.

Abuse Serves Some Higher End Second, abuse may be justified even when it is not seen as deserved. In particular, individuals may claim that the abuse serves some higher, typically human, end—such as the protection of human jobs, health, and life. Meat eaters point to the alleged health benefits of meat: benefits actively promoted by the meat industry. Livestock producers and slaughterhouse workers argue that their work is necessary to satisfy the need for meat. They further claim that the use of more humane methods in their work might jeopardize their economic position. Animal researchers claim that their work saves human lives. Hunters claim that hunting protects wilderness areas and, in some cases, protects livestock and people from diseased or otherwise threatening animals (Cartmill, 1993). People who euthanize animals claim they are performing a valuable community service (Owens, Davis, and Smith, 1981). And abusers of several types have justified their behavior in religious terms, claiming that it has divine approval (Herzog and McGee, 1983).

Animal abusers, in fact, have been rather creative in pointing to the higher ends served by their activities. Cockfighters, for example, argue that the bravery and tenacity of the gamecock is a superb model for humans: cockfighting is claimed to build character and foster courage in humans. Further, it has been claimed that cockfighting is a family sport: the labor involved in raising gamecocks is said to keep kids off the street and out of trouble. Some hunters describe their hunting as a spiritual or religious experience that serves to bring them closer to the natural world, including the animals they kill. Even the fur industry has found a higher purpose for its calling, linking the right to wear fur to the value we place on the freedom of expression.

Abuse Prevents Even Greater Suffering by Animals   A variation on the above justification is the claim that certain types of animal abuse may prevent even greater suffering on the part of animals. There are two versions of this justification. First, it is claimed that while particular animals suffer from the treatment they receive, they would suffer *more* if not so treated. People who euthanize animals sometimes claim that these animals would suffer more if permitted to live (Owens *et al.*, 1981). People who work in animal labs sometimes point out that the animals they work with are fortunate to have been bred for experimental purposes, otherwise they would never have existed at all (Arluke, 1988). Cockfighters sometimes point out that while their birds may die in battle, they have excellent care for most of their lives—far better than that received by nonfighting birds (Darden and Worden, 1996). Sec-

ond, it is claimed that the abusive behavior directed at particular animals is designed to prevent even greater suffering among *other* animals. Hunters and trappers, in particular, claim that they prevent overpopulation and degradation of the environment—thereby saving many animals from starvation and disease.

Condemnation of the Condemners   Fourth, many animal abusers excuse their behavior by pointing to the questionable or immoral behavior of those who criticize them—especially animal rights activists. Animal abusers do not justify their behavior, but they excuse it by essentially arguing that their behavior is no worse than that of others—especially those who attempt to take the moral high ground by criticizing them. On the one hand, animal rights advocates have been accused of supporting animal abuse; for example, by wearing leather products or using products tested on animals. On the other hand, animal rights activists are sometimes said to care more about animals than people. In its most extreme form, animal activists are portrayed as dangerous radicals who engage in violence against animal researchers and who would rob us of our freedoms. In less extreme form, animal activists are portrayed as overly sentimental and misguided—caught up in their affection for animals and oblivious to human problems and concerns. Animal abusers may also attempt to excuse their behavior by pointing to other forms of animal abuse that are more widely practiced and/or not as strongly condemned. Animal experimenters, for example, may point to the massive abuse in the meat industry. Animal abusers may also point to the existence of abusive practices involving humans—cockfighters, for example, may claim that their activities are little different than boxing.

Denial/Diffusion of Responsibility   Finally, animal abusers may attempt to justify or excuse their behavior by denying or minimizing their responsibility for it. Some claim that we are by nature predators and therefore have no choice but to engage in activities like meat consumption and hunting (Cartmill, 1993). Unlike most justifications, this one minimizes rather than accentuates the differences between human and non-human animals. Some blame others for the abusive behavior in which they engage, claiming that they were following the orders of others or that others created the conditions which make their abusive behavior necessary. For example, those who euthanize animals blame society for creating a situation in which animals must be killed. And many believe that their role in abuse is small, perhaps inconsequential. This belief is fostered by the fact that they are just one of many who contribute to abuse, that their contribution is indirect, and/or that their contribution is limited to just one portion of the abuse process.

Perceived Benefits of Abuse Outweigh the Costs

Animal abuse is also a function of its perceived benefits and costs for the individual. Singer (1975) states that "the interests of animals are allowed to count only when they do not clash with human interests" (p. 220). When clashes do occur, any feelings of guilt are dealt with by distancing oneself from the consequences of one's actions or claiming that conditions justify abuse. These devices, then, merely play a secondary role in abuse: they originate out of self-interest and simply make it easier for individuals to act in their self-interest. In fact, it has been suggested that the primary reason we show any concern for animals at all is because we believe that it is in our self-interest to do so: we desire to protect our (animal) property and we fear that the abuse of animals will "brutalize" humans and thereby lead to crimes against people.

This view may be somewhat overstated: people may sometimes act against their self-interest. Survey data suggest that most people do *not* think of animals in primarily utilitarian terms, but rather have a more humanistic or moralistic orientation toward them (Kellert, 1980). Further, many people report that they would oppose animal abuse even in situations where such opposi-

tion would result in a substantial loss of benefits to people (Kellert, 1980). There are numerous instances of people and organizations acting in what appears to be an altruistic manner toward animals (Arluke, 1988). One's moral concerns, then, may sometimes take precedence over the perceived benefits of animal abuse. For most people, however, it is probably the case that such moral concerns are too weak or too flexible to effectively counter self-interest (see Hills, 1993).

The costs of most forms of animal abuse are low. Internal costs—such as guilt—can be neutralized through a variety of beliefs/justifications/excuses. The external costs are likewise low. Formal sanctions for most forms of abuse are nonexistent, they are rarely implemented when they do exist, and they are typically mild in form when imposed (see Sherry, 1994). Informal sanctions are also uncommon. Animals are typically unable to protect themselves from abuse since they have less power than most humans. In fact, the extreme dependence of many animals on humans makes them especially easy targets for abuse. Informal sanctions from humans are also unlikely. Abuse is easily hidden from view, and animals are generally unable to solicit aid from others or identify their abusers. Many forms of abuse are socially acceptable, and condemnation for socially unacceptable forms of abuse is often mild. This partly reflects the low status of animals and the fact that many animals are viewed as private property—and therefore off limits to outside interference. If anything, there are often costs associated with *nonabusive* behavior—such as the difficulty of finding food and products that do not contain animal ingredients.

Several major benefits of animal abuse can be listed, with the most obvious being material in nature. The animal industry is the second largest in the United States behind the automobile industry (Plous, 1993). Enormous numbers of people make money, directly and indirectly, from the abuse of animals. This includes people in the following industries: meat, egg and dairy; fur; biomedical; pet; entertainment (horse racing, dog racing, circuses, rodeos, zoos, aquaria, etc.);

cosmetic and pharmaceutical; hunting and fishing; and food service. In addition to being a source of income, animal abuse satisfies certain other material needs—including the needs for food, clothing, shelter, and products tested on animals.

Animal abuse may also be a source of status or prestige. Among other things, it has been suggested that one's status may be enhanced (or displayed) by wearing animal furs or other animal products; possessing certain types of animals—like certain breeds of dog (see Savishinsky, 1983); eating certain types of animals; killing or dominating certain types of animals; and raising certain types of animals, like successful gamecocks. Related to this, it has been suggested that animal abuse may be a mechanism for demonstrating one's masculinity since it often exemplifies such "masculine" traits as aggression, domination, and the suppression of feeling. Animal abusers' reasons for abuse include a desire to impress others with their capacity for violence, improve their aggressive skills, and compensate for feelings of weakness or vulnerability by exercising total power and control over animals (Kellert and Felthous, 1985).

The abuse of animals also provides "psychic benefits." The use of animals for entertainment purposes provides pleasure to large numbers of people. Likewise, animal abuse (or the conditions surrounding such abuse) is a source of pleasure for many hunters, fishers, cockfighters, and others (Cartmill, 1993). It has been suggested that animal abuse is a common mechanism for the expression of anger and frustration, with several studies noting that animals are often the victims of scapegoating—especially in families characterized by abuse (Deviney *et al.* 1983).

A Note on Opportunities for Abuse Abusive behavior is a function of both disposition and opportunity. This is especially true when it comes to direct forms of abuse. Two individuals may be similarly disposed to engage in the abuse of companion animals, but the individual who owns a companion animal is obviously more

likely to commit abuse. Likewise, there are large differences in the opportunity to participate in such direct forms of abuse as hunting, cockfighting, and animal experimentation—with such differences being partly a function of social location (e.g., occupation, social class, area of residence). The opportunities for indirect forms of abuse are generally more widespread. Most people are in situations where they can easily purchase meat and products tested on animals, although differences in social location may have an impact on the amount and types of such purchases. Opportunities for visiting zoos, aquaria, rodeos, circuses, etc. may be more heavily affected by social location.

Factors Having a Direct and Indirect Effect on Animal Abuse

Animal abuse is said to be a direct function of three factors:

1. awareness of the abusive consequences of our behavior for animals;
2. the extent to which we believe that abuse is justified; and
3. the perceived benefits and costs associated with abuse.

These factors vary between and within individuals. Variation in these factors can be used to explain why some individuals are more abusive than others, and why the abusive behavior of particular individuals varies over time and between situations.

Individual Traits

Those individual traits said to cause crime may also cause animal abuse through their effect on the above three factors. Such traits include impulsivity, sensation-seeking, and irritability, as well as more general traits such as low self-control. The individual low in self-control has been described as "impulsive, insensitive, physical (as opposed to mental), risk-taking, short-sighted, and non-verbal" (Gottfredson and Hirschi, 1990: 90). It seems reasonable to suppose that such an individual would be less aware of the abusive consequences of their actions for animals, less willing to grant animals moral consideration, and less aware of and concerned about the negative personal consequences of their actions. Further, such an individual would be more likely to take advantage of the benefits of animal abuse.

While a range of individual traits may affect animal abuse, the trait of empathy is often singled out for special consideration. Many individuals are said to have trouble empathizing with the pain felt by animals and so are more likely to engage in abuse. Certain data suggest that there is a strong link between empathy and animal abuse or at least attitudes regarding animal abuse (Broida *et al.*, 1993).

Socialization

Socialization regarding animals and related issues may affect animal abuse—indirectly through the above three factors and perhaps also directly. Most individuals in the United States are socialized in ways that foster certain types of animal abuse, particularly the consumption and use of animal products and—to a lesser extent—the use of animals for entertainment purposes. This socialization takes place through the family, school, peer group, religious institutions, media and other agencies. The key features of the socialization process are the models we are exposed to, the reinforcements and punishments we receive, and the beliefs we are taught.

First, people we like and respect consume animals, wear and use animal products, and are entertained by animals. Second, we are led to participate in these activities at an early age and soon find them reinforcing. They function as both unconditioned reinforcers (e.g., meat, leather clothing) and conditioned reinforcers (e.g., through their association with social approval). It has been argued that our consumption of meat has an especially profound effect on us, since it pits us against animals in a fundamental way and thereby leads to distancing behavior on the one hand and justifying beliefs on the other (Singer, 1975). Third, we are taught beliefs that

promote animal abuse, including the justifying and other beliefs listed above (e.g., farm animals lead happy lives, animals do not feel pain, meat is an essential part of a healthy diet, certain animals possess undesirable traits, various types of animal abuse benefit us). Finally, we are kept ignorant of the ways in which many animals are treated and of information which might challenge our behavior toward them.

While most individuals are socialized in ways that foster the above types of animal abuse, there is still some variation in the exposure to agents promoting abuse and in the strength of the message that is presented. For example, some individuals are highly committed members of religious denominations that directly promote abuse or present beliefs highly conducive to abuse, while others are nonreligious or are members of denominations more favorably disposed to animals (Bowd and Bowd, 1989). Further, there may be significant variation in socialization regarding other types of abuse—like the abuse of companion animals, animal research, and hunting. For example, Zahn-Walker *et al.* (1985) found considerable variation in the ways that parents treated companion animals. Some parents clearly used such animals as scapegoats for family and personal problems; this was especially true in "volatile, angry" families. Other parents treated companion animals with respect and affection. The children, in turn, imitated the behavior of their parents. There was also much variation in the extent to which parents praised and rewarded the child's nurturing behavior toward animals and how much teasing they tolerated. Some parents found their children's aggression or abuse "cute," while others would make serious efforts to stop such abuse. Data also suggest that some parents expose their children to and reinforce them for participation in forms of abuse like hunting and cockfighting (e.g., Herzog and Borghardt, 1988). Likewise, data suggest that certain subcultural groups support specific forms of abuse—like cockfighting and hunting. Such groups are typically male, and accounts suggest that animal abuse may be a method for accomplishing gender in these groups (see Hawley, 1993).

Our behavior toward animals, however, is also shaped in a more indirect fashion. Liberal beliefs may be important because of their emphasis on tolerance for diversity and support for those in need, while feminist beliefs may be important for their emphasis on caring and nurturance. Among other things, such beliefs might increase one's awareness of animal suffering, one's willingness to grant moral consideration to animals, and the perceived costs of abuse. If we focus on specific types of animal abuse, we may find that additional beliefs and attitudes are important. For example, certain data suggest that one's views regarding science may have a strong effect on one's support for animal research. Those with a lot of faith in science and technology are more likely to support animal research, presumably because they believe that such research will reap important benefits (Broida *et al.*, 1993).

The Role of Companion Animals

The above discussion has focused on the socialization of the individual by other humans. It has been suggested, however, that companion animals may also influence the individual's propensity for animal abuse. While we may not want to classify such influence under the category of "socialization," many have argued that it is nevertheless quite important. In fact, the development of the animal welfare movement over the last 200 years is also said to be partly a function of the spread of companion animals. Several studies describe the close relationship individuals often develop with their companion animals; they are commonly loved and viewed as members of the family. It has been argued that our close association with such animals has made us more aware of their unique personalities, increased our opinion of their cognitive abilities, and sensitized us to the pain and suffering they sometimes experience. The media has also been said to contribute to this process through their anthropomorphic portrayal of certain animals, like deer and lions. This, in

turn, has led us to grant greater moral consideration to them (and possibly other animals).

Strain

Strain or stress may also directly and indirectly lead to animal abuse, particularly socially *unacceptable* forms of abuse.

This is most obviously the case with strain caused by animals. Animals may interfere with the achievement of valued goals (e.g., monetary success) or engage in other negative behaviors (e.g., attack us or damage our property). As a result, we may become angry, feel that abuse is deserved or necessary for some higher end, and conclude that abuse is of personal benefit. We may then engage in abuse for revenge and/or personal gain—justifying our behavior in the process. Animals are also frequently viewed as threats to our economic livelihood or health. For example, concern over endangered species may halt development, animals may threaten crops or livestock, or they may pose a direct threat or nuisance to people. Such strain may also promote abuse.

Strain that is *not* caused by animals may also foster socially *unacceptable* animal abuse. First, strain may create a general propensity for abuse by reducing one's awareness of the abusive consequences of one's behavior, one's willingness to grant animals moral consideration, and one's concern with social sanctions. These effects are a function of the fact that strained individuals are typically angry/frustrated and preoccupied with their own problem. Second, animal abuse may function as a convenient mechanism for coping with strain in certain situations. Strained individuals may engage in animal abuse to reduce strain, seek revenge against those who have placed them under strain, or manage the negative emotions associated with strain. For example, they may kill or threaten the companion animals of those who have wronged them in an effort to change their "negative" behavior or obtain revenge. Such actions are often reported in cases of family violence. Also, as indicated above, it has been suggested that animal abuse may be a vehicle for accomplishing masculinity. Finally, several researchers have noted that strained individuals may use animals as scapegoats, the implication being that they provide a safe target for the discharge of aggressive feelings. These arguments also suggest that strain is most relevant to socially unacceptable forms of abuse—since socially accepted forms of abuse like meat consumption are generally not good vehicles for controlling others, seeking revenge, or accomplishing masculinity.

In certain special situations, however, strain may *reduce* the likelihood of all or certain forms of abuse. This seems most likely to occur when strained individuals perceive that both they and abused animals are the victims of a common enemy and experience similar forms of abuse (some minimal level of empathy and moral consideration for animals would also seem necessary). In such cases, empathy and moral consideration for animals may be heightened and individuals may feel that it is in their self-interest to end abuse. These arguments may explain the participation of the English working class in the antivivisection movement during the 1800s. Members of the working class thought that they too were victims of the medical establishment and they found it easy to identify with the experiments being performed on dogs (Finsen and Finsen, 1994). And these arguments may help explain the participation of some feminists in the animal rights movement, with these feminists arguing that both female and animal oppression have their roots in male domination and are similar in certain ways (Adams and Donovan, 1995).

Level of Social Control

One's level of social control may influence the likelihood of socially *unacceptable* abuse. In this connection, social control can be measured in terms of the individual's attachment to conventional others (we do not want to incur the disapproval of people we like), commitment to conventional institutions like school and work (we do not want to jeopardize such commitments through deviance), and supervision by others. (Beliefs regarding the acceptability of abuse have

already been discussed.) Individuals high in these forms of social control should be less likely to engage in socially unacceptable forms of animal abuse, since they are more likely to perceive the costs of such abuse to be high.

Level of social control should have little or no impact on socially *acceptable* forms of abuse, since such abuse is not likely to threaten one's attachments and commitments or result in social sanction. In fact, one might argue that *low* social control will *reduce* rather than increase the likelihood of socially acceptable abuse, since the individual is less influenced by those who support abuse. The pervasive and entrenched nature of socially acceptable abuse (e.g., eating meat, going to the circus), however, makes this unlikely in most cases.

The relevance of social control theory to animal abuse can be extended by examining attachments to *animals,* especially companion animals, as well as attachments to people. Our attachment to companion animals may reduce animal abuse not only by altering our beliefs regarding animals (as indicated above), but by raising the costs of abuse for us. It is more difficult to hurt someone we like and value, partly because we are better able to empathize with their pain and partly because we feel they are less deserving of abuse (Plous, 1993).

It is important to note, however, that attachment to animals does not work in entirely the same way as attachment to people. If we are attached to conventional people, like parents and teachers, we are less likely to harm these people *and others.* We are less likely to harm others because our parents and teachers might find out and think badly of us. It is unlikely that we avoid abusing *other* animals because our companion animals might find out and think badly of us. As a consequence, attachment to a particular animal may not be very effective in preventing the abuse of other animals.

The Nature of the Animal

The above factors are also a function of the nature of the animal under consideration. A key dimension in this area is the similarity of the animal to us on the phylogenetic scale. Similar animals are liked more, shown more concern/empathy, given greater moral consideration, and blamed less for their transgressions (Zahn-Walker *et al.*, 1985). Other important traits of the animal include its aesthetic appeal (including "cuteness"), utility for us, the actual or perceived threat it poses for us, and the cultural and historical importance of the species (e.g., bald eagles). Such traits also influence our concern/empathy for animals and the moral consideration we grant them.

Social Position

Social position includes one's gender, age, race, occupation, education, income, urban/rural location, and region. These variables may sometimes have a direct effect on awareness of abuse, justifying beliefs, and perceived benefits of abuse, but they most often affect these factors through their effect on individual traits, socialization, strain, and social control.

Gender Women are more opposed to animal abuse, are more involved in the animal rights movement, and are less likely to engage in animal abuse (Herzog *et al.*, 1991; Jasper and Nelkin, 1992). Data (Gallup and Beckstead, 1988; Pifer, 1996) suggest several reasons for this; among other things, women:

a. show more empathy/concern for animals;
b. show greater affection for many animals;
c. take a less utilitarian/dominionistic orientation toward animals;
d. grant greater moral consideration to animals;
e. have less faith in science and technology; and
f. hold more liberal and feminist beliefs.

There has been some speculation about the origin of the gender differences noted above, with the most common argument being that gender influences one's socialization. Among other things, women are socialized in ways that foster a nurturant, caring orientation—while men are socialized to develop a more instrumental, dominionistic orientation.

Other Socio-Demographic Variables Data suggest that opposition to animal abuse is greater among whites (versus African Americans), the well educated (with the exception of attitudes toward animal research), young adults (although young children have little concern for the rights and protection of animals—see Kellert, 1985), Pacific Coast residents (especially compared with Southerners), and people in occupational categories that do not directly involve abuse (see Kellert, 1980, 1985). Income is weakly related to animal attitudes (Kellert, 1983) and data on rural/urban residence are somewhat mixed, although the best data suggest that urban residents are more opposed to animal abuse (Kellert, 1980).

The relationship between these variables and animal abuse can be explained in several ways. Most notably, all of these variables may be associated with differences in socialization. Well-educated individuals, for example, may be more likely to learn about animal abuse and be exposed to beliefs that discourage abuse—such as liberal and feminist beliefs.

Certain of the above variables may also have a direct effect on awareness of abuse, justifying beliefs and perceived benefits of abuse. Rural individuals, for example, may perceive more benefits from abuse given their greater direct dependence on animals as a source of livelihood. The same is obviously true for individuals in certain occupational categories, like slaughterhouse workers.

It should be noted that certain of the findings reported above may not match those in other countries. For example, Kellert (1993) found that education is unrelated to animal attitudes in Japan, even though it is related to attitudes in the United States and Germany. The least industrialized and urbanized countries generally have the lowest levels of opposition to abuse. This may be a function of the more utilitarian attitude toward animals often found in rural areas. Related to this, it has been suggested that concern for animals is something of a luxury; we care about animals when we can afford to do so.

Conclusion

The theoretical model presented in this paper (summarized in Figure 8.1) integrates previous discussions of the causes of animal abuse and builds on such discussions by drawing on the leading crime theories. Certain key points should be emphasized regarding this model and areas for further research.

- While the model refers to animal abuse in general, certain variables in the model may be more relevant to some types of abuse than others. Socially acceptable abuse often involves indirect harm and is almost always seen as necessary or serving some compelling human interest. Socially unacceptable abuse is more likely to be direct, intentional, and unnecessary (as commonly defined). Individual traits (e.g., low self-control, empathy), strain, and social control were said to be most relevant to socially unacceptable forms of abuse. Ignorance regarding the consequences of our behavior was said to be most relevant to those socially acceptable forms of abuse that involve the indirect infliction of harm.
- The model only attempts to depict the causal relationships between the variables at a gross level. Some attempt was made to describe the effect of the exogenous variables on the intervening variables. However, little attempt was made to describe how the intervening variables may affect one another, except to say that individuals who perceive high benefits from abuse may be more inclined to distance themselves from abuse and develop moral justifications for abuse. Likewise, little attention was devoted to the relationships between the exogenous variables. Strain caused by animals, for example, might reduce one's attachment to animals. Finally, little attention was devoted to possible interaction effects. For example, strain caused by animals is most likely to lead to animal abuse when such abuse is seen as justified.
- The model does not discuss the macro-level determinants of animal abuse. As indicated, the model attempts to explain individual differences in the disposition to abuse, and such differences are explained largely in terms of the individual's traits, experiences, and social location. Even a cursory reading of the abuse literature, however, makes clear the absolutely key role that social and cultural forces play in the overall explanation of abuse. Among other things, the western religious/philosophical tradition provides much cultural support for animal abuse. Likewise, the profits to be made from animal abuse in our economic system are another major source of abuse. In particular, the desire to maximize profits provides much incentive for abuse, while the resultant profits from abuse have created a powerful set of actors who work for the continuation and expansion of abuse. Ideally, more work will be done at both the macro- and micro-levels, with the eventual goal of an integrated theory of animal abuse.

References

Adams, Carol J., and Josephine Donovan (1995). *Animals and Women*. Durham, NC: Duke University Press.

Arluke, Arnold B. (1988). "Sacrificial Symbolism in Animal Experimentation: Object or Pet?" *Anthrozoös* 2:98–117.

Baldwin, Elizabeth (1993). "The Case for Animal Research in Psychology," *Journal of Social Issues* 49:121–31.

Benton, Ted (1993). *Natural Relations*. London: Verso.

Bowd, Alan D., and Anne C. Bowd (1989). "Attitudes Toward the Treatment of Animals: A Study of Christian Groups in Australia," *Anthrozoös* 3:20–4.

Braithwaite, John, and Valerie Braithwaite (1982). "Attitudes Toward Animal Suffering: An Exploratory Study," *International Journal for the Study of Animal Problems* 3:42–9.

Broida, John, Leanne Tingley, Robert Kimball, and Joseph Miele (1993). "Personality Differences between Pro- and Anti-Vivisectionists," *Society and Animals* 1:129–44.

Cartmill, Matt (1993). *A View to a Death in the Morning*. Cambridge, MA: Harvard University Press.

Darden, Donna K., and Steven K. Worden (1996). "Marketing Deviance: The Selling of Cockfighting," *Society & Animals* 4:211–31.

DeViney, Elizabeth, Jeffrey Dickert, and Randall Lockwood (1983). "The Care of Pets within Child Abusing Families," *International Journal for the Study of Animal Problems* 4:321–9.

Finsen, Lawrence, and Susan Finsen (1994). *The Animal Rights Movement in America.* New York: Twayne.

Fox, Michael (1990). *Inhumane Society.* New York: St. Martin's.

Gallup, Gordon G., and Jason W. Beckstead (1988). "Attitudes Toward Animal Research," *American Psychologist* 43:474–6.

Gottfredson, Michael R., and Travis Hirschi (1990). *A General Theory of Crime.* Stanford, CA: Stanford University Press.

Hawley, Fred (1993). "The Moral and Conceptual Universe of Cockfighters: Symbolism and Rationalization," *Society & Animals* 1:159–68.

Herzog, Harold A., Jr., and Gordon M. Borghardt (1988). "Attitudes Toward Animals: Origins and Diversity," in Andrew N. Rowan (ed.), *Animals and People Sharing the World*, pp. 85–100. Hanover, NH: University Press of New England.

Herzog, Harold A., Jr., and Sandy McGee (1983). "Psychological Aspects of Slaughter Reactions of College Students to Killing and Butchering Cattle and Hogs," *International Journal for the Study of Animal Problems* 4:124–32.

Herzog, Harold A., Jr., Nancy S. Betchart, and Robert B. Pittman (1991). "Gender, Sex Role Orientation, and Attitudes Toward Animals," *Anthrozoös* 4:184–91.

Hills, Adelma M. (1993). "The Motivational Bases of Attitudes Toward Animals," *Society & Animals* 1:111–28.

Jasper, James M., and Dorothy Nelkin (1992). *The Animal Rights Crusade.* New York: Free Press.

Kellert, Stephen R. (1980). "American Attitudes Toward and Knowledge of Animals: An Update," *International Journal for the Study of Animal Problems* 1:87–119.

Kellert, Stephen R. (1983). "Affective, Cognitive, and Evaluative Perceptions of Animals," in Irwin Altman and Joachim F. Wohlwill (eds.), *Behavior and the Natural Environment*, pp. 241–67. New York: Plenum.

Kellert, Stephen R. (1985). "Attitudes Toward Animals: Age-Related Development Among Children," in Michael W. Fox and Linda D. Mickley (eds.), *Advances in Animal Welfare*, pp. 43–60. Boston: Martinus Nijhoff.

Kellert, Stephen R. (1993). "Attitudes, Knowledge, and Behavior Toward Wildlife Among the Industrial Superpowers: US, Japan, and Germany," *Journal of Social Issues* 49:53–69.

Kellert, Stephen R., and Alan R. Felthous (1985). "Childhood Cruelty toward Animals among Criminals and Noncriminals," *Human Relations* 38:1113–29.

Kellert, Stephen R., and Miriam O. Westervelt (1981). *Trends in Animal Use and Perception in 20th Century America.* Washington: US Government Printing Office.

Mason, Jim (1985). "Brave New Farm?" in Peter Singer (ed.), *Defense of Animals*, pp. 89–107. Oxford: Basil Blackwell.

McCaghy, Charles H., and Arthur G. Neal (1974). "The Fraternity of Cock-fighters: Ethical Embellishments of an Illegal Sport," *Journal of Popular Culture* 8:557–69.

Olson, Kathryn M., and G. Thomas Goodnight (1994). "Entanglements of Consumption, Cruelty, Privacy, and Fashion: The Social Controversy Over Fur," *The Quarterly Journal of Speech* 80:249–76.

Owens, Charles E., Ricky Davis, and Bill Hurt Smith (1981). "The Psychology of Euthanizing Animals: The Emotional Component," *International Journal for the Study of Animal Problems* 2:19–26.

Pifer, Linda K. (1996). "Exploring the Gender Gap in Young Adults' Attitudes about Animal Research," *Society & Animals* 4:37–52.

Plous, S. (1993). "Psychological Mechanisms in the Human Use of Animals," *Journal of Social Issues* 49:11–52.

Rollin, Bernard E. (1990). *The Unheeded Cry.* Oxford: Oxford University Press.

Savishinsky, Joel S. (1983). "Pet Ideas: The Domestication of Animals, Human Behavior, and Human Emotion," in Aaron Honori Katcher and Alan M. Beck (eds.), *New Perspectives on our Lives with Companion Animals*, pp. 112–31. Philadelphia: University of Pennsylvania Press.

Serpell, James (1986). *In the Company of Animals.* New York: Blackwell.

Sherry, Clifford J. (1994). *Animal Rights: A Reference Handbook.* Santa Barbara, CA: ABC-CLIO.

Singer, Peter (1975). *Animal Liberation.* New York: Avon.

Vermeulen, Hannelie, and Johannes S. J. Odendaal (1993). "Proposed Typology of Companion Animal Abuse," *Anthrozoös* 6:248–57.

Waggoner, Martha (1997). "No-kill Controversy Tears at Animal Shelters," *Atlanta Constitution*, 20 April, 2M.

Zahn-Walker, Carolyn, Barbara Hollenbeck, and Marian Rodke-Yarrow (1985). "The Origins of Empathy and Altruism," in Michael W. Fox and Linda D. Mickley (eds.), *Advances in Animal Welfare*, pp. 21–41. Boston: Martinus Nijhoff.

Arnold Arluke
Jack Levin
Carter Luke
Frank Ascione

The Relationship of Animal Abuse to Violence and Other Forms of Antisocial Behavior

Previous research has often assumed a "violence graduation hypothesis" whereby animal abusers are expected to work their way up from harming animals to harming people. The strong form of the graduation hypothesis suggests that the presence of cruelty to animals at one developmental period predicts interpersonal violence at a later developmental period. From this viewpoint, violence toward animals comes first and is subsequently generalized to humans. According to this form of the hypothesis, the 5-year-old who abuses animals is on the way to becoming an elementary school bully, aggressive adolescent, and adult violent offender. This simplistic model belies more complex associations that may exist between animal abuse and violence. For example, making this assumption has led researchers to ignore the possibility that aggressive individuals instead might begin with violence toward humans and later move on to animals or might restrict their violence to human victims.

A general form of the graduation hypothesis is actually codified in the *Diagnostic and Statistical Manual of Mental Disorders* (DSM; American Psychiatric Association [APA], 1994). The adult personality disorder most closely related to violent behavior is antisocial personality disorder (APD) and its diagnosis has, as a prerequisite, the presence of conduct disorder (CD) prior to age 15. The first area of concern listed under the APD diagnostic criteria is "failure to conform to social norms with respect to lawful behaviors as indicated by repeatedly performing acts that are grounds for arrest" (APA, 1994, p. 649). Although aggressiveness is also listed as a symptom of APD, there is no specific mention of animal abuse. This contrasts with the diagnostic symptoms for CD, which include cases where a child or adolescent "has been physically cruel to animals" (APA, 1994, p. 90). Physical cruelty to animals is one of 15 separate symptoms listed under the CD classification.[1]

Since Macdonald (1961) first proposed his triad of childhood characteristics—enuresis, firesetting, and cruelty toward animals—as symptomatic of violence proneness in later life, investigators have sought to document and clarify the relation between animal abuse and interpersonal violence. Aside from a few case studies, the early evidence has been less than compelling. Many researchers who followed Macdonald did not find a significant association between cruelty to animals and violence against people. In a controlled study of personal histories, Macdonald (1961, 1968) himself failed to establish that violent psychiatric patients were significantly more likely than nonviolent psychiatric patients to have abused animals.

By contrast, more recent research has purported to find supporting evidence for the hypothesis that aggressive individuals are also abusive toward animals. For example, Kellert and Felthous (1985) uncovered significantly more childhood cruelty toward animals among "aggressive criminals" than among either "nonaggressive criminals" or "noncriminals." More specifically, they found that 25 percent of aggressive criminals, 5.8 percent of nonaggressive criminals, and none of the noncriminals had abused animals five or more times in childhood. Although they did not study childhood cruelty toward animals, other researchers have found strong associations between aggressive behavior and animal abuse. Ascione (1998) found that 71 percent of battered women in a shelter who owned a pet reported that their assaultive male partners had threatened to harm or had actually harmed the family pet, and Renzetti (1992) reported that 38 percent of pet-owning abused women in lesbian relationships claimed their abusive partners mistreated their pets.

An interesting exception to these recent studies is the research by Miller and Knutson (1997) who provide less enthusiastic support for the link between animal abuse and violence. Using self-reports, they reportedly failed to find a substantial association between past experiences of animal abuse and physical punitiveness ($r = .13, p < .05$), and noted that past experiences of animal abuse did not differentiate the four groups of offenders they had classified (e.g., homicide, violent, sex, and other offenses). Although Miller and Knutson (1997, p. 59) conclude that their data were "not consistent with the hypothesis that exposure to animal cruelty is importantly related to antisocial behavior or child maltreatment," they themselves urge caution about interpretation of their findings. First, they note that base rates of some exposure to animal cruelty were quite high in this incarcerated sample (i.e., 71 percent reported some exposure). This also was the case in a second study they conducted with 308 undergraduates in which 68.9 percent of males and 33 percent of females reported some exposure to animal cruelty (this gender difference was statistically significant). Second, Miller and Knutson (1997) note that the distribu-

tion of scores on the composite measure of exposure to animal cruelty was positively skewed (i.e., most respondents scored in the low range) and leptokurtic (i.e., more sharply peaked than bell shaped). Because these characteristics indicate a restricted range of scores, correlational analyses were less likely to yield significant results.

The present study was designed to test the violence graduation hypothesis against the deviance generalization hypothesis according to which animal abuse is simply one of many forms of antisocial behavior that can be expected to arise from childhood on. Social deviance theorists argue that a wide range of criminal behaviors are positively correlated with one another either because one form of deviant behavior leads to involvement in other forms of deviance or because different forms of deviance have the same underlying causes. In other words, individuals who commit one form of deviance are likely to commit other forms as well, and in no particular time order. When applied to animal abuse, the deviance generalization hypothesis makes no assumptions as to time-order, allowing for the possibility that animal abuse might occur either before, after, or concurrently with antisocial behavior directed at humans. In short, if the deviance generalization hypothesis is correct, animal abuse will correlate just as strongly with nonviolent criminal behavior as it will with interpersonal violence, and animal abuse will be as likely to occur after interpersonal violence toward humans as before it.

We investigated official records of criminality in a sample of animal abusers who had come to the attention of the Massachusetts Society for the Prevention of Cruelty to Animals (MSPCA). Using Vermeulen and Odendaal's (1993) and Arluke and Luke's (1997) classifications of animal abuse, *cruelty* was operationally defined as any investigated case where an animal had been intentionally harmed physically (e.g., beaten, stabbed, shot, hanged, drowned, stoned, poisoned, burned, strangled, driven over, or thrown).

Chart review of MSPCA records from 1975 to 1986 revealed 153 participants who were prosecuted for at least one form of animal cruelty listed above. There were 146 male and 7 female participants. The mean age of abusers was 31 years, although ages ranged from 11 to 76 years. Of the abused animals, 69 percent were dogs, 2 percent were cats, and 9 percent were birds, wildlife, horses, or farm animals.

Simultaneously, a search was conducted for case controls that would closely match the neighborhoods of abusers. Neighborhoods, by definition, tend to be homogenous in terms of socioeconomic status and related characteristics; city or suburban blocks rarely differ by income or property levels, and many observers have commented on the racial and ethnic segregation of America's neighborhoods. Case controls were matched by gender, socioeconomic status, and age by randomly picking an individual of the same sex, same age range (by decade), and same street. If a street match could not be obtained, an appropriate individual was used from an adjacent street.

Using state computerized criminal records, both abusers and controls were tracked in the state's criminal justice records system. This tracking identified each participant's adult criminal record in the state of Massachusetts and the results were coded according to Douglas and his colleagues' (1992) classification of criminal offenses (i.e., violent, property-related, drug-related, public disorder, and/or others). Because juvenile records are sealed in Massachusetts, we could not obtain criminal records for participants younger than age 17.

Results

The graduation hypothesis was tested in two ways. Whereas the weak form of the hypothesis predicts an association between abuse and violence, the strong form suggests that animal abuse is uniquely related to violence toward humans as opposed to other forms of deviant behavior. Thus, by comparing animal abusers with control participants, we examined the extent to which animal abuse was correlated with several antisocial behaviors, including but not limited to violence. However, even if a strong and unique relationship were detected between abuse and violence, this would constitute a necessary but not sufficient condition to demonstrate the core of the graduation hypothesis; namely, that animal abuse subsequently leads to violence. Therefore, we also directly tested the sequential relationship between these two variables.

Results obtained in the present study indicate that animal abusers were significantly more likely than control participants to be involved in some form of criminal behavior, including violent offenses (Chi square = 68.24, df = 1, p < .0001). More specifically, 70 percent of those who abused animals also committed at least one offense, where this was true for only 22 percent of the control participants; in other words, abusers were 3.2 times more likely to have some criminal record when compared with control participants.

As predicted by the violence graduation hypothesis, there was at least an association between abuse and violence. Table 9.1 shows that

TABLE 9.1   Abusers and Controls Who Committed Various Offenses

	Abusers		Controls	
	n	Percentage	n	Percentage
Violence	57	(37)	11	(7)
Property	67	(44)	17	(11)
Drug	57	(37)	17	(11)
Disorder	57	(37)	18	(12)

NOTE: The total number of offenses is greater than 153 because some offenders committed more than one type of offense. Percentages were calculated from a base of 153 offenders and 153 control participants.

37 percent of the abusers, but only 7 percent of the control participants, had committed a violent crime (Chi square = 73.70, $df = 1, p < .0001$). Thus, abusers were 5.3 times more likely to have a violent criminal record than control participants.

However, abuse was not only associated with violence. In contrast to predictions from the graduation hypothesis and in line with the deviance generalization hypothesis, abusers were significantly more likely to commit a host of other types of antisocial acts as well. In particular, they were four times more likely to be arrested for property crimes (Chi square = 71.34, $df = 1, p < .0001$), three and a half times more likely to be arrested for drug-related offenses (Chi square = 70.17, $df = 1, p < .0001$), and three and a half times more likely to be arrested for disorderly behavior (Chi square = 70.09, $df = 1, p < .0001$).

To examine the time order of animal abuse and violent offenses, abusers were studied who had been arrested for at least one criminal act ($N = 106$) included in Douglas's (1992) offender classification. This subgroup was then broken down into violent offenses that occurred either before or after abuse and other crimes that occurred either before or after abuse. Of course, we could only examine the temporal order of antisocial behavior reported in official offense records; some offenders may have committed undetected antisocial acts. Nevertheless, if the graduation effect applied, then participants should have been more likely to commit animal abuse before rather than after committing a violent crime.

As shown in Table 9.2, the graduation hypothesis could not be supported from an analysis of the sequence between animal abuse and antisocial behaviors including violence: Animal abuse was no more likely to precede than follow either violent offenses (Chi square = 1.42, $df = 1, p > .05$) or nonviolent offenses (Chi square = 2.66, $df = 1, p > .05$). It should also be noted that overall, only 16 percent of the abusers studied graduated to subsequent violent crime. Indeed, as shown in Table 9.2, there actually was a tendency, although not statistically significant, for animal abuse to follow rather than precede nonviolent offenses.

Discussion

Even though we could not test the graduation hypothesis from childhood to adulthood, we do provide some data indicating that graduation, from late adolescence through adulthood, does not happen. If graduation does not occur in adulthood, it is reasonable to speculate that it also does not occur in childhood. Rather than being a predictor or a distinct step in the development of increasingly criminal or violent behavior, animal abuse, as shown in these results, is one of many antisocial behaviors committed by individuals in society, ranging from property to personal crimes. At least in the general population, the deviance generalization hypothesis seems to be a more accurate characterization of animal abuse than the violence graduation hypothesis.

Despite our findings and the mixed results of prior researchers, the graduation hypothesis continues to be espoused by concerned lay people and professionals alike. There are many thought-provoking and heart-felt newspaper and magazine

TABLE 9.2   Sequence for the Relationship of Abuse and Antisocial Behavior

	Violence		Other Crimes		
	n	Percentage	n	Percentage	Total
Abuse precedes	24	(42)	19	(39)	43
Abuse follows	33	(58)	30	(61)	63
Total	57	(100)	49	(100)	106

articles, editorials, essays, speeches, discussions, summit reports, and commentaries on the abuse-violence link that emphasize the generality of the graduation hypothesis. Why does this thinking persist when it does not have strong and consistent empirical support?

First, some animal advocates advance the graduation hypothesis as a way to further public concern for animal mistreatment. If animal cruelty can be shown to be a strong predictor of violence, then judges, child care workers, law enforcement officials, and the general public might take animal abuse more seriously than they now do. The emphasis on cruelty to animals in animal welfare organizations' public education efforts, in many ways, mirrors strategies that have been enlisted by child welfare organizations. Gordon (1989) noted that, at the turn of the century, child welfare agencies often highlighted the most egregious cases of child physical abuse despite the fact that the majority of their cases involved child neglect. This is understandable because child physical abuse cases are more likely to capture the attention and garner the support of the public.

Second, the graduation hypothesis is an appealing model for the many individuals interested in combating violence in society. Finding a single magic bullet would increase the possibility for intervention and prevention of violence. Despite the understandable wish for such a magic bullet, the link between animal abuse and violence does not appear to be so simple. Close adherence to the graduation assumption neglects more complex or subtle connections, which may bear more empirical fruit than thus far uncovered by researchers.

Third, a type of phylogenetic reasoning that is common in our culture underlies the graduation hypothesis. Graduation is assumed to be from animals to humans, with the abuser practicing or desensitizing himself to aggression against humans by beginning with phylogenetically "lesser" beings. Although commonsensically appealing, such an approach ignores the possibility of alternative kinds of graduation or

progression. For example, graduation may not be from animals to humans at all, but from distant to intimate targets. If so, we may be just as likely to find cases where offenders are violent to humans before they abuse animals, when the former are strangers and the latter are intimates. The child who tortures his own puppy may have already been violent toward fellow children who are more distant or strange to him than his own dog. The family pet or even that of a neighbor, after all, may be regarded as more "human" than a strange person. Thus, there may be some sort of graduation—not necessarily from animals to people, but from remote to intimate targets. Laboratory experiments provide indirect evidence for this idea. In one study (Milgram, 1974), participants were more willing to inflict greater pain on human targets that were more removed from them than they were with targets that were physically closer. This may also apply to cases where antisocial but not violent behavior toward strangers (e.g., vandalism of cars) is followed by abuse of familiar (although not necessarily intimate) animals, perhaps belonging to neighbors.

Fourth, the graduation hypothesis has been presumably supported by anecdotal stories of animal torture in the early lives of serial murderers. Cases such as these, where animal abuse seems directly tied to interpersonal violence, abound in the literature on serial homicide and are often cited as evidence by humane organizations for the graduation hypothesis. Because the abuse-violence link has not received extensive research attention, it is understandable that animal welfare organizations have emphasized high-profile cases where animal abuse appears related to interpersonal violence. Animal abuse may desensitize a perpetrator, may represent a form of rehearsal for the abuse of humans, and, if undetected, may embolden the perpetrator about his ability to escape the authorities and consequences for his acts. Although these accounts are held up as compelling evidence for the graduation hypothesis, there is evidence that many multiple killers, including some of the most notorious, did not as children abuse animals. For example, it is commonly thought that the young Jeffrey Dahmer tortured animals. However, there is no evidence that Dahmer abused animals, only that he was fascinated with dead animals and collected road kill. In other cases, the purported link between animal abuse and violence is reversed. In an analysis of woman battering, Jacobson and Gottman (1998) note that animal abuse is often a component of the emotional abuse suffered by battered women. When physical abuse decreases, emotional abuse may increase. Animal abuse may thus serve as a "reminder" that physical battering is still available as a control strategy. Although information is lacking about the temporal ordering of animal abuse and physical attacks on women, it is clear that animal abuse may follow physical attacks. As a further example of this, interviews with executed serial killer Arthur Gary Bishop discovered that Bishop was so distressed by the abduction, torture, and murder of his first child victim, that he was pursuing ways of "de-escalating." Bishop's "solution" was to acquire nearly 50 puppies from animal shelters and pet shops, take them home, and torture and kill them. Instead of reducing his need for violence, Bishop found that he so enjoyed the tortured cries of the animals, it helped motivate him to abduct, torture, and kill more children. Indeed, if one goes by anecdotal reports alone, there are even occasional multiple murderers who appear to exhibit marked compassion toward animals. For example, the Australian Martin Bryant, who in April 1996 was arrested for the deaths of 35 people, was a known "animal lover" who kept 30 to 40 cats and dogs in his home.

Even if true, the animal abuse-serial killer link does not help us understand the vast majority of animal abusers who are not as troubled. Many people who abuse animals do not become violent; they have the symptom but do not get the disease. Most, if not all, serial killers very likely were conduct disordered as children and adolescents, but only a minuscule proportion of conduct disordered children are likely to develop into such offenders. As noted by a colleague who

works with juvenile fire setters (M. Chappuis, personal communication, March 23, 1998), every adult arsonist he has encountered had a childhood history of fire setting, yet very few fire-setting children progress to adult arson. Clearly, we need to learn more about the variables that lead some abusers to later violence and not others.

Our findings should not dishearten those people who seek to rally society's interest in animal abuse. On the contrary, there is much to rally around. People who commit a single known act of animal abuse—oftentimes far less torturous and sadistic than the individuals examined in classic studies in the literature, such as those by Kellert and Felthous—are more likely to commit other criminal offenses than matched participants who do not abuse animals. As a flag of potential antisocial behavior—including but not limited to violence—isolated acts of cruelty toward animals must not be ignored by judges, psychiatrists, social workers, veterinarians, police, and others who encounter cases of abuse in their work. Moreover, a link might exist between animal abuse and violence, but future research needs to tease out how often and why a subset of animal abusers subsequently commit adult violent behavior. For now, there must be a moratorium on painting a broad stroke of violence over most cases of abuse; treating the latter as a magical bullet will only hurt the cause of those who genuinely champion the protection of animals.

Note

1. Unfortunately, researchers have not tried to tie the presence of cruelty to animals as a conduct disorder (CD) symptom to the probability of antisocial personality disorder (APD) in adults. If the strong form of the graduation hypothesis were viable and a sufficient sample of APD clients could be located, many clients would likely display cruelty to animals as part of their CD symptomatology. Furthermore, a prospective study of children identified as conduct disordered and who display cruelty toward animals as part of their symptomatology should display interpersonally violent behavior in adulthood and be more likely to be classified as APD than children who do not display animal abuse.

References

American Psychiatric Association (APA). (1994). *Diagnostic and statistical manual of mental disorders* (4th ed.). Washington, DC: Author.

Arluke, A., and C. Luke (1997). Physical cruelty toward animals in Massachusetts. *Society & Animals, 5,* 195–204.

Ascione, F. (1998). Battered women's reports of their partners' and their children's cruelty to animals. *Journal of Emotional Abuse, 1,* 119–133.

Douglas, J., Burgess, A., Burgess, A., and R. Ressler. (1992). *Crime classification manual.* New York: Lexington.

Gordon, L. (1989). *Heroes of their own lives: The politics and history of family violence.* New York: Penguin.

Jacobson, N., and J. Gottman (1998). *When men batter women: New insights into ending abusive relationships.* New York: Simon and Schuster.

Kellert, S., and A. Felthous (1985). Childhood cruelty toward animals among criminals and noncriminals. *Human Relations, 18,* 1113–1129.

Macdonald, J. (1961). *The murderer and his victim.* Springfield, IL: Charles C. Thomas.

Macdonald, J. (1968). *Homicidal threats.* Springfield, IL: Charles C Thomas.

Milgram, S. (1974). *Obedience to authority.* New York: Harper and Row.

Miller, K., and J. Knutson (1997). Reports of severe physical punishment and exposure to animal cruelty by inmates convicted of felonies and by university students. *Child Abuse & Neglect, 21,* 59–82.

Renzetti, C. (1992). *Violent betrayal: Partner abuse in lesbian relationships.* Newbury Park, CA: Sage.

Vermeulen, H., and J. Odendaal (1993). Proposed typology of companion animal abuse. *Anthrozoös, 6,* 248–257.

Clifton P. Flynn

Battered Women and Their Animal Companions

Battered Women and Animal Abuse

In the family violence literature, the connection between animal abuse and domestic violence, until very recently, only had appeared secondarily, as anecdotal data. As family members, companion animals, like women and children, are vulnerable to abuse. The characteristics of families, including privacy and the stress associated with the high level of interdependence, can result in violence against human and nonhuman members. Anecdotal data have revealed evidence of animal abuse in studies of battered women, child abuse, lesbian battering, and sibling abuse. Companion animals should be added to the list of so-called "hidden" victims of family violence (Gelles, 1997).

Ascione (1998) was the first to examine the pet abuse in the lives of battered women. In a study of clients at a battered women's shelter in Utah, 71 percent of the women with companion animals reported that their pets had been threatened, abused, or killed by a male partner. One woman in five delayed seeking shelter due to her concern for her pet's safety.

In an effort to replicate and extend Ascione's findings, I surveyed 107 clients at intake at a South Carolina shelter for battered women (Flynn, 2000). Nearly half of the women with pets—46.5 percent—reported that their partners had threatened and/or harmed their animals.

The survey data clearly revealed that their animal companions were important sources of emotional support to the women as they coped with their violent relationship. Interestingly, this was especially true if the pets had been abused.

Almost 75 percent of all women and 90 percent of women whose pets were abused said that their pets were at least somewhat important as a source of emotional support. This finding suggests that the batterers may have targeted animals precisely because of the strong bond between woman and animal. In part, such behavior could occur out of jealousy. It could also occur as a cruel attempt to inflict hurt on the woman. What better way to abuse one's partner emotionally than physically to abuse an individual to whom she is close to—in this case, her companion animal?

Women continued to worry about their animal companions after coming to the shelter, particularly if their pets also had been abused. This concern was likely well founded, given that about half of the women reported that their pets were residing with their abusive partner. Twenty percent of the women with pets, and 40 percent of those whose pets had been harmed, said they delayed seeking shelter out of concern for their pet.

The Current Study

Following the initial quantitative study of the role of pets in the lives of battered women, a smaller qualitative study was undertaken. Ten clients with companion animals from the same battered women's shelter were interviewed. With one exception, none of these women had been at the shelter during the earlier study. To protect their identities, the names of the women and their family members have been changed in this report.

The study focused on the following questions. First, what was the nature of the companion animal abuse? How was the animal cruelty used by the batterers to control, hurt, or intimidate their partners? Second, what was the relationship between the women and the companion animals? What role did the pets play in the lives of these women and their families? More specifically, what role did the companion animals play emotionally as abused women attempted to cope with their violent relationships? How were the pets affected by the women's victimization?

Extent and Nature of Pet Abuse

Kinds of Abuse

Eight of the ten women had companion animals—all were either cats or dogs—who were threatened or abused by their male partners. Two women—Casey and Mary—had more than one animal victimized. Each had two cats and a dog who were abused.

Ashley was the only woman whose animal was threatened several times, but never physically abused. Yet threats should not be dismissed as trivial or minor. According to Ashley, age 30, her boyfriend had threatened as recently as the day before the interview to call the dog pound. On other occasions, he had reportedly said that he was going to "kill that little bastard," and had warned her that "the next time you go away you better take him or he's gonna take up missin.'"

For the other seven women, their animals were not so lucky. The cats and dogs in these women's families suffered numerous and varied forms of maltreatment, including physical, sexual, and psychological abuse, and in one case, death. Sadly, Mary and her companion animals suffered abuse in multiple marriages.

Psychological Abuse   For many animals, having to witness their human female companions being assaulted was extremely stressful. This was an indirect form of emotional abuse. A few women reported more direct forms of psychological aggression. Andrea's husband would sometimes stomp his foot in the face of Boomer, their dachshund, in order to terrify and intimidate him. Jerri's husband once shot at their dogs—and at her—and fortunately missed all of them.

Physical Abuse   Unfortunately, the women's male partners committed a variety of forms of physical violence against family companion animals. Two women had cats that were abused. Casey's two cats were often "smacked" and kicked, and routinely slung off of the bed by her husband. Laura had witnessed her husband fling her cat across the room. The abused companion animals of the remaining five women were dogs. Three women, Jane, Andrea, and Karen, reported that their dogs had been kicked by their husbands. Karen's husband had kicked her chow off the porch. Boomer, Andrea's dachshund, had been kicked and flung across the room. He had also been intentionally left outside by Andrea's husband. Jerri reported that her husband hit their dogs fairly frequently, and fed them gunpowder in order to "make 'em mean."

The worst abuse, by far, was suffered by Mary's companion animals over the course of three marriages. All three husbands had physically abused various companion animals, and her first two husbands had each sexually abused Belinda, her Boston terrier. Her current husband has abused their cat, by throwing her and by backhanding her off of the table.

Her second husband intentionally ran over Belinda on his motorcycle, and then buried her alive. Later, according to Mary, he sacrificed Belinda as part of a satanic ritual. She also had a Doberman named Hans who was beaten up by her husband. In one horrible incident, her husband became enraged when both Hans and Belinda tried to intervene while he was assaulting Mary. To retaliate, he tried to hang Belinda by tying a clothesline wire around her neck, nearly choking her to death. Mary had to cut her down to free her.

Interpreting Males' Animal Abuse: Intentions and Effects

Power and Control According to Adams (1995), male batterers abuse animals as part of their deliberate strategies to control their female partners. Controlling these women by hurting, terrorizing, and intimidating them was a primary purpose of males' animal abuse. Andrea recognized this motive for her husband's abuse of Boomer, saying ". . . I think he uses the dog big time to hurt us. . . . "

Laura recounted the time her husband "picked the cat up and slung it across the room" because "he knew it would hurt me to see my cat fall." Jerri believed that her husband knew that he was hurting her and her son when he was hurting their dog. When asked if her husband would sometimes hit the dogs to try to show her who was boss, she replied, "He say [sic] he control me and the dogs and little Maurice, too."

A partner's attempts to control and hurt them (and sometimes their children) through their animals indicated that their pets may have been seen by the men as extensions of the women. Andrea stated this directly, saying, "So, yeah, I mean and it was like an extension of me, you know? And you know, maybe he abused the dog cause he couldn't, didn't want to go to jail for abusing me, I guess."

In other words, pets may have served as scapegoats. Andrea felt her husband "used the dog instead of us . . . as his punching bag." She went on to say that her husband

> would sometimes do to Boomer what he wished he could do to us, . . . there was plenty of times that we were in the middle of a huge fight and Boomer would just get in the way—just get in the way accidentally. He'd swat at him, kick him, or he'd go like this with his boot, you know, stomp it really loud, you know, right next to Boomer's face so that Boomer would run, you know. And the dog didn't even do anything, so I really felt like he was tryin to intimidate the dog as much as he would try and intimidate the family, you

know? So, in essence I guess he treated, uh, the dog just like family, too. . . .

Some of the women felt that their husbands' jealousy of the relationship the women had with the animals had contributed to the pet abuse. Casey, talking about her husband, said, "And he's even accused me of treatin the cats better than him." And later, she reported him saying, "'You think more of them cats than you do me,' which is true, yeah," she added.

Overall, the batterers' attempts to dominate and control the women through their pets illustrated the larger role of traditional gender role stereotypes held by these men. More than one woman spoke of her partner's beliefs in male dominance. Karen indicated that her husband believed that he, and men in general, were the head of the household, and should be in charge. She felt like he believed that "he was supposed to have all control and supposed to know every time, where it went and decide where it went. Not KNOW where it went; DECIDE where it went."

Ashley expressed similar sentiment about her boyfriend. "He just thinks he's supposed to be the boss. He wants to control me. He says I'm supposed to stay home while he goes out all day ramblin' around."

In some cases, as with wife abuse, it may have been the men's failure to live up to masculine expectations, especially with regard to providing for their families, that contributed to the pet abuse. Of the four men who were unemployed, all were abusive to their companion animals.

In at least one case, experiences with animals may have served to heighten traditionally masculine expressions of dominance and aggression. Karen insightfully connected her husband's violence with the aggressive animals he has had—including a Doberman, a pit bull/boxer mix, and snakes—both growing up and as an adult.

> . . . The animals that Greg had when I met him [hesitation], were mean, ferocious, and scary animals, . . .

Now his pit bull, the pit bull boxer, it was a mixed-breed dog, he had it at the same time that he had the Doberman. And they were in his parents' backyard, and when it came to feedin' time in that house, they were both on chains and it was all him and his daddy could do—and his daddy's a big man—it was all they could do with hoe handles and rake handles to keep them dogs from tearin' each other apart come feedin' time.

When asked if she saw any connection between her husband having aggressive dogs and his aggression toward her, Karen replied, "When he had those aggressive dogs, he was more aggressive to me as opposed to when he had the horse and, he wasn't as physically abusive. It didn't feel like he hit as hard either. You know [long hesitation]. Of course, maybe that was just cause I was gettin immune to the pain."

Effects on Children Of the eight women whose pets were abused, seven had children. Four women—Jerri, Andrea, Jane, and Casey—reported that their children had witnessed their companion animals' victimization. Like their mothers, the children were both angered and terrified by their fathers' or stepfathers' cruelty toward their beloved companion animals. Casey describes her son Jared's reaction when his stepfather kicked their cat, Trouble, across the room.

> He [Jared] just looked at me like, you know, "please don't let. . ." He didn't say anything. He just looked at me like, "please don't let him do my cat that way!" And he just stood there in fear like he wanted to go get his cat but, you know, we were all headed out the door, and he just kind of stood there in fear, and I said something to Steve and he said, "Well, he [Trouble] don't need to go outside. I won't never catch him to get him back in!"

Andrea's children witnessed her husband abuse Boomer, their dachshund. She said that it "upset both of them, but especially Shawn . . . ." When asked if her sons ever tried to protect Boomer from her husband, Richard, she responded,

And the kids most of the time were afraid of Richard, so they never got in the way. They would, Shawn would just be quiet about it and give Richard dirty looks, you know. But when he'd go out and Richard would sometimes say, "don't go out and get him, don't call him. Let him come, he'll come home when he wants to." So Richard wouldn't even want Shawn to go out and coddle him because, that's what he called it, because, you know, [Richard] would say things like "he [Boomer] was bad. You need to let him just be out there by himself. If he gets run over or whatever, it's HIS fault or it's HIS problem!"

How were Andrea's children affected by Richard's maltreatment of Boomer?

> I think it affected them the same way it affected them when they saw Richard be abusive to us, you know, is that, you know, here's someone we love, you know, is a part of our family to us, just like one of my children, that dog is. I've had him for a long time and he's part of my family. And, um, same for the boys. They LOVE that dog, and for them to see it, you know, it's hurtful and then to know they can't protect him because Richard's bigger and stronger, and um, you don't want him to do that to YOU, you know, and it's kinda like. . . [long hesitation]. So, I mean, they were just kinda stuck, yeah. I think it affected them a lot.

So children were also victimized by the abuse of the companion animals in ways that often parallel the effects of wife abuse on children. Not only was a loved one, a valued member of the family being harmed, but they were powerless to do anything about it at the time, and often prevented from comforting the animal immediately following the abuse. In general, the abuse contributed to a climate of control, intimidation, and terror for children, women, and animals.

Animals' Responses to Women's Victimization

Comforters

It was clear from the interviews that, because of their close relationship with their companion animals, the animals were very important emotionally to the women following a violent episode. Some indicated that their pets could sense that something was wrong, and that, as a result, they provided comfort and unconditional love.

For Andrea, having her dachshund Boomer around after she had been assaulted was like having her children there. "... Same as my kids, you know, it's like having them around just makes you know that everything is okay, you know. No matter what, you're gonna be all right."

Jane, whose pets were abused by both her first and current husbands, said that "a lot of times after me and Stanley [first husband] got into it, I'd go out in the yard and, where we had the dogs at, they all come and crawl up and sit beside me and put their head in my lap like they knowed somethin was wrong, you know." Later, she said, "You know, they make me feel like [hesitation] I was needed for somethin anyway."

Talking with their companion animals following an argument or a battering incident was comforting to these women. Brenda, when asked if she ever talked to Mutt, her chow, after being hit by her husband, replied,

Oh yeah, he's there for me. If we get into an argument, I'll go outside and sit there because there's like, when he chops the wood, there's like a bench you can sit on. It's right next to Mutt and I'll sit there, and then Mutt will just come and sit next to me with his chain cause he's strong enough. He'll sit there and he'll look at me like, "What's wrong?" And I'll start talkin to him and he's like, "It's okay." And he'll lay his little head right here on my lap and I'll start pettin him. And he'll look at me like, "Ah, that feels so good."

As many who share lives with companion animals have attested, one of the major rewards for the women is the unconditional love that animals bestow upon them. Jane described a night when her current husband had been, in her words, in "one of his foul moods." Her Chihuahua, Killer, got up in her lap and began to lick her. "I said, 'You love mama whether anybody else does or

not, don't ya, Killer?' And he'd just whine, you know. And then he curled up and laid down right here like a baby would, on my chest and went to sleep."

Unfortunately, there were times when some women were unable to be with their pet following an abusive episode, because the animal was terrified and in hiding. When Andrea was asked about whether Boomer, her dachshund, was ever a source of comfort and support after an incident, she said, "Well, sometimes I, I would have liked to have him been, but he was so afraid that he wouldn't come out." Later, she acknowledged that Boomer was "very, very important to me when he was around. When I couldn't get him to come out because he was too scared, then I didn't have that comfort, but yeah, he was very comforting to me."

Protectors

It was not at all unusual for an animal to attempt to protect a woman when she was being abused. Mary, Laura, Ashley, and Andrea all reported protective responses from their animals. Laura reported that her Himalayan cat, Gizmo, once tried to get to her husband.

Eddie hit me and that cat jumped at Eddie. [Long hesitation] The only cat I know of that had ever protected its master. Cause, um, when he jumped, I grabbed him 'cause I knew Eddie would kill him. And, uh, he wouldn't let Eddie around me for like four or five hours. I'd get up and go to the kitchen and he'd be on my heels.

Ashley recounts how Darlene, her golden retriever mix, responded to her husband's physical taunts.

I'd be sittin in the left front room next to the front door, and he'd come by me going to the bathroom or whatever and he'd slap me on the head—just not hard enough to hurt me, but hard enough to annoy me. And Darlene, the little retriever mix, she, every time he stands there for a moment, she gets up on him pushing him away, or crawls up in my lap where he can't get to me. She won't let, doesn't want him to come too close to me. . . .

On a few occasions, Boomer tried to protect Andrea from her husband by snarling and barking at him. But her husband would slap at Boomer, causing him to flee the scene, making him unavailable to give or receive emotional support. Sometimes an animal's attempt to intervene in a battering episode led to the animal's victimization. Mary's dog, Belinda, tried to defend Mary during an assault by her second husband and was nearly killed.

Emotional Responses to Witnessing Women's Abuse

Whether or not they were trying to protect her, witnessing a woman's abuse was often very emotionally upsetting for her animal companion. Similar to symptoms of stress in humans, women reported several physical manifestations of stress in their pets when the animals witnessed her abuse, including shivering or shaking, cowering, hiding, and urinating. In the only violent episode after acquiring Sparky, Laura believed he was affected by observing it.

> He would just shy away and wouldn't come to us. It took him about 30 minutes for him to come to me, which I'm always the first one he'll go to anyway, and it took him 30 minutes. I don't know whether he just decided he wasn't afraid or, you know, sensed that I was upset and came to me because of it, but [brief hesitation] he shied away. He stayed up under the chair. Even got a "Begging strip" out and he didn't want it, and that's not like Sparky—his popcorn and his "Beggin' Strips."

Sometimes just shouting by the batterer was troubling to the animals. "Well, he claims he couldn't love a child as much as he loves Darlene [golden retriever mix]," Ashley explains, "but when he raises his voice and carrying on like a lunatic, it upsets Darlene, and I keep tellin' him, 'lower your voice—you're upsetting Darlene! Don't yell like that!' He'll say, 'I don't give a damn' and just keeps on."

Thus, even just by yelling at his partner, he inflicts multiple forms of psychological damage on both woman and animal. The verbal abuse hurts her directly, but it also upsets her animal companion. And that victimizes her in yet another way.

Jerri identified the mutual nature of harm with regard to violence in her relationship. She understood that when her husband abused her dogs, he was hurting her and their son, as well. But she also understood that his violence toward them was harmful for the dogs to witness. . . . When he'd be hurtin' us, he'd be hurtin' the dogs, too, cause they'd sit there and look, you know, like they're sayin,' 'why he jumpin' on them— they ain't did nothin'. They'd be actually barkin' at him and stuff."

After an abusive episode, Ashley describes trying to calm down Darlene, who "panics. She actually starts shivering." When asked if you could really see the physical reaction, Ashley replied, "Uh-huh. She comes up and lays across me and a 60-pound dog does not belong in your lap, and she sits there and curls up to me, and I get her big head in my hands and I just rub her and talk real softly to her and she calms down, but he just keeps yackin' and yackin' at the top of his voice."

These examples reveal an interesting dimension to domestic violence involving companion animals. It is important to see that both women and animals are victimized. On the one hand, animals are harmed emotionally when they observe their human female companions abused. On the other hand, women are simultaneously emotionally victimized, as they are forced to worry about the animal's well-being, both in the midst of and immediately following a violent episode.

Leaving Companion Animals Behind

Delayed Leaving Due to Animals

Earlier studies of shelter women have found that about one-fifth of women delayed coming to the shelter out of concern for the welfare of their companion animals (Ascione, 1998; Flynn,

2000b). Such delays mean that both women and animals remain at risk for additional abuse. Among this sample, four women—Andrea, Ashley, Laura, and Casey—indicated that they delayed leaving their batterers because they were worried about their pets. For example, Laura said that she "found out about this place [the shelter], but, um, I couldn't leave Sparky um 'cause I was afraid he'd kill her. So, soon as I found Sparky somewhere to stay, I came." Andrea echoed those feelings, saying, "Yeah. I might have left sooner if I would have had a place for him [Boomer] to go—probably would've left quite a while sooner."

Ashley said she would have come one month sooner if not for her concern about what would happen to Scooter and Darlene. Casey delayed even longer, waiting about two months before leaving her abuser. Casey explained, "Steve is not the kind of guy you can just leave. He'll hunt you down. You can't just leave him. You gonna have to go to the Safe Homes. And see, I started callin' here in January and February—several weeks ago, but the cats, I just didn't know what to do with the cats, or I would've been in here. If I didn't have those animals, I would've been here."

Each of these women spoke about how they wished that the shelter could somehow accommodate their animals. Andrea, who fortunately had found someone to care for Boomer while she was at the shelter, talked about how "great" it would be if the shelter had a place for pets.

When asked if she would have brought Scooter and Darlene if the shelter had accepted pets, Ashley said, "Oh yeah, even if I had to bring a mop and my own broom and cleaning solution. I'd a brought 'em." Laura expressed similar sentiments, saying, "If they tell me I could bring my dog, I'd walk [and get him.]"

The women also miss the emotional support of their companion animals during this very difficult time in their lives. Laura put it this way: "To me, they ought to let us bring our pets because that's the one thing we could get the help from. When nobody else wants a hug or wants to be around you, they don't care. Just love 'em and feed 'em."

Miss, Worry About Animals

Having to leave their companion animals behind is extremely upsetting for most of these women. Since the women tended to view their pets as children, as family members, it is easy to understand their worry and concern. Some women were lucky enough to find caretakers for their animals. An elder in Andrea's church volunteered to keep Boomer for her. Laura had a friend who was willing to provide a temporary home to Sparky. Karen's cat, Sammy, was living at their old house, which has since been abandoned by Karen's husband.

The companion animals of Casey, Jane, and Ashley, however, were still with their (both the women's and the animals') abusers. This caused a great deal of concern for a variety of reasons. Ashley was worried that her husband might not be feeding her animals what they should be eating. But beyond that, she was also receiving threats that he might take Darlene, their golden retriever mix, away from her. Such concerns demonstrate how companion animals can be used by batterers to control, hurt, and manipulate women even after they have left home.

Ashley's account of this struggle sounded like divorcing parents in a custody fight. She was considering letting her husband visit her dogs, especially Darlene, because she believed that was important for both of them.

> Well, in a way it is [like a custody battle] because we both been [sic] with her since she was just a baby. And just like, 'cause I was kept from my father, I mean I'm very against that idea unless it's harmful. . . . So I am thinking about changing my mind about that! Letting him see her when he wants to.

Interestingly, in the case of Jane and Ashley, it appears that the main reason that their pets had remained with the male batterers was that the batterers had developed relationships with the animals that the women were trying to respect, and that led them to be less concerned about future abuse. This may be due to the fact that the prior animal abuse was not as frequent or severe as in some of the other relationships.

On the other hand, Andrea and Laura "knew" their husbands would hurt their animals, and that knowledge led them to "foster" their pets before coming to the shelter. According to Andrea, "I KNOW Richard would've done something to him because he's just, he was just SO mad that I knew something would happen if I wasn't careful. So, I was really, really worried. I almost didn't leave until the next day because I didn't know what to do with him. . . ." Later in the interview, she explained why she was convinced her husband would have harmed Boomer if she had left him there.

> . . . I think he would have hit him and kicked at him and whatever, you know. . . . Maybe not right away, but whenever he got mad, you know, he thought about it and got mad, you know, maybe thought about us leaving or whatever and, "hey, you stupid dog—you're still here!" I can just see him because he's like that. . . .

But knowing that Boomer was now safe didn't cause all of the worrying to stop. Among other things, Andrea was still worried that Boomer may have picked up bad habits, or was being spoiled, or that his "foster parents" may be becoming attached to Boomer and wouldn't want to give him back.

Because the women missed their animal family members terribly, they often made great efforts to check on and sometimes visit their companions. Laura said that she checked on Sparky every day. Andrea, who was planning to take her children to visit Boomer soon, had different kinds of worries about visiting Boomer.

> . . . I'm just afraid when I go see him that I won't be able to leave him, you know, or that he's going to want to come with me and try to hop in my car, and I would be really, really upset. . . . I KNOW he's going to be upset when I leave . . . but the kids really want to see him so we'll probably drive out there fairly soon and visit with him.

Including Animals in Future Plans

The importance of companion animals in the women's lives is highlighted by their efforts to incorporate the animals into their plans for the future. Andrea, Karen, and Casey all talked about wanting to find a place to live where they could have pets. Yet they worried about whether they would be successful, given that many apartment complexes either do not allow pets, or if they do, impose additional charges, such as pet deposits and/or higher rents.

So, even after the women, their children, and their animals are safe, many women still fear losing their valued animal companions when they begin rebuilding their lives following their abusive relationships.

Discussion

Interviews with battered women who have companion animals provide support for the gendered nature of violence in families, and reveal the symbolic role of pets in families, and the symbolic interaction between humans and animals. There was little doubt that, for the most part, these women considered their companion animals to be members of the family, referring to them as their children, their "babies." Unfortunately, the domestic violence literature in general, and feminist scholarship in particular, make it clear that weaker, less powerful members of families—women and children—are at risk of being assaulted by stronger, more powerful members—men. Now companion animals can be added to the list of potential victims of male violence in intimate relationships.

Men employed many forms of abuse, including threatening to harm or give away beloved companion animals, hitting, kicking, beating, choking, and in one case, even killing them. Often this animal abuse was used to control, hurt, or intimidate their female partners, and sometimes, their children. This harm to their animal companions added to the stress and terror they were already experiencing as victims of domestic violence themselves.

Men's use of violence against their partners' companion animals is consistent with feminist explanations that have stressed the role of patriarchy and the connection between gender, power, and control in understanding violence in intimate relationships. The work of Adams (1994, 1995) extends this analysis to include animals along with women and children among the victims of male violence.

If companion animals are thought of as family members, and if women and animals are both targets of abuse, then each may turn to the other for comfort and support, and even protection, during and after a battering episode. In addition, both women and animals are victimized by violence toward the other. A man's violence toward an animal also hurts his partner (and children), just as his violence toward her also hurts the animal. These interviews help shed light on the multidimensional nature of domestic violence.

Concern for the safety and welfare of their pets led some women to delay leaving their batterers, one by as much as two months. Even after leaving they continued to worry about their animals, check on them frequently, and visit them whenever possible. If at all possible, women were committed to finding a place to live after leaving the shelter that would allow them to have all members of their family living with them—including their nonhuman members.

Given the significant role that animals play in the lives of some battered women, it becomes critical for professionals who serve them to be aware of and acknowledge the importance of women's relationships with their pets. Shelter staff need to inquire about companion animals at intake, and take seriously women's emotional turmoil related to missing and worrying about their animals. Previous research by Ascione, Weber, and Wood (1997) has shown that although shelter staff are often aware of animal abuse in their clients' families, typically by their batterers, few shelters actually provided services related to this issue. Shelters could develop foster programs that could provide temporary homes for clients' pets, or better yet, create animal hous-

ing facilities on site. Perhaps the local animal shelter could house women's animals while they were in the shelter. Providing a foster home for pets becomes particularly important considering that some women delay coming to the shelter since they cannot bring their animals with them.

Provisions should be made for women to check on their animals, both for the sake of the animals and the women. Prior research has found that pets of battered women have received lower levels of regular and emergency veterinary care than animals of nonabused women. Shelters could establish arrangements with veterinarians whereby medical services for their animals could be performed either free of charge or for a reduced fee.

Clinicians need to respect the relationship women have with their companion animals. Counselors need to understand that another family member has been left behind, one who may be at risk for abuse and/or neglect, and that both woman and animal are likely to be suffering as a result of their separation. Finally, when shelter staff help their clients prepare to leave the shelter, they should make every effort to help find housing for the women where their pets are also welcome.

References

Adams, C. J. (1994). Bringing peace home: A feminist philosophical perspective on the abuse of women, children, and pet animals. *Hypatia, 9,* 63–84.

—— (1995). Woman-battering and harm to animals. In C. J. Adams and J. Donovan (eds.), *Animals and women: Feminist theoretical explorations* (pp. 55–84). Durham, NC: Duke University Press.

Ascione, Frank R. (1998). Battered women's reports of their partners' and their children's cruelty to animals. *Journal of Emotional Abuse, 1,* 119–133.

Ascione, F. R., Weber, C. V., and D. S. Wood (1997). The abuse of animals and domestic violence: A national survey of shelters for women who are battered. *Society & Animals, 5,* 205–218.

Flynn, C. P. (2000). Woman's best friend: Pet abuse and the role of companion animals in the lives of battered women. *Violence Against Women, 6,* 162–177.

Gelles, R. J. (1997). *Intimate violence in families,* 3rd ed. Thousand Oaks, CA: Sage.

PART FOUR

Wild(life) Encounters

Introduction

Anthropologists were the first social scientists to study wildlife by documenting the nature and importance of animals in tribal cultures. Ethnographic research in the nineteenth and early twentieth centuries examined the material use of animals for food, clothing, or shelter, and the symbolic use of animals as totems. Sociologists and others interested in human-animal relations have been slower to study the social meaning and context of wildlife, instead largely focusing on companion animals and, to a lesser, extent, the exploitation of animals in general. However, a small, but robust social science literature is emerging on human-wildlife relations (e.g., Dizard 1999; Herda-Rapp and Goedeke 2005). This literature asks how modern society defines the meaning of wildlife and, in so doing, creates, perpetuates, blurs, or transcends boundaries between civilization and the wild, manmade environment and nature, and human and animal.

Typically, people think of these meanings and boundaries as "factual"—fixed and invariant in place and time. Consider which animals are regarded as wild, and which as tame. At an early age, children learn by watching animated movies, reading fairy tales, and listening to their parents that a "wild animal" can be a tiger in the jungle, an elephant in a zoo, a squirrel living in the backyard of a suburban home, an ownerless dog that roams the neighborhood, or a mean-spirited, raunchy person looking to pick a fight in a bar. As social designations, "wildness" comes to mean distance and danger with "tameness" its converse. Many learn what a "tame" animal is by owning one themselves. Parents often acquire pets for their children who themselves in turn attribute personlike qualities to these animals and protect them from the dangers that lurk outside in the world of nature. The result is that children come to view what constitutes a wild or tame animal as a hard and fast "fact" whose meaning is given—external to human culture and social process. Yet we know that sociological "facts" can vary because in different places and times people will assign them different meanings.

Thus, what at one time a group regards as wild can at another time be regarded as tame. For example, our conception of primates developed dramati-cally in the twentieth century, so that their place in the modern order has changed from being exotic and wild to being tame and almost human. Anthropologist Susan Sperling (1988) claims that several factors account for this shifting view. As postwar America grew increasingly interested in the complex cognitive and social abilities of animals, images of primates in particular were remodeled to become more humanlike. Anthropological models of evolution started replacing "primitive" human groups, such as the Trobriand Islanders, with nonhuman primates—making the latter our "ancestors." These models along with observational studies of primates were disseminated to the public in magazines like *National Geographic*, nature shows on television, or in movies like *Gorillas in the Mist*, giving the impression of extreme similarity between the species. Baboon troops, for instance, were uncritically viewed as microcosms of human society because they too had social characteristics, such as a division of labor. Compounding the effect of this research were field studies, like those of Jane Goodall's, in which chimpanzee subjects were given human names and their personalities described in human terms. Additional anthropomorphizing came from researchers who studied the acquisition of language by apes and treated their animals like foster children who could talk and live in human settings. The consequence, contends Sperling, was the obliteration of the border between humans and nonhumans.

With such boundary blurring, it is not surprising that what were once wild animals may now be regarded as pets. A case in point is a project that allowed volunteers to assist with research and conservation efforts with wild orangutans in Borneo (Russell 1995). Some people had expected and desired to have a "cuddly" experience with these animals. They did; they experienced the apes as "children" in their interactions with confiscated infants, which were to be sold as pets but were being rehabilitated in a clinic. Although they were initially forbidden to have physical contact with the infants, many of the tourists expressed an intense desire to hold them. Many "oohed" and "aahed" when seeing the animals and commonly described them as "cute" or as "sweet little ones." When permitted physical contact, all the tourists felt very fortunate to have had the opportunity, saying that it "profoundly" affected them. Some tourists even competed for the affections of certain infants, as they sought to "babysit" them or were reluctant to break off contact because they felt "needed" by the young animals. No longer seen as alien or strange creatures as they might have been years ago, these primates were related to in the only way that made sense to these tourists. They defined the primates as pets or as quasi-family members of human society.

In fact, some wild animals are literally transformed over time into pets, of a sort. Elizabeth Lawrence (1990) contends that the twentieth century witnessed a remarkable transformation of wild bears into tame and civilized stuffed teddy bear dolls that hardly resemble their natural forebears. Although the teddy bear is obviously an inanimate object—a doll—it is now often seen and treated as though it were a companion animal. Lawrence goes so far as to say that teddy bears nearly become people. Child and adult owners attribute personalities, thoughts, feelings, and behaviors to their teddy bears and report that their dolls make them feel comfortable. In return for the dolls' unconditional affection, owners cherish them. This conversion of nature into culture, according to Lawrence, has resulted in a counterpart of oppositions between the teddy bear and the living bear. The former is tame, dependent, dependable, neutered, civilized, humanized, and sanitized, while the latter is wild, unpredictable, uncontrolled, aloof, and dangerous. Lawrence's analysis highlights the power of social constructions to alter what we think of as normal or natural.

For example, what are animals in zoos? They are animals that most of us will never see in their "natural" state, but can only read about or imagine. Taken from their natural context, these animals are put in a human frame, while their natural habitat is transformed into our dream of a human-animal paradise (Sax 1997). They become creatures of leisure—given food rather than hunting and fighting for live game among themselves. Even the "prey" is transformed so that it cannot be identified as a specific animal—meat is thoroughly butchered—and zoo animals are not allowed to eat fellow captives. Zoo animals also live in harmony, never struggling over territorial matters

with other animals. They live in an environment built by humans: a constructed world that shrinks entire continents into acres and often combines different species in the same exhibit, even though they may live far apart in their normal climatic zone.

The artificiality of this zoological paradise renders invalid the traditional dichotomy of wild versus domestic animals. There, symbols of captivity, such as cages and cold cement floors, increasingly are being eliminated, while animals in nature are being carefully observed and controlled through devices such as concealed cameras and radio collars. Because of modes of modern captivity, animals can be closely approached and admired in ways that are impossible in the wild. This proximity means that humans are not unobtrusive to zoo animals. Although it is not known exactly how their behavior changes, one study found that instead of ignoring or being habituated to visitors, zoo animals respond to and interact with them; for instance, these animals are often encouraged by the public to beg, despite signs warning to the contrary. What zoo visitors see, then, is a culturally falsified version of how these animals actually behave in the wild.

The result is often a captive wild animal that is regarded as a human in animal skin. Perhaps one of the best examples of this transformation is the giant panda. Many of the panda's physical features—the round head, large eyes, vertical posture—facilitate anthropomorphizing it. The panda is not a distant animal but becomes a cuddly friend endowed with a human personality, needs, and emotions. Once an animal is perceived in this manner, the distinction crumbles between what we regard as wild and tame. Thus, visitors often have a fondness for zoo animals, and even aquarium sea life, sometimes naming them, adopting them, giving them tea parties, or playing with and touching them in children's zoos and aquaria petting tanks. Even the killer whale "Shamu" is regarded by visitors as something like a pet (Davis 1997). For their part, animal handlers often form even closer relationships with individual zoo animals, treating them as companion animals.

This constructionist approach underlies several key questions about the interaction of humans with wild animals. First, why have modern western societies become so emotionally interested in wildlife—or at least certain kinds of wild animals? The emotional regard for wildlife is a contemporary western phenomenon. Early nineteenth century sentimentalization of farm animals and pets did not extend to wild animals (Isenberg 2002). Not until the late 1800s or early twentieth century did signs emerge of a growing emotional connection to and romantic interest in wildlife and the wilderness, expressed in highly successful publications such as Jack London's *The Call of the Wild*. Underlying these signs of interest in wildlife was an unstated, but real, desire to close the boundary between what was natural and what was human.

Interest in wildlife escalated toward the end of the twentieth century. Attendance at zoos and aquaria continued to grow (exceeding that of all sporting events combined), viewing of media edutainment programs about wild animals sharply rose, volunteer efforts to save and protect endangered species drew increasing support and fervor, and organized efforts to directly experience—or even to touch—wild animals, sometimes in their natural habitat, showed mounting popularity. For many people, the desire to close the human-wildlife gap evolved into wanting to deny or transcend it. Movies, television, and print media encouraged this desire by furthering widespread popular fascination for certain, heavily anthropomorphized wild animals, such as dolphins and nonhuman primates, and then by showcasing one-on-one encounters with them in which humans appear to communicate directly and personally with their interspecies co-equal. This passion has created a tourist industry of people hungry for such encounters with certain—near mythic—wild animals. Lofty expectations for these encounters include idyllic, peek experiences that some believe cure chronic diseases and provide transcendent spiritual experiences. However, the very loftiness of these expectations, and their foundation in heavily anthropomorphized media constructions of wildlife, may make actual encounters less personally transformative than hoped for by many.

A second question asks how we should regard wildlife that already exists in our human habitat, when they are not regarded with the same awe as dolphins, for example. Instead of fascination for these creatures, or passion to have one-on-one contact with them, they are often viewed as problems or pests in our backyards, streets, or parks. To wit, officials in New York City recently declared "war" on pigeons because of their unsightly and unsanitary droppings. There are, of course, residential encounters with wildlife that are greeted with awe, as happens when there is a rare moose sighting in an upper-middle-class suburb of Boston. And for every family that does not want deer walking through the backyard, there is another that welcomes such visits.

These varied responses again show the plasticity of wild animal constructions. A case in point involves a deer intrusion in a small Oregon town. An injured fawn strayed into a backyard and was subsequently cared for and raised as a pet by a family for six years—it was named (Snowball), brought into the house for the first year, talked to, pet, fed, and played with. But city officials and wildlife managers that oversaw hunting and residential zoning initially refused to consider Snowball and her meaning to her human hosts. The owner did not have a permit to raise wildlife, which was illegal under state law. Officials said that Snowball could only remain if her pen's gate could be unlocked, so she could be free to roam, to which her owner demurred, fearing for the deer's welfare. From the authorities' perspective, there was no other way to process the issue—Snowball could not be kept like a penned dog in the neighborhood, and if someone could afford a hunting license, given that she was a wild animal, the deer could have been dispatched. Failing to free Snowball led officials to propose her euthanasia. Public outcry ensued over the possibility that authorities would seize Snowball from the family and kill her. Responding to pressure, Oregon's Fish and Wildlife Department declined to do this, although it did seize the deer in search of other options for her future placement.

Such wildlife encounters are important to examine because they expose our distinctions between human versus nonhuman, pet versus wildlife, person versus property, and show how these distinctions easily crumble if we change the situation or the participants. These distinctions are important because they influence how—or even whether—we interact with wild animals not only in the wilderness but in our cities and suburbs. Yet it is interesting that urban theorists, scholars, and planners do not address these local wildlife interactions, or animals more generally, whether experienced with antipathy as annoying vermin or awe as a welcome guest. In fact, wildlife is completely disregarded in discussions of urban development and growth, in which animals are treated as nonexistent. However, scholars and activists are starting to call for rectifying this oversight. If wildlife can be refactored into our human settlements, we can live more as kin with other species. The result might spiritually benefit humans while protecting animals.

A final question asks to what extent our interest in preserving the wilderness per se affects our interest in the plight of particular wild animals. With never-ending urban expansion into wetlands, forests, and other land uninhabited by humans, wildlife takes on added importance as a proxy for our heightened concern for the loss of wilderness. In other words, concern for endangered species, or for that matter any wild animal, may be symptomatic of a broader worry over the failing health and shrinking size of our environment. If animal populations are decreasing, the answer to reverse this trend is not always as simple as adding new animals or encouraging their mating. Reversing this problem may call for new environmental policies that prevent human use of or intrusion into the natural habit of wild animals.

Susanna Curtin's article explores what it is like to swim with dolphins and why so many people are drawn to this experience. This rapidly growing form of tourism has enormous appeal to people, whether they swim with captive or wild dolphins. Because of the dolphin's almost mythic status in modern western societies, people set high expectations for these encounters. People come with "virtual capital" about what dolphins—and their experiences with them—should be like from watching television programs and reading about them. This capital leads to extensive anthropomorphizing of dolphins and unrealistic expectations of swimming with them. While people are enthralled by their contact with dolphins, it fails to meet unrealistic expectations. This is true for those who expect a life-changing experience and those, in particular, who swim with captive dolphins because these contacts seem artificial, brief, and too

focused on the trainers. Nevertheless, this novel interspecies connection, involving touch and closeness, provides a "peak experience" to most swimmers. Being in their presence uplifts people because of the dolphin's perceived beauty, grace, agility, intelligence, power, facial expressions, and humanlike attributes.

Tackling an opposing question, the next article by Jennifer Wolch asks why we have ignored "common" wildlife living in our cities. She invites us to bring the nonhuman animal world back into geography, urban thinking, and everyday life. She argues that exotic and domestic animals should not be privileged over common animals who live in cities and with whom people do not interact everyday. To do this, we need to treat all animals as subjects rather than objects, thereby bringing the animal's subjective experience into our understanding of and interaction with them. Acknowledging the animal's standpoint recognizes kinship and difference with them and encourages respect, friendship, and reciprocity. The concept of "zoöpolis" embraces this idea and affirms that we can and should bring animals back into city life and urban thought. But to "renaturalize" cities, we must consider how animals are affected by urbanization, how city residents interact with animals, how animals adapt to cities, and how cities currently deal with urban animals. Carrying out this agenda brings us closer to living as kin with animals in our urban habitat.

Robert Granfield and Paul Colomy, in the final article, show how general anxiety over diminishing wilderness can fuel public dismay over the loss of wildlife. In 1995, an elk was shot and killed by a poacher in a Colorado park. Although the elk—known by his frequent visitors as Samson—was treated by many people as a beloved pet and friend, the intensity and extent of public clamor and anger over the incident was initially hard to explain. According to Granfield and Colomy, Samson was ecopomorphized; qualities associated with the environment—its magnificence—were attributed to Samson. He became a symbol of the evaporating wilderness outside Denver; emotional distress over Samson's death was symptomatic of a larger worry about never-ending urban expansion and intrusion into pristine land. Response to

Samson's loss demonstrates that our thinking about wild animals can sometimes dissolve traditional boundaries that separate us from animals, and civilization from wilderness.

References

Davis, S. 1997. *Spectacular Nature: Corporate Culture and the Sea World Experience.* Berkeley: University of California Press.

Dizard, J. 1999. *Going Wild: Hunting, Animal Rights and the Contested Meaning of Nature.* Amherst, MA: University of Massachusetts.

Herda-Rapp, A. and T. Goedeke. 2005. *Mad About Wildlife: Looking at the Social Conflict Over Wildlife.* Leiden, The Netherlands: Brill.

Isenberg, A. 2002. "The Moral Ecology of Wildlife." In N. Rothfels, ed., *Representing Animals*, 48–64. Bloomington, IN: Indiana University Press.

Lawrence, E. 1990. "The Tamed Wild: Symbolic Bears in American Culture." In *Dominant Symbols in Popular Culture.* Bowling Green University Popular Press.

Russell, C. 1995. "The Social Construction of Orangutans: An Ecotourist Experience." *Society & Animals* 3:151–170.

Sax, B. 1997. "The Zoo: Prison or Paradise?" *Terra Nova* 2(1):59–68.

Sperling, S. 1988. *Animal Liberators: Research and Morality.* University of California Press.

Susanna Curtin

Swimming with Dolphins

Introduction

There is an unmistakable, ill-defined and inexplicable attraction between us and dolphins. Over time, however, the fascination for them and the postmodern belief that interacting with dolphins improves physical and "spiritual" well-being has turned into a rapidly expanding worldwide tourist activity, with a proliferation of opportunities to swim with captive and wild dolphin populations throughout the world. Such tourist activities have capitalized on the tendency of dolphins, either as individuals or as groups, to apparently enjoy interacting with people.

According to Hughes (2001), the majority of dolphin tourist attractions occur via the captive display, training and performances of animals before a paying audience. The Marine Studios in Florida were the first to develop "dolphin dressage" in 1938. This was the beginning of the trained dolphin acts that are increasingly prevalent today in tourist locations throughout the world (WDCS, 2005). Large, themed marine parks such as Discovery Cove and Sea World in Florida have provided the blueprint for facilities to offer opportunities for a small number of tourists to enter the dolphin pools to touch, play and swim with the dolphins.

The information available, however, suggests that in the United States alone there are around 18 swim-with-dolphin facilities compared with only four 10 years ago. Cruise ship passengers and other tourists can now swim with dolphins at more than 30 marine attractions throughout the Caribbean, double the number that existed 5 years ago. Similar development is occurring in European mass tourist destinations such as Spain, the Algarve, the Canary Islands, as well as in Egypt, the Middle East and Asia. According to Frohoff and Packard (1995), 40,000 people swam with captive dolphins in 1990. Since then, Kestin (2004, p. 5) reports that Sea World alone attracted 11 million visitors in 2003, although how many of these visitors swam with the dolphins is difficult to ascertain.

As well as these contrived marine settings, there is a burgeoning "swim with wild dol-phins" industry in many natural locations throughout the world. In fact, wherever there are resident pods of dolphins, appropriate sea conditions and a critical tourist mass, small- and medium-sized operators offer trips to watch and swim with dolphins. Swimmers are generally placed in the water nearby, can swim freely around the dolphins or are told to hold onto ropes from which they can safely experience the dolphin encounter.

There are many historical accounts of interaction between wild dolphins and humans which can be used to place the development of this "new" industry in context. Orams (1997) identifies many different geographically dispersed cultures where dolphins have become mythical or god-like symbols such as the Maori in New Zealand, the Greeks and Romans and prehistoric Africans. Here, stories about dolphins that have formed regular and long-term relationships with people are scattered throughout history. Typically, these include symbiotic fishing arrangements, general touching, playing, communication and interaction.

113

However, the most common form of interaction between dolphins and humans occurs on boats where dolphins often approach vessels to surf on the bow-wave and stern-wake. Surfers, too, often meet dolphins who surf alongside them in brief and unpredictable encounters (personal observation). Such behavior appears to be associated with the dolphins' curiosity, play and, possibly, movement from one place to another using waves to assist them. This charming performance helps consolidate the stories and myths which society has constructed; myths such as Flipper, the eponymous star of the well-known 1960s television series.

Popular representations of animals in the media typically have anthropomorphic overtones, creating a rather Disney-like portrayal of the dolphin. Consequently, this may affect tourist perceptions of the animal kingdom, which is then carried over into tourist behavior. Amante-Helweg (1996) refers to the anthropomorphic tendencies by tourists to interpret and experience the interaction with dolphins by relating their behaviors and attributes to those of humans. In Ryan's (1988) matrix for classifying animals, dolphins appear in the "safe" and "human-oriented" categories and corresponds to Woods' (2000) and Kellert's (1989) contention that preferred animal species tend to be large, aesthetically pleasing, considered intelligent, and have a history of association with humans.

Although such interactions may benefit us, they do not always bode well for the dolphins. Denying the dolphins the freedom of the seas and the natural way of life that is their birthright is questionable. Yet swimming with dolphins in captivity is currently deemed a number one "must do" tourist activity. Indeed, swimming with cetaceans, particularly dolphins, consistently produces a strong positive emotion from holidaymakers, who claim that for them, the highlight of their holiday was fulfilling a lifelong ambition to swim with dolphins.

Tourist Experiences

Wildlife experiences can be defined as "the mental, spiritual and psychological outcomes" resulting from the wildlife tourism experience (Schanzel and McIntosh, 2000, p. 37); that is, the ultimate value that people place on such experiences, or as Dilthey (1985, p. 59) describes it, "the emotional reverberence of an experience." DeMares and Krycka (1998) go a step further and claim that wild animal encounters trigger peak experiences and transcendent consciousness; transcendent because the persona of the experiencer is not dominant, almost that the experience, always spontaneous, is so intense that it overrides the normal state of "being."

The aim of this article is to gain an insight into the human–dolphin attraction and recollections of a swim-with-dolphin experience. Frohoff (1998), a biological scientist, acknowledges the tremendous emotional and spiritual effects that human–animal encounters have on people, but is concerned that these encounters are difficult to explain and impossible to measure.

The primary question was open-ended: What is it like to swim with dolphins? Also, inherent in the discussions were other *a priori* questions such as the attraction of dolphins, the emotions experienced prior and post-dolphin interaction and the relative importance of the holiday activity in relation to other holiday pursuits.

An advertisement was placed on a university website calling for respondents who had swum with either captive or wild dolphins while on holiday, and who would be prepared to engage their time for the duration of the research and be willing to describe their experiences using narratives, photographs and anecdotes. A total of 14 people responded, 11 women and 3 men; 5 who had swum with wild dolphins: Paula, Lucy, Victoria, Isobel and Peter; and 9 who had swum with dolphins held in captivity. Laura, Anna, Sharon, Dorothy, Christine, Teresa, Sue, Christopher and Mike (names have been changed to protect anonymity).

The interviews were recorded and transcribed, allowing a systematic approach to data reduction based on the clustering of invariant meaning units into themes. Most of the themes are apparent in both groups of respondents; those who had swum with dolphins in the wild (SWD) and those who had swum with dolphins in captivity (SCD). However, on closer analysis, some discrete themes emerged with the SWD respondents.

Recalling and Sharing

The opportunity to reflect on, analyze, and share experiences immediately after an intense human–dolphin interaction seems to consolidate the experience and transform it into a cherished memory. Anecdotal evidence suggests that dolphin experiences add value to the lives of visitors long after their on-site activity. It leads to pleasant memories that can be shared with significant others. Taking photographs or digital video film is a common way to capture the experience and to facilitate this sharing. Photographs were extremely important for all of the SCD respondents, most of whom used them later either as screensavers or placed them in prominent places around the home and workstation.

According to Hunt *et al.* (1992), animal interactions encourage and stimulate conversations. This is an example of animals as "social lubricants" (Hunt *et al.,* 1992, p. 247) and photographs can facilitate this also once back home. Anna's account confirms this: "I have of photographs of it (swimming with dolphins) everywhere on my walls at home, in my office—all over the place—it's a good talking point or icebreaker."

Associated with this is the need to experience shared memories between the respondents and immediate loved ones, particularly children: "I wanted to provide this experience. It was just something I could give to my daughter which you can't put a value on really" (Teresa). "It would be a really important experience for the children as well" (Dorothy).

Once in the water with the dolphins, the respondents' focus was on the satisfaction of seeing loved ones enjoying themselves: "I was really concentrating on my daughter having a good time" (Christopher). "I think that I got most joy at seeing my children and my husband because I knew he was so desperate to do it and as I say, the look of pure joy on their faces gave me as much

pleasure as me being there in with the dolphins themselves; to see their pleasure and their joy and their obvious happiness about it was equally important" (Dorothy).

For the SWD respondents, the experience was profoundly personal, yet the satisfaction would have been, or was, enhanced by sharing experiences with loved ones: "It was definitely a one-to-one thing, yes. Had it been my husband there or my children with me, then that would have enhanced it in fact" (Lucy). Therefore, sharing the experience in the water was far greater than telling the story to someone who had not had the same experience. "I wanted to talk about it with my husband who had also experienced it. But still telling others afterwards that we'd swum with dolphins is also important as it keeps the experience alive" (Isobel).

Such holiday experiences gather significance as they are relived and retold. Travel is often composed of many different and new experiences, sometimes too many to take in at the time. As Peter explains: "You don't really appreciate what you are doing at the time—backpacking for example, is an experience overload. That's why when we come back home we relive it over and over again."

Also, the realization that you have fulfilled a long-held ambition takes time to sink in. This feeling was not unique and confirms Van Manen's (1990) and Dilthey's (1985) contention that experiences cannot be fully grasped in their immediacy. As Mike confirms: "Swimming with dolphins seems more significant now when I look back."

Moreover, the process of remembering and retelling stories allows the feelings to be brought to the present. As Laura puts it: "When I look back and reflect upon it, I get the same wonderful feeling that I got when I was in the water with them."

Attributes of the Experience

Swimming with dolphins in captivity tends to follow a very similar format regardless of the location. Swimmers, usually in groups of up to 12 people, are given a time slot in which to arrive at the dolphinarium. They are first given a talk and/ or shown a video which provides a small amount of interpretation, as well as how to behave when you are in the water with dolphins, particularly on how to touch them and how to restrain from any sudden movement or noise.

Nail polish, jewelry, and rings are removed and the swimmers enter the dolphin pool donned with wetsuits and life jackets. The time spent in the pool varied from place to place, and also the type and price of program that was purchased. This ranged from a 10-minute "taster" to being a "trainer for a day." However, 20 to 40 minutes seemed to be the norm.

Once in the pool, swimmers are asked to stand either in a line or in a circle whereby one, or sometimes two or three, dolphins swim slowly past. There is an opportunity to stroke the dolphins and to see how they feel. After this introduction, several tricks are performed. These included jumping over poles held by two swimmers, kissing, waving, and splashing. But the highlight for SCD respondents is the feeling of being dragged along while holding onto the dolphin's fins. Of course, each maneuvre with individual swimmers represents a photo opportunity and an additional income stream for the parks.

Some people noticed that the dolphin's behavior appeared to affirm their perceptions regarding gentleness and intuition. Sue, Deirdre, and Anna noticed that they were either "sillier" or "more gentle" around younger or smaller children. For some SCD respondents, the dolphin's size was overwhelming, especially when coupled with their speed, agility and obvious power. This could be "surprisingly scary" (Sue).

The dolphins are controlled by the trainers using food rewards, hand signals, and whistles. The entire experience is totally mediated from beginning to end, with very little time for one-to-one interaction. For most SCD respondents, this amount of control and lack of spontaneity detracted from the overall experience: "I would have preferred to have spent more time with them. It feels like you are constantly waiting on the side while other people take their turn" (Anna). "It

would have been better if it had just been me and the dolphin" (Sue). "It wasn't really a natural experience. All the swimmers were very herded. It was very stage-managed and controlled. It was very regimented, not at all spontaneous" (Sharon). Conversely, for the more cautious and less-confident swimmers, the amount of control made their experience more comfortable.

There is a sound body of literature (Beardsworth and Bryman, 2001) that purports that tourists want to experience the feeling of wilderness or wild animals in a contrived, safe environment. This trait was highly noticeable in the SCD respondents, particularly those who had visited the large marine parks where you could also snorkel alongside fenced areas which contained sharks, stingrays, and exotic fish.

Awareness of a dolphin's strength, power, and animal impulsiveness also made swimming with wild dolphins less attractive: "I'd be more afraid in the wild because there would be no one there to control them" (Laura). "I don't like the open sea. I would like to swim with them in the wild, but I know that I would be afraid. Fear of the sea and unpredictability" (Sue).

Although there were simmering anxieties in the SWD respondents, there was no doubt that respondents who had swum with wild dolphins (SWD) had a completely different experience to those who had swum with captive dolphins (SCD). They all felt the experience, although always disappointingly brief, to be much more significant. "It felt like we were really lucky to experience their world " (Isobel). This supports Franklin's (1999) contention that there is a deeper enjoyment of seeing wild animals in their natural setting. The element of uncertainty makes any dolphin encounter all the more special, as contact was seen to be due to the dolphin's own volition and was, in some cases, perceived to be symbolic of a greater connection, "almost like equal beings" (Lucy).

The Attraction of Dolphins

Several authors consider why some species are more sought after than others (Barstow, 1986;

Shackley, 1996; Woods, 2000; Tremblay, 2002). Freeman and Kreuter (1994) suggest that this is particularly evident in the desire to see sea mammals and primates. Observers, they claim, can connect with the curiosity, playfulness, social habits, and the desire to interact with humans. Sharing human attributes has also been a feature of the literature (Amante-Helweg, 1996; Franklin, 1999); however, dolphins appear from this research to be more attractive than primates, whose appearance and behavior is more akin to our own.

Cochrane and Callen (1998) ponder whether at some stage in our evolutionary path our pathways crossed and that the memory of this affinity lives in our subconscious. Certainly, why we find the seas so inviting raises some pertinent questions in respondents: "I remember bending down and whispering to it, telling him (the dolphin) how gorgeous he was. Then I felt silly. Are we psychically attuned? Have we come from dolphins? Have we evolved from the sea? You read these things don't you?" (Sue).

The belief that dolphins are nonaggressive creatures also heightens the attraction: *"no way would I go into a cage full of chimpanzees—I would feel a lot more nervous of them than going in the ocean with dolphins . . . and maybe that's it—that might be because they aren't as aggressive and I think that's why we are attracted to them"* (Lucy).

Conversely, almost all respondents knew that dolphins were not the gentle, harmless, "doe-eyed" creatures they are often portrayed to be. This created a certain amount of tension in some instances both in captivity and in the wild, and particularly in perceptions of swimming with wild dolphins as "they are not always gentle—they can be aggressive" (Dorothy). "They are powerful animals, just the size, shape and bulk of them—if they wanted to cause you some harm they could" (Anna).

The most significant attraction, however, was the perception of intelligence; all respondents referred to this. Many people have highlighted the dolphin's unfathomed intelligence as a source of awe and wonderment. Can this ex-

plain the potent influence they exert on the human psyche?

The notion that dolphins might be as intelligent as we are has long captured the human imagination. In order to determine the nature of this intelligence, scientists have probed the animals' brains, testing their ability to learn and understand various orders. But the quest to determine the dolphins' intelligence is riddled with pitfalls, as they have embarked on a completely different evolutionary path to our own; therefore, we are not comparing like for like (Cochrane and Callen, 1998). However, the fact that they could be trained to respond to human command was a signifier to the SCD respondents, as likening dolphins to dogs was very apparent: "they were like very responsive 'puppies'" (Sue).

Their aesthetic beauty is obviously a critical factor. "They're such graceful, agile creatures" (Isobel) and "the way they open their mouths they seem to have a permanent smile" (Sue). The sounds that dolphins make are also universally attractive. "They are just lovely. If you put your ear into the water you could hear them click. It was just a wonderful, wonderful experience" (Anna).

There was a significant awareness of dolphin-assisted-therapy programs, and several SCD respondents made reference to the healing attributes associated with dolphins: "I've seen lots of documentaries which talk about their sonar communication and pioneering research with children with disabilities such as cerebral palsy" (Laura).

Webb and Drummond (2001) provide some evidence for the therapeutic benefits of human–dolphin interaction, concluding that swimming with dolphins in the ocean reduced anxiety levels and increased feelings of well-being. There is a suggestion that the brain's reticular activating system, which controls arousal, attention, and awareness, may be affected by dolphin echolocation sound emissions, possibly accounting for reports of swimmer well-being (Webb and Drummond, 2001). This is supported by organizations such as Scope (2005) in the UK, who claim that dolphin acoustic emissions may bring about modifications in human brainwave activity, aiding relaxation, and reducing stress and pain. However, they warn that this is still only speculation.

Peak Experience

Nevertheless, these creatures have the remarkable power to uplift the human spirit; simply being in their presence seems to evoke feelings of profound happiness and often a state of euphoria (Cochrane and Callen, 1998). This heightened state after swimming with the dolphins might be explained in terms of Maslow's (1970) "peak experience" and examined by DeMares and Krycka (1998), who reveal that human–dolphin encounters incorporate all the identified elements of the human emotional peak: intention, reciprocity, connectedness, aliveness, and harmony. Wilson (1984), too, suggests that novel encounters with animals enhance the likelihood of an emotional peak in humans.

Defining what constitutes a peak experience is a matter of some conjecture. DeMares and Krycka (1998, p. 161) describe it as "a complex human experience which is transcendent in nature, beyond normal enthusiasm." Contact with animals, particularly wild ones, has long been recognized to be among the triggers for a peak experience, but has since been largely unstudied.

Clearly, there are positive human attributes associated with viewing and swimming with cetaceans, which fit the notion of a peak experience. Indeed, Orams (1997, p. 300) reveals that nearly a third of the visitors who take part in the wild dolphin feeding program at Tangalooma beach resort in Australia claimed that the experience was one of "their most enjoyable experiences ever"; such is the intensity of wonderment and emotion. Respondents who had swum with captive dolphins were more likely to regard it as the highlight of their lives:

> I was on a complete high—I think that the high lasted the whole holiday. It still, even now, when I reflect on it, I still have that same amazing feeling that is almost indescribable. It's just

fabulous—it just brings back so many wonderful memories. I just love it (Dorothy).

> I can't think of any other experience that made me feel this way—the excitement and adrenalin (Laura).

However, this was not the case for everyone, especially those who had built up higher expectations: "I had an experience in my head and it didn't match it, but it didn't stop it being a wonderful experience. I had expected it to be a life-changing experience and it wasn't. We are led to believe that it is a life-changing experience" (Sue).

SWD respondents also tended to rank it fairly highly, but not totally exceptional. On closer analysis, this may be explained in terms of tourist typologies. This set of respondents was more likely to be adventurous and undertake independent travel, as opposed to a packaged holiday in a popular destination where there are contrived tourist attractions. The type of travel usually undertaken also corresponded to the fact that SCD respondents were less likely to have ever seen dolphins in the wild, which made the possibility of seeing them up close in captive situations even more attractive.

Nonetheless, it rather depended on the quality of the SWD experience. Isobel was the only respondent to have encountered them by chance, as opposed to being on an organized trip. Her experience was profoundly different; it was in clear blue, warm water, and the dolphins stayed closer for a much longer period of time: "It was a serendipitous experience, much better than I had ever imagined. I was overwhelmed. It was definitely a highlight of my life." Her experience was more akin to DeMares and Krycka's respondents, who tended to have prolonged encounters in the wild where eye contact can be better maintained.

Connectivity, Closeness, and Touch

According to DeMares and Krycka (1998), one finds connection with another being when one sees oneself reflected in the other being's eyes.

Making eye contact was a profound experience for both sets of respondents, but particularly to SWD respondents: "I don't know what the connection is . . . it's just a recognition . . . that's what I felt—you know it was that . . . that it had come back to see me and that's what surprised me was that it was being curious about us—and there was definitely eye contact" (Lucy).

Another way of making a connection is through touch. Touch, both human to human and human to animal, has profound psychological, physiological, and behavioral effects. In reaching out and touching another being, we make contact and affirm bonds with others. Touch is seen to benefit infants and elderly patients, and stroking animals is known to have several health benefits. According to Franklin (1999), pet ownership has become prominent in society since the 1960s due to the raised awareness of the health and therapeutic benefits of pet keeping.

Research suggests that stroking pets is associated with better recovery from illness and lower instances of depression (Akiyama *et al.*, 1986). Further papers explore the use and value of pets in child development, particularly in respect of gaining empathy for others, containing aggression, and dealing with loss (Levinson, 1980). Touch is also a way of exploring and understanding our immediate environment. "Being close and touching things seems to trigger something . . . When somebody says dolphin to me—I always think of the Monkey Mia dolphin. When you are up close to something you can see the shape of it, different colours and markings—somehow it makes it more real" (Peter).

It follows, therefore, that to reach out to safe-oriented animals, or to crave proximity, is an instinctive human behavior. Indeed, proximity to wildlife has been identified as a key feature of the wildlife tourist experience. Being able to touch a dolphin was a considerable motivation, especially for the SCD contingents.

Well that's what we went for— to be able to touch a dolphin—yes that was important, it helped you to almost bond ... it's a very personal experience. If they hadn't allowed us to touch the dolphin and to learn more about him while we were in the water there would have been no context to it (Teresa).

However, this desire to touch was less apparent for the SWD respondents for a number of reasons, particularly the context in which they saw them and the notion of "wildness": "These are wild animals and I respect that. I didn't want to touch them, not because I was scared, but because they deserve their own space and human interference should be minimal. We could probably have touched them as they kept swimming close by and looked like they wanted to play. But there was no need to touch them; just being in the water with them was overwhelming" (Isobel).

This was sometimes associated with the sea conditions and the setting or environment in which they were encountered. Remoteness, sea conditions, and sea visibility heightened the notion of wildness, which lessened the need to touch. In these conditions, there was a heightened sense of vulnerability and anxiousness. "At one time I thought oh God that's going to touch me—it's quite you know as you see it coming closer, closer" (Lucy).

Virtual Capital

The "truth" of such an encounter can often be far removed from a tourist's perception of what the experience will be like: *"I had an experience in my head and it didn't match it"* (Sue). Much of the literature focuses on the tourist gaze; however, it is the phase that precedes the gaze that is so fascinating: what creates the perception that this is a place or activity worthy of gazing upon? Such notions are socially constructed and are based on deep-rooted perceptions of our world. In Deruiter and Donnelly's (2002) discussion of socialization, they claim that values and attitudes toward wildlife are passed down through the "stories" presented by families, cohorts, education, and media. This notion is neatly confirmed by Lucy: "A lot of it is to do with the collective psyche—because we all sort of think dolphins are special—because a lot of us do, everybody else does."

Beardsworth and Bryman (2001) contend that representations of wild creatures in literary, artistic, and symbolic terms have become ever more elaborate and sophisticated. They suggest that the typical television viewer's primary mode of engagement with the wild is through highly processed and skillfully edited representations of wild animals both in cartoon and live format. This suggests that swim-with-dolphin tourists come to the activity with a large stock of knowledge and images assembled from sources such as television, film, and advertising. This they term virtual capital (Beardsworth and Bryman, 2001, p. 99).

Embedded in this virtual capital is a strong tendency toward anthropomorphism, which is hardly surprising given the "Disneyfication" of animals and their kingdom. These notions provide the basis of a consumer's knowledge, perceptions, and expectations, and to consolidate this—certainly in the Disneyized zoo context—the anthropomorphism and sentimentality are reinforced by the presentation of animal performances, in which creatures are invited to exhibit apparently human motivations, attributes, and actions (e.g., training dolphins to wave at the audience or kiss swimmers). These behaviors mimic human actions and portray a sense of fun and games, which is another primary attraction of the species.

Such anthropomorphism is not always perceived in a negative light. Franklin (1999) proposes that it has the ability to make people aware of the extent to which they share their life worlds with members of other species, and is a way of actually exploring possibilities for empathy, mutuality, and coexistence.

Animal Sensitivities and Dissonance

SWD respondents demonstrated strong feelings about the ethics of keeping dolphins in captivity. They tended to be less anthropocentric than their SCD counterparts in that they did not perceive the dolphins were there for their own entertainment: "I won't swim with captive dolphins because I don't believe that the dolphins should be captive" (Lucy). "It's like turning them into Alton Towers—you know it's a play thing and they are not—they're wild animals" (Christine).

In this respect, SCD respondents demonstrated cognitive dissonance. All had concerns regarding captivity, yet they tried to reduce this concern by accentuating the positives and denying the negatives. Festinger (1957) suggests that dissonance, being psychologically uncomfortable, motivates the person to reduce the dissonance and leads to avoidance of information likely to increase it; the greater the magnitude of dissonance, the greater the desire to reduce it.

> Beforehand, my husband and I had a conversation and I wondered. Do you think it is wrong? But it was like they were children playing. I honestly didn't feel that they were distressed. They were quite happy to do it. They were well maintained and cared for. Not at all treated like circus animals (Sue).

Franklin (1999) and Hughes (2001) maintain that a strong ethical shift has taken place from an exploitative view of animals to a more caring one. As a result, animal performances in circuses are perceived as being rather distasteful. This is partly reflected in this research; however, despite their concerns, most respondents seemed to enjoy participating in the dolphin's tricks and that such tourist opportunities are gaining popularity.

Desmond (1999, p. 197) highlights the "emphasis placed in Sea World's performances on the animals' love of their trainers." This, he claims, reinforces the emotional expressivity of both trainer and sea mammal. This emotion is then conveyed to the swimmers. Beardsworth and Bryman (2001, p. 96) refer to this as emotional labor, exhibited when animals are induced to perform behaviors that can be interpreted by the audience as indicative of an emotion: friendliness, humor, and mischief. This was very prevalent in the SCD cases, where there is a firm belief that "the dolphins love their trainers and the trainers love them" (Laura).

Despite the high level of enjoyment on the day, further reflection highlighted areas of disappointment. Furthermore, the highly staged nature of the experience failed to meet the ideal picture of human–dolphin interaction. All SCD respondents were dismayed that "it wasn't really a natural experience. Everything I've read and seen gave me a sense that it would be mystical and I could imagine that happening in a less-controlled situation" (Sue).

Conclusions

For the respondents involved in this study, swimming with dolphins was a very satisfying, important, and memorable holiday activity. Although it was universally referred to as a "highlight" of the holiday, only two respondents claimed it as being a highlight of their life, or a peak experience. Perhaps this was due to the nature of the environment and the brevity of their experience. Despite this, making a connection, whether through touch or eye contact or by simply sharing their space, was deemed to be a magnificent and incredibly important aspect of the encounter.

There was a general feeling that dolphins should not really be held in captivity, but the desire to interact with them overturned the concerns of the SCD respondents. Upon reflection, there is evidence of cognitive dissonance, which is relieved by concentrating on the emotional labor of the trainers toward the dolphins, their level of care, and the conservation efforts that presumably their visit supports.

In most SCD and SWD cases, the respondents' experiences did not meet their prior expectation or ideals based upon the virtual capital that swimmers bring to the experience. These ideals are often heavily anthropomorphic and unrealistic, yet they contribute a significant perception of what it is like to swim with dolphins. Disappointments in captive situations were mostly due to the highly "staged" and impersonal nature of the program, as well as the short period of contact time. Similarly in the wild, respondents were often thwarted in their attempts to get close to the dolphins and to maintain contact for an ideal length of time.

Postmodern animal sensitivities might deem it prudent for marketers and popular media to "rewrite" the virtual capital—emphasizing the dolphin's actual attributes rather than its human ones and providing the tourist with more realistic, fundamental knowledge of dolphin behavior.

References

Akiyama H, Holtzman JM, Britz WE. 1986. Pet ownership and health status during bereavement. *Omega* 17: 187–193.

Amante-Helweg V. 1996. Ecotourists' beliefs and knowledge about dolphins and the development of cetacean ecotourism. *Aquatic Mammals* 22: 131–140.

Barstow R. 1986. Non-consumptive utilisation of whales. *Ambio* **15**(3): 155–163.

Beardsworth A, Bryman A. 2001. The wild animal in late modernity. *Tourist Studies* 1(1): 83–104.

Cochrane A, Callen K. 1998. *Beyond the Blue: Dolphins and Their Healing Powers.* Bloomsbury Publishing Plc: London.

DeMares R, Krycka K. 1998. Wild animal triggered peak experiences: transpersonal aspects. *The Journal of Transpersonal Psychology* 30(2): 161–177.

Deruiter DS, Donnelly MP. 2002. A qualitative approach to measuring determinants of wildlife value orientations. *Human Dimensions of Wildlife* 7: 251–271.

Desmond JC. 1999. *Staging Tourism: Bodies on Display from Waikiki to Sea World.* University of Chicago Press: Chicago, IL.

Dilthey W. 1985. *Poetry and Experience. Selected Works.* Vol. 5, Princeton University Press: Princeton, NJ.

Festinger L. 1957. *A Theory of Cognitive Dissonance.* Row, Peterson: Evanston, IL.

Franklin A. 1999. *Animals and Modern Cultures: A Sociology of Human-Animal Relations in Modernity.* Sage Publications: London.

Freeman MMR, Kreuter UP (eds). 1994. *Elephants and Whales: Resources for Whom?* Gordon and Breach Science Publishers: Basel, Switzerland.

Frohoff TG. 1998. Beyond species. In *Intimate Nature: The Bond Between Women and Animals,* Hogan L, Metzger D, Peterson B (eds). Ballantine Publishing: New York.

Frohoff TG, Packard JM. 1995. Human interactions with free-ranging and captive bottlenose dolphins. *Anthrozoös* 8(1): 44–53.

Hughes P. 2001. Animals, values and tourism—structural shifts in UK dolphin tourism provision. *Tourism Management* 22: 321–329.

Hunt SJ, Hart LA, Gomulkiewicz R. 1992. The role of small animals in social interactions between strangers. *Journal of Social Psychology* 132: 245–256.

Kellert SR. 1989. Perceptions of animals in America. In *Perceptions of Animals in American Culture,* Hoage RJ (ed.). Smithsonian Press: Washington DC.

Kestin S. 2004. *Captive Mammals Can Net Big Profits for Exhibitors. Part 3: Park Business.* Available at www.sun-sentinel.com/news/sfl-dolphins-money (accessed 13 April 2005).

Levinson BM. 1980. The child and his pet: A world of nonverbal communication. In *Ethology and Nonverbal Communication in Mental Health*, Corson SA, O'Leary Corson E (eds.). Pergamon Press: Oxford.

Maslow A. 1970. *Religions, Values and Peak Experiences.* Viking Penguin: New York.

Orams MB. 1997. Historical accounts of human–dolphin interaction and recent developments in wild dolphin based tourism in Australasia. *Tourism Management* 18(5): 317–325.

Ryan C. 1988. Saltwater crocodiles as tourist attractions. *Journal of Sustainable Tourism* 6(4): 315–327.

Schanzel HA, McIntosh AJ. 2000. An insight into the personal and emotive context of wildlife viewing at the Penguin Place, Otago Peninsula, New Zealand. *Journal of Sustainable Tourism* 8(1): 36–53.

Scope. 2005. Available at www.scope.org.uk (accessed 10 June 2005).

Shackley M. 1996. *Wildlife Tourism.* International Thomson Business Press: London.

Tremblay P. 2002. Tourism wildlife icons: Attractions or marketing symbols. *Journal of Hospitality and Tourism Management* 9(2):164–180.

Van Manen M. 1990. *Researching Lived Experience.* The Althouse Press: Ontario, Canada.

WDCS. 2005. *The Whale and Dolphin Conservation Society (WDCS).* Available at www.wdcs.org/dan/publishing.nsf/allweb (accessed 20 June 2005).

Webb NL, Drummond PD. 2001. The effect of swimming with dolphins on human well-being and anxiety. *Anthrozoös* 14(2): 81–85.

Wilson EO. 1984. *Biophilia* Harvard. University Press: Cambridge, MA.

Woods B. 2000. Beauty and the beast: Preferences for animals in Australia. *Journal of Tourism Studies* 11(2): 25–35.

ARTICLE 12

Jennifer Wolch

Zoöpolis

Why Animals Matter (Even in Cities)

The rationale for considering animals in the context of urban environmentalism is not transparent. Urban environmental issues traditionally center around the pollution of the city conceived as human habitat, not animal habitat. Thus the various wings of the urban progressive environmental movement have avoided thinking about nonhumans and have left the ethical as well as pragmatic ecological, political, and economic questions regarding animals to be dealt with by those involved in the defense of endangered species or animal welfare. Such a division of labor privileges the rare and the tame, and ignores the lives and living spaces of the large number and variety of animals who dwell in cities. In this section, I argue that even common, everyday animals should matter.

The Human-Animal Divide: A Definition

My position on the human-animal divide is that animals as well as people socially construct their worlds and influence each other's worlds. The resulting "animal constructs are likely to be markedly different from ours but may be no less real."[1] Animals have their own realities, their own worldviews; in short, they are *subjects,* not objects. This position is rarely reflected in ecosocialist, feminist, and anti-racist practice, however. Developed in direct opposition to a capitalist system riddled by divisions of class, race/ethnicity, and gender, and deeply destructive of nature, such practice ignores some sorts of animals altogether (for example, pets, livestock) or has embedded animals within holistic and/or anthropocentric conceptions of the environment and therefore avoided the question of animal subjectivity. Thus, in most forms of progressive environmentalism, animals have been objectified and/or backgrounded.

Thinking Like a Bat: The Question of Animal Standpoints

The recovery of animal subjectivity implies an ethical and political obligation to redefine the urban problematic and to consider strategies for urban praxis from the standpoints of animals. Granting animals subjectivity at a theoretical, conceptual level is a first step. Even this first step is apt to be hotly contested by human social groups who have been marginalized and devalued by claims that they are "closer to animals" and hence less intelligent, worthy, or evolved than Anglo-European white males. It may also run counter to those who interpret the granting of subjectivity as synonymous with a granting of rights and object either to rights-type arguments in general or to animal rights specifically. But a far more difficult step must be taken if the revalorization of animal subjectivity is to be meaningful in terms of day-to-day practice. We not only have to "think like a mountain" but also to "think like a bat," somehow overcoming Nagel's classic objection that because bat sonar is not similar to any human sense, it is humanly impossible to answer a question such as "what is it like to be a bat?" or, more generally," what is it like to be an animal?"[2]

But is it impossible to think like a bat? There is a parallel here with the problems raised by standpoint (or multipositionality) theories. Standpoint theories assert that a variety of individual human differences (such as race, class, or gender) so strongly shape experience and thus interpretations of the world that a single position essentializes and silences difference, and fails to

123

challenge power relations. In the extreme, such polyvocality leads to a nihilistic relativism and a paralysis of political action. But the response cannot be to return to practices of radical exclusion and denial of difference. Instead, we must recognize that individual humans are embedded in social relations and networks with people similar or different upon whom their welfare depends. This realization allows for a recognition of kinship but also of difference, since identities are defined through seeing that we are similar to, and different from, related others. And through everyday interaction and concerted practice, and using what Haraway terms a "cyborg vision" that allows "partial, locatable, critical knowledge sustaining the possibility of webs of connection called solidarity,"[3] we can embrace kinship as well as difference and encourage the emergence of an ethic of respect and mutuality, caring and friendship.

The webs of kinships and difference that shape individual identity involve both humans and animals. This is reasonably easy to accept in the abstract (that is, humans depend upon a rich ecology of animal organisms). But there is also a large volume of archeological, paleoanthropological, and psychological evidence suggesting that concrete interactions and interdependence with animal others are indispensable to the development of human cognition, identity, and consciousness, and to a maturity that accepts ambiguity, difference, and lack of control. In short, animals are not only "good to think" (to borrow a phrase from Lévi-Strauss) but indispensable to learning how to think in the first place, and how to relate to other people.

Who are the relevant animal others? I argue that many sorts of animals matter, including domestic animals. Clearly, domestication has profoundly altered the intelligence, senses, and life ways of creatures such as dogs, cows, sheep, and horses so as to drastically diminish their otherness; so denaturalized, they have come to be seen as part of human culture. But wild animals have been appropriated and denaturalized by people too. This is evidenced by the myriad ways

wildlife is commercialized (in both embodied and disembodied forms) and incorporated into material culture. And like domestic animals, wild animals can be profoundly impacted by human actions, often leading to significant behavioral adaptations. Ultimately, the division between wild and domestic must be seen as a permeable social construct; it may be better to conceive of a *matrix* of animals who vary with respect to the extent of physical or behavioral modification due to human intervention, and types of interaction with people.

Our ontological dependency on animals seems to have characterized us as a species since the Pleistocene. Human needs for dietary protein, desires for spiritual inspiration and companionship, and the ever-present possibility of ending up as somebody's dinner required thinking like an animal. This aspect of animal contribution to human development can be used as an (anthropomorphic) argument in defense of wildlife conservation or pet keeping. But my concern is how human dependency on animals was played out in terms of the patterns of human-animal interactions it precipitated. Specifically, did ontological dependency on animals create an interspecific ethic of caring and webs of friendship? Without resurrecting a 1990s version of the Noble Savage—an essentialized indigenous person living in spiritual and material harmony with nature—it is clear that for most of (pre) history, people ate wild animals, tamed them, and kept them captive, but also respected them as kin, friends, teachers, spirits, or gods. Their value lay both in their similarities with and differences from humans. Not coincidentally, most wild animal habitats were also sustained.

Re-Enchanting the City: An Agenda to Bring the Animals Back In

How can animals play their integral role in human ontology today, thereby helping to foster ethical responses and political practices engendered by the recognition of human-animal kinship and difference? Most critically, how can such responses and practices possibly develop in places where everyday interaction with so many kinds of animals has been eliminated? Most people now live in such places, namely cities. Cities are perceived as so human-dominated that they become naturalized as just another part of the ecosystem, that is, the human habitat. In the West, many of us interact with or experience animals only by keeping captives of a restricted variety or eating "food" animals sliced into steak, chop, and roast. We get a sense of wild animals only by watching "Wild Kingdom" reruns or going to Sea World to see the latest in a long string of short-lived "Shamus."[4] In our apparent mastery of urban nature, we are seemingly protected from all nature's dangers but chance losing any sense of wonder and awe for the nonhuman world. The loss of both the humility and the dignity of risk results in a widespread belief in the banality of day-to-day survival. This belief is deeply damaging to class, gender, and North-South relations as well as to nature.

To allow for the emergence of an ethic, practice, and politics of caring for animals and nature, we need to renaturalize cities and invite the animals back in, and in the process re-enchant the city. I call this renaturalized, re-enchanted city *zoöpolis*. The reintegration of people with animals and nature in zoöpolis can provide urban dwellers with the local, situated, everyday knowledge of animal life required to grasp animal standpoints or ways of being in the world, to interact with them accordingly in particular contexts, and to motivate political action necessary to protect their autonomy as subjects and their life spaces. Such knowledge would stimulate a thorough rethinking of a wide range of urban daily life practices: not only animal regulation and control practices, but landscaping, development rates and design, roadway and transportation decisions, use of energy, industrial toxics, and bioengineering—in short, all practices that impact animals and nature in its diverse forms (climate, plant life, landforms, and so on). And, at the most personal level, we might rethink eating habits, since factory farms are so environmentally destructive *in situ*, and the Western meat

habit radically increases the rate at which wild habitats are converted to agricultural land worldwide (to say nothing of how one feels about eating cows, pigs, chickens, or fishes once they are embraced as kin).

While based in everyday practice like the bioregional paradigm, the renaturalization or zoöpolis model differs in including animals and nature in the metropolis rather than relying on an anti-urban spatial fix like small-scale communalism. It also accepts the reality of global interdependence rather than opting for autarky. Moreover, unlike deep ecological visions epistemically tied to a psychologized individualism and lacking in political-economic critique, urban renaturalization is motivated not only by a conviction that animals are central to human ontology in ways that enable the development of webs of kinship and caring with animal subjects, but that our alienation from animals results from specific political-economic structures, social relations, and institutions operative at several spatial scales. Such structures, relations, and institutions will not magically change once individuals recognize animal subjectivity, but will only be altered through political engagement and struggle against oppression based on class, race, gender, and species.

Beyond the city, the zoöpolis model serves as a powerful curb on the contradictory and colonizing environmental politics of the West as practiced both in the West itself and as inflicted on other parts of the world. For example, wildlife reserves are vital to prevent species extinction. But because they are "out there," remote from urban life, reserves can do nothing to alter entrenched modes of economic organization and associated consumption practices that hinge on continual growth and make reserves necessary in the first place. The only modes of life that the reserves change are those of subsistence peoples, who suddenly find themselves alienated from their traditional economic base and further immiserated. But an interspecific ethic of caring replaces dominionism to create urban regions where animals are not incarcerated, killed, or sent off to live in wildlife prisons, but instead are valued neighbors and partners in survival. This ethic links urban residents with peoples elsewhere in the world who have evolved ways of both surviving and sustaining the forests, streams, and diversity of animal lives, and enjoins their participation in the struggle. The Western myth of a pristine Arcadian wilderness, imposed with imperial impunity on those places held hostage to the International Monetary Fund and the World Bank in league with powerful international environmental organizations, is trumped by a post-colonial politics and practice that begins at home with animals in the city.

Ways of Thinking Animals in the City

An agenda for renaturalizing the city and bringing animals back in should be developed with an awareness of the impacts of urbanization on animals in the capitalist city, how urban residents think about and behave toward animal life, the ecological adaptations made by animals to urban conditions, and current practices and politics arising around urban animals. Studies that address these topics are primarily grounded in empiricist social science and wildlife biology. The challenge of trans-species urban theory is to develop a framework informed by social theory. The goal is to understand capitalist urbanization in a globalizing economy and what it means for animal life; how and why patterns of human-animal interactions change over time and space; urban animal ecology as science, social discourse, and political economy; and trans-species urban practice shaped by managerial plans and grassroots activism.

Animal Town: Urbanization, Environmental Change, and Animal Life Chances

The city is built to accommodate humans and their pursuits, yet a subaltern "animal town" inevitably emerges with urban growth. This animal town shapes the practices of urbanization in key ways (for example, by attracting or repelling people/development in certain places, or influencing animal exclusion strategies). But animals are even more profoundly affected by the urbanization process under capitalism, which involves extensive denaturalization of rural or wild lands and widespread environmental pollution. The most basic types of urban environmental change are well-known and involve soils, hydrology, climate, ambient air and water quality, and vegetation. Some wild animal species (for example, rats, pigeons, cockroaches) adapt to and/or thrive in cities. But others are unable to find appropriate food or shelter, adapt to urban climate, air quality, or hydrological changes, or tolerate contact with people. Captives, of course, are mostly restricted to homes, yards, or purpose-built quarters such as feed lots or labs, but even the health of pets, feral animals, and creatures destined for dissecting trays or dinner tables can be negatively affected by various forms of urban environmental pollution.

Metropolitan development also creates spatially extensive, patchy landscapes and extreme habitat fragmentation that especially affects wildlife. Some animals can adapt to such fragmentation and to the human proximity it implies, but more commonly animals die *in situ* or migrate to less fragmented areas. If movement corridors between habitat patches are cut off, species extinction can result as fragmentation intensifies, due to declining habitat patch size, deleterious edge effects, distance or isolation effects, and related shifts in community ecology. Where fragmentation leads to the loss of large predators, remaining species may proliferate, degrade the environment, and threaten the viability of other forms of wildlife. Weedy, opportunistic and/or exotic species may also invade, to similar effect.

Such accounts of urban environmental change and habitat fragmentation are not typically incorporated into theories of urbanization under capitalism. For example, most explanations of urbanization do not explicitly address the social or political-economic drivers of urban environmental change, especially habitat fragmentation. By the same token, most studies of urban environments restrict themselves to the scientific measurement of environmental-quality shifts or describe habitat fragmentation in isolation from the social dynamics that drive it. This suggests that urbanization models need to be reconsidered to account for the environmental as well as political-economic bases of urbanization, the range of institutional forces acting on the urban environment, and the cultural processes that background nature in the city.

Efforts to theoretically link urban and environmental change are at the heart of the new environmental history, which reorients ideas about urbanization by illustrating how environmental exploitation and disturbance underpin the history of cities, and how thinking about nature as an actor (rather than a passive object to be acted upon) can help us understand the course of urbanization. Contemporary urbanization, linked to global labor, capital, and commodity flows, is simultaneously rooted in exploitation of natural "resources" (including wildlife, domestic and other sorts of animals) and actively transforms regional landscapes and the possibilities for animal life—although not always in the manner desired or expected, due to nature's agency. Revisiting neo-Marxian theories of the local state as well as neo-Weberian concepts of urban managerialism to analyze relations between nature and the local state could illuminate the structural and institutional contexts of, for example, habitat loss/degradation. One obvious starting place is growth machine theory, since it focuses on the influence of rentiers on the local state apparatus and local politics; another is the critique of urban planning as part of the modernist project of control and domination of others (human as well as nonhuman) through rationalist city building and policing of urban interactions and human/animal proximities in the name of human health and welfare. Finally, urban cultural studies may help us understand how the aesthetics of urban-built environments deepen the distanciation between animals and people. For instance, Wilson demonstrates how urban simulacra such as zoos and wildlife parks have increasingly mediated human experience of animal life. Real live animals can actually come to be seen as less than authentic since the terms of authenticity have been so thoroughly redefined. The distanciation of wild animals has simultaneously stimulated the elaboration of a romanticized wildness used as a means to peddle consumer goods, sell real estate, and sustain the capital accumulation process, reinforcing urban expansion and environmental degradation.

Reckoning with the Beast: Human Interactions with Urban Animals

The everyday behavior of urban residents also influences the possibilities for urban animal life. The question of human relations with animals in the city has been tackled by empirical researchers armed with behavioral models, who posit that, through their behavior, people make cities more or less attractive to animals (for example, human pest management and animal control practices, urban design, provision of food and water for feral animals and/or wildlife). These behaviors, in turn, rest on underlying values and attitudes toward animals. In such values-attitudes-behavior frameworks, resident responses are rooted in cultural beliefs about animals, but also in the behavior of animals themselves—their destructiveness, charisma, and charm, and, less frequently, their ecological benefits.

Attitudes toward animals have been characterized on the basis of survey research and the development of attitudinal typologies. Findings suggest that urbanization increases both distanciation from nature and concern for animal welfare. Kellert, for example, found that urban residents were less apt to hold utilitarian attitudes, were more likely to have moralistic and humanistic attitudes, suggesting that they were concerned for the ethical treatment of animals, and were focused on individual animals such as pets and popular wildlife species.[5] Urban residents of large cities were more supportive of protecting endangered species; less in favor of shooting or trapping predators to control damage to livestock; more apt to be opposed to hunting;

and supportive of allocating additional public re-sources for programs to increase wildlife in cities. Domestic and attractive animals were most pre-ferred, while animals known to cause human property damage or inflict injury were among the least preferred.

Conventional wisdom characterizes the re-sponses of urban residents and institutions to local animals in two ways: (1) as "pests," who are implicitly granted agency in affecting the urban environment, given the social or economic costs they impose; or (2) as objectified "pets," who pro-vide companionship, an aesthetic amenity to property owners, or recreational opportunities such as bird-watching and feeding wildlife. Al-most no systematic research, however, has been conducted on urban residents' behavior toward the wild or unfamiliar animals they encounter or how behavior is shaped by space or by class, pa-triarchy, or social constructions of race/ethnicity. Moreover, the behavior of urban institutions in-volved in urban wildlife management or animal regulation/control has yet to be explored.

How can we gain a deeper understanding of human interactions with the city's animals? The insights from wider debates in nature/culture the-ory are most instructive and help put behavioral research in proper context. Increasingly, na-ture/culture theorizing converges on the convic-tion that the Western nature/culture dualism, a variant of the more fundamental division be-tween object and subject, is artificial and deeply destructive of Earth's diverse life-forms. It vali-dates a theory and practice of human/nature re-lations that backgrounds human dependency on nature. Hyperseparating nature from culture en-courages its colonization and domination. The nature/culture dualism also incorporates nature into culture, denying its subjectivity and giving it solely instrumental value. By homogenizing and disembodying nature, it becomes possible to ig-nore the consequences of human activity such as urbanization, industrial production, and agro-industrialization on specific creatures and their terrains. This helps trigger what O'Connor terms the "second contradiction of capitalism," that is,

the destruction of the means of production via the process of capital accumulation itself.[6]

The place-specific version of the nature/cul-ture dualism is the city/country divide; as that place historically emblematic of human culture, the city seeks to exclude all remnants of the coun-try from its midst, especially wild animals. As we have already seen, the radical exclusion of most animals from everyday urban life may disrupt de-velopment of human consciousness and identity, and prevent the emergence of interspecific webs of friendship and concern. This argument filters through several variants of radical ecophilosophy. In some versions, the centrality of "wild" animals is emphasized, while the potential of tamer ani-mals, more common in cities but often genetically colonized, commodified, and/or neotenized, is questioned. In other versions, the wild/tame dis-tinction in fostering human-animal bonds is min-imized, but the progressive loss of interspecies contact and thus understanding is mourned. Cor-poreal identity may also become increasingly destabilized as understandings of human embod-iment traditionally derived through direct experi-ence of live animal bodies/subjects evaporates or is radically transformed. Thus what we now re-quire are theoretical treatments explicating how the deeply ingrained dualism between city (culture) and country (nature), as it is played out ontologically, shapes human-animal interactions in the city.

The ahistorical and placeless values-attitudes-behavior models also miss the role of social and political-economic context on urban values and attitudes toward animals. Yet such val-ues and attitudes are apt to evolve in response to place-specific situations and local contextual shifts resulting from nonlocal dynamics, for ex-ample, the rapid internationalization of urban economies. Deepening global competition threat-ens to stimulate a hardening of attitudes toward animal exploitation and habitat destruction in an international "race to the bottom" regarding environmental/animal protections. Moreover, globalization sharply reveals the fact that under-standings of nature in the West are insufficient to grasp the range of relationships between people and animals in diverse global cities fed by international migrant flows from places where nature/culture relations are radically different. Variations on the theme of colonization are being played back onto the colonizers; in the context of internationalization, complex questions arise concerning how both colonially imposed, indigenous, and hybrid meanings and practices are being diffused back into the West. Also, given globalization-generated international migration flows to urban regions, we need to query the role of diverse cultural norms regarding animals in the racialization of immigrant groups and spread of nativism in the West. Urban practices that appear to be linked to immigrant racialization involve animal sacrifice (for example, Santeria) and eating animals traditionally considered in Western culture as household companions.

An Urban Bestiary: Animal Ecologies in the City

The recognition that many animals coexist with people in cities and the management implications of shared urban space have spurred the nascent field of urban animal ecology. Grounded in biological field studies and heavily management-oriented, studies of urban animal life focus on wildlife species; there are very few ecological studies of urban companion or feral animals. Most studies tend to be highly species- and place-specific. Only a small number of urban species have been scrutinized, typically in response to human-perceived problems, risk of species endangerment, or their "charismatic" character.

Ecological theory has moved away from holism and equilibrium notions toward a recognition that processes of environmental disturbance, uncertainty, and risk cause ecosystems and populations to continually shift over certain ranges varying with site and scale. This suggests the utility of reconceptualizing cities as ecological disturbance regimes rather than ecological sacrifice zones whose integrity has been irrevocably violated. In order to fully appreciate the permeability of the city/country divide, the heterogeneity and variable patchiness of urban habitats and the possibilities (rather than impossibilities) for urban animal life must be more fully incorporated into ecological analyses. This in turn could inform decisions concerning prospective land-use changes (such as suburban densification or downzoning, landscaping schemes, transportation corridor design) and indicate how they might influence individual animals and faunal assemblages in terms of stress levels, morbidity and mortality, mobility and access to multiple sources of food and shelter, reproductive success, and exposure to predation.

Scientific urban animal ecology is grounded in instrumental rationality and oriented toward environmental control, perhaps more than other branches of ecology since it is largely applications driven. The effort by preeminent ecologist Michael Soulé to frame a response to the postmodern reinvention of nature, however, demonstrates the penetration into ecology of feminist and postmodern critiques of modernist science. Hayles, for instance, argues that our understanding of nature is mediated by the embodied interactivity of observer and observed, and the positionality (gender, class, race, species) of the observer. Animals, for example, construct different worlds through their embodied interactions with it (that is, how their sensory and intellectual capabilities result in their worldviews). And although some models may be more or less adequate interpretations of nature, the question of how positionality determines the models proposed, tested, and interpreted must always remain open. At a minimum, such thinking calls for self-reflexivity in ecological research on urban animals and ecological tool-kits augmented by rich ethnographic accounts of animals, personal narratives of nonscientific observers, and folklore.

Finally, scientific urban animal ecology is not practiced in a vacuum. Rather, like any other scientific pursuit, it is strongly shaped by motives of research sponsors (especially the state), those who use research products (such as planners), and ideologies of researchers themselves. Building on the field of science studies, claims of scientific ecology must thus be interrogated to expose the political economy of urban animal ecology and biodiversity analysis. How are studies of urban animals framed, and from whose perspective? What motivates them in the first place—developer proposals, hunter lobbies, environmental/animal rights organizations? Sorting out such questions requires not only evaluation of the technical merits of urban wildlife studies, but also analysis of how they are framed by epistemological and discursive traditions in scientific ecology and embedded in larger social and political-economic contexts.

Redesigning Nature's Metropolis: From Managerialism to Grassroots Action

A nascent trans-species urban practice, as yet poorly documented and under-theorized, has appeared in many U.S. cities. This practice involves numerous actors, including a variety of federal, state, and local bureaucracies, planners, and managers, and urban grassroots animal/environmental activists. In varying measure, the goals of such practice include altering the nature of interactions between people and animals in the city, creating minimum-impact urban environmental designs, changing everyday practices of the local state (wildlife managers and urban planners), and more forcefully defending the interests of urban animal life.

Wildlife managers and pest-control firms increasingly face local demands for alternatives to extermination-oriented animal-control policies. In the wildlife area, approaches were initially driven by local protests against conventional practices such as culling; now managers are more apt to consider in advance resident reactions to management alternatives and to adopt participatory approaches to decision-making in order to avoid opposition campaigns. Typically, alternative management strategies require education of urban residents to increase knowledge and understanding of, and respect for, wild animal neighbors, and to underscore how domestic animals may harm or be harmed by wildlife. There are limits to educational approaches, however,

stimulating some jurisdictions to enact regulatory controls on common residential architectures, building maintenance, garbage storage, fencing, landscaping, and companion-animal keeping that are detrimental to wildlife.

Wild animals were never a focus of urban and regional planning. Nor were other kinds of animals, despite the fact that a large proportion of homes in North America and Europe shelter domestic animals. This is not surprising given the historic location of planning within the development-driven local state apparatus. Since the passage of the U.S. Endangered Species Act (ESA) in 1973, however, planners have been forced to grapple with the impact of human activities on threatened/endangered species. To reduce the impact of urbanization on threatened/endangered animals, planners have adopted such land-use tools as zoning (including urban limit lines and wildlife overlay zones), public/nonprofit land acquisition, transfer of development rights (TDR), environmental impact statements (EISs), and wildlife impact/habitat conservation linkage fees. None of these tools is without severe and well-known technical, political, and economic problems, stimulating the development of approaches such as habitat conservation plans (HCPs)—regional landscape-scale planning efforts to avoid the fragmentation inherent in project-by-project planning and local zoning control.

Despite the ESA, minimum-impact planning for urban wildlife has not been a priority for either architects or urban planners. Wildlife-oriented residential landscape architecture remains uncommon. Most examples are new developments (as opposed to retrofits), sited at the urban fringe, planned for low densities, and thus oriented for upper-income residents only. Many are merely ploys to enhance real-estate profits by providing home-buyers, steeped in an anti-urban ideology of suburban living emphasizing proximity to "the outdoors," with an extra "amenity" in the form of proximity to wild animals' bodies. Planning practice routinely defines other less attractive locations which host animals (dead or alive), such as slaughterhouses and factory farms, as "noxious" land uses and isolates them from urban residents to protect their sensibilities and the public health.

Wildlife considerations are also largely absent from the U.S. progressive architecture/planning agenda, as are concerns for captives such as pets or livestock. The 1980s "costs of sprawl" debate made no mention of wildlife habitat, and the adherents to the so-called new urbanism and sustainable cities movements of the 1990s rarely define sustainability in relation to animals. The new urbanism emphasizes sustainability through high-density and mixed-use urban development, but remains strictly anthropocentric in perspective. Although more explicitly ecocentric, the sustainable cities movement aims to reduce human impacts on the natural environment through environmentally sound systems of solid-waste treatment, energy production, transportation, housing, and so on, and the development of urban agriculture capable of supporting local residents. But while such approaches have long-term benefits for all living things, the sustainable cities literature pays little attention to questions of animals per se.

Everyday practices of urban planners, landscape architects, and urban designers shape normative expectations and practical possibilities for human-animal interactions. But their practices do not reflect desires to enrich or facilitate interactions between people and animals through design, nor have they been assessed from this perspective. Even companion animals are ignored; despite the fact that there are more U.S. households with companion animals than children, such animals remain invisible to architects and planners. What explains this anthropocentrism on the part of urban design and architectural professions? Social theories of urban design and professional practice could be used to better understand the anthropocentric production of urban space and place. Cuff, for example, explains the quotidian behavior of architects as part of a collective, interactive social process conditioned by institutional contexts including the local state and developer clients; not surprisingly,

design outcomes reflect the growth orientation of contemporary urbanism. More broadly, Evernden argues that planning and design professionals are constrained by the larger culture's insistence on rationality and order and the radical exclusion of animals from the city. The look of the city as created by planners and architects, dominated by standardized design forms such as the suburban tract house surrounded by a manicured, fenced lawn, reflects the deep-seated need to protect the domain of human control by excluding weeds, dirt, and—by extension—nature itself.

Environmental designers drawing on conservation biology and landscape ecology have more actively engaged the question of how to design new metropolitan landscapes for animals and people than have planners or architects. At the regional level, wildlife corridor plans or reserve networks are in vogue. Wildlife networks and corridors are meant to link "mainland" habitats beyond the urban fringe, achieve overall landscape connectivity to protect gene pools, and provide habitat for animals with small home ranges. Can corridors protect and reintegrate animals in the metropolis? Corridor planning is a recent development, and we need case-specific political-economic analyses of corridor plans to answer this question. Preliminary experience suggests that at best large-scale corridors can offer vital protection to gravely threatened keystone species and thus a variety of other animals, while small-scale corridors can be an excellent urban design strategy for allowing common small animals, insects, and birds to share urban living space with people. However, grand corridor proposals can degrade into an amenity for urban recreationists (since they often win taxpayers' support only if justified on recreational rather than habitat-conservation grounds). At worst, corridors may become a collaborationist strategy that merely smooths a pathway for urban real-estate development into wilderness areas.

A growing number of urban grassroots struggles revolves around the protection of specific wild animals or animal populations, and around the preservation of urban wetlands, forests, and other wildlife habitat due to their importance to wildlife. Also, growing awareness of companion-animal wants and desires has stimulated grass-roots efforts to create specially designed spaces for pets in the city, such as dog parks. But we have very little systematic information about what catalyzes such grassroots trans-species urban practices or about the connections between such struggles and other forms of local eco/animal activism. It is not clear if grassroots struggles around animals in the city are linked organizationally either to larger-scale environmental activism or green politics, or to traditional national animal welfare organizations, suggesting the need for mapping exercises and organizational network analyses. Ephemeral and limited case-study information suggests that political action around urban animals can expose deep divisions within environmentalism and the animal welfare establishment. These divisions mirror the broader political splits between mainstream environmentalism and the environmental justice movement, between animal rights organizations and environmentalists, and between groups with animal rights and groups with animal welfare orientations. For example, many mainstream groups only pay lip service (if that) to social justice issues, and so many activists of color continue to consider traditional environmental priorities such as wildlands and wildlife—especially in cities—as at best a frivolous obsession of affluent white suburban environmentalists, and at worst reflective of pervasive elitism and racism. Local struggles around wildlife issues can also expose the philosophical split between holistic environmental groups and individualist animal rights activists; for example, such conflicts often arise over proposals to kill feral animals in order to protect native species and ecosystem fragments. And reformist animal welfare organizations such as urban humane societies, concerned primarily with companion animals and often financially dependent on the local state, may be wary of siding with animal rights/liberation groups critical not only of state policies but also the standard practices of the humane societies themselves.

The rise of organizations and informal groups acting to preserve animal habitat in the city, change management policies, and protect individual animals indicates a shift in everyday thinking about the positionality of animals. If such a shift is underway, why and why now? One possibility is that ecocentric environmental ethics and especially animal rights thinking, with its parallels between racism, sexism, and "speciesism," have permeated popular consciousness and stimulated new social movements around urban animals. Other avenues of explanation may open up by theorizing trans-species movements within the broader context of new social movement theory, which points to these movements' consumption-related focus; grass-roots, localist, and anti-state nature; and linkages to the formation of new sociocultural identities necessitated by the postmodern condition and contemporary capitalism. Viewed through the lens of new social movement theory, struggles to resist incursions of capital into urban wildlife habitat or defend the interests of animals in the city could be contextualized within larger social and political-economic dynamics as they alter forms of activism and change individual-level priorities for political action. Such an exercise might even reveal that new social movements around animals transcend both production and consumption-related concerns, reflecting instead a desire among some people to span the human-animal divide by extending networks of caring and friendship to nonhuman others.

Toward Zoöpolis

Zoöpolis presents both challenges and opportunities for those committed to eco-socialist, feminist, and anti-racist urban futures. At one level, the challenge is to overcome deep divisions in theoretical thinking about nonhumans and their place in the human moral universe. Perhaps more crucial is the challenge of political practice, where purity of theory gives way to a more situated ethics, coalition building, and formation of strategic alliances. Can progressive urban environmentalism build a bridge to those people struggling around questions of urban animals, just as reds have reached out to greens, greens to feminists, feminists to those fighting racism? In time- and place-specific contexts where real linkages are forged, the range of potential alliances is apt to be great, extending from groups with substantial overlap with progressive environmental thinking to those whose communalities are more tenuous and whose focuses are more parochial. Making common cause on specific efforts to fight toxics, promote recycling, or shape air-quality management plans with grassroots groups whose raison d'être is urban wildlife, pets, or farm animal welfare may be difficult. The potential to expand and strengthen the movement is significant, however, and should not be overlooked.

The discourse of zoöpolis creates a space to initiate outreach, conversation, and collaboration in these borderlands of environmental action. Zoöpolis invites a critique of contemporary urbanization from the standpoints of animals but also from the perspective of people, who together with animals suffer from urban pollution and habitat degradation and who are denied the experience of animal kinship and otherness so vital to their well-being. Rejecting alienated theme-park models of human interaction with animals in the city, zoöpolis instead asks for a future in which animals and nature would no longer be incarcerated beyond the reach of our everyday lives, leaving us with only cartoons to heal the wounds of their absence. In a city re-enchanted by the animal kin-dom, the once-solid Enchanted Kingdom might just melt into air.

Notes

1. Barbara Noske, Humans and Other Animals, London: Unwin Hyman, 1989.

2. Thomas Nagel, "What Is It Like to Be a Bat?" *The Philosophical Review* 83, 1974.

3. Donna Haraway, "Situated Knowledges: The Science Question in Feminism and the privilege of Partial Perspective," in *Simians, Cyborgs, and Women: The Reinvention of Nature,* New York: Routledge, 1991.

4. "Shamu" was the name used for a series of killer whales who performed in a major U.S. marine theme park.

5. Stephen R. Kellert, "Urban Americans' Perspectives of Animals and the Natural Environment," *Urban Ecology* 8, 1984.

6. James O'Connor, "Capitalism, Nature, Socialism: A Theoretical Introduction," *Capitalism, Nature, Socialism* 1, 1988.

Robert Granfield and Paul Colomy

The Transformation of Wildlife Law in the Vanishing Wilderness

Introduction

Sociologists have given scant attention to the subject of wildlife crime and law. Although there has been empirical examination of environmental issues in the sociology of law, interest had not extended to the subject of wildlife law and criminalization. This lack of detailed socio-legal analysis may be due to the secondary status that has been accorded to rural issues and animal issues. For instance, crimes perpetrated against wildlife, such as poaching or the illegal killing of game animals, have been typically seen as folk crimes. These crimes have little moral stigma associated with them and, though violations are not generally approved, such crimes are relatively numerous and often treated as unimportant by law enforcement authorities. However, the enforcement of wildlife law may be in the process of flux for a variety of reasons.

First, the animal rights movement has gained considerable strength and popularity over the past several years. There has been growing opposition to the use of animals in experiments and efforts to protect animals from human exploitation and persecution have moved into the legal arena. In Boulder, Colorado, for example, a new law restricts killing and displacing prairie dogs, a species considered by many to be a growing urban nuisance, thereby according them rights to land use; citizens and businesses are encouraged to live in peaceful coexistence with their rodent brethren. Similarly, in Denver a law passed in 2002, dubbed "Westy's Law" in honor of a cat that was tortured by two teenage boys, makes cruelty to animals a felony punishable by up to three years in prison and up to $100,000 in fines. In California, Proposition 197, which would have reopened a hunting season on mountain lions, was narrowly defeated in 1996. Most remarkably, in Germany animals have recently been accorded legal rights under that country's constitution. On an international level, increased public attention has been given to the unethical treatment of animals for food production as well as to the commercialization of big game hunting.

A second reason for the growth of interest in wildlife and other animal issues may be due to the rise of animal "edu-tainment" programs, that is, television programs such as *Discovery*, *Animal Planet*, *The Crocodile Hunter* and others that deal with non-human animal issues. There is even a television program called *Busted* that is like the *Cops* of the non-human animal world in which daring game wardens, wildlife law enforcement agents and animal rescue officials do battle with unsavory poachers and assorted animal abusers. Perhaps a more global reason for the increasing attention to the legal issues involving animals has to do with increasing urbanization and growth within the rural landscape. Sampson and Groves (1989) have indicated that increased population growth is associated with an increase in deviance, either real or constructed. During periods of growth, old accepted practices may give way to new legal regulations. What was once considered a form of normal deviance such as the case of poaching becomes redefined as a significant malfeasance.

In this article, we present a preliminary analysis of the transformation of wildlife law and consider how law emerges out of, or is constituted within, local, concrete, and historically specific situations. Specifically, the subject of this chapter is the recent enhancement of legal sanctions associated with hunting and game laws in Colorado. Although poaching of game animals, for the most part, is on the fringe of public consciousness, it continues to persist in advanced industrial society. Some observers have argued that poaching has become increasingly attractive, particularly in light of the expanding market for trophies.

In the sociological literature the subject of poaching has received some limited attention. However, much of this research tends to focus on the neutralization techniques employed by poachers to account for their crime (Eliason and Dodder 1999). By contrast we explore how one incident of poaching led to the collective mobilization of a community and passage of more punitive legislation.

Method

In the fall of 2002, the authors initiated an investigation into the 1995 poaching of a large bull elk in Estes Park, Colorado, known as "Samson." In-depth interviews were conducted with several Estes Park residents familiar with the poaching incident, as well as law enforcement officials who investigated the case.

In addition to these sources, we conducted an extensive analysis of the various newspaper accounts and follow-up stories on the case. More than 200 newspaper stories about Samson were analyzed. These articles were used mainly as a way of providing information pertaining to the broader context surrounding the case.

In addition, we employed observational strategies as part of this study. Each of the authors visited Estes Park where they paid particular attention to the actual and symbolic presence of elk in the community. We toured the grounds of the YMCA where Samson was killed, visited shops that displayed Samson artifacts, and walked the town with residents and tourists observing the elk herd as they wandered through

the busy streets. We also attended the annual "Elk Fest," which provided information on hunting and featured simulated elk hunting video games, talks from local wildlife experts and law enforcement officials and a guided tour in open-bed trucks to view the elk that had taken up residence at a local golf course. The Elk Fest also offered a memorial to Samson whose head is displayed each year at the festival to "educate" visitors on the evils of poaching.

Finally, the authors collected legislative information on Samson's Law that was contained in archives located at the State House in Denver. We not only reviewed drafts of the law but we also "dubbed" audio-tapes from the assorted legislative committee hearings.

Killing an Icon

Milton Estes first visited the Estes Valley on a hunting trip in October of 1859 and described it as a paradise. Soon others came from the east to trap, hunt and view the scenery. Ranching and tourism provided a livelihood for most of the 200 citizens recorded in the 1900 census. The two principal sources of commerce in the area, ranching and tourist hunting, eventually took a toll on the elk population in Estes Park, reducing it to a tiny fraction of its original size by 1910. To sustain the tourist economy, a group of concerned citizens brought in elk from Yellowstone National Park to replenish the local herd, twenty-five in 1913 and another twenty-five in 1915. The Rocky Mountain National Park was established in 1915 and the town of Estes Park, nestled at its base, was incorporated just two years later. Because of conservation efforts to protect the herd, the population of elk grew rapidly. The herd also grew because there were no longer natural predators such as wolves to control them. By 1945 a reduction and management system was enacted to limit damage to the landscape from elk.

The town of Estes Park has continued to grow both in terms of people and in elk over the years. The human population has more than tripled since 1970, reaching the current population of nearly 10,000 people. Over the past decade, the town has extended its geographical borders farther and farther into wilderness areas as housing developments, golf courses, restaurants, coffee shops, motels, and strip malls have appeared, transforming the landscape into an increasingly upscale mountain retreat for the financially well-heeled. The elk population has grown as well to an estimated 4,000 animals, each of which is considered to be a rightful citizen of Estes Park. This number is much higher than what game experts refer to as the carrying capacity of the local environment.

Every year thousands of hunters descend upon the Estes Park area hoping for the opportunity to bring down a large elk. Although female elk were considered attractive by hunters in years past because of the higher quality of their meat, hunters have increasingly sought out large male "bull" elk as their quarry, primarily for the antlers or "rack" that drape their head. Because of the increasing value of trophy-sized animals to both sportsmen and commercial hunters, poaching or the illegal taking of an animal has been a relatively common occurrence in the area. Although the people of Estes Park oppose poaching, little has been done over the years to prevent it from occurring. In interviews, several people commented that Estes Park was known as a relatively safe haven for poachers and that when poachers were apprehended, fines were nominal and the county court judge refused to impose stiff fines.

All this changed on November 11, 1995, when late in the afternoon in Estes Park a single arrow shot from a crossbow ended the life of a large male elk. The elk that was killed, however, was no ordinary elk. Local residents knew this elk as "Samson." Samson was thought to be the largest bull elk in the Estes Valley and was well-known throughout the region and beyond as a national celebrity who had been photographed by thousands of Estes Park guests.

Weighing approximately 1,000 pounds and estimated to be about 12 years old, Samson was an 8 × 9 point elk who, over the years, had become like a mascot to the community, particularly people at the local YMCA camp where Samson spent most of his winter months. It was on the YMCA grounds that a commercial poacher from nearby Lakewood, Colorado, who reportedly had a $10,000 offer for Samson's head, approached to within ten yards of the icon to deliver the fatal shot.

As news of Samson's death spread, phone calls came in from around the country. The story of his killing was covered by the local and national media including *Headline News* and *U.S.A. Today*. Producers at *Court TV* had even made plans to televise the trial had it not been settled. More recently, *Animal Planet* aired the story of Samson, complete with a re-enactment of the crime, on its popular *Busted* program.

In interviews with residents of the area, as well as in the many newspaper articles and accounts of his death that were printed over the next several weeks, Samson was "ecopomorphized." We use this term as a way of describing the meaning this animal had for citizens in relation to the surrounding environment. While anthropomorphization implies that individuals attribute human qualities to animals, ecopomorphization suggests that individuals attribute ecological qualities to animals. Samson was frequently described as "awe-inspiring," or "majestic" and "noble." These images were very romantic and reminiscent of the wilderness imagery discussed earlier. Local people also anthropomorphized Samson by attributing agency to him. As one local resident commented, "He (Samson) enjoyed having his picture taken. He was a wild animal who had this affinity for people and this place. He felt safe here [at the YMCA]." Another commented that Samson "was always a willing model for photographers and if he got tired of posing he never complained. He was aware of his fame and importance." One resident who often illegally fed Samson described him as a "neat friend," and another described his death as a deep "personal loss."

News of Samson's death spread rapidly throughout the town of Estes Park. A local radio announcer stayed on the air the entire day to report breaking news to residents as well as to take calls from angry and distraught citizens. Within days of the elk's death, residents began holding town meetings calling for stiffer sentencing for poachers and increased law enforcement in the area. One individual inquired into whether a class action suit against the poacher could be filed because wildlife is the property of the state and because there were several victims who could claim damages. Some people even went so far as to suggest that the poacher should be put to death.

Death threats were taken seriously by local law enforcement agents who refused to release the name of the poacher to the press for fear of reprisals. As a result of this decision citizens perceived local law enforcement as not acting quickly enough to prosecute the poacher. There was much consternation. Letters and petitions demanding the prosecution and punishment of the offender to the full extent of the law poured into the offices of district attorney and county judge.

Most residents and law enforcement personnel in the area agreed that the killing of Samson was the biggest single event to have taken place in Estes Park in the past decade. The district attorney responsible for prosecuting the case claimed that, in all of his years of prosecutorial work in the region, he had never witnessed anything that came close to the kind of moral outrage expressed in the Samson case. In an interview, he explained:

> We had a case very close in time [to the Samson case], probably within a year or two, where a baby was left in a car and the mother forgot the baby was in the car. It was a hot day and the baby died. We had more calls and letters showing outrage and sympathy in the Samson case than we did in that case. We often commented about that around the table, you know, what and where are our real sentiments and priorities?

It was in this context of moral outrage and widespread indignation that Samson's Law was

proposed and eventually accepted in the State of Colorado.

The Origins of Samson's Law

In interviews, many of those who led the charge for the enactment of a new law indicated that they did not want Samson's death to be in vain. Many residents were disappointed by the fact that, although initial discussion of the punishment for the poacher involved possible fines of up to $100,000 and a lengthy jail term, the final sentence was significantly less than their expectations. The poacher eventually plead guilty to a series of wildlife violations including hunting without a license and the willful destruction of wildlife and paid $6,000 in fines and spent 90 days in jail.

A number of memorials were erected to honor Samson. For example, visitors to Estes Park are now greeted by a larger-than-life bronze statue of the elk. In addition, each year Samson's head and antlers are displayed during the annual Elk Festival. Tourists may also purchase reproductions of his image on postcards, posters and tee shirts. Also, the Colorado Division of Wildlife adopted Samson's image for its official state logo. But perhaps the most significant tribute was the passage of Samson's Law.

Samson's Law, as it is widely known in Colorado, adds a surcharge for "illegally taking" (the legal phrase for "poaching") select, "trophy-sized" animals. The statute defines trophy status for each species included in the bill—bull elk, mule deer buck, whitetail deer buck, bull moose, bighorn sheep, mountain goat and pronghorn antelope. The definitions of trophy-class wildlife are based on the tenth edition of Boone and Crockett's *Records of North American Big Game* (1988) record book and use a minimum antler/horn standard. A trophy pronghorn antelope, for example, must have a horn length of 14 inches or more; a trophy bull elk must have at least six points on one antler; and a horn length of one-half curl qualifies a bighorn sheep as a trophy. The surcharge for trophy poaching varies by species, and these variable rates are tied to the estimates of the "cost of replacement." Replacement costs, in turn, represent the average amount paid for guides, licenses, airfare/travel, skinning and other processing and taxidermy fees. In accord with these costs, the law stipulates that poaching a trophy-sized pronghorn antelope, for instance, will incur a surcharge of $4,000 (that is added to the existing fine of $700); illegally taking a trophy bull elk (like Samson) incurs a surcharge of $10,000 (on top of the existing fine of $1,000); and poaching a trophy bighorn sheep incurs a surcharge of $25,000 (added to an existing fine that ranges from $1,000 to $100,000). The revenue generated by the surcharge goes to the local town, city or county where the citation is issued.

State Senator Mark Udall, a Boulder-based Democrat whose family has long been involved with environmental and wildlife issues and whose district includes Estes Park, initially introduced the bill to the Colorado General Assembly in 1997. Despite public support the bill was voted down, a victim of partisan politics according to its proponents. Udall was a Democrat and a freshman to boot, and his measure was killed quickly in the Republican-controlled legislature. The following year Udall enlisted a powerful Republican co-sponsor, Senator Tilman Bishop of Grand Junction, while also securing the support of other influential Republicans in both chambers. With key Republicans in tow and important alterations to the original measure, the bill was approved and signed into law in 1998.

In his introductory remarks to the Assembly, Udall initially attempted to distance the measure from Samson and what he termed "legislation by anecdote." But by then Samson had become the state's most infamous instance of poaching and Udall's reticence notwithstanding, his colleagues repeatedly brought the bill back to the big bull elk, peppering Udall and the director of the Colorado Division of Wildlife (DOW), David Croonquist (who testified at length during the legislative hearings) with questions about Samson and the penalties imposed on the poacher. For legislators, and the public at large,

Samson was the "poster animal" for trophy poaching, supplying not only a shared point of reference for discussion but a primary impetus for "doing something" about the problem.

Legislators were not alone in making Samson a touchstone for Udall's bill. Local papers, including the *Denver Post*, the *Rocky Mountain News*, the *Estes Park Trail Gazette*, the *Coloradoan* (in Fort Collins) and the *Reporter-Herald* (in Loveland), consistently referred to Samson's Law in their news stories and editorials. So did DOW, which, in a 1998 release circulated to lawmakers and wildlife organizations during the legislative session, offered the following explanation of the measure's origins and purpose (Lewis and Smith 1998):

> The bill was written in response to the poaching of Samson, the spectacular bull elk which freely roamed the area around Estes Park. Randall Francis, the man who shot Samson, received a sentence of only three months in jail and a $6,000 fine for the wanton act. That sparked a storm of protest around Estes Park, as well it should have. It's more than appropriate to stiffen penalties for those who think nothing of slaughtering wildlife simply because they want a hunting trophy. That's why Mark Udall introduced a bill to establish harsher penalties for trophy poaching.

By the 1998 session, Udall's reservations about legislation by anecdote had dissipated, and both he and (co-sponsor) Bishop frequently referred to Samson as the prototypical trophy the bill sought to protect from poachers.

According to the bill's proponents, the harm associated with trophy poaching is both symbolic and material. When testifying before the House Committee on Agriculture, Livestock, and Natural Resources, Udall characterized trophy wildlife as a "symbol of our way of life here that's so special about Colorado." Similarly, Jo Evans, a lobbyist representing several hunting and conservation groups, described trophy-class animals as "the largest, the best, and the most beautiful." Poaching such animals constitutes "a crime against the people of Colorado whose wildlife it is." Diane Gansauer, Executive Director of the Colorado Wildlife Federation, depicted these animals as "invaluable," portraying them as an essential part of America's "national treasury" and as "crown jewels."

In addition to their symbolic value, trophy wildlife was presented as a significant economic asset, attracting tourists and hunters from across the country. Focusing specifically on hunting, Udall and Bishop noted that it represents a $1.6 billion industry in Colorado. And the vast majority of those who testified at the legislative hearings represented organizations whose core constituency was hunters, and these witnesses hammered home the point that poachers endanger this industry by depriving legitimate sportsmen, who often pay significant licensing fees, from the opportunity to legally hunt trophy animals.

The proponents of Samson's Law also wanted to ensure that penalties for poaching would be administered. Proponents sought to reduce judicial discretion in cases where an individual had been found guilty of poaching. The bill's proponents felt that some judges had not taken wildlife crime seriously in the past and had used their discretion to impose minimal fines, if any at all. The language of Udall's bill sought to remedy this perceived problem by effectively eliminating judicial discretion.

The Context of Legal Action

What explains the level of moral outrage about the loss of Samson the elk to the point that a new law was enacted to honor his memory? Interestingly, the moral outrage over the case and the ensuing law occurred at a time when wildlife violations were on the decline. According to DOW statistics, the number of violations associated with the illegal taking of big game (elk, mountain lions, big horn sheep, etc.) had been declining since the early 1990s. In 1991, the DOW reported a total of 669 big game violations while in 1995, the year of Samson's death, only 392 big game violations were assessed.

Movements to enact legislation often occur independent of statistical evidence of rising problems. For example, drug laws, including National Prohibition, have often symbolized and represented broad-based fear and anxiety associated with a changing society. Gusfield (1963), in his classic study of prohibition, maintained that the coercive reform movement to transform alcohol laws represented the social elite's fear of transition; they felt that their status was eroding within a rapidly changing social and cultural landscape. The point is that law emerges in a social and cultural context that is significantly broader than the problem or issue it is designed to address. As with other legislation geared toward affecting social control, the Colorado poaching law addressed a problem that was in reality on the decline.

So why was the law passed? In life and, particularly, in death Samson embodied a meaning that was beyond his own distinctive stature as a large bull elk. Residents and tourists who knew and visited Samson as well as the legislators who passed Samson's Law imbued him with a meaning that embodied the very essence of the wilderness. Although he was most certainly human-habituated and relatively tame, a fact that may have contributed to his demise, people envisaged in him their own projections of the wilderness. Animals frequently connote a sense of place for people. In their recent book on geographies of human and animal encounters, Philo and Wilbert (2000:11) comment that:

> Zones of human settlement are envisaged as the province of pets or companion animals, zones of agriculture activity are envisaged as the province of livestock animals, and zones of unoccupied lands beyond the margins of settlement and agriculture are envisaged as the province of wild animals.

Thus, the human construction of animals is wrapped up with the human construction of place. As Scarce points (2005), communities are defined differently by different groups. In his study of the reintroduction of wolves into Yellowstone National Park, Scarce found that reactions to wolf reintroduction in the area depended on the relationship individuals had with the area itself. Long-term residents tended to see the reintroduction of wolves as a sign of uncertainty while the newcomers viewed wolves as a benefit for recreational purposes. In each case, the definition of the wolf was mediated by the individual's construction of place.

To the people of Estes Park as well as many legislators, gazing upon the elk is akin to gazing upon the wilderness itself. It is this wilderness aesthetic that brings both residents and tourists to the Estes Park region. However, the landscape of the American wilderness has all but vanished from the scene. In towns across the West, growth and development have transformed wilderness into zoos without bars. In Estes Park, growth and development have been so widespread that residents and tourists view elk, not from some remote area in a nearby forest, but from the green on one of the two championship-sized golf courses that have been recently constructed.

Game officers and residents complain about the increasing numbers of road kills of elk, elk-facilitated traffic jams and elk walking through the town with, as one game officer put it, "arrows in their butts." There has also been an increasing commercialization of hunting in the area where local ranchers will either herd elk onto their private land or raise them in order to sell private property hunting licenses. This has transformed hunting into what one interviewee described as a "slaughter." As this resident explained in an interview:

> January around here is a sad time. It's a mass slaughter of elk. It's gotten to the point where people shoot from the side of the road. Last year there was a guy who had killed an elk and was field dressing the critter right across the street from a school bus stop where children were waiting. I don't disapprove of hunting, but this isn't hunting. Things have really changed in this town.

The wilderness is largely a myth within American society, although it continues to evoke powerful imagery. It is very likely that the wilderness image has become even more potent in the wake of increasing urban development and the resulting loss of the natural environment. The Estes Park elk known as Samson was part of this wilderness narrative kept alive in order to maintain a kind of separation between the sacred and profane, between the wilderness and civilization. The killing of Samson and the passage of Samson's Law were played out on a field of a transforming social landscape. As one resident we interviewed insightfully commented, "the killing of Samson was the killing of an idea; an idea that brought people here. We thought we were immune to this sort of thing."

The residents of Estes Park and legislators who led the charge to pass Samson's Law and to memorialize him in other ways were, in addition to mourning a unique elk, responding to a felt crisis associated with the challenge to their ideology of the wilderness. The effort to further criminalize poaching might actually be seen as an example of "governing through crime," a phrase that is used to describe crime rhetoric and increasing criminalization as a response not to crime itself but rather to what Scheingold (1998) refers to as a general feeling of malaise and marginalization associated with a sense of crisis in society.

In a related way, Boeckman and Tyler (1997) have argued that citizens who feel that the moral and social cohesion that holds society together is declining tend to be more supportive of punitive public policies. In their research on the public support for "three-strikes" legislation, the authors argue that rather than actually fearing crime, crime becomes a mobilizing theme for the public who feels a sense of foreboding—a feeling that social conditions and underlying social values have become too precarious and uncertain. In a similar way, proponents of the Samson bill used law not only as a way of asserting a claim that the current criminal justice system is inadequate for not protecting them against poachers, but also as a way of reaffirming their own vision of the wilderness that is under attack on several fronts. The law was also a way to articulate its supporters' particular vision of human-animal relationships. The killing of Samson not only became a mobilizing event for many of those who found the commercial poaching of these animals offensive, but also a symbol for the loss of the wilderness.

Discussion and Conclusion

This article offers insight into the degree to which nature and wildlife are socially constructed and act as powerful boundary markers for certain groups. While framed as a problem-solving instrument, Samson's Law served as a boundary marker, establishing and reaffirming several boundaries. First, it legally inscribed a hierarchical distinction between the more highly prized trophy-class animals and their somewhat less valued, normal-sized brethren. Though this dichotomy resonates in a very general way with many casual human observers' appreciation for unusually large wildlife, the detailed specifications of trophy-status incorporated in the bill clearly reflect characteristics celebrated by the hunting community.

Second, affirming a particular iteration of the broader, longstanding distinction between "good" and "bad" animals, the bill protected "non-predator" trophy-sized wildlife while excluding equally spectacular (in size) "predators." The 1997 bill had sought to shield large bears and mountain lions from poachers, but speaking on behalf of ranchers and farmers, members of the House Committee on Agriculture protested that these animals sometimes prey on livestock and occasionally threaten human life as well. Ranchers and farmers had a right to protect their cattle and families from predators of whatever size. Deferring to these interests, the 1998 bill deleted bears and mountain lions from the list of protected wildlife.

Third and perhaps most significantly, the bill affirmed a bright line between legitimate hunters and poachers. Pitched at a symbolic level, legislators and those who testified on the

bill's behalf reasserted a radical moral contrast between these two groups. Within the legislative hearings, the hunter was characterized in an idealized, reverential way, as a man (usually, though, lawmakers were well aware that the number of women hunters is growing) who rigorously adheres to both the formal (and often complicated) rules and regulations established by the Division of Wildlife as well as the informal but vitally-felt ethos of the hunting community. The hunter personified values of restraint, conservation, safety, concern for others in the field, respect for law and legal authorities, and a deeply-felt connection to animals. The hunter's project was lauded for its positive contribution to wildlife management. By contrast, the poacher was vilified, and he (no mention was made of female poachers) was vilified most vociferously by those who testified on behalf of organizations whose principal constituencies were hunters. During legislative hearings, poachers were portrayed as selfish and greedy, motivated either by the prospect of large, illegitimate profits or unseemly ego enhancement. They had no respect for the law or legal authorities nor did they exhibit much regard for hunters or their ethos. Poachers were seen as exceedingly dangerous, posing a threat not only to wildlife but, to (non-poaching) humans who might inadvertently encounter them in the wild. They were criminals with no respect for the law. Unlike hunters, poachers cared not at all for the animals they killed and were often satisfied with the rack alone, leaving the rest of the animal to rot on a secluded hillside.

No legislator (or testifying non-legislator) contested this idealized symbolic contrast. But after affirming this contrast, lawmakers (and others) reflected on more practical features of hunting and enforcing rules against poaching. This "practical rationality" parsed away (but did not challenge) the ideal-typical contrast between poachers and hunters. This leavening of symbolism with practicality was prompted both by a recognition of the difficulties even the well-intentioned confront in following the letter of the law (against poaching) and by a certain level of distrust some hunters harbor toward the Division of Wildlife. These concerns prompted legislators, particularly those who were hunters and/or whose constituencies included hunters, to advise DOW officials about using common sense in law enforcement.

Legislators and several witnesses held that not all poaching is equally deplorable. The target of the law was decidedly not subsistence poaching, the illegal taking of an animal for its meat. In this vein, a few legislators recollected their own dirt-poor youth when dire economic circumstances compelled them to poach for groceries. Mark Udall, the bill's principal sponsor, explicitly noted that the target of his bill was not "the man with the family back home in December driving a lonely county road to take a doe for some meat in the freezer for the rest of the winter." Legislators also noted that accidents sometimes occur in the field, with an illegal take occurring when a bullet travels through an intended, legal target and inadvertently striking another animal for which the hunter has no license.

Also animating this practical rationality was a certain level of distrust some legislators expressed toward the DOW. Though the relationship between the Division and hunters is generally cooperative, with a sizeable portion of the Division's budget coming from the fees and licenses paid by hunters and anglers, the Division's law enforcement function introduces an inherent tension between its officers and hunters. Hunters complain that DOW managers sometimes enforce laws against poaching in an overly zealous way, and some legislators told the DOW representative testifying in support of the bill about calls he had received from hunters complaining about the officious way they had been treated by DOW officers.

Referring to past incidents where antipoaching regulations had been applied too rigidly, another legislator wanted assurance from the DOW that the proposed bill would be enforced with common sense and compassion. In this vein, the DOW official was reminded, several times, about an infamous incident during the 1990s in the San Luis Valley where an officer, working undercover, had befriended a largely impoverished, immigrant community that partially relied on poaching for subsistence. After the officer relayed these findings to his superiors, DOW launched what many considered a SWAT-like raid on the community. Though legally justifiable, this heavy-handed approach provoked considerable resentment toward DOW, not only in the Valley but throughout the State of Colorado. Legislators wanted assurances from DOW that passage of the Samson bill would not be taken as license for another San Luis Valley.

The elk of Estes Park have much more to fear than the occasional poacher. Development tracts that shrink corridors for elk to move, ranchers who herd elk on their lands so they can be harvested and citizens who are increasingly unwilling to share their space with these animals represent more urgent dangers. Samson's Law constructs the threat to elk and wildlife in a traditional way, by assigning blame to an old enemy, the poacher. Historically, this enemy is well known: a lower class and commercially motivated "outsider" and "nonhunter." However, this law will do little to reduce the modern threats that confront these animals and the wilderness they represent.

Wildlife managers face an increasingly difficult and complex social environment. While the Samson Law was initially cast as an attempt to validate wildlife as a natural asset, interests and constituencies that were removed from the original outcry concerning Samson's death inevitably shaped the law. Initially pushed by constituencies who viewed elk like Samson as valuable for their own sake as a part of nature and wanted them protected, the Division of Wildlife officials were eventually instructed by legislators and hunting groups to enforce the Samson Law with commercial and recreational interests in mind. The law erected symbolic boundaries in ways that meant that the elk would not be made safe in their own right, but made safe for hunters and other commercial interests to continue to kill elk legally. Despite the fact that the initial impulse surrounding the death of Samson involved a deeply-felt expression of community loss associated with the decline of nature due to growth and development, the law re-defined this sense of loss in a way that supported the interests and worldviews of the traditional communities associated with hunting and ranching.

While many community members in the town of Estes Park where Samson roamed may feel vindicated with the passage of the law, the law may do little to reduce the majority of poaching cases. Although the law has created new standards for poaching enforcement on the books, wildlife officials are still nevertheless faced with enforcing the law. Based on the evidence in this article, it is likely that wildlife enforcement officials will apply the law narrowly to cases of poaching that do not offend hunting or other commercial interests.

References

Boeckmann, Robert, and Tom Tyler. 1997. "Three Strikes and You Are Out, But Why? The Psychology of Public Support for Punishing Rule Breakers." *Law and Society Review* 31:337–365.

Boone and Crockett Club. 1988. *Records of North American Big Game: A Book of the Boone and Crockett Club.* Missoula, MT: Boone and Crockett Club.

Eliason, Stephen, and Richard Dodder. 1999. "Techniques of Neutralization Used by Deer Poachers in the Western United States: A Research Note." *Deviant Behavior* 20:233–252.

Gusfield, Joseph. 1963. *Symbolic Crusade: Status Politics and the American Temperance Movement.* Urbana: University of Illinois Press.

Lewis, Cameron, and Bud Smith. 1998 (February 6). "Make Poachers Pay." *Wildlife Report: News from the DOW's North Region.* Fort Collins: Colorado Division of Wildlife.

Philo, Chris, and Chris Wilbert. 2000. "Animal Spaces, Beastly Places: An Introduction." In *Animal Spaces, Beastly Places: New Geographies of Human-Animal Relations,* ed. C. Philo and C. Wilbert. New York: Routledge.

Sampson, Robert, and B. Groves. 1989. "Community Structure and Crime: Testing Social Disorganization Theory." *American Journal of Sociology* 94:774–802.

Scarce, R.K. 2005. "More Than Mere Wolves at the Door: Reconstructing Community Amidst a Wildlife Controversy." In *Mad About Wildlife: Looking at Social Conflict Over Widlife,* edited by A. Herda-Rapp and T. Goedeke, Netherlands: Brill Academic Publishers.

Scheingold, Stuart. 1998. "Constructing the New Political Criminology: Power, Authority and the Post Liberal State." *Law and Social Inquiry* 23:857–895.

PART FIVE

Science

Introduction

what constitutes the appropriate use of animals is constantly being questioned by animal advocates and debated by the general public. Hunting, intensive agriculture, and circuses, for example, all have their vociferous critics who see these practices as unnecessary and cruel. Yet nowhere is the use of animals more contested than the laboratory. The use of animals in scientific research has a long history—and also a long history of opposition (Rurke 1987). Today, most people in Western countries are familiar with newspaper articles expounding upon the alleged cruelty of a particular lab, or the suffering of particular kinds of animals. Whatever moral stance we take on the issue, we know the story well. Controversy over the scientific use of animals is part of modern life (Rudacille 2000).

Several sociological issues underlie this controversy and shape how people think about this issue. First, there is the question of how we define the meaning of lab animals, both inside and outside science. The lay public tends to anthropomorphize lab animals, giving them human thoughts and feelings. The chimp given skin grafts for experimentally induced burns not only feels physical pain but is perceived as "suffering" in humanlike ways. The cow implanted with a mechanical heart stays for weeks alone in a small room, so it must be "lonely." The caged rabbit seeing blood drawn from other animals must be "terrified." Once attributed human thoughts and feelings, lab animals in the public's eye become individual animals with unique personalities—perhaps akin to the way many people regard their own pets. This view is not surprising, since the lay public makes sense of the scientific use of animals from the modern perspective of people whose contact with and knowledge of animals is largely based on their experience owning pets, visiting zoos, exterminating vermin, sighting occasional backyard birds, and watching television shows about wildlife. But this view starkly contrasts with that held by people who experiment on animals.

To scientists and technicians, lab animals are tools to be used to produce knowledge, test drugs, or refine procedures. Lynch's (1988) study of neuroscientists' laboratory work with rats notes the contrast in scientists' speech between what he called the naturalistic animal—that is, the animal of common sense, the kind with which most of us are familiar—and the analytic animal. The latter type of animal can be turned into data. So, if scientists comment that "that was a good animal," they are not necessarily referring to the behavior of the animal when it was alive, but to the way that its brain tissue has turned out once the scientists have made slices of its preserved brain. The "animal" here refers to the product of a series of experimental procedures.

The definition of lab animals as tools is built into the subculture of science (Birke, Arluke, and Michaels 2007). It begins with the socialization of novice scientists who undergo a process of desensitization to the emotional responses that many people have to the act of cutting into an animal body. Facing up to the first experience of dissecting a fetal pig in high school, or to the first experience of "dog lab" in medical school, means coping with conflicting emotions (Solot and Arluke 1997). Students must find ways of adjusting, of getting through the process, to come out the other side as part of a professional community of scientists, doctors, or veterinarians. Defining lab animals as tools is one of the most important techniques to manage such conflict.

Students who eventually work full time in laboratories—as research technicians, postdoctoral students, or as principal investigators—experience various organizational practices that reinforce the definition of lab animals as tools. Animals are seen as objects before they arrive in labs, when grant proposals list them under the "supplies" section, note their future death as the protocol's final step, and justify their selection as the best "model" for studying human problems. When they arrive, new animals are given an identifying code that indicates such information as the principal investigator of the study, the experiment's number, and the animal's number. A laboratory bulletin board might have a card posted that lists the lab's current experimental animals, reading "Dogs, 2-5-07, 1831, 9672, 9570, 1913."

Additionally, it is difficult for staff members, especially principal investigators, to get to know lab animals as individuals because they are separated most of the time from labs, kept in caretaking facilities until they undergo experimental procedures or tests.

A second issue underlying the debate is the individual scientist's perspective toward experimenting on animals. Critics usually portray lab scientists as unfeeling about their use of animals. Their only concerns, it is argued, are to produce more knowledge, maintain funding to support their research, and build a reputation through publishing. It is true that most scientists see themselves as addressing a specific problem rather than studying the animals used. Yet, whatever the scientific questions addressed, that work necessarily centers on the animal in the lab and how its place there is understood. Few take the issue lightly. But they do generally believe that there is a greater good that can justify the use of animals—such as potential medical advances or gains in knowledge about how bodies work. It is for that reason they endeavor to come to terms with using animals in ways that would, outside the lab, be considered unethical. For most researchers, the use of animals in potentially painful research can be justified with two caveats: (1) the research is justified, they argue, if the knowledge gain is great enough (trivial knowledge is not justification enough), and (2) if the animals are well cared for and care is taken to ensure anesthesia where appropriate (Hart 1998).

However, believing in a greater good does not necessarily relieve practitioners from criticism. Researchers are only too well aware of the growth in public concern about animals, and in public perceptions of science in general. They know that their opponents believe it is simply wrong to experiment on animals because they indubitably suffer when they are used. And they know that their opponents do not believe that scientists take adequate care of lab animals: on the contrary, opponents tend to suggest that animals suffer unnecessarily at the hands of an uncaring scientific profession.

The portrayal of scientists as indifferent to the use and possible suffering of lab animals is simplistic and belies a more complex reality (Blum 1994). For some laboratory personnel, the question of using and experimenting on animals is a daily ethical dilemma. Like other professional identities, being a scientist is both something one always is, and something that at times one is not. A person may define himself or herself as a scientist—and accept its ethics and practices—yet define himself or herself as something other—with different ethics and practices—outside the lab (going home, for example, to the family dog). Having two conflicting perspectives toward the use of animals makes for some ambivalence. For example, the "official" definition of lab animals as tools may be difficult for scientists and technicians to apply when in their labs. The term animal has a multitude of meanings in our culture, including those meanings derived from science itself, all of which impinge on how scientists—or the wider public—perceive animal experiments. Scientists, like everyone else, must make sense of what they do not only in light of the ongoing public controversy and in light of the many meanings given to animals in society at large, but also in light of their own personal experience and relationships with animals. The result is that, especially with certain species, such as nonhuman primates, domestic animals, and even some rodents, lab workers on the job may not always be able to see these animals as mere tools.

A more accurate picture of laboratory scientists and technicians suggests that they experience a general feeling of uneasiness, or even contradiction, about their use of animals. Four aspects of animal experimentation cause uneasiness, especially among technicians because they usually have more direct contact with lab animals than do scientists. First, if laboratory personnel form strong attachments to lab animals, they can feel conflict between their nurturing and the experimental manipulations they perform. Most staff members learn to curtail these attachments. Second, the "sacrifice" of lab animals becomes routinized and stripped of special meaning for many lab workers, making killing uncomfortably rote. Third, scientists and technicians sometimes encounter outsiders who are critical of animal experimentation and ridicule them for doing this work, so they may avoid telling outsiders about their work or take an educational approach to deal with these awkward encounters. Finally, many lab workers report some ethical uneasiness about doing certain types of experiments or using certain kinds of animals.

A third issue underlying controversy over the scientific use of animals has to do with the public's uneasiness about the power of science and technology. Lay perceptions of science include awareness of its benefits alongside uncertainty, or even anxiety, over its potential harm. Although a number of researchers have argued that increased "public understanding of science" would lead to greater acceptance, the opposite is often the case. This general public ambivalence becomes particularly salient around the more "exotic" biomedical uses of animals. For example, the rapid growth in biotechnology concerns many lay people, not the least for its potential power to alter "nature." Altered animals (genetically engineered agricultural animals, for example, or the production of animals with human genes to provide some product of clinical value) have a particularly salient role here. Not only do these animals raise all the issues suggested laboratory and agricultural practice in general, but they offer new challenges as they seem to threaten the boundary of what is human.

These issues are explored in the following selections of *Between the Species*. Mary Phillips looks at how scientists perceive laboratory animals and use them in experiments that entail pain or suffering. Historically, treatment for pain relief has varied according to the social status of the sufferer. In the nineteenth century, certain groups of people— uneducated, poor black or Indian males, Irish and German immigrants, or alcoholics and drug users— were viewed as less sensitive to pain than other people, leading to amputations without anesthesia. Phillips found a similar tendency to make arbitrary distinctions affecting pain relief in her ethnographic study of animal research laboratories. The administration of pain-relieving drugs for lab animals differed from standard practice for humans and, perhaps, for companion animals. Although anesthesia was used routinely for surgical procedures, its administration was sometimes haphazard. Analgesics, however, were rarely used. Most scientists never thought about using analgesics and did not consider the subject worthy of serious attention. While they agreed readily that animals are capable of feeling pain, such assertions were muted by an overriding view of lab animals as creatures existing solely for the purposes of research. As a result, it was the exceptional scientist who was able to focus on anything about the animal's subjective experience that might lie outside the boundaries of the research protocol.

The next selection presents a very different picture of animal researchers. Harold Herzog captures the ethical complexities of both animal scientists and their critics by drawing on his own experiences in labs. He recounts his predicament as a graduate student when, in the face of having to boil alive various animals, he found himself unable to do so to a mouse after having done it to worms and a snake. And peers shared his struggle with the moral consequences of animal experimentation, one of whom had become attached to the cats he had to kill. He traces this moral dilemma to several sources. One source is a paradox—the more a species biologically resembles humans, the more useful it is for studying human medical problems—but the more a species resembles us biologically, the more likely it experiences similar mental states. Another source is inconsistency— the moral status of animals does not depend on their species, intelligence, or degree of suffering, but on how we label different members of the same species. With mice, for example, our actions toward them will vary, depending on whether they are seen as pests, food, or research subjects. Herzog goes on to note that those who oppose animal experimentation are also morally ambiguous. Having such different perspectives complicates communication between scientists and their critics.

The last selection by Donna Haraway examines the controversy surrounding the bioengineering of animals. Haraway, a cultural theorist, has shifted her attention from genetic technology, primates, and cyborgs, to dogs. As her work on cyborgs explored the intersection of human and machine, this article illuminates the relationships of humans and dogs, shedding light on both species. Instead of condemning biotechnology, Haraway makes an effort to embrace it. She looks at "breed activists" or lay dog lovers whose passion for the breed leads them deep into scientific research and activism, such as Linda Weisser and Catherine de la Cruz, who are activists and breeders of Great Pyrenees. They set out to reduce the incidence of canine hip dysplasia in this breed by trying to get breeders of these dogs to use an open health and genetics registry that would lead to better breeding practices. Other efforts to promote healthier breeding are also examined, such as the Canine Diversity Project web site that educates breeders to the dangers of inbreeding. But the leap from canine diversity to dog cloning is not as long as one might think, according to Haraway, with both rooted in the motivation to "save the endangered [fill in the category]." She discusses why it is reasonable to have a project to clone "Missy," a northern California dog who, as a mutt, is an endangered species of one.

References

Birke, L., A. Arluke, and M. Michaels. 2007. *The Sacrifice: How Scientific Experiments Transform Animals and People.* West Lafayette, IN: Purdue University Press.

Blum, D. 1994. *The Monkey Wars.* New York: Oxford University Press.

Hart, L. 1998. *Responsible Conduct with Animals in Research.* New York: Oxford University Press.

Lynch, M. 1988. "Sacrifice and the Transformation of the Animal Body into a Scientific Object: Laboratory Culture and Ritual Practice in the Neurosciences." *Social Studies of Science* 18:265–289.

Rudacille, D. 2000. *The Scalpel and the Butterfly: The Conflict Between Animal Research and Animal Protection.* Berkeley: University of California Press.

Rurke, N. 1987. *Vivisection in the Historical Perspective.* London: Croom Helm.

Solot, D., and A. Arluke. 1997. "Learning the Scientist's Role: Animal Dissection in Middle School." *Journal of Contemporary Ethnography* 26:28–54.

Mary T. Phillips

The Researcher's Perception of Pain

For several decades after its discovery, anesthesia was withheld in a large proportion of surgical operations. According to records unearthed by Pernick and discussed in his fascinating study of nineteenth-century attitudes toward pain, about 32 percent of all major limb amputations performed at the Pennsylvania Hospital from 1853 to 1862 were done without anesthesia. Pernick gives a comparable figure for amputations done at New York Hospital during the 5 years following the introduction of ether there (Pernick, 1985, p. 4).

The reasons for this drew upon a complex ideology of pain that attributed sensitivity to pain selectively, according to social status (sex, race or ethnic origin, age, education, social class) and personal habits (especially alcohol and drug use), as well as the nature of the surgical operation. People considered most sensitive to pain (and therefore the most likely to receive anesthesia) were women, the educated and wealthy classes, whites (except for recent immigrants), children and the elderly, and people with no history of alcohol or drug abuse. Their social opposites—males, the uneducated, the poor, "savages" (meaning blacks and Indians), Irish and German immigrants, young adults, and alcoholics—were considered least likely to need anesthesia because of their relative insensitivity to pain.

Down at the bottom of the hierarchy of sensitivity, along with the lower classes, was the place of animals. Silas Weir Mitchell, nineteenth-century physician and pioneer in neurology, wrote: "[I]n our process of being civilized we have won, I suspect, intensified capacity to suffer. The savage does not feel pain as we do; nor, as we examine the descending scale of life, do

animals seem to have the acuteness of pain-sense at which we have arrived" (JAMA, 1967, p. 124).

This hierarchical view of life, so much a part of the nineteenth-century ethos of colonialism, casts differences of skin color and class and culture (and species, the extreme case) as unbridgeable chasms. Such a perspective did not foster much empathy for the suffering of others, as this episode from the history of anesthesia illustrates. "The descending scale of life," however, is a metaphor from a bygone age. Already in the Victorian era (a time of great humanitarian and antivivisectionist movements), the scope of empathy was growing. Social historians have remarked upon the dawning, at about this time, of a distinctly modern sensitivity to the feelings of a widening circle of others. By the turn of the century, social station was no longer considered a relevant consideration in the decision to administer anesthetic drugs. Today we would no more condone operating on a Native American without anesthesia than we would condone calling him or her a savage.

If we were to document the use of anesthesia in veterinary surgery over the past century, we would probably find a pattern similar to that of the less fortunate classes of humans. Animal surgeons in the nineteenth century were slow to adopt surgical anesthesia, in spite of a strong campaign by the British antivivisection movement to counter the belief that animals were insensitive to pain (Pernick, 1985, p. 178). Antivivisectionist pressure prompted the British Association for the Advancement of Science to publish guidelines in 1871 that contained a requirement for the use of anesthetics in experimentation, but a study by

Stewart Richards (1986; 1987) suggests that even the authors of these guidelines often did not follow them. John Scott Burdon Sanderson, who was one of the authors of the 1871 guidelines, omitted any mention of anesthesia in describing many experiments in his *Handbook for the Physiological Laboratory* (1873). Richards' detailed analysis of the *Handbook* reveals that about 15 percent of the potentially painful experiments did not specify the use of any anesthetic.

Nevertheless, the use of anesthesia for all major surgery, both animal and human, is now routine. This says something about how attitudes have changed, but it is hardly the end of the story. In a 3-year study of animal research laboratories in New York, I found that the administration of pain-relieving drugs to animals used in scientific experiments differs considerably from the standards for human patients—and, I suspect, for pets in veterinary hospitals. As will be seen, researchers tend to view lab animals as somehow different from other animals, belonging to an altogether distinct category of being.

Methods and Procedures

This report is based on an ethnographic study of laboratories located in two research institutions in the New York City area. At one of the institutions (hereafter referred to as the Institute), participants were selected using a random sampling technique, weighted to assure adequate representation of behaviorists and of those using species other than mice and rats. At the other, smaller institution (hereafter referred to as the University), every eligible researcher was selected. A total of 27 scientists in 23 laboratories participated in the study, for an overall participation rate of 77 percent of those selected.

From January 1985 through November 1987, I spent hundreds of hours observing experiments on rats, mice, hamsters, toads, birds, rabbits, cats, monkeys, and fish. I took notes during these observations, from which I later typed a detailed account of each session. After several weeks or months (or, in one case, years) in a given laboratory, I interviewed the lab's participants.

Anesthesia in Animal Research

Until the passage of the Laboratory Animal Welfare Act (PL 89-544) in 1966, experimenters in this country had free rein to do whatever they wanted to animals in their laboratories. Even after 1966, researchers were not required to use anesthesia or any other pain-relieving drugs, since the Act was primarily intended to ensure that animals purchased by scientific laboratories were not stolen pets. The legislation also established some minimum standards for the humane care of animals awaiting experimentation. However, it covered only facilities that used dogs and cats, and it expressly exempted from regulation the treatment of animals "during actual research or experimentation."

The Act has been amended three times: in 1970, 1976, and 1985. The 1970 amendments changed its name to the Animal Welfare Act (dropping "Laboratory"), extended coverage to zoos and circuses and to many more species, and inserted a provision requiring "the appropriate use of anesthetic or tranquilizing drugs, when such use would be proper in the opinion of the attending veterinarian of such research facilities." This was backed by a requirement (still in effect) that each research facility covered by the Act submit an annual report to the government showing how many animals of each species were used in experiments during the previous year, how many of these animals received pain-relieving drugs; and how many animals were used in painful experiments without receiving any pain relief. The report must include an explanation for any instances of the latter. These annual reports are public record, available by request under the Freedom of Information Act.

In 1985, the pain-relief provisions were strengthened somewhat. An explicit prohibition was placed on the use of paralytic drugs without anesthesia (once a popular procedure in vision research), and more authority was vested in the facility's veterinarian to make decisions about pain relief. In addition, the 1985 amendments required that an Institutional Animal Committee be established at each facility to review experiments that might involve pain, and to ensure that research meets all the standards of the Act, including these other new provisions: that the principal investigator consider alternatives to painful procedures; that animal pain and distress be minimized; and "that the withholding of tranquilizers, anesthesia, analgesia, or euthanasia when scientifically necessary shall continue for only the necessary period of time."

Compliance with the NIH guidelines, first published in 1963, is mandatory for researchers receiving NIH funds—and that means the majority of them (USDHHS, 1985). Moreover, the NIH guidelines cover *all* warm-blooded animals used in research, thus filling a gap left by the Animal Welfare Act's exclusion (until recently) of mice, rats, and birds from its coverage.

The cumulative effect of these regulations and guidelines is constraining, despite the loophole that allows scientists to withhold anesthesia when "scientifically necessary." I observed no instances in which surgery was performed on unanesthetized animals, and without exception researchers told me they would consider it unacceptable to do so. Legal, political, and technical/scientific reasons for using anesthesia are overwhelming, quite aside from the ethical qualms that many researchers expressed. They feared the consequences of breaking the law and bringing down the wrath of animal advocates. They pointed out that it is more convenient to operate on anesthetized animals than on struggling ones. In addition, scientists have come to appreciate the many ways in which pain and stress can alter physiological functions and thereby affect the validity of research results. The clincher, perhaps, is that most reputable scientific journals will not publish results of painful research done on unanesthetized animals. One researcher told me frankly that he had wanted to curarize some monkeys without anesthesia for vision experiments, but he was deterred by the knowledge that he could never get the work published.

However, none of these rules or regulations can prevent a researcher from becoming inattentive or careless in monitoring an animal's level of anesthesia during surgery. While one laboratory I visited had an elaborate array of equipment to monitor the physiological state of the cats and monkeys undergoing surgery there, many scientists who worked with rats and mice relied on nothing more than the animal's general appearance. Unlike human operating rooms, animal laboratories have no full-time anesthesiologist standing by whose sole responsibility is to administer and monitor the anesthesia. Sometimes, during very long experiments, anesthetized animals are even left alone for hours at a time.

One morning when I arrived at a neuroscience laboratory to observe the finale of an experiment on a cat that had begun the day before, I found the investigators sitting around glumly. They had worked until about 1:00 am the night before, they told me, leaving the cat anesthetized with a combination of drugs (urethane and surithal) administered continuously through a vein. When a graduate student arrived the next morning at about 6:00 am, the cat was dead. There is no reason to suppose that the cat ever gained consciousness, but if it had, its open wounds would have caused intense suffering. Leaving anesthetized animals unattended through the night was standard practice in this laboratory, and is apparently so in many neuroscience labs, where experiments often last for 36 hours or longer. The intention is never to cause pain (nor, certainly, to kill the animal prematurely), but it is implausible to believe it never happens.

In another laboratory, I was present when a rat regained consciousness during brain surgery. The rat was one of 20 given brain transplants on one day by a team consisting of the senior investigator (study participant), a postdoctoral fellow, the facility's veterinarian, and an undergraduate student. The procedure was for the veterinarian to inject each rat with anesthetic (chloropent, a commercially available drug containing pentobarbital and chlorohydrate) about 10 minutes prior to surgery. Then an incision was made in the top of the rat's head, the skin drawn back, and a drill used to make a small hole in the skull. Into this opening the researcher injected a tiny amount of material that had been extracted from the brain of a rat fetus a few hours earlier. The incision was then closed with surgical staples and the rat was placed on a warming pad to recover. The whole procedure took about 20 minutes.

My notes for the afternoon show that at 2:35 pm, the postdoctoral fellow began drilling into the skull of a rat, which immediately began to squirm and struggle. The rat's hind legs began scrambling in a coordinated running movement, eventually running right off the small cardboard box being used as a makeshift operating platform. While its hind quarters were hanging over the edge of the platform, the rat's head was still held firmly in place by ear bars, part of the stereotaxic device that keeps the animal's head correctly aligned for precise placement of the drill. The researcher kept on working on the skull, paying no attention to the rat's frantic struggles. After several minutes of this, the rat managed to kick over the box-platform, making it impossible for the researcher to continue. At that point, he asked the veterinarian for more anesthesia, which the latter immediately injected. The researcher righted the box, repositioned the rat on it, and at once resumed drilling. The rat again struggled until half of its body had slipped off the box. The researcher continued drilling for about 30 seconds, then once more repositioned the rat. By this time— it was 2:45, ten minutes after the rat's first movements—the booster dose of anesthesia had taken effect, and the animal became quiet, and remained so for the duration of the surgery. During all this time, the senior investigator, seated a few feet away performing an identical operation on another rat, did not look up from his work. The others paid no attention, either. They all acted as though nothing unusual or untoward was going on.

I asked the senior investigator about this incident when I interviewed him some 3 months later. I described what I had seen, and asked if he thought the rat had been in pain. He replied that "in that kind of situation, it's probably more uncomfort than anything else." But then he asked, rhetorically, "Is it worthwhile giving a general anesthetic to prevent the animal from feeling those two minutes of pain that would be involved in surgery and risk killing the animal?" He continued, explaining at some length the statistical probability of accidents due to anesthetic overdose. Out of every 20 animals, he said, one or two are likely to be more resistent to the anesthesia than the others. But "99 percent of the animals that die before you want to terminate them, it's because of anesthetic." "I think that in order to eliminate all pain," he concluded, "the chances are that you would be killing a lot more animals."

This scientist did not seem very convinced, himself, that the rat felt "more uncomfort than anything else." But the question was not really important for him. Much more important was the possibility of losing data by inadvertently killing animals with too much anesthesia. The risk is not that animals might die—they were all to be killed a week or two later—but that they might die "before you want to terminate them." In this passage, the scientist has subtly clothed his interest in the success of his experiment in the nobler garb of concern for the animal's life.

Analgesia in Animal Research

In spite of these kinds of lapses, there is a wide consensus among researchers that anesthetics should be used in pretty much the same situations as for humans, and in practice this is usually followed. At any rate, researchers have virtually no latitude in deciding when to administer anesthetics. Analgesics—painkillers, such as aspirin— are an entirely different matter. The use of analgesics in animal research, in practice, if not in theory, is left almost entirely to the discretion of the investigator. For this reason, the administration of analgesics can provide us with a far more sensitive indicator of the view of animal pain and suffering held by scientific researchers than can the use of anesthetics.

On the face of it, the federal regulations require the use of analgesics no less than anesthetics. The Animal Welfare Act mandates that "animal pain and distress [be] minimized, including adequate veterinary care with the appropriate use of anesthetic, analgesic, tranquilizing drugs, or euthanasia" (1966, PL 89-544 Sec. 13 [3][A]) and that "in any practice which could cause pain to animals—(i) that a doctor of veterinary medicine [be] consulted in the planning of such procedures; (ii) for the use of tranquilizers, analgesics, and anesthetics" (1966, PL 89-544 Sec. 13 [3] [C] [i,ii]). The NIH *Guide* is more specific. It states: "Postsurgical care should include observing the animal to ensure uneventful recovery from anesthesia and surgery; administering supportive fluids, analgesics, and other drugs as required . . ." (USDHHS, 1985, p. 38).

Analgesics are routinely given to human patients following surgery, and in fact a number of commentators have made much of modern Westerners' dependence on painkillers (e.g., Illich, 1976; see also Pernick, 1985, pp. 233–234). In the animal laboratories, however, analgesics were rarely used. No one (with the possible exception of some animal welfare advocates) considers this a violation of the regulations, but rather a (more or less) legitimate interpretation of the "appropriate use" and "as required" clauses. Whereas the regulations were invariably interpreted to require anesthesia for surgery, they were not construed to require analgesic drugs under any specific conditions. Analgesics were considered—when they were considered at all—to be a matter for individual judgment.

In the 23 laboratories I visited, I never saw an analgesic administered, although two researchers reported regular analgesic use: monkeys were said to be given Tylenol (acetaminophen) after brain surgery in one laboratory; and rats that had had brain surgery in another laboratory were reportedly given Talwin (pentazocine, a potent nonnar-

cotic analgesic), at the veterinarian's suggestion. I was not present immediately after surgeries in either laboratory, but I have no reason to doubt these reports.

In a third laboratory, the senior investigator told me that he gives postoperative rats an aspirin in their water "all the time." (He later modified this claim to "sometimes," and, when pressed, "not normally.") However, this laboratory chief had his graduate students do all the surgeries, and the student I had observed not only did not administer aspirin, but she told me that she never did so because aspirin is not appropriate for rats. It was her belief that "there just are no analgesics appropriate for rats." In a fourth laboratory, monkeys received no analgesics after head surgery at the time of my visits, but both scientists interviewed here stated their intention to begin the use of opiates for this purpose soon.

It should be noted that in five laboratories there was really no opportunity to administer analgesics, either because the animals were killed while still under surgical anesthesia or because nothing that would normally be considered painful was done to them. This discussion, which assumes that the question of whether or not to administer an analgesic is an applicable one, should be understood to refer only to the remaining 18 laboratories. In most of the latter, major survival surgery provided a situation in which one could reasonably wonder if an analgesic might be appropriate.

The majority of researchers interviewed for the present study who did not administer analgesics appeared surprised when I asked about them. Some answered as though they thought I meant anesthetics; others said the idea had never occurred to them; many assured me that their animals did not seem to need painkillers; a few, like the graduate student performing rat surgery, thought none was available; and a sizable proportion added that, in any event, they would not want to introduce the unpredictable effects of a new variable into their research results.

The following interview excerpts are drawn from many that illustrate these themes:

MTP: Do the rats suffer much coming out of anesthesia, after the surgery?

Researcher: Well, I can imagine they have a headache.

MTP: Do they ever get analgesics?

Researcher: Um [pause] No, I don't think so. Of course, they are certainly anesthetized for surgery. Um [trails off]

MTP: Is that something you've ever given any thought to?

Researcher: I've never given it any thought. I'm not sure I would, anyway. I give *myself* as few drugs as possible, even when I'm in pain . . . That's tricky, to dwell on that issue. One could turn down all sorts of alleyways of thought.

MTP: Is there any pain recovering from that surgery [rats recovering from ovariectomies]?

Researcher: I would imagine that after *any* surgery there must be some pain. They don't seem to show any discomfort. They eat as well. They drink as well. They walk around as well as before. But I can't ask them.

MTP: Do you ever use, or have you ever considered using, analgesics?

Researcher: No, we don't use that.

MTP: Is there any particular reason?

Researcher: I think simply because it would add another variable to the experiment. And because you don't see the animal in any apparent discomfort.

Most researchers had never sought a veterinarian's advice on this subject, and the last quoted above even seemed amused by the idea. Yet they had had very little training in this area, and often admitted ignorance about available drugs. The only scientist who did consult a veterinarian—an endocrinologist who was worried about the poor appearance of her rats after surgery—was advised to administer a painkiller, a practice that she told me had since become routine in her laboratory (this was the laboratory in which I was told Talwin was given). In only two other laboratories were discussions about the

issue reported to have taken place, and in both cases the decision was subsequently made to give analgesics. Elsewhere, the question was not treated as worthy of serious discussion.

Inaccurate beliefs were sometimes given as reasons for not considering analgesics. For instance, a scientist told me that he could not give cats morphine-related analgesics, because "cats don't tolerate morphine drugs." Another told me that "Demerol drives [cats] crazy; they go bananas if you give them Demerol." In fact, a standard veterinary manual recommends Demerol (the trade name for meperidine, a morphine-like narcotic) and other opioids, such as buprenorphine, for cats (Flecknell, 1987). In another laboratory, a neuroscientist assured me that the nembutal anesthesia he used in monkey surgery had an analgesic effect that lasted for "half a day" after the animals regained consciousness. On the contrary, the veterinary manual states that one of nembutal's undesirable characteristics is its *poor* analgesic activity (Flecknell, 1987, p. 35). Recovery from nembutal anesthesia (as from other barbiturates) is prolonged, causing the animal to remain groggy for hours afterwards; that effect may have led the researcher to think, mistakenly, that nembutal is also an analgesic.

I do not mean to imply that all of the animals were in pain after the surgical operations I observed or that they *should* have been given painkillers. I am not claiming a privileged position from which to judge such matters. In fact, I was amazed, just as some scientists said they were, by how active and normal many of the animals appeared as they emerged from anesthesia. (On the other hand, there were also some that looked miserable.) However, at the time of my field work, there was growing discussion of this issue in the animal science and veterinary literature. Experts in the field of animal pain were pointing out that pain may be present in spite of an animal's "normal" appearance (Dawkins, 1980), and many were urging the use of analgesics, especially after surgery. Manuals and papers with advice on appropriate drugs and dosages for various species were readily available (e.g., Heidrich and Kent, 1985). The new climate of opinion was summed up in one pain specialist's comment that "one of the psychological curiosities of therapeutic decision making is the withholding of analgesic drugs, because the clinician is not absolutely certain that the animal is experiencing pain. Yet the same individual will administer antibiotics without documenting the presence of bacterial infection. Pain and suffering constitute the only situation in which I believe that, if in doubt, one should go ahead and treat" (Davis, 1983, p. 175).

This attitude toward analgesics can be found in at least two sets of interdisciplinary animal research guidelines drawn up by organizations with a broad representation (including veterinarians and pain specialists). One, adopted at an international conference on animal research held under the auspices of the World Health Organization and UNESCO, stated that "Postoperative pain should be prevented or relieved by analgesics" (CIOMS, 1983, VIII). The other is the New York Academy of Sciences' *Interdisciplinary Principles and Guidelines for the Use of Animals in Research, Testing, and Education*, which states that "Post-surgical analgesia must be provided appropriate for the type of surgical intervention" (NYAS, 1988, p. 5).

It is against this background that one must consider the almost total lack of interest in animal analgesia that I found among researchers. The subject was being treated very seriously by specialists in veterinary medicine and pain, while researchers in the laboratories included in this study were ignoring it. The point being made here is not so much that analgesics were withheld, but that so few researchers even considered the subject worth thinking about.

USDA Data on Pain in Animal Experimentation

Statistics compiled by the United States Department of Agriculture show that nationwide, scientists report that the majority of research animals are not exposed to painful or distressing procedures: the percentage of animals in this category has ranged from about 58 percent to 62 percent in recent years. Of the others, most received "appropriate pain relief." The percentage of animals reported to have actually experienced pain or distress, without any pain relief, ranges from about 6 percent to 8 percent each year. These figures are provided by the animal facilities themselves, in the annual reports mentioned earlier that are required under the provisions of the Animal Welfare Act.

For the years 1985 to 1987, University scientists reported *no* animals subjected to "pain or distress without administration of appropriate anesthetic, analgesic, or tranquilizer drugs" (Category D) during all three years. Researchers are required to attach explanations for all Category D cases; the explanations attached to the Institute's reports for these years reveal that none of the experiments in Category D was performed in any laboratory included in this study. We can only conclude that *not one* investigator included in the present study reported *any* instances of unrelieved pain for *any* of the experiments performed during this three-year period. These experiments included not only many instances of major survival surgery (with no post-operative analgesics), but also mice injected with cobra venom, LD-50 tests in which rats died from large doses of a toxic substance, and cancers in mice and rats. No anesthetics or analgesics were administered in these nonsurgical situations.

Category D experiments go unchallenged by the USDA as long as a "brief explanation" for withholding pain-relieving drugs is attached. It is possible that for some investigators this is simply too much trouble, but judging from the attachments to the Institute reports, an explanation acceptable to the USDA requires precious little thought or effort. The following samples are typical, and constitute about a third of all the explanations attached to the Institute reports for 1985 to 1987:

- Dogs are used to study treatment of heart worms.
- Rats are used in studies of aortic occlusion and Trypansoma [*sic*] infection. (Annual Report, 1985)

• Fourty[sic]-four rabbits were required for use in a study of Toxic Shock Syndrome prevention. (Annual Report, 1987)

In 1987, an atypical explanation also was submitted:

• Sixty-three hamsters were decapitated without prior anesthesia as anesthesia would alter neuroendocrine data. (Annual Report, 1987)

The last is atypical because it alone mentions *why* no anesthesia could be administered; the others simply state the general type of research that was done. The hamster explanation is also noteworthy for another reason: I saw scores of rats and mice decapitated without anesthesia at both the University and the Institute, as well as unanesthetized mice killed by cervical dislocation or a blow to the head. And yet none of these researchers made any entries in Category D on their annual reports.

Since the USDA data reflect only the scientists' own evaluations of animal pain and distress in their research, these figures cannot be used to "prove" that there is very little painful experimentation. All they show is that researchers *report* very little painful experimentation. When the biomedical research establishment uses USDA figures uncritically to refute complaints about animal pain, as the American Medical Association did in a recent white paper, one cannot but wonder if the authors are really as unsophisticated as all that. The AMA paper smugly states, "The fact that most experiments do not expose animals to pain was confirmed by a report issued by the Department of Agriculture . . . " (AMA, 1989, p. 17). This gives the impression that the USDA conducts independent evaluations using standardized criteria, which is far from the case.

One can easily understand why scientists might not want to fan the flames of the animal research controversy by reporting many Category D animals. Animal rights activists can easily obtain copies of these reports under the Freedom of Information Act—just as I did—and target individual research facilities for harass-

ment. These fears probably underlie some decisions to report animals in Category B (no pain or distress) rather than Category D; and to put all animals that received anesthetics in Category C (pain relieved by drugs), regardless of whether analgesics had been withheld. However, the researchers I studied appeared convinced—and they clearly hoped that by opening their laboratories to me, I would also become convinced—that nothing painful or distressing was going on.

Over and over researchers assured me that in their laboratories, animals were never hurt. "I love animals. . . . I would not feel that I'm doing the right thing if I would do anything to animals that is not being done to human beings," said one. "I do believe in not causing pain to them," said another. "We certainly aren't inflicting pain on the animals," said a third. Another insisted, "I limit the kinds of experiments that I think about [doing] to those that are not going to cause pain and suffering to the animal."

Scientists could tell me these things with apparent conviction because they defined pain and suffering very narrowly. "Pain" meant the acute pain of surgery on conscious animals, and almost nothing else. Most felt that their humane obligations were fulfilled when they relieved that pain with anesthesia. Although the USDA reporting forms refer to "pain or distress" and ask for information regarding "anesthetic, analgesic, or tranquilizer drugs," no annual report for any of half a dozen research facilities that I examined ever included a Category D explanation of why analgesics were not administered. As we have seen, one certainly cannot assume that this is because analgesics always *were* administered.

Conclusions

The scientists I studied were full participants in "the modern sensibility." There were no latter-day Cartesians among them who claimed that animals do not feel pain. The majority of them had pets at home, with whom they seemed capable of empathizing enormously. But their pets were individuals whom they knew by name, and whom they would *never* use in an experiment. Laboratory animals were (usually) nameless, deindividualized creatures, whose sole purpose in life was to serve in a scientific experiment. Researchers continually made distinctions between lab animals and pets, on the one hand, and between lab and wild animals on the other.

Although researchers always acknowledged the ability of animals to feel pain, this knowledge remained an abstraction for most. Scientists rarely saw any pain or suffering in their labs. Their view of lab animals as statistical aggregates overshadowed any perception of an individual animal's feelings at any given moment. And when I went beyond the issue of physical pain to ask about psychological or emotional suffering, many researchers were at a loss to answer. Typical was the comment of one neuroscientist who, when asked about possible boredom of monkeys kept in bare metal cages, answered with a palpable lack of interest: "We can speculate about these things, but I think it's pointless." Another responded more impatiently: "Oh, how would anybody know that? I mean, *any*body? How could *any*body know that? There's a danger of being anthropomorphic about anything. I just, I wouldn't even venture a guess."

The savage and the drunk of yesteryear find their counterpart in the twentieth-century laboratory, but not because of any simple belief that the lab animal is insensitive to pain. Laboratory animals are categorized and perceived as distinctive creatures whose purpose and meaning is constituted by their role as bearers of scientific data. Researchers believe that all animals are *capable* of feeling pain, but what they actually *see* when they look at lab animals is a scientific objective, not the animal's subjective experience. The result is that it rarely occurs to them to consider whether an animal is in pain, is suffering—or whether it is feeling anything at all, outside the boundaries of the research protocol.

References

American Medical Association (AMA). (1989). Use of Animals in Biomedical Research: The Challenge and Response. AMA White Paper. Available from the AMA, 535 N. Dearborn St., Chicago, IL 60610.

Animal Welfare Act. (1966, 1970, 1985). 7 U.S.C., 2131-2157. PL 89-544, Aug. 24, 1966, 80 Stat 350-353; as amended by PL 91-579, Dec. 24, 1970, 84 Stat 1560-1565; PL 94-279, Apr. 22, 1976, 90 Stat 417-423; and PL 99-198, title XVII, subtitle F, Dec. 17, 1985, 99 Stat 1645-1650. Reprinted in Phillips and Sechzer 1989, pp. 179–197.

Council for International Organizations of Medical Sciences (CIOMS). (1983). Proposed International Guiding Principles for Biomedical Research Involving Animals. Ms. prepared at XVIIth CIOMS Round Table Conference, Geneva, Dec. 8–9.

Davis, L. E. (1983). Species Differences in Drug Disposition as Factors in Alleviation of Pain. In R. L. Kitchell *et al.* (eds.), *Animal Pain: Perception and Alleviation* (pp. 161–178). Bethesda, MD: American Physiological Society.

Dawkins, M. S. (1980). *Animal Suffering: The Science of Animal Welfare.* New York: Methuen.

Flecknell, P. A. (1987). *Laboratory Animal Anesthesia: An Introduction for Research Workers and Technicians.* London: Academic Press/Harcourt Brace Jovanovich.

Heidrich, J. E., and G. Kent (1985). Use of Analgesics after Surgery in Animals. *J. Am. Vet. Med. Assoc. 187*, 5, 513–514.

Illich, I. (1976). *Medical Nemesis: The Expropriation of Health.* New York:Pantheon Books.

Journal of the American Medical Association (JAMA). (1967). Untitled. *199*, 9, 124. Reprinted from *JAMA* 18 (Jan. 23, 1892):108.

New York Academy of Sciences (NYAS). Ad Hoc Committee on Animal Research. (1988). *Interdisciplinary Principles and Guidelines for the Use of Animals in Research, Testing and Education* (pamphlet). New York: New York Academy of Sciences. Reprinted in Phillips and Sechzer 1989, pp. 200–234.

Pernick, M. S. (1985). *A Calculus of Suffering: Pain, Professionalism, and Anesthesia in Nineteenth Century America.* New York: Columbia University Press.

Richards, S. (1986). Drawing the Life-Blood of Physiology: Vivisection and the Physiologist's Dilemma, 1870–1900. *Annals of Science 43*, 27–56.

Richards, S. (1987). Vicarious Suffering, Necessary Pain: Physiological Method in Late Nineteenth-Century Britain. In N. A. Rupke (ed.), *Vivisection in Historical Perspective* (pp. 125–148). London: Croom Helm.

United States Department of Agriculture, Animal and Plant Health Inspection Service (USDA-APHIS). (1982–1986). *Animal Welfare Enforcement: Report of the Secretary of Agriculture to the President of the Senate and the Speaker of the House of Representatives.* National Technical Information Service, Springfield, VA.

United States Department of Agriculture, Animal and Plant Health Inspection Service (USDA-APHIS). (1982–1987). Annual Reports of Research Facilities. USDA-APHIS, Federal Building, Hyattsville, MD.

United States Department of Health and Human Services (USDHHS). Public Health Service. National Institutes of Health. (1985). (Revised). *Guide for the Care and Use of Laboratory Animals.* NIH Pub. No. 85-23. Bethesda, MD: National Institutes of Health.

Harold Herzog

Human Morality and Animal Research

The ethical complexities of scientific research using animals first hit me during my second year of graduate school. I had been assigned to work in the laboratory of a chemical ecologist who was studying the skin chemistry of animals. Part of my job was to make molecular extracts from earthworms. Live worms were immersed in distilled water that had been heated to 180 degrees. After 2 minutes, their bodies were removed and the remaining liquid centrifuged and frozen for later analysis. I had performed this procedure several times and had come to view it as another lab chore, one that I did not particularly enjoy, but that caused me no particular moral discomfort. The worms died almost instantly when dropped into the near-boiling water. And, after all, they were just worms.

One afternoon I was asked to do something different. A scientist at another university was undertaking similar studies on desert animals and had arranged for some of his chemical analysis to be done in our laboratory. Shortly thereafter a large cardboard box arrived air express from Utah containing a veritable menagerie: several kinds of insects, a pair of pale scorpions, a lizard about six inches long, a small snake, and a lovely gray mouse. The task of converting the animals to vials of clear liquid was delegated to me.

I had dumped more than a few live lobsters into boiling pots with nothing more than the slightest moral twinge, and I did not expect to be bothered by the procedures. For some reason, it made sense to start with the smallest and most primitive of the animals. I began with the crickets, which, like the worms, died almost immediately when I dropped them into the hot distilled water. No problem. Next, the arthropods. In the

several days that they had been in the lab, I had come to like the scorpions. They had more body mass than the insects and took a little longer to die when I dropped them in the beaker. I began to wonder about what I was doing.

The lizard was the first vertebrate. My stomach turned queasy, I began to sweat, and my hands shook when I dropped it into the near-boiling water. The lizard did not die quickly. It thrashed about in the hot liquid for 10 or 15 seconds before becoming still.

The snake was an elegant racer probably about a year old. I have always been fascinated by snakes. I collected them as a kid, and I still deal with them as one of the handful of comparative psychologists who study ophidian behavior. I drank a slow cup of coffee between the lizard and the snake, putting off the inevitable as long as I could. More shaky hands, a sweaty brow, a queasy stomach. More thrashing reptile reduced to an inert carcass and molecules suspended in solution.

Something was clearly wrong. I was not upset by a logical pang of conscience telling me that I was doing something immoral; it was years later that I was drawn to philosophical treatises by animal advocates. No, my response was purely visceral, a physical nausea akin to the body's involuntary shudder in response to the odor of putrification.

Finally, the mouse. I weighed the mouse, poured the appropriate amount of distilled water into the beaker, and lighted the Bunsen burner. As the water approached the 180 degree mark, it dawned on me that I simply could not "do" the mouse. I turned off the flame and, with trepidation and relief, walked into the office of the laboratory manager, thinking that my career as a graduate student was over. I said that I had made almost all of the extracts, but that I would not do the mouse. Much to his credit, the supervisor did not ask me to continue. He wound up boiling the mouse.

I have thought about my predicament that day many times over the years. I am now struck by the similarity between my task that afternoon and the plight of the subjects in Stanley Milgram's infamous obedience experiments. The hapless participants in his studies were instructed to administer a series of electrical shocks of increasing intensity to other subjects in an adjacent room. As all introductory psychology students know, the majority of people in the experiment administered levels of shock that they thought would be extremely painful, if not lethal. Like Milgram's subjects, I was confronted with a series of escalating choice points, based on phylogenetic status rather than shock intensity. The difference between the Milgram experiment and my situation was that in his study the shocks were a ruse; the subjects were really confederates of the experimenter. In my laboratory, the animals really died.

I was not the only member of my graduate school cohort who struggled with the moral consequences of their research. My friend Ron Neibor had a bigger problem than I did. He worked with cats. The focus of Neibor's dissertation was how the brain reorganizes itself after injury, a topic that was, unlike my explorations in chemical ecology, quite relevant to human health and well-being. Neibor did not choose cats because of any special curiosity about feline behavior. I suspect he would rather have worked with mice or rats. Cats, unfortunately, were the best model for the neural mechanisms that were his real interest. He employed a time-honored neuroscience technique; he surgically destroyed parts of the brains of his animals and observed the recovery of behavioral function over a period of months.

The problem was that Neibor liked his cats. His study lasted over a year, during which time he became quite attached to the two dozen animals in his control and experimental groups.

Even on weekends and holidays he would drive to the lab, release his cats from their cages and play with them for hours. (This was long before federal regulations decreed that a few laboratory species be given the opportunity for daily exercise.) He thought of them as individuals. He talked about them, and he treated them more like pets than research animals.

His experimental protocol required that he confirm the location of the neurological lesions in animals in the experimental group through examination of their brain tissue. Part of this procedure, technically referred to as perfusion, is not pleasant under the best of circumstances. Each animal is injected with a lethal dose of anesthetic. Formalin is pumped through its veins via the heart, and the head is severed from the body. Heavy steel pliers are used to chip away the skull so that the hardened brain can be extracted and sliced into thin sections for microscopic analysis.

It took several weeks for Neibor to perfuse all of the cats in the experimental group. His personality changed. A naturally genuine and warmhearted person, he became tense, withdrawn, shaky. Several graduate students working in his lab became concerned about his mental state, and they offered to perfuse his cats for him. Neibor refused, unwilling to dodge the moral consequences of his research. He did not talk very much during the weeks he was "sacrificing" his cats. Sometimes I noticed that his eyes were red, and he would look down as we passed in the halls.

These incidents provoked me to ask myself questions that I continue to struggle with two decades later. Is there really a difference between researchers who kill mice in the name of science and the legions of good people who smash their spines with snap traps or slowly poison them with D-Con because they prefer not to share their houses with small rodents? Why was it easy for me to plunge the crickets into hot water, hard for me to do the same with the lizard, and impossible for me to do it to the mouse? Was it a matter of size, phylogenetic status, nervous system development, or simply attractiveness (the mouse was really cute)? Would Neibor's plight have been any different if his experimental subjects had been rats? What were the relative roles of logic and sentimentality underlying the moral confusion that nagged Neibor and me?

The moral problems of animal researchers can be traced to Charles Darwin, who, incidentally, had personal qualms about vivisection. The Cartesian argument that humans and animals are fundamentally different was persuasive in the seventeenth century. To Descartes, animals were biological machines. Thus early physiologists interested in the mechanics of blood circulation had no more ethical qualms about nailing a live dog to a board prior to dissection than we might about ripping memory chips from a balky computer. Evolution, on the other hand, implies phyletic continuity—not just in anatomy and physiology, but also in behavior and mental experience. And, in the halls at the annual meeting of the Animal Behavior Society, there is serious talk these days of deception, intention, and consciousness among chickens and monkeys. (One of the ironies of the animal-research debate is that animal-rights activists often invoke recent discoveries about the mental capacities of animals when arguing against the very research that has uncovered these abilities.)

There are ethical implications to the notion of phylogenetic continuity of mental experience. An obvious paradox arises—the more a species is like us in its physiology, the more useful a model it is for human biomedical problems. But, precisely *because* a species resembles us biologically, the more likely it is that it experiences similar mental states. In short, the more justified the use of a species on scientific grounds, the less justified is its use on moral grounds.

There is a related problem that I struggle with as an animal researcher. I call my version "E.T.'s dilemma," though the central issue has been described under other labels by ethicists. At the end of Steven Spielberg's well-known film, E.T.'s mother returns to Earth to retrieve her errant son, a lovable alien who has spent several days running around southern California with his

new friend, Elliot. There is a sentimental parting scene. Elliot pleads with E.T. "Stay?" he asks. E.T. wistfully shakes his head and croaks to Elliot, "Come?" But, both know that each must return to his own world. E.T. and his mother take off back to Zork, and Elliot returns to life in the suburbs.

Suppose for a minute that the film ends differently. Again, Elliot declines the invitation to join E.T. The extraterrestrial, however, does not take no for an answer. He grabs the boy by the arm and drags him kicking and screaming into the ship. The doors close, and they zoom off to Zork. An AIDS-like epidemic has struck the home planet, and humans are the best animal model. The question is: Does E.T. have the right to abduct Elliot to be used as the subject of research aimed at developing a vaccine to protect the Zorkians? Clearly, they are intellectually and spiritually advanced over humans. (E.T. fashioned a phone out of junk to call home and made a dead flower blossom.) Research with animals is based on the premise that a "superior" species has the right to breed, kidnap, or kill members of "lesser" species for the advancement of knowledge. Though it violates my moral intuition, I see no way around the conclusion that E.T. has the right to abduct Elliot for his research. To do otherwise gives credence to the charge by animal-activist philosophers like Peter Singer and Tom Regan that our use of animals reflects self-serving speciesism, pure and simple.

The problem raised by E.T. is essentially that of ethical consistency. But, we do not have to turn to hypothetical space aliens to find inconsistencies associated with animal research. Take, for example, the moral status of mice in research facilities. Several years ago, I spent a sabbatical year working in the Laboratory of Reptile Ethology at the University of Tennessee. The laboratory is located on the third floor of the Walters Life Sciences Building, a state-of-the-art facility that houses about fifteen thousand mice each year along with a smattering of other research animals. The mice are housed in antiseptic rooms in the basement and are cared for by a fully certified staff. As is standard practice at universities receiving federal funds, each project involving animal subjects is reviewed by the University of Tennessee Institutional Animal Care and Use Committee, whose members are charged with weighing the potential benefits and costs of the experiments. All of the mice in the building belong to the same species, and they appear virtually identical. In terms of moral status, however, they belong to quite different categories.

The vast majority of the mice in Walters are good mice, the subjects of the hundreds of biomedical and behavioral experiments conducted by faculty, postdoctoral researchers, and graduate students working in the building. I suspect that the bulk of this research is directly or indirectly related to the solution of biomedical problems that afflict our species. Though they do not have any voice in the matter, these animals live and die for our benefit. They are now covered under the federal Animal Welfare Act and are entitled to a certain legal status not granted the mice in your home or even to your dog. (A judge in Oklahoma once threw out a charge against a cockfighter, ruling that roosters were not covered under the state animal-cruelty statutes because chickens were not animals. Lest we judge the judge too harshly, note that the Animal Welfare Act in essence also denies that mice and rats are animals, as they are excluded from coverage under the act. Recently a federal judge ruled that the exclusion of rodents under the law, while convenient for the research community, was arbitrary and illogical, although this matter is currently under appeal.)

There are also bad mice in Walters. The bad mice are pests, free-ranging creatures that can occasionally be glimpsed scurrying down the gleaming fluorescent corridors. These animals are a potential threat in an environment in which there is a premium on cleanliness and in which great care is taken to prevent cross contamination between rooms within the animal colony. These animals must be eliminated.

The staff of the animal facility has tried a number of different techniques to eradicate the bad mice. Household snap traps were found ineffective, and the staff was reluctant to use poison for fear of contaminating research animals. "Sticky traps" came to be the preferred method of rodent capture. Sticky traps are squares of cardboard coated with adhesive and imbued with a chemical mouse attractant, hence their alternate name, glue boards. The traps are placed in areas that pest mice frequent and are checked each morning. When a mouse steps on the trap, there is no escape; it only becomes more stuck as it struggles to free itself. Even though there is no poison embedded in the adhesive, over half of the mice found on the traps are dead, the result of struggle and stress. The rest are immediately killed by the staff.

Death by glue board is not humane, and I suspect that most animal-care committees would be reluctant to approve a study in which mice were glued to pieces of cardboard and left overnight. Thus there exists a peculiar situation in which treatment that is unacceptable for one category of animals is prescribed for animals of the same species that are of a different *moral* type. The irony of the situation is further compounded by the source of the bad mice. The building does not have a problem with wild mice invading the premises. The pests are virtually always good mice that have escaped, an inevitability in a facility housing many thousands of animals. As a staff member once said to me, "Once an animal hits the floor, it is a pest."

There is a third category of mice in the building, which is neither good nor bad. This category consists of mice that are food. The laboratory in which I worked specializes in the study of snake behavior. Most of the research animals were garter snakes, which thrive on a diet of worms and small fish. We did, however, keep some rat snakes and small boa constrictors, which need mammalian prey in order to thrive, and these mammals were mice ranging in size from newborns ("pinkies") to adults. Animal-care committees do not typically regulate the use of mice as snake food. After all, many reptiles will only eat live prey. Not providing them with an adequate diet of live rodents would ultimately result in their starvation, a clear violation of our ethical responsibilities.

In some experiments the role of a mouse as food or subject becomes clouded. Suppose Professor X wants to study the anti-predator strategies of mice. She plans to introduce live mice into a rattlesnake's cage and videotape the encounters between predator and prey. Now from the point of view of the mouse, there is little difference between being dropped into a rattler's cage for the purpose of being eaten or for the purpose of a study of its defensive responses. From a legal point of view, however, these are quite different situations. If Professor X presents the mouse to the snake simply to provide her research animal with its weekly meal, she does not need to secure prior permission from the animal-care committee. If her motivation is to study how the mouse defends itself, she had best begin filling out the request forms. In this case, the moral and legal status of the animal hinges not on species, brain size, or even the amount of suffering it might be expected to experience, but on its label—pest, food, or research subject.

Animal-rights activists will no doubt take satisfaction in knowing that I am not alone in squirming when these issues come up over beers late at night at scientific conferences. But animal activists have their own problems with moral coherence. I suspect that it was my own unease with these issues that compelled me to venture out of ethology, my academic home territory, and foray into ethnology. I became interested in the lives and worldviews of animal activists— people who would like to put scientists like me out of business, people who change their lives because of an idea. For three years, I attended animal-rights demonstrations and meetings, accumulated philosophical treatises and political pamphlets, and, most important, interviewed several dozen activists in their homes.

This essay is not the place to describe the methods and results of these studies. Suffice it to say that the animal activists I interviewed rarely fit the stereotypes in which they are sometimes cast by scientists, and I was impressed by their intelligence, sincerity, and dedication. One aspect of my findings, though, is germane here. For many activists the effort at consistency between belief and behavior affected almost all aspects of their lives—what they wore and ate, who their friends and lovers were, their thoughts during the day and dreams at night. This effort took many forms. Several spoke of feeling guilty when they drove their cars down the street, knowing that the tires were made from animal products and that bugs would inexorably be squashed on their windshields. One man told me of his love of softball. But, while he had found an adequate plastic glove, there was no getting around the fact that good softballs are covered with the skin of cattle and horses. In describing her attempts at consistency, one activist told me, "I don't use toxic chemicals on my dog to get rid of fleas. Instead I try to pick them off and release them outside. I know they do not feel pain or anything, but I feel it is important to be consistent. If I draw the line somewhere between fish and mollusks, it isn't going to make sense."

But just like animal researchers, animal activists can rarely escape the moral ambiguities inherent in even seemingly benevolent relations with other species. Take pets. I was introduced to the moral problems of pet keeping in a curious manner. A friend of mine who is an animal activist told me that she had received a complaint about me from a fellow activist. She was told that I was procuring kittens from our local animal shelter and feeding them to Sam, my son's pet boa constrictor. My first response was laughter at a groundless charge. Sam was just a baby snake, much too small to swallow even the littlest kitten. The incident did, however, provoke me to consider the ethics of feeding the animals we keep in our homes as pets.

The person who made the charge against me has four cats that wander at will in her house and in the surrounding woods. Domestic cats, no less than their larger cousins, are carnivores. Unlike humans and even dogs, they need meat to live healthy and happy lives. My accuser was a vegetarian for whom, in the language of the movement, "meat stinks." Prisoners of their biological constitution, her cats did not share her personal aversion to flesh. Thus, while diligently avoiding the meat counter for herself, she was, nonetheless, obligated to ponder the relative merits of the flesh of cow, turkey, horse, and fish when selecting meals for her pets. Even bags of dried cat food are advertised as containing fresh meat. She was driven by love of her cats to become an unwitting participant in the factory farm system that she was fighting.

Feline dietary habits are related to another moral quagmire—the predation problem. Cats like to kill things. They are inveterate hunters even if amply supplied with the tastiest of commercial fare. Two ecologists recently asked a group of English cat owners to record as best they could the number of mammals and birds that their pets killed over a period of months. They concluded that the five million domestic cats in Britain kill at least seventy million small animals each year, an average of fourteen prey animals per cat. There are about sixty-five million pet cats in the United States, and I do not have to spell out the dangers these animals represent to the birds, chipmunks, and lizards of America. It is even possible that more furry and feathered creatures die in the claws of cats owned by animal activists than in all of the research laboratories in the United States. The predation problem is particularly acute for cat owners who, with all good intentions, offer handouts to wild birds. With sunflower seeds and beef suet, they inadvertently lure their avian friends to within a pounce of their coldly efficient pets.

Other moral complexities confront animal advocates who choose to enjoy the comfort of "companion animals." Like it or not, most pets are subservient creatures, ultimately maintained for the amusement and comfort they afford their owners. This fact has not escaped more sophisticated activists who struggle with the moral implications of *owning* a member of another species. This issue was addressed by one of the activists I interviewed.

Question: Do you have pets now?

Answer: No.

Question: For philosophical reasons?

Answer: Yes. Absolutely. I would love to have a pet. I grew up with the companionship of a dog and a cat and know that it is a real special thing. But I also think that it is wrong. Animals are not here for our happiness. Up until recently I had a parrot. I would leave him free to fly around my room. One day I just looked at him and said to myself, "This is wrong. It wants to be free." I just took it out in the backyard and let it go—even though it was hand-fed and trained and I knew it wouldn't survive in the wild. Since then I have thought that letting him free was not the best thing for the bird—though I felt really good when it flew up and into a tree for the first time it had ever been able to fly really high. It was great, amazing. I was really happy to see that. I assume that he probably starved to death. It may have been more something that I was doing for myself than for the bird.

Enough said.

Animal activists use the phrase "the dreaded comparison" when pointing out the similarity between the rhetoric used by nineteenth-century advocates of slavery and twentieth-century defenders of animal research. But the animal-rights movement may have its own "dreaded comparison" in the issue of abortion. Several years ago I attended a public lecture given by Ingrid Newkirk, co-founder of People for the Ethical Treatment of Animals. Her formal presentation was followed by the obligatory question-and-answer period that was dominated by hostile challenges from animal husbandry students from a local agriculture college. Newkirk, as might be expected from one who spends considerable time in public forums, easily handled the questions and comments from the more skeptical members of the audience. Predictably, the issue of where one draws the proverbial line was thrown at the speaker ("Ms. Newkirk . . . Do you think flies and mosquitoes have rights?"). Her answer was direct: "We are concerned with *all innocent life.*"

I thought about her answer while returning home that night. At some point during the long drive it occurred to me that there might be a natural affinity between the two social movements in our society that proclaim support for the rights of the innocent. I began to query my interviewees about their attitudes toward abortion. Of the two dozen animal activists I interviewed, all but two supported "a woman's right to choose." Some of the activists were completely comfortable with their stance on abortion; in some cases they simply denied that there is any association between the two issues. ("I simply fail to see the connection between abortion and animal rights.") Others found their own pro-choice views problematic ("Oh, please don't ask me about abortion. I am so confused about it"). In only one case did a person tell me that he had shifted from "pro-choice" to "pro-life" as a result of his beliefs about the moral status of animals.

I should not have been surprised at this pattern. There have been a half-dozen or so sociological studies of the animal-rights movement. All have reported two salient demographic facts. Somewhere between two-thirds and three-fourths of animal activists are women, and, as a group, they tend to identify with the liberal side of the political spectrum. Liberal women rarely ally themselves with the right-to-life movement.

The divisiveness of the abortion issue among animal activists is illustrated by the following exchange between animal-rights activists, which recently arrived in my office through the miracle of electronic mail. It was posted on AR-TALK, an animal-rights computer bulletin board:

Message: I'd be very surprised if there isn't a positive correlation between "in favor of animal rights and protection" and "pro-choice attitudes" for the simple reason that intelligent, reasonable, and humane people will tend to support both.

Response 1: In other words, for intelligent, reasonable, and humane people, the unborn human child doesn't even count as much as an animal and thus deserves no protection?

Response 2: I would like to put in my own two-cents' worth. I agree with those who want to

keep the abortion issue out of AR-TALK. I am not against open discussion of the issue of abortion, but it is *not* the same question as whether animals have "rights," whether humans are or are not to have pets, eat meat, experiment with animals, etc.

Though a pro-choice advocate myself, I find the supposition that a person and a pigeon share more in terms of moral status than a person and a six-month-old fetus troubling, if not bizarre. Some of the major philosophical thinkers behind the animal-protection movement such as Peter Singer, Tom Regan, and Steven Sapontzis do a reasonable job of arguing that there is a moral distinction between the interests of animals and those of a fetus. But the intellectual shucking and jiving of the philosophers notwithstanding, I would not be surprised to find that pro-choice animal activists sometimes feel the same nagging discomfort I experience late at night when contemplating the fate of Elliot in the scaly hands of E.T.

I once heard Andrew Rowan, the author of *Of Mice, Models, and Men*, say, "The only thing consistent about human-animal relations is paradox." Twentieth-century history offers a splendid example of "Rowan's Principle"—the Nazi animal-protection movement. Though not generally known, Adolf Hitler came close to being an animal-rights activist. A strict vegetarian, he objected to vivisection and once stated that hunting and horse racing were the "last remnants of a dead feudal world." His views on the treatment of animals were apparently shared by many of the Nazi ruling elite. Heinrich Himmler was "hysterical" in his opposition to hunting, and in one of history's great ironies, Hermann Göring wrote, "I will commit to concentration camps those who still think they can continue to treat animals as property."

This obscure historical footnote was brought to light in a remarkable paper published recently in the journal *Anthrozoös* by Arnold Arluke and Boria Sax, respectively an anthropologist and a linguist. In methodical and chilling fashion, Arluke and Sax chronicle the rise of the animal-protection movement that flourished in Germany in the 1930s and

1940s under the leadership of the Nazi party. Strict laws governing animal research and the slaughter of animals for food were enacted. An endangered-species act was passed by the German legislature. The Nazis sponsored an early international conference on animal protection. The list goes on.

What are we to make of a culture in which government officials were more concerned with the treatment of lobsters in restaurants than genocide, in which vivisection was abhorred, yet torturous medical "experimentation" on humans was condoned? Surely, Nazi animal protectionism is paradoxical. Not so for Professors Arluke and Sax. They argue that when one understands the cultural and intellectual milieu of pre-war Germany, the contradictions of Nazi animal advocacy become more apparent than real. They write, "Our analysis raises what is to most contemporaries a troubling and unsavory contradiction, namely, that Establishment concern for animals in Nazi Germany was combined with disregard for human life. This paradox vanishes, however, if we see that the treatment of animals under the Third Reich really tells us about the treatment of humans and the cultural rules and the problems of human society."

While I admire the elegance of their analysis, I beg to differ. We can indeed follow the twisted logic that enabled the Nazis to construct a moral taxonomy in which some animals were endowed with higher moral status than some people. But does this really cause the paradox of a humane Hitler to vanish? Not for me. I suggest that Nazi animal protectionism is the ultimate paradox, one that we *should not* explain away for it may be the central metaphor haunting all of our relations with other species. Is a vegetarian Hitler any more paradoxical than the pain physiologist who administers electrical shocks to devocalized beagles in the quest for a better analgesia during the day but who is met at the door by his faithful cocker spaniel when he returns home from his laboratory? Or the animal-rights/vegetarian cat owner?

Neither animal researchers nor animal activists inhabit a tidy moral universe. The different worldviews of animal-rights activists and scientists often make communication between scientists and activists about as productive as discussions between evolutionary biologists and creationists. In words that apply all too aptly to the animal-research issue, Mary Midgely described the difficulty of discussion between moral vegetarians and meat-eaters: "The symbolism of meat-eating is never neutral. To himself, the meat-eater seems to be eating life. To the vegetarian, he seems to be eating death. There is a kind of gestalt-shift between the two positions which makes it hard to change and hard to raise questions on the matter at all without becoming embattled."

Animal-rights supporters are often portrayed by their opponents among scientists as hyper-emotional and anti-intellectual Luddites who value puppies and baby seals over healthy human children. Research with animals, says the scientist, is rarely more painful than the pervasive cruelty of nature. Besides, it is our only avenue for alleviating the disease and pestilence that afflicts our own and other species.

Not so, claims the activist. Scientists are cold and unfeeling, so blinded by years of socialization in laboratories and classrooms that they cannot see the suffering before their eyes or hear the cries of their innocent victims. For researchers, animals are Cartesian automata, objects to be used in the unending quest for fame, federal funds, and trivial knowledge. Biomedical research does not relieve suffering. It causes it. Further, animal research doesn't work—you cannot generalize from mice to men. And the scientific use of non-consenting individuals, be it animals or humans, is an ill-gotten gain. Whether it works or not is irrelevant.

In reality, both are right—and wrong. True, most biomedical scientists I know aspire to tenure, full professorships, editorial boards, and a share of federal research funds. But they are drawn to animals from curiosity (not a trivial motive for scientists), a desire to make human life better, or a genuine reverence for the natural world.

True, too, many animal activists tend to empathize viscerally with the suffering that they see as the result of situations unfairly perpetrated on the innocent. It is also true that experiments on kittens and dogs are more likely to bring out the protesters than research on snakes. But in my view it is a mistake to dismiss the moral sensibilities of animal activists as "mere emotionalism." The philosophical underpinnings of the movement are rooted in cold, rigorous logic and are not as easy to refute as many scientists like to think. Contrary to stereotype, most activists do not scarf down cheeseburgers at McDonalds between demonstrations or wear leather shoes. Indeed, they labor under a particularly heavy personal moral burden.

Disagreements about the treatment of animals in research ultimately stem from our tendency to think simply about complex problems. Decisions about the use of other species are extraordinarily intricate, rooted more in the peculiarities of human psychology than in pure reason. Inevitably, the result is paradox and inconsistency. It is a complicated world for all but the true believers.

When asked where I stand on the animal-research issue, I have taken to responding with Strachan Donnelley's phrase, "the troubled middle." Granted, the troubled middle is not a comfortable place to be. But, for most of us, neither are the alternatives.

Donna J. Haraway

Cloning Mutts, Saving Tigers

Two points need to be highlighted at the outset. First, responsible dog breeding is a cottage industry, made up largely of amateur communities and individuals. These people are not scientific or medical professionals, but they breed modest numbers of dogs at considerable cost to themselves over many years and with impressive dedication and passion. Second, "lay" people who breed dogs are often solidly knowledgeable about science, technology, and veterinary medicine, often self-educated, and often effective actors in technoculture.

The efforts of Linda Weisser and Catherine de la Cruz, West Coast health activists and breeders of Great Pyrenees livestock guardian dogs, to reshape the habits of Pyr breeders in dealing with canine hip dysplasia are good examples of this technosavvy and its biological-ethical demands. Weisser insists that the moral center of dog breeding is the breed, that is, the dogs themselves, as both specialized kinds and as real individuals to whom all the participants in Pyr worlds have an obligation. The obligation is to work so that the dogs and their people flourish over as long a time as possible. Hers is an "other-centered" ethics of a resolutely antiromantic sort that despises both anthropomorphism and anthropocentrism as a framework for practicing "love of the breed."

What counts as "improving the breed" in dogland is controversial, to say the least. But since the founding in 1966 of the Orthopedic Foundation for Animals (OFA), a closed registry and voluntary diagnostic service addressing the problem of canine hip dysplasia, standards of good breeding practice require at least X-raying potential mates for the soundness of their hips. This practice, however, even coupled with conscientious breeders' mating only dogs whose hips

are rated good or excellent by OFA, cannot seriously reduce the incidence of this complex genetic-developmental condition for two reasons. First, the registry is voluntary and closed. Breeders cannot get the records of problems in someone else's dogs, and breeders with a questionable dog do not have to get an X-ray to be able to register that dog's offspring with the American Kennel Club or other registry. Second and just as bad, if only potential mates are X-rayed and archived, then the rest of the relatives (littermates, aunts and uncles, and so forth) go unrecorded. People like Weisser and de la Cruz argue that open registries with complete pedigrees and fully disclosed health records for as many relatives as possible, all accessible to the community of practice, are needed. That is what biological-technical-ethical "love of the breed" requires.

This is also far from standard current practice. How can a community be led to a better practice, especially when something like full disclosure of genetic problems can lead to terrible criticism and even ostracism by those with too much to hide or those who simply do not know any better? First, an open registry in the United States for canine genetic diseases exists. The Institute for Genetic Disease Control in Animals (GDC, www.vetmed.ucdavis.edu/gdc/gdc. html), founded in 1990 at the University of California at Davis veterinary school, is modeled after the Swedish Kennel Club's open registry. GDC tracks several orthopedic and soft tissue diseases. Listing suspected carriers and affected animals and maintaining breed-specific registries and research databases as well as all-breed registries, the GDC issues a KinReport™ to individuals with a valid reason for inquiring. However, GDC faces a problem that could end the service in the near future: too few dog people use the registry, and the organization is in financial trouble. In 2001, in coalition with progressive breeders and breed groups, GDC launched a major effort to develop a grassroots advocacy program to support its work. It needs five thousand breeders and owners who will use the service and work to promote the open registry.

Weisser and de la Cruz are among the most active Great Pyrenees breeders working to get their peers to use GDC instead of a closed registry. Biology and ethics are lived in concert in this emergent dogland biosociality. What an open registry implies, however, makes for an uphill battle. In August 2001, de la Cruz got "quarterly reports from both OFA and GDC. Discouraging. There were 45 Pyrs listed as cleared by OFA and only *three* from GDC. . . . I would think any breeder would be proud to be able to point to a product of her breeding and say, 'That dog is producing sounder dogs than the breed average.' Instead we continue to see ads for the numbers of champions produced, the number of shows won. . . . I would love to hear from other breeders. Why don't you use the GDC?" (Great Pyrenee Discussion List [Pyr-L@apple.ease.lsoft.com], 17 August 2001). There followed one of many extended discussions on Pyr-L, along with behind-the-scenes work, in which de la Cruz, Weisser, and a few others educated, exhorted, and otherwise tried to make a difference for their breed. The GDC is not a technical fix; it is a biologically and technologically sophisticated, whole-dog approach that requires difficult changes in human practice for dog well-being. Despite Weisser's and de la Cruz's well-earned, enviable alpha-bitch status, they may lose this battle, and dogland may lose the whole apparatus of the GDC.

Meanwhile, the gold rush for commercially viable parental verification DNA markers and DNA tests for individual genetic diseases goes on with gusto, with all the collaborations of biotech companies, academic institutions, and individual researchers that we know from two-legged geneticists. This is an example of the distance between an ethics of flourishing and the rhetoric of bioethics prevalent in dogland, where gene-as-code (and gene tests for diagnosis and gene therapies as solution) holds sway, as it does in so much current technoculture.

The point of introducing Weisser and de la Cruz's struggle for the open registry is not only to support their effort, in my less-than-neutral ethnographic posture, but also to stress the technosavvy of "lay" dog people as they live within genetic biosociality. They read widely, are knowledgeable about international dog cultures, take on-line genetics courses from a major veterinary school, follow medical and veterinary literatures, support wolf reintroduction projects, keep track of Pyrs who might protect livestock on adjoining ranches, engage in conservation politics broadly, and otherwise live well-examined lives in technoculture. Their expertise and action are planted in the soil of generations of particular dogs, whom they know in intimate detail as kin and kind. What do such people do when they meet emergent demands not only to deal with genetic disease but also to breed for canine genetic diversity in the context of global biodiversity science and politics?

Saving Tigers

In spite of the long history of population genetics and its importance for the modern theory of natural selection, genetic diversity concerns are news—and hard-to-digest news—for most dog people. Why? Genetics culture for both professionals and nonprofessionals, especially but not only in the United States, has been shaped by medical genetics. Human genetic disease is the moral, technoscientific, ideological, and financial center of the medical genetics universe. Typological thinking reigns almost unchecked in this universe, and nuanced views of developmental biology, behavioral ecology, and genes as nodes in dynamic and multivectorial fields of vital interactions are only some of the crash victims of high-octane medical genetics fuels and gene-jockey racing careers.

Evolutionary biology, biosocial ecology, population biology, and population genetics (not to mention history of science, political economy, and cultural anthropology) have played a woefully small role in shaping public and professional genetic imaginations and all too small a role in drawing the big money for genetic research. In dog worlds, my preliminary research turns up millions of dollars in grants going into genetic disease research, though this is peanuts compared to the dollars funneled into genetic research in organisms such as mice that conventionally are models for human diseases. Dog genetics gets more money as it is shown that genome homologies make canines ideal for understanding human conditions such as narcolepsy, bleeding disorders, and retinal degeneration. I find only thousands of dollars (and lots of volunteer time from professionals and lay collaborators) going into canine genetic diversity research.

The pioneering scientists in canine genetic diversity in the early 1980s were Europeans such as the Austrian Walter Schleger and the Swede Per-Erik Sundgren. The most demanding draft policy for regulating breeders' practices in the interest of genetic diversity was the Central Breeding Policy of the Dutch Kennel Club (15 March 2001). Unlike the American Kennel Club's *AKC Gazette*, the Swedish Kennel Club's *Hundsport* regularly discusses popular sire effects and damage to dogs from inbreeding (the interbreeding of closely related individuals) and linebreeding (the interbreeding of individuals within a single line of descent).

The emergence of genetic diversity concerns in dog worlds makes sense as a wavelet in the set of breakers constituting transnational, globalizing biological and cultural diversity discourses, in which genomes are major players. The emergence since the 1980s of biodiversity discourses, environmentalisms, and sustainability doctrines of every political color on the agendas of nongovernmental organizations and of institutions such as the World Bank, the International Union for the Conservation of Nature and Natural Resources, and the Organization for Economic Cooperation and Development has been crucial. The notoriously problematic politics and the natural-cultural complexity of diversity discourses require a shelf of books, some of which have been written. I am compelled by the *irreducible* complexity—moral, political, cultural, and scientific—of diversity discourses, including those leashed to the genomes and gene pools of purebred dogs and their canine relatives in and out of "nature."

The last few paragraphs are preparation for logging onto the Canine Diversity Project website, www.magma.ca/~kaitlin/diverse.html, originally owned by Dr. John Armstrong, a lover of standard and miniature poodles and a faculty member in the Department of Biology at the University of Ottawa, who died on 26 August 2001. Armstrong widely distributed his analyses of the effects of a popular sire and a particular kennel on standard poodles. Also owner of the listserv CANGEN-L, or the Canine Genetics Discussion Group, dedicated to canine genetics and especially genetic diversity concerns, Armstrong conducted collaborative research with dog health and genetics activists to study whether longevity is correlated to the degree of inbreeding. Their conclusion: it is. Aiming, according to his introductory sentence, to draw dog breeders' attention to "the dangers of inbreeding and the overuse of popular sires," Armstrong started the Canine Diversity Project website in 1997. It is used by at least several hundred dog people of many nationalities, and from January 2000 to June 2001, it registered more than thirty thousand log-ons.

Linda Weisser has been a frequent visitor to and a vociferous advocate of this website, but she is not a true believer in all the positions that the population biologists on CANGEN-L advocate. Her complexity is as interesting as that of the diversity discourses she evaluates in the light of her experience with her breed. Along with Weisser and other dog people, I have learned a tremendous amount from the website. I appreciate its quality of information, the controversies it has engaged, its care for dogs and people, its range of material, and its commitments to issues. Professionally, I am also acutely alert to the semiotics—the meaning-making machinery—of the Canine Diversity Project website.

Animated by a mission, the site draws its users into its reform agenda. Some of the rhetorical devices are classic American tropes rooted in popular self-help practices and evangelical Protestant witness, devices so ingrained in U.S. culture that few users would be conscious of their history. For example, right after the introductory paragraph with the initial link terms, the website leads its users into a section called "How You Can Help." The question is like those of advertising and preaching—Have you been saved? Have you taken the Immune Power pledge (to quote the slogan from an ad for a vitamin formulation in the 1980s)? Or, as the Canine Diversity Project puts the query, "Ask the Question—Do you need a 'Breed Survival Plan'?" This is the stuff of subject-reconstituting conversion and conviction discourse.

The first four highlighted linkage words in the opening paragraphs of the website are "popular sires," a common term for many years in purebred dog talk about the overuse of certain stud dogs and the consequent spreading of genetic disease; "Species Survival Plans," a term that makes a new link for dog breeders to zoos and the preservation of endangered species; "wild cousins," which places dogs with their taxonomic kin and reinforces the consideration of purebreds within the family of natural (in the sense of "wild") and frequently endangered species; and "inherited disease," in last place on the list and of concern primarily because a high incidence of double autosomal recessives for particular diseases is an index of lots of homozygosity in purebred dog genomes. Such high incidences of double recessives are related to excessive inbreeding and linebreeding and especially to overuse of popular sires, which are diversity-depleting practices. But, as I read it, the soul of the website is diversity itself in the semiotic framework of evolutionary biology, biodiversity, and biophilia, not diversity as an instrument for solving the problem of genetic disease. These two values are not mutually exclusive; they are complementary. But priority matters. In that sense, "breeds" become like endangered species, inviting the apparatus of apocalyptic wildlife biology.

Constructed as a teaching instrument, the website constructs its audience as engaged lay breeders and other committed dog people. These are the subjects invited to declare for a breed survival plan. Secondarily, scientists might learn from using the site, but they are more teachers here than researchers or students. Nonetheless, the site features plenty of boundary objects linking lay and professional communities of practice. Further, a website by its nature resists reduction to single purposes and dominating tropes. Links lead to many places; these paths are explored by users within the webs spun by designers, but rapidly spiraling out of such control. The Internet is hardly infinitely open, but its degrees of semiotic freedom are many.

"Popular sires" is sufficiently recognized that the linking term would appeal to most dog people open to thinking about genetic diversity. For one thing, the link keeps *dogs* as the principal focus of attention and does not launch the user into a universe of marvelous creatures in exotic habitats—creatures whose utility as models for dogs is hard for many breeders to swallow, even those interested in such nondog organisms and ecologies in other contexts. "Species Survival Plans," on the other hand, opens up controversial metaphoric and practical universes for breeders of purebred dogs and, if taken seriously, would require major changes in ways of thinking and acting. The first obvious point is that "survival plans" connote that something is endangered. The line between a secular crisis and a sacred apocalypse is thin in American discourse, where millennial matters are written into the fabric of the national imagination, from the first Puritan City on a Hill to *Star Trek* and its sequelae. The second obvious point is that the prominent role given to species survival plans on the Canine Diversity Project website invites a reproductive tie between natural species and purebred dogs. In this mongrelizing tie, the natural and the technical keep close company, semiotically and materially.

To illustrate, I will dwell on the material on my computer screen in the spring of 2000 after

I clicked on "Species Survival Plan" (SSP) and followed up with a click on "Introduction to a Species Survival Plan." I am teleported to the website for the Tiger Information Center, and, appreciating a face-front photo of two imposing tigers crossing a stream, I encounter a paper titled "Regional and Global Management of Tigers," by R. Tilson, K. Taylor-Holzer, and G. Brady. Lots of dog people love cats, contrary to stereotypes about folks being either canine or feline in their affections. But tigers in the world's zoos and in shrunken "forest patches spread from India across China to the Russian Far East and south to Indonesia" *are* a leap out of the kennel and the show ring or herding trials. I learn that three of the eight subspecies of tigers are extinct, a fourth is on the brink, and all the wild populations are stressed. Ideally, the goal of a survival master plan for an endangered species is to create, out of existing animals in zoos and some new "founders" brought in from "nature," viable, managed, captive populations to maintain as much of the genetic diversity as possible for all of the extant subtaxa of the species. The purpose is to provide a genetic reservoir for reinforcing and reconstituting wild populations. A practical SSP, "because of space limitations generally targets 90% of genetic diversity of the wild populations for 100–200 years as a reasonable goal." I am in love with the hopefulness of that kind of reasonableness. The "zoo ark" for tigers has to be more modest because resources are too few and needs too great.

An SSP is a complex, cooperative management program of the American Zoo and Aquarium Association (AZA). What does developing and implementing an SSP involve? The short answer is, a long list of companion species of organic, organizational, and technological kinds. A minimum account of such companion species includes the World Conservation Union's specialist groups who make assessments of endangerment; member zoos with their scientists, keepers, and boards of governors; a small management group under the AZA; a database maintained as a regional studbook, using specialized software such as SPARKS (Single Population

and Records Keeping System) and its companion programs for demographic and genetic analysis, produced by the International Species Information System; funders; national governments; international bodies; local human populations; and, hardly least, the animals in danger. Crucial operations within an SSP are measurements of diversity and relatedness. One wants to know "founder importance coefficients" as tools for equalizing relative founder contributions and minimizing inbreeding. Full, accurate pedigrees are precious objects for an SSP. Mean kinship (MK) and kinship values (KV) rule mate choice in this sociobiological system. "Reinforcing" wild species requires a global apparatus of technoscientific production in which the natural and the technical have high coefficients of semiotic and practical inbreeding.

Purebred dog breeders also value deep pedigrees, and they are accustomed to evaluating matings with regard to breed standards, which is a complex, nonformulaic art. Inbreeding is not a new concern. What, then, is so challenging about an SSP as a universe of reference? The definitions of populations and founders are perhaps first. Discussions among engaged breeders on CAN-GEN—that is, people sufficiently interested in questions of genetic diversity to sign on and post to a specialized listserv—show that dog people's "lines" and "breeds" are not equivalent terms to wildlife biologists' and geneticists' "populations." The behavior associated with these different words is distinct. A dog breeder educated in the traditional mentoring practices of the fancy will attempt, through linebreeding with variable frequencies of outcrosses, to maximize the genetic or blood contribution of the truly "great dogs," which are rare and special. The great dogs are the individuals that best embody the type of the breed. The type is not a fixed thing but a living, imaginative hope and memory. Kennels are recognized for the distinctiveness of their dogs, and breeders point proudly to their kennel's founders, just as breed club documents celebrate the breed's founders. The notion of working to equalize the contributions of *all* the founders, in the population geneticists' sense, is truly odd in traditional dog breeders' discourse. Of course, an SSP, unlike nature and unlike dog breeders, is not operating with adaptational selectional criteria; the point of an SSP is to preserve diversity as such as a banked reservoir.

The SSP is a conservation management plan, not nature, however conceptualized, and not a breed's written standard or a breeder's interpretation of that standard. Like an SSP, a breed standard is also a large-scale action blueprint, but for other purposes. Some breeders talk of those purposes in capital letters as the Original Purpose of a breed. Others, less typological, are attuned to dynamic histories and evolving goals within a partly shared sense of breed history, structure, and function. These breeders are keenly aware of the need for selection on the basis of many criteria as holistically as possible in order to maintain and improve a breed's overall quality and to achieve the rare, special dogs. They take these responsibilities seriously, and they are not virgins to controversy, contradiction, and failure. They are not against learning about genetic diversity in the context of the problems they know or suspect their dogs face. Some breeders—a very few, I think—embrace genetic diversity discourse and population genetics. They worry that the foundation of their breeds might be too narrow and getting narrower.

But the breeder's art does not easily entertain adopting the mathematical and software-driven mating systems of an SSP. Several courageous breeders insist on deeper pedigrees and calculations of coefficients of inbreeding, attempting to hold those coefficients down wherever possible. But the breeders I meet are loathe to cede decisions to anything like a master plan. They do not categorize their own dogs or their breed primarily as biological populations. The dominance of specialists over local and lay communities in the SSP world does not escape dog breeders' attention. Most of the breeders I overhear squirm if the discussion stays on a theoretical population genetics level and if few of the data come from dogs rather than from, say, a Malagasy lemur

population, a laboratory-bound mouse strain, or, worse still, fruit flies. In short, breeders' discourse and genetic diversity discourse do not hybridize smoothly, at least in the F1 generation, the first generation resulting from the cross. This mating is what breeders call a "cold outcross," which, they worry, risks importing as many problems as it solves.

There is much more to the Canine Diversity Project website than the SSP links. If I had space to examine the whole website, many more openings, repulsions, inclusions, attractions, and possibilities would be evident for seeing the ways in which dog breeders, health activists, veterinarians, and geneticists relate to the question of diversity. The serious visitor to the website could get a decent elementary education in genetics, including Mendelian, medical, and population genetics. Fascinating collaborations between individual scientists and breed club health and genetics activists would emerge. The differences within dog people's ways of thinking about genetic diversity and inbreeding would be inescapable as the apocalyptic and controversial Jeffrey Bragg's "evolving breeds" and Seppala Siberian sled dogs meet John Armstrong's more modest standard poodles (and his more moderate action plan, "Genetics for Breeders: How to Produce Healthier Dogs") or Leos Kraal's and C. A. Sharp's ways of working in Australian shepherd worlds. Links would take the visitor to the extraordinary code of ethics of the Coton de Tulear Club of America and this breed's alpha-male geneticist activist, Robert Jay Russell, as well as to the on-line documents with which the Border collie website teaches genetics relevant to that talented breed. The visitor could follow links to the molecular evolution of the dog family, to updated lists of gene tests in dogs, to discussions of wolf conservation, to taxonomic debates, to accounts of a crossbreeding (to a pointer) and backcross project in dalmatians to eliminate a common genetic disease, and to reports of the importation of new African stock in basenjis to deal with genetic dilemmas. One could click one's way to discussions of infertility, stress, and herpes infections or follow links to endocrine disrupter discourse for thinking about how environmental degradation might affect dogs, as well as frogs and people, globally. Right in the middle of the Canine Diversity Project website is a bold-type invitation to join the listserv CANGEN-L, where a sometimes rough-and-tumble exchange among lay and scientific dog people has stirred up the website's pedagogical order.

So dogs, not tigers—and breeds, not endangered species—dominate on the Canine Diversity Project website. But the metaphoric, political, scientific, and practical possibilities of those first links to species survival plans attach themselves like ticks on a nice blade of grass, waiting for a passing visitor from purebred dogland. The emergent ontologies of biodiversity naturecultures are laced with new ethical demands. In many ways, the expertise and practices of dog breeders are in a relation of torque with the discourses of genetic diversity. Kin and kind mutate in these emergent apparatuses of dog (re)production. Whether companion species will flourish is at stake.

Cloning Mutts

A well-funded, media-savvy, commercially venturesome project to clone a mutt in a major agribusiness-linked U.S. university would seem to lie at the opposite end of the spectrum from the scientific and ethical practices emergent in canine genetic diversity worlds. Yet similar issues are at stake: What kinds of collaborations will produce the relevant expertise and make the decisions for the biosocial evolution of companion species in technocultural dogland? What constitutes an ethic of flourishing—and for which members of the companion species community? Unlike the world represented by the canine open health registry debates or the genome diversity discourses, the dog cloning world is a surreal mix of state-of-the-art reproductive technoscience, inventive ethics, New Age epistemological pranksterism, and marketing extravagance.

The Missyplicity Project began in 1998 with a $2.3 million grant for the first two years from a wealthy anonymous donor to three senior researchers at Texas A&M University and their collaborators from several other institutions. The project has an elaborate website (www. missyplicity.com) with comments from the public; stories about the mixed-breed dog, Missy, that is to be cloned; a list of research objectives; an account of home adoption and dog training programs for the surrogate bitches used in the research ("All of our dogs have been trained using only positive reinforcement through clicker training"); and a state-of-the-art code of bioethics.

Marketing is never far from the dog cloning project, and advertising is an easy, if cheap, window onto the trading floor in cultural futures in dog geneticism. In advance of the actual ability to clone a dog, Animal Cloning Sciences, Inc. (ANCL), claims, over a picture of an elderly white woman holding her beloved terrier, "You no longer have to look forward to heart-rending grief at the death of your pet. If you preserve your pet's DNA now, you will have the option to clone your pet and continue your pet's life in a new body" (www. animalcloningsciences.com). Alien identity transfer experiments were never so successful, even on *The X-Files.* Promising cloning technology for companion animals "soon," ANCL offers cryopreservation of cells today at $595. The less said about avoiding grief in intimate relationships, including cross-species ones, the better.

Another company offering cell cryopreservation, Lazaron BioTechnologies, started by two embryologists and a business associate at the Louisiana Business and Technology Center on the campus of Louisiana State University, in a *DogWorld* ad urged readers to take tissue samples from their dogs before it was too late, so that they might "save a genetic life." This is something of an advance on pro-life rhetoric before the Age of Genes™. At the top of its website, Lazaron describes itself as "saving the genetic life of valued animals" (www.lazaron.com). Never has value had more value, in all its kinds. Bioethics "enterprised up" flourishes here, where profit meets science, conservation, art, and undying love-on-ice.

Both companies deal in agricultural and endangered species as well as companion animals, and the link to "saving endangered species" lends a value cachet not to be despised. We met this enhancement in dog genome diversity contexts, and it has now become a boundary object joining conservation and cloning discourses.

Thus, cloning dogs could have a scientific appeal for dog breeders. Prizewinning writers on canine genetics and health, as well as breeders themselves, the statistician John Cargill and the immunologist Susan Thorpe-Vargas argue the merits of dog cloning to preserve genetic diversity. They write that the depletion of genetic diversity might be mitigated if it were possible to clone desirable dogs rather than try, through excessive linebreeding and overuse of popular sires, to duplicate those dogs' qualities. Cryopreservation and cloning could be tools in the effort to manage the genomes of small populations in the best interests of the breed or species.

High seriousness characterizes the rhetoric of the website of Genetic Savings and Clone, Inc. (GSC; www.savingsandclone.com), the only cryopreservation tissue and gene bank directly associated with cloning research, beginning with the Missyplicity Project. After buying out Lazaron in 2001, GSC put pets, livestock, wildlife, and assistance and rescue dogs all on its agenda. The company's perception of ethical, ontological, and epistemological emergents is fascinating. Large investment, best science, and academic-business collaboration feature prominently; GSC does not see itself as a "vanity" cloning and biobanking endeavor. Its bioethics statement endorses an extraordinary collage of progressive commitments: GSC pledges itself to maximize public knowledge and keep as proprietary only the minimum needed for its business goals. Transgenic alterations will be made only under strict scrutiny by the GSC Advisory Board. Biological weapons—figured as attack dogs!—will not be produced, nor will GSC's animals enter the food chain as genetically modified organisms (GMOs). No information will be knowingly shared with those attempting human cloning. GSC promises to raise

its animals in "traditional" and not "factory farm" conditions. "This means that the animals will spend part of every day grazing and interacting with humans and other animals—rather than being constantly isolated in sterile pens" (www. savingsand-clone.com/ethics). GSC even pledges itself to organic farming methods and to other ecologically conscious practices.

So GSC's traditionally raised, cloned animals and surrogate mothers will have plenty of organic produce in their diets. Irony has little chance in the context of such high ethical seriousness. True, we must take the company's word for everything; no public power intrudes into this corporate idyll. Still, as the song goes, "Who could ask for anything more?"

We do, in fact, get even more in the Missyplicity Project itself. Its goals foreground the basic knowledge of canine reproductive biology crucial to repopulating endangered species (for example, wolves), birth control for feral and pet dog populations, and "replicating specific, exceptional dogs of high societal value—especially seeing-eye and search-and-rescue dogs" (www.missyplicity. com/goals). How will they ever make a buck, one wonders? Perhaps a merger with Amazon .com?

Missyplicity's scientific founding team is a microcosm of crosscutting technoscience at institutions such as Texas A&M University, a "land- sea- and space-grant institution" with twenty-four hundred faculty members and a research budget of $367 million (www.tamu.edu/ researchandgradstudies, 1996 figures). Mark Westhusin, the principal investigator, is a nuclear transfer specialist with an appointment in the Department of Veterinary Physiology and Pharmacology. He has a large lab and numerous publications from cloning research on agriculturally important mammals. The embryo transfer specialist is Duane Kraemer, Ph.D., D.V.M. "He and his colleagues have transferred embryos in more different species than any other group in the world" (www.missyplicity.com/team). Kraemer is a cofounder of Project Noah's Ark, an international effort to bank the genomes of numerous wildlife species in case they become further endangered or extinct. Kraemer wants to get mobile satellite labs around the world that could perform needed in vitro fertilizations and cryopreservation (www3.cnn.com/EARTH/9509/hartebeast). Project Noah's Ark originated in the mid-1990s from Texas A&M students' "concerns for the world's endangered species" (www.tamu.edu/researchandgradstudies/scicoa98/tamu2.html).

"Saving the endangered [fill in the category]" emerges as the rhetorical gold standard for "value" in technoscience, trumping and shunting aside other considerations of the apparatus for shaping public and private, kin and kind, animation and cessation. "Endangered species" turns out to be a capacious ethical bypass for ontologically heterogeneous traffic in dogland.

Where better could I turn for edification on this issue than to a solemn public program sponsored by Stanford University's Ethics in Society Program? On 12 May 2000, Lou Hawthorne, the chief executive officer of GSC and coordinator of the Missyplicity Project, spoke on the panel "The Ethics of Cloning Companion Animals." Also on the panel were two Stanford philosophy professors, a professor of theology and ethics at the Pacific School of Religion, and Lazaron CEO Richard Denniston, who is also director of the LSU Embryology Biotechnology Laboratory. During questions after the formal presentations, someone asked how the Missyplicity Project, with its mongrel subject, affected purebred dog breeders. Reaching for the gold standard, Denniston called mutts "an endangered species of one"! Hawthorne more modestly said that GSC was a "celebration of the mutt," because these one-of-a-kind pooches could not be bred to type.

A talented polemicist and media expert, Hawthorne might be seen as a trickster in the American tradition so well understood by Herman Melville, P. T. Barnum, and New Age savants. Hawthorne is also a thoughtful and complex actor in cross-species technoscience. A trickster tests the goodness of reasoning and valuing, perhaps showing up the baseness of what

passes for gold in official knowledges or at least tweaking the certainties of the pious, those "for" or "against" a technoscientific marvel. A savvy operator in twenty-first-century America would also like to make some money, preferably lots of it, while saving the Earth. Joseph Dumit sees such figures as being engaged seriously with "playful truths." Not innocent truths—play is not innocent, just not convincingly adult. Play opens up degrees of freedom in what might seem fixed. I read Hawthorne as a master player in technoscience, whose not inconsiderable earnestness is overmatched by his trickster savvy.

At Stanford, Hawthorne staged his discussion of the Missyplicity Project's code of ethics with an origin story and a travel narrative. He began as a Silicon Valley media and technology consultant with no knowledge of biotechnology or bioethics. In July 1997 his "rich and anonymous client" asked him to explore the feasibility of cloning his aging mutt. This study led to many and marvelous places in biotechnology land, including the conference "Transgenic Animals in Agriculture" in August 1997 in Tahoe City, California. There Hawthorne heard about animals as "bioreactors" that could be manipulated without moral limit. He emerged "with two epiphanies": that Missyplicity would need a strong code of bioethics, "if just to distance ourselves from the giddy, anything-goes attitude of most bioengineers" (preprint of presentation), and that his lack of scientific training might be an advantage.

Like many other Western seekers, Hawthorne arrived in the East. Returning to his experience in filming a documentary on Zen Buddhism in 1984, he retrieved "a core value of Buddhism—borrowed from Hinduism—*ahimsa,* commonly translated as 'non-harming.' *Ahimsa,* like most Buddhist ideas, is a koan, or puzzle without clear-cut solution, which can only be fully resolved through a process of personal inquiry. . . . I decided to put non-harming at the top of the Missyplicity Bioethics Code" (preprint). His search led to a way to live responsibly in emergent technocultural worlds, where kin and kind are unfixed.

Hawthorne's explication of the code reveals a wonderful collage of transactional psychology (all the partners—humans and dogs—should benefit) ; Buddhist borrowings; family values ("at the completion of their role in the Missyplicity Project, all dogs should be placed in loving homes"); no-kill animal shelter policies; and birth control discourses ("how many dogs could we save from death—by preventing their births in the first place—through the development of an effective canine contraceptive?"). If Margaret Sanger had been a dog activist, she would be proud of her progeny. Animal rights, disability rights, and right-to-life discourses have echoes in the Missyplicity code, with practical consequences for how the canine research subjects get treated—that is, as subjects, not objects. No matter how many trips are made to the East, in its soul Western ethics is riveted to rights discourses. In any case, if I were a research dog, I would want to be at Texas A&M in the Missyplicity Project, where the Zen of cloning is more than a slogan. Besides, that is where "best science" lies. As Hawthorne noted, cloning dogs is harder than cloning humans. Missyplicity is against cloning those bipeds anyway, and as a reward, Missy's companion species get to do more leading-edge research.

The clincher in Hawthorne's savvy presentation at Stanford, where making money is no stranger to producing knowledge, is his introduction of Genetic Savings and Clone, Inc., "which is based in College Station, Texas, but [which] also heavily leverages the internet." Distributed networking is not limited to neural nets and activists. GSC "represents the first step toward commercializing the enormous amount of information being generated by Missyplicity." There is a backlog of demand for private cloning services. Hawthorne speculates that the price of cloning a pet dog (or cat—a project that succeeded in 2002 with the birth of CC, or Copy Cat) will "fall within three years to under $20,000—though at first it may be ten times as much."

Not surprisingly, these figures lead Hawthorne to great works of art, those conserved, one-of-a-kind creations. "I'd like to end with this thought: great companion animals are like works of art. . . . Once we've identified these masterpieces, then arguably it's not just reasonable but imperative that we capture their unique genetic endowments before they're gone—just as we would rescue great works of art from a burning museum." Science, business, ethics, and art are the familiar renaissance partners at the origin of technopresence, where "evolution intersects the free market; those who can afford it will save what they like and leave the rest to burn" (preprint). Even as he mobilizes the resources for bringing cloned dogs into the world, Hawthorne playfully tweaks official truths in his well-funded trickster boosterism in the "Museum of Mutts" (preprint).

Let me return for a moment to the more homely metaphors of Linda Weisser and her less dazzling work to get Pyr people to use an open health and genetics registry and to try to whelp only dogs that will improve the breed, helping the kin and kind of companion species to flourish. Immersed in emergences of many kinds, I do not oppose dog cloning in principle, and I see more than a little of value in practice in the Missyplicity Project—without that fire at the end of things. I am firmly on the side of endangered tigers—and the people who inhabit the nations where the big cats (barely) live. Genetic diversity is a precious pattern for dogs as well as people, and cats *are* like dogs. The crucial issues remain, as always, attending to the details. Who makes decisions? What is the apparatus of production of these new sorts of being? How can we stay on Linda Weisser's science-savvy riverbank while choking on the ether of the techno-present? If "saving the endangered [fill in the blank]" means personally and collectively cleaning the rivers so that the earth's always emergent kin can drink without harm or shame, who could ask for anything more?

PART SIX

Agriculture

Introduction

It is within the system through which animals are transformed into "livestock"—in which animals are bred, reared, transported, slaughtered, marketed, and consumed—that the cultural ambivalence about nonhuman animals and their place in human society is perhaps most clear. While the emergence of agricultural and pastoral culture some 11,000 years ago in the Near East is often hailed as an advancement of "civilization," it does not appear to be an unmixed blessing for humankind. The anthropologist Jared Diamond calls the movement from hunting and gathering to a dependence on agriculture and animal husbandry "the worst mistake in the history of the human race" (quoted in Budiansky 1992: 37). Studies of modern hunter-gatherers show that this form of subsistence provides more than adequate levels of protein and calories and members of these tribal cultures spend relatively little time acquiring food. On the other hand, paleontological studies indicate that members of early agricultural communities suffered from malnutrition, a variety of infectious diseases, and osteoporosis and other problems related to physical stress. The average life expectancy for members of these more "advanced" societies was 19 years (see Budiansky 1992: 19–41).

Domestication is central to agricultural/pastoral societies. Most basically, domestication involves removing animals from the wild and through ongoing interaction making them unafraid of humans. Essentially, this means that domestic animals are under the control of human beings, incorporated into human society, and defined as objects to be owned by humans (Ingold 1994). Typically, this process of removal from the wild and incorporation into human social life has been seen as originating when Mesolithic peoples adopted infant wild animals and transformed them into "pets." Steven Budiansky (1992) offers an interesting counterargument when he maintains that domestication is an outcome of a coevolutionary process in which association with humans was as much chosen by animals as it was forced upon them. In short, close association was evolutionarily advantageous for both humans and animals. Humans offered food, protection, and other benefits while animals provided food, hunting assistance, and protection.

This movement from hunter-gatherers to farmer-herdsmen meant that humans moved from seeing animals as equals to viewing them as subordinates. The dominance and control of animals came to be central to human association with them. At the same time, this transformed orientation toward animals was an ambivalent one as close association with animals prompted people also to come to view them as individuals worthy of affection (see Tuan 1984). In her ethnographic study of Scottish farmers, sociologist Rhoda Wilkie (2005) stresses the ambiguity of the relationship between farmers and their "livestock." On the one hand, sheep, pigs, and cattle are commodities. On the other hand, farmers commonly come to develop emotional connections to their animals. The emotional ambivalence inherent in this relationship is most troubling when it comes time to slaughter the animal. Wilkie quotes a "hobby farmer's" description of the emotional trauma she feels when taking the sheep she has come to view as pets to be slaughtered.

> The worst thing that happened with sheep and myself was when I had two pet lambs . . . and they were so *pet* that they followed me to get them into the box to take them to be killed. . . . And I think that's the worse thing I have ever done to sheep. . . . I knew they had to be killed but it was the way that they trusted. I led them into their death. . . . I found that very difficult to live with. . . . (I)t hurts still to think of it. . . . (Wilkie 2005, 227)

The ambivalence felt by those closely associated with livestock animals is also encountered among those who have rarely, if ever, seen a live pig, cow, or other source of "meat." As seen in the selections in this part, the principles of vegetarianism/veganism are highly emotional components of the ethical orientation of the some 2 to 10 percent of Americans who follow this dietary path (Moore 2007). The decision to avoid animal flesh and/or any animal-related food products is based on various arguments. Some vegetarians stress the health advantages provided by a meat-free diet. Those who consume animal flesh risk physical problems as they ingest significant quantities of saturated fat and the hormones and antibiotics that are routinely given to animals in factory farms. Another reason for avoiding meat focuses on the environmental consequences of factory farming. This perspective stresses the inefficiency inherent in devoting cropland and grain crops to animal feed (in the United States, around 70 percent of grain is fed to livestock [Moore 2007, 48]), the deforestation involved in creating cropland, and the environmental problems of animal excrement and other pollutants related to industrial farming.

The most common argument for a vegetable-based diet is grounded in moral and ethical concerns. To varying degrees, this perspective stresses that nonhuman animals (10 billion of whom are killed and eaten each year in the United States [*The Week*, February 8, 2008, 16]) are sentient beings who possess an inherent right to life and who should not be subjected to pain and suffering. Commonly, "claims-makers" for vegetarianism use graphic depictions of commercial slaughterhouses to generate the revulsion that could prompt some to alter their dietary lifestyles (see Lesy 1989, 71–87, 115–132).

Yet another rationale for not eating animal flesh or using animal-based products involves stressing the interconnections between the social definition and treatment of animal-objects and other forms of oppression. As seen in the selection by Winders and Nibert that follows, this approach sometimes implicates factory farming, meat production, and meat eating as central to, and supportive of, the inequalities inherent in capitalist economic organization. Exploitation of nonhuman animals is presented as parallel to the oppression of subordinate racial and class groups (see Nibert 2002, Spiegel 1989).

As seen in the selection by Adams, feminist concerns with gender oppression have also come to play a role in vegetarianism and the larger issue of animal rights. Ecofeminists stress the basic interconnection between humans and nature and oppose the interrelated oppressions of animals, people of color, women, and nature. They critique the environmental effects of technology and see environmental problems as resistant, if not impervious, to traditional political solutions. As Birkeland (1993) describes the ecofeminist perspective, it

> is a value system, a social movement, and a practice, but it also offers a political analysis that explores the links between androcen-

trism and environmental destruction. It is "an awareness" that begins with the realization that the exploitation of nature is intimately linked to Western Man's attitude toward women and tribal cultures. . . . Ecofeminists believe that we cannot end the exploitation of nature without ending human oppression, and vice versa. . . . To ecofeminists, values and action are inseparable: one cannot care without acting. (18–19)

From this (somewhat romanticized) perspective then, women historically have had a closer relationship to nature and animals and, like animals, have traditionally been dominated by men. This perspective leads ecofeminists to be strongly supportive of animal rights and to draw connections between violence against animals and violence directed toward women and children within families (see the selection by Flynn in this volume).

This fairly direct relationship between human-on-human violence and violence toward animals is commonly drawn by animal rights activists as well as ecofeminists (e.g., Ascione 1993, Flynn 1999). It is important to note that, while this connection is commonsensically compelling, it has been called into serious question by a number of scholars (e.g., Arluke *et al.* 1999, Tallichet, Hensley, and Singer 2005).

The selections in this part stress these oppressive elements of the human-animal relationship. The article by Bill Winders and David Nibert takes on what feminist anthropologist Barbara Noske (1997) refers to as the "animal industrial complex." Their critique of the contemporary phenomenon of meat eating is grounded in an economic and political analysis. In short, they see New Deal style capitalism and the agricultural policies this approach has generated since the end of World War II as being responsible for Americans' dietary reliance on meat. Price supports and advances in agricultural technologies resulted in an overproduction of corn, wheat, and soybeans. In order to deal with this surplus, farm and governmental organizations promoted meat production and meat eating as effective means of dealing with the oversupply of grain. In turn, the authors maintain that the expansion of meat production led to more oppressive and inhumane living conditions for those animals whose flesh was destined to be on the nation's dinner tables. Further, increased dietary reliance on animal products led to more oppressive working conditions for those employed in the meat industry and to environmental degradation as livestock production on factory farms had a negative impact on water and other natural resources. Clearly, the authors are horrified by the consequences of the system they describe for the lives of nonhuman animals. It is a system that transforms sentient beings into "meat" and animals into "product." Capitalism, the authors emphasize, leads directly to animal oppression.

This political critique of meat eating is continued in Carol Adams' "The Feminist Traffic in Animals." Adams uses the issue of whether or not meat products should be served at feminist conferences to focus a discussion of vegetarianism as a political issue. Feminists who continue to consume meat ("animalized protein") and animal products such as eggs, milk, and cheese ("feminized protein") are complicit in the oppression of animals; they are "traffickers" in a producer-consumer relationship that revolves around disposable bodies. Adams, like Winders and Nibert, emphasizes how linguistic terms (e.g., "meat" instead of "animal muscle tissue") and other cultural factors help to separate us from the fact of killing and eating other sentient beings. In this she draws a striking parallel between human sexual, racial, and ethnic oppression and the oppression of nonhuman animals.

This focus on meat production and consumption as a form of cruel oppression is continued in Barbara McDonald's article on becoming a vegan. As she presents it, the career of the vegan is fraught with potential emotional and relational conflicts. The conversion to veganism is a learning process in which one is precipitated into considering the lifestyle change by a cathartic realization that cruelty to animals is central to the animal-oriented diet. This realization prompts the person to examine his or her self, to acquire more information about veganism and, eventually, to convert to the new ideological position and dietary lifestyle. This choice to become vegan, in turn, often leads to "marginalization" as newly converted vegans find it necessary to reorient their relationships with friends and family members who continue to support what they have now come to see as a cruel and oppressive dietary lifestyle.

References

Arluke, A., Levin, J., Luke, C., and F. Ascione. 1999. "The Relationship of Animal Abuse to Violence and Other Forms of Antisocial Behavior." *Journal of Interpersonal Violence* 14:963–975.

Ascione, F. 1993. "Children Who Are Cruel to Animals: A Review of Research and Implications for Developmental Psychopathology." *Anthrozoös* 6:226–247.

Birkeland, J. 1993. "Ecofeminism: Linking Theory and Practice." In G. Gaard, ed., *Ecofeminism: Women, Animals, and Nature*, 13–59. Philadelphia: Temple University Press.

Budiansky, S. 1992. *The Covenant of the Wild: Why Animals Chose Domestication*. New York: Morrow.

Flynn, C. 1999. "Animal Abuse in Childhood and Later Support for Interpersonal Violence in Families." *Society & Animals* 7:161–172.

Ingold, T. 1994. "From Trust to Domination: An Alternative History of Human-Animal Relations." In A. Manning and J. Serpell, eds., *Animals and Human Society*, 1–22. New York: Routledge.

Lesy, M. 1989. *The Forbidden Zone*. New York: Anchor.

Moore, H. 2007. "Animals as Food: Veganism." In M. Bekoff, ed., *The Encyclopedia of Human-Animal Relationships*, 46–49. Westport, CT: Greenwood Press.

Nibert, D. 2002. *Animal Rights, Human Rights: Entanglements of Oppression and Liberation*. Lanham, MD: Rowan and Littlefield.

Noske, B. 1997. *Beyond Boundaries: Humans and Animals*. Montreal: Black Rose Books.

Spiegel, M. 1989. *The Dreaded Comparison*. New York: Mirror Books.

Tallichet, S., Hensley, C., and S. Singer. 2005. "Unraveling the Methods of Childhood and Adolescent Cruelty to Nonhuman Animals." *Society & Animals* 13:91–108.

Tuan, Y. 1984. *Dominance and Affection*. New Haven: Yale University Press.

Wilkie, R. 2005. "Sentient Commodities and Productive Paradoxes: The Ambiguous Nature of Human-Livestock Relations in Northeast Scotland." *Journal of Rural Studies* 21: 213–230.

Bill Winders
David Nibert

Expanding "Meat" Consumption and Animal Oppression

Animal rights activists decrying the abuse of animals frequently cite the direct consumption of animals as food. Billions of other animals are "produced" in deplorable conditions, brutally killed and eaten by relatively elite groups of humans. Such critiques tend to focus on the ethics and morality of such practices, but often overlook social structural forces—such as the integral links between a "free market" economy and government economic policies and the consumption of other animals as food.

In this article, we examine the links between New Deal-inspired U.S. agricultural policy and the expansion of animal oppression after 1945. U.S. agricultural policy encouraged increased "meat"[1] consumption to help reduce the oversupply of feed grains, in particular, corn. This policy expanded the oppression of animals in two ways. First, the consumption of animals obviously increased, which meant that more animals were slaughtered. Second, animals considered "food" experienced increasingly oppressive conditions: large feeding lots, diets of feed grains rather than pasture, the use of growth hormones, shorter life spans, chemically-altered growth patterns and assembly-line style slaughter. "Livestock" production became increasingly scientific and used more technology. We argue that the expansionary and profit-driven market economy underlay each dimension of animal oppression, and that this development is fueled and maintained by state policies.

The expansion of "meat" consumption has not only increased harm to animals but also to the environment, to workers and to consumers'

health. This entanglement of oppression envelops many oppressed groups and demonstrates the reach of capitalism's harm and the wide-ranging effects of state policies. Underlying U.S. agricultural policy are the capitalist imperative of expansion and the issue of power.

Capitalism, the State, and Agriculture

Twentieth century U.S. agricultural policy emerged out of the economic turmoil of the 1920s and 1930s, when the capitalist "free market" forces fueled mechanization and concentration of agricultural production—and wreaked havoc on farmers' incomes. Overproduction in cotton, grains and feed was at the root of this crisis. Agricultural prices fell dramatically between 1926 and 1932: corn fell from 74 cents a bushel to 32 cents and wheat from $1.22 a bushel to 38 cents, and cotton from 13 cents a pound to 6 cents (Hosen, 1992:272). Likewise, gross farm income fell from about $14 billion in 1929 to $6 billion in 1932 (Hosen, 1992:270). Agricultural production and rural communities were devastated by the market chaos.

The Agricultural Adjustment Acts (1933, 1938)—the core of Great Depression-era, New Deal policies—attempted to remedy this overproduction with supply management principles. This legislation was composed of two key policies: price supports and production controls. Price supports were essentially guaranteed minimum prices for certain commodities, but farmers were required to agree to programs to limit their production in order to receive the guaranteed prices. These policies had two goals: (1) to reduce the supply of agricultural commodities, such as grains; and (2) to raise farm incomes. While New Deal agricultural policy was successful at the second goal, it failed miserably at the first. In fact, the combination of price supports and production controls actually encouraged greater productivity, leading to growing surpluses.

While corn production and productivity were relatively stable during the 1920s, they skyrocketed after 1940. Wheat and soybean productivity demonstrated similar trends. Corn yields increased from an average of 26 bushels per acre from 1925 to 1929, to 39 bushels from 1948 to 1952, to 62.5 bushels from 1960 to 1964. The combination of price supports and production controls provided the incentive for this "second agricultural revolution." Federal policy limited farmers in the acreage they could use for production, not in the amounts they could produce. Since farmers received artificially high prices on what they did produce, they optimized their profits by intensifying their production on limited acreage.

New technologies such as mechanization, chemical fertilizers and hybrid seeds (for corn) were central to this development (Matusow, 1967; Rasmussen, 1962). Government price supports facilitated the industrialization of agriculture by infusing previously cash-strapped farmers with increased incomes that allowed many to purchase new technology that increased productivity. Government payments to farmers totaled almost $6.5 billion from 1935 to 1945, about $3.6 billion from 1946 to 1956, and about $19.4 billion from 1957 to 1967 (USDA, 1967:570, Table 690). Total farm income increased from about $10 billion in 1935 to $25 billion in 1945 to $33 billion in 1955 to $45 billion in 1965 (USDA, 1967:570, Table 690).

As farmers invested in new technologies, production expenses increased steadily: from $5 billion in 1935 to $13 billion in 1945, to $22 billion in 1955, and to $31 billion in 1965 (USDA, 1967:570, Table 690). This in turn facilitated the concentration of farming, since not all farmers had the resources to keep up with such technology. Ironically, the advent of much of the new technology that presented problems for supply management policies was facilitated by the state: ". . . while the CCC [Commodity Credit Corporation] was fighting surpluses, the research bureaus of the Department [of Agriculture] were developing ever more effective ways of increasing yields" (Matusow, 1967:127).

The supply management policies that emerged out of the New Deal, combined with increased capacity from new technologies, spurred dramatic increases in productivity (per acre) and overall production. Surpluses of grains became a chronic problem. Supply management largely failed to control production; farmers began searching for alternative solutions to the oversupply problem, and expanding meat consumption was an attractive option.

Economic Power and State Policy

While World War II and the postwar reconstruction in Europe helped to consume the U.S. grain surplus during a limited period, most farm organizations feared an eventual return of overproduction. Nonetheless, some farm organizations—such as the American Farm Bureau Federation—opposed further supply management policies and argued that the answer was to increase the demand for and consumption of agricultural goods. Controlling production effectively stifled the expansionary tendency in capitalism and potentially limited profits, which was not in these organizations' interests. The solution was obvious: increase "meat" consumption.

Corn farmers, in particular, advocated this avenue. Allan Kline, president of the AFBF, testified before Congress in 1949: "We are interested in trying to develop policies and programs which will avoid burdensome surpluses in feed grains by encouraging the translation of increased feed production into greater livestock production" (U.S. House, 1949:436). The two main agricultural commodities of the Corn Belt—corn and soybeans—were the basis of "livestock" feed. The idea here, in the late 1940s, was that there was ample room to expand "meat" consumption.

Focusing on "meat" consumption was an especially efficient manner of controlling grain surpluses. Kline pointed out that "it takes seven times as many acres to feed a people on livestock products as it takes if people eat grain" (U.S. House, 1949:437). Corn farmers could expand—rather than limit—their production if the number of "livestock" animals increased.

This option was also appealing to farmers since "meat" production is "high value" production, yielding greater profits than grain production. This was especially true in the Corn Belt, where producers undoubtedly benefitted from expanding "meat" consumption: "Corn producers. . . do not get their farm income directly from the sale of their crop. After all, between 85 and 90 percent of corn produced is sold in the form of livestock and livestock products" (Testimony of Kline, U.S. House, 1949:438). Furthermore, as Matusow (1967:136) notes, "Since demand for meat is elastic (that is, sales rise more than proportionally as prices fall), many hog farmers saw no advantage in limiting supply to keep prices high." Thus, corn producers favored policies that would facilitate expanded grain production to be used for "livestock."

As a supplement to the supply management policies, the state began to promote "meat" production and consumption in two important ways. First, the state supported the production of "pork" through price supports. This encouraged farmers to expand their hog "production." Second, the state supported and conducted research to make "livestock" production more efficient, more industrialized. Just as it had with crop production, the research bureaus of the USDA promoted the industrialization and modernization of "livestock" production. Land grant universities also conducted research to improve the productivity of "livestock" production. Consequently, industrial production of other animals for human consumption expanded dramatically after 1945. The number of cows slaughtered in the U.S. increased from about 21 million in 1945 to about 43 million in 1975. Yet, this increase does not reflect that the size (weight) of cows slaughtered also increased significantly during this period. More cows were slaughtered, but they were also larger cows to make the process more profitable.

As production increased, so too did the consumption of "meat." While per capita consumption of pigs remained relatively constant during this period, per capita consumption of cows increased significantly beginning in the 1950s. Per capita consumption of chickens increased gradually until the late 1970s, when consumption increased more rapidly.

Skaggs (1986:166) points out that this increase in per capita meat consumption occurred as the U.S. population expanded greatly: by 1976, ". . . the population had increased by 64 percent, to an estimated 218 million persons, from about 132.5 million in 1945. Thus, not only had the number of red-meat eaters increased, but, individually, they ate more red meat." Even had per capita meat consumption remained constant, the significant population growth meant that the number of animals raised and slaughtered for human consumption would have increased dramatically as well.

Maurer (2002:14–15, emphasis in original) points out that as "meat" consumption increased, "the *type* of meat has gradually shifted—from pork to beef and now from beef to poultry." As we discuss shortly, this shift from "beef production to "poultry" production meant a general increase in animal oppression in this industry. Maurer (2002) also observes that consumers' choice of "meat" is shaped largely by price (e.g., the price of "pork" relative to that of "beef" or "poultry"). The trends in the treatment of other animals that we discuss below—trends that have seen the oppression of other animals greatly increase—are a function of competition within capitalist markets. Changes in the methods and structure of "meat" production result from competition to cut costs, increase production and lower prices relative to other "meats."

"Meat" consumption increased in the second half of the twentieth century, both in the United States and in other affluent nations. For example, Japanese "meat" consumption increased dramatically: "From 1965 to 1995, Japan saw annual meat consumption rise from 6.4 kg to 30.7 kg per inhabitant" (MHR Viandes, 1997). World "beef" consumption increased from less than 20 kg per person in 1950 to almost 40 kg per person in 2000 (Worldwatch Institute, 2003). "Poultry" production and consumption have seen the most significant increase.

This increase in consuming other animals as food helped to alleviate the problem of increased amounts of grain—grain that might feed millions of humans around the world. The expansion in the consumption of other animals also is central to the economic value of U.S. agricultural production. Cash receipts for cows and pigs increased along with production. Durrenberger and Thu (1996:409) note that "Pork production . . . is a cornerstone of Iowa's agriculturally oriented economy." The higher profitability of "meat" versus grain production underlies the expansion *of* "meat" consumption.

In response to the crisis of overproduction in agriculture in the Great Depression, the state created supply management policies, which ultimately proved ineffectual. Increased "meat" consumption then became the primary solution for growing grain surpluses, helping to reduce surpluses and raise profits. Yet, this solution to problems of capitalist agriculture has had devastating effects on other animals that have endured the industrialization of "livestock" production.

Expanding Oppression

As U.S. agribusiness and the state wrestled with overproduction and the capitalist imperative for growth, their solutions and policies intensified the levels of various oppressive arrangements. Suffering inflicted on other animals grew as their consumption as food increased. As more animals were killed in slaughterhouses, workers in the "meat" industry suffered as well, as quests for in-creasing profits also led to attempts to reduce labor costs. The expansion of the "meat" industry led to the displacement of subsistence farmers, indigenous humans, free-living animals and other vulnerable groups in Third World nations. Moreover, consumers of "meat" are paying a high price for this oppressive and destructive diet in their own quality of health.

Raising Other Animals as Food

The conditions of other animals raised for "meat" have undergone dramatic changes since 1945. As noted, the supply management policies increased farm income and capital, allowing farmers with large operations to invest in corporate-friendly technologies (e.g., chemical fertilizers, tractors) for crop production as well as for "livestock" production. Increasingly, factory farms replaced traditional methods of producing "meat." Between 1945 and 1960 chickens, turkeys and pigs largely disappeared from pens and pastures in rural areas and moved indoors to more confined, streamlined, and centralized operations—called *concentrated animal feeding operations*, or CAFOs. These "scientifically" developed living arrangements are nothing short of diabolical, considering the nature of pigs. Finsen and Finsen (1994:11) observes:

> When given the opportunity, pigs form stable social groups, build communal nests, use dunging areas at a distance from their nests, and lead an active life rooting in woodlands. In intensive farms, however, most of these activities are impossible. (1994:11)

Pigs raised for consumption face torturous confinement in CAFOs, and many "do not see the light of day" (Durrenberger and Thu, 1996:410). In such crowded, sterile and unnatural confinements their experiences—from their eating to the quality of their air to their exposure to artificial light—are entirely controlled (and largely automatically controlled, at that) to maximize their physical size before they are cruelly transported to slaughterhouses to be killed.

Female pigs confined for the purpose of continually birthing piglets are imprisoned in such tiny enclosures that they cannot even turn around. When actually giving birth and nursing their young, female pigs are forced into farrowing pens that impair even further their ability to move—restraints that many struggle against for hours. In many instances, shortly after their birth baby pigs are raised on a robot "autosow" so that their real mother can be re-inseminated so she will "produce" a new litter even faster. The lives of such female pigs are thus reduced to "reproductive machines" (Fox, 1990:26–27). Such control, as abnormal and stressful as it is for them, has been crafted to coordinate pig birth and "production" with the "meat" market, which centers on steady, constant production. Michael W. Fox notes, "Such conditions would shock muckrakers like Upton Sinclair far more than anything they actually envisioned at the Chicago abattoirs in the early 1900s" (Fox, 1990:30).

Since 1945, most chickens also have endured conditions of extreme confinement, deprivation, and misery. Like pigs, chickens have no opportunity to experience any kind of life that is natural to them. Chickens confined for purposes of egg production are crowded into minuscule "battery cages" that are stacked from floor to roof. The tiny cages—each of which imprison four to five birds—have slanted, wire floors to permit automatic retrieval of the chickens' eggs.

Pathological behavior that is produced by such confinement is offset somewhat by keeping the chickens in darkness, or near darkness, a great deal of the time and by cutting off the chickens' beaks—an exceedingly painful procedure. Frequently female chickens are subjected to "forced molting," a process in which they are totally deprived of food for about two weeks and forced to live in darkness. While such treatment results in increased egg laying in some chickens, for others it produces a slow, agonizing death. Chickens typically live for 7 years or more in natural settings, but in battery cages exist for only 12 to 24 months. Those birds that survive the horrors of the battery cage will experience gruesome

deaths in slaughterhouses when their productivity as egg-laying machines declines. The rough handling they experience, from battery cages to the "disassembly line," results in broken bones in 30 to 40 percent of those who make the trip.

Male chicks are considered mere byproducts of efforts to create more disposable "battery hens" and pulled from the rest. They are then subjected to brutal death by suffocation or crushing, ground up into "feed," and frequently fed to the female chicks. Other chickens have been bred as "broilers" or "meat" producers. These birds have been modified by "science"—much of it by way of large, state land-grant universities in the United States—to grow rapidly so they can be sent to slaughterhouses and killed within 6 to 8 weeks of their birth. Many are so grotesquely deformed, due to techniques to increase the amount of "breast meat" per bird, that they cannot walk—or even stand. "Today's eight-week old chickens carry seven times more breast muscle than nine-week old chickens of twenty-five years ago" (Marcus, 1998:109).

Unlike pigs and chickens, the flesh of cows was traditionally consumed by the more affluent in society, due to the high financial costs associated with their production as food. However, state-facilitated grain surpluses reduced the cost considerably, by providing affordable feed. The drop in the cost of production facilitated the rise of mass consumption of "ground beef" and the emergence of the "hamburger culture."

Raised as "beef cattle," calves are taken from their mothers and transported to feed lots, where their size is increased as quickly as possible. These separations are traumatic experiences for both the calves and their mothers. The emotional sensitivity of cows strikes many who witness such separations. Gold (1995:33) brings an example of the suffering of "farm animals" to light in the following moving passage about a calf.

> One stockman related how some calves will actually die from "homesickness" when they are sold on to another farm. He explains how on

one occasion he was called to look at a sick cow, fourteen days after having sold her. He found that she "lay—unable to rise, emaciated and with horribly sunken eyes," seven though "she had good food and fresh water in front of her." The cow was loaded onto a lorry and taken on a three-hour journey to her original "home." Once there she was hauled from the "flat-out" position in which she lay so that she could face out from the lorry. The stockman describes what happened next:

"Well, miracle of miracle: she opened her eyes, recognized her surroundings, struggled to her knees and scrambled down the ramp to the ground. Once there, she accepted a drink of water from a pail, then shook her lungs and let out a roar. A cow in the byre close by answered her."

Gold notes that the calf made a speedy recovery. These sensitive individuals, all relegated to the social position of "beef cattle," are transported to crowded and barren feed lots where they are fed corn-rich diets, usually laced with growth-enhancing hormones. Such diets are unnatural for cows and produce serious digestive problems—which are usually treated with large doses of antibiotics. The cows frequently are subjected to painful castration, dehorning, and branding before they are cruelly prodded and forced into trucks for transportation to the slaughterhouse.

Cows exploited for their milk are increasingly confined to small corrals—usually with little shade from the sun—or in barns with slanted floors. They are impregnated to facilitate a continuous flow of their milk. Like their brothers in the feedlots, their diets are carefully engineered to maximize milk production and minimize infection. Once their production of milk ebbs, they are sent to slaughterhouses where they will be invisibly transformed into "ground beef." Most of their male calves will be subjected to the horrible fate of the "veal" crates to live isolated and immobilized for about 16 weeks before sent to slaughter.

The move toward industrializing livestock production centered around manipulating other animals and their environments for the purposes of increasing efficiency, economies of scale and profitability. This is the full commodification of animals as goods to be bought and sold in the most productive and efficient manner—according to market demands (Polanyi, 1944). Behind this commodification were the state policies that facilitated the grain surpluses, which both permitted and required the expansion of "meat" consumption and the industrialization of "livestock" production.

Conclusion

The dramatic expansion in grain and soybean ("livestock feed") production after 1945 created an economic and political problem: what should be done about the resulting surpluses? Farm organizations, especially those based in the Corn Belt, pursued expanded use of the crops for "livestock" production. This policy choice set "meat" production in a direction funded in part by state policies in the form of price supports: agricultural industrialization. The result was that greater and greater numbers of other animals were raised in increasingly artificial and oppressive environments; more other animals were slaughtered for consumption, to the detriment of humans in core nations; workers in "meat" production suffered from deteriorating conditions; and these conditions were exported throughout the world economy, displacing masses of humans and other animals and rapidly increasing the rate of environmental devastation and resource depletion. (While some of the worst forms of mistreatment of other animals in agriculture have been ameliorated somewhat by reforms in Europe, agribusiness in the United States has largely forestalled similar legislation and regulations here.)

Significantly, such conditions exist to a large degree because of the definition of other animals as commodities and as food, a social construction exacerbated by the fundamental processes of the capitalist market—the drive for profit, expansion and capital accumulation—and the state's role in supporting that market. Without acknowledging this link between capitalism and animal oppression, both animal rights and human rights activists will face increasingly greater obstacles in alleviating all the various forms of entangled oppression.

Note

1. Words and expressions that are disparaging to other animals and euphemisms that tend to disguise the reality of oppression (such as the term "meat," which disguises the reality that other animals' dead bodies are used for food) are placed in quotation marks. While this may make the text somewhat awkward at times, it is much preferable to using smoother language that implicitly supports oppressive arrangements.

References

Durrenberger, E. Paul, and Kendall M. Thu. 1996. "The Expansion of Large Scale Hog Farming in Iowa: The Applicability of Goldschmidt's Findings Fifty Years Later." *Human Organization* 55(4): 409–416.

Finsen, Lawrence, and Susan Finsen. 1994. *The Animal Rights Movement in America: From Compassion to Respect.* New York: Twayne Publishers.

Fox, Michael W. 1990. *Inhumane Society: The American Way of Exploiting Animals.* New York: St. Martin's Press.

Gold, Mark. 1995. *Animal Rights: Extending the Circle of Compassion.* Oxford: Jon Carpenter Publishing.

Hosen, Frederick E. 1992. *The Great Depression and the New Deal.* Jefferson, NC: McFarland & Company.

Marcus, Erik. 1998. *Vegan: The New Ethics of Eating.* Ithaca, NY: McBooks Press.

Matusow, Allen J. 1967/1970. *Farm Policies and Politics in the Truman Years.* New York: Antheum.

Maurer, Donna. 2002. V*egetarianism: Movement or Moment?* Philadelphia: Temple University Press.

Polanyi, Karl. 1944/1957. *The Great Transformation: The Political and Economic Origins of Our Time.* Boston: Beacon Press.

Rasmussen, Wayne D. 1962. "The Impact of Technological Change in American Agriculture, 1862–1962." *Journal of Economic History* 22 (Dec.) 578–591.

Skuggs, Jimmy M. 1986. *Prime Cut: Livestock Raising and Meatpacking in the United States, 1607–1983.* College Station, TX: Texas A&M University Press.

United States Department of Agriculture (USDA). Various Years. *Agricultural Statistics.* Washington, D.C: Government Printing Office.

United States House of Representatives. 1949. "General Farm Program." Hearings before the Special Subcommittee of the House Committee on Agriculture. 81st Congress, 1st Session. Washington, D.C.: Government Printing Office.

MHR Viandes. 1997. *Meat Consumption in Japan.* May 1997. Accessed at: www.mhr-viandes.com/en/docu/docu/d0000217.htm.

Carol J. Adams

The Feminist Traffic in Animals

Should feminists be vegetarians? This question has appeared more and more frequently in recent years. Claudia Card offers one opinion: "Must we all, then, be vegetarians, pacifist, drug-free, opposed to competition, anti-hierarchical, in favor of circles, committed to promiscuity with women, and free of the parochialism of erotic arousal? Is this too specific? These values are not peripheral to analyses of women's oppressions."[1]

Many believe that feminism's commitment to pluralism should prevail over arguments for vegetarianism. This position sees pluralism as applying only to an intraspecies women's community. It defends personal choice as an arbiter of ethical decisions and limits pluralistic concerns to those of oppressed human beings. Pluralism is used to depoliticize the claims of feminist vegetarianism.

This article offers an interpretative background against which the depoliticizing of feminist moral claims on behalf of the other animals can be perceived. Since feminists believe that the personal is political, it appears that many do not think their personal choice of animal foods reflects a feminist politics. But what if the values and beliefs imbedded in the choice to eat animals are antithetical to feminism, so, that, in the case of meat eating, the personal *is* political? Feminist theory offers a way to examine and interpret the practice of eating animals that removes vegetarianism from the category of "lifestyle" choice. In this chapter I provide a feminist philosophical exploration of the claim that animal rights should be practically enacted through all-vegetarian conferences by examining the dialectic between "the political" and "the natural."

The eating of animals is the most pervasive form of animal oppression in the Western world, representing as well the most frequent way in which most Westerners interact with animals. It carries immense environmental consequences in addition to the destruction of six billion animals yearly in the United States alone. Yet those living in the United States do not require animal flesh to ensure adequate nutrition; indeed, evidence continues to accumulate that "meat" eating is actually injurious to human health. Lastly, this topic provides an opportunity to respond to anti animal rights statements by feminists.

Defining the Traffic in Animals

Through the use of the phrase "feminist traffic in animals," I wish to politicize the use of animals' bodies as commodities. The serving of animal flesh at feminist conferences requires that feminists traffic in animals—that is, buy and consume animal parts—and announces that we endorse the literal traffic in animals: the production, transportation, slaughter, and packaging of animals' bodies.

Trafficking in animals represents a dominant material relationship in our culture. The animal-industrial complex is the second-largest industry, and the largest food industry, in the United States. Currently 60 percent of American foods come from animals, including eggs and dairy products (or "feminized protein") and animal corpses (or "animalized protein").[2] These terms disclose that the protein preexists its state of being processed through or as an animal; in other words, vegetable protein is the original protein. Trafficking in animals relies on this vegetable protein as well, but requires that it be the raw material, along with animals, for its product. Feminized protein and animalized protein come from terminal animals.

For feminists to traffic in animals, we must accept the trafficking in ideas, or the ideology, about terminal animals. These ideas form the superstructure of our daily lives, a part of which involves the presumed acceptability of this traffic. The difficulty is that the coercive nature of the ideological superstructure is invisible and, for trafficking to continue, must remain invisible.

When I use the phrase "traffic in animals," I deliberately invoke a classic feminist phrase, appearing in works such as Emma Goldman's "The Traffic in Women," and Gayle Rubin's "The Traffic in Women: Notes on the 'Political Economy' of Sex."[3] By choosing the word "traffic," I imply that similarities in the treatment of "disposable" or "usable" bodies exist.

To "traffic in animals" involves producers *and* consumers. Whatever "objects" we determine to be worth purchasing become included within our moral framework, and the production of these objects, too, becomes a part of such a framework, even if this aspect remains invisible. While numerous books on the animal-industrial complex are available,[4] they rarely are cited in feminist writings other than those by vegetarians, thus ensuring the invisibility of trafficking in animals for those who do so. The phrase "traffic in animals" is an attempt to wrest discursive control from those who wish to evade knowledge about what trafficking entails.

Discursive Control and Ignorance

No objective stance exists from which to survey the traffic in animals. Either we eat them or we do not. Not only is there no disinterested observer, but there is no impartial semantic or cultural space in which to hold a discussion. We live in a "meat"-advocating culture. Conflicts in meaning are resolved in favor of the dominant culture. Whatever our individual actions, the place from which we stand to survey the eating of animals is overwhelmed by the normativeness of "meat" and the (supposed) neutrality of the term "meat."

The contamination of the discursive space in which we might discuss the matter of cross-species consumption is further complicated by ignorance. Vegetarians know a great deal more about the material conditions that enable "meat" eating than "meat"-eaters do. But discursive power resides in those with the least knowledge. Lacking specific information regarding the topic, the people with the most ignorance set the limits of the discussion. Thus, when Ellen Goodman argues that "people make choices in these matters [animal rights] from the first time they knowingly eat a hamburger or catch a fish," she is making an epistemological claim without defining it. She also assumes that this claim dispenses with the challenges of animal rights. What exactly do "meat"-eaters know? That a hamburger is from a dead animal? The details of the literal traffic in animals that has brought the dead animal into the consumer's hands? Goodman implies that people have specific knowledge about "meat" production that in reality they do not have and usually do not want.

Discursive Privacy

It is necessary to politicize the process of obtaining animal bodies for food by using terms like "trafficking" because of the prevailing conceptual divisions of our culture. The context for talking about our use of animalized and feminized protein is one of rigid separation between "political," "economic," "domestic," and "personal."

The result of this social division is that certain issues are banished to zones of discursive privacy rather than seen as foci of generalized contestation. For instance, purchasing, preparing, and eating food is cast as a private-domestic matter. A similar separation exists between "economic" and "political."

Thus, while issues associated with *marketing* and *purchasing* dead animals become privatized to the domestic sphere of individual choice, issues involving the *production* of animals are *economized*, such as when the rise of "factory farms" is attributed solely to the demands of the market, or it is argued that we cannot interfere with the prerogatives of the animals' "owner."

When issues are labeled "domestic" or "economic," they become enclaved, shielded from generalized contestation, thus entrenching as *authoritative* what are actually only *interpretations* of issues. Furthermore, "since both domestic and official economic institutions support relations of dominance and subordination, the specific interpretations they naturalize tend, on the whole, to advantage dominant groups and individuals and to disadvantage their subordinates."[5] This is precisely what happens with the consumption of animals' bodies: it has been naturalized to favor the dominant group—people—to the disadvantage of the other animals.

As feminism demonstrates, the divisions between politics, economics, and domestic issues are false. The problem that an analysis such as mine faces is that these divisions continue to be accepted even by many feminists when the issue is animals; and the response by dominant groups is to banish the issue back to a zone of discursive privacy. When the issue is people's oppression of the other animals, this tendency to enforce discursive privacy when issues are being politicized is further complicated. Another social division exists—that between nature and culture.

We do not think of the other animals as having social needs. Since animals are ideologically confined to the realm of nature, making any sort of social claim on their behalf already introduces dissonance into established discourses. It appears that we are confusing the categories of nature and culture. But this in itself is a cultural classification enabled by predetermined ideologies that maintain a narrow, uncontextualized focus. Thus, any feminist animal rights position—by which I mean any argument for the freedom of the other animals from use by human beings—must challenge what has been labeled "natural" by the dominant culture.

Ideology: Hiding the Social Construction of the Natural

Any debate about the place of animals in human communities occurs within a cultural context and a cultural practice. Here ideology preexists and imposes itself on individual perceptions, so that what is actually a problem of consciousness—how we look at animals—is seen as an aspect of personal choice and is presented as a "natural" aspect of our lives as human beings. Claiming human beings to be predators like (some of) the other animals (fewer than 20 percent of animals are actually predators) is an example of naturalizing the political. Distinctions between people's carnivorism and carnivorous animals' predation are ignored in such a claim: human beings do not need to be predators, and there is no animal counterpart to human perpetuation of the grossly inhumane institutions of the animal-industrial complex. Nel Noddings summons natural processes when she states that "it is the fate of every living thing to be eaten,"[6] implying a similarity between the "natural" process of decay and the activity of slaughterhouses (which remain unnamed). Eating animals is also naturalized by the glamorization of hunting as an essential aspect of human evolution or as representing the true tribal relationship between indigenous people and animals, even though gathering cultures could be hearkened to as well. The result is that exploitation of animals is naturalized as intrinsic to people's relationships with the other animals. The "naturalization" of the ways in which we are socialized to look at animals affects how we act toward animals—that is, if we see animals as "meat," we eat them. Thus we can read in a letter responding to an article on "political correctness": "None of us has the whole picture. For one woman, vegetarianism is an ethical imperative; for another, eating meat is part of the natural world's give and take."[7]

Attempts to make the ideology and the material reality of "meat" production visible, to denaturalize it, result in responses by feminists who through further promulgation of the superstructure and its importance for individual, or certain groups of, feminists, uphold the trafficking in (traditional) ideas about animals and actual trafficking in animal flesh. "Meat" is thus an *idea* that is experienced as an *object*, a *relationship* between humans and the other animals that is rendered instead as a *material reality* involving "food choices," a social construction that is seen as natural and normative. When we see the concept of species as a social construction, we are enabled to offer an alternative social construction that is morally preferable, one that recognizes animals as a subordinated social group, rather than naturally usable.

To understand why feminists defend their trafficking in animals, we must perceive the dialectic that is at work between the "political" and the "natural."

Naturalizing the Political: I

In a "meat"-advocating culture, decisions that are actually political are presented as "natural" and "inevitable." When Ellen Goodman argues that "we acknowledge ourselves as creatures of nature" in "knowingly" eating a hamburger or catching a fish, she presumes that her readers share with her an understanding that "creatures of nature" eat dead bodies. She also assumes that we will find it acceptable to be likened to the other animals when the issue is the consumption of animal flesh, even though so much of human nature (and justification for such consumption) is precisely defined by establishing strict notions of differentiation between humans and the other animals. Two prevalent conceptualizations assist in the naturalizing of the political choice to use animals as food and explain Goodman's confidence in her defense of such actions.

The Case of the False Mass Term

The existence of "meat" as a mass term contributes to the naturalizing of the phenomenon of eating animals' bodies. Mass terms refer to things like water or colors; no matter how much you have of it, or what type of container it is in, water is still water. You can add a bucket of water to a pool of water without changing it at all. Objects referred to by mass terms have no individuality, no uniqueness, no specificity, no particularity.

When we turn an animal into "meat," someone who has a very particular, situated life, a unique being, is converted into something that has no distinctiveness, no uniqueness, no individuality. When you add five pounds of hamburger to a plate of hamburger, you have more of the same thing; nothing is changed. But if you have a living cow in front of you, and you kill that cow, and butcher that cow, and grind up her flesh, you have not added a mass term to a mass term and ended up with more of the same. Because of the reign of "meat" as a mass term, it is not often while eating "meat" that one thinks: "I am now interacting with an animal." We do not see our own personal "meat"-eating as contact with animals because it has been renamed as contact with food. But what is on the plate in front of us is *not* devoid of specificity. It is the dead flesh of what was once a living, feeling being. The crucial point here is that we make some*one* who is a unique being and therefore not the appropriate referent of a mass term into some*thing* that is the appropriate referent of a mass term. We do so by removing any associations that might make it difficult to accept the activity of rendering a unique individual into a consumable thing. Not wanting to be aware of this activity, we accept this disassociation, this distancing device of the mass term "meat."

Ontologizing Animals as "Naturally" Consumable

The prevailing ideology ontologizes animals as consumable, as mass terms. This ontology is socially constructed: there is nothing inherent in a cow's existence that necessitates her future fate as hamburger or her current fate as milk machine. However, a major way in which we circumvent responsibility for terminal animals' fate at the hands of humans is to believe that they have no other fate than to be food, that this is their "natural" existence. As a result, certain positions regarding animals' ontology—that is, the normativeness of "meat" eating—are embraced by people across the divisions of race, class, and sex. Unless some factor dislodges these positions and brings about consciousness, these positions will continue to be held and, when under attack, fiercely defended as natural, inevitable, and/or beneficial.

The existence of "meat" as a mass term contributes to the ontologizing and thus "naturalizing" of animals as intrinsically consumable. The ideology becomes sanctioned as eternal or unalterable, rather than suspect and changeable. To be a pig is to be pork. To be a chicken is to be poultry. When Nel Noddings raises the issue of the possible mass extinction of certain domesticated animals if humans were to stop eating them, she is reproducing this ontology. She continues to see the animals as being dependent on their relationship to us, as literally existing (only) for us. To be concerned about whether animals can live without our needing (eating) them continues their ontologized status as exploitable. Indeed, it clearly evokes this ontology: without our needing them, and implicitly, using them as food, they would not exist.

Warehousing animals (the term I prefer to "factory farming") is inevitable in a "meat"-advocating, capitalist culture such as ours. It has become the only way to maintain and meet the demand for flesh products that currently exists and must be seen as the *logical outcome* of this ontology. Warehoused animals account for 90 to 97 percent of the animal flesh consumed in the United States. Thus, those who argue that warehousing is immoral but alternatives to obtaining animal flesh are acceptable deny the historical reality that has brought us to this time and place. They conceive of some "natural" practice of flesh consumption that is free from historical influence, that is essentially atemporal and thus apolitical. Thus they naturalize the political decision to eat other animals.

Politicizing the Natural: I

Animal rights discourse refuses to see the consumption of dead animals as a natural act and actively asserts it to be a political one. It does so by refusing to accept the discursive boundaries that bury the issue as "natural" or "personal." In doing this, animal rights discourse exposes a matrix of relations that are usually ignored or accepted as implicit, the matrix that I call trafficking in animals, by proposing three interrelated arguments: other species matter, our current ontology of animals is unacceptable, and our current practices are oppressive.

Other Species Matter

Central to the process of "naturalizing" the political is the human/other dialectic in which "human" de facto represents white (human) maleness and "other" represents that which white human maleness negates: other races, sexes, or species. The process that Zuleyma Tang Halpin observes in scientific objectivity is generalizable to the view of anyone in a dominant position in a class-, race-, sex-, and species-stratified culture: "The 'other,' by definition, is the opposite of the 'self,' and therefore comes to be regarded as intrinsically of lesser value."[8] Caroline Whitbeck identifies this as a "self-other *opposition* that underlines much of so-called 'western thought.'"[9] This opposition has been identified in ecofeminist discourse as a set of dualisms: culture or nature, male or female, mind or body, and, importantly, human or animal. In the prevailing dualistic ontology, equation of any human group with the other animals serves to facilitate the humans' exploitation. As Halpin points out, "Even when groups labeled 'inferior' are not explicitly equated with women, they are often compared to animals, usually in ways designed to make them appear more animal than human (using white males as the prototype of humanity)."[10]

What we have for the most part in feminism is a species-specific philosophical system, in which (an expanded) humanity continues to negate the other animals precisely because their otherness is located in the natural sphere. This species-specific tendency in feminist philosophy is evident, for instance, in Elizabeth Spelman's important article "Woman as Body." After discussing the equation of women, slaves, laborers, children, and animals with the body and how this equation facilitates their oppression, she goes on to offer theoretical redress only for the human animals so oppressed.[11] Barbara Noske points out that "as yet there exists in our thinking little room for the notion of a non-human Subject and what this would imply."[12] Nancy Hartsock wonders "why there must be a sharp discontinuity between humans and [the other] animals. Is this too an outgrowth of the masculinist project?"[13] As if in reply, Noske suggests that "even if there is such a thing as a species boundary between ourselves and *all* animals, might this discontinuity not exist on a horizontal level rather than on a vertical and hierarchical level?"[14] A species-neutral system would recognize each animal as a person, "and to some extent as an Alien person."[15]

Our Current Ontology of Animals Is Unacceptable

Resisting the current ontology of animals as consumable is central to animal rights. Once the human-animal division is perceived to be as corrupt and as inaccurate as the other dualisms closely examined by ecofeminism, the re-Subjectification and denaturalization of animals can occur. This involves accepting them ontologically on their own terms and not on the basis of our interests. The current ontology requires that we acquiesce to the hierarchical structure that places humans above animals and defines "human" and "animal" antithetically. The current ontology continues to subordinate nonhuman nature—in this case the other animals—to people's whims.

The ontology of animals that accompanies animal rights theory involves distinguishing between reforms of certain practices that accept animals as usable and abolition of these practices. The goal is not bigger cages, but *no* cages; not bigger stalls, but *no* veal calves; not mandated rest

stops, but *no* transporting; not careful placement of downed animals into front-loader buckets, but *no* system that creates downed animals; not "humane" slaughter, but *no* slaughter. Reform of the current system still subordinates animals to humans. Reform situates itself within the issue of animal *welfare* rather than animal rights, and the concern becomes the *appropriate* use of animals rather than the elimination of humans' use of animals. Often when feminists respond to animal rights, they attempt to dislodge the ontological claims of animal rights and argue for the reformist acceptance of animals' exploitation. Ellen Goodman argues for the "intelligent, responsible use of animals." Mary Zeiss Stange wants hunters to "promote positive public images of animal use and welfare, as opposed to animal protectionism."[16] In upholding the dominant ontology, the promotion of responsible use of animals grants charity where liberty is needed.

What is required is both an acceptance of the ontological integrity of those who are different from the "normative" human and a recognition of animals' consciousness and cultures. As much as men's accounts of women's lives have been partial, false, or malicious lies, so too have humans' accounts of the other animals' lives. In resisting the "naturalization" of animals, we need, as Noske argues, to develop an anthropology of the other animals that encounters them on their terms. A false generosity only serves to restrict animals to the natural realm that enables their ontologizing as usable.

"Predation" Is Oppressive

Claiming that human consumption of the other animals is predation like that of carnivorous animals naturalizes this act. But if this predation is socially constructed, then it is not a necessary aspect of human-animal relations. Instead it is an ongoing oppression enacted through the animal-industrial complex.

Using the three-part definition of oppression proposed by Alison Jaggar,[17] we can see its applicability to the experience of the victims of the traffic in animals.

First, the "oppressed suffer some kind of restriction on their freedom."[18] Terminal animals suffer literal constraints upon their freedom: most are unable to walk, to breathe clean air, to stretch their wings, to root in the dirt, to peck for food, to suckle their young, to avoid having their sexuality abused. Whether warehoused or not, all are killed. They are not able to do something which is important for them to do, and they lack the ability to determine for themselves their own actions.

Second, "oppression is the result of human agency, humanly imposed restrictions."[19] Humans have a choice whether to eat animals or not. Choosing to purchase flesh at a supermarket or have it served at a conference represents human agency; such human agency requires that the other animals lose their freedom to exist independently of us.

Third, "oppression must be unjust."[20] Injustice includes the thwarting of an individual's liberty because of her or his membership in a group that has been targeted for exploitation. From the perspective of human-skin privilege, the oppression of other animals is seen as just, even though it arises from targeting for exploitation specific groups—in this case, the other animals. In a species-neutral philosophical system, such as the one that I believe is integral to ecofeminism, human skin should not be the sole determinant of what is moral. Viewed from a philosophical system that rejects the intertwined human/animal and subject/object dualisms, humans' treatment of terminal animals is unjust. Beverly Harrison proposes that "no one has a moral right to override basic conditions for others' well-being in order to have 'liberty' inconsistent with others' basic welfare."[21] This is what people are doing when they traffic in animals. As Alice Walker observes, "The oppression that black people suffer in South Africa—and people of color, and children face all over the world—is the same oppression that animals endure every day to a greater degree."[22]

Naturalizing the Political: II

In response to efforts to re-Subjectify the other animals and label our treatment of them as oppression, people who do not wish to give up human-skin privilege seek ways to banish animal rights discourse from the political realm, to reprivatize and re-"naturalize" it. Reprivatization defends the established social division of discourses—that is, the personal is not the political, the natural is not the social, the domestic is not the political—thus denying political status for animal rights. For instance, when Ellen Goodman contends that animal rights are "unnatural," she implicitly accepts discursive boundaries she otherwise finds disturbing. If animal rights are unnatural, then animal oppression is natural; if it is natural, it is not political. She is attempting to encase the debate once again in discursive privacy. Or, when a feminist refers to the "so-called animal liberation movement,"[23] she implicitly denies political content to this movement. When Nel Noddings claims that domestic animals do not have meaningful relationships with other adult animals nor do they "anticipate their deaths,"[24] she delimits their lives within the sanctity of the "natural," which it is presumed we can identify (and control), rather than the social. It may be reassuring to believe that animals have no social network and do not object to their deaths; however, these beliefs are possible only as long as we do not inquire closely into the lives of animals as subjects. Then we see that certain cultural structures facilitate these efforts at depoliticizing and renaturalizing animals' oppression.

Feminist theorist Nancy Hartsock observes that ruling-class ideas "give an incorrect account of reality, an account only of appearances."[25] Our discourse about animals has been determined largely by the appearance of "meat" in animals' marketable form—T-bone, lamb chops, hamburger, "fresh" chickens—an appearance positing that "meat," like George Eliot's happy women, has no history. As long as "meat" has no past, its identity will come only from the constructed context of appetites and appearances. This permits what I call the flight from specificity.

The flight from specificity favors generalities instead of engaged knowledge, mass terms over individual entities. To be specific would require confronting the actual practice and the meaning of what is done to animals. Generalities safely insulate one from this knowledge, keeping debates at a predetermined, unbloodied level. Most frequently they do not pinpoint the victim, the perpetrator, or the method. Just as most feminists would recognize that the statement "Some people batter other people" is imprecise—who and how left undefined—so is the statement "We eat 'meat.'"

When, for instance, in her defense of eating animals, Nel Noddings refers to ensuring that domestic animals' "deaths are physically and psychically painless,"[26] she presumes that such a practice exists and that we all sufficiently understand what she means so that we can *agree* that such a practice either exists or is attainable for terminal animals. In this view, ignorance about the act of slaughtering prevails, though it remains unexposed. In fact, such a practice neither exists nor is attainable.

Another example of the flight from specificity occurs when the term "meat eating" is applied transhistorically, transculturally, implying that the means by which "meat" is obtained have not changed so much that different terms are needed, or else that the changes in the means of production are immaterial to a discussion.

How can the flesh obtained from mass-produced, warehoused, terminal animals in any way duplicate the flesh eaten by the ancestors when they were alive, when a different material reality constructed the meaning of "meatballs"? "Meat" is not an ahistorical term, though it functions here as though it were, as representation. Surely the ancestors know that "pork" obtained from a twentieth-century warehoused animal—who was pumped full of chemicals, who never saw the light of day until transported to be butchered, whose relationship with other animals, including mother and/or children was curtailed, and who never rooted in the earth—is not at all the "pork" they ate.

In each of these cases, terms such as "painless" or "meatballs" or "pork" convey little specific knowledge about the production of "meat."

Those aspects unidentified or misidentified are then presumed to be unproblematic or inconsequential. The result of this discursive control is that "meat"-eaters can set the limits on what sort of information about "meat" eating is allowed into a discussion.[27]

The meanings that are established regarding "meat" are almost always general, rarely specific. They recognize neither the specific animal killed to be food, nor the specific means for raising, transporting, and killing this animal. This flight from specificity regarding "meat" production bars from the discourse matters that in other areas of feminist theory are considered the basis for making ethical decisions: material reality and material relationships.

Feminist Defenses of Trafficking in Animals

Before examining specific feminist defenses of trafficking in animals, some general problems of discursive control must be identified. Feminists, like nonfeminists, generally seek to banish animal rights by reprivatizing decisions about animals and renaturalizing animals' lives as subordinate to humans'. In this, several factors function in their favor. They assume that their predefined understanding of the issue is adequate: for example, that it is correct to label animal rights as being in opposition to pluralism because their definition of pluralism excludes animal rights. Any predefined feminist principle that is established as in opposition to animal rights requires closer examination: does it presume that the socially authorized forms of feminist debate available for discussing this issue are adequate and fair? To paraphrase Fraser, does it fail to question whether these forms of public discourse are skewed in favor of the self-interpretations and interests of dominant groups (including human females)—occluding, in other words, the fact that the means of public discourse themselves may be at issue?[28]

Hidden ethical stances prevail even in pluralistic feminisms. In an evolving community of individuals who share ideas and goals for changing patriarchal society, some values are so given, so taken for granted, that we never examine them. For instance, we agree that cannibalism is not a legitimate way to obtain nutrition, even though human flesh can be very tasty. Cannibalism is not a question of individual tastes, appetites, autonomy, or ritual; it is a forbidden activity whose forbiddenness appears obvious to almost everyone, and therefore this forbiddenness disturbs very few. Clearly this is not so when it comes to eating nonhuman animal flesh. In this case the flesh is considered both tasty and acceptable, based on a decision individuals and cultural traditions have made about nutrition and ethics. To suggest that nonhuman animal flesh be forbidden disturbs many.

The differing ethical stances regarding the flesh of human animals versus the flesh of nonhuman animals illustrates that the issue is not whether a community can forbid an action but who is to be protected from being consumed. Since a community-wide vegetarianism is seen as problematic but a community ban on cannibalism is a given, it is obvious that theorizing about species is at this point in time receiving different discursive space from theorizing about race, class, gender, and heterosexism.

Politicizing the Natural: II

A species-exclusive philosophy establishes human and animal as antithetical categories, and naturalizes human beings' use of the other animals. In contrast, a species-neutral philosophy would not exaggerate differences between humans and the other animals, or imply that singular human evils such as warehousing animals or rape represent some residual "natural" or "animal-like" tendency. As the "natural" is politicized and labeled "oppression," "meat" will no longer be an idea that is experienced as an object. Trafficking will be destabilized by consciousness and solidarity.

The Politics of Consciousness

Consciousness of oppression requires responses. Alison Jaggar observes that to "talk of oppression

seems to commit feminists to a world view that includes at least two groups with conflicting interests: the oppressors and the oppressed"[29]—or, to put it more bluntly in the terms of this article, "meat"-eaters and their "meat." Paulo Freire suggests that we can respond to these conflicting interests either as critics/radicals, for whom "the importance is the continuing transformation of reality," or as naive thinkers/sectarians, who accommodate "to this normalized 'today.'" Naive thinkers/sectarians accept prevailing ideological barriers and discursive boundaries; critical consciousness can find no hold here: "sectarianism, because it is myth-making and irrational, turns reality into a false (and therefore unchangeable) 'reality.'"[30]

The alternative to this accommodation of and mythicizing of reality is to accept the process of radicalization, an actual engagement in the efforts to transform concrete reality. This transformation aligns one with the oppressed rather than the oppressor, the "meat" rather than the "meat"-eater.

Breaking down ideological boundaries requires that those who are the oppressors must stop "regarding the oppressed as an abstract category,"[31] must stop seeing "meat" as a mass term.

The Politics of Solidarity

Critical consciousness makes us aware of ourselves as oppressors. It transforms our understanding of a reality in which the political has been naturalized. Trafficking in animals oppresses them, ontologizing them as "beings for another." In other words, trafficking in animals makes us oppressors.

The necessary precondition for animals to be free is that there be no trafficking in animals' bodies. The ontology will not collapse upon itself until the actions that the ontology upholds—for example, "meat" eating—are stopped, and until we stop being animals' oppressors.

Notes

1. Claudia Card, "Pluralist Lesbian Separatism," in *Lesbian Philosophies and Cultures,* ed. Jeffner Allen (Albany: State University of New York Press, 1990), 139.

2. See Carol J. Adams, *The Sexual Politics of Meat: A Feminist Vegetarian Critical Theory* (New York: Continuum, 1990), 80–81.

3. Emma Goldman, "The Traffic in Women," in *The Traffic in Women and Other Essays on Feminism* (New York: Times Change Press, 1970); Gayle Rubin, "The Traffic in Women: Notes on the 'Political Economy' of Sex," in *Toward an Anthropology of Women,* ed. Rayna R. Reiter (New York and London: Monthly Review Press, 1975), 157–210. See also Janice Raymond, "The International Traffic in Women," *Reproductive and Genetic Engineering* 2, no. 1 (1989): 51–70.

4. See C. David Coats, *Old MacDonald's Factory Farm: The Myth of the Traditional Farm and the Shocking Truth About Animal Suffering in Today's Agribusiness* (New York: Continuum, 1989); Jim Mason and Peter Singer, *Animal Factories* (New York: Crown Publishers, 1980); John Robbins, *Diet for a New America* (Walpole, N.H.: Stillpoint, 1987).

5. Nancy Fraser, *Unruly Practices: Power, Discourse and Gender in Contemporary Social Theory.* (Minneapolis: University of Minnesota Press, 1989), 168.

6. Nel Noddings, "Comment on Donovan's 'Animal Rights and Feminist Theory,'" *Signs* 16 (1991): 420.

7. Susanna J. Sturgis, "Arsenal of Silencers," *Sojourner: The Women's Forum*, December 1991, 5.

8. Zuleyma Tang Halpin, "Scientific Objectivity and the Concept of the 'Other,'" *Women's Studies International Forum* 12 (1989): 286.

9. Caroline Whitbeck, "A Different Reality: Feminist Ontology," in *Women, Knowledge, and Reality: Explorations in Feminist Philosophy*, ed. Ann Garry and Marilyn Pearsall (Boston: Unwin Hyman, 1989), 51.

10. Halpin, "Scientific Objectivity," 287–88.

11. Elizabeth V. Spelman, "Woman as Body: Ancient and Contemporary Views," *Feminist Studies* 8 (1982): 109–31.

12. Barbara Noske, *Humans and Other Animals* (London: Pluto Press, 1989), 157.

13. Nancy C. M. Hartsock, *Money, Sex, and Power: Toward a Feminist Historical Materialism* (Boston: Northeastern University Press, 1983, 1985), 302, n. 9.

14. Noske, *Humans and Other Animals,* 125.

15. Ibid., 138.

16. Mary Zeiss Stange, "Hunting—An American Tradition," *American Hunter,* January 1991, 27.

17. See Alison M. Jaggar, *Feminist Politics and Human Nature* (Totowa, N. J. Rowman & Littlefield, 1988), 6–7. Thanks to Nancy Tuana for her suggestion of Jaggar's text.

18. Ibid., 6–7.

19. Ibid.

20. Ibid.

21. Beverly Harrison, *Making the Connections: Essays in Feminist Social Ethics*, ed. Carol S. Robb (Boston: Beacon, 1985), 255.

22. Ellen Bring, "Moving Towards Coexistence: An Interview with Alice Walker," *Animals' Agenda* 8 (April 1988): 6–9.

23. Stange, "Hunting," 26.

24. Noddings, "Comment," 421.

25. Hartsock, *Money, Sex, and Power*, 9.

26. Noddings, "Comment," 421.

27. This problem is discussed at length in Adams, *Sexual Politics of Meat*, 63–82.

28. Fraser, *Unruly Practices*, 164.

29. Jaggar, *Feminist Politics and Human Nature*, p. 7.

30. Paolo Freire, *Pedagogy of the Oppressed* (New York: Penguin, 1972, 1978), 65.

31. Freire, *Pedagogy of the Oppressed*, 29.

Barbara McDonald

Becoming Vegan

Vegans are people who object to the use of non-human animal products for food, cosmetics, clothing, and vivisection—virtually all invasive activities involving nonhuman animals. In the United States, adopting such a lifestyle is a major change from the normative practice and ideology of human dominance over nonhuman animals. Veganism appears to be related to a propensity toward alternativism in other areas of life, and eschewing the use of all animal products represents a lifestyle change that necessarily involves all areas of life. How do people make such a remarkable change? A possible explanation might be offered by Mezirow's transformation theory (Mezirow, 1991), which predicts that such lifestyle change will follow a ten-step process that pivots on dialogue, reflection, and action.

Mezirow's transformation theory has been widely discussed in adult education as an explanation of how adults learn to make major lifestyle changes. The ten steps, which Mezirow says can occur in any order, include a disorienting dilemma, self-examination, and critical assessment of assumptions. They also include recognizing that discontent and transformative experiences are shared, exploring new options, planning a course of action, acquiring new skills and knowledge, trying new roles, renegotiating relationships and building new ones, and reintegrating the new perspective into one's life. A central triad, upon which the ten steps depend, includes critical reflection, democratic dialogue, and reflective action.

As part of a larger study, I discovered that Mezirow's theory does not explain the process of learning to become vegan (McDonald, 1998). The research presented here is in answer to the question, "How do people learn to become vegan?"—the first question in my investigation of Mezirow's transformation theory.

Becoming vegan represents a major change in lifestyle, one that demands the rejection of the normative ideology of speciesism. With only 3 percent of Americans claiming they had not used animals for any purpose within the previous 2 years (Duda and Young, 1997), veganism represents an alternative ideology and lifestyle. How do people learn about this alternative ideology, and how do they learn to change their lifestyle?

Method

As a practicing vegan, I wanted to employ a perspective and methodology that would enable me to use my own experience to enhance understanding of how other vegans have learned; yet I wanted the story to be their own. My adoption of veganism, following years as a vegetarian and animal rights activist, was triggered by the loss of a long-time canine companion. My journey as a vegan in mainstream society and my familiarity with the personal and social issues surrounding veganism informed the interview protocol and data analysis.

However, because I wanted to know the path that others had traveled, I chose a phenomenological perspective. Typically in phenomenology, the researcher attempts to remove his or her biases from the research. To enable the incorporation of my own understanding, I chose heuristics, a modification of phenomenological methodology (Moustaskas, 1990). Heuristics explicitly recognizes the impossibility of neutrality in research and enables the researcher to study phenomena with which he or she has had intense experience.

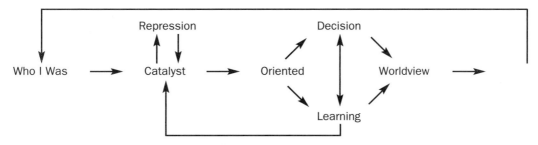

FIGURE 19.1   The Process of Learning to Become Vegan

I used a naturalistic design to collect interview data from twelve vegans. Purposeful sampling was used, beginning with the June 1996 nationwide March for the Animals in Washington, DC. I employed snowball sampling to further identify vegans from a small core of vegans identified at the March. To increase the probability of interviewing committed vegans, I interviewed only those who had been vegan for at least one year. I used an unstructured interview protocol, with the primary purpose of allowing each participant to share the story of how he or she learned to adopt a vegan lifestyle. Although I asked for clarification or elaboration regarding their learning, most of my contribution to the interviews was to keep the participants from straying away from their stories.

Findings

The Process of Learning to Become Vegan

The process of learning to become vegan was rooted in the individuals' sense of who they are and how they fit in the world. During the learning process, the individual passed through a number of experiences diagrammed schematically as a general process of learning to become vegan (Figure 19.1). The elements are described below and defined in Table 19.1.

Each individual came to the learning event with a unique personal and cultural history, identified in this study as *who I was.* These histories shaped their original worldviews and, for most of the participants, influenced their learning to become vegan. For example, most of the participants claimed to have been "animal people" all their lives, which they felt may have helped them become more receptive to information about animal cruelty.

Information on cruelty served as a *catalyst* to one of two reactions. In two cases, individuals reported a reaction interpreted as *repression.* These participants put the information in the back of their minds until a later time, when another catalytic event facilitated its recall. A second, more

TABLE 19.1   Elements of the Vegan Learning Process

Who I Was	— The background and experiences that made the participant who they were prior to the learning experience
Catalytic Experience	— The experience that introduced the participant to some aspect of animal cruelty, and resulted in repression or becoming oriented
Repression	— The repression of knowledge
Becoming Oriented	— The intention to learn more, make a decision, or do both
Learning	— Learning about animal abuse or how to live as a vegetarian or vegan
Decision	— Making the choice to become vegetarian or vegan
Worldview	— The new perspective that guides the vegan's new lifestyle

common reaction was to become *oriented* in one of two ways: either to *learn* more about animal cruelty or to *decide* to become vegetarian or vegan and, subsequently, to learn more about animal cruelty and how to live as a vegetarian or vegan.

The participant typically spent a fair amount of time, even years, learning about animal cruelty or how to live as a vegetarian or vegan. If oriented to learn about cruelty but undecided about becoming a vegetarian or vegan, the participant made the decision after a period of learning about animal cruelty.

Over time, the participant adopted a *worldview* characteristic of vegans, represented by a belief in the equality of human and nonhuman animals. This worldview became the foundation for an ethically-based praxis. The following discussion examines each stage of the process in more detail.

Participants' Testimonies

Who were these people before they became vegans? Most of the participants had a prior love of nature and of "pets" but did not see the connection between their companion animals and food animals. Before becoming vegan, most of the participants felt that they had always been compassionate and caring to nonhuman animals, but they had compartmentalized their compassion. Will described it this way:

> We consider ourselves to be animal people, and compassionate, but it was cats and dogs, and pets, and you always felt compassion for them, but that was kind of compartmentalized, in that you didn't really think about the rest of the animal kingdom.

Although most of the participants had always been "animal people," they had not made the connection between nonhuman animals and the food they ate. Lucille, Lanny, Cary, Roger, Lisa, Will, and Maire all expressed amazement that they had not seen the connection. Cary, for example, said,

> When I saw hamburgers or steaks, I never put two and two together. I used to eat tongue,

which is a Jewish delicacy. I never even knew what it was. It's that disguised. Even though they say the word tongue, I never knew it was that.

Lena, atypical of the participants, said that she did not have a strong affection for animals when she was young. Nevertheless, she recalled numerous events involving companion animals during her childhood. Janet observed that childhood affection for animals is not exceptional: "I remember I was heartbroken when my pet frog [died]. Absolutely devastated me. But I don't think that's anything unusual. I think other children were the same way."

Catalytic Experiences

Catalytic experiences presented information to the participant about animal cruelty and resulted in further action. Participants usually encountered more than one catalytic experience. The catalytic experience triggered one of two responses. Most participants became oriented to further learning about animal abuse. Alternatively, a few participants repressed the information, only to have it resurface at a later time. Most participants who became oriented to further learning did not make an immediate decision. These participants became open to learning about animal abuse and eventually made the decision to give up animal products.

For Lanny and Lisa, the catalytic experience was akin to a religious conversion. Lanny, who had learned about animal cruelty but had not yet decided to go vegetarian, made the decision one day while sitting reflectively in a bottomland pasture. Lanny's life had not been turning out as he thought it might, and he had gone outside to think about it. While he was thinking, he looked up and exchanged a long and pensive gaze with a buck standing on the hill above him. He said,

> I just decided not to eat meat anymore. Just all of a sudden, that afternoon, for whatever reason, whether it was a force that made me decide, I don't know. But, it was that instant that I decided to give up meat.

Lisa converted to veganism after watching a video on animal cruelty. She described her reaction to the video this way:

> I watched the video. It was almost like, it was like they say, the curtain was pulled back. The truth was made known. I felt like I had been born again. It was like there is no turning back now. Now I know the cruelty that exists.

The catalytic experience was often, but not necessarily, emotional. An intense emotional reaction to the catalytic experience usually also included a cognitive interpretation that enabled the participant to immediately comprehend, as well as feel, the consequences of the new knowledge of animal abuse. Cognition typically manifested recognition of the power relationship between human and nonhuman animals and was fed by negative emotions, such as guilt, sadness, and anger.

Rarely was a decision made or did learning occur without an interaction between emotions and cognition. Participants often described their understanding as immediate, exemplified by Michelle's statement: "I thought, my God, I just didn't realize what things went on, I really didn't."

The emotions felt during the catalytic experience were typically negative ones: pain, shock, guilt, sadness, or depression. Lisa, like Michelle, cried as she first learned about animal cruelty. Lena told about her emotional reaction to a video about vivisection, saying, "It affected me so dramatically. It just broke my heart. I have never had [anything] to [have] such an effect."

Emotions seem to have been one of the major defining characteristics of the more memorable catalytic experiences. The decision to become vegan following a period of vegetarianism was more often rational. Will and Maire, for example, spent a lot of time discussing veganism before they decided to make the decision. Maire noted that they "really consterned over [becoming vegan]. That ended up being a big decision, a big conversation, with us." Drew, who examined animal rights literature for about a month before making his decision, said his decision was "mostly rational. I just decided I did not

want to contribute to the big . . . meat machine anymore . . . I would not say it was emotional."

Becoming Oriented

Following a catalytic experience, the participants became oriented to further learning. For some, this orientation included making a decision to go vegetarian or vegan. For others, the orientation was toward learning about animal abuse, how to live a new lifestyle, or both. Becoming oriented provided clear direction for the participant.

When a participant became oriented toward learning about animal abuse or about living a vegetarian or vegan lifestyle, the decision was made consciously and purposefully. As Lanny noted, information about animal cruelty is "not front page news." Learning about animal abuse and how to live a marginalized lifestyle required a clear commitment to learn. Lisa's words describe this commitment: "There's no turning back. Now I know the cruelty that exists. I've been learning and studying and reading ever since." Will and Maire were disturbed by the brutality of the Harp seal hunts, which they learned about from a TV special: "We were really shocked at that, and so we started getting more information about [animal cruelty]."

Learning

Becoming oriented and open facilitated learning about animal abuse, how to live a vegetarian or vegan lifestyle, or both. Participants became self-directed, goal-directed learners. Learning about animal abuse and learning a new lifestyle was, in retrospect, guided by an ethical praxis of compassion. As they learned, participants became more convinced of the moral rightness of their direction. Lisa assuredly pronounced,

> I feel like I have been born again. I feel like I am still on a path to enlightenment. . . . It's been a spiritual transformation for me. It was like, yes! God has led me to this.

Participants learned through reading, thinking, talking, and becoming involved in animal rights or vegetarian-related activities. Dialogue was one strategy attempted to learn, teach, or cope with the stress of adapting to their emerging perspective and lifestyle. Often, conversations with others were one-sided, heated, or fraught with the intention to persuade. Many of the participants' families and friends argued with or trivialized the vegetarian or vegan decision, and eventually everyone stopped discussing it.

For most participants, lack of support from family and friends caused hurtful feelings. Lanny's family, for example, won't discuss his diet with him anymore. After they argued for a period of time, Lanny sadly concluded, "Yeah, it did hurt a great deal, that they would not accept me and the choices I made."

Some of the participants were able to discuss what they were learning with family and friends. This happened most often when the family member or friend was open-minded, sympathetic to the vegetarian or vegan position, or was also a vegetarian or vegan. Drew's wife and her grandmother, for example, were vegetarian before Drew met them. Cary's family was supportive, as long as he could prove he was getting the appropriate nutrients. Sean's parents had experimented with vegetarianism, and his words reveal how support may facilitate learning:

> For about five years of my life, my parents were very strict vegetarians. I was a young 13, 14, 15 years old. I was rebellious. I'm gonna eat meat. They switched back and saw that I was getting a little curious about vegetarianism, and they had so much literature and so many books and so much to say. So it was really helpful, getting that from your parents.

Reading was a primary way of learning for every participant. For those like Michelle and Sean, reading was the main and almost exclusive source of information. Sean explained,

> After being vegetarian for less than a year, I was just so curious as to why people take it to a further extent such as veganism. So I started reading a lot of books by John Robbins and Peter Singer, who are some of the top authors that speak on factory farming, animal liberation,

and veganism. It attracted me so that I wanted to take it to the next step.

The participants used literature both to learn and to teach. One of their most frequently used ways of educating was giving literature about animal cruelty to others. Participants learned through experience that dialogue was usually ineffective as a method of teaching others. Lena gave an example:

> The guy who is my mechanic, apparently I took him something on vegetarianism a while back, but when I was in there the last time he said, You gave me some stuff on vegetarianism a while back. I don't know what I did with it. I really wasn't ready for it then, but could you send me some more stuff. I'm really considering this.

Most of the vegans also learned through some form of animal rights activism. Lena became active in a vegetarian society, where she writes a newsletter and sits on the board of directors. Drew became well-informed by preparing for appearances on radio and television shows. Cary was elected to the leadership of an animal rights organization. Janet lobbies state legislatures for animal protection legislation. For example, Janet and a friend, "along with some animal activists . . . worked to get [the mandatory spay and neuter law] passed." All these activities required the vegan to be well informed.

Making the Decision to Eliminate Animal Products

The decision to become a vegetarian or a vegan was made either immediately after a catalytic experience and the orientation to such a lifestyle or following some period of learning. If the decision was made temporally close to the catalytic experience, it was typically more emotional than if it was made after a period of learning. Typically, the vegan decision was made after a period of learning, in which the logical inconsistency of being in favor of animal rights but continuing to eat animal products was pondered. As they reflected, talked, read, and became active, the vegetarians-turned-vegan recognized this logical inconsistency between their beliefs and their actions. Lanny explained,

> I would think about being a vegetarian but still using milk or still putting cheese in stuff. I would learn more and then decided, where do you draw the line? What's the difference? So why not cut out all animal products, not just in food, but in clothing, in my house, you know, live a truly cruelty-free lifestyle.

The decision to become a vegetarian or a vegan was often seen in retrospect as a fit. Reflecting on the decision to go vegetarian, Will commented that becoming vegan "was something that [we] just had to do." Roger, Lisa, Franz, and Michelle also noted that the decision to be vegan, in retrospect, was inevitable. It felt comfortable, and once made, was final.

The Transformed Worldview

The vegans' transformed worldviews were shaped by a felt connection with nonhuman animals and with nature, the moral rightness of veganism, and by experiencing the world as a vegetarian and vegan. Advocating for the welfare and rights of animals became a dominant purpose of the transformed worldview. A central feature of this worldview was that animals were no longer viewed as food. Lanny, for example, explained why Indians do not eat cows, even though there is hunger in India: ". . . they understand that that cow is not food. It is a being. And to them, a holy being. So, I would be that way now myself."

Other features of this worldview were that animal protection extended to all areas of life. Major changes had to be made in virtually every area. Maire noted this necessity, explaining that even a vegan's wardrobe and accessories had to be renovated. Lanny, Lisa, Lena, and Franz described an affection for the nonhuman world that extended to caring for nature. Lena commented,

> It's like I have a much, much greater respect, certainly for all living things, and of course plant life. I don't even want to pull weeds

really. It's sort of like, why do I have to kill this weed? It has a right to be there.

The participants especially expressed a feeling of connectivity with nonhuman animals. Often, that connection was made tangible by the animals' ability to feel pain. Almost every participant mentioned the recognition of this close association with human feeling. Cary expressed this shared ability to feel pain as a bond between human and nonhuman animals: "The dogs, the cows, they certainly feel pain, and yeah, that's a big thing. I mean, it's like a bond."

The vegans in this study experienced a major shift in their worldview. They transformed themselves from people who used animals for convenience, desire, or a perceived necessity to people who, in Lena's words, live by the "general philosophy [of] harmlessness to all." This philosophy was expressed as an ethical praxis in the way they live their lives. By becoming vegan, they rejected the normative ideology of animal domination by taking a different path and by educating others whenever they had the opportunity. They resisted institutional power by choosing cruelty-free products and by engaging in protests and other activism. They accepted personal relationships by ceasing to argue with friends, family, and acquaintances. Instead, they gently tried to educate when they could, and otherwise they taught by example.

As they moved through the process of learning to become vegan, participants had to reintegrate themselves into society. Although at times they felt like removing themselves from society, they knew that they could serve the animals best by facing the challenges of being vegan in a sometimes-hostile society.

As marginalized individuals, most of these vegans sought the comfort of solidarity in fellowship with others who feel as they do. But between those times of fellowship, they had to reconcile their philosophy and lifestyle with the need to maintain their marriages, friendships, and family and work lives. Each of the participants in this study had either done this or was in process of doing so. Lisa, the newest of the vegans I interviewed, was continuing to find her place in society. She said, "I'm still confused. I'm still working through all of this."

Although each story is unique, the vegans followed the same general path from an omnivorous to a vegan lifestyle. A common outcome of the vegan lifestyle was a desire to educate others about animal cruelty. Although the vegans had been through the process, they felt frustrated by the inability to communicate what they had learned. Often rebuffed, or worse, for their efforts, they modified their approach to become less invasive and feel more accepted by others.

Discussion

If one of the goals of vegans is to educate others, we must better understand how people learn to become vegan. To better understand the adoption of a vegan perspective, it is important to identify commonalities in the stories of individuals experiencing such change. This research indicates that for these vegans, a common path emerged that, although generalized, also allowed for the telling of individual stories. Models such as the one constructed can guide educational efforts. Before this model is adopted, however, it should be further explored with a larger sample of vegans. One of its limitations is its psychological emphasis. It does not give voice to the rich social milieu in which these vegans learned. Further analysis, which was beyond the scope of this article, revealed psychological experience inextricably embedded in social relations and the dominant ideology of human superiority.

As noted, Mezirow's transformation theory did not explain adequately the learning process of vegans. Transformation theory overestimates the role of democratic dialogue, as these vegans found little opportunity for such dialogue. Transformation theory also pivots on the individual's critical reflection on assumptions. I found little evidence for such reflection in the narratives of these vegans. Finally, as noted in other critiques, Mezirow's transformation theory fails to account

for the power of the normative ideology to shape the learning and practice of vegans over time.

Noteworthy Points

Considering the findings of this research, a number of points are noteworthy. First, this was a study of successful and committed vegans. They are the ones who listened, considered, and accepted the information about animal cruelty as truth. Although two vegans described repressing such information for a time, this research does little to shed light on the important phenomenon of repression. Repression may be a key factor in why many individuals hear about animal cruelty but do not act. More research is needed on why and how information about animal cruelty is repressed or ignored by otherwise sensitive and caring individuals.

A second point to emerge from this research is the importance of both logic and emotion in the learning of vegans. For some vegans, logic was the primary cognitive tool used to process information. For others, affect and emotion guided the learning process. For most vegans, the importance of logic and emotion varied across time. More often, emotional trauma appeared initially, followed by rational consideration of information. Veganism, therefore, was more often a rational decision, especially if it had been preceded by a vegetarian lifestyle. For every vegan, however, both logic and emotion played a role in the learning process. Recent reports from neuroscience, such as the work of Damasio (1994), support this finding, highlighting the mutually supportive roles of emotion and reason. Educational efforts for veganism, therefore, should acknowledge the value in recognizing both, while recognizing that individuals will likely respond more to one over the other and, in time, may even change their receptiveness to one over the other.

Another consideration is the importance of openness as a critical characteristic of eventual acceptance. Openness is probably related to an orientation to learn, as well as to the resurfacing of repressed information. It is easy to identify those individuals who are immediately open to learning about veganism and more difficult to know which individuals will eventually allow their repressed emotions and logic into their conscious thoughts.

The Willingness to Learn

That initially resistant people can recall repressed information about animal cruelty with a new willingness to learn and that most of the vegans in this study reported a lifelong fondness for nonhuman animals indicate that people may have a biologically or socially instilled connection to nonhuman animals. Janet, one of the vegans in this study, thought that most children feel a bond with nonhuman animals.

Wilson (1993) would agree with Janet. He stated that people have an "innately emotional affiliation . . . to other living organisms" (p. 31). Kellert (1996) concurred, but added that this affiliation is a reflection of values rooted in "weak biological tendencies . . . requiring learning and experience if they are to become stable and consistently manifest" (p. 26). Thus, Kellert argued, affection toward animals may be latent in almost everyone. In American society today, however, he noted that people have less opportunity for learning and experiences that enable those tendencies to be manifested.

If Kellert is correct, a transformation to veganism may be one manifestation of the innate biological affiliation with life. Others, however, are not as sure. Grier (1999) proposed that the child-animal bond was a construction of American Victorian society in an effort to instill the values of kindness and civility in boys. Nevertheless, few would argue that in today's society children typically feel a connection to nonhuman animals. This connection may be rekindled as an adult by a recognition of that bond.

Another important finding to the vegan movement is the centrality of reading to the learning of vegans. These vegans learned from books, cookbooks, newsletters, magazines, brochures, and other written information. Pivotal to the success of such information is its perception as being

true. Recognizing this potential pitfall in educating non-vegans, Phillips (1999) recently called for all vegan-related information to be "impeccably accurate" (p. 1). This study indicates that when people accept animal cruelty information as true, they are compelled to either act on it, repress it, or deal with the moral implications of knowingly supporting cruelty to nonhuman animals.

Finally, learning about veganism was separated into two conceptually different tasks. These tasks correspond to what Mezirow (1991), borrowing from Habermas, called communicative and instrumental learning. Communicative learning has to do with ideas, such as the idea of institutionalized animal cruelty, animal rights, and veganism. Instrumental learning concerns the skills needed to live a vegan lifestyle, such as how to cook, order food in restaurants, and read ingredient labels. Participants indicated the centrality and interdependence of both kinds of learning to their vegan journey. Thus, if others are to be successfully educated about the vegan lifestyle, they must understand the ideological basis for veganism as well as learn the tools for living a vegan lifestyle.

References

Damasio, A. R. (1994). *Descartes' error: Emotion, reason, and the human brain.* New York: Avon.

Duda, M. D., and K. C. Young (1997). *Americans' attitudes toward animal rights, animal welfare, and the use of animals* (Report). Harrisonburg, VA: Responsive Management.

George, K. P. (1994). Should feminists be vegetarians? *Signs, 19* (Winter), 405–434.

— (1995). Reply to Adams, Donovan, and Gaard and Gruen. *Signs,* 21 (Autumn), 242–260.

Kellert, S. R. (1996). *The value of life: Biological diversity and human society.* Washington, DC: Island Press/Shearwater Books.

McDonald, B. (1998). *A comparison of Mezirow's transformation theory with the process of learning to become an ethical vegan.* Unpublished doctoral dissertation, University of Georgia, Athens.

Mezirow, J. (1991). *Transformative dimensions of adult learning.* San Francisco: Jossey-Bass.

Moustakas, C. (1990). *Heuristic research: Design, methodology, and applications.* Newbury Park, CA: Sage.

Phillips, C. (1999). Getting our facts straight. *Vegan Outreach, 8* (3), 1.

Rozin, P., Markwith, M., and C. Stoess (1997). Moralization and becoming a vegetarian: The transformation of preferences into values and the recruitment of disgust. *Psychological Science, 8* (March), 67–73.

Stepaniak, J. (1998). *The vegan sourcebook.* Los Angeles: Lowell House.

Strauss, A., and J. Corbin (1990). *Basics of qualitative research: Grounded theory procedure and techniques.* Newbury Park, CA: Sage.

Walker, C. (1995). Meet the new vegetarian. *American Demographics, 17* (January), 9–11.

Wilson, E. O. (1993). Biophilia and the conservation ethic. In S. R. Kellert and E. O. Wilson (eds.), *The biophilia hypothesis* (pp. 31–41). Washington, DC: Island Press/Shearwater Books.

PART SEVEN

Entertainment and Education

Introduction

Animals have been, and continue to be, central to human entertainment. They have been the focus of artistic representations from prehistoric cave paintings to the contemporary dog photographs of William Wegman. Animals have been involved in human competitions from ancient blood sports to the dog and horse races of today. Animals have been central features of popular culture from the folk tales of tribal cultures to the animated film now showing in your local theater. Captive animals have been collected and exhibited since the menageries of Egyptian royalty assembled some 4,000 years ago to the modern zoological gardens ostensibly devoted to the preservation of species and the edification of visitors. Animals are, in short, central to the way that humans spend their leisure time, symbolize and pass on important beliefs, and demonstrate their dominance over nature.

The place of animals in sport is of particular importance. Within sociology, sport is defined as a form of play that is set apart from everyday life. It is organized, involves physical exertion, is governed by established rules, and is intended to provide the participants with some form of emotional satisfaction. For both participants and spectators, sport offers excitement and entertainment.

Animals are connected with human sporting activities in three major ways. Some sports involve animals competing against other animals. Other sporting activities pit humans against animals. Finally, various sports entail humans cooperating with animals—in essence, forming human-animal teams that compete against each other (see McFadden 2007). While hunting originated as a means for acquiring food, it developed into what is the most ancient form of animal-related sport. It is particularly interesting in that it frequently involved human-animal cooperation directed at locating and killing other animals. The use of dogs in fox hunts (see the selection by Marvin in this volume) or to locate, flush, and retrieve the bodies of "game" birds are obvious examples.

While debates over hunting as a form of human cruelty or a historically viable, and even beneficial, activity have raged for centuries (see Hummel 1994), social distaste for "pit sports" in which animals fight each other (commonly to the death) has been, and is, wide-

spread. The sociological literature on cockfighting (e.g., Darden and Worden 1996) and dogfighting (Forsyth and Evans 1998), for example, clearly illustrates the conventional definition of these activities as forms of collective deviance and the important role this negative definition has in forming and maintaining closely knit subcultures of practitioners and fans. Blood sports in which animals battle humans—Spanish bullfighting, for example—are the focus of similar controversy as some see the activities as part of the national heritage and others see them as especially brutal examples of cruelty toward animals (see Mitchell 1991).

Pitting animals against each other in races as opposed to mortal combat is considerably less controversial. When either racing alone, as in dog racing, or teamed with a human partner, as in horse or dog sled racing, these animal contestants are commonly regarded as valuable resources in the social world surrounding the competition and are treated with at least a certain degree of care and consideration. However, these sporting activities, like those involving the shedding of animal blood, are also the focus of some controversy and form the core of a social world composed of intensely involved participants (see Case 1991).

Another area of social life in which nonhuman animals play a significant entertainment role is in popular culture. Animals typically have been portrayed in painting, sculpture, and other forms of both folk and fine art (see Clark 1977), and they are key elements in films, television shows, and pictorial materials such as comics. The reason for the common presentation of animals in popular cultural materials has, in part, to do with one of the key features of popular culture as a commercial product. Confronted by commercial uncertainty, creators of popular culture are never entirely sure what materials will be monetarily successful. As a consequence, the craft system that manufactures popular culture (Hirsch 1972) relies on two major mechanisms in the search for commercial success. First, the system operates on a principle of overproduction as far more materials and thematic elements are produced than can be reasonably marketed. These product examples are filtered by important "gatekeepers" in the popular cultural production system (e.g., film producers, artists and repertoire [A and R] personnel in record companies, studio heads in companies that produce television programming) in the hopes of eventually finding a successful product. Secondly, and most important for our discussion here, the cultural production system operates on the principle of formulaic reproduction as materials and themes that are now popular or have proved to be commercially successful in the past are duplicated and recycled in the hopes that these materials and themes hold the key to commercial success. The dominance of reality shows in current TV programming and the release of numerous sequels to films that draw large audiences are blatant examples of this process (see Sanders 1982). Animals—their lives in domestic settings or the wild, their adventures with humans, or as monstrous threats to human welfare, for example—are central to a formulaic convention that has proven to be perennially successful (see Baker 1993). The many animated films and somewhat more realistic films produced by the Disney studios (see Whitley 2008) offer testimony to the importance of animals and their exploits with or without people as popular cultural themes.

Although it is overtly intended to prompt consumers to purchase particular objects or experiences, memorable advertising has entertainment value and commonly features nonhuman animals from Tony the Tiger, through Morris the Cat, to the Geico gecko. In their discussion of animals in television commercials, Magdorff and Barnett (1989) maintain that animals portrayed in advertising not only draw viewer interest but are also used to connect products with consumers' self-definitions. As they observe:

> The use of animals, both animated and real, in many TV ads is directly related to the ability of the animals to evoke powerful responses in viewers—animals become "as-if" representations of the viewer's idealized self-image, in terms of both positive attributes and desired relationships. Animals are particularly appropriate male and female symbols to Americans because, unlike people in some other societies, Americans tend to believe that animals, especially mammals, have families similar to human families. Pets are often seen as members of the family. Animals are also important symbols for advertisers because Americans tend to believe that certain attributes are characteristic of certain kinds of animals. . . . The fastest way to make a point in a TV spot is to use a visual image

whose meaning viewers agree upon. Using stereotypical animals in commercials is a standard tactic. . . . (94)

For most of us, zoos offer the major setting in which we encounter animals other than the companion animals who share our everyday lives. Historically, collections of wild animals have been privately owned by those with considerable wealth and social status. The first modern zoos were established in Europe in the mid-eighteenth century and in the United States a century later (the Philadelphia Zoo opened in 1874). In addition to being settings where families can engage in recreational activities, zoos are intended to have an educational purpose as visitors observe the animals and read the instructional information provided. Recently, zoos have stressed conservation as a major function as a wide variety of animal species have disappeared from or become extremely rare in the wild, and zoos have focused more directly on fostering breeding programs (see Beardsworth and Bryman in this volume, Hanson 2002, Malamud 1998). A number of writers dispute the standard argument advanced by zoo administrators and other advocates that zoos do not exploit animals and that, in fact, zoos advance the interests of the animal species in captivity. Most basically, these objections focus on zoos as cruel (and immoral) in that they are paternalistic and deprive of their freedom animals who are healthy and would be better off in the wild (see Zamir 2007).

In addition to their instructional role in zoos, animals are also employed in conventional educational settings. Dead animals are dissected, small animals are confined in classroom cages, and family pets are brought into school and displayed. The ostensible purpose of this use of animals is furthering the education of students. Gene Myers (1998) provides an especially rich description of the role animals played in the nursery school he observed. Myers emphasizes that in this educational setting, interactions with animals taught students how to relate to others and how to express their thoughts and feelings. Most importantly, he describes how playful interactions with animals helped the children develop a self—an understanding of who they were in relationship to others. Hirschman and Sanders (1997) make a similar point in their content analysis of a sample of animal-centered

films directed at children. They maintain that mo-
tion-picture narratives about animals constitute socializing devices as they present animals behaving
in appropriate and socially desirable ways.

The selections included in this part focus on the
matters briefly outlined above. "Greyhound Racing"
deals with dog racing and connects this form of entertainment to the larger issue of violence in sports.
The authors center their discussion on the views of
the sociologist Norbert Elias (1994) who maintained
that violent sports are a consequence of and a mechanism for the advancement of social civility. In brief,
Elias believed that sporting violence helped to displace and redirect real-life violence and thereby was
beneficial to the order and cohesion of society. Atkinson and Young offer examples of the abusive elements of greyhound racing and contend that
participants in the racing world interact in a culture in
which the mistreatment and killing of the dogs are
cast as understandable, tolerable, and necessary elements of the sporting activity.

The authors of the next article use the concept of
"Disneyization" to focus their discussion of the zoo.
First and foremost, this means that the zoo provides
a commodified experience that is removed from the
authentic context of animals, nature, and wildness.
Visitors are provided with a sanitized and themed animal experience as they are guided and instructed by
employees who are required to repress their real feelings or to display feelings they are not experiencing
but that are seen as necessary by administrators in
order to provide attendees with a positive encounter.
The commodification of the zoo experience is further
"Disneyfied" as visitors are encouraged to purchase
products that carry representations of iconic animals
while advertising the zoo itself.

The final selection deals with how the natural
world of animals is presented on the Discovery
Channel. Pierson emphasizes that animals are
highly anthropomorphized in these programs—the
animals are presented as thinking and behaving
much like humans. Making a similar point as made
by Hirschmann and Sanders (1997) in their discussion of animals in film, the author sees nature
shows on the Discovery Channel as instructing viewers about appropriate gender relationships, the acceptability of "natural" hierarchies, and the "proper"
relationship between humans and nature.

References

Baker, S. 1993. *Picturing the Beast: Animals, Identity and Representation*. Manchester, UK: Manchester University Press.

Case, C. 1991. *Down the Backstretch: Racing and the American Dream*. Philadelphia: Temple University Press.

Clark, K. 1977. *Animals and Men: Their Relationship as Reflected in Western Art from Prehistory to the Present Day*. New York: Morrow.

Darden, D., and S. Worden. 1996. "Marketing Deviance: The Selling of Cockfighting." *Society & Animals* 4(2):211–231.

Elias, N. 1994. *The Civilizing Process*. Oxford: Basil Blackwell.

Forsyth, C., and R. Evans. 1998. "Dogmen: The Rationalization of Deviance." *Society & Animals* 6:203–218.

Hanson, E. 2002. *Animal Attractions: Nature on Display in American Zoos*. Princeton, NJ: Princeton University Press.

Hirsch, P. 1972. "Processing Fads and Fashion: An Organization-Set Analysis of Cultural Industry Systems." *American Journal of Sociology* 77:639–659.

Hirschman, E., and C. Sanders. 1997. "Motion Pictures as Metaphoric Consumption: How Animal Narratives Teach Us to Be Human." *Semiotica* 15:53–80.

Hummel, R. 1994. *Hunting and Fishing for Sport*. Bowling Green, OH: Bowling Green University Popular Press.

Magdorff, J., and S. Barnett. 1989. "Self-Imaging and Animals in TV Ads." In R. J. Hoage, ed., *Perceptions of Animals in American Culture*, 93–100. Washington: Smithsonian Institution Press.

Malamud, R. 1998. *Reading Zoos: Representations of Animals and Captivity*. New York: New York University Press.

McFadden, C. 2007. "Sport and Animals." In M. Bekoff, ed., *The Encyclopedia of Human-Animal Relations*, 1321–1325. Westport, CT: Greenwood.

Mitchell, T. 1991. *Blood Sport*. Philadelphia: University of Pennsylvania Press.

Myers, Eugene. 1998. *Children and Animals*. Boulder, CO: Westview Press.

Sanders, C. 1982. "Structural and Interactional Features of Popular Culture Production: An Introduction to the Production of Culture Perspective." *Journal of Popular Culture* 16:66–74.

Whitley, D. 2008. *The Idea of Nature in Disney Animation*. Hampshire, UK: Ashgate.

Zamir, T. 2007. The Welfare-Based Defense of Zoos. *Society & Animals* 15:191–201.

Michael Atkinson
Kevin Young

Greyhound Racing and Sports-Related Violence

The Ancient Egyptians, Romans, and Greeks revered the greyhound, the world's oldest pure-bred dog, as a companion, hunter, and religious icon; and such reverence seems to have lasted through the Middle Ages. By the turn of the eighteenth century, colonial expansion led to transformations in the "distinguished" cultural status of the greyhound. Greyhounds were used less for hunting game and more for taming colonized peoples of the New World. For example, greyhounds were employed by British and French explorers to aid in the slaughter of native populations in the Caribbean and, soon after, throughout the southern Americas. Relatively shortly thereafter, however, greyhounds were transported to North America for more "civilized" purposes.

English aristocrats introduced greyhound coursing—a baiting contest in which two dogs chased and sought to kill a hare in an open meadow—to North America (circa 1840s), and exposed popular audiences to the breed through dog shows. By the mid-1800s, a strong tradition of coursing had emerged on the United States plains. With more access to the dogs via expanding breeding networks in the United States, working classes established their own tradition of coursing in the 1920s that would eventually supersede the dogs' use for show purposes or for traditional coursing contests. After a series of failed attempts to create a bloodier coursing culture, Owen Patrick Smith helped establish the first modern greyhound racetrack in 1910 in Oakland, California. Smith, an engineer, developed the electronic lure—a device he called the "Inanimate Hare Conveyor"—to "pacify" the event. By the 1930s, working-class crowds flocked to makeshift racetracks across the southern United States where sports betting was legal. Races were billed as humane versions of traditional coursing, and as more culturally and economically accessible events than upper-class horse racing. Until the 1990s, greyhound racing served as a staple of American sports-betting culture, ranking as the sixth most popular spectator sport during the period.

Although academic attention is limited, the long-term transformation of greyhounds from revered companions to sporting commodities has not escaped public scrutiny. Indeed, modern greyhound racing is beleaguered by spectator dissatisfaction and social protest, perhaps partly as an outcome of increasing social, and particularly youth, sensibilities to questions of animal stewardship in the modern era. With ethical concerns raised by groups such as the Society for the Prevention of Cruelty to Animals (SPCA), People for the Ethical Treatment of Animals (PETA), and the Animal Liberation Front (ALF), greyhound racing has fallen into moderate disrepute in North America. Since 1993, dozens of tracks have closed in the 16 U.S. states still permitting greyhound racing, although these have been primarily business decisions in response to rapidly declining profits.

In this connection, the economy of dog racing has negatively impacted treatment practices. Amid widespread industry decline, accounts of animal abuse and neglect in the surviving racing figuration have expanded. Consequently, U.S. adoption and rescue agencies such as Wings for Greyhounds, Second Chance for Greyhounds, Operation Greyhound, and the Greyhound Protection League have helped place retired racers in private homes, and militant antiracing groups continue to call for the outright termination of the sport. A dominant discourse surrounding contemporary greyhound racing challenges the alleged pervasiveness of the violence, abuse, and neglect some dogs suffer, but few sociologists have empirically interrogated these claims, or how abusive practices are rationalized within this sport-entertainment culture.

According to the National Greyhound Association (NGA), there are, on average, approximately 34,000 racing greyhounds born in the United States each year, and 28,000 registered to race every year. Estimates suggest that approximately 50,000 to 60,000 greyhounds are used as racers in the United States annually. At the time of writing, 46 tracks were in operation in 16 U.S. states, generating over $100 million in revenue per year. In the past 10 years, many of the racetracks have expanded their operations to include races simulcast over the Internet in order to reach gaming populations around the world. However, there are other, more sobering racing statistics. For instance, estimates published by the Greyhound Protection League suggest that nearly 30,000 young greyhounds are killed in North America every year when they are no longer able to win or place. Approximately 5000 to 7000 farm puppies are culled annually, and more simply "go missing" without being registered to an owner.

The sheer number of greyhounds killed in the industry (either as a result of early identification as unsuitable racers, or through lackluster results on the track) represents only the end result of abuse and violence in the sport, just as only some of the food products ending up in the supermarket are merely the final stage of tolerated and sanctioned violence against farm-raised livestock. Clearly, closer inspection of the varied forms of violence against greyhounds is required.

In particular, we argue that four major types of violence are faced by some racing greyhounds in North America: breeding violence, training violence, housing violence, and disposal violence. All require closer scrutiny.

In this article, then, greyhound racing is examined as a type of "blood sport." In making this case, we are not suggesting that the kinds of graphic and intentional cruelty associated with baiting, pit, and fighting animal sports characterize greyhound racing. Nor are we suggesting that the entire racing figuration engages violence and cruelty toward greyhounds. Indeed, members of the North American figuration regularly suggest that violence and neglect are anomalies in the sport rather than the rule. There is ample empirical evidence indicating that dogs at many North American tracks are prized and handled carefully as legitimate athletes. Still, we are interested in placing greyhound racing along a broad continuum of potentially harmful animal sports, which, while clearly distinct from, for example, cockfighting and bearbaiting in its intent and inevitably severe outcomes, nevertheless *systematically* produces abuse, neglect, and harm in its animal participants.

Although generally disregarded as a legitimate subject of sociological inquiry, our view is that animal abuse, exploitation, and victimization in mainstream western sport/leisure pastimes warrant far more serious sociological investigation than it has received to date. Following Young's (2001) call to conceptually expand our understanding of forms of sports-related violence (SRV)—as "potentially harmful acts that cannot easily be separated from the sports process and that only begin to make sense when the socially, culturally and historically embedded character of sport is closely scrutinized" (2001: 4)—this article employs aspects of figurational sociology (Elias, 1994) to interpret certain social constructions of, and rationalizations offered about, both demonstrated and alleged cases of greyhound abuse at North American racetracks. Attention is directed to how the treatment of greyhounds in breeding, training, housing, and disposal practices may be framed by centrally positioned stakeholders within the dog racing figuration (e.g., breeders, dog owners, track operators, and fans) as legitimate, tolerable, or accidental SRV. By exploring selected accounts of greyhound mistreatment at U.S. racetracks, it is argued that the "mimetic" potential and exciting significance of greyhound racing as a spectator sport masks the physical pain and trauma many greyhounds experience in racing environments.

Greyhound Racing as Sports-Related Violence

Although much has been written about abusive and victimizing forms of violence in mainstream sports, violence against animals is, at best, haphazardly inserted into analyses of violence *occurring in and around* the sports field. Identified by Young (2001) as a "blood sport" in his matrix of SRV, contests pitting animals against one another in a combative manner, or involving potentially harmful animal pursuits for the entertainment of participants or spectators, may be linked, in both ideology and practice, to more mainstream sport and SRV activities. Since greyhound athletic contests, first through coursing and then through formalized racing, symbolically resemble killing-based competitions, they represent a clear example of exciting significance for audiences. Greyhound racing involves the cultural quest for contests representing blood-letting in a controlled manner, and does so in a way which effectively exploits the participants. In Stebbins's (1997) terms, the sport is, in these respects, a clear form of "tolerable" deviance.

Although research on animals and animal abuse in sports is considerably underdeveloped by sociologists, figurationalists such as Dunning (1999) and Sheard (1999) have illustrated how sports involving animals in the UK have become less violent over the course of civilizing processes. Sports involving animals are understood as forms of "killing (or hurting) by proxy," wherein social desires to witness, and indeed actively participate in, violent forms of hunting may be explored. In considering the social history of greyhound hunting and coursing, figurational sociology offers considerable insight into how the greyhound has featured in "civilizing" events and practices.

Empirical accounts of animal abuse in North America and continental European sport typically take a radically different tack than figurational studies. Analyses of dogfighting (Forsyth and Evans, 1998), cockfighting (Darden and Worden, 1996), rodeo (Rollin, 2001), and bullfighting (Mitchell, 1991), for instance, give less conceptual attention to the *systematic process* of violence in animal sports, or the centrality of violence in western cultures more broadly. Instead, authors tend to examine *individualistic* or *situational* constructions of animal abuse in deviant sport subcultures. Rationalizations of and subcultural perspectives toward animal abuse are interrogated, and detailed descriptions of violence are offered. Rarely, however, is more than one interpretive standpoint introduced into these undertheorized analyses. Grounded conceptualizations of animal abuse/violence in sport are thus developed from rather limited perspectives.

In addition to these research trends, empirical investigations of animal blood sports have been tied only loosely to emerging academic and political discourses on the ethical and moral treatment of animals. As Regan (1983) noted some time ago, the exploitation of animals in a full range of social spheres should be comparatively analyzed in order to grasp how their mistreatment figures into everyday human group life. This study of greyhound racing is, then, an attempt to highlight how sociological theory and analysis may help advance a case for heightened ethical standards in sports figurations for animal participants; *and*, to build conceptual links between animal blood sport violence and the suffering of animals in other spheres, as well as SRV more generally.

By building on figurational sociology, and incorporating Young's (2001) figurationally sensitive conceptualization of violence in sport, greyhound racing is examined as a historically produced and highly contested form of SRV. The brands of SRV embedded in certain greyhound racing cultures are conceptualized as hyper-versions of the mimetic violence found in other sports cultures, and extreme outcomes of the objectification of animals. In the process of understanding how violence against animals may be explained as mimesis, we suggest that the racing figuration represents a complex web of social interdependencies involving players located at a number of levels. In its most basic mode, the racing figuration is held together on an ongoing basis through the notion of mimetic violence. Rather than naively assuming that violence occurs only situationally at the hands of those directly administering dogs at the track, or as a product of only a handful of individuals involved in the sport, we conceive of contributors operating at various levels of the racing figuration, including spectators who may or may not fully comprehend the ways dogs are prepared and treated before and after their track performances, as complicit in its maintenance.

We contend that in order to understand the social processes involved in greyhound racing as SRV, we must examine: 1) how greyhound racing is managed as a form of mimesis; 2) how greyhound racing emerges as SRV; 3) the contexts, conditions and ideologies of violence against greyhounds in creating exciting significance in the sport; and, 4) the current trends in greyhound racing.

Greyhound Racing as Mimesis

An undercurrent in Elias's work (e.g., 1994) on long-term civilizing processes is that modern western figurations have produced relatively unexciting social environments. The general pacification of figurations over time resulted in a collective need to devise and institutionalize cultural activities that strike a balance between personal pleasure and restraint. As outward displays of emotion are largely pushed behind the scenes of social life in many cultures, individuals learn to pursue a range of activities that elicit exciting significance under highly controlled circumstances.

Elias and Dunning (1986) note that sport provides an interactive context within which a moderate degree of violence is both permissible and encouraged, allowing individuals to participate in activity which is less condoned or, indeed, strictly taboo in other social settings. Sport, for example, is predominantly a social institution rationalized in terms of the virtues of competition and physicality (i.e., as part of character building), while providing a source of temporary liberation from diffuse social codes curtailing violence and uncontrolled affective outburst. In figurational terms, sports contests provide an interactive opportunity which allows a "controlled decontrolling of emotional controls" among participants and spectators (Elias and Dunning, 1986).

Elias and Dunning (1986) and Dunning and Rojek (1992) further suggest that one of sport's primary roles within complex figurations is to "de-routinize" social life. Constrained by dense chains of interdependency, individuals are socially expected to engage in (and learn to internalize the merits of) predictable and emotionally restrained behavior. Sport is a social theater in which spectators are deliberately aroused by the tension balances created through athletic contests.

Sports like greyhound racing may be considered mimetic because they deliberately resemble warlike competition. They are socially and emotionally significant to individuals because they elicit a level of excitement, while structured by an understanding that the outcome of the "battle" is not as perilous to the participants as a genuine war. Hence, sport spectators are excited by the often rough and violent competitive exchange between the participants, yet feel neither guilt nor repugnance in watching the battles since they are not perceived as real.

The social history of greyhounds exemplifies how animals have been inserted into the mimetic sporting pastimes of westerners. From early coursing to later racing traditions, greyhounds have been prized for their ability to hunt one form of game or another. The long-term custom among European and North American upper classes of using the hounds to track game as recreation unintentionally made them ideal animals for violent-looking forms of dog racing in the United States among the working and lower middle classes. Aligned with broader civilizing processes, athletic contests involving greyhounds came to symbolize a diffuse habitus categorized by affective restraint, and the pursuit of exciting (mock violent) social activities. Concretely, through the formation of the International Greyhound Association in 1926, racing developed a sporting and civilized façade, as rationalized association rule structures and specified outcomes minimized, even obscured, the often harsh experience of the races. In these ways, violence is not mocked in the sport merely to provide "bread and circuses" for spectators; rather, this mock hunt became carefully structured by codified rules of physical engagement.

Clearly, for enthusiasts and insiders, greyhound racing is also thrilling given the speed of the races. The greyhound is a formidable runner, reaching speeds in excess of 45 km/hour. Coupling the image of the hunt implicit in a staged race with the considerable pace at which it occurs, a greyhound race is undeniably *exciting* on a sensory basis. As former breeder Jim remarked: "I've been to every sport you can think of, and nothing beats the hounds. The dogs were born to race and, when you see them flying down the track, you think to yourself, this is what God intended. . . . It's poetry in motion; it's grace, art, and beauty." Yet the sport is culturally exciting on economic grounds too. Despite historical concerns regarding the rigging of races in both the United States and abroad, the unknown nature of race outcomes provides considerable uncertainty and excitement. Gaming culture, a central component in greyhound racing in the United States, latched onto the sport early on, enhancing its meaning vis-à-vis the spectators' ability to reap financial success from the contests. With race rules in place, structured techniques for betting on the races developed. Following the formation of race cards, published biographies of individual racers, "scientific" means of predicting the outcomes of races, and considerable purses at each track, the

mock violence grew in social significance. It is perhaps no surprise that in an era of North American prohibition (1920s), the popularity of this legal vice expanded considerably. Over the course of the twentieth century, gambling has grown as an increasingly central part of the sport. Clearly, spectators do not attend races or closely follow television, Internet, or radio broadcasts only for the mimetic excitement of watching the dogs race. Their financial investment is also central—so much so, that it is difficult to conceive of greyhound racing as a popular cultural pursuit without gambling.

Also noteworthy here, as part of the same process of rationalization, is the historically pervasive view that animals neither experience pain as humans do (i.e., reflexively or emotionally), nor should be appreciated as sentient entities with moral rights. Indeed, western cultural habituses from the Middle Ages onward seem to routinely conceive of animals as incapable of experiencing or communicating even base, self-reflective emotions such as anxiety and fear. Consequently, some individuals in the animal sports figuration tend to adopt a "don't ask, don't tell" standpoint when it comes to animal suffering; dominant views appear to adhere to the following logic: "we do not believe animals feel pain or should be morally protected from victimization, but neither do we wish to observe the actual violence occurring on farms, in laboratories, or in zoos." Apparently, sports audiences concur that if we do not see animals being openly victimized in sport—even though we may anticipate its occurrence in the inevitable back regions of such activities—animal sports, including the bloodiest versions, can be rationalized as simply, and tolerably, mimetic.

An undercurrent of sport as mimesis has historically flourished in the greyhound racing figuration, as in other animal-oriented sports cultures, perhaps as a result of the relative lack of victim vocalization and representation within the racing community. Prior to the 1990s, few historical accounts of greyhound racing include voices of concern for the safety of the dogs. As nonhuman competitors (and thus, again, beings without emotions), greyhounds do not possess the communicative resources to recount or oppose their experiences with pain. For this reason and others, as long as the physical trappings of rough competition (i.e., anxiety, pain, and injury) are hidden from spectators, the sport is not problematized as victim-producing and thus retains its acceptability in the public sphere. Coupled with a wider cultural objectification of dogs as chattel, and speciesist understandings of violence against nonhuman living creatures, it is perhaps no surprise that few have historically considered greyhounds as victims of anything; almost no one has considered greyhound racing as a component of a larger matrix of abusive and violent practices related to sport.

Violence and Abuse in Greyhound Racing

The contemporary greyhound racing phenomenon is formed through the interweaving of action between seemingly disparate players operating at different levels of the figuration. Before discussing exactly what constitutes "violence" in greyhound racing, it is necessary to understand something about how violence in the sport occurs through the cooperative endeavours of insider role players.

Using another animal blood sport as a comparison, even though a bull dies at the hands of a single matador, the bull arrives in the ring through the cumulative efforts of numerous social actors operating at multiple levels of the bullfighting figuration. Simply put, many more than just the bull and matador are involved in the social organization of an event which may be perceived as exciting, sporting, and tolerable, and it is clear that considerable numbers of persons are required to support the figuration and stage the bullfights. For the purposes of this article, of interest are the ways in which actors come together in the greyhound figuration to produce and rationalize abuse and violence against racing dogs. As a means of drawing the conceptual linkages between the major players in the sport, Figure 20.1 provides an overview of the figuration.

In Figure 20.1, individuals are placed in one of three main categories, representing their roles in the racing figuration. *Context players* are those responsible for establishing the supply of, and demand for, the races. These individuals aggressively normalize the sport in varied social spheres, and often act as the primary definers of greyhound racing. For the most part, they are responsible for circulating the following kinds of techniques of neutralization (Sykes and Matza, 1989): the dogs are treated humanely; racing is

Context players	Conditions players	Regulation players
• Track owners – local and international • Track promoters, scouts, and marketers • Spectators • Gamblers • Betting establishments • Betting industries and tourism services	• Breeders • Trainers • Dog owners • Kennel owners • Track workers • Veterinarians • For hire "disposers" • Medical organizations • Universities and research centers • Hunters	• State legislators • NGA and other greyhound associations • Antiracing groups • Animal rights activists • Adoption and rescue agencies • Private adopters and foster families

FIGURE 20.1 The Greyhound Racing Figuration

healthy and exciting for the dogs; the sport is exhilarating for the audience; and, the sport represents a suitably monitored cultural pursuit.

Through such processes of covert facilitation and rationalization, context players form the basis of the greyhound racing economy, supplying the structural resources (i.e., tracks and promotional industries) and financial resources (i.e., breeding and wagering monies) needed to fuel the industry. Crucially, context players may rarely, if ever, come into contact with the greyhounds involved in racing. For them, the dogs are commodities to be bought and sold or bet upon; it is in this connection that we should understand their affective detachment from the racers.

By contrast, *conditions players* are more directly involved in actual physical harm to the dogs. From breeders to trainers to medical organizations who experiment on ex-racers, conditions players represent the unseen members of the figuration. They operate very much in Goffman's back regions, overseeing the daily care and handling of the racers. A striking parallel may be found in circus/carnival cultures. Here, there is also a contrast between what is seen in the front stage of an animal showcase, and the type and degree of care occurring in the backstage by handlers and trainers after the audience has gone. As demonstrated below, conditions players are also complicit in the abuse of dogs, when it occurs.

Regulation players are the members of the figuration responsible for policing any alleged abuse against racers. From state regulators (who establish gaming laws and animal abuse codes) to police to national greyhound associations (such as the American Greyhound Council) to animal rights advocates, these individuals/groups pursue a mandate to regulate and control "unwanted" forms of abuse in the sport. Historically speaking, it is clear that this mandate has been exercised somewhat passively, at least in the U.S. racing figuration.

Violence against Greyhounds

Our research inquiries convince us that it is almost impossible to ignore how some racing greyhounds endure entire lives of pain and abuse. For the dogs themselves, their suffering is not physically mimetic or rational; rather, it is real, and "put there" by human actors who are all too aware of the painful outcomes of neglect and abuse, and who choose to rationalize them in terms of the aforementioned principles of financial motives, exciting significance or tolerated customs. We outline four principal ways in which a greyhound might suffer through involvement in the business of racing.

Breeding Greyhounds encountering abuse as part of their racing careers typically do so at an early stage. Among other forms of neglect, breeders may kill or simply abandon puppies they deem to be unsuitable for racing, or dogs that "wash out" after failing to succeed in events at local racing schools—estimates received from informants place this number at approximately one in 10 dogs bred every year. This process is referred to in the industry as "farm culling."

Reports of improper, suspect, or flagrantly inhumane housing facilities abound in the southern United States (i.e., the location of some of the most financially unstable tracks in the entire U.S. racing industry), with dogs reportedly being left chained outdoors or to roam without proper feeding or care. As part of the breeding process, in some rare cases, the dogs are trained using live animals such as hares as bait (an illegal practice in all states sanctioning greyhound racing). Transportation of the dogs from breeders to their eventual owners (kennel owners at tracks or other private owners/syndicates) may also prove perilous. Over a dozen cases of transportation-related deaths have been reported since 1993 by greyhound advocacy groups. Deaths may occur when greyhounds are left unattended in small caravans or wagons in extreme heat conditions. In such cases, the dogs die of either heat exhaustion or dehydration. Dogs placed in these positions tend not to be the most successful in the figuration, yield few pay-offs for owners, and are not identified as desirable breeding stock; thus, they are funnelled out of the contexts of best care in the figuration. While these cases may seem minor or statistically small in number given the thousands of dogs at work in the industry, they are legitimate indicators of how the dogs are viewed as expendable commodities and not as sentient beings with their own pain barriers and rights.

For the most part, information on farm culling rarely surfaces in contemporary racing discourses. Context players, especially those policing the lower-rung tracks, far too infrequently question how greyhounds arrive at the tracks, or interrogate the conditions in which they have lived.

Regulation players do intervene on occasion to sanction repeat offenders, but typically with a tokenistic temporary license suspension or a written warning. As in so many other deviancy contexts, offenders are constructed as isolated "bad apples," and as unrepresentative of the industry as a whole. Regulation players, in this process, adopt the role of primary public definer of greyhound neglect by promoting the perspective of rarity. Furthermore, members of the most respected tracks in the United States often discredit the publicly identified deviants in the business, and pejoratively label them as "bottom feeders." Yet others prefer to "turn a blind eye" and continue to work within the system, rather than against it. These people are more concerned with taking care of the animals after they emerge from the track, and often realize that they have little agency to meaningfully contest apparent problems in the industry. As a result of such interpretive positions, allegations of greyhound abuse are maintained in the back regions of the figuration, or disregarded in more public venues as merely atypical or exaggerated versions of rather less sensational truth.

Training and Racing   The on-track training and racing of greyhounds may also lead to significant physical abuse and harm. While it is commonly suggested by trainers, and indeed set as precedent through the racing of the dogs over time, that each dog should be raced two or three times per week, track averages can reach up to six or seven times per week, and vary enormously. Information provided by former track workers and other insiders (verified by actual racing cards posted) indicate that some dogs may be raced up to three times the recommended level.

From overuse and the intensity of the races themselves, pain and injury inevitably occur. As with human athletes, some greyhounds live through pain on a daily basis—broken bones, torn ligaments or muscles, back and neck injuries, lacerations, and facial abrasions caused by muzzling are common. Here, the question might be raised as to why owners and operators would allow their investments to be injured or placed in harm's way. In practice, there is a simple economic equation in place. Treatment of the animals often proceeds on a cost–benefit basis; if a successful racer is injured, and the injury is "economically minor" (as assessed against what a successful racer may yield on a yearly basis), medical intervention will result. But since many dogs "crash out" after two or three years of racing and there is a surplus of younger dogs to promote to regular racing tracks, owners may find it more economical to run an injured racer until it can no longer perform, after which it is relegated to a lower grade track where it will likely finish its career.

As part of their daily training, greyhounds require a substantial amount of food. Rather than feeding the dogs a high-caliber diet, some low-budget tracks utilize what has been termed "4-D" (dead, dying, downed, diseased) meat to minimally sustain the greyhounds' nutritional requirements and athletic bodies. Such meat is often rife with *E. coli* toxins and may not be sold commercially according to USDA standards. It is illegally purchased for pennies per pound, and its consumption may lead to a skin condition in the dogs referred to disconcertingly by handlers as "Alabama rot" (a condition featuring open lesions and ulcers) or an intestinal problem referred to as "blow-out" (which includes chronic vomiting and diarrhea leading to death from dehydration). Insider estimates suggest that from 15 to

20 percent of racing greyhounds have consumed 4-D meat at some point in their careers. In Ernie's words: "You know that saying, 'not even fit for a dog?' Well the food we used to give them takes that saying to a whole new level. The so-called 4-D meat is disgusting, for sure, but [Alabama] 'rot' is the worst thing I've ever seen in an animal."

Other greyhounds are allegedly injected with anabolic steroids such as methyl testosterone to improve their on-track performance. Further still, and as indicated by recent allegations against greyhound tracks in Florida, some greyhounds are also injected with cocaine as a performance-enhancer or pain-killing agent. Dogs may not be neutered or spayed in order to maintain a high level of energy and their potential as breeding dogs. Yet, to curb the sexual activities of some dogs, they may also be chained in pens away from one another, or metal devices may be inserted into their genitalia to prevent "energy wasting" coitus.

Again, these sorts of practices, pushed behind the scenes of everyday life in the greyhound figuration, provide evidence of how greyhounds in contexts of economic and social neglect may be treated. As part of the mimetic process, this backstage behavior is undertaken to lower the overhead costs of the races, and is hidden from public view to avoid scandal and critical inquiry. This is especially evident at the poorer tracks, and in regions where the business has been threatened by other gaming industries.

Conditions players, including track handlers and workers, certainly witness the type of treatment described here, but often fear reprisal from track owners or trainers if they voice concern. Thus, containment of these insider power tensions seems to be quite normative in the industry. In the process, the focus of greyhound-related discourses is shifted to the front stage excitement of the races, and away from the often dubious, and occasionally shocking, treatment the dogs may receive behind closed doors.

Housing   The housing of greyhounds at racetracks often reflects a similar cost-cutting, low-overhead mentality and, in terms of the use of sometimes brutally inhumane care methods, further objectifies the dogs. At any given time, a greyhound track may house up to 1,000 dogs in a complex of kennels. A kennel operator is in charge of all dogs in a specific kennel (anywhere from 10–100-plus dogs). The dogs are often kept in rows of stacked cages, for space considerations (sometimes, a cage may be only 24 inches in width), and may be housed and/or muzzled for up to 22 hours per day. Also, the more dogs that can be squeezed into cramped kennel spaces, the more races can be run every day, thus increasing track efficiency and revenue. Without opportunity to adequately socialize, the dogs are literally "left alone together." They are "turned out" several (1–4) times per day to urinate/defecate, and usually once to eat and receive water. Due to this stacking approach to kennelling, the wire mesh structure of the kennels, and lack of proper flooring in each, greyhounds at the bottom rows are showered with the waste of others. At some of the more disreputable tracks, music is blasted in the kennels to drown out the incessant barking or whining of the dogs.

Under such conditions, some greyhound kennels become infested with fleas and ticks. As a result, greyhounds from particular tracks carry skin, blood, heart, and respiratory diseases such as canine ehrlichiosis, *Ehrlichia equui*, canine babesiosis, and Rocky Mountain spotted fever.

Furthermore, due to poor sanitary conditions at the low-budget tracks, greyhounds may suffer from hookworm, tapeworm, whipworm, and giardia. In the past 6 years, outbreaks of "kennel cough" at several American racetracks have killed several dozen greyhounds. On-track conditions, however, may be no kinder to the dogs. Many die each year from on-track collisions and falls (often, smaller females are trampled in races with large males), or are electrocuted by electrical lure systems.

Release   Recently circulated stories of release or the retirement of racers have prompted close scrutiny of the racing industry in the United

States and other countries (e.g., Ireland, the UK, and Spain). When racers no longer win, they are downwardly discarded through the racing system (i.e., at tracks of lower status and grade). When they have finally reached the end of this career spiral, and are no longer financially worthy of housing at any racing level, they must be replaced and disposed of. While increasing numbers of greyhounds are now fostered out through developing greyhound adoption agencies such as Wings for Greyhounds, thousands of racing hounds are also "euthanized" annually. Once again, and reflective of the profit-based culture of greyhound racing, their disposal may be brutal and painful.

Disposal of the dogs varies considerably, but two noticeable trends (other than adoption) are evident in "dumping" processes. First, greyhounds may be individually killed following their retirement as racers. Colloquially referred to as "going back to the farm," a greyhound's life may be ended in a rather unceremonious manner.

Although such disposal methods are clearly not industry standard, racing greyhounds in the United States may be bludgeoned, hanged, starved to death, abandoned in a field or woods, decapitated, electrocuted (this is known as a "Tijuana hotplate"), sold to local fishermen (to be used, for example, as shark chum) or a local hunter, or sold to a medical laboratory for research purposes. Reports of tracks employing the services of a for-hire killer, who will terminate the life of a greyhound for a small fee, are not uncommon. Further, and again disconcertingly, since race hounds are tattooed upon registration, their left ears may be removed to prevent identification.

While some may claim that in other mainstream "pet cultures," animals are routinely put to death at an "early" age (i.e., due to illness, changing social circumstances of care for the owners, or simply because the pet is no longer wanted), it is the serial use of greyhounds for economic purposes and their subsequent replacement by more lucrative counterparts (as part of a "civilized sporting culture") that is distinctive in

the greyhound figuration. While farm animals are also slaughtered for economic purposes to produce the food we eat and are also quickly replaced, the euthanizing of family pets does not occur under such rational-economic circumstances or in order to help reproduce a branch of the entertainment industry.

An even more disturbing microtrend is the mass killing of racing hounds. Since the mid-1990s, antiracing organizations have reported the discovery of so-called "killing fields" of dog carcasses in the United States and Europe (especially Spain). Greyhounds have been found dead in rural grasslands, tied to railway tracks, or stacked in local dumpsters. Medical laboratories and a handful of U.S. universities have been identified as mass murderers of greyhounds, and the entire racing industry has been labelled by groups like PETA as abusive and inhumane in its treatment methods in these respects.

In light of such evidence, it is clear that episodes of abuse in the greyhound figuration occur through a multilayered constellation of actors' efforts. While one individual may starve a dog, fail to treat a racer's wounds, feed it spoiled food, or euthanize it inhumanely, numerous others are complicit in these acts through conscious acquiescence or simply turning a blind eye. Each of the (contexts, conditions, and regulation) players performs a contributory role—although clearly a different role—in the process of greyhound abuse, with physical acts of neglect and violence as the end result of their actions. Animal abuse is not unique to the world of greyhound racing but, rather, representative of numerous contexts in which animals suffer from selective mistreatment in the name of sport.

Discussion: Challenge and Change in the Greyhound Figuration

Recently, scores of adoption agencies have brokered the placement of greyhounds in family homes across North America and Europe. Once a fledging movement, like-minded individuals have collectively placed an estimated 80,000 dogs in private residences away from the track (www.gpl.com). Despite widespread stories of physical and psychological abuse, the accounts of adopters suggest that, once nurtured and cared for, ex-racing greyhounds may become placid family pets. Staunch antiracing critics, however, question the long-term merit of the adoption movement, claiming that such involvement in the figuration, while well intended, inadvertently helps reproduce the racing industry. With new *outlets* for the disposal of dogs, it is argued, the racing figuration will continue to produce and abuse a new *reservoir* of racers each year. Furthermore, the adoption movement, which must by necessity be part of the racing figuration (and only rarely voices concerns about the treatment of dogs), may act as an abuse-facilitator by downplaying rumors/images of brutality and inhumanity surrounding other segments of the figuration. Indeed, most Web pages maintained by U.S. racetracks promote the adoption movement as a fully integrated wing of the industry.

Despite the noticeable decline in the U.S. greyhound industry and progressive attempts to remedy abuse/violence issues in it, lines of comparison between neglect in greyhound racing and the systematic mistreatment of animals in other settings such as laboratories (for experimentation), zoos (for gaze), factory farms (for mass consumption), pet stores (for companionship), and hunting fields (for sport killing) can be drawn. For instance, the conceptual figuration of factors described in this article may be compared with a plethora of other contexts where animals are subject to neglect, abuse, or violence. Each contains its own indigenous *context, conditions*, and *regulations players*, performing various roles in the abuse/violence process. In some cases, figurations appear to be composed of a modest number of actors participating individually or in small groups (such as in hunting cultures), while others (such as bullfighting or rodeo) more expansively include larger and more complex chains of participants who directly and indirectly contribute to harm against animals which also

becomes rationalized and normalized. Significantly, and as with the U.S. greyhound figuration, women continue to slowly change the face of context, condition, and regulation player spheres in these animal sport arenas, but the figurations remain, for the most part, strongly gendered and specifically masculinist social settings.

Sociologists of sport have significantly increased our understanding of the meaning of human sports participation and the way it may intersect with forms of harm, abuse, and victimization, but they have not paid attention to the meaning of animal participation and its potentially abusive outcomes. While the extent, form, and meaning of abuse and violence in the sport are hotly contested within the racing figuration, and while not everyone in the figuration is indifferent to or a violator of animal rights, that new stories of abuse surface on a regular basis cannot be denied. In this connection, the racing industry must confront and more publicly account for its treatment of animals if it wishes to hold on to a share of the gaming/sports market and contemporary sports culture more generally. Policy positions released by groups such as the National Greyhound Racing Association indicate that the racing figuration is consciously striving to rid the industry of any abusive practices and admonish serious offenders in the sport. As part of this accountability process, sociological interrogations of violence against animals in sport, and its subsequent social construction, should be extended. We must break free of the rather simplistic notion that on-track action involving greyhounds is the only context of risk in the sport, and move toward a line of inquiry acknowledging how risk during races may co-exist with neglect and violence occurring in the back regions of the sport. In this regard, it also seems sociologically prudent to continue to explore the ways in which little known or seldom seriously considered abusive animal practices that, again, cannot be separated from the sports entertainment business (such as abuse in greyhound racing), interface with more familiar articulations of sports-related violence.

References

Darden, D., and S. Worden (1996) "Marketing of Deviance: The Selling of Gamefowl," *Society & Animals* 4(2):27–44.

Dunning, E. (1999) Sport Mattecs: Sociological Studies of Sport, Violence, and Civilization. London: Routledge.

Dunning, E., and C. Rojek (1992) *Sport and Leisure in the Civilising Process.* London: Macmillan.

Elias, N. (1994) *The Civilizing Process.* Oxford: Basil Blackwell.

Elias, N., and E. Dunning (1986) *Quest for Excitement: Sport and Leisure in the Civilizing Process.* Oxford: Basil Blackwell.

Forsyth, C., and R. Evans (1998) "Dogmen and the Rationalization of Deviance," *Society & Animals* 6:157–86.

Mitchell, T. (1991) *Blood Sport: A Social History of Spanish Bullfighting.* Philadelphia: The University of Pennsylvania Press.

Regan, T. (1983) *The Case for Animal Rights.* Berkeley: University of California Press.

Rollin, B. (2001) "Rodeo and Recollection: Applied Ethics and Western Philosophy," *Journal of the Philosophy of Sport* 23:1–9.

Sheard, K. (1999) "A Stitch in Time Saves Nine: Birdwatching, Sport, and Civilising Processes," *Sociology of Sport Journal* 16:181–205.

Stebbins, R. (1997) *Tolerable Differences: Living with Deviance.* Whitby: McGraw-Hill.

Sykes, G., and D. Matza (1989) "Techniques of Neutralization: A Theory of Delinquency," in D.H. Kelly (ed.) *Deviant Behavior,* pp. 104–11. New York: St Martin's.

Young, K. (2001) "Toward a More Inclusive Sociology of Sports-Related Violence," paper presented at North American Society for the Sociology of Sport, San Antonio, TX, 31 October–November.

Alan Beardsworth and Alan Bryman

The Disneyization of Zoos

Introduction

How salient is the concept of the wild animal in the late modern, urban consciousness? Perhaps it is a good deal more prominent than first considerations might lead us to conclude. Certainly, the sheer volume and variety of images of wild animals in the mass media might provide us with a broad indication of the continuing interest our species has in the other species with which it shares the global environment. But the mass media, of course, are not our only sources of ideas about other species. The overall purpose of this article is to consider the ways in which humans engage with wild animals, and to focus attention on one particular institution that brings them together, the zoo. This exercise is undertaken in order to consider the proposition that this institution, in the late modern context, is undergoing a crucial structural and ideological transformation.

The zoo is of particular significance in a late modern context because it represents an intersection of both the "zoological gaze" (Franklin, 1999) and the "tourist gaze" (Urry, 1990). As Franklin observes, the zoo has been very much neglected in the burgeoning literature on leisure and tourism. This is surprising on at least three accounts. First, the zoo is very much part of the tourist trail. In their publicity, zoos present themselves as tourist destinations and regional tourist brochures emphasize the zoo as a tourist attraction. Second, as this article will explore, zoos have been undergoing considerable change in western societies, partly in response to shifts in attitudes to the display of captive animals. The connection between these changes and the predilections of late modern tourists is of considerable interest in terms

of changing sensitivities concerning wild animals and the "wild" in general. Third, several writers have pointed to the emergence of the "post-tourist," someone who seeks instant pleasures in the artifices created for his or her delectation (Rojek, 1993; Urry, 1990). The modern zoo constitutes an interesting site for the exploration of this kind of idea, since several of the changes that it is undergoing reveal affinities with the concept of post-tourism. Consequently, the zoo is a neglected but potentially fruitful area of enquiry.

The Zoo in Its Cultural and Historical Context

The practice of assembling collections of captive wild animals appears to date from the early phases of the formation of hierarchically organized, agriculture-based civilizations. Thus, in their comprehensive overview of the historical development of animal collections, Mullan and Marvin (1999) start with the sacred menageries linked to religious observances in ancient Egypt, and connect these institutions to the practice of keeping temple animals found in other ancient cultures.

They go on to describe early examples of the creation of large enclosed parks within which collections of wild animals were kept (for example in China), and describe those menageries in ancient Rome which were open to the public, as well as those whose purpose was to provide animals for amphitheatres. Mullan and Marvin's account also makes clear the importance of such collections as displays of power and status for high-ranking individuals, and the role of gifts of exotic wild animals in diplomacy. Certainly, by the late medieval and early modern period, what Mullan and Marvin term "princely menageries" appeared to be widespread in Europe, with particularly notable examples at Versailles in France, Schönbrunn in Austria, and the Tower of London in England (Mullan and Marvin, 1999: 101–3).

However, perhaps the most crucial development these authors describe is the expanding scientific logic behind the menagerie, particularly from the beginning of the eighteenth century onwards. Certainly, crucial landmarks are the founding of the world's first national menagerie in Paris in 1793, and the founding of the Zoological Society of London along with the opening of the Zoological Gardens in London in 1827 (Mullan and Marvin, 1999: 107–9). From these beginnings, public collections were established in urban locations around Europe and in the United States. The "zoo" as an attraction for a mass audience was firmly established by the beginning of the twentieth century.

Running through the historical development of the menagerie in its varied forms we can discern two crucial underlying themes: the theme of the *gaze* and the theme of *power*. The main aspect of the power dimension is largely self-evident. Within the artificial confines of the menagerie or zoo, almost total control is exercised by humans over the animal's movements and activities, with minimal opportunity for the animal to exercise its own preferences and priorities. As Mullan and Marvin (1999: 68) put it ". . . exhibition is a process of power." Parallels with prisons and mental hospitals inevitably spring to mind, with the zoo readily classifiable as an example of a "total institution" (Goffman, 1968), but an institution with animal rather than human inmates. However, in an important sense, the menagerie is also an expression of human superiority over other humans, since the exhibition of exotic animals may well be employed as a demonstration of the prestige and power of an individual (such as a monarch) or some corporate entity (for example a city or state).

But in such contexts, the exercise of power is intimately bound up with the process of surveillance (Foucault, 1979). In other words, the *powerless* are at all times subject to the gaze of the *powerful*, subject (irrespective of their own preferences) to constant scrutiny, monitoring and examination. For example, confined animals may be subjected to a scientific gaze or more specifically, a zoological gaze. That is, they become objects of analysis in the discourses of such disciplines as ethology, parasitology, reproductive biology, animal nutrition and so on. More generally, they become the objects of a kind of recreational gaze on the part of the general public who form the principal audience for the zoo's presentations. Of course, this recreational scrutiny of confined wild animals can be seen as one example of what Urry (1990) terms the "tourist gaze," by which he means the way in which many leisure activities, which are separated from the mundane settings of home and work, are shaped and framed by the act of *looking*. For humans, the visual predominates, and organizes experience. There are parallels here with what Mulvey (1981) has termed the "male gaze," referring to the ways in which many printed, film and electronic media make available images of women as objects of gaze for men. Women are thus seen as the passive objects of male scrutiny through the processes of representation. (Of course, the male gaze can also be catered for more directly through the *presentation* of women in such locations as strip clubs and lap-dancing bars.) Indeed, in her discussion of the zoo as an institution that "inscribes various human representational and material strategies for domesticating, mythologizing and aestheticizing the animal universe," Anderson (1995: 276) reinforces this point strongly. She argues that the gaze of the "rational male subject" has established itself as the generic human gaze, objective and all-encompassing. This dominance is, in turn, seen as based upon the denial or exclusion of competing possibilities.

However, it is manifestly the case that in recent decades the rationale behind the zoo has been undergoing a transformation. As early as the eighteenth century, fundamental shifts were taking place in western culture concerning the relationship between humans and the natural world. By the latter half of the nineteenth century, moral attitudes toward animals had become more sensitized to the idea of human/animal kinship. By the latter part of the twentieth century, social scientists like Fiddes (1991) were arguing that a shift from an exploitative to a "caring" view of animals and their environments has led to far-reaching changes in both attitudes and practices. Certainly, within a philosophical context, a substantial body of argument has emerged laying powerful emphasis on animal rights and animal welfare issues. In such a situation, the zoo as a site for the exercise of naked power over animals, and as a location for the indulgence of an unashamedly recreational gaze upon its captive inmates, becomes less and less appealing, and more difficult to justify. This process is almost certainly compounded by changes in public perception induced by the enormous increase in the anthropomorphized portrayal of animals in printed, film and electronic media.

Hence, the zoo is being recast and re-invented, with an attempt being made to switch the emphasis from entertainment to education, conservation, and animal welfare. However, the process of making zoos less overtly custodial and more "natural" (that is, the creation of quasifications not of animals per se, but of their native habitats) is arguably as much for the benefit of human visitors' sensibilities as a response to animals' needs. Inevitably, such observations must remain largely speculative, as empirical studies of zoo visitors remain relatively scarce (see for example Altman, 1998; Heinrich and Birney, 1992; Morgan and Hodgkinson, 1999).

Thus we arrive at the contention that the zoo, in its late modern manifestation, is moving toward a fundamentally new form. This contention, in turn, leads us directly into a consideration of the main focus of this article, the process of Disneyization.

The Disneyization of the Zoo

In spite of anxieties among the general public about animal captivity and perhaps because of the changes that many zoos have introduced, zoo visiting remains an important and popular leisure pursuit. Some well-known figures are frequently deployed to make this point: for example, according to World Zoo Organization estimates, there are some 10,000 zoos worldwide, which are visited by around 619 million people annually. The number of visitors to zoos in the United States and Canada exceeds the combined annual attendance of baseball, American football, and hockey.

We are proposing that one way of understanding the changes that are occurring in many western zoos is through the concept of *Disneyization*. This notion was proposed by Bryman (1999) as a parallel idea to Ritzer's (1998) influential thesis that society is undergoing a process he calls "McDonaldization." Disneyization is a parallel concept to McDonaldization in that the processes that are constitutive of the two terms frequently co-occur in relation to particular institutional spheres. Indeed, it may be that zoos exhibit certain manifestations of McDonaldization, but that is not an issue that is central to the present discussion. However, before discussing in detail the concept of Disneyization, it is important to distinguish it from the related notion of *Disneyfication*. The latter term is invariably applied to the impact of a Disney approach to cultural products, such as folk tales and novels. It is usually employed in a pejorative way to indicate a process of infantilization and vulgarization of the original content. By contrast, *Disneyization* is a more neutral term employed to describe the impact of Disney theme park principles on a range of organizations and institutional settings. The modern zoo, we argue, is a prime example of an institutional form which is increasingly subject to Disneyization.

In general terms, then, Disneyization can be seen as:

> . . . the process by which *the principles* of the Disney theme parks are coming to dominate more and more sectors of American society as well as the rest of the world. (Bryman, 1999: 26; emphasis in original)

Disneyization, then, refers to the diffusion of the principles of the Disney theme parks. The principles (which will be outlined below) cannot necessarily be attributed solely to the Disney theme parks themselves since they largely predate the opening of Disneyland—the first Disney theme park—in 1955. Instead, the Disney theme parks embody and exemplify the principles of Disneyization, though it is also the case that the extensive admiration for many of their business, presentational, and representational practices has meant that there has been widespread adoption of these principles by other organizations. In a sense, we can identify two related but distinguishable forms of Disneyization: first, *structural* Disneyization, which reflects a complex of underlying changes of which the Disney theme parks are exemplars, and second, *transferred* Disneyization, where the Disney principles from one sphere (the Disney theme park) are translated into another sphere.

The idea of Disneyization subsumes four trends or principles, which are as follows:

1. theming
2. dedifferentiation of consumption
3. merchandizing
4. emotional labor

The possible significance and relevance of the idea of Disneyization for zoos will be the focus of discussion below, but first each of these principles requires some elaboration.

Theming

A theme may be viewed as a master narrative that is appended to institutions and exhibits. Theming can be said to be a feature of many zoos in two major senses. First, there is evidence of growing theming within zoos, so that areas or collections are themed in a more abstract way than the conventional presentation of animals in categories like monkey house, lion and tiger house, and so on. The second sense in which theming can be said to be occurring in relation to zoos is that, in the process of reconstructing their institutional identities, zoos are theming themselves at the corporate level. Each of these senses will now be examined.

First, an example of theming within zoos is to be found in Jungle World in Bronx Zoo, which opened in 1985 and which is often regarded as an exemplar. The various components are intended to represent Asian rainforest, mangrove swamp, and scrub forest. Thus the zoo architecture and flora are no longer neutral but are in effect quasi-fications of natural habitats. Another example is the Lied Jungle at Henry Doorly Zoo in Omaha, which was influenced by the Bronx Zoo development, and similarly places animals within a wider ecosystem context. The Ford African Rainforest in Zoo Atlanta and the Thai Elephant Forest and Rain Forest at Woodland Park Zoo in Seattle are further instances of this process.

The whole of Busch Gardens in Tampa, Florida, is themed around Africa and includes a massive area containing free-roaming animals in zones like the Myombe Reserve. The Sea World theme parks are basically zoos/aquariums for various forms of marine life and their exhibits are themed in several different ways: Penguin Encounter, Tropical Rain Forest, Tropical Reef, Key West, and Pacific Point Preserve. It seems conceivable that this penchant for theming will accelerate following the opening in 1998 of the Animal Kingdom in Walt Disney World in Florida. Initially, the bulk of the park was themed on the African Savannah. Guests travel on a Kilimanjaro safari and visit areas like the Harambe Village. The publicity this venture has attracted and its sheer scale are likely to provide food for thought among zoo managers, a point to which we will return below.

In part, theming inside the zoo is a product of public unease about the sight of captive animals in cages. Placing animals in contexts in which they could roam more freely is much more consistent with modern sensibilities and attitudes to animals in captivity. However, theming was not a *necessary* accompaniment to this shift. Theming, for example in terms of an African motif, is largely extraneous to the removal of cages, since the backdrops can be, and indeed often still are, neutral in their connotations, although it could be argued that re-creating for wild animals their "natural" habitats provides a more comfortable environment for them. The evidence that the animals somehow benefit from such environments is unclear, and some commentators suggest that they are designed to enhance the sense of well-being of the zoo visitor more than that of the animal (Anderson, 1995: 290–291; Croke, 1997: 76–84). Nevertheless, what Bostock (1993: 113) terms the "aesthetic of the naturalistic" appears to have a powerful appeal for contemporary zoo designers and architects. It is plausible to argue, therefore, that this form of theming, that is the production of quasifications of "natural" environments, may be primarily for the benefit of humans. It is they who can relish and enjoy the carefully crafted artificiality of such settings. For the inmate animals, such artifices, which Desmond (1999: 164) has usefully termed "faked organic realisms," are in themselves beyond comprehension.

The second sense in which zoos are becoming themed is that they are seeking to reinvent themselves in an institutional and cultural sense, in the light of changing public sensibilities concerning the capture and caging of animals, and changing conceptions of the relationships between humans and nature. This trend suggests a growing theming *of* the zoo as a corporate form. Increasingly, zoos publicize and justify themselves not as repositories of animals to be gawked at, but as agencies dedicated to education and to the preservation of rare and nearly extinct species. As Dibb (1995: 263) notes from her examination of UK zoos and wildlife parks, as a result of changes in public opinion regarding captivity in zoos, "the role of wildlife facilities in protecting endangered species and encouraging breeding programmes is increasingly pushed to the fore."

Some zoos, like Marwell in Hampshire, have adopted this conception of their mission more or less from the outset. Others have essentially themed along these lines and in the process reinvented themselves. What was the Bronx Zoo is no longer the Bronx Zoo; since 1993 it is the

Bronx Wildlife Conservation Park. This follows a decision by the New York Zoological Society to rebrand it—and the three other zoos under its jurisdiction—in this way. Likewise, the Sea World parks place great emphasis on their role in rescuing and breeding rare marine mammals like the manatee.

Unsurprisingly, the motifs of species conservation plus education are major components of Disney's Animal Kingdom's raison d'étre too. The Disney corporation states that: "inspiring a love of animals and concern for their welfare is the underlying theme, both subtle and obvious, throughout the Animal Kingdom" (quoted in Tomkins, 1998: 9). This remark nicely sidesteps the fact that one of its lands is sponsored by McDonald's and the park itself sells vast quantities of steaks, burgers, hot dogs, and chicken nuggets and is built on former wetlands. However, its director of animal operations, who was lured from the famous San Diego Zoo, has stated that he would not have taken on the task unless he was "sure Disney was a 100 per cent committed to conservation" (quoted in Churchill, 1998: 3).

This growing unease about the use of the depiction "zoo" and the substitution of alternative terms stressing conservation and education are in themselves components of the turn toward theming. However, it has to be acknowledged that some commentators are sceptical about the application of new master narratives of education, science, and species conservation (for example Jamieson, 1995; Malamud, 1998). Nevertheless, the theming of zoos in terms of these master narratives is a continuing process, as is the internal theming of the zoo in terms of quasifications.

Dedifferentiation of Consumption

Dedifferentiation of consumption means "the general trend whereby the forms of consumption associated with different institutional spheres become interlocked with each other and increasingly difficult to distinguish" (Bryman, 1999: 33). This process reveals itself in such trends as the ways in which theme parks and shopping malls increasingly shade into one another, or the way hotels/casinos in Las Vegas append theme park attractions. It is in these settings that the process we have termed quasification can take on its most impressive and significant forms, in that the quasifications often serve to conceal further the boundaries between consumption spheres. What is more, in the case of the Mirage hotel/casino in Las Vegas, real tigers and other large cats are presented in zoo-inspired quasifications of "natural" settings.

Disney's Animal Kingdom is an extreme in this respect and it is hardly surprising that a Disney location should be a major site of this aspect of the Disneyization of zoos. In placing a zoo in the midst of Walt Disney World, which comprises theme parks, water parks, nearly 20 hotels, six golf courses, and numerous restaurants, including one of the Rainforest Café chain in the Animal Kingdom and a hotel very close to it, the dedifferentiation of consumption in relation to zoos is magnified. Like Busch Gardens, West Midlands Safari Park, and several other zoos, it includes theme park attractions within its grounds. The Animal Kingdom has a thrill ride tellingly called "Countdown to Extinction." Busch Gardens has numerous thrill rides which are organized in terms of African lands, and Sea World in Orlando has a flume ride called "Voyage to Atlantis." Some theme parks, like Drayton Manor in the UK, incorporate a zoo amid the various rides and attractions. Aqualeon, just outside Barcelona in Spain, combines a water park with the display of wild animals, as well as shows which actively involve some of these animals. We see in these examples a tendency for the distinction between zoo and theme park to become blurred.

A further aspect of this issue is the fact that the large American zoos (Animal Kingdom, Busch Gardens, Sea World) include extensive shopping and eating facilities. While most zoos cannot match this provision because of their much smaller scale, it is conceivable that these features will become more prominent and will gradually supplant the standard café or tea room and small gift shop at the exit. Cain and Merritt (1998) point to the growing commercialism of

American zoos and aquariums and the significance of restaurants and gift shops selling soft toy animals and other merchandise as part of that strategy. The authors even suggest that zoo managers need to be more aware of the ways in which such institutions can be developed as businesses. This leads smoothly to the next dimension.

Merchandising

All of the large American zoos mentioned above sell very extensive ranges of merchandise—T-shirts, baseball caps, wallets, pens and pencils, and so on. However, there is evidence that this feature is becoming much more widespread. The director of Zoo Atlanta, Terry Maple, has argued that such merchandise is important because it produces revenue and also provides publicity and enhances the zoo experience. He has written that "we must be prepared to provide our supporters, partners, and guests with specialized bumper stickers, pins, T-shirts, ties, and coffee mugs" (Maple and Archibald, 1993: 79–80). In addition, he proclaims that in his own zoo, "we adopted some of the techniques and methods commonly used by entertainment and amusement enterprises, like Disney World and Six Flags" (Maple and Archibald, 1993: 89). The growing commercialism of zoos previously referred to is likely to increase the range of merchandise on offer. Merchandising is reinforced through the creation of representations of "iconic" animals (such as tigers, manatees, giant pandas) and other species seen as threatened with extinction or as having a particular magnetism. Such representations can then be directly incorporated into merchandise items. Thus, the presentation of animals and animal performances by zoos can feed directly into the generation of commoditized images, which can have considerable commercial potential. As Desmond (1999: 148) observes, the commodification of wild animals is ironic in that they are invariably depicted as symbols of pristine nature and therefore as beyond the clutches of a commoditized world. However, surrounding the zoo with an aura of research, conservation, and education helps to legitimate this commodification and helps to resolve the irony.

Emotional Labor

Emotional labor refers to the individual worker's control of the self, a control which is geared to expressing socially desired emotions in the course of service transactions. Emotional labor is increasingly anticipated by customers in the course of service encounters, but it can also cause the worker some distress because of the need to express "unreal" emotions (Hochschild, 1993). This is the one area where specific evidence is sparse, largely because zoo employees have not often been the focus of research on zoos. There is a growing expectation of good customer service and since the interface with the public is a component of this, it would not be too unwise to predict a growing tendency toward the use of emotional labor as zoos become more commercialized, but this is an area that clearly requires further investigation. Indeed, Dibb (1995: 270) reports that encouraging staff to demonstrate "a positive attitude toward customer service" is a preoccupation for managers of zoos and wildlife parks in the UK.

When such service is *not* forthcoming, the effects can create a highly negative response. Certainly, visitors will notice that emotional labor is definitely a feature of the Sea Worlds and Busch Gardens, and it seems likely in view of the Disney Corporation's renown for its ever-smiling, ever-helpful "cast members" that emotional labor will also be a feature of Disney's Animal Kingdom.

Davis's (1997) study of Sea World in San Diego makes explicit reference to emotional labor as a feature of the park. She writes: "Sea World employees must be friendly, cheerful, helpful, and always smiling to a vast throng of stroller-pushing pedestrians" (Davis, 1997: 90).

Also, as noted above, there is evidence that many zoos have taken specific note of the entertainment orientation to education at Disney theme parks. It seems likely that the infusion of emotional labor has been a component of this

borrowing of Disney ideas. What is more, in the zoo setting, the possibility exists that emotional labor can take a distinctive form, particularly in relation to environmentalist ethics and conservationist appeals. On the one hand, emotional labor may be used to induce a sense of guilt (in relation to environmental degradation, species extinction, etc.). On the other hand, it may be used to induce a "feel-good factor" in the minds of visitors, predicated on the proposition that by visiting the zoo and buying its merchandise, they are participating, however indirectly, in the lofty ideals of species and habitat protection.

Of course, zoos frequently enlarge the field of emotional labor by conscripting their animal inmates, particularly the large mammals, into the performative realm that such labor inhabits. As Desmond notes: "Zoos have experimented with ways of getting the animals to do something, to perform a behavior, to move, so that people will be more interested" (1999: 172). In effect, human emotional labor can be simulated when the animals are induced to display behavior that can be interpreted by the audience as indicative of an emotion, such as friendliness, humor, or mischievousness (as when the killer whale Shamu soaks the first ten rows of the audience in Sea World's Shamu show). Such displays are not only spectacular performances in themselves, but also serve to increase the attractiveness of merchandise and souvenirs based on the animals concerned. Desmond also argues that the emphasis placed in such performances on the animals' "love" of their trainers, further serves to enhance the plausibility for the audience of these displays of apparent emotional expressivity (Desmond, 1999: 197).

The "Wild" as Theme

There are clearly far-reaching implications to the argument that zoos may no longer be in a position to base their continued existence upon the notion of wild animals as mere exhibits for public entertainment. As we have seen, alternative rationales and justifications have been brought into play, emerging out of practices and discourses relating to education and conservation. However, principles like conservation and education have to be marketed to a public whose primary orientation to the zoo probably remains that of entertainment. One solution to this problem is to package the principles themselves as themes. Entertaining and diverting themes then become the vehicles through which lay members of the public are enlightened, and through which zoo professionals can achieve their broader goals.

Of course, over and above the theming of education and conservation, the "wild" itself becomes a theme. Wildness as theme can be seen in a variety of other contexts, such as the elevation for touristic consumption of the whale as a creature with both real and imagined traits and the display of wild animals in tourism safari brochures. In both these cases, the theming may conflict with traditional values regarding these creatures, such as the whale as a fishery resource or large wild terrestrial mammals as game or pests.

"Wildness" is also re-invented and reformulated, rendered "playful" and engaging through the powerful quasification technologies developed for use in other themed leisure settings. Thus the zoo, as a form and an actual location, provides the potential for the creation of spectacular and appealing attractions by quasification designers and engineers. Once the wild has been commoditized in this way (perhaps most popularly in its African form) it becomes available for safe and easy consumption. By these means, even the dangerous and threatening aspects of "wildness" are themselves sanitized and rendered harmless and entertaining. Moreover, the notion of the wild as theme shares with conservation imagery what Anderson (1995: 289) has called "the inchoate public lament for lost natures." Thus, zoos simultaneously commoditize the wild (and wild animals in particular) and pander to public anxieties about the erosion of the natural world in the face of urbanization, industrialization, and the spread of technology.

This process of the commoditization of the wild is enhanced and supported by the fact that zoo themers can rely upon the extensive supply of relevant "virtual capital" (Beardsworth and Bryman, 1999) their visitors will bring to the zoo. By virtual capital is meant the large stock of knowledge and images assembled by the individual from sources like television, film, and advertising, plus a capacity for playful responses to mediated and simulated images. The complexes of representations and depictions contained in the individual's stock of virtual capital will enable him or her to make sense of, and appreciate the entertainment value of, the presentations, representations and quasifications contained within the themed zoo. This effect is particularly intense in relation to the Disneyization process. Within the Disney idiom, there are powerful currents of anthropomorphism and sentimentality in the depiction of animals (both in live action and cartoon contexts), and these currents themselves become incorporated into the virtual capital of consumers of Disney cultural and commercial products. In the Disneyized zoo context, the anthropomorphic and "sentimental" expectations brought into the setting by the visitor may then be catered for by the presentation of animal performances in which creatures are invited to exhibit apparently human motivations, attributes, and actions.

It seems plausible to suggest, then, that the themed zoo represents the next step in the evolution of the menagerie, as it moves into its late modern form. Indeed, museums in general, and natural history museums in particular, might also be seen as moving in this general direction. However, zoos face a problem not encountered by museums: live animals are considerably more difficult to present and manage than are quasified ones! This is of particular significance in that, in the themed zoo, the animal inmates inevitably become more than the exhibits of a traditional zoo. Increasingly they will be "staged" as attractions in quasified entertainment settings. In a very real sense, they will become "workers" or "cast members" in the playgrounds created by the leisure industry. This will be particularly true for those "charismatic" animals the public is especially drawn to.

However, captive wild animals require fundamentally different forms of control and management, as compared with domesticated animals (even though, with captive breeding some wild species may become, effectively, semi-domesticated). Of course, the contrasts are even greater when captive animals are compared with their human co-workers, with very different requirements in relation to feeding, resting, control of behavior, health and safety issues, and so on. Thus, extracting the required performance from an animal "cast member" may entail elaborate forms of training and manipulation. With these factors in mind, it is clear that in certain settings requiring close contact with the public and regularity of performance, animatronic quasifications of zoo animals are likely to be employed.

In the context of the Disneyization thesis discussed above, the question also arises as to whether zoo animals can be trained to perform, or rather mimic, the emotional work that is expected of human employees. Such training is clearly feasible, and has a long tradition in such settings as circuses, fairs, and stage performances. That this kind of performance by animals entails the mere semblance of emotional engagement may not be a stumbling block as regards the reactions of visitor/customers, as such semblance may also apply, albeit in a rather different sense, to the performances of human cast members.

Conclusion

In this article, it has been suggested that many modern zoos are becoming Disneyized. The process is both direct and indirect with respect to the Disney theme parks. The popularity of the parks and their innovative approach to education and the provision of information have undoubtedly had a direct impact. Equally, the process is indirect: many of the processes described as indicators of Disneyization precede the parks, but also as those processes become absorbed into the economy and the culture an imitation bandwagon is set up. However, the arrival of what is in effect a Disney zoo—its Animal Kingdom—is likely to encourage

comparisons with non-Disney establishments and may provide an additional spur to the direct Disneyization of zoos in general. As a result, zoos may enter a phase of what might be termed *imitative* Disneyization as the Disney zoo becomes an explicit model for future designs and directions. This development is in addition to the two other processes of Disneyization (that is, *structural* and *transferred*) that were discussed above.

What is more, since the Disneyized zoo locates animal presentation and animal performance in highly elaborate quasified settings, it could be that we are also witnessing a basic shift in the object of the tourist gaze. There exists the probability that the exhibition of animals will become subordinate to the staging of elaborate quasifications of the "wild." Rather than the animals being the primary attraction, the settings themselves will become the main objects of the visitor's entranced and admiring gaze. Hence, the themed zoo becomes the location in which urban humans can experience a quasified form of the "wild" with maximum comfort, convenience, and safety. These developments are very much in tune with the theme park and its emergence as a tourist destination.

There can be no doubting the central role of tourism in the economy and culture of late modern societies. However, in the post-tourist context the consumers of tourism experiences do not necessarily demand that those experiences be authentic. Rather, they seek out experiences which are entertaining, compelling, and effectively staged. Hence, the four modes of engagement with wild animals which we have outlined above increasingly become geared to entertainment as a means of attracting the post-tourist. The zoo, as the primary institution of wild animal presentation, thus becomes more and more entertainment-orientated, and if it seeks also to do educational "work" on its clients, such work will increasingly be disguised as entertainment. Emotional labor facilitates this process by providing a form of interactional glossing which serves to smooth the transition between education and diversion.

There are, however, more subtle appeals inherent in the theme park configuration of the zoo.

For example, threatening aspects of the wild can be neutralized and sanitized in such settings. In contrast, such sanitization may be much more difficult to achieve for active encounter seekers, even for those who purchase professionally guided encounters on a commercial basis. What is more, through its theming and entertainment motifs, this new configuration can offer an accessible and palatable model of humankind's continuing ability to exercise power over nature. That power, once conceived of as a right to exploit, has now been transmuted into a duty to manage and conserve. Thus the theme of conservation, delivered as part of a "fun day out," becomes a reassuring legitimation of the continued existence of one of the earliest forms of total institution, the menagerie.

References

Altman, J.D. (1998) "Animal Activity and Visitor Learning at the Zoo," *Anthrozoös* 11 (1): 12–21.

Anderson, K. (1995) "Culture and Nature at the Adelaide Zoo: At the Frontiers of 'Human' Geography," *Transactions of the Institute of British Geographers* 20: 275–294.

Beardsworth, A., and A. Bryman (1999) "Late Modernity and the Dynamics of Quasification: The Case of the Themed Restaurant," *The Sociological Review* 47: 228–257.

Bostock, S. St C. (1993) *Zoos and Animal Rights: The Ethics of Keeping Animals.* London: Routledge.

Bryman, A. (1999) "The Disneyization of Society," *The Sociological Review* 47: 25–47.

Gain, L.P., and D.A. Merritt (1998) "The Growing Commercialism of Zoos and Aquariums," *Journal of Policy Analysis and Management* 17: 298–312.

Churchill, D. (1998) "Beware, It's a Jungle Out There," *The Times* (Weekend section) 28 March: 3.

Croke, V. (1997) *The Modern Ark.* New York: Scribner.

Davis, S.G. (1997) *Spectacular Nature: Corporate Culture and the Sea World Experience.* Berkeley: University of California Press.

Desmond, J.C. (1999) *Staging Tourism: Bodies on Display from Waikiki to Sea World.* Chicago, IL: University of Chicago Press.

Dibb, S. (1995) "Understanding the Level of Marketing Activity in the Leisure Sector," *Service Industries Journal* 15: 257–275.

Fiddes, N. (1991) *Meat: A Natural Symbol.* London: Routledge.

Foucault, M. (1979) *Discipline and Punish.* Harmondsworth: Penguin.

Franklin, A. (1999) *Animals and Modern Culture: A Sociology of Human–Animal Relations in Modernity.* London: Sage.

Goffman, E. (1968) *Asylums: Essays on the Social Situation of Mental Patients and Other Inmates.* Harmondsworth: Penguin.

Heinrich, C.J., and B.A. Birney (1992) "Effects of Live Animal Demonstration on Zoo Visitors' Retention of Information," *Anthrozoös* 5: 113–121.

Hochschild, A. (1983) *The Managed Heart.* Berkeley, CA: University of California Press.

Jamieson, D. (1995) "Zoos Revisited," pp. 52–66 in B.G. Norton, M. Hutchins, E.F. Stevens, and T.L. Maple (eds.), *Ethics on the Ark: Zoos, Animal Welfare, and Wildlife Conservation.* Washington, DC: Smithsonian Institution.

Malamud, R. (1998) *Reading Zoos: Representations of Animals and Captivity.* New York: New York University Press.

Maple, T., and E. Archibald (1993) *Zoo Man: Inside the Zoo Revolution.* Atlanta, GA: Longstreet.

Morgan, J.M., and M. Hodgkinson (1991) "The Motivation and Social Orientation of Visitors Attending a Contemporary Zoological Park," *Environment and Behaviour* 31: 227–239.

Mullan, B., and G. Marvin (1999) *Zoo Culture,* 2nd ed. Urbana: University of Illinois Press.

Mulvey, L. (1981) "Visual Pleasure and Narrative Cinema," in T. Bennett *et al.* (eds.), *Popular Television and Film.* London: British Film Institute.

Ritzer, G. (1998) *The McDonaldization Thesis.* London: Sage.

Rojek, C. (1993) *Ways of Escape: Modern Transformations in Leisure and Travel.* London: Macmillan.

Tomkins, R. (1998) "Fair Game for a Gentle Savaging." *Financial Times,* 25 April:9.

Urry, J. (1990) *The Tourist Gaze.* London: Sage.

David P. Pierson

Representations of the Animal World on the Discovery Channel

During a 1996 cable TV marketing conference, leading cable network executives reinforced the notion that "effective branding means cultivating a network identity around a narrowly targeted concept with global appeal" (Littleton 56). Whether a cable network offers 24-hour news programming or classic Hollywood movies, the central goal of successful cable branding is to become recognized as a worldwide authority in a content field. Along with MTV and other cable networks, the Discovery Channel has sought to establish a global brand image based on its perceived authority in educational and nonfictional documentary programming. "A brand is something that can be appreciated universally," said Greg Moyer, chief executive and creative officer of Discovery Communications. The market strength of Discovery's brand has allowed it to extend its cable and satellite networks into 155 countries, and to expand its worldwide audience to over 231 million homes (Eisenberg 54). According to the National Cable Television Association's 2002 ranking of the top 20 cable TV networks, the Discovery Channel ranked fifth, with 86.1 million subscribers, just ahead of TNT (Turner Network Television; Park 282).

While this information illustrates many of the corporate and economic determinants of the Discovery Channel's programming, it does not really explain how the network produces and schedules programming that effectively engages its diverse array of viewers. In fact, Discovery explicitly and tacitly develops a recognizable "identity" across the range of its programming. Discovery also taps into a wide range of available social discourses, and reworks, structures, and shapes them into TV programs and program schedules that enable viewers to create a multiplicity of meanings from them. To understand this practice, this study analyzes a week of prime-time (8:00–11:00 p.m. EST) nature programming on the U.S. Discovery Channel to determine the specific thematic discourses that are represented.

Analyzing a week of prime-time nature programming yielded the thematic discourse of nature, or the natural world as familiar domain. The Discovery Channel's nature programming engages its viewers and creates an identifiable cable identity because the discourses are already a recognizable part of a viewer's social and imaginative worlds. These discourses do not exist just in Discovery's nature programming, but are in fact represented in many other social and media forms. Evaluating animals through human moral values (good, evil, lazy) is also represented in Hollywood films (e.g., *The Lion King*), circuses, children's books, songs, and other popular cultural forms.

This thematic discourse can be further divided into four subcategories: nature and gender, anthropomorphism, nature and social structure, and social conceptions of nature. Finally, this study concludes with a brief statement of the ideological and social implications of these discourses in understanding nature and the environment.

Nature and Gender

One of the most consistent cultural patterns present in Discovery's nature programs and in nature programs in general is the concept of gender. One of the central assumptions made within early feminist scholarship is that there is a distinct difference between sex and gender; while biological sex is natural and innate, gender (masculinity and femininity) is a cultural construct. Feminist scholarship maintains that biological sex differences cannot account for the range of social meanings attached to gender and to the distribution of power and social position between men and women. But despite the overwhelming weight of academic theories and scholarship behind this perspective, the majority of people still tend to conceive of gender differences as natural and innately given, and that, beyond sexual differences, there is an underlying essential gendered dichotomy between men and women. This assumption is so ingrained in our social consciousness and social institutions that to perceive otherwise carries with it undeniable social and political implications (Coltrane 45).

In the examined segment of Discovery's nature programs, traditional nineteenth-century Romantic Rousseauian images of self-sacrificing motherhood are reproduced. These images of female animals implicitly reinforce Jean Rousseau's discourse concerning the biological destiny (and institutional role) of human females to become mothers, to care for their children, and to preserve the integrity of their families for the survival of the human species. In the *Wild Discovery* episode "Great Siberian Grizzly" (July 28, 1998), for example, a mother grizzly leads her three bear cubs from their winter hibernation den on a long trek to a salmon-filled lake for the summer, and then makes the perilous journey back to the den before the descent of winter. The mother bear's maternal instincts are featured in a number of familiar scenarios, from nursing her young cubs to fearlessly protecting them from being attacked by adult male bears. The bear is also represented as the self-sacrificing mother when she delays her

brood's agonizing, snow-swept journey back to the den for a day to care for one of her weakened cubs. The program's voice-over narration highlights her sacrificial behavior: "mothers risk everything to give a fallen cub a chance."

Discovery's nature programs also offer traditional images of physically and sexually aggressive mature male animals, images that tend to reinforce the biological essentialism of Robert Bly and other followers of the men's movement. Bly's work relies on figures from ancient Greek, Roman, and Native American mythologies to construct their masculine ideals; these social ideals generally rest on the timeless categorization of "Man-the-Hunter" and spiritual wanderer-seeker of new knowledge (Coltrane 45–46). In these gendered conceptions of ancient and past cultures, women were mainly relegated to domestic and nurturing roles in society. As with Bly's conception of human males, Discovery's male animals are represented as combative and competitive with other males, and disassociated from the process of raising their offspring.

In the *Wild Discovery* episode "Whitetail Country," the voice-over narration explains that a strict social structure governs a herd of whitetail deer. This rigid power structure dictates that subordinate bucks must avoid eye contact with dominant bucks. These dominant bucks use their superior size to intimidate any rivals and to maintain their dominant positions. On a rare occasion, a buck intent on defending his doe must participate in a one-on-one antler fight with a rival buck. While the loser of the fight must leave the area, the "victor buck" is said to strengthen the genetic lineage of the deer population. In *The Science of Whales*, the narration points out that a similar power structure exists with whales: one male challenges another established male for mating rights with the female. As with the bucks, the male whales fight against each other with a series of brutal head butts until the other dies or leaves the area. And, as with the bucks, the consequence of this violent encounter is that the male is "rewarded" with the mating rights with the females. While these episodes accurately present a central facet of the existing social and power structures within these species, their continued stress on the more aggressive and power-related practices of the males tends to perpetuate the social perception that all male animals (including humans) are predominantly "wild males" at heart.

Anthropomorphism

Margaret King, in her analysis of Disney's True-Life nature films, asserted that one of the central themes of these films is the anthropomorphizing of the entire spectrum of nature, including animal and plant life. The broad template of human social organization, with its inscribed concerns, morals, and values, is imposed on the natural world. Disney extends its anthropomorphic slant by creating animal "stars" and providing them with names, often human names—for example, *Flash, the Teenage Otter* (1965) and *Perri* (1957), a film biography of a squirrel. A central anthropomorphic technique is to construct the film's central animals as empathic "characters" with clearly discernable personalities (King 64–65).

This anthropomorphic penchant for constructing animals into characters is also present in Discovery's nature programs. For example, the *Wild Discovery* episode "Great Siberian Grizzly" is primarily structured by two simultaneous storylines. The main story concerns a mother grizzly bear, her three cubs, their long springtime trek to a salmon-filled lake, and their perilous snowy journey back to the winter den. The secondary story concerns an adolescent bear's crucial life struggle to master the art of catching salmon in order to put on enough body weight to survive the long winter hibernation. Both of these storylines follow a familiar chronological narrative as they trace the animal's progression from springtime back to the winter den. Through the continual incorporation of intimate close-up shots accompanied by a voice-over narration that details the animal's specific behavior and motivations, these animals are effectively transformed into dramatic characters for the viewing audience. While this episode does describe the activities of other wildlife in the Russian region of the Kamchatka Peninsula, it primarily presents dual narratives featuring the mother grizzly and her cubs, and the vital life lessons of a single adolescent bear. Though the Discovery Channel stops short of personally naming its animals and does portray them in a less sentimental manner than Disney, many of its nature programs focus on the storylines of one or more animals.

Another anthropomorphic technique is to use familiar human terms to describe acts of nature. In the *Wild Discovery* episode "Baboons" (July 26, 1998), the voice-over narration characterizes baboons in such morally judgmental terms as "criminals," "beggars," and "victims." The program's narrative involves the social, economic, and environmental problems associated with the baboon population within a Kenyan national park. The narrative highlights the baboons' destructive damage to local crops that border the park. In the first segment, the visual rhetoric and narration construct the moral image of these baboons as "raiders" committing a "crime" by "stealing" corn in the fields. The baboons' transgression against humans is further reinforced by a dramatic sequence in which the animals invade a village home and damage private property in their search for food.

This tendency of anthropomorphizing animals includes the way in which individual animals in nature programs are constructed and perceived by viewers. The majority of animals in nature programs tend to fall within the confines of the cuteness/repulsiveness dichotomy. On the one hand, certain animals (e.g., lions, bears, and whales) are valued for their aesthetic beauty and form. In addition, humans are attracted to animals, such as bear and lion cubs, that share the same evolutionary juvenilization of biological features as human infants. Such features include large eyes and a protruding cranium. But animals that have an adult alien appearance, lack the proper juvenilization of their biological features, and employ senses outside of human abilities are generally associated with negative values that may be translated into emotional reactions like disgust and repulsion. Stephen Kellert asserts that the list of species disliked by Americans includes "the cockroach, mosquito, rat, wasp, rattlesnake, bat, vulture, and shark" (21).

Despite these negative connotations, Discovery's annual "Shark Week," which features a week of prime-time programming centered on the shark, has been one of the channel's most popular and enduring program specials. Papson points out that the box office success of *Jaws* in 1975 elevated the great white shark to "celebrity status," and "the great white was given both personality and internationality" (68). Following *Jaws* were several feature films and TV documentaries that featured the shark as their main subject of interest. The gradual aesthetization of the shark in the 1970s as a beautiful but deadly predator signaled a cultural change of perception of the animal. Papson argues that aesthetization, or the practice of culturally appreciating the shark as an art object, was essential for the shark's survival and protection by humans (73).

The cuteness/repulsiveness dichotomy can be found in many of Discovery's prime-time nature programs. When a young bear cub dies in "Great Siberian Grizzly," his death is not only a family tragedy, but also represents a preordained form of spiritual death. The voice-over narration poetically explains that when the young cub dies, his "soul will return to the Kamchatka mountains." In effect, this small bear cub is granted the same level of spirituality normally reserved for humans and their deities.

But while bear cubs are valued to the extent of being endowed with spiritual souls, other animals are so reviled and physically repulsive that we tend to associate them with moral "evil." In Discovery's *Movie Magic* episode "Snakes, Snakes and More Snakes" (July 28, 1998), several experts discuss why most people are scared of snakes. One theorizes that people unconsciously fear snakes because of their disturbing tube shape and their ability to swallow their victims whole. He states that snakes are like "traveling esophaguses." Despite the program's best efforts to demystify the ratio-

nale behind people's dread of snakes, it still continues to emphasize the same negative attributes that are socially attached to the animals.

Nature and Social Structure

One of the most prevalent themes in nature programs is a persistent stress on nature's intrinsic hierarchal structure; in Discovery's nature programs, this structure is often referred to as the "Great Chain of Being." In this chain, the natural world is conceived as part of the grand scheme of the universe, in which every living thing is connected to each other, and there is a natural hierarchical ordering of things from the lowest form of existence to the highest and the most perfected, or God. Directly below God are humans, followed by the other warm-blooded forms of life. Because all language is metaphoric to "outside of skin" reality, conceiving of nature as a Great Chain of Being, a Newtonian mechanism, or a living social organism becomes an operative way by which to know and understand nature. Unfortunately, there is always the tendency among some scientists, environmentalists, and members of the public to confuse the metaphoric reality for the material reality of the natural world.

Because humans have a historical penchant for imposing their own social organization onto the natural world, it should come as no surprise that nature is conceived as a familiar social world. Nature's perceived hierarchal social structure mirrors the socioeconomic stratification governing twenty-first-century modern capitalism. And just as human society is represented as a patriarchal social structure in which dominant males compete for power within an increasingly social Darwinistic global capitalist system, a similar power struggle exists among dominant whitetail deer males who compete for social and genetic dominance within a single herd. While the perceived common-sense rewards for dominant humans includes social, economic, and sexual success, the spoils for the dominant whitetail bucks include a "harem" of does and the continuation of their genetic heritage.

Another familiar discourse often associated with modern capitalism is that of gambling. Capitalism is frequently perceived as a complex, risky game of identifiable winners and losers in which a majority of new business ventures fail every year. A similar gambling discourse is used to explain why some species survive over others. In Discovery's *The Extinction Files* (July 27, 1998), despite the program's determined scientific discourse, the narration frequently employs the discourse of gambling to remind viewers that species' evolution and extinction are primarily driven by chance and luck. For instance, during the late Cretaceous period, the demise of the dinosaurs and the mass extinction of 76 percent of the species on Earth provide a forum for the mammals to emerge as winners and assume center stage in the evolutionary game. Although evolutionary changes are never absolutes and in fact involve a certain level of indeterminacy, the program's reliance on a gambling discourse to represent the evolutionary process as a type of natural lottery tends to validate conventional evolutionary thinking.

Social Conceptions of Nature

According to King, one of the central issues posed in the nature film is defining the proper relationship between humans and nature. King asks what types of relationships are possible other than the older exploiter/exploited model. These relationships involve a number of relevant issues, including hunting and preservation, conservation and animal husbandry, and protecting select animal and plant species (King 61). But before one can address these issues, one must first define nature.

Phil Macnaghten and John Urry suggested that most people take for granted that strictly speaking, there is no such thing as one single identifiable "nature"; there are only natures. There are three primary ways in which contemporary Western cultures have conceptualized nature: (1) nature as a field of scientific inquiry and human management, (2) nature as a threatened realm, and (3) nature as a sacred realm filled with great moral and spiritual powers.

The first conception of nature constructs it as an open-air laboratory or a field for scientific inquiry that can be managed and controlled through modern science and conservation. Macnaghten and Urry point out that in the early part of the twentieth century, there were tensions between preservationists who desired to leave nature in its original wild state, and ecologists who were apt to regard nature and nature reserves as sites for scientific inquiry. By the end of World War II, there emerged a consensus among the Western scientific community that wildlife and conservation issues could be incorporated within the new rational, planned order (38–40). Because one of the main components of modern science is empirical observation, surveillance becomes one of the primary tasks of the scientist studying the natural world. Surveillance is necessary not only for the rudimentary function of counting, categorizing, and describing all forms of animal and plant life, but also for using this information to make conservationist decisions about whether to alter nature's natural habitat or its biological conditions.

This conception of nature is represented in many of Discovery's nature programs. In Discovery's *Jaws in the Mediterranean* (July 29, 1998), for example, natural scientists rely on numerous methods to survey the "shark ecology" of the great white shark in the waters of the Mediterranean Sea. These methods include measuring the size of small sharks at a local village fishmonger's market to studying the great white's available food supply of seals and dolphins. Later in the episode, the scientists continue their surveillance efforts by tagging blue sharks in order to track their growth and migration patterns.

The second concept is nature as a threatened realm. This concept can be seen in the public concern over endangered species, the idea of nature as an exhaustible resource worthy of conservation, and the perception of nature as a pure and healthy body being constantly threatened by human-made pollution (Macnaghten and Urry 22). This conception is represented in many of Discovery's nature programs; humans are implicitly represented as having ultimate power and control over nature. Unchecked, this control often becomes a destructive force.

In the episode "Baboons," the narrator exemplifies the extent of this control when he solemnly asserts that "humans have altered the world beyond all recognition." In the *Wild Discovery* episode "The Island of the Apes" (July 29, 1998), the African villagers' seasonal damming of a river to dig for diamonds has disastrous environmental consequences for the indigenous fish and the spotted-neck otter. Later in the episode, the viewer also learns that "monkey hunting" is not only a big business in neighboring Sierra Leone, but also that the hunters are threatening the very survival of the primate population on the tiny island of Tiwai. Although this episode depicts the detrimental effects of poaching on the island, it does not describe the broader social, political, and economic contexts that make this so-called monkey trade possible. In conceiving of nature as a threatened realm, one frequently finds oneself torn between assuming a position of impotence in the human destruction of nature, and taking the more active role of being a preservationist or steward to it. Discovery, despite its general statements concerning the need for protecting threatened animal and plant species, does not address how viewers can take a more active role in this preservationist process.

The third concept is nature as a sacred realm filled with great moral and spiritual power, a place to be enjoyed and worshiped by all humans. Nature is represented as an inexhaustible resource for moral, physical, and spiritual healing (Macnaghten and Urry 22–23).

In Discovery's nature programs, nature is sometimes represented as a great eternal moral and spiritual entity. In "Siberian Grizzly," the episode's picturesque visual rhetoric and narration work together to present the animals of Kamchatka as being a part of the Great Chain of Being, including every creature from "bear to eagle." The death of an animal is seen as just a part of this great cycle: "salmon are the lords; they die so others can live." This emphasis on the

Great Chain reinforces the "naturalness" of the hierarchal social structure that pervades modern capitalist human society. At the end of the episode, the narrator calls on humans to learn from this great cycle in Kamchatka, a near eternal place where one encounters "innocent animals" that have existed since the Ice Age. He states that the "great bears can teach us so much we have forgotten." This episode conceives nature as an all-knowing, godlike teacher with the inexhaustible capacity to restore and renew humankind's place within the universe. In this conception, humans are humbled into being just one of nature's creatures. The central danger in perceiving nature as an eternal entity is that one easily overlooks the impact that humans continue to have on the natural world through industrial development and pollution.

Conclusions

What are the ideological and social implications of Discovery's nature programs' perceptions of the natural world as a familiar domain? While these programs do provide factual information about animals, they also rely on the "human template of character" to perceive animals in moral and normative terms, and to engage their viewers on a dramatic and emotional level. These programs also tap into the viewer's knowledge of human social organization to impose this hierarchal social order on the "animal kingdom." The animal world is represented as a highly dramatic realm filled with close-knit families, external conflicts, and intense competitions—in other words, a world not unlike the one inhabited by Discovery's middle-class suburban viewers. For the most part, these social representations of the animal world tend to reinforce the dominant social and cultural conceptions of social class and gender in the human world. William Timberlake asserts that while no complete objectivity exists in describing nonhuman behavior, there are ongoing discussions in the natural sciences about constructing a "provisional objectivity, the value of limited anthropomorphism, the value of models, and whether one can take an animal's view without turning it into a human one" (85). Unfortunately, Discovery's nature programs do not investigate these discussions concerning language and its representational role in studying animal behavior. Timberlake states that though "anthropomorphism can contribute to the study of (animal) behavior, alone it leads inevitably to the realm of human social relations, not to the realm of understanding (animal) behavior" (85).

Works Cited

Coltrane, Scott. "Theorizing Masculinities in Contemporary Social Science." *Theorizing Masculinities*. Ed. Harry Brod and Michael Kaufman. Thousand Oaks, CA: Sage, 1994. 39–60.

Eisenberg, Daniel. "TV's Unlikely Empire." *Time* 3 Mar. 2003: 54–56.

Kellert, Stephen. "Perceptions of Animals in America." *Perceptions of Animals in American Culture.* Ed. R. J. Hoage. Washington: Smithsonian Institution, 1989. 5–24.

King, Margaret J. "The Audience in the Wilderness." *Journal of Popular Film & Television* 24.2 (1996): 60–68.

Littleton, Cynthia. "Cable Targets Global 'Niche' Brand." *Broadcasting & Cable* 1 July 1996: 56–57.

Macnaghten, Phil, and John Urry. *Contested Natures.* London: Sage, 1998.

Papson, Stephen. "'Crossing the Fin Line of Terror': Shark Week on the Discovery Channel." *Journal of American Culture* 15.4 (1992): 67–81.

Park, Ken. "Top 20 Cable TV Networks, 2002." *World Almanac & Book of Facts, 2003.* New York: World Almanac Books, 2002.

Timberlake, William. Rev. of *Images of Animals: Anthropomorphism and Animal Mind*, by Eileen Crist. *Quarterly Review of Biology* 75.1 (2000): 85.

PART EIGHT

Health and Welfare

Introduction

There are many reasons why veterinary medicine has become a key profession—comparable to medicine and law—in contemporary society. Over the years, veterinary research and practice have made innumerable contributions to both animal and human welfare. Various changes in society also have served to bolster the importance of the veterinary profession in America. The increasing numbers of farm animals and pets has meant greater demand for veterinary services. And the increasing willingness of the public to view animals as moral beings, rather than mere chattel, has meant raised client expectations of veterinary care.

Compared with the medical and legal professions, veterinary medicine, in the last few decades, has undergone enormous change as the society around it has changed. Veterinary medicine has been part of a cultural shift in thinking about the moral status and importance of its patients—the animals for whom veterinarians care for and treat—and in the demographic and political background of its practitioners. Once a predominantly male profession that favored the treatment of farm over domestic animals, veterinary medicine has dramatically transformed itself into a female profession concentrating on the care of companion animals (Slater and Slater 2000). In fact, more and more students entering veterinary schools will be the harbingers of change within the profession since they bring a new perspective toward animals, according greater importance to animal health and welfare and expecting veterinarians to share these values and perhaps become advocates for animals in the public arena.

In the wake of this rapid change, there is marked ethical confusion about how best to treat animals. Indeed, the field of veterinary medicine is unequaled among the professions for having ethical tensions among its practitioners and students (Herzog, Vore, and New 1989). While veterinarians have increasingly become advocates for animals—seeing them as having significant moral status, approaching that of humans—the general public often does not always share this moral perspective and sometimes see animals as having less moral value than humans or even as having greater moral value than humans. This moral confusion or contradiction presents itself, on a daily basis, to veterinarians who must negotiate these differences while balancing their own moral views about animals. The work of laboratory animal veterinarians—who must balance the needs of biomedical researchers against those of experimental animals—is a prime example of this moral complexity (Carbone 2004), although it occurs throughout the profession in virtually every practice.

This collision of varying moral perspectives is evident in the work of veterinarians when they encounter and deal with requests for elective surgical practices, such as declawing, ear and tail docking, or unnecessary euthanasia. Many of these practices—not long ago unquestioned—are now having their morality and fate challenged by people who see these practices as unnecessary if not cruel (Atwood-Harvey 2005). For example, this sentiment led to a 2003 city ordinance prohibiting declawing in West Hollywood. Veterinarians are certainly aware of these challenges—and may sympathize with them. They are, after all, trained to relieve animal suffering and may feel ambivalent and conflicted if they carry out these practices. Despite growing opposition to practices like declawing and docking, and mounting concern over unnecessary euthanasia, veterinarians usually carry out these requests. Some even challenged the West Hollywood ordinance, claiming that it was unconstitutional to ban declawing.

How do we explain this apparent contradiction? If veterinarians defined controversial owner requests as morally ambiguous and painful, it would be difficult, if not impossible, to carry them out. That they end up carrying out these requests—or even opposing their ban—in part speaks to veterinarians' professional socialization. Veterinary schools socialize students to distance themselves from their own agency and the subjects of their actions, so they can manage ambiguity when encountered in future practice. This informal education, reinforced in the workplace after graduation, gives veterinarians tools to lessen such conflict and not feel remorse or guilt. One tool is linguistic. Using misleading euphemisms makes it psychologically easier to consider and carry out certain procedures for veterinarians and their clients, rather than referring to them more accurately, but in less-sanitized ways. "Declawing" sounds much better than chopping off the first knuckles. Another tool is for veterinarians to see the decision to perform controversial practices as one made by clients or directors of veterinary hospitals. The legal status of the client's animal as property means that ultimate responsibility for its care rests with the client. For veterinarians working in a clinic or hospital, the facility's director can also be seen as having the final word in such cases. These, and other coping tools, enable veterinarians who are uneasy meeting the wishes of clients to continue to meet their demands in morally ambivalent situations.

That veterinarians carry out these controversial requests also speaks to the economic pressure of running a successful practice. Whether they work in one-person practices, small clinics, or large hospitals, income is largely generated through clients who pay for veterinary care, making veterinarians dependent on clients' income. They must please their clients, ideally in ways that will make them return for future visits, while also serving the interests of their animals. The result—given the marginal position of animals under law, and the owner's ability and willingness to pay for certain services—is that the latter can unilaterally make decisions that privilege human over animal interests. Economic realities can trump the veterinarian's moral uneasiness.

Like the veterinary profession, the animal sheltering community has experienced significant growth and change in the past century in terms of its missions to protect animals and serve its human clients. In the mid-1800s, there were neither animal shelters nor a declared animal overpopulation problem, even though stray animals existed. As concern grew over the spread of rabies, animal control departments were created to capture and kill roaming dogs. Stray dog and cat populations continued to grow and efforts to control them, like licensing, failed; the absence of spaying or neutering exacerbated this problem. Public outcry over what was perceived as cruel mass killing by city pounds led to the formation of the first shelters, shortly after the Civil War. Here, workers tried to find homes for stray animals and, if this failed, they were euthanized in ways considered humane for that period.

The twentieth century witnessed growing numbers of humane societies that continued to fight a never-ending battle of re-homing animals and euthanizing those they could not. Post–World War II America experienced a rapid growth of pet ownership, leading to an explosion in the dog and cat population and an influx of animals being turned into shelters because pets were too much trouble, did not fit with a changing lifestyle, or for a multitude of other reasons. As shelter populations increased and the availability of adopters decreased, shelter staff were forced to euthanize animals that were potentially adoptable. Periodically, existing methods of euthanasia were terminated in favor of new methods deemed more humane, as concern mounted over large numbers of animals being euthanized—with yearly estimates ranging in the millions. Although there has been some decrease in the number of animals surrendered and euthanized in shelters each year, the euthanasia of healthy animals remains a major problem. Several strategies to deal with the animal overpopulation problem have emerged in recent decades.

A more progressive attitude emerged in the 1970s with shelters taking an aggressive and preventive approach to pet overpopulation. Public education programs, combined with strict adoption standards and follow-up programs, sought to ensure that animals would stay in responsible homes. Sterilization requirements were instituted to ensure that adopted animals would not add to the overpopulation problem. Shelters also started to provide support for pet owners who might be considering the surrender of their animals, by offering such services as free pet training or animal behavior advice. The thinking was that people might be able to keep troublesome animals in the home if only they had some help and guidance. And in many communities, animal welfare organizations began to work with animal control agencies to better deal with the problems of stray and injured animals. Despite these efforts to control animal overpopulation, estimates of the numbers of animals euthanized yearly in shelters have ranged from 6 to 10 million (e.g., Olson and Moulton 1993).

A different approach to pet overpopulation also surfaced in the later half of the twentieth century, as very different ethical perspectives emerged regarding "humane" killing (Palmer 2006). Some shelter workers and animal advocates decided to deal with this problem in ways other than euthanasia, except in the most extreme cases in which animals are too sick to be helped or too aggressive to be put in homes. "No-kill" proponents see the fundamental problem as a *person* problem—one of changing the nature of shelter work so that workers can have a professional identity uncontaminated by the contradictions posed from conducting frequent euthanasia, especially if the animals are potentially adoptable. That conducting such euthanasia entails considerable moral stress is well documented (Reeve *et al.* 2004). Evidence of this changing emphasis from animals to people can be seen in the public justifications of shelters that have abandoned their prior "open-admission" policies for no-kill approaches. When the ASPCA (American Society for the Protection of Cruelty to Animals) did so, a *New York Times* headline proclaimed: "A.S.P.C.A. Plans to Give Up Job Killing New York Strays." The text elaborated that killing 30,000 to 40,000 strays had obscured the ASPCA's mission and image. Instead, of being perceived as an animal killer, the ASPCA, as a no-kill shelter, could have the image it wants—that of an animal care and adoption agency.

Traditional, open-admission shelters have a different conception of the fundamental "problem." They see the problem as an *animal* problem— one of managing pet overpopulation—and argue that the no-kill approach does not solve this problem but rather shifts the responsibility for euthanasia to another shelter or agency. So the problem still stands. The result is that tension has mounted within the shelter community between two apparent camps advocating either open-admission or no-kill. To be clear, these tensions are not new to the humane community. They always have existed, lurking in the cultural background of shelters and animal control offices everywhere. The difference now is that because of the no-kill movement, these doubts, concerns, or questions have been brought to center stage to be challenged and reconsidered by some, and defended and explained by others. To wit, one recent article about this polarization, entitled "Killing Ourselves Over the Euthanasia Debate," cataloged "hurtful criticisms" lobbed by each side "accusing the other of not caring for animals in the 'right' way" (Dowling and Stitley, 1997).

The selections in this part examine the social worlds of veterinary medicine and animal sheltering. Joanna Swabe's selection describes the practical ethics and contradictions of veterinarians. Studies of ethics fall into two categories. *Prescriptive* ethics is a branch of philosophy that focuses on the development of moral principles that can guide people when they encounter morally problematic situations. By contrast, *descriptive* ethics is a branch of the social sciences that examines what people actually think and do when confronting moral problems. Using the latter approach, social scientists have only recently begun the difficult and challenging task of unpacking the actual ethical thinking of professionals at work. Swabe's article is an important addition to the study of descriptive ethics among professionals. By shedding significant light on this process, her work will be of particular value to scholars, including educators who want to examine the ethical underpinnings of professional education, moral philosophers who want to inject a healthy dose of reality into their studies, sociologists who want to better understand the moral conflicts and contradictions of professionals, and veterinarians who want insight into how their field is rife with moral uneasiness, if not struggle, for both practitioners and clients alike.

The next two selections explore how, and with what consequences, shelter workers have dealt with the animal overpopulation problem. Leslie Irvine's article examines the cross communication between animal shelters and their clients over how to deal with unwanted pets. She argues that animal shelters "think" differently about this problem than do persons in everyday life. Shelters portray pets as life-long commitments and provide resources to enable owners to keep animals in their homes should problems arise, such as dog aggressiveness. However, much of the public simply wants to get troublesome pets out of their homes because they are moving, have developed pet allergies, or cannot cope with the pet's behavior, to name some of the more common excuses. Alternatives to surrender, such as treating a pet's health or behavior problem through services often provided by shelters, are not generally considered because people lack information about animals. Without proper information, people have unrealistic expectations about a pet's behavior and needs. As owners blame the problems on the pets themselves, rather than their own ignorance, they gradually detach themselves from their animals, thereby setting the stage for surrender. While shelters make it relatively easy for people to surrender their animals because that enhances their community image, doing so makes it less likely that owners will do anything to remedy their pet's problems.

Arnold Arluke's selection explores the roots of a different tension in the animal sheltering community—that among shelter workers themselves. The reason why the controversy between open-admission and no-kill approaches defies a quick fix is that it touches on the defining issue of what it means to be a shelter worker. No-kill followers see themselves as forging or "rediscovering" their humane identity as opposed to open-admission workers who are accused of forgetting their mission and getting lost in the overwhelming job of euthanasia. Carrying out euthanasia is thought to be an "endlessly demoralizing activity" that stops workers from focusing on their core purpose—bringing an end to the killing of these animals. To no-killers, the work of open-admission shelters is not the work of a "humane society." They argue that open-admission shelters need to rethink their mission and identity, so they can become no-kill themselves and "get out of the killing business." The result of such "identity work" has significant consequences because it not only affects how shelter workers will regard themselves in the future; it will determine the fate of innumerable homeless animals.

References

Atwood-Harvey, D. 2005. "Death or Declaw: Dealing with Moral Ambiguity in a Veterinary Hospital." *Society & Animals* 13:315–342.

Carbone, L. 2004. *What Animals Want: Expertise and Advocacy in Laboratory Animal Welfare Policy.* New York: Oxford University Press.

Dowling, J., and C. Stitley. 1997. "Killing Ourselves Over the Euthanasia Debate." *Animal Sheltering* Sept–Oct:4–15.

Herzog, H., Vore, T., and J. New, Jr. 1989. "Conversations with Veterinary Students: Attitudes, Ethics, and Animals." *Anthrozoös* 2:181–188.

Olson, P., and C. Moulton. 1993. "Pet (Dog and Cat) Overpopulation in the United States." *Journal of Reproduction & Fertility* 47:433–438.

Palmer, C. 2006. "Killing Animals in Animal Shelters." In Animal Studies Group, ed., *Killing Animals*, 170–187. Urbana: University of Illinois Press.

Reeve, C., Spitzmuller, C., Rogelberg, S., Walker, A., Shultz, L., and O. Clark. 2004. "Employee Reactions and Adjustment to Euthanasia-Related Work: Identifying Turning-Point Events Through Retrospective Narratives." *Journal of Applied Animal Welfare Science* 7:1–25.

Slater, M., and M. Slater. 2000. "Women in Veterinary Medicine." *JAVMA* 217:472–476.

Joanna Swabe

Veterinary Dilemmas

Introduction

The relationship between humans and domesticated animals is replete with contradictions. It can be characterized by both intimacy and exploitation. Our conduct toward other animals is often seen in very black and white terms: some species we keep and use for food; upon others we lavish affection. In reality, however, the borders are rather more nebulous. While dogs are commonly kept and cherished as pets, they may also be severely maltreated and abandoned by their owners, or employed for sporting or scientific research. Similarly, an animal destined for the dinner plate may receive a great deal of respect, care and affection throughout its lifetime, and will not be treated at all as if it were merely an animate unit of production. We must therefore avoid making sweeping statements about the relationship between ourselves and other animals. One dog owner may dote upon his dachshund, another may beat his. As Arluke and Sanders (1996, 4) have pointed out, "One of the most glaring consistencies" in our interactions with other animals "is inconsistency." It is largely for this reason that we should be cautious when referring to the small domesticated animals in our homes and gardens as "companion animals." Frequently, this descriptor will fit the bill, but not always.

The ambiguity and ambivalence that typically characterize our relationship with domesticated animals are most clearly reflected in settings in which human-animal interactions play a central role. Perhaps the best settings within which ambiguity and ambivalence in the human-animal relationship can routinely be observed are those involving veterinarians. Veterinary settings provide interesting fora within which one can observe both a wide range of human-animal interactions and the professional activities of the veterinarian, who is, in essence, a mediator between the human and animal world.

Veterinarians are engaged in a broad spectrum of activities involving animals, ranging from the treatment of domesticated animals, both large and small, to meat inspection, wild animal medicine, laboratory animal science, veterinary pharmaceutics, and public health management. However, when one thinks of veterinarians, one generally conjures up images of Herriotesque animal doctors who rescue and care for sick and injured animals. To this we can perhaps partially owe the plethora of literature, films, documentaries, and television series that have been produced highlighting and endearing the role of the veterinarian to wider society. The popular image of the kindly animal doctor has become firmly fixed in our collective imagination and has been repeatedly reinforced by the images that are routinely broadcast into our living rooms: the TV vet, be he real or fictional, is a familiar sight to all. More often than not, the television program makers have tended to focus upon the work of small animal practitioners, rather than upon the veterinarians who take care of food-producing animals. There are several factors that may explain this apparent preference. First, the sight of small, furry, pet animals is a particularly appealing one to viewers, capable of eliciting the kind of "cute response" (Serpell, 1996) that can make the program popular and attain high viewing figures. Second, in our modern, urbanized, industrial society, people seem to be more readily able to identify and empathize with—and prepared to watch—the plights of both pet animals and their owners than those of livestock and farmers. The veterinary treatment of large animals and the environments in which—particularly intensively farmed—animals are kept may often appear distasteful and would confront audiences—often looking for light entertainment, rather than enlightenment—with the origins of their food.

Small animal practitioners are also the topic of this article, although, as will become clear, they do not and cannot always live up to either the romantic paragons of fiction or televised heroism. This article is based largely upon sociological research that I conducted in a variety of veterinary practices in both urban and rural settings in The Netherlands. By spending several months in the field as a participant observer, I was able to involve myself in the ongoing, daily world of the veterinarians whom I studied. This article will examine—from a sociological perspective—some of the routine transactions and procedures that were observed and discussed with veterinarians during my ethnographic study of veterinary practice. Furthermore, it will illustrate how the contradictions that pervade the human-animal relationship are clearly visible in veterinary situations, and will draw attention to some of the dilemmas with which veterinarians are routinely confronted, which may conflict with the interests of their animal patients.

A Brief History of Small Animal Medicine

Historically speaking, the diseases and afflictions of dogs and cats have received very limited veterinary attention. Unlike horses and livestock, whose inherent economic and nutritional value has motivated human attempts to preserve their health and cure their disease, these small domesticates and their attendant diseases—with the notable exception of rabies—have posed little threat to the human economy or public health. In centuries past, dogs and cats simply did not warrant the therapeutic attentions of medical science: while useful creatures—for protection, pest control and companionship—they were essentially of little economic value and easily replaceable. Instead, early medical scientists tended to view small animal species—particularly those of the canine variety—in quite a different light as the highly suitable subjects for the experimental study of anatomy and physiology; dogs were, after all, cheap, abundant, and easy for the experimenters to control. Furthermore, small animals—or, rather, parts or by-products of them—provided useful ingredients for the medical pharmacopoeia of the past.

There is evidence that small animals sometimes received a degree of therapeutic attention and care, generally in accordance with their usefulness. In the agriculturally based society of ancient Rome, for example, shepherd and guard dogs played an important role in protecting humans and their livestock and property. During the Middle Ages, hunting and falconry enjoyed great popularity among the nobility of feudal Europe. The care of hunting hounds and birds became increasingly important and demanded the attentions of specialist animal attendants who could oversee the health and care of these valued creatures.

In 1783, the first popular work specifically devoted to the diseases of the dog appeared. During the early nineteenth century, additional works dedicated exclusively to the veterinary treatment of canine disease were published. The prevailing view at that time was that animal medicine was not only greatly inferior to human medicine, but also that the horse was the *only* species of animal that was believed to deserve *any* veterinary medical attention whatsoever.

Yet, while the fledgling veterinary profession failed to acknowledge the importance of directing its attention to the diseases of dogs and other small animals, the increasing popularity of the practice of pet-keeping throughout nineteenth-century western European society revealed that there was a growing market for professional advice on this very subject. Although the market for canine veterinary services gradually expanded within Britain, the question remained of whether veterinary school–educated veterinarians possessed the competence and skills necessary to treat dogs. Veterinary education continued to remain—as it had always done—firmly focused upon the treatment of horses and—to a much lesser extent—livestock species. In the majority of nineteenth-century textbooks that were produced to assist veterinary training, the dog and its complaints generally only received a cursory mention. By the mid- to late nineteenth century, the market for specialist canine veterinary services also emerged within mainland Europe and North America. Small animal medicine was, however, still very much in its infancy; it was only during the course of the twentieth century that it would come of age.

At the turn of the twentieth century, the veterinary profession was still largely ambivalent toward studying and treating pet animals and their diseases. The increasing sentimentality toward animals at this time, particularly among the urban middle classes, seems to have been quite alien to most veterinary practitioners, who only saw profit, both in monetary and societal terms, in treating creatures of clear economic value. This attitude was also echoed throughout the veterinary schools of Europe that continued to regard the study and treatment of small animals with considerable disdain. The veterinary profession had after all striven hard throughout the nineteenth century to elevate itself far above the "vulgar" level of gelders and blacksmiths and wished to be taken seriously as a scientifically enlightened and socially useful profession. These educated veterinarians did not now wish to lower themselves by tending to, what they essentially regarded as, "useless" animals.

One of the chief consequences of this attitude was that, at least until the dawn of the twentieth century, there was comparatively little knowledge of, or concern for, the nature and pathology of small animal disease. Until this time, veterinary attention to this subject seems to have been justified only when the study of small animal disease was seen as instrumental to increasing the understanding of the pathology of horses or food-producing animals. More signifi-

cantly still, most of the advancement that occurred in understanding the diseases and physiology of small animals occurred indirectly through scientific research aimed at understanding and improving human health. For example, experiments conducted on dogs led to the understanding of the process of endocrine secretion in humans, eventually resulting in the isolation of insulin during the 1920s. It was, however, to take many years before such discoveries were actually applied in the treatment of dogs and cats.

Yet, while pet animals were regarded with contempt by the veterinary establishment, they nonetheless crept insidiously into the veterinary schools as patients. From the late nineteenth century onward, increasing numbers of small animals and birds were brought by their owners to the veterinary schools for treatment at out-patient clinics, eventually necessitating accommodation for animals requiring hospitalization.

However, in spite of both the increasing numbers of pet animals requiring treatment, and the emerging medical technologies and innovators able to provide it, the rise of small animal medicine during the twentieth century perhaps owes more to the invention of the internal combustion engine than anything else. The rise of motorized transport led to the inevitable decline of the importance of the horse in European society. This development had its greatest consequences for the urban veterinary practitioners who had, until then, made their living by tending the horses of private citizens, local businesses, and the local municipality. However, as the horses that pulled the carriages, wagons, carts, trams, and even the fire-brigade were replaced by motorized vehicles, the urban veterinarians were left with little local work other than meat inspection. Thus, it was more by accident than design that the veterinary practitioners of the early twentieth century set aside their contempt for small animals and instead began to earn a living from them.

After the First World War, increasing numbers of practices devoted, often exclusively, to the veterinary treatment of small animals were established in urban areas, generally deriving their income and clientele from the more affluent middle-class members of the community. Some small animal clinics were also established in association with animal protection organizations and the newly emerging animal sanctuaries to provide veterinary care for pet animals. This trend accelerated after the end of the Second World War. The increased material affluence of postwar society has not only influenced our tendency to keep pets, but has also provided us with the means to go to considerable lengths to ensure their lives are happy and healthy ones. During the subsequent 50 years or so, an entire industry evolved to provide and service pet animal needs. From the breeders who produce tailor-made animals to the pet food manufacturers who feed them, there are considerable profits to be made by exploiting our attachments to small animals and encouraging people to keep them as pets. The veterinary world was also part of this development, and consequently small animal medicine rapidly became the most progressive area within veterinary medicine; it also became a rather profitable one.

Veterinary Dilemmas

To understand the nature of veterinary work, one must forget the popular image of the animal doctor, battling to save the lives of sick and injured animals. Although activities such as saving accident victims and helping animals in labor are the most fulfilling and challenging part of their work, veterinarians spend a large proportion of their time performing extremely routine tasks. In the practices studied, the bulk of routine veterinary work tended to be preventive, rather than curative. In fact, animals that had been taken to the veterinarian to be vaccinated against infectious disease or to be treated for parasitic infection accounted for the highest proportion of visitors to regular surgery hours. Such routine consultations tended to be rather unspectacular. This is in sharp contrast to the kind of veterinary consultations that are filmed and broadcast for popular television viewing.

The management of animal reproduction is also a priority on the everyday veterinary agenda. The veterinarian is responsible for helping to control the size of animal populations and overseeing the (re)production of healthy pet animals. This work includes neutering pet animals and providing obstetric and post-natal care. The neutering of pet animals accounted for the largest proportion of surgical procedures observed in each practice. Further, the veterinarian is also entrusted the task of "routine animal maintenance." In other words, he or she is responsible for the repair, rehabilitation, or destruction of sick and injured animals. Aside from this, the veterinarian will also treat dermatological conditions, advise on appropriate animal care, nutrition and housing, provide counsel with regard to behavioral problems, attend to dental problems, and other matters relating to animal health and welfare.

The procedures that veterinarians are asked to perform and the decisions that they are required to make can present a host of practical, moral, and ethical problems. In some instances, they may be legally restricted from performing particular surgical interventions, such as declawing cats or debarking dogs, and can avoid having to deal with the ethical implications of such procedures. In many situations, however, the veterinarian's own personal judgment is relied on and he or she must make weighty decisions as to what course of action should be taken. There are, of course, basic guidelines that the veterinarian is professionally obliged to conform with. For example, Article 1 of the Dutch Veterinary Code states that a veterinarian should act in accordance with:

(a) the benefit of the health and welfare of the animal and the interests of the owner;
(b) public interest and general veterinary interests;
(c) the benefit of public health and environmental hygiene;
(d) the position and function of veterinary medicine in society.

The first of these principles is the most problematic for veterinarians. The interests of the animal and its owner are not always reconcilable. The course of action that a veterinarian must take is often dependent upon the species or breed with which he or she is dealing and its economic or emotional value, irrespective of the nature of the medical complaint and whether or not it can be successfully treated. Frequently, the veterinarian is well aware that material considerations may overshadow the actual treatability of an animal's condition.

Notwithstanding such guidelines, the veterinarian is still required to perform surgery and make decisions that those more idealistically involved with animal welfare issues may question. Even within small animal medicine, the veterinary treatment that an animal receives may often be guided by practical and financial considerations, rather than sentiments or idealism. The veterinarian must be aware of the client's ability or willingness to pay for services rendered. A consequence of this is that certain decisions and procedures—as distasteful as they may seem to some—are standard to veterinary practice. The following discussion considers some of the procedures and decisions that are routine to small animal practice.

To Kill or Cure?

There is great variety in the value that people place on small animals in our society. Some pet animals are treated as cherished members of the family for whom no time, energy, and expense are to be spared, whereas others may be neglected, abandoned, or abused. One cannot, therefore, make generalizations about pet owners' attachments to their animals and the lengths that they may be prepared to go to in order to preserve their pets' health. Indeed, the attitudes of owners with regard to paying for and deciding to proceed with veterinary treatment vary greatly. For some animal owners the decision to go ahead with a life-saving operation or drug therapy is a highly emotive and problematic one; for others, it is very simple and is decided purely upon pragmatic grounds. Furthermore, an animal's condi-

tion need not actually be life-threatening for a decision to end its life to be made.

In small animal practice, ending an animal's life is commonly known as euthanasia. This term is seen as particularly problematic when used to refer to healthy animals being killed—from a moral point of view—unnecessarily. Animal rights philosophers, such as Tom Regan (1983), have strongly objected to the use of the term euthanasia as a blanket description for the deliberate killing of pet animals. They argue that the term is entirely inappropriate unless certain conditions are met: first, that the animal is killed by the most painless means possible; second, that the individual who ends its life truly believes that a painless death is in the animal's own interests; and finally, that the individual who euthanizes it is motivated to euthanasia out of a concern for the animal's interests, good, or welfare (Regan, 1983: 110–111). In veterinary practice, euthanasia is simply defined and understood as the "act of inducing a painless death" (Tannenbaum, 1989: 209). This term is, however, only deemed appropriate to the deliberate killing of pet animals and horses: food-producing animals are simply slaughtered, not euthanized. Both of these terms in themselves say much about societal attitudes to, and treatment of, animals.

Unlike the majority of their clients (unless they are involved in farming, hunting, or abattoir work), veterinarians are accustomed to death, for they are routinely required to euthanize animals in the course of their work. Dealing with the death of animals is an almost unavoidable part of the job. The task of performing euthanasia is, however, not one veterinarians relish for it is inherently problematic: first, because performing it can bring serious ethical and personal dilemmas to the fore, and, second, because of the possible emotional responses of the client whose animal is being euthanized. Although a veterinary education provides the practitioner with all the necessary clinical and diagnostic skills, many veterinarians are inadequately trained to deal with client emotion and pet loss.

The veterinarians I studied tended to deal with euthanasia consultations in a very *ad hoc* manner. Their sensitivities toward clients' feelings varied greatly, depending to a large extent on their own ability to empathize, and on their individual social and communicative skills. It is, however, essential that the clients' emotional needs are adequately met and responded to in the event of euthanasia. Indeed, the veterinarian has a vested interest in keeping his or her clients happy, for contented clients are likely to return to the practice with other animals in the future. In recent years, professional journals and organizations have attempted to provide practical suggestions about how veterinarians should deal with both the procedure of euthanasia itself and their clients' (and their own) emotional responses to it. Articles and books designed to explain euthanasia to pet owners and help people to deal with it more adequately have also recently begun to appear on the market (e.g., Quackenbush, 1985). Many veterinary colleges operate pet loss support services, such as telephone hotlines for bereaved animal owners. Others have a professional psychologist or social worker on hand for grief counseling.

Pet animals are often accorded an almost quasi-human status. Sometimes they have even been treated as substitutes for people or other human relationships. While this may be so in extreme cases where, for example, acute grief may follow the demise of an animal, it is more plausible that the majority of pet owners' relationships with their pets are supplementary to human contact rather than substitutes for it, animals perhaps offering a kind of relationship that people do not provide and that must, therefore, be sought elsewhere. Nevertheless, people can often be rather attached to—or feel a responsibility toward—their pets, and when these animals become ill, veterinary treatment is frequently sought. The nature of the actual veterinary treatment that can be provided is often dependent, however, on the client's willingness or ability to pay for it and/or the degree to which he or she is prepared or able to care for the animal at home as part of the des-

ignated therapy. Conditions such as diabetes, for example, may remain untreated if a client is reluctant to administer regular insulin injections or to maintain a strict dietary regimen for his or her pet. Similarly, if an animal requires a costly operation that the owner cannot afford or is unwilling to pay for, its condition may not be treated. Such action may be detrimental to the animal's welfare, although this will depend on the exact nature of its predicament. If an animal's well-being is likely to be seriously compromised by a lack of surgical or therapeutic intervention, euthanasia may be the only available and affordable option.

Veterinarians are, however, often reluctant to end an animal's life unnecessarily, particularly when the animal is young and/or stands a good chance of making a full recovery. Often they will try to dissuade the client from choosing euthanasia, and will attempt to make alternative financial arrangements, such as payment by installments, for any necessary surgery or drug therapy. This reluctance to unnecessarily terminate animal life is also typified by veterinary responses to requests to euthanize animals with behavioral problems, especially when these animals are otherwise physically healthy. When an animal's aggressive behavior is seen to endanger the health and safety of humans and other pets—and often when all other alternatives such as obedience training and muzzling have been exhausted—euthanasia will generally be seen to be a viable and ethically defensible course of action. However, requests to euthanize animals are commonly made by pet owners when the animal and its behavior have simply become an inconvenience to them.

A prime example of this relates to feline elimination problems. Inappropriate elimination, most particularly house soiling by urination, is a behavioral problem that motivates many requests to have cats "put down." Months and even years of continually soiled furniture and carpets may drive cat owners to seek a final solution to their problem, but sometimes just one mistake on the part of the cat is enough for it to be condemned to death by its owner. There may well be a physical and treatable cause for such inappropriate feline elimination behavior, such as diabetes, bladder or urethral inflammation, or bladder damage. Alternatively, such elimination may be related to territorial marking, though it may also occur when the cat is dissatisfied with its litter tray or is unhappy for some other reason. In the event of the latter, the owner's negligence or ignorance of the cat's needs is frequently singled out as the root cause of the problem. Even though the owner may be deemed responsible, the veterinarian is still presented with the dilemma of whether or not he or she should accede to the client's request to have the animal euthanized. The modification of the owner's behavior toward the animal may provide a solution to these elimination problems. However, it is often the case that once the animal has become a nuisance, the owner will wish to get rid of it by any means possible. When faced with the dilemma of being asked to euthanize a healthy, though behaviorally problematic, cat, veterinarians are often inclined to look for alternative solutions, such as re-housing the animal.

At the other extreme, small animal practitioners may be faced with pet owners who are resolute in their refusal to consider euthanasia as a viable option, in spite of the fact that having the animal euthanized may be both in their interests financially, and in the interests of the animal's welfare. Some pet owners will be prepared to spend substantial amounts of money (that they cannot necessarily afford) to keep their beloved animals alive and well for as long as possible. However, when an animal's quality of life is significantly reduced and all reasonable therapeutic options have been exhausted, veterinarians will logically conclude that euthanasia is the best and kindest course of action. Getting the owner to consent to it is another matter altogether. Pet owners may insist that the veterinarian attempts a new course of treatment or that the animal undergoes another operation before abandoning hope. Frequently, clients in this situation will refuse to accept the veterinarian's judgment and will go elsewhere to seek a second opinion. Although it may be economically profitable for the veterinarian to do as the client requests, the question remains whether it is morally defensible to do so, especially when such intervention may only extend an animal's life by a matter of weeks, or may cause unnecessary stress or pain.

In this regard, the extension of the use of medical treatments, such as chemotherapy, to small animal medicine from human medicine has raised serious ethical questions about the extent to which one should go to preserve animal life. Few animal tumors, for example, can be cured by chemotherapy. Although animals will generally tolerate chemotherapy fairly well, the majority of patients will only experience a temporary or partial remission from their symptoms; this will, at least in the short term, prolong survival and improve the quality of life. Nevertheless, given that chemotherapy is often not curative—and also because the use of cytotoxic drugs may be potentially harmful—the ethics of employing such a treatment may still be disputed. The use of such medical treatments may also be questioned if profit can be made from them. There may, therefore, be a potential risk of financial considerations influencing the course of treatment that the veterinarian advises, particularly if the client is willing and able to pay for it.

For all the compassion that they may often have for both their animal patients and human clients, the inescapable fact remains that most veterinarians operate their practices as businesses: essentially, animals are more lucrative to them alive than dead. The decision to kill or cure can thus often be quite arbitrary, irrespective of medical indications. One terminally ill pet may be kept alive by all means possible, while another perfectly healthy animal may be euthanized simply because the owner has requested that this service be provided. This state of affairs clearly illustrates not only the ambivalence that exists within the human-animal relationship, but also ethical dilemmas with which the small animal practitioner is routinely faced in weighing the animal's, client's, and his or her own interests.

Animal Mutilation

If an animal does not satisfy human requirements, it is simply altered, either through a process of selective breeding or by surgical intervention. Selective breeding enables specific and desirable characteristics, be they physical or behavioral, to be "artificially" generated. Human interference in the genetic makeup of other species has inevitably led to great problems for animal well-being, particularly when mutant genes, which, if left up to nature would probably die out, are deliberately selected to change an animal in order to produce a new breed. Sometimes, such deliberate selection can seem fairly innocuous, for instance when genes are selected to produce a particular coat color. But more often than not, genes are selected to produce specific facial features (e.g., ones that are paedomorphic), shape, and size that are attractive to humans, yet can seriously impair the animal's well-being. The extent of human intervention through breeding can be illustrated by looking at the great diversity within one particular species: the dog. Today, after centuries of selective breeding, an adult dog can weigh between 2 and 80 kg, in contrast to the wolf, the wild species closest to dogs, whose natural body weight can vary between 20 and 50 kg, or heavier still in the case of Canadian timber wolves.

Along with selective breeding, surgical interventions to alter the appearance or functioning of an animal are also sometimes performed. In recent years, procedures such as tail-docking, ear cropping, declawing, and debarking have come under increasing attack. The freedom for small animal practitioners to perform such procedures has, in some instances, been greatly restricted, since these surgical interventions have been deemed by professional bodies or legal statutes to be an unacceptable infringement of the animal's interests. It should also be noted that the aforementioned surgical alterations are seldom performed for any therapeutic purpose, but rather they are done entirely for cosmetic purposes or for the convenience of the owner.

Tail-docking is probably the oldest form of mutilation. It is thought that it originally developed as a practical measure to allow working dogs to perform their tasks more efficiently. Furthermore, during the Roman era, it was believed that tail-docking would afford a degree of protection against canine rabies. As the primary function of such animals as workers has largely been supplanted by their roles as companions, this practice has become more embedded in notions of how each breed should appear physically; the functional aspects of tail-docking have faded or have been lost to history. Today, tail-docking is generally viewed as a purely cosmetic mutilation that has a negative impact on the animals. Dogs use their tails to communicate with others. Opponents to tail-docking have therefore argued that it is cruel since it deprives the docked animal of this function. Similarly, ear cropping is also objected to, not only because it is unnecessary, apart from an aesthetic point of view, but also because it is of no direct benefit to the animal and, again, like tail-docking, it deprives the animal of the ability to communicate fully with others. Although both practices are forbidden in The Netherlands, one can frequently observe dogs on the streets whose ears have clearly been trimmed and whose tails have been docked. These procedures are thus performed illegally, often by non-veterinarians and without adequate anaesthetic or pain-killers.

Similarly, the declawing of cats and "debarking," that is, the devocalization of dogs, are banned in The Netherlands, although these procedures, particularly the former, are widely and commonly performed in other western countries, particularly in the United States. In The Netherlands, legal and professional regulations stipulate that these surgical procedures can only be performed if they are the only viable alternative to euthanasia. Veterinary ethicists and animal welfare experts consider both procedures to be an infringement of the animal's integrity, and to prevent it from behaving naturally. Furniture-destroying cats and incessantly barking dogs might be a nuisance to their owners, but operating on them to solve the problem has been deemed unacceptable since such surgery is considered to be against the interests of animal well-being. All of the surgical procedures described deprive pet animals of performing natural behaviors. In recognition of this, they have—at least in The Netherlands—been severely restricted, and veterinarians (should) no longer perform them unless they are of therapeutic value—for instance when a dog's tail is broken. The dilemma of whether or not veterinarians should perform such procedures has been taken out of their hands by the legislators. In this instance, the interests of the animal have been placed above those of the owner. Yet, even where animal mutilations have been severely restricted, veterinarians may still be faced with having to deal with clients who wish such surgical interventions to be performed. Where these mutilations are perfectly legal, the matter is left up to the veterinarian's own conscience and/or economic interests. To some extent, it is also a question of supply and demand. Even though a veterinarian may find such mutilations unnecessary or distasteful, if he or she is not prepared to provide the service, clients may be lost to competitors who will.

The final pet animal mutilation that will be considered here is neutering. This commonplace surgical alteration of animals is deemed unproblematic by veterinarians, although it quite clearly alters the natural function of the animal in a similar fashion to those interventions performed for aesthetic reasons. Within small animal practice, neutering is the most common surgical intervention performed upon pets. Neutering is, however, sometimes viewed by animal owners as a violation of an animal's natural right to procreate and bear young. Consequently, it is often only performed after an animal has had one litter and has briefly experienced its natural "privilege." There appears to be little scientific evidence to support this belief that animals should bear at least one litter before being sterilized. It has been widely argued that, since it is unlikely that the animal will have any concept of what it is missing, neutering does it no harm. In view of the surplus of pet an-

imals and the problem of pet abandonment, it is logical that pet procreation and population be controlled. Since pets cannot voluntarily control their own fertility, human owners are required to take responsibility for them by having them neutered. The veterinarian's task is both to educate his or her clients as to the wisdom of taking neutering as a course of action, and to perform the surgery itself. Neutering is also sometimes advised by small animal practitioners as a means of hindering the onset of various disorders of the reproductive organs to which various breeds of animal are often prone. It has also been employed more recently as a means of encouraging dangerous breeds, such as pit-bull terriers, gradually to die out.

The desire to prevent unwanted litters often provides the grounds for the neutering of an individual animal, but neutering is also often performed entirely for the owner's convenience. Uncastrated tomcats, for example, habitually spray pungent urine, which is both offensive in smell and often damages furniture and carpets. When castrated, they largely stop this undesirable behavior and can become far more sedate and submissive. In short, a castrated cat tends to make a more ideal pet than one left fully intact. Neutering is often performed this way as a form of behavioral control since it often makes animals less aggressive and reduces their proclivity to stray or fight with other animals. It could thus also be said that by neutering their animals, humans have ensured that their pets will never, in a sense, really grow up. In other words, they will retain more infantile behavioral characteristics that seem to be particularly attractive to humans, they will not become sexually active, and they will better appeal to human idealizations of what pets should be. Moreover, the control of animal sexuality, in addition to the restriction of pet animals' eating, hunting, and toileting behavior, could be viewed as an attempt to "civilize" them, to regulate and constrain their natural functioning so that it is no longer offensive to us. The "natural" behavior of pet animals has been transformed so that it bears greater semblance to that of humans and, as a consequence, it is not so reminiscent of our own suppressed animality. It can, however, easily be argued that pet neutering is performed in the interest of the animals themselves, as much as in the interest of humans, given that the excess of pets causes much distress and suffering to many thousands of unwanted animals each year. In this way, the neutering of pets can be justified as a necessary and fairly harmless evil, as long as it is performed using anaesthetic in as sterile conditions as possible. For both veterinarians and their clients alike, neutering is the most defensible mutilation that a pet animal can undergo. Indeed, the fact that it is not commonly perceived as a mutilation speaks volumes about the acceptability of the practice.

Conclusion

The contradictions and ambivalence in the relationship between humans and animals are clearly embedded in routine veterinary practice. These ambiguities, as this article has sought to illustrate, find expression in the kinds of dilemmas with which small animal practitioners are faced during the course of their everyday work. To some extent, the legal and ethical parameters of their profession help to determine the course of action that they may take in dealing with the requests and demands of their clients. However, it seems that the action taken, particularly when it comes to either preserving or ending the life of an animal, is often highly dependent upon the veterinarian's discretion, and the client's wishes or ability to pay for treatment. As suggested above, a variety of factors may influence the decision-making

process; financial gain for the veterinarian sometimes ranks among them. The notion that profit may possibly influence veterinary decision making undoubtedly conflicts strongly with the collective image of the kindly animal doctor that we hold. Yet, we should remember that providing a veterinary medical service for pet animals is not just about animal doctoring, but is—at least as far as private practice goes—also about running a viable business. This does not, of course, necessarily exclude compassion, humanity, or the adherence to ethical standards, but it does mean that the activities and work of veterinarians should not be over-romanticized. The fact remains that veterinary professionals are often faced with difficult dilemmas when dealing with their animal patients and human clients. In deciding the course of action to take, practical and financial considerations may well often outweigh sentiment and idealism.

References

Arluke, A., and C.R. Sanders. (1996). *Regarding Animals.* Philadelphia: Temple University Press.

Quackenbush J. (1985). *When Your Pet Dies: How to Cope with Your Feelings.* New York: Simon & Schuster.

Regan, T. (1983). *The Case for Animal Rights.* London: Routledge & Kegan Paul.

Serpell, J. (1996). *In the Company of Animals: A Study of Human–Animal Relationships.* Cambridge: Cambridge University Press.

Tannenbaum, J. (1989). *Veterinary Ethics.* Baltimore: Williams & Wilkins.

Leslie Irvine

How Shelters "Think" about Clients' Needs and Unwanted Pets

The organizations charged with ameliorating social problems tend to "think," as Mary Douglas (1986) put it, in certain ways. I use the notion of institutional "thinking" as a metaphor for the interpretive practices that become apparent in organizational discourse. Institutions "think" for those within their purview by providing models through which experience is processed. As a guiding metaphor, institutional "thinking" reveals how an organization's discourse and activities help to reproduce characteristic definitions of and solutions to social problems. From within an organization, a solution to a social problem "is only seen to be the *right* one if it sustains the institutional thinking that is already in the minds of individuals as they try to decide" (Douglas 1986:4, my emphasis). For example, in Jaber Gubrium's (1992) study comparing two treatment facilities for family problems, he finds that the "overriding contrast between the two institutions lies in their images of domestic disorder" (p. 18). One facility defines domestic disorder as a problem of authority; the other uses emotional terms. Nevertheless, "whatever background differences or similarities patients and families bring to the organizations," Gubrium writes, "and regardless of the administrative differences or similarities encountered in the settings, these images sort the particulars" (1992, 19). Because the template of institutional thinking frames social problems selectively, the solutions offered do not necessarily address the problems *as experienced* by persons outside the institutional purview. Institutional thinking ignores salient aspects of the conditions persons may associate with the problem in everyday life, which later emerge through the cracks, as it were, of the "organizationally embedded" solutions (Gubrium 1992).

The concept of "social problems work" (Holstein and Miller 1993) refers to a cluster of activities that are associated with institutional thinking. Social problems work encompasses the claims-making activities that were the original focus of analyses of the social construction of social problems. It also includes the interpretive and rhetorical work involved in the production and reproduction of "collective representations" (see Holstein and Miller 1993), or the "typifications" of social problems. For instance "crack babies," "abused wives," "victims of crime," "welfare mother," and "alcoholic" are all collective representations that offer us an understanding of conditions and categories of people beyond those we personally experience (see Loseke 1999). Because social problems work involves creating new typifications and elaborating distinctions that produce new understandings of existing social problems, it has a role in the production of culture. Analyses of social problems work extend the claims-making approach developed by Malcolm Spector and John Kitsuse (1973) to show how these interpretive activities "are related to other social, cultural, and political processes, particularly, how claims-making may perpetuate or change prevailing patterns of action and relationship in society" (Miller and Holstein 1989, 4).

Social problems work not only creates *problems* and poses *solutions*, but also "produces" *clients* in particular ways. For example, Donileen Loseke examines how workers in a shelter for abused wives define some women as "battered" and thus as "appropriate clients" for their services (1989, 2001). J. William Spencer (1994) turns attention away from workers and examines the role of clients in institutional thinking. He develops the term "client work" to highlight ways that homeless clients construct their biographies to cast themselves as worthy of the services of the Homeless Assistance agency. These studies show how service organizations perpetuate their own definitions of the problem and those affected by it.

This study examines social problems work within the institutional setting of an animal shelter. Specifically, it compares the way one shelter "thinks" about why people give up unwanted animals with how clients see their reasons for doing so. The term used for the process of giving up an animal is "surrender." This, in itself, represents some of the social problems work that takes place within sheltering. Although clients are abandoning their animals, the gentler term of "surrender" helps produce an image of the "good" client, in contrast to those who leave their animals to fend for themselves. Through this rhetorical practice and others, shelters frame the problem of unwanted pets in ways that encourage public support for their efforts. That frame, however, ignores aspects of the problem that do not fit within its borders.

This article draws on data collected and analyzed through emergent inductive techniques. The primary source is over 300 hours of ethnographic research at a humane society which I will refer to as "The Shelter." This private, nonprofit organization offers adoptions, veterinary services, humane education, dog training, and cat behavioral consultations, and serves as headquarters for the city's animal control services and welfare investigations. The Shelter takes in animals regardless of age, breed, or condition. It is among a small but growing number of shelters in the country that do not euthanize healthy animals. However, it is *not* a "no-kill" facility; animals are put to death if they are considered unadoptable due to serious, untreatable health or behavior problems. A well-run Foster Care program provides temporary housing for very young puppies and kittens and for animals who would be killed in other facilities because they are not immediately adoptable. The Shelter takes in approximately 5,000 unwanted animals per year, which is a low number within the animal welfare industry. About 85 percent end up in new homes.

In 1998, I began working as one of The Shelter's volunteers. A year later, intrigued by the dynamics of the place, I gained permission to study the surrender process. I moved into what Peter and Patricia Adler (1987) call a "complete membership role." I continued working as a volunteer, but also began observing surrenders, recording notes, and examining them regularly in search of emergent themes and patterns. Eventually, I began interviewing clients who surrendered animals. The Shelter generously helped me recruit interviewees by attaching an information and consent form to the surrender paperwork. This resulted in 40 in-depth interviews on surrender decisions. Meanwhile, I also observed Shelter workers and talked with them about their experience and understanding of the surrender process.

Constructing the Problem of Unwanted Pets in the United States

At the time of the Civil War, there was no such thing as a "homeless pet" and, consequently, no "animal shelters." To be sure, unowned dogs and cats wandered the streets and countryside. However, homeless animals did not constitute a social problem until claims-makers began the work of portraying them as such. During the nineteenth century, fear of rabies prompted American city governments to authorize the capture of roaming animals, particularly dogs. Municipalities authorized local constables and the infamous "dog catchers" to hunt and catch stray dogs, often for a bounty. In addition, many American (and European) cities implemented dog licensing laws.

Similar efforts to establish cat licensing laws failed, and the practice of licensing dogs accomplished little. The regulations usually applied to dogs over 6 months of age and effectively restricted ownership to those who could afford the fees. To avoid paying the licensing fees, many people simply let their dogs loose once they passed the endearing puppy stage. Consequently, in most towns and cities, packs of dogs ran free and colonies of cats abounded, creating numerous potential and actual troubles. The lack of spaying or neutering greatly compounded the problem.

City pounds held animals for a prescribed period and killed the unclaimed by drowning or electrocution or sold them in quantity to vivisectors. Although the cities' efforts had reduced the numbers of roaming animals, the middle class in particular objected to the cruelty and mass killing through which this was accomplished. Early histories of the humane movement document the horrors of the city pounds, and the image of the "dog catcher" itself speaks to the demonization of the agents of animal control.

In the 1860s, two Philadelphia women, Elizabeth Morris and Annie Waln, began going around the city picking up and sheltering strays. Morris and Waln found homes for those they could and chloroformed the others, which was a more humane method than those used in the pounds. In 1874, the two started the first Animal Rescue League. At about the same time, Caroline White, another Philadelphian, was similarly infuriated at the city's role in supplying animals for vivisection. White had spearheaded the formation of the Pennsylvania Society for the Prevention of Cruelty to Animals (PSPCA).

The establishment of the first shelters prompts three observations about social problems work. First, it highlights how social problems claims-making establishes the link between the contemporaneous *moral climate* and the *timing* of problems construction. Concurrent social problems work during the late nineteenth century, such as the founding of the American Society for the Prevention of Cruelty to Animals (ASPCA) and antivivisection organizations, fo-

mented concern from an ethical or moral standpoint about humans' treatment of animals. Prior to this, there was no belief system (or none with enough popular support) defending the welfare of stray dogs and cats. Second, and related to this, the emergence of the first shelters reveals *fragmentation* within a moral climate. Fragmentation means that people will often "unite at the extremes" (Loseke 1999:180) of social problems, making them the points where claims-making will be most effective. In the context of animal welfare, not everyone would agree on the particulars of animals' moral standing, but most would disapprove of torture and suffering. The audience *united at the extreme*—agreeing that killing needed to be humane—so this was where the claims were most successful. Third, the creation of the first shelters reveals the construction of *victims* and *villains*, two necessary components of defining a condition as a social problem (see Loseke 1999). The animals were those most harmed by the inhumane killing, but within the moral climate of the humane movement, the horrors of the city pounds also diminished humanity itself. The city governments and "dog catchers" responsible for the killing were the villains, but the people who let their animals wander were implicated as well.

The phenomenon of "uniting at the extremes" and the construction of villains and victims combined to give "audience members neat and tidy images" of the animal problem (Loseke 1999:94). The resulting simplistic image framed the problem and assigned blame, but simultaneously obscured the complexity of the underlying conditions. This situation would endure into the present.

Reconstructing the Popular Frame: Piggybacking

As Loseke explains, one effective strategy for expanding claims about social problems involves constructing a new problem as a different instance of an existing one (1999:82). An example of this strategy, known as piggybacking, is apparent in how claims about civil rights for African Americans made it easier for *subsequent* groups to make claims about *their* right to equality. Piggybacking nicely describes the ways that animal welfare claims-makers expanded the frame around the problem of *stray animals* to include a new version of the problem of *unwanted pets.*

Although stray animals continued to populate shelters throughout the twentieth century, facilities *also* began taking in litters of puppies and kittens for whom their human guardians were unable to find homes. The innocence of puppies and kittens made them the ideal "victims," epitomizing the "deserving" shelter animal. In terms of piggybacking, taking in puppies and kittens was simply an effort to reduce the troublesome strays of the future. As the population of shelters consequently changed, the social problems work within sheltering shifted its practices, from solving the problem of stray animals to reducing reproduction. In the 1970s, a nationwide campaign to educate the public about the need for sterilization gradually reduced the flow of litters into shelters. Joint claims-making efforts on the part of the American Veterinary Medical Association, The American Humane Association, The Humane Society of the United States, The American Kennel Club, and The Pet Food Institute framed the problem as one that would respond to education about sterilization and free or discounted spay and neuter clinics. In addition, legislation began to require the sterilization of adoptable animals in shelters so that no dogs or cats who left a shelter could contribute to the problem that had led them there in the first place.

Thirty years later, shelters continue to receive an unending supply of animals, but the population dynamics have changed again. To be sure, sterilization remains a core aspect of the social problems work within sheltering; witness the "Spay and Neuter" stamps released by the U.S. Postal Service in 2002. Whereas positive strides in sterilization have reduced the numbers of litters, the new majority of shelter animals are adults who failed to become the kind of pets for which their guardians had hoped. This has resulted in another institutional reframing of the "problem" of unwanted animals. In the 1990s,

sheltering organizations began to consider what else (besides sterilization) could "stop the flow of animals into the building" (Lawson 2000:10). The local culture of animal sheltering framed its task as increasing the likelihood that people would keep their dogs and cats for life. This expanded the scope of social problems work to include educating the public about animal health, behavior, and training. As part of this effort, shelters began remaking themselves as resource centers and not just last resorts. In order to draw people in to seek these resources, shelters sought to become more pleasant places for human *and* nonhuman animals.

A large part of this makeover addressed the image of shelters as death chambers. Until roughly the 1990s, the institutional discourse of sheltering portrayed putting unwanted animals "to sleep" as an act of mercy. The moral climate changed when claims-makers within sheltering began to voice opposition to the mass killing. This prompted new efforts to re-home a greater number of animals. Shelters have had to stop "waiting patiently for customers to come to them and instead develop more aggressive adoption strategies" (Brestrup 1997:44). Increasing adoptions meant stepping up public relations efforts, including making adoptable animals more visible through newspaper photos, websites, and bringing them to the people (at community events), rather than waiting for people to come to them.

The animals remained the victims in the reframed "problem" of unwanted pets, but the new claims required a new villain. If shelters were to market themselves as resource centers, then the new villain must be the person who does not use those resources. More specifically, the new villain is an irresponsible, unloving person who does not bring the unwanted animal to a shelter. Shelter workers warn the public of the fates that await animals "on the streets," or, worse still, when they are offered "Free to a Good Home." Such ads often bring people in search of dogs, in particular, to sell to dealers who then sell them to medical research labs. The images of the uncertainty animals will face when they are not surrendered to a shelter parallel successful cases of claims construction that depict the "horrifying consequences" other types of victims will face (Loseke 1999:86). Similar horror stories include the cases of "missing children" (Best 1990), "abused children" (Johnson 1995), and "abused wives" (Loseke 1989, 1992).

The production of the villain implies the concurrent production of the "good" shelter client. Evidence of this production appears in the way shelters train workers to accept the reasons that guardians offer for surrender without criticism. If surrenderers feel guilty, the logic goes, they will avoid shelters, and animals will face "horrifying consequences." The local culture of shelters thus "creates" guardians who surrender dogs or cats as those who are doing the right thing for the animals. To "produce" clients as the "good" ones, The Shelter trains workers not to judge, criticize, or even ask probing questions about surrenders, but to take only the necessary information. The intake paperwork requires only a brief, single reason for the surrender, and the computer program that generates it does not allow for lengthy accounts. Indeed, the software forces staff members to select the best reason from options on a pull-down menu. The application of formal rationality in this way promotes the predictability that bureaucracy requires. However, the social problems work involved in sustaining the image of "good" clients may also perpetuate the problem that shelters set out to solve. To examine how this occurs, I turn to the empirical data.

Guardians' Accounts of Surrender Decisions

Reducing the surrender decision to a single reason allows for tracking of the frequency with which guardians offer particular reasons. Many of the organizations and groups seeking solutions to the problem of unwanted animals have made use of such data. However, interviews with guardians reveal that basing solutions on surrender data is problematic because the reasons for surrender follow institutionally embedded formulas. Relying on statistical data reproduces institutional thinking that ignores or even

exacerbates the conditions that lead guardians to surrender.

Judging by frequency of occurrence, I found that the top three reasons offered by guardians for the surrender of dogs and cats were moving, allergies, and behavior problems. The latter category included such things as incompatibility with other animals in the household (commonly mentioned among dogs *and* cats) and elimination problems (common among cats). Thus, according to frequency of occurrence, a major cause of homeless animals is that guardians were moving into places that either did not allow animals or limited the number of animals allowed. It would then seem that making rental housing pet-friendly could go a long way toward solving the problem of homeless animals. Indeed, this is precisely what The Shelter has tried to do. Like many shelters across the country, The Shelter makes available, both on paper and on-line, a list of "Animal Friendly Housing" in the area. Yet, when I asked guardians what steps they had taken to locate housing that would allow their animals, the answer usually boiled down to "none."

The reasons people offer for relinquishment reveal only a partial picture of the decision process. Through interviews, I found that multiple circumstances contribute to the decision to surrender an animal. This finding is consistent with other qualitative studies of surrender (see DiGiacomo, Arluke, and Patronek 1998). This finding also resonates with Loseke's (2001) discussion of the complexity of the lived experience of battered women. In her study of a battered women's shelter, the problem that is institutionally categorized as a "failed relationship" is experienced by many women as "many simultaneous, interrelated, and vaguely defined troubles" (p. 108). Similarly, a single reason such as "Moving" might have been the one *recorded* for surrendering an animal, but this categorization was the product of the interpretive demands of The Shelter's intake paperwork. In a case of what Gubrium and associates (1989) call the "tyranny of forms," the paperwork makes demands on the staff members who complete them, requiring brief, standardized accounts of complex situations. However, my interviews unearthed numerous factors that contributed to the decisions, attesting to what Loseke calls the "messiness" of lived experience. For example, in this interview excerpt, a guardian (G) who surrendered her cat because she was moving reveals other reasons for her decision:

G: I could have taken her with me, but I would have had to pay the pet deposit.

LI: How much was it?

G: One hundred dollars.

LI: A month or a year?

G: No, just a one-time thing, along with the security deposit. An extra $100.

LI: And you'd get it back when you moved again?

G: Well, yeah, if there was no damage. But anyway, she was really bothering me, the way she'd wake me up early all the time. I loved her and all, but she was bugging me. And she sheds all the time, too. I mean, there's fur all over everything!

The woman's unwillingness to take the cat with her presents a more complex picture than does a simple, "I'm moving." The cat's early morning hours had been "bugging" her and she objected to the shedding—both normal, inevitable aspects of life with cats. The move presented an opportunity to weigh her relationship with the cat, and, in this case, it was not worth $100.

People who surrendered animals because someone in the household had allergies revealed similar bundles of reasons that defy the narrative conventions of the surrender paperwork. I interviewed a woman who surrendered a cat to whom she had become allergic and heard a medically unlikely "quasi-theoretical" explanation (Hewitt and Hall 1973). Quasi-theories impose order on otherwise inexplicable situations. In this case, the woman explained that she had recently moved several times, but at the time of the interview, she "had a good situation" sharing an apartment with a female roommate who also had a cat. The woman denied any previous symptoms of allergies. She explained that her allergies had oc-

curred because the two cats did not get along, and because her cat was the aggressor. The stress of that situation had, she claimed, made her allergic. I asked if she had seen a doctor about her symptoms, and she had not. Because there was still a cat in the household, I asked how the allergies were since she had surrendered *her* cat. She said she no longer had symptoms because the stress that had brought them on had disappeared. Although allergies are idiosyncratic immune responses, it is highly improbable that a fleeting sensitivity such as this could occur. Because allergens remain in an environment long after an animal leaves it, surrendering a cat will seldom bring immediate relief. Moreover, although many people claim that they are only allergic to certain cats, the research suggests that even "different breeds of cats seem to be strongly related allergenically" (Joneja and Bielory 1990:158). In short, a hypersensitivity to *one* cat will usually produce an allergic reaction to *other* cats, as well.

Like the woman in the above example, other guardians who surrendered an animal because of moving or allergies also admitted to having additional animals still at home. This concurs with the national studies, which report that 17 percent of guardians who surrendered one or more animals because of allergies had one or more remaining dog, cat, or both at home. More importantly, these guardians gradually revealed that the surrendered animal had done something to prompt the surrender, perhaps had urinated on the carpet or fought with another animal in the house. Similarly, in nationwide studies, 33 percent of those who surrendered dogs for reasons such as moving or allergies *also* reported a "nonaggressive behavioral problem in the dog surrendered" (Scarlett et al. 1999:45). In addition, most guardians had procrastinated about the surrender for some time, allowing bad situations to worsen until something eventually tipped the scales.

Blaming the Victim

Although The Shelter offers numerous alternatives to surrender, adopting one or more of them would require understanding and defining the problem, isolating one problem from others, and accepting an uncertain outcome of, say, training or treatment. For example, a guardian who locates pet-friendly housing might find that her cat's urination problems continue in the new place, or the animals who remain at home after the surrender of the "troublemaker" might have been fighting for some other reason all along. Many guardians simply prefer surrender, which contrasts dramatically with The Shelter's thinking about a lifetime relationship with an animal.

Most people did not consider alternatives to surrender because of a lack of basic knowledge about animals, which results in an inflated estimation of one's expertise. The lack of knowledge also produces unrealistic expectations about what animals are like and what they need. In interviews, I found that most dog guardians mistakenly thought that a female dog could not be spayed while in heat and that neutering a male dog before adulthood would stunt his growth. In research sponsored by the National Council on Pet Population Study and Policy, a majority of people (61 percent) surrendering animals thought, incorrectly, that dogs and cats should mate at least once before being sterilized (or they did not know whether this was true). Only about 20 percent of those surrendering cats were aware that females are seasonally polyestrous, meaning that they can go into heat and bear several litters over a season. Among those surrendering dogs, 43 percent did not know how often female dogs experience estrus (the answer is twice a year). About half of those relinquishing dogs or cats also thought (incorrectly) that animals misbehave to spite their guardians.

Inadequate knowledge led to a failure to seek information and treatment for animals' health or behavior problems, much of which was available through The Shelter. Although many guardians had taken their animals to a vet upon first acquiring him or her, few had consulted vets further once behavioral problems appeared, *even when the problems seemed health related*. Moreover, many of the behavior problems occurred among animals who were sexually intact at the time of

surrender, but few guardians associated the two factors.

Few guardians had consulted behaviorists or trainers, both of whom are readily available in the area. In addition, most of the surrendered dogs had received no training, which is consistent with the findings of other studies. The Shelter offers a free "Canine Behavior" seminar and six months of feline behavioral counseling with each adoption. Yet these resources go woefully underused. Because no one can be *required* to use them, guardians who choose not to do so miss learning even the basic knowledge that might allow them to keep a newly adopted animal in their home. For instance, a woman returned a dog whom she had adopted just two weeks earlier, saying she could not housebreak him. When asked if she had tried crate training the dog, which is The Shelter's endorsed method for ensuring successful house-breaking, she said she had never heard of it. In saying so, she revealed that she had neither attended the seminar nor read the material included in her adoption packet, as both convey how-to instructions on the topic and information about The Shelter's crate rental program. Instead, she explained that she had repeatedly rubbed the dog's nose in his urine and feces—an ineffective method that will apparently take generations to disappear.

Because many people considered their existing stock knowledge about animals accurate and sufficient, they lay the blame for behavior problems on the animal. When a dog or cat does not behave correctly, guardians assume there must be something wrong with the animal and they become emotionally disconnected from the animal as time goes on. Guardians in this position often used the language that Sanders (1999) calls "unlinking."

Unlinking is lay social problems work, in that it rhetorically casts the "problem" as the animal's rather than the person's. Moreover, unlinking language indicates that the animal's behavior is so threatening to the guardian's self-image that he or she has disengaged from any emotional and relational connection with the animal. For example, a man I interviewed had surrendered a large dog who pulled constantly on his leash. The family had hoped the dog would be a companion for the young son, who, as it turned out, was not strong enough to walk him. However, no one took any steps to teach the dog to walk without pulling.

Most people simply did not know about the resources available to them as alternatives to surrender. In the case of allergies, interventions such as shots and prescription medications can help tremendously. Yet, no one I interviewed had considered these; to the contrary, most expressed horror at the idea of shots or being "on medications." However, there are also products (Allerpet-C® for cats, and Allerpet-D® for dogs) to wipe on an animal's coat that neutralize the allergenic proteins. Most pet supply stores stock them (including The Shelter's) and I have also seen them in grocery stores, yet no one who surrendered an animal because of allergies had heard of them. Measures such as keeping the animal out of the bedroom, combined with thorough vacuuming of carpets and brushing of the animal (by a nonallergic person) can help. Granted, this requires commitment. Nevertheless, most people did not know of and hence had not tried any of these ameliorative measures.

The failure to seek information or assistance was particularly striking in the context of behavioral problems. Few people who surrendered dogs for aggression to other dogs had consulted with a behaviorist. The Shelter offers training classes and the trainers will do private consultations for specific problems, but most people I spoke with neither made use of these resources nor consulted their veterinarian during routine visits. This is particularly striking in light of evidence indicating that frequency of visits to a veterinarian is associated with decreased risk of relinquishment among dogs (Patronek *et al.* 1996b). Instead of seeking advice, however, many people simply surrendered their dogs, Tusing unlinking language such as, "We just don't know what to do."

Many of the alleged behavior "problems" in dogs and cats stemmed from guardians' ignorance about breed characteristics or developmentally normal behaviors. For instance, several guardians defined their dogs' behavior problem as "hyperactivity." Because many of the surrendered dogs were under 2 years old, these guardians held unrealistic expectations of the behavior and exercise requirements of young dogs. This was also the case when people acquired herding breeds or dogs with high prey drives and then surrendered them for chasing the household cat.

I also found a consistent failure to use resources among people who surrendered cats for the most common feline behavioral problem: urinating outside the litter box. This behavior is often due to urinary tract problems, but few guardians who surrendered cats had even taken the step of seeing a veterinarian. Cats, especially males, are subject to a number of urinary tract problems, but most of them are treatable or manageable with medication or a change in diet. When urination becomes painful, cats, perhaps associating the pain with the litter box, will try to find a less painful place to go. However, only half of the guardians who surrendered cats for litter box problems had *ever* taken their cat to a veterinarian.

Some cats' elimination problems stemmed from guardians' failure to respect the cat's need for cleanliness and consistency. The following interview excerpt offers a good example of a guardian's lack of awareness:

G: [The cat] started peeing on my bed. On my bed! I mean, I love her, but I can't have her peeing on my bed!!

LI: When did it start?

G: Well, I first noticed it when we got [another female cat]. Then my daughter brought home this other cat that her boyfriend couldn't keep, so it started right when the other cat came, and by the time we had a third, she had just about ruined my bed.

LI: How many litter boxes do the cats have?

G: Just one.

LI: How often do you clean it?

G: About twice a week, usually.

LI: Where do you keep it?

G: It's down in the basement. That's another thing. It used to be in here in the hallway, but once we got more cats, the traffic was— they were always underfoot, so we moved it. We moved it a couple of times, and then settled on keeping it in the basement. Then they started fighting on the basement stairs when they had to pass each other to go down there, but it's the best place for us because it's out of the way. It was a real mess.

The woman had no idea that the number of cats in a household affects behavior, as does the cleanliness of the litter box, its location, and the type of litter used. Since *any* basic cat care book would contain this information so vital to a cat's well-being, this woman's situation shows how ill prepared she was to have a single cat, much less several of them. Her case is illustrative of many in which the institution provides ample information about animals' needs, but the clients toward whom that information is directed do not see the problem as one solved by information.

Conclusion

In claiming that institutions such as The Shelter "think" differently than clients do about social problems, this article raises an implicit question about differences in perspectives on social problems. I have used the term institutional "thinking" as a guiding metaphor, but can illuminate the dynamics that make the metaphor work. In particular, my analysis shows how institutional thinking produces versions of problems (and solutions) that are at odds with the lived experiences of people outside the organizational setting that ostensibly deals with those problems.

In this instance, I have shown how institutional discourse characteristics of The Shelter do not necessarily comport with accounts and descriptions offered by shelter clients. This may be a frequent upshot of institutional thinking more generally. For example, institutional or organizational discourse crafted by bureaucrats or policymakers may portray problems like homelessness or welfare reform in terms which do not strongly resonate with the terms through which actual lived experience is understood. This may lead to disjunctures over what is deemed "necessary" to solve putative problems. As Loseke argues, the complexities of lived experience may not be convincingly captured in institutional formulations, leading to "discursive disjunctions" between incompatible systems of meaning (Loseke 2001: 123). As we have seen in the circumstances confronting shelter workers and their clients, such disjunctions can lead to confusion, conflict, and failure to resolve problems.

This article highlights three aspects of organizational discourse that produce institutional thinking that is at odds with the experience of clients. The first of these is a series of paradoxes that apply to the relationship between social progress and social problems, in general. These paradoxes highlight the ways that institutional insiders must navigate among contradictory assumptions and evidence about the problems with which they deal.

First, Best (2001) calls attention to the *paradox of perfectionism*. By this, he means that looking toward the elusive goal of eliminating social problems can obscure actual progress in ameliorating them. In the context of sheltering, focusing on the failure to eradicate the problem of unwanted pets means overlooking significant accomplishments in areas such as sterilization and humane education. Second, the *paradox of proportion* means that "reducing large problems makes smaller problems seem relatively larger" (Best 2001:1). For example, the establishment of the first shelters reduced the significant hazards associated with roaming animals in cities. However, doing so pushed smaller problems, such as sterilization and animal behavior, to center stage. Third, the *paradox of proliferation* "'encourages recognition of a larger number of problems'" (Best 2001:1). Within the realm of sheltering, the problem of unwanted animals has proliferated into problems of behavioral management, humane education, sterilization, veterinary care, animal-friendly housing, and others discussed in this article. Fourth, the *paradox of paranoia* means that the perceived number and size of social problems fosters intense fear and suspicion. Just as the rhetoric following 9/11 spawned new fears of terrorism and suspicion of suspected terrorists, the rhetoric of sheltering exacerbates concerns over the infinite horrors that await animals around every corner, even at the hands of their human caretakers.

To these four, I add the *paradox of popularization*. This refers to framing social problems in ways that win popular support but exacerbate or ignore aspects of the problem that do not fit the frame. The popular framing of social problems from rape to child abduction depicts these crimes as occurring in the streets. However, data reveal that family members or dates, not strangers, commit most rapes, and parents are most often responsible for child abductions. Framing problems differently might lead to better solutions, but the public might be less amenable to such frames. Moreover, the framing sets the institutional thinking in motion and, once started, the attendant social problems work is hard to stop or reverse.

The institution of sheltering thinks about the animal problem in terms of providing practical solutions to a public that is cast as sharing similar concerns. Moreover, those who are not receptive to such solutions and would prefer to "get rid of" their animals can do so and maintain their moral identities as the "good" ones. Making surrender easier for guardians is effective social problems work, in that it enhances the organization's image in the community, but it decreases the likelihood that guardians will take any steps to improve things. Because shelters unquestioningly absorb the results of the public's irresponsibility, they may protect *people* more than they do *animals*. Shelters essentially say to the public, "We will take in your canine and feline mistakes and inconveniences, and we will shield you from the 'dirty work' that takes place here." In most shelters today, the majority of animals are not sickly strays or litters of puppies and kittens, but healthy,

unwanted, adult pets. About 80 percent of these animals do not find new homes. Instead, they are humanely killed. Although precise estimates are impossible because the number of shelters in the United States is unknown, indications are that shelters kill as many as two million dogs and four million cats annually (Patronek *et al.* 1996a, 1996b). This makes shelter killing the leading cause of death among dogs and cats. Alternative framing might better address the conditions that create the problem of unwanted animals, but the guilt such frames might heap on the public would drive them away. Instead, the existing institutional "thinking" courts public support but reproduces numerous aspects of the problem. Even an apparently positive step such as building a new, efficient, light-flooded shelter could reproduce the problem. If clients see the setting as appealing, this may decrease the negative emotional response toward the animals' circumstances, and thereby decrease the motivation to adopt.

The paradox of popularization contributes to what I call the *paradox of permutation*. This refers to the transformation of good clients into bad ones. A client is defined as "good" for surrendering an animal when a problem occurs. However, from the perspective of the institution, most problems can be solved using The Shelter's resources and solutions. The key institutional problem is that clients do not use the resources provided. Thus, the "good" client who surrenders a problematic animal is simultaneously a "bad" client who remains ignorant despite the efforts of the institution. This is evident in the hostility and resentment the staff manifests toward clients "backstage." Not surprisingly, The Shelter attracts employees who consider themselves animal lovers (see also Arluke and Sanders 1996; Balcom and Arluke 2001; Frommer and Arluke 1999). Many workers who have moved repeatedly and kept their animals often find it hard to imagine why others would not do the same. Similarly, those who have solved or managed behavioral problems cannot understand why others would not want to do so, as well. For them, the commitment to an animal may mean making compromises in where one lives, or choosing an animal over a boy- or girlfriend. The *paradox of permutation* thus reinforces the already significant disconnect between the institutional and public definitions of the problem and its solutions.

A final paradox I will add is the *paradox of progression*. It describes how one social problem develops into others. Social problems organizations, once established, seldom go out of business. Instead, they find new problems or "piggyback" new versions onto existing ones. For example, when the problem of roaming animals diminished, the treatment of unclaimed strays became problematic. When shelters offered a solution to *that* problem, the *new* problem became one of uncontrolled breeding. When sterilization reduced breeding, the problem became one of unwanted pets. If this is so, then the unwanted pet problem might someday be resolved, resulting in a new set of concerns that occupy shelters and justify their existence.

A second aspect of organizational discourse that produces institutional thinking that differs from the experience of clients is the "descriptive tyranny of forms" (Gubrium, Buckholdt, and Lynott 1989). As I have said, the descriptive demands of paperwork increase bureaucratic efficiency but run roughshod over the complexity of the narratives offered by clients. Gubrium and associates (1989) point out that description is seldom if ever "precisely representational of whatever it describes" (p. 212). Social problems workers often recognize the "contradictions between what they claim to know and what a form descriptively demands" (p. 212).

Third, institutional thinking is also buttressed by the extent to which clients use legitimating rationales. Thus, an account of the surrender of an animal might begin with moving, but go on to incorporate allergies. By placing blame for our actions on factors such as moving or allergies, the avowal of motives mitigates responsibility for our conduct, and in doing so reduces blame. Motive talk restores our own sense of self-approval. In this way, motives are similar to the "techniques of neutralization" examined by Gresham Sykes and David Matza (1957). These neutralize negative

attributions and help clients to "save face," but they also incapacitate the social controls intended to check the problem. For instance, in the context of The Shelter, rationales such as moving or allergies cloak the conditions for surrender in culturally accepted terms. The client neutralizes disapproval from *others* and thereby maintains his or her sense of *self*-approval. In this way, the resources that The Shelter and other organizations offer go underutilized, for the rationalizing client can explain how they *really* did not apply to him or her.

The disjuncture between institutional "thinking" and lived experience calls attention to how social problems organizations are themselves the products of ongoing social problems work. Successful claims-making means that workers within such organizations see problems and clients in particular ways. These organizational frames cannot capture the complexity of clients' lived experience. As a result, workers and clients compete over definitions of reality. The outcome of the competition can have important consequences. It can prevent help-seeking or even cause outright denial of problems when individual cases do not match up with organizational frames. In the end, then, the social problems work associated with the problem of unwanted dogs and cats has implications far beyond the concern for pets and their people.

References

Adler, Patricia A., and Peter Adler. 1987. *Membership Roles in Field Research.* Newbury Park, CA: Sage.

Arluke, Arnold, and Clinton R. Sanders. 1996. *Regarding Animals.* Philadelphia, PA: Temple University Press.

Balcom, Sarah, and Arnold Arluke. 2001. "Animal Adoption as Negotiated Order: A Comparison of Open versus Traditional Shelter Approaches." *Anthrozoös* 14:135–50.

Best, Joel. 1990. *Threatened Children.* Chicago: University of Chicago Press.

———. 2001. "Social Progress and Social Problems: Toward a Sociology of Gloom." *The Sociological Quarterly* 42:1–12.

Brestrup, Craig. 1997. *Disposable Animals: Ending the Tragedy of Throwaway Pets.* Leander, TX: Camino Bay Books.

Coleman, Sidney H. 1924. *Humane Society Leaders in America.* Albany, NY: American Humane Association.

DiGiacomo, Natalie, Arnold Arluke, and Gary Patronek. 1998. "Surrendering Pets to Shelters: The Relinquisher's Perspective." *Anthrozoös* 11: 41–51.

Douglas, Mary. 1986. *How Institutions Think.* Syracuse, NY: Syracuse University Press.

Frommer, Stephanie S., and Arnold Arluke. 1999. "Loving Them to Death: Blame-Displacing Strategies of Animal Shelter Workers and Surrenderers." *Society & Animals* 7:1–16.

Gubrium, Jaber. 1992. *Out of Control: Family Therapy and Domestic Order.* Newbury Park, CA: Sage.

Gubrium, Jaber F., David R. Buckholdt, and Robert J. Lynott. 1989. "The Descriptive Tyranny of Forms." pp. 195–214 in *Perspectives on Social Problems,* vol. 1, edited by J. Holstein and G. Miller. Greenwich, CT: JAI Press.

Hewitt, John, and Peter Hall. 1973. "Social Problems, Problematic Situations, and Quasi-Theories." *American Sociological Review* 38:367–74.

Holstein, James A., and Gale Miller, eds. 1993. *Reconsidering Social Constructionism: Debates in Social Problems Theory.* New York: Aldine de Gruyter.

Johnson, John M. 1995. "Horror Stories and the Construction of Child Abuse." pp. 17–31 in *Images of Issues: Typifying Contemporary Social Problems,* edited by J. Best. New York: Aldine de Gruyter.

Joneja, Janice Vickerstaff, and Leonard Bielory. 1990. *Understanding Allergy, Sensitivity, and Immunity: A Comprehensive Guide.* New Brunswick, NJ: Rutgers University Press.

Lawson, Nancy. 2000. "Teaching People and Their Pets." *Animal Sheltering* 23 (March–April):7–17.

Loseke, Donileen R. 1989. "Creating Clients: Social Problems Work in a Shelter for Battered Women." pp. 173–94 in *Perspectives on Social Problems,* vol. 1, edited by J. Holstein and G. Miller. Greenwich, CT: JAI Press.

———. 1992. *The Battered Woman and Shelters.* Albany, NY: State University of New York Press.

———. 1999. *Thinking about Social Problems: An Introduction to Constructionist Perspectives.* New York: Aldine de Gruyter.

———. 2001. "Lived Realities and Formula Stories of 'Battered Women.'" pp. 107–26 in *Institutional Selves: Troubled Identities in a Postmodern World,* edited by J. Gubrium and J. Holstein. New York: Oxford University Press.

Miller, Gale, and James A. Holstein. 1989. "On the Sociology of Social Problems." pp. 1–16 in *Perspectives on Social Problems,* vol. 1, edited by J. Holstein and G. Miller. Greenwich, CT: JAI Press.

Patronek, Gary J., Lawrence T. Glickman, Alan M. Beck, George P. McCabe, and Carol Ecker. 1996a. "Risk Factors for Relinquishment of Cats to an Animal Shelter." *Journal of the American Veterinary Medical Association* 209:582–8.

———. 1996b. "Risk Factors for Relinquishment of Dogs to an Animal Shelter." *Journal of the American Veterinary Medical Association* 209:572–81.

Sanders, Clinton R. 1999. *Understanding Dogs: Living and Working with Canine Companions.* Philadelphia: Temple University Press.

Scarlett, Janet M., Mo D. Salman, John G. New, Jr., and Philip H. Kass. 1999. "Reasons for Relinquishment of Companion Animals in U.S. Animal Shelters: Selected Health and Personal Issues." *Journal of Applied Animal Welfare Science* 2:41–57.

Spector, Malcolm, and John I. Kitsuse. 1973. "Social Problems: A Re-formulation." *Social Problems* 21:145–59.

Spencer, J. William. 1994. "Homeless in River City: Client Work in Human Service Encounters." pp. 29–45 in *Perspectives on Social Problems,* vol. 6, edited by J. Holstein and G. Miller. Greenwich, CT: JAI Press.

Sykes, Greshman, and David Matza. 1957. "Techniques of Neutralization." *American Sociological Review* 22:664–70.

Arnold Arluke

Hope and Conflict in the Social World of Animal Sheltering

Throughout much of the twentieth century, a nagging sense of inauthenticity has plagued workers in animal shelters and produced a caring/killing paradox. On the one hand, they have a core professional identity of being humane, good-hearted "animal people" who want the very best for their charges. Most not only have histories of multiple pet ownership but also of being "supernurturers," caring for stray and injured animals while feeling a strong attachment to animals in general. On the other hand, people in animal shelters destroy millions of animals each year for lack of space or ill health. Workers have always detested doing this because it seems wrong to euthanize so many animals that could be kept alive if only adopters were found and because the act itself is so antithetical to their nature.

In the past, shelter workers lived with the moral tension of killing animals by relying on various institutional coping devices that reduced this stress and normalized killing. Typically, shelter workers saw themselves as compassionate people who put animals out of misery in a humane fashion while blaming the general public for being guilty and responsible for causing the killing. Most shelter workers denied that their killing or "euthanasia" was cruel and did not see it in the same light as harm rendered to animals in labs or farms, even when they euthanized animals that might be adoptable, let alone those that were young, attractive, and healthy. They just saw no other option for handling the enormous numbers of animals brought by the public to shelters. Workers were thus able to maintain their humane, animal-person identity, despite or even because of their euthanasia of animals.

Until the last decade, shelter workers could sustain this humane self-image because little if any organized criticism claimed that euthanizing, per se, was cruel. When criticism occurred it tended to be case specific, focusing on which animals were euthanized, how it was done, and whether the shelter was honest in sharing this with the public. Individuals in the community who were distressed by euthanasia informally communicated their concern. Negative comments came mainly from passing remarks made by friends or strangers who lamented killing animals and lauded the "nice" shelters that did not euthanize. Even apparently positive remarks intended to be empathetic, such as "I could never do your job," were often taken as slams against the humaneness of shelter workers. In this context, the dominant paradigm in the shelter community defined euthanasia as a necessary evil because animals were considered unadoptable or there was insufficient space to house them. Although a few shelters offered an alternative to this paradigm by restricting admission of unadoptable animals and billing themselves as "no-kill" shelters, they did not represent a serious threat to the continuation of "open-admission" thinking about euthanasia in which virtually all animals were taken, but some would be euthanized because the shelter deemed them unadoptable or lacked sufficient cage space.

This began to change in 1994 when the Duffield Family Foundation created Maddie's Fund, which through the lure of financial support, sought to revolutionize the status and well-being of companion animals by championing the "no-kill" movement. Some shelters have embraced the "no-kill" philosophy and have become the vanguard of this movement, designating entire cities or states as "no-kill." No longer possible to ignore or discount as an outrageous idea, this movement has spurred debate at the national level about the proper role of euthanasia in shelter practice.

Criticism of euthanasia has steadily mounted in frequency and fervor from the no-kill movement, challenging the idea that euthanasia is humane and raising the suspicion that those doing it might be cruel to animals and themselves. Indeed, revealing more than mere suspicion, 2003 saw the first court case involving a shelter worker being charged with cruelty because she euthanized seven cats as part of her job that might have otherwise been adopted. The accused, nicknamed "Killer Kelly," by some of her co-workers, was thought to have been too quick to euthanize these animals, ignoring posted notes by her peers to "not kill the kittens!" In her defense, Kelly said that although overcrowding often left her no choice but to euthanize animals, the decisions were heart-wrenching and made only after supervisors approved them (Murray 2003).

These criticisms have strained the ability of conventional shelters and humane organizations to psychologically protect workers from the charge that euthanasia is a form of cruelty. Instead of preventing cruelty, which their mission maintains, they are now seen as causing it. How do no-killers use the implication of cruelty as a way to reclaim emotions long absent in shelter work? Although the charge that euthanasia is cruel is first and foremost an animal issue, at another level the charge is about what shelter workers should or should not feel. It is about caring for animals the way "animal people" ought to, instead of being cruel to them, in the eyes of no-kill proponents. They are tired of feeling guilty

because they kill animals, tired of having so little hope for animals, and tired of holding back their attachments to animals for fear of being hurt. In short, no-killers deny that they are "animal killers" and strive to get back in touch with feelings they consider to be "natural" for anyone who cares so much about animals and wants so desperately to rescue those in need. That the accusation of cruelty serves as a stepping stone for no-killers to find and experience their authentic self, and the feelings that go with it, is this article's focus.

To study how no-killers do this, I carried out 200 hours of observation and 75 formal interviews in shelters, animal control offices, and sanctuaries in two communities on opposite coasts of the United States. These institutions have taken different approaches to the use of euthanasia, in one case seeing it as necessary and humane while in the other as inappropriate and inhumane. I also attended the national meetings of the major humane organizations having conflicting opinions about this matter, examined press accounts and shelter publications relating to euthanasia, and combed Internet news groups that discussed shelter issues.

Giving Second Chances

The implication that shelter workers are cruel if they do not save animals is understandably provocative and elicits countercharges of cruelty. Open-admissionists claim that they are the ones who save animals because they take the needy and less desirable animals turned down by no-kill programs. One open-admission shelter defender writes in an editorial, "The Door Remains Open," that "no-kill shelters seldom operate programs to rescue sick and injured animals off the streets," suggesting that animals in need are turned away (Savesky 1995, 2), while open-admission shelters "rescue sick and injured animals every day . . . dogs hit by cars, cats tangled in debris, animals injured by other animals, victims of all sorts of accidents." In addition, no-kill shelters, according to this author, "often turn away older animals, those with minor health or behavioral problems, or those that they otherwise classify unadoptable." Moreover, this author adds that "no-kill shelters seldom investigate and prosecute complaints of cruelty and neglect" (Savesky 1995, 2). By contrast, this editorial argues that many of these animals have a greater chance of being adopted in open-admission shelters.

Open-admissionists also argue that no-killers are cruel because they "warehouse" animals past the point where they should be "humanely euthanized," keeping them in shelters for long periods, sometimes with inadequate care, socialization, and housing. "The Humane Society of the United States has files of cases on 'no-kill' shelters from which they've had to rescue neurotic, sick animals that were kept in desperate conditions," writes one critic in an article discussing the "confinement" of shelter animals in "pet warehouses" (Phalan-Dahmen, n.d.). Another claimed that some no-kill shelters keep animals so long they develop "that nervous thing, like dogs spinning, or some of the barking sounds like suffering to me. They are just unhappy and crying." And another critic of warehousing points out after visiting a no-kill shelter: "It was spotless . . . they had air conditioning, climbing trees, toys and good food. But when you walked in, they were all over you. I had cats attached to my legs and arms, on my shoulders and my head. I had scratch marks for a week after that but not from aggression. These cats were starved for human contact. That's what breaks my heart about these places" (Donald 1991, 4).

Strengthening their allegation of cruelty, open-admissionists claim that warehousing can cause physical harm to shelter animals. This critique is echoed in a popular magazine article that reports the reactions of a 4-H group leader after visiting one no-kill shelter, "Dogs limping around with mange and open sores. Others gasping for air or dragging broken legs, struggling to fight off vicious packs in the large communal pen. 'I might as well have taken them to a horror show'" (Foster 2000). The reporter who authored this article refers to the "atrocious conditions" at some no-

kill facilities and the "luckless inmates" that are "condemned" to "filth" and "suffer" from long-term caging. Indeed, one open-admissionist claims that the "quality of care of animals is horrific. They [no-kill] need to do it right and have some standard of care." To illustrate, he points to a no-kill facility that asked his shelter to take 110 animals to reduce overcrowding. A visit to this no-kill alarmed him because he discovered that it was very cold, a mere "semblance" of a building, having dead animals strewn throughout.

Such charges, especially if unanswered, challenge the ability of no-killers to maintain their hope for animals and, without hope, their claim to an authentic identity, free from cruelty, becomes precarious. That they continue to be heartened reflects their ability not only to reject but transform these charges into further hope.

Most vehemently deny "warehousing" of animals. One advocate speaks of her frustration with people who misconstrue the meaning of no-kill as a preference for keeping animals alive in unpleasant or unhealthy circumstances. "I don't know if there is any sane person who would agree with a warehouse-kind-of-life, like an animal collector, is better than death. I don't think anybody is arguing that except for an extremely small subset of people who are not in the mainstream of the no-kill movement." They claim that if adverse "warehousing" exists, it is very rare and at a facility other than their own. Indeed, it is common to point to the few very well-funded no-kills where "lavish" surroundings include "luxury suites for animals, replete with toys, TVs, and playrooms" that are not excessive but "important for the animals" to reduce their stress and make them "healthier and happier. So the toys and playrooms are not frivolous. They're just what the doctor ordered."

Charges of warehousing, however, are extremely threatening to the no-kill quest for authenticity because they raise the specter of cruelty and undermine their hopefulness. Through their language, no-killers redefine these extended stays as hopeful and humane, although "less than ideal" (Foro 2001). For one, there is a lot of talk about maintaining the "quality of life" of animals. As one worker claims, it "is as good if not better than the placements at many open admission shelters. I know a good many dogs in suburbia who don't get walked, have minimal veterinary care, don't get socialized, they don't get patted much by their owners, they're in the yard." No-killers also find hope in the language used to describe physical and mental problems in animals housed for long periods in shelters. For example, in one such facility, animals with behavior problems, sufficient to justify euthanasia in open-admission shelters, were described as only having "issues." "Issues" conjures up psychological problems in humans that can be lived with and managed, as opposed to more troubling behavior that is difficult to tolerate and control. In one case, a shelter dog had a history of snapping at children and was spoken about as "having an issue with children." The solution was to work on ridding the dog of that "issue," while also seeking childless adopters who could keep the dog away from children.

Fighting the Good Fight

Asserting the humaneness of extended stays is necessary to counter charges of cruelty, but it is not sufficient to ensure a hopeful experience. More important to building their new identity is for no-killers to feel they are championing individual animals, or as one no-kill advocate notes: "We dare to think that every individual life does matter . . . that *that* individual's life *actually* matters." This means they will "fight the good fight" for each animal that comes their way, expending as much time, labor, and money as necessary to ensure that the animal—likely euthanized in an open-admission shelter—is cared for, loved, and hopefully adopted.

No-killers fight the good fight by attempting to "rescue" animals, on and off the job, believing that it is always worth "trying" to find a home for every animal. One worker compares this desire to rescue animals to the attitude of emergency room personnel who are trying to save human lives: "That's like giving up on a patient that you know you can save. It's like triage. You are working in an ER . . . a patient comes in, if he came in ten minutes earlier you would have gotten him. That's how I have to look at what I do. It's very ER-ish. You have to want to save the next one. And that's why we are here and not in an animal care and control facility. We pour everything into an animal. We invest it all." However, it becomes progressively more difficult to fight the good fight when no-killers try to rescue animals with increasingly adverse medical and psychological conditions. Yet they remain hopeful. As one worker says, her facility's goal is to try to make ever sicker animals into adoptable ones: "We are raising the bar for what we can handle medically or behaviorally. We've got animals with chronic health conditions. We've got aggressive dogs. We are trying to rehabilitate them so they can be made adoptable."

Workers who violate this rescue ethos are often isolated from their peers, teased, or seriously ridiculed. They are seen as too "rigid" with intake selections, turning away animals that would then be killed, or too "eager" to call for and endorse the euthanasia of shelter animals. In one no-kill shelter, a kennel manager was called "Dr. Kevorkian" by staff members because she put down a 10-year-old dog that tried to bite, but was regarded as very adoptable by most workers. She feels that some dogs should be put to sleep, while most workers in her shelter do not. In a different no-kill shelter, there is strong internal pressure on intake workers to accept as many dogs as possible from the nearby animal control office, regardless of their bad or "spooky" behavior or poor condition; otherwise they likely will be euthanized. For example, after an intake worker refused an aggressive, 6-month-old dog offered to her shelter, several co-workers chided her and called her a "murderer" for doing this; more politely, some peers criticized her in general for being the "most conservative" temperament tester in the shelter." "I am the bad guy," she sadly noted.

This logic means that no-kill facilities can rescue animals from open-admission shelters, who by implication manage animals in ways that cause them to need saving. Reflecting this view, one no-kill proponent makes the following plea: "If you consider that we cannot save them all, what difference does one make? You ought to know the joy of the one who is saved. Mourn those we cannot save. It is a eulogy to their being. Do not let their loss be in vain. Please . . . rescue a shelter animal today!" Open-admissionists are offended by the notion that their animals need rescuing, since this implies they are unnecessarily killing animals, and they think it is wrong to fight the good fight for individual animals, since this misuses limited resources. They argue that if no-killers "rescue" with their hearts, they neglect the "bigger picture." To them, it is more important to attack the overpopulation problem by euthanizing unadoptable animals than to indulge one's need to feel hopeful. This means always accepting surrenderers' animals, despite workers' frustration and anger with them, fearing what might happen to animals not left at the shelter. This criticism is commonly expressed when people point to the number of animals turned down by shelters having a rescue ethos because they have insufficient resources to keep taking more animals. To open-admissionists, this is a management problem—a combination of poor resource allocation and bad judgment that allows workers to be self-indulgent. Such shortsighted policies are thought to benefit workers, offering them emotional gratification at the expense of animal welfare. They say that relating to shelter animals with one's heart makes it harder for no-killers to acknowledge "suffering" in their animals because doing so raises the possibility of euthanasia. Having such a narrow definition of suffering delays what open-admissionists see as necessary euthanasia, in turn causing more suffering.

Viable Pets

In order to fight the good fight, no-killers must be able to see all of their charges as viable pets that can be kept and loved in homes, each animal having the potential for a good life for itself and its guardians. The identity forsaken by no-killers is one that turns its backs on animals that are less

than "perfect," euthanizing many that could be placed in homes if given behavioral or medical attention, as well as time and careful placement. One no-kill worker elaborates this view: "Where do you draw the line? Does everything have to be pristine and perfect, and you kill everything else? We want to give animals a chance that we think ought to be given a chance. I mean, the Blackies and the Willies out there, they would be killed because they are not perfect, and I see this wonderful pet that would make a great companion for someone and I think they are worth investing the resources into." Another no-killer explains, "There are a lot of self-proclaimed experts who will tell you that this or that dog is unadoptable, don't even bother trying. And we don't accept that. You can get terrifically good outcomes . . . it's a question of when can you and when can't you. The jury is out on our animals until we have exhausted all reasonable attempts."

No-kill trainers believe they can rehabilitate most problem animals, including those exhibiting aggressiveness. One trainer compares this challenge to working with criminals, concluding that both can be rehabilitated if people try hard enough. "If you've gotten people who've committed certain levels of crime, can they be rehabilitated? If you gave them the right counseling, can you turn them around or is it always in them? I would submit that the right kind of effort hasn't been tried." Indeed, the belief that any shelter animal is a viable pet extends deep into no-kill culture. In one shelter, the desire to see animals as viable pets even extends to avoiding certain common words, such as "adoptable," that suggest some might not cut muster and make it into a home. A worker explains why his organization does not use the word adoptable. "A kitten with two legs who is four weeks old is adoptable to a person who wants to adopt her. Adoptability is only about who wants this animal. It is not about you judging, to sit back and say, 'This darling animal is adoptable.' No. Adoptability is only judged by the adopter. We had a dog who was thirteen years old. This one had no front legs. She gets around. She kisses everyone. And she was placed."

However, seeing all their charges as viable pets can be difficult in no-kill shelters because some animals are far from the well-behaved, healthy, and attractive pet desired by most adopters. In fact, critics charge that no-kill shelters downplay or conceal problems in animals to get them adopted. "They (counselors/trainers) are soft-peddling the issue . . . they are couching it in a less scary way for the client," according to one worker. For instance, "excuses" are made for the bad behavior of animals, as in the case of a dog whose "guarding behavior" around food was "explained away" by pointing to how little it had been given to eat. Making excuses for bad behavior sometimes is combined with failing to disclose information to adopters about the dangerousness of aggressive animals. One worker spoke about "the betrayal the public would feel if they were aware that the shelter they trusted has made them the subject of an experiment in placing rehabilitated biting dogs, an experiment with so many failures." Uncomfortable with her own shelter's policy, she reported "incredible feelings of guilt" making it "hard to sleep at night" because she felt "complicity" in adopting out unsafe animals to clients from whom information about these problems was hidden. Upset by this problem, another worker described a shelter that was being sued for adopting out a Rottweiler that was known to have already killed one dog, only to have it subsequently knock down its new owner and kill her pet dog. The same worker also claimed that this shelter did not tell potential adopters that another dog had bitten seven volunteers. In response to such shelter actions, the worker said, "That is the main reason I had to resign from volunteering with the rescue group I was working with. They adopted out any and all dogs, no matter their history and worst of all, did not tell adopting families if the dog had bitten previously."

Perfect Adopters

Fighting the good fight rests on the belief that there is a suitable adopter for every rescued animal. However, the drive to save difficult-to-adopt animals severely reduces the pool of potential adopters, since it takes a very special person to be the right match for an animal with behavioral or veterinary problems, let alone finding a person who wants one that is old or unattractive. No-kill workers convince themselves that a perfect adopter exists for virtually every one of their charges. Having this view justifies keeping animals for a long time as adoption staff search for the right person for each animal.

This search can be particularly trying when dogs are highly aggressive, needing to be muzzled and constantly monitored. When a no-kill worker was asked who would be an appropriate adopter for such challenging animals, she said a dog trainer would eventually come to the shelter and take home one of these dogs. "How many dog trainers come through our doors looking for a dog? That's the problem. We can see that. It's not that there is no owner in the world who can do it, it's that there is no owner who wants them or can take them right now. In the right hands they would be okay." She acknowledged, without apparent irony, that no such adopter had visited her shelter since she arrived there 3 years earlier.

No-kill culture buttresses the belief that a perfect adopter exists for each animal. Rescue narratives circulate among workers that talk about shelter animals that make it into good homes and "live happily ever after" because they have been saved, despite many medical or psychological problems. Hopefulness pervades these stories because shelter workers correct the animal's problem and find the right kind of owner. The rescue tale is especially prevalent in no-kills because it speaks to that culture's wish for happy endings and denial of euthanasia. The latter's subtext is that it is wrong to euthanize an animal because, if given a chance, it can find a loving home. Less commonly relayed, but serving to support their hopefulness, are tales about failed or missed rescues, typically at open-admission shelters. These stories describe animals declined at intake because of ill health, bad behavior, or unattractiveness that could have been rehabilitated and adopted if they had been in a no-kill facility.

This culture also helps workers cope with and explain adoptions that apparently fail because animals are returned to the shelter. When this happens, it can be a problem to maintain the belief that animals end up with the right owners and "live happily ever after." These apparent failures, if not addressed, can disillusion workers and question their no-kill identity. In these hope-threatening instances, workers learn to blame adopters for whatever problems they were having with the animals. One adoption counselor, who disagrees with this strategy, describes this attitude: "When animals are returned for the very problems they had, the attitude of the people in the dog division is always anger at the client . . . they did something stupid, they blame the client. If I gave the client a dog that was almost guaranteed to bite, and then the dog is brought back, the training department will say, 'Gee, Fluffy was returned.' 'Why?' 'Well, he bit the aunt who came over to visit.' 'Well, she must have done something. She must have startled him. Boy, what a jerk.' That's the attitude."

Organizational measures ensure robust adoption rates and maintain workers' sense of rescuing animals. If good adopters can be found for most animals, then no-kill shelters should have extremely high adoption rates. Open-admissionists challenge this, calling the claim that no-kill shelters adopt out 100 percent of their animals a "smart marketing strategy." Instead, they argue that no-killers create high adoption rates by only taking very adoptable animals in the first place, leaving the "burden" of euthanizing rejected animals to open-admission shelters. Critics allege that no-kill shelters "take in the 'movie star' dogs and cats, the pretty ones they know they can place in new homes, and turn away the rest" (Caras 1997, 17). "They are strays, 'too old,' unsocialized, injured, or diseased. They are considered unadoptable by no-kill shelters so they are brought to us" (Bogue 1998). One person compares this self-serving policy to a private high school that always has impressive SAT scores because it only accepts bright students in the first place. Some no-kill shelters are even "pickier,"

even rejecting animals with extremely minor problems. As one open-admissionist contends: "If an animal has the tiniest patch of flea allergy, dermatitis, which is curable, they say no if they want to. Bad teeth, they say no if they want to. Any animal they can say no to, they are going to say no. They don't take many that need treatment." All these manipulations, some charge, enable the "no-kill propagandists" through "deception" to produce very high rates of adoption and low rates of euthanizing.

Even after taking an animal, critics charge that no-killers can reclassify an animal's status in order to maintain a high adoption rate. They claim that no-kill shelters use a "changeable" classification of animals, such that a placeable animal could be reclassified as unplaceable if the animal were not adopted. This enables the no-kill shelter to say that no adoptable animals are killed and to assert that a "huge" percentage of their "placeable" animals are adopted (Stark 1993). Some feel that this classification "game" is so incredibly capricious as to make the very notion of no-kill "a joke." One worker said that even "color" could be used as a reason to classify an animal as "unadoptable" if there are too many similar looking animals together in a shelter, such as tiger striped kittens. "I could make distinctions any way I want . . . their rates are meaningless."

Challenging back, some no-kill shelters contend that their save rates would be higher if they did not have so many difficult and unadoptable animals. Denying that they are "picky," no-killers claim to take many animals that are not the "cream of the crop." As one worker says: "One of the things that gets hurled at us, I mean I become so defensive even if there is no attack, is the charge that we set the bar so high medically or behaviorally, therefore almost anybody can label themselves no-kill." Another no-kill worker concurs, "We get only the worst here, everybody thinks we take only the best dogs here . . . we get the worst of the worst. If you are looking for a behavior case, we are probably the shelter to go to. It's harder for me to find a family dog in our shelter than it is in most because we are taking the ones no one else takes."

No-kill culture makes it possible for workers to feel hopeful. It does so even though some of their very steps to rescue and save animals come perilously close to the antithesis of their identity—cruelty. Despite criticisms that could easily threaten their hope, most no-killers cling tenaciously to the belief that almost every shelter animal, regardless of disability, age, or unattractiveness, can be successfully placed if given sufficient time. The focus on the welfare and fate of individual animals, combined with the knowledge that euthanasia is very unlikely, allow no-killers to indulge their desire to have emotionally deep and complex relationships with shelter animals, even though permanent guardians will probably adopt them. Feelings engendered by these relationships are an essential component of the humane identity sought by no-killers, an identity untainted by suggestions of cruelty. Like blamelessness and hope, they experience these sentiments by constructing them as they carry out their everyday shelter jobs.

Dividing the Community

Cruelty is a pivotal concept for no-killers to define and assert a new identity. However, the quest for authenticity creates tension *between* the no-kill and open-admission camps as well as *within* the former group. Although Durkheim (1912) and others (e.g., Heeren 1983) argue that social groups create unity through sharing emotions in group rituals and practices, emotions play an equally important role in separating people from one another. For example, victims of disasters develop a strong unity with fellow victims (Fritz 1961), but experience conflict with outsiders. Boundaries go along with any shared feeling. Pride can lead to an increase in social cohesion (Retzinger 1991), but a more cohesive group may be more likely to be in conflict with outsiders. Similarly, anger also can unify victims who share that anger, but that emotion may lead to dissociation with others.

By disavowing their own cruelty and seeing it in others, no-killers manage emotions in ways that divide the shelter community; their pursuit of authenticity compromises the solidarity of the larger group. One way they do this is to transform open-admissionists into dirty workers. Their jobs are seen as distasteful, if not discrediting, casting a moral pall around those who do this work. They are "less" of a person, morally and emotionally, because of what they do, making them a modern form of untouchables—a caste of people symbolically contaminated and best avoided or pitied because they are associated with unpopular, unpleasant, or unclean tasks. Predictably, open-admissionists resent doing the dirty work. By being forced to euthanize so many animals, they shoulder all the moral, emotional, and aesthetic heartaches that are part of euthanasia. The no-killers "let others do the killing for them," as one worker notes. This point is made patently clear in one editorial in which the author argues that the harm of a no-kill facility is that "it punishes shelters that are doing their very best but are stuck with the dirty work. It is demoralizing and disheartening for humane workers who would do almost anything to stop that heartbreaking selection process. Humane workers who are brave enough to accept that dirty work deserve better than that" (Caras 1997, 17). Open-admission workers deplore dirty-work delegation by no-kill shelters and call for "sharing the burden. As long as there is euthanasia to be done, our resentment is that we shouldn't be doing it all. We should all be doing the good stuff and the bad stuff." Despite these protests the distinction remains, and open-admissionists are shamed by the stigma that no-killers create for them.

A second way that no-killers divide the shelter community is to portray open-admissionists as powerful people who defend the status quo and muffle dissent from the powerless who challenge tradition. In their quest for a humane identity, free of any trappings of cruelty, no-killers create a heightened sense of embattlement or even persecution that further cements boundaries between them and open-admissionists. This identity is empowering because it has an outlaw quality that makes it an attractive and powerful label for no-kill workers who feel alienated, misunderstood, and excluded from the humane powers that be. In particular, poorly endowed, small no-kill shelters cling to the outlaw image because it symbolically represents their powerlessness in an animal community dominated by a few large and powerful national organizations. Believing that they are disempowered frames their camp as "anti-establishment," relative to open-admissionists (Foro, n.d.). For one, they feel ignored, misunderstood, and criticized at national conferences sponsored by open-admissionists. One no-killer, angry at the reaction she receives, explains: "I don't like being dissed and demonized. So many people there were very resentful of us. We were like getting slammed, shielding ourselves from the rotten vegetables being thrown at us. That feeling was very pervasive there [at national meeting]." When it comes to planning and running their own conferences, no-killers feel that attempts to get open-admission support and participation fall on deaf ears. One spokesperson claims that open-admissionists do not even return her phone messages inviting them to take part or asking for conference advice. In this conflicted environment, no-kill shelters that seek to reconcile differences and eliminate distinctions risk being seen as sellouts. The charge made by some that a leading and highly visible no-kill shelter has "sold out" to the Humane Society of the United States (HSUS) because it has increased the number of animals it euthanizes, from almost none to a few, speaks to the current identity-conferring importance of boundaries in the humane community.

There also is tension within the no-kill ranks because institutional guile is used to pursue authenticity. Like all workers, no-killers are normatively constrained to display "appropriate" feelings for specific contexts. In shelters, they are guided to feel guiltless, hopeful, and safely attached to animals. However, some resist these collective sentiments because they "feel wrong" to them at the same time that peers are exalted by these feelings, as new identities can do for people. Instead, they value emotions prohibited by their organizational culture. These sequestered feelings make no-killers question the identity expected of them; they do not always blame open-admissionists, feel hopeful about their charges' prospects, or enter into deep and complex relationships with them.

Instead of blaming others, some no-killers resist the oppositional identities of no-kill versus open-admission. When individual no-killers speak informally with peers or with the author, their political and rhetorical guards are lowered enough to admit to more overlap in their identities than they would concede in a public forum. They know the emotional party line about what they are supposed to feel, but this does not resonate with them. With their guard down, they talk about shelter workers in general in ways that are less polarized and more sympathetic than one might expect given the public rhetoric over the nature of their "real" occupational identities. Clearly, such rhetoric is used more for public consumption and posturing than it is an accurate reflection of the feelings and actions of everyday workers. If permitted to air their thoughts, stark and inflammatory distinctions blur or fade. Workers "see through" the collective search for authentic shelter identity by identifying with open-admissionists or feeling like they are fellow travelers—more alike than not in basic values relating to the care of animals. At these times, no-killers acknowledge that they feel like open-admissionists, expressing common rather than conflicting sentiments about basic issues and concerns faced by everyone in the shelter world. Other movements, particularly those whose mission and effectiveness call for crafting just the right emotions for followers, also experience this kind of resistance, as in the case of pro-life and pro-choice supporters; when confronted one-on-one, their differences are less pronounced than is their public rhetoric.

To illustrate, some no-killers express solidarity with open-admissionists. They have sympathy and pity for those who have to euthanize animals, or even work in shelters that do this, because the emotional toll of killing causes staff to "suffer." More than sympathizing with them, these no-killers identify with open-admissionists who are assumed to have the same compassion as they do for animals, but simply work in the wrong place. One speculates that open-admissionists resent those who work in well-endowed no-kill shelters. She explains: "It's a horrible thing to have to euthanize animals every day. I feel fortunate that I am working in an organization where we don't have to do that. They [open-admissionists] have the same amount of compassion that we have, but because they have fewer resources, they can't do what we do. I can understand why they are resentful. And that is where this [tension] is coming from."

In addition to not blaming open-admissionists, no-kill resisters are less likely to embrace the rescue ethos expected of them. They oppose fighting the good fight for each animal admitted to the shelter and dispute that just the right adopter exists for every shelter animal. Resisters consider even the "best" shelters to be unhealthy, if not destructive, environments for animals, and express feelings for shelter animals that are far from the hope and optimism central to no-killers' authentic identity and its "feeling rules." They agree that, in an ideal world, shelters would not exist or, if they did, would only serve as temporary way stations to rehabilitate and home needy animals. In the words of one no-kill worker, even her own "nice" shelter is "still" a shelter: "In some cases, I really wonder about the animal's quality of life. I think 500 days is our longest-term animal right now. They get walked and handled by staff, but I wonder about their quality of life. Granted, we are a nice shelter, but we are still a shelter." Another no-kill worker concurs with this sentiment, saying: "We've had dogs here for a year or two and you look at when they came in versus when they went out or were put to sleep, and they get worse not better. Shelters aren't always great places for dogs. And the longer they are here, the more likely we are to make them

worse." And yet another no-kill worker expresses similar misgivings about virtually any shelter confinement, even in the best facilities: "I don't care how wonderful we make it for them, they are still institutionalized. Caretakers are there for 30 minutes to an hour and then you are alone . . . not able to do any of the innate things that you as a dog are supposed to be doing. None of those needs are being fulfilled." No-kill resisters also stop themselves from forming deep relationships with shelter animals. These workers refuse to become closely attached to shelter animals, as is more common in open-admission shelters, and do not openly grieve the loss of individual animals that are euthanized. To these resisters, no-kill has less to do with getting in touch with one's true identity and more to do with indulging certain feelings at the expense of proper animal care.

This resistance creates conflict among workers. Sometimes, dissenters are marginalized by dismissing their objections and labeling them "problem children," "difficult employees," not "team members," or the like. They are expected to adjust to the job (i.e., accept and play by the rules for expressing no-kill emotions and identity), become silent, or leave, but these expectations may fail. In larger facilities, there are cliques devoted to such dissent. Alienated from their own shelter's feeling rules, they outwardly challenge them. Within some no-kill shelters, these cliques lead to debates about the appropriateness of their own facility's stance on euthanasia when that issue is raised for certain animals, but this dissent is usually contained to specific incidents or cases rather than generalized to broader shelter practice. Nevertheless, some degree of tension permeates these shelters as workers question the propriety of their facility's feeling rules and debate what constitutes cruelty.

Whether the ambiguously provocative notion of cruelty creates tension within the no-kill world or between it and the open-admission camp, the tension is a struggle over the right way to feel about doing shelter work and the proper way to think about one's identity. At a certain level, this struggle goes beyond tensions within individual shelters. No-killers' pursuit of an authentic identity, and the feelings that go with it, present a crisis to the shelter world akin to the impact of disasters on communities. While there is no destruction of physical property, there is destruction of an idea—that the long-accepted method of disposing of unwanted animals is now seen as a cruel practice. Although disasters typically unify survivors and lead to greater cohesion, one exception parallels what has happened in the shelter community. After the 1973 flood in Buffalo Creek, West Virginia, the connections among residents were transformed from what had been a very close and personal coal-mining community into one in which residents felt distrust and isolation. The failure to restore these family-like bonds made Buffalo Creek an exception, since most communities reestablish their former ties in the aftermath of disaster. Erikson (1976) argues that the huge loss of life and property contributed to this transformation, but that Pittston Corporation's culpability was a leading cause. Before the flood, residents were dependent and relied on this coal mine operating company, but found themselves blaming Pittston for inadequately securing dams that held back millions of gallons of water filled with residue from mined coal. Residents mourned the loss of their former community. Like the Buffalo Creek flood, the no-kill perspective has divided the community that had long existed among shelter workers, changing how they think and feel about each other. With the introduction of the idea of no kill, the vast majority of shelter workers suddenly are thought of as cruel; 5 million deaths each year are seen as avoidable rather than inevitable, as previously thought. As with the Buffalo Creek flood, the no-kill idea has created culpability within the shelter world; open-admissionists have become the guilty party. In the years following the flood, Buffalo Creek's community never returned. Former ties were severed and never restored, leaving a disintegrated community behind. This may not be the fate of the shelter world, but after cruelty became an issue for workers—escaping it or being accused of it—their sense of solidarity was dealt a serious blow. Now challenged by two camps, each vying for what constitutes a "true" shelter worker, the unified community that once existed is no more.

References

Bogue, G. 1998. "Shelters Need to Join Forces to Stop Killing." *Contra Costa Times.*

Caras, R. 1997. "Viewpoints." *Animal Sheltering* Sept–Oct:16–17.

Donald, R. 1991. "The No-Kill Controversy." *Shelter Sense* Sept: 3–6.

Durkheim, E. 1912. *The Elementary Forms of Religious Life.* Paris: F. Alcan.

Erikson, K. 1976. *Everything in Its Path.* New York: Simon and Schuster.

Foro, L. 2001. Personal correspondence, September 17.

Foro, L. n.d. "Know the Thrill of No-kill–Retreat, Hell!" Online Doing Things for Animals.

Foster, J. T. 2000. "A Fate Worse than Death: Are 'No-Kill' Shelters Truly Humane?" *Reader's Digest,* 20 July.

Fritz, C. 1961. "Disasters." In R. Merton and R. Nisbet, eds., *Contemporary Social Problems,* 651–94. Beverly Hills, CA: Sage.

Heeren, J. 1983. "Emotional Simultaneity and the Construction of Victim Unity." *Symbolic Interaction* 22:163–179.

Murray, B. 2003. "Ex-Animal Shelter Worker on Trial for Killing 7 Cats." *The Star Ledger,* April 11.

Phalan-Dahmen, L. n.d. "Why Isn't the SPCA a 'No-Kill' Shelter?"

Retzinger, S. 1991. *Violent Emotions: Shame and Rage in Destructive Conflicts.* Newbury Park: Sage.

Savesky, K. 1995. "The Door Remains Open." *Paw Prints,* pp. 2–3.

Stark, M. 1993. Unpublished document. NY: The Fund for Animals, Inc.

PART NINE

Healing

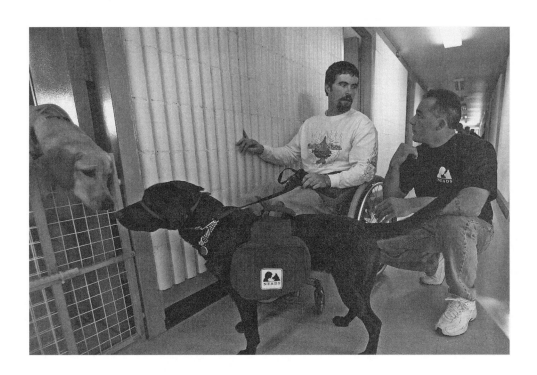

Introduction

In recent years, there has been an explosion of studies trying to document the many ways that animals benefit human well-being. Varying species, from dolphins to dogs, have been studied for their therapeutic impact on populations of varying age, from young child to geriatric, for an endless list of personal, clinical, and social problems. The result is that animals are no longer considered mere companions; they are now viewed as significant contributors to our physical, mental, and community health.

It seems highly likely that interacting with animals—sometimes even in cursory ways with nonpets—can improve the physical well-being of humans. Some of the earliest studies in this area found that something as simple as sitting near a fish aquarium in a physician's waiting room could lower blood pressure. But some of the most dramatic results came from studying pet owners. Studies of companion dogs suggest that their owners benefit medically, sometimes in dramatic ways (see Wilson and Turner 1998). For example, dog ownership has been shown to provide significant cardiovascular benefits, such as survival after myocardial infarction as well as reduction of high blood pressure and cholesterol levels. In addition, dog owners, compared with nonowners, are less likely to visit their doctor, be on medication for heart problems and sleeping difficulties, report illnesses, and deteriorate in health after losing a spouse. An important public policy implication is that pet ownership probably reduces national health expenditure. Even brief exposure to unfamiliar dogs, or those that one does not own, has been shown to reap important physical benefits to humans. Contact with an unfamiliar dog provides cardiovascular benefits to young adults and children and drops cranial pressure of coma patients.

Animals also can enhance human psychological well-being. Pet ownership has been linked to the reduced incidence of a number of emotional and mental disorders, including depression, stress, and grief. For example, among single people, dog companions are a welcome relief from loneliness, while among childless couples, they are love objects on which to lavish parenting urges. Dog ownership also provides a buffer

against stress. For AIDS patients, dog companionship reduces depression, while for children, dogs make it easier for them to cope during stressful times. In the latter case, as noted in Gail Melson's work on children and animals (2001), studies have found that 75 percent of children between the ages of 10 and 14 claimed that they turned to their pet when feeling upset, and many of these children said that, at these times, they preferred the company of their pet to that of other children. Even brief encounters with unfamiliar dogs seem to have mental health benefits. In laboratory experiments, such encounters make children feel safe and create a sense of intimacy (Beck and Katcher 1983), while among nursing home residents, these encounters appear to sometimes improve socialization, reality orientation, engagement, affect and mood, anxiety level, attention span, humor, acceptance, relaxation, and ease of conversation (Perelle and Granville 1993).

There is also mounting evidence that animals may benefit communities (Wood *et al.* 2007). Pets can facilitate social approach, contact, and interaction. Dog walkers, for instance, bump into people and their dogs trigger conversation among strangers and casual acquaintances. Pets also encourage reciprocity between neighbors; feeding or taking care of pets when owners are away is returned with favors and a sense of goodwill and trust. Pet owners also are more likely than nonowners to be civically engaged, concerned, and active in their local community. And pet ownership makes for feelings of safety among neighbors because they see people outside walking their dogs instead of seeing empty streets and parks. Clearly, pet keeping contributes to community health.

However, everyday pet ownership is not the only way that animals can heal. Animals have been used in more deliberate and therapeutic ways. The modern therapeutic use of animal interactions is usually traced to eighteenth-century philanthropic groups in Europe that advocated the use of animals in mental institutions. However, more widespread use of animal-assisted interventions (AAIs) did not occur until the 1960s following the publication of a book of case studies and anecdotes by Boris Levinson (1969) about the benefits of using dogs in counseling sessions.

Levinson's work also encouraged the application of AAIs to combat a variety of mental health and community problems, such as reducing aggressive and violent behavior. Antiviolence interventions can range from obedience training of dogs to care and feeding of horses. They can be highly structured interactions, referred to as animal-assisted therapy (AAT), in which clients carry out set tasks toward designated animals while being closely monitored by mental health workers; or they can be unstructured interactions, referred to as animal-assisted activities (AAA), in which clients choose how and when they will play with or nurture various animals without adult supervision or with the supervision of non-clinicians. It is believed that these interventions can instill positive attitudes and behaviors, such as empathy and responsibility, in "at-risk" or incarcerated children, adolescents, and young adults by providing them a safe and nonthreatening environment to work through their troubled past. Those receiving AAIs, in theory, are not only provided the added comfort of an animal while working through the therapeutic process necessary to deal with their issues, but are given the opportunity to unlearn the cycle of violence to which they have been exposed.

Despite the unequivocally positive media attention they usually get, AAIs can only be described as a promising tool to combat violence (Kruger, Trachtenberg, and Serpell 2004). While most practitioners who provide these interventions are convinced that they "work," much of their supportive evidence is anecdotal. Few empirical studies have evaluated the extent to which AAIs can positively shape the behavior of problem children and youth. When studied, researchers claim that AAIs can teach knowledge about animals to participating youth, reduce aggression and recidivism, curb anxiety and depression, improve vocational skills, and enhance social skills, such as empathy, decision making, patience, task concentration, and interpersonal communication. However, these results must be cautiously approached because they come from poorly designed studies that lack features such as control groups or adequate samples.

Even if we accept that everyday pets or therapeutic animal interventions can heal many human

woes—running from ill health to antisocial behavior— it is still unclear how or why they do this. Understanding what it is about AAIs that make them therapeutic and facilitate health benefits could have important policy implications. For example, if it is discovered that certain mechanisms are more effective for certain types of problems or subjects than are other mechanisms, then programs can tailor the implementation of AAIs to best achieve their therapeutic goals.

Several mechanisms have been theorized to explain the positive effects of animals on people—although not all can be designed into AAIs or enhanced by program directors. Some scholars believe that there is a biological reason why animals benefit us. Dogs, for example, need walking and such exercise may contribute to physical health. A different biological explanation—the biophilia hypothesis (Kellert and Wilson 1993)—argues that humans have an innate drive or need to be in the presence of animals and nature; denying this connection may be bad for physical and mental health. While we should be cautious against overidealizing people's natural affinity for animals, a number of studies suggest that their positive effects on people have at least some biological basis. For example, researchers report that infants follow strange animals with their eyes and smile at them or try to touch them and that young children nearly all want pets or animals in their lives, express love for them by age 3, express an especially strong solidarity with dogs, watch them with rapt attention despite distractions or demands, and if denied such companionship or contact, will seek it out by sharing other people's pets.

Others believe that psychological mechanisms explain AAIs' positive affects. Pet ownership, for example, may mitigate isolation and lack of social support, both thought to be risk factors for cardiovascular disease. Pets also may have a positive effect on owners because they can provide a nonjudgmental "audience" that, unlike most parents or even friends, offers people a confidant or partner with whom they feel safe. Further positive effects may occur because pets represent safety, comfort, love, and stability, thereby providing owners emotional reassurance and support when facing stress. For example, very young children may spontaneously turn to their pets when they feel sad or afraid.

Other researchers think that the underlying mechanism is sociological, suggesting that there is something about the distinct kind of relationship that emerges between people and animals that accounts for its therapeutic benefit. Recent evidence suggests that relationships between people and animals are very complex, and not all may confer health benefits (Franklin *et al.* 2007). For example, one study found that people who felt close to their dogs made fewer physician visits and took less medication than those people who did not feel close to their dogs. Such findings suggest that the critical health benefit may not be from ownership per se, but from the relationship's closeness that evolves between people and their animals.

To examine how close relationships develop and why they have therapeutic benefits, researchers will need to go beyond existing, but deficient, explanations for human-animal relationships. According to Franklin and his coauthors (2007), substitutive explanations claim that companion animals fill in for missing relationships with significant others, such as friends and family; in other words, animals are replacements for people's support, solidarity, and loyalty, but do not in themselves bring anything unique to the relationship. Anthropomorphic explanations argue that humans project meanings, emotions, and thoughts onto companion animals and assume reciprocal perspectives, concluding in the animal's love for the human. But this is an asymmetrical exchange that denies the animal's communicative competence and agency. To understand why animals can sometimes facilitate human health, we need to capture the relationship itself that emerges, dialectically, between humans and animals and to entertain that this relationship can be hybridic or fused in ways not currently understood.

The selection by Deborah Wells reviews evidence for the many ways that dogs contribute to human health. When it comes to physical health, dog ownership seems to reduce the frequency of minor physical problems, like colds or headaches, as well as prevent more serious problems, like coronary heart disease. Dogs also help people recover from serious medical ailments, like heart attacks; they may even alert people about the onset of serious diseases like cancer, epilepsy, or diabetes. In terms of mental health benefits, dogs can reduce stress and depression from events like divorce or bereavement, and serve as social lubricants by facilitating interaction with other people. Dogs are now used for therapeutic benefit in private therapy, nursing homes, hospitals, programs for at-risk children, and prisons. Despite methodological problems with research on the therapeutic value of animals, and the risk of disease or injury from dogs, Wells concludes that dogs, in particular, can make a significant contribution to human well-being.

Despite the potential for animals to improve the physical, mental, and community lives of humans, researchers have not explored why such contact may be good for us. Gennifer Furst explores this question in the second selection. Taking a sociological approach, she argues that AAIs can transform people, not through the acquisition of individual cognitive skills, such as empathy, but through the experience of new relationships, both with animals and other people. To examine the transformative role played by human-animal relationships, Furst studied two animal programs in prisons where inmates socialized and trained dogs for future work or home placement. Prisoners assigned human-like features to their dogs, seeing them as thinking, intelligent individuals who were emotionally giving and who played social roles in their lives. These attributions, whether empirically true or not, served as the fodder for relationships to emerge and be experienced between the prisoners and their dogs. Importantly, these new relationships led to comments from other people that indicated a changed and positive perception of the prisoners as worthy and reformed as well as changed self-perceptions by prisoners who redefined themselves more positively because of these animal relationships. Armed with this new identity, it is possible that these prisoners would be buffered from a future of criminal activity.

The final selection, by Douglas Robins and his co-researchers, suggests how pets can benefit the community. Based on participant observation with dog owners who gathered twice daily in a city park, Robins—with his dog—found that pets facilitate interaction and relationships among previously unacquainted people. As a new dog walker, Robins was solicited by regulars to initially engage in "small talk" about dogs. Over time, more familiarity led to invitations for him to unleash his dog. Ultimately, Robins was made to feel like one of the regulars—sharing interests and activities in a spot the dog walkers claimed in the park as their territory. Of course, this study is at the shallower end of the continuum of interaction and social lubrication—dog walking prompted greetings among strangers and encouraged the formation of casual friendships and social networks. There may be more far-reaching community benefits of animal ownership than those reported in this study. While casual acquaintances formed through pets do not always lead to meaningful social networks and support, on balance, it seems likely that pets also influence our perception and experience of neighborhood and community in complex and meaningful ways by prompting reciprocity, trust, and civic engagement.

References

Beck, A., and A. Katcher. 1983. *New Perspectives on Our Lives with Companion Animals*. Philadelphia: University of Pennsylvania Press.

Franklin, A., Emmison, M., Haraway, D., and M. Travers. 2007. "Investigating the Therapeutic Benefits of Companion Animals." *Qualitative Sociology Review* 3:42–58.

Kellert, S., and E. Wilson. 1993. *The Biophilia Hypothesis*. Washington, DC: Island Press.

Kruger, K., Trachtenberg, S., and J. Serpell. 2004. *Can Animals Help Humans Heal? Animal-Assisted Interventions in Adolescent Mental Health*. Philadelphia: Center for the Interaction of Animals and Society, University of Pennsylvania School of Veterinary Medicine.

Levinson, B. 1969. *Pet-Oriented Child Psychotherapy*. Springfield, IL: Charles C. Thomas.

Melson, G. 2001. *Why the Wild Things Are: Animals in the Lives of Children*. Cambridge: Harvard University Press.

Perelle, I., and D. Granville. 1993. "Assessment of the Effectiveness of a Pet-Facilitated Therapy Program in a Nursing Home Setting." *Society & Animals* 1:91–100.

Wilson, C., and D. Turner (eds.). 1998. *Companion Animals in Human Health*. Thousand Oaks, CA: Sage.

Wood, L., Giles-Corti, B., Bulsara, M., and D. Bosch. 2007. "More than a Furry Companion: The Ripple Effect of Companion Animals on Neighborhood Interactions and Sense of Community." *Society & Animals* 15:43–56.

Deborah L. Wells

Domestic Dogs and Human Health

Recent years have witnessed a surge of interest in the relationship between companion animals and human health. While a wide variety of species (e.g., cats, rabbits, birds) have been shown to offer therapeutic value to humans, the domestic dog has been employed considerably more in experimental and applied settings than any other animal. Despite this, most articles in this area have focused on the relationship between human health and pets as a generic group, rather than concentrating specifically on the dog alone.

This article provides an overview of research that has explored the relationship between the domestic dog and human well-being. The article examines the value of dogs for both physical and psychological human health, focusing on new advancements in the area, including, for example, the role of dogs as early warning systems for human disease and as therapists for people in institutions such as prisons.

Dogs and Physical Health

The notion that "pets are good for us" is by no means a new one, but it is only relatively recently that any scientific attention has been devoted to the relationship between companion animals and physical well-being in humans. While not without its methodological weaknesses or criticisms, this research has shown that the domestic dog may be able to *prevent* us becoming ill, *facilitate* our recovery from ill health, and *predict* certain types of underlying ailment.

Dogs as Preventers of Ill Health

A small number of studies have explored the relationship between pet ownership and general

physical well-being in a bid to determine whether companion animals can prevent ill health. This work tends to suggest that pet owners, as a group, are a healthier cohort of individuals than are nonowners. Dogs may be particularly valuable as preventers of ill health. Serpell (1991), for example, followed up dog and cat owners for 10 months following the acquisition of their pet from an animal rescue shelter. Significant reductions in the frequency of minor physical ailments (e.g., headaches, colds, hay fever, dizziness) were noted for both types of pet owner 1 month following their animals' acquisition. Dog owners maintained this decrease in health problems 10 months later; cat owners, by contrast, did not.

While Serpell explored relatively minor physical ailments, other researchers suggest that dogs may be able to prevent more serious medical problems, such as coronary heart disease. For instance, Anderson and colleagues (1992) interviewed 5,741 people attending a screening clinic for coronary heart disease in Melbourne and discovered that the risk factors for this disease were significantly lower for dog (and other pet) owners than those who did not own a companion animal, particularly for males. More recently, Dembicki and Anderson (1996) found lower levels of serum triglycerides (high levels of which are associated with increased risk for heart attacks) in senior citizens who owned a dog or other type of pet.

Dogs as Facilitators to Recovery from Ill Health

Not only may dogs prevent us from becoming ill, they may also facilitate our recovery from certain types of ailment. Most of the research in this area has explored the ability of dogs to facilitate recovery from relatively serious physical problems, specifically coronary heart disease. Interest in this area stemmed from work by Erika Friedmann and colleagues (1980), who reported that dog (and other pet) owners were significantly more likely to still be alive 1 year after a heart attack than nonowners. While this work has been criticized for its statistical methods and lack of control for other potential risk factors, for example social support, personality type, and socioeconomic status (see Bergler, 1988), it remains one of the most widely cited studies in the field.

More recently, Friedmann and Thomas (1995) replicated their earlier work and extended it to a larger number of participants with improved measures of cardiovascular physiology and psychosocial status. The study revealed that different species may hold different health advantages, with dogs serving as stronger facilitators to recovery from ill health than cats. Dog owners were roughly 8.6 times more likely to still be alive 1 year after a heart attack than those who did not own a dog. Cat ownership, by contrast, was not only unrelated to survival rate, but cat owners were actually more likely to have died in the year following their heart attack than were nonowners.

The question remains as to how dogs might be able to protect their owners from ill health or, for that matter, facilitate recovery from something as serious as myocardial infarction. A number of mechanisms may be at play. Dogs may, for example, be able to promote their owners' psychological health (see later), a factor that can contribute significantly to physiological well-being. Dogs may also be able to shield their owners from stress, one of the major risk factors associated with ill health. The action of stroking and/or talking to a dog, for example, has repeatedly been shown to cause transient decreases in human blood pressure and heart rate. Moreover, the mere presence of a dog can help to lower autonomic responses to stressful situations.

It is also possible that dogs may contribute indirectly to long-standing physical health. This species, unlike other companion animals, needs to be exercised. The relationship between physical fitness and physiological well-being is well established. The increased physical activity that typically accompanies the ownership of a dog (see Serpell, 1991) may thus explain, to some degree, the greater health advantages experienced by the owners of such pets.

Obviously, the mechanisms underlying the ability of dogs to prevent, and facilitate recovery from ill health are complex, and much further research is needed before firm conclusions can be drawn. The possibility that there is a noncausal association (i.e., no correlation) between dogs and human health must also be acknowledged at this point in time (McNicholas and Collis, 1998).

Dogs as Predictors of Ill Health

Recently, researchers have become interested in exploring whether dogs might be able to serve as early warning systems for certain types of physical ailment in humans, for example cancer, epilepsy, and diabetes.

Cancer Detection In 1989, Williams and Pembroke reported a case in the *Lancet* of a Border Collie/Doberman Pinscher crossbreed sniffing repeatedly at a mole on its owner's leg; the lesion later turned out to be malignant. Similar anecdotal reports have since appeared in newspapers (Dobson, 2003) and scientific journals (Church and Williams, 2001).

That some dogs can detect cancerous masses is perhaps not surprising given their acute sense of smell. Tumors typically produce odorous compounds that are released into the air through routes including breath and sweat. The dog, with its olfactory acuity, may be able to detect these compounds, even in minute quantities.

While some dogs may have an innate ability to detect the odor of cancerous tumors, it appears that many dogs can be trained to perform this feat. In the first study of its kind, Willis and colleagues (2004) successfully trained six dogs of mixed breed to identify people with bladder cancer using a discrimination task. As a group, the dogs correctly identified urine samples from patients with bladder cancer on 22 out of 54 occasions—mean success rate of 41 percent. The authors hope that modifications to their training regime will result in improvements in the success rate of the dogs in their future studies.

Seizure Detection Evidence now suggests that certain dogs may be able to sense spontaneously oncoming epileptic seizures in humans. Until recently, the notion that dogs could detect human seizures was based on little other than anecdotal report, and attempts to assess the validity of claims that dogs have innate seizure-alerting powers were relatively inconclusive (Edney, 1991, 1993). However, recent work has shown that some dogs can indeed detect oncoming seizures, and moreover, that many animals can be successfully trained to monitor their human owners for outward signs of an imminent seizure and to react in an appropriate manner (e.g., barking or pawing) if a seizure is predicted (Strong and Brown, 2000; Strong et al., 2002).

The mechanisms underlying the ability of dogs to anticipate seizures in humans is still unknown and warrants investigation. However, observations of dogs by trainers and surveys of alert dog owners suggest that seizure alerting is primarily based on visual cues such as facial expressions, postures, and general behavior as opposed to, for example, olfactory or auditory cues (Kirton et al., 2004). That said, it is possible that other physiological cues such as muscle tension, respiratory signs, and perspiration might also be monitored by dogs using visual, auditory, or olfactory senses.

While seizure-detection dogs hold enormous potential for those with epilepsy, the danger of using untrained animals as alert systems has been highlighted (Strong and Brown, 2000). Moreover, it has been suggested that while every dog may be able to detect seizures, not all animals respond appropriately to oncoming seizures, and hence careful selection and training is important (Dalziel et al., 2003).

Hypoglycemia Detection There is now some evidence to suggest that dogs may be able to detect hypoglycemia, a common and hazardous complication of diabetes. Lim and associates (1992), for example, indicated that over one-third of dogs living with diabetic owners have been reported to show changes in their behavior during their owners' hypoglycemic episodes. Dogs may even be able to warn owners of impending hypoglycemia before symptoms are noticed by those whose awareness of the condition is mostly intact (Chen et al., 2000).

While it is unclear exactly how dogs may be able to detect hypoglycemia, odor cues have been proposed as the most plausible explanation (Chen et al., 2000). One dog, for example, was reported to exhibit hypoglycemia-alert behavior when its owner was asleep and presumably emitting no cues other than olfactory ones. Increases in sweating have been repeatedly noted in hypoglycemic individuals (McAulay, Deary, and Frier, 2001); it is likely that dogs can detect these changes in the chemical composition of their owners' sweat using their acute sense of smell. Research is now required to determine whether dogs can be trained to alert their owners to the onset of hypoglycemia in the same way that they can be trained to anticipate oncoming seizures or sniff out cancer.

Dogs and Psychological Health

Dogs may not only be able to facilitate certain aspects of physiological health in humans, they may also contribute to the psychological well-being of people. Over the years, research has shown that animals, and in particular dogs, can ameliorate the effects of potentially stressful life events (e.g., bereavement, divorce), reduce levels of anxiety, loneliness and depression (Folse et al., 1994), and enhance feelings of autonomy, competence, and self-esteem (Beck and Katcher, 1983). Many of these psychological benefits may arise directly from the companionship that dogs offer people. Their greeting rituals, naturally affectionate disposition, loyalty, and widely perceived ability to love unconditionally may all serve to promote feelings of self-worth and self-esteem.

Dogs may also help to promote psychological well-being indirectly, through the facilitation of social interactions between people. Domestic dogs have long been noted for their socializing role. For example, Messent (1983), McNicholas and Collis (2000), and, more recently, Wells (2004) have all shown that walking with a dog results in a significantly higher number of chance conversations with complete strangers than walking alone. Younger dogs and those with a reputed good temperament tend to act as stronger social lubricants than older animals or those that have received more negative public attention (Wells, 2004). The social lubrication effect may be particularly apparent with, and useful for, disabled individuals with service animals (see later).

Dogs as Therapists

Recognition of the fact that dogs can bolster psychological well-being in humans has resulted in their wide-spread use as therapists. In the 1960s, Boris Levinson, an American child psychologist, noted that his patients developed a rapport with his dog, Jingles, and were more inclined to respond positively to therapy in his presence. Levinson postulated that the dog served as a social catalyst, facilitating a safe channel for the discussion of subconscious worries and fears (Levinson, 1962, 1969). Levinson's theories have been supported by a wealth of subsequent studies exploring the role of dogs as pet-facilitated therapists in hospitals, nursing homes, and other settings.

Dogs in Hospitals and Nursing Homes   Pet-assisted therapy has been employed for numerous years in hospitals and residential nursing homes. Corson and others were among the first to assess the utility of dogs in these types of settings. In their original study, 47 withdrawn and uncommunicative patients in a psychiatric unit were allowed to interact with self-chosen dogs on a daily basis. Five of the patients were noted to have im-

proved markedly by the end of the study, and at least some psychological improvement was seen in all of the participants. While this study was heavily reliant on individual case histories and lacked rigorous control, more scientifically robust experiments have subsequently revealed similar findings to these earlier results. Salmon and Salmon (1982), for instance, found that the presence of a residential dog in a nursing home resulted in "happier," more "alert," and more "responsive" patients, as assessed by staff reports. More recently, Bernstein and associates (2000) discovered that animal assisted therapy in the form of visits from rescue-sheltered dogs (and cats) facilitated social interactions (particularly long conversations) between residents of nursing homes. Numerous other authors have reported similar patterns of positive results in settings such as residential homes and hospital wards (e.g., McCabe *et al.,* 2002; Moody, King, and O'Rourke, 2002).

While none of the above studies are without their methodological problems, as a whole they tend to suggest that the presence of a dog in an institutional setting can help to facilitate many of the psychological benefits discussed earlier (e.g., increased self-esteem), break the vicious cycles of loneliness that many people experience, and encourage social interactions and communication between patients and staff.

Pet-facilitated therapy programs involving dogs are now relatively commonplace across the UK, Europe, and North America.

Dogs and the Disabled   Dogs have been widely employed as assistants for the disabled for numerous years. Perhaps the best-known type of assistance dog is the Guide Dog for the Blind. First established in 1931, the British Guide Dog Association has managed to help over 21,000 blind and partially sighted people through the provision of a carefully matched and trained assistance animal. More recently, dogs have been trained, both in the UK and farther afield, to provide assistance to people with other types of disability including, for example, hearing difficulties (e.g., Hearing

Dogs for Deaf People), mobility problems (e.g., Dogs for the Disabled) and epilepsy (e.g., Support Dogs, see earlier).

In addition to achieving the goal for which they were purposely trained (i.e., to enhance the physical capabilities of their owners), assistance dogs have been shown to contribute significantly to the psychological well-being of their owners. Such animals can dramatically decrease the feelings of isolation that many with physical disabilities are prone to, and help to improve social confidence, self-esteem, independence, and social identity (Allen and Blascovich, 1996; Sanders, 2000).

Assistance dogs can also act as strong social catalysts, helping to normalize relationships with other people. Hart and colleagues (1987), for example, reported that wheelchair users received a median of eight friendly approaches from unfamiliar adults per shopping trip when they were accompanied by their service dog, but typically only one friendly approach if the animal was not present. Similar findings have been reported by others (e.g., Eddy et al., 1998).

It must be noted that assistance dogs are not without their complications. Owners of such animals have reported a variety of drawbacks including unwanted interference from members of the public, time and financial pressures, and travel complications (Hart et al., 1995). The death of an assistance animal, or termination of an assistance partnership, can also present problems, particularly given the close bond of attachment that can develop between many owners and their service animals (Nicholson, Kempwheeler, and Griffiths, 1995). Overattachments can also present problems for the animals themselves. Scott and Beifelt (1976), for example, noted signs symptomatic of separation anxiety (e.g., vocalization and destructiveness) in at least 21 percent of guide dogs separated from their owners. More recently, Davis and associates (2004) reported behavior problems as the greatest burden to assistance dog placement in the pediatric population. Concerns regarding the physical welfare of assistance dogs have also been voiced (Serpell, Coppinger, and Fine, 2000). Raising owner awareness and expec-

tations prior to animal placement, in addition to postplacement check-ups, may be the most useful strategies for overcoming these types of problems.

Dogs in Prisons   Recently, institutions such as prisons have started to employ animals, including dogs, in a therapeutic capacity. Similar to those residing in other institutions, prison inmates can suffer from loneliness, denied responsibility, and low self-worth. A wide variety of animal-based therapy schemes have thus been introduced to penal institutions, particularly in the United States, in a bid to enhance psychological welfare and rehabilitate previous offenders. Participants are required to look after the animal in their care, and in many cases train it for a specific purpose, for example, as an assistance dog for the elderly or physically disabled (e.g., Hines, 1983).

Research to explore the utility of dogs employed in this type of context is relatively limited, although that conducted has yielded largely positive results. Bustad (1990), for example, established a dog training program at a correctional center for women and reported increased levels of self-esteem in the participating inmates. Improvements in the behavior of incarcerated, violent male juveniles, and their respect for authority, social interaction, and leadership have also been noted following the introduction of abandoned and abused dogs with the program Project Pooch (Merriam-Arduini, 2000).

People in the UK have been much slower to consider the introduction of dogs (or other animals) to prisons than in the United States, although the positive results arising from the research in this area suggest that it is only a matter of time before similar programs are commonplace in British penal institutions.

Conclusions

This paper has provided an overview of research that has explored the relationship between the domestic dog and human health. Taken together, the studies suggest that dogs can have prophylactic and therapeutic value for people. It must be borne in mind that not all of the studies carried out in this area have been methodically robust. The lack of longitudinal designs and standardized measures, which assess diverse areas of functioning, makes it difficult to draw finite conclusions. It must also be remembered that dogs can pose an enormous risk to human health, spreading zoonoses, causing allergies, bites and, in extreme circumstances, even death. That said, the risks that dogs pose to human well-being can be reduced to an acceptable minimum through proper selection, training, veterinary care, and control. The dog should not be regarded as a panacea for ill health in humans. Nonetheless, the findings from this overview suggest that this particular companion animal can contribute to a significant degree to our well-being and quality of life.

References

Allen, K., and J. Blascovich. (1996). The value of service dogs for people with severe ambulatory disabilities—A randomized controlled trial. *Journal of the American Veterinary Medical Association*, 275, 1001–1006.

Anderson, W. P., Reid, C. M., and G. L. Jennings. (1992). Pet ownership and risk factors for cardiovascular disease. *Medical Journal of Australia*, 157, 298–301.

Beck, A., and A. Katcher. (1983). *Between pets and people: The importance of animal companionship*. New York: G. P. Putnam.

Bergler, R. (1988). *Man and dog: The psychology of a relationship*. Oxford: Blackwell Scientific.

Bernstein, P. L., Friedmann, E., and A. Malaspina. (2000). Animal-assisted therapy enhances resident social interaction and initiation in long-term care facilities. *Anthrozoös*, 13, 213–223.

Bustad, L. K. (1990). Prison programs involving animals. In L. K. Bustad (Ed.), *Compassion, our last great hope* (pp. 72–73). Renton, WA: Delta Society.

Chen, M., Daly, M., Natt, S., and G. Williams. (2000). Non-invasive detection of hypoglycaemia using a novel, fully biocompatible and patient friendly alarm system. *British Medical Journal*, 321, 1565–1566.

Church, J., and H. Williams. (2001). Another sniffer dog for the clinic? *Lancet, 358*, 930.

Corson, S. A., and E. O'Leary Corson. (1980). Pet animals as nonverbal communication mediators in psychotherapy in institutional settings. In S. A. Corson and E. O'Leary Corson (Eds.), *Ethology and nonverbal communication in mental health* (pp. 83–110). Oxford: Pergamon Press.

Dalziel, D. J., Uthman, B. M., McGorray, S. P., and R. L. Reep. (2003). Seizure-alert dogs: A review and preliminary study. *Seizure, 12*, 115–120.

Davis, B. W., Nattrass, K., O'Brien, S., Patronek, G., and M. MacCollin. (2004). Assistance dog placement in the pediatric population. Benefits, risks, and recommendations for future application. *Anthrozoös, 17*, 130–145.

Dembicki, D., and J. Anderson. (1996). Pet ownership may be a factor in improved health of the elderly. *Journal of Nutrition for the Elderly, 15*, 15–31.

Dobson, R. (2003, April 27). Dogs can sniff out first signs of men's cancer. *Sunday Times*.

Eddy, J., Hart, L. A., and R. P. Boltz. (1988). The effects of service dogs on social acknowledgements of people in wheelchairs. *Journal of Psychology, 122*, 39–45.

Edney, A. T. B. (1991). Dogs as predictors of human epilepsy. *Veterinary Record, 129*, 251.

Edney, A. T. B. (1993). Companion animal topics: Dogs and human epilepsy. *Veterinary Record, 132*, 337–338.

Folse, E. B., Minder, C. C., Aycock, M. J., and R. T. Santana. (1994). Animal-assisted therapy and depression in adult college students. *Anthrozoös, 7*, 188–194.

Friedmann, E., Katcher, A. H., Lynch, J. J., and S. A. Thomas. (1980). Animal companions and one year survival of patients after discharge from a coronary care unit. *Public Health Reports, 95*, 307–312.

Friedmann, E., and S. A. Thomas. (1995). Pet ownership, social support, and one year survival after acute myocardial infarction in the cardiac arrhythmia suppression trial (CAST). *American Journal of Cardiology. 76*, 1213–1217.

Hart, L. A., Hart, B. L., and B. Bergin. (1987). Socializing effects of service dogs for people with disabilities. *Anthrozoös, 1*, 41–44.

Hart, L. A., Zasloff, R. L., and A. M. Benfatto. (1995). The pleasures and problems of hearing dog ownership. *Psychological Reports, 77,* 969–970.

Hines, L. M. (1983). Pets in prison: A new partnership. *California Veterinarian, 5,* 7–11.

Kirton, A., Wirrell, E., Zhang, J., and L. Hamiwka. (2004). Seizure-alerting and -response behaviors in dogs living with epileptic children. *Neurology, 62,* 2303–2305.

Levinson, B. M. (1962). The dog as co-therapist. *Mental Hygiene, 46,* 59–65.

Levinson, B. M. (1969). *Pet-oriented child psychotherapy.* Springfield, IL: Charles C. Thomas.

Lim, K., Wilcox, A., Fisher M., and C. I. Burns-Cox. (1992). Type 1 diabetics and their pets. *Diabetic Medicine, 9* (Suppl. 2), S3–S4.

McAulay, V., Deary, I. J., and B. M. Frier. (2001). Symptoms of hypoglycaemia in people with diabetes. *Diabetic Medicine, 18,* 690–705.

McCabe, B. W., Baun, M. M., Speich, D., and S. Agrawal. (2002). Resident dog in the Alzheimer's special care unit. *Western Journal of Nursing Research, 24,* 684–696.

McNicholas, J., and G. M. Collis. (1998). Could Type A (coronary-prone) personality explain the association between pet ownership and health? In C. C. Wilson and D. C. Turner (Eds.), *Companion animals in human health* (pp. 173–186). Thousand Oaks, CA: Sage.

McNicholas, J., and G. M. Collis. (2000). Dogs as catalysts for social interactions. Robustness of the effect. *British Journal of Psychology, 91,* 61–70.

Merriam-Arduini, S. (2000). *Evaluation of an experimental program designed to have a positive effect on adjudicated violent, incarcerated male juveniles age 12–25 in the state of Oregon.* Unpublished doctoral dissertation, Pepperdine University.

Messent, P. R. (1983). Social facilitation of contact with other people by pet dogs. In A. H. Katcher and A. M. Beck (Eds.), *New perspectives in our lives with companion animals* (pp. 37–46). Philadelphia: University of Philadelphia Press.

Moody, W. J., King, R., and S. O'Rourke. (2002). Attitudes of pediatric medical ward staff to a dog visitation programme. *Journal of Clinical Nursing, 11,* 537–544.

Nicholson, J., Kempwheeler, S., and D. Griffiths. (1995). Distress arising from the end of a guide dog partnership. *Anthrozoös, 8,* 100–110.

Salmon, P. W., and I. M. Salmon. (1982). *A dog in residence: A companion animal study undertaken at the Caulfield geriatric hospital.* Joint Advisory Committee on Pets in Society (JACOPIS), Melbourne, Australia.

Sanders, C. R. (2000). The impact of guide dogs on the identity of people with visual impairments. *Anthrozoös, 13,* 131–139.

Scott, J. P., and S. Beifelt. (1976). Analysis of the puppy testing program. In C. J. Pfaffenberger, J. P. Scott, J. L. Fuller, B. E. Ginsburg, and S. W. Beifelt (Eds.), *Guide dogs for the blind: Their selection, development and training* (pp. 39–75). New York: Elsevier.

Serpell, J. A. (1991). Beneficial effects of pet ownership on some aspects of human health and behaviour. *Journal of the Royal Society of Medicine, 84,* 717–720.

Serpell, J. A., Coppinger, R. and A. H. Fine. (2000). The welfare of assistance and therapy animals: An ethical comment. In A. Fine (Ed.), *Handbook of animal-assisted therapy* (pp. 415–431). London: Academic Press.

Strong, V., and S. W. Brown. (2000). Should people with epilepsy have untrained dogs as pets? *Seizure, 9,* 427–430.

Strong V., Brown, S., Huyton, M., and H. Coyle. (2002). Effect of trained seizure alert dogs on frequency of tonic-clonic seizures. *Seizure, 11,* 402–405.

Wells, D. L. (2004). The facilitation of social interactions by domestic dogs. *Anthrozoös, 17,* 340–352.

Williams, H., and A. Pembroke. (1989). Sniffer dogs in the melanoma clinic? *Lancet, 1,* 734.

Willis, C. M., Church, S. M., Guest, C. M., Cook, W. A., McCarthy, N., *et al.* (2004). Olfactory detection of human bladder by dogs: Proof of principle study. *British Medical Journal, 329,* 712–716.

Gennifer Furst

How Prison-Based Animal Programs Change Prisoner Participants

Animal-assisted activities (AAA) and animal-assisted therapy (AAT) have been incorporated into a growing range of programs (Arluke, 2008). People with various physical and emotional needs interact with (e.g., train, groom, pet) an assortment of animals (e.g., dogs, horses, llamas) in many different settings (e.g., prisons, nursing homes, schools). While there is mounting evidence of the effectiveness of AAA and AAT (see Becker, 2002; Fine, 2000; Wilson and Turner, 1998), "studies so far have only provided solid statistical proof of the benefit, not an explanation for it" (Franklin *et al.*, 2007, p. 44). Franklin and his coauthors suggest that research consider the distinct contributions of the nonhuman animal to the relationship formed with the person.

Previous studies have found that people view their pets as individual beings (Alger and Alger, 1997, 2003; Sanders, 1993, 2003). The social identity the animal takes on is then able to influence the humans' self-identity (Sanders, 1993). A changed self-identity, where a person is redefined, both by self and others as a prosocial transformed individual, has been found to have implications for criminal desistance (Maruna, 2001). It may be that the unique, largely nonverbal nature of the human-animal interaction is particularly suited to affect prison inmates' self-concepts.

In order to explore why animal interventions are apparently so successful, this article considers how one type of intervention—the prison-based animal program—affects participants. Evidence of the expanding role of animals in society can be found inside correctional facilities across the globe. Animals are increasingly being incorporated into several different types of prison programming. Prison-based animal programs (PAPs) have primarily been implemented by departments of correction in order to provide a service to the external community, such as having inmates train and/or care for animals for adoption or service use in the community (Furst, 2006).

Although the programs are viewed as successful from a service perspective, the benefits to inmates have largely been ignored or considered an unintentional, secondary outcome of the program. Similarly, while PAPs are appealing on an intuitive level, and are consistently regarded as successful according to anecdotal information, researchers have failed to examine the underlying mechanisms that may account for their success.

This article argues that the development of relationships—between prisoners and their dogs, and prisoners and other humans—is at the core of such success. Research suggests that a new view or sense of oneself is necessary for successful transformation or desistance from crime. Successful desistance from criminal activity, or "making good" (Maruna, 2001), may be dependent on a changed self-identity. It has been argued that this new prosocial sense of self requires both social reaction and personal experience (Maruna *et al.*, 2004).

Prison-based animal programs may affect how a person labels him/herself and is labeled by

others. Inmates may engage in a process of assigning the animals with which they work a humanlike identity, similar to that of traditional pet
owners (Alger and Alger, 1997; Sanders, 1993).
Once established, this unique relationship may
then result in the prosocial relabeling of ex-
offenders. The animal is viewed by participants
in such a way as to influence their sense of self
and, at the same time, participants are viewed differently by both themselves and others because of
the relationship with the animal.

The present research describes how PAP
participants undergo self-transformation from
their relationships with the dogs. First examined
is the extent to which PAP participants attribute
a humanlike identity to the dogs, which in turn
is able to influence their self-concept. Based on
Bogdan and Taylor's (1989) research on humans and Sanders (1993) extension to human-
animal relationships, PAP participants are
found to assign four aspects of selfhood to program dogs by perceiving them as thinking intelligent beings, as individuals, as emotionally
giving, and as having a social role. Second examined is the extent to which these relations
with dogs affect a new self-identity as a result of
both personal experiences and feedback from
others. A process of relabeling appears to occur
whereby participants come to perceive themselves as noncriminal or rehabilitated, and others—both humans and the dogs—treat the
participants as such. Finally, the implications of
the findings for facilitating desistance from
crime are briefly outlined.

Interview data were collected from inmates
at two separate prisons who were volunteering in
their facility's PAP. The first program, in a maximum-security facility for females (housed in a
low-security area of the compound), pairs offenders with puppies who are socialized in preparation
for advanced training in explosives detection. At
the time of the interviews in spring 2005, there
were 13 dogs and 22 inmates participating, 15 as
primary handlers and 7 as backup handlers.
Among the 15 primary handlers interviewed, ages
ranged from 24 to 50 years old. Seven participants

identified themselves as white, five as black, and
one each as Hispanic, Native American, and bira-
cial. The average length of program participation
was 22.4 months and ranged from 6 to 60 months.

The second program, in a medium-security
facility for males aged 17 to 25 in the same northeastern state, pairs offenders with greyhounds
rescued from being destroyed after the end of a
racing career (usually 2–3 years) who are socialized for placement as pets in homes in the community. At the time of the interviews, there were
7 dogs and 18 inmates participating—7 primary
handlers, 7 backup handlers, and 4 trainees. Individual interviews with each of the 7 primary
handlers and a focus group with 14 participants
were conducted at the facility. Among the primary handlers, ages ranged from 21 to 33 years
old. Six participants identified themselves as Hispanic and one as black. The average length of
program participation was 18.1 months and
ranged from 9 to 36 months.

Prison-Based Animal Programs

Prison-based animal programs, while grounded
in well-developed knowledge regarding the therapeutic potential of human-animal interactions,
do not have the treatment of participants (inmates) as their primary goal. Prison-based animal
programs have been implemented by departments of correction largely to provide a service to
the community by having inmates care for and
train animals (Furst, 2006). The benefit to the
participants and the positive press the facility inevitably receives are considered collateral.

Early PAPs

While contemporary PAPs are typically viewed
by administrators as volunteer or work assign-
ments, the first program to introduce animals to
a maximum-security population had a more traditional, therapeutic approach. The program at
Lima State Hospital for the Criminally Insane
(currently Oakwood Forensic Center) in Ohio
was started after the unit director was impressed
with how the usually solitary and unresponsive

patients coordinated their efforts to hide and feed an injured wild bird one of them had found (Lee, 1987). As a result of this observation, additional small animals including fish and rabbits were introduced to the ward. After 1 year, the unit was compared with another at the facility without animals. While there was some concern for the safety of the animals, the findings indicated that patients in the unit with pets required "half as much medication, had drastically reduced incidents of violence and had no suicide attempts during the year-long comparison. The ward without pets had eight documented suicide attempts during the same year" (Lee, 1987, p. 232).

The first formal PAP was implemented by Sister Pauline Quinn in 1981 at the Washington Corrections Center for Women, a maximum-security prison in Tacoma, Washington (see Quinn, 2004). Through the People Pet Partnership program, inmates participated in 11 weeks of courses taught at Tacoma Community College. In addition to the classroom instruction, they received hands-on lessons with local shelter dogs in training, grooming, and job-seeking skills (Hines, 1997). Through the efforts of the program participants, a number of homeless dogs were made more adoptable and several were sent on for more advanced training working with people with disabilities. Administrators noted that they found some participants were more cooperative than previously, while others said the women learned self-control. Although some were initially apprehensive about the safety of the animals, the administrators reported that the inmates quickly become concerned for the animals' welfare (Hines, 1997).

At the same time at Lorton Prison in Virginia, Leo Bustad, a veterinarian, established a program built around a prison chapter of the national People-Animals-Love group (Arkow, 1998; Beck and Katcher, 1996; Graham, 2000; Hines, 1997). In this pet adoption program, inmates were paired with animals they could keep if transferred or released. In an evaluation conducted several years after it began, Moneymaker

and Strimple (1991) found that participants reported significant reductions in feelings of isolation and frustration. Participants had fewer disciplinary infractions and demonstrated "considerable change in their outlook toward others and their sense of self-worth, as well as their sense of achieving a better goal in life" (p. 148).

Contemporary PAPs

Prison-based animal programs are found in the United States, Canada, England, Scotland, Australia, and South Africa (Lai, 1998). In addition to using a wide variety of animals, these programs also encompass a range of designs as well, including but not limited to, having participants care for livestock or injured wildlife, care for and adopt out pets, or receive training and certification in animal grooming/handling/care.

Furst (2006) documented the trend in programming through a national survey of state departments of correction and found the programs exist in most states but most common are those having a community service design involving the socialization of animals that would otherwise be destroyed, including dogs and wild horses, which are then adopted out to the community. Also, most of the programs are relatively new, having being established after 2000 (Furst, 2006). While dogs are most common, animals used in PAPs include wild animals, farm animals, and other domestic animals such as cats. Open-ended responses regarding how the programs benefit participants overwhelmingly indicated the sense of responsibility instilled. Other commonly identified benefits of the programs included job skills, meaningful work, and positive impact on patience, anger management, and self-esteem.

There is currently a considerable demand for work and service dogs, particularly in the United States after September 11, 2001, as they are increasingly being used by law enforcement agencies. In service animal socialization programs, puppies or dogs are taught basic commands; the most successful animals go on to specialized training. The U.S. Veterans Administration is currently studying PAPs as a way to fulfill the growing need for assistance animals created by the rising number of veterans who are returning home with significant physical injuries (Strom, 2006). These sociopolitical conditions have created a market in which prison inmates, due to the availability of their time, make ideal candidates to conduct the intensive and time-consuming work required to prepare animals to go on to specialized training.

Selfhood in Others

Several contemporary theorists have described the process by which humans attribute identity to other humans, even when their interactions lack a verbal, shared language. Bogdan and Taylor (1989), for example, have studied how nondisabled people, in the course of interacting with severely disabled people, define the latter's humanness and define the other as a human with a unique self. According to Bogdan and Taylor (1989), "the nondisabled view the disabled people as full-fledged human beings. This stands in contrast to the dehumanizing perspectives often held by institutional staff and others in which people with severe disabilities are viewed as nonpersons or sub-human" (p. 138).

Bogdan and Taylor identified four aspects of the nondisabled person's perspective that enable the maintenance of a human identity for the severely disabled person. First, the nondisabled person attributes thinking to the disabled person. Despite usually significant physiological limitations, the disabled person is regarded as intelligent, even if unable to fully communicate thoughts. Second, the disabled person is viewed as an individual with a unique personality comprised of likes and dislikes, feelings and motives, a life history, and a physical appearance. Third, the nondisabled person regards the disabled person as reciprocating or contributing to the relationship. In addition to companionship and the opportunity to meet others in the community, the nondisabled person may derive a "sense of accomplishment in contributing to the disabled other's well-being and personal

growth" (Bogdan and Taylor, 1989, p. 144). Finally, the disabled person is given a social place and regarded as a "full and important member" and participates in the "rituals and routines of the social unit" (p. 145).

Sanders' (1993, 2000) research extends that of Bogdan and Taylor to human-animal relationships. He found that through "routine, intimate interactions with their dogs, caretakers come to regard their animals as unique individuals who are minded, empathetic, reciprocating, and well aware of basic rules and roles that govern the relationship" (1993, p. 207). According to Sanders, the same four features identified by Bogdan and Taylor are used by people to construct a subjective identity for their pets. Pet owners attributed thinking to the animals and regarded their animals as intelligent and having free will. Frequently, they cited "their dogs' play activities, and the adjustments they made while being trained. The dog's purposive modification of behavior was seen as indicating a basic ability to reason" (1993, p. 213). Pet owners also viewed their dogs as individuals with "unique personal tastes. Informants typically took considerable pleasure in talking about individual likes and dislikes in food, activities, playthings, and people" (pp. 215–216). In addition to the "subjective experiences" described above, pet owners reported that "they frequently understood their relationships with the animals as revolving around emotional issues. . . . One indication of the intensely positive quality of their relationship with their animals were the owners' perceptions that their dogs were attuned to their own emotions and responded in ways that were appropriate and indicated empathy" (p. 218). Given the value placed on the relationship, it should be no surprise that dog owners reported "they actively included their animals in the routine exchanges and the special ritual practices of the household" (p. 219). Sanders thus concluded that the preceding are "categories of evidence used by dog owners to include their animals inside the ostensibly rigid but actually rather flexible boundaries that divide minded humans from mindless others" (p. 221).

It should be noted that Alger and Alger (1997, 2003) extended Sanders' findings on dog owners to cat owners and found a similar process of viewing cats as minded actors.

Dog as Thinking, Intelligent Being

Unlike traditional pet ownership, the main purpose of the relationship in the PAPs is the training of the dogs. For the female participants, successful training meant the dogs would go on to specialized explosives training; for the male participants, the dogs would be adopted by families. The participants' discussions of their dogs reflected this focus. Many participants were enthusiastic about describing their dog's intelligence and special skills. Through their participation, the women have learned that the dogs have innate abilities; the dogs were bred specifically to excel at their training and are usually the offspring of previously successful working dogs. One female participant told how her dog progressed through the program more quickly than any other dog, which she attributed to his nature as a particularly gifted and intelligent creature, and denied she had any special ability as a trainer.

Participants believe that their dogs have free will and claim to control their own behavior in light of their animals' perceived independence. More than half of the female sample said they were less angry and more patient as a result of their participation. "I was angry," said one woman, "and this is slowing me down and has taught me to be calm. We go at the pace of the puppy." Three male respondents also reported increased impulse and/or emotional control. For example, according to one participant, "I think before I react. I'll think, 'Why is the dog acting that way?' and then I do something."

Dog as an Individual

Program animals are regarded as unique creatures by participants. All keep records of their dogs' individual progress. Women create a "Puppy Book" that follows the dog's development from a puppy and accompanies the dog upon leaving the facility. The book contains samples from the dogs' first nail clipping and grooming as well as the dogs' baby teeth and pictures of them dressed for various holidays (e.g., Christmas and Easter) and in paper birthday hats during celebrations. During a tour of the participants' dormitory where they live with the dogs, two participants proudly shared their Puppy Books with the researcher. One woman commented that the books are much like the baby book she kept as a new parent. In the program at the male facility, participants keep a written journal about their dogs that is given to the adopting family. Participants include information such as how the dog progressed with training, the dog's favorite toys and tricks, and any behavioral quirks, such as chewing certain objects, that the dog may still possess. In addition, during interviews at both facilities, participants consistently introduced the researcher to the dog after introducing themselves.

Dog as Emotionally Giving

There was agreement that the dogs provided emotional support to the participants. According to one female, "To come to a place with no hope or joy and get unconditional understanding is amazing." Another said, "He doesn't criticize me or talk back or want to pick a fight. No matter what I say, here is here for me." Another woman described her relationship with her dog as "better than any I'll have with a person." Approximately half of all respondents identified the companionship of the dog as the major benefit of participation.

Participants reported that their interactions with their dogs help alleviate their depression or improve their mood. As one woman emphatically stated, "These puppies make me happy." According to another participant, "I have my 'jail days' when I'm depressed and angry but I see that little face and the wagging tail and they're happy to see you and it just can't be a bad day." Another said the program has given her "happiness and a purpose to life." The ability of the dogs to fulfill participants' emotional needs was demonstrated by the woman who reported that she no longer gets "upset with my kids for not writing enough; I just talk to my best friend here [referring to the dog]."

The male program participants reported receiving similar emotional support from the dogs. One male participant reported, "I took Anger Management and Behavior Modification Therapy but they weren't as helpful as this program. I can show real emotion toward the dog. I have better sessions with the dog than I do with the doctor I see here in therapy. I'm more comfortable with the dog." Another male participant said, "I let my barrier down with the dogs because they're not gonna judge me." According to another male participant, "I will talk to him after a tough call with my daughter; it definitely helps with stress." And another said simply, "I talk to my dog—she is better than a person." Thus, participants from both programs indicated having emotional needs met through their interactions with their dogs.

Dog as Having a Social Role

Participants support the idea that the dogs they work with take on social roles in their lives. They recognized their dogs' ability to serve as social facilitators; participants told of increased communication with fellow participants, other inmates, and staff and administrators regarding their dogs. According to one female participant, other women "will ask about your dog when you wouldn't usually talk to them." Participants in both programs reported conversations about the dogs' health and training progress as common topics. Another female related that, when she was seen walking the prison grounds without her dog, who was recuperating in the cell after being spayed, "everyone was asking where she was. They were all worried about her, and if something bad had happened to her." This participant also said that others "all greet her before me when we're walking around grounds." Describing increased interaction with facility staff and administrators, one woman said, "We talk more about the dogs and they'll ask how they're doing. I talk to them about her health and stuff." In addition, the dogs increase communication between participants. Among the female participants, one woman said, "We share concern over the dogs." A male respondent noted, "We have more trust with each other in the group." A second participant reported that "we get along for the dogs. If you took the dogs away we wouldn't be a community." Another participant agreed and said, "Without the dogs we wouldn't talk to each other as much."

Participants also reported the dogs had positive effects on their relationships with family members. One woman claimed that her dog work was interesting to her mother and made for conversation when they would talk on the phone or visit at the prison. Another reported that her children are "less anxious about me being locked up. They get to see the dog when they visit and they'll even request a specific dog for me to bring." Male participants also reported that their families are interested in the dogs and they discuss the dogs with their families. According to one, "When my family calls me they check up on the dogs and me."

Another indication of the extent to which the dogs take on social roles for participants is the sadness they anticipated when their dogs leave the facility. "I do experience sadness with the program. It is tough to leave them; it's like separating from my kids all over again," according to one woman. (As with most programs, the two programs included here work to quickly pair the participant with another dog.)

Relabeling

Prison-based animal program participants assign their dogs a humanlike social identity. This newly constituted human-animal relationship may transform inmates' sense of self. Maruna *et al.* (2004) refer to this new self-definition as relabeling, which they contend is necessary for successful desistance from crime. They argue that desistance depends on a two-step process involving both social feedback and personal, or agentic, experiences. The first stage, or primary desistance, refers to any break or interruption in criminality, while the second stage, or secondary desistance, occurs when the individual comes to assume the role of a transformed or changed person. The authors point to recent research that finds persistent desistance entails recognizable changes in personal identity. They propose that secondary desistance may best be achieved when the desisting person's change in behavior is acknowledged by others and mirrored back to the individual. They go on to note that the source of this new, prosocial label is significant and might be most effective when coming from authority figures. The authors suggest that "if the relabeling were to be endorsed and supported by the same social control establishment involved in the 'status degradation' process of conviction and sentencing (e.g., judges or peer juries), this public redemption might carry considerable social and psychological weight for the participants" (p. 275). In PAPs, prisoners have been carefully chosen to participate in a rewarding opportunity where prison staff and administrators and members of the community interact with participants as responsible and worthy of the chance they have been given. As a result of participating in the program, prisoners can receive feedback from others that reflects the transformed self-identity they experience internally.

To examine whether PAP participants' relationships with program dogs led to relabeling or development of a prosocial identity, evidence was gathered to see whether they received feedback from others who recognized such change and whether they regarded their own efforts in the PAP as having brought about this change. According to participants, they were treated differently by those around them; interactions with prison staff and administrators indicated they recognized the participants as reformed. Participants also identified their own efforts in the process of redefinition; they reported having experiences that supported a changed self-concept.

Social Feedback

More than half of the participants reported receiving better treatment from the staff since entering the program. According to one woman, "The COs treat us differently because we're doing something special and worthwhile. We get a little bit of respect." Another participant indicated that "the dog makes me different from other inmates and I'm in better standing with the officers. I've been complimented by officers who had been tough on me before." Another participant said COs "treat you more humanely; you're not just a number."

Family members also served as a source of positive feedback for many participants. One woman said, "My family loves it. I talk to them about the dogs on the phone. My mom always asks me about them. My family focuses on the dog when they come visit. They're proud of me and they see the changes in me." Another participant indicated that her family members have "come to admire what I do. I work hard whether it is freezing or hot outside. They admire my dedication and see I have gone above and beyond what I need to do in here."

Participants are aware that, in this process of change, others' views of them are important, as demonstrated by the woman who said, "Raising dogs for law enforcement means a lot. Being an inmate doesn't make us evil." Another participant may have captured the essence of the "looking-glass self" when she noted that "this gives me more credibility with others on my journey to being a whole and trusted person again."

The prison's director and deputy director confirmed the participants' reports of how staff members viewed them. Asked to identify any changes she has seen in the women, the director said they "develop trust, love, and confidence" and that participation fosters "growth and pride." She stated that she has seen the women "rise above their limitations" as well as become less aggressive. She also noted that the program is an opportunity for "the community to recognize the value of people who are incarcerated." Both the director and the deputy director agreed that participants put their own needs aside and cooperate for the sake of the dogs, as well as to remain in the program. They also concurred that the most positive aspect of the program is the personal growth of the women who participate.

Agentic Experiences

Participants claimed they achieved emotional growth as a result of their involvement in the program. More than half of the sample said they were less angry and more patient as a result of their participation. "I'm more relaxed and not as tense," said one woman. Several participants said the program has led them to be more aware of their emotions and more connected to those around them. One woman reported, "I have seen an enormous change in my emotions. Before, I didn't show much emotions. I'm not a people person. But the dogs make my emotions more active. I worry about them if they are hurt during play or whatever. It is truly a big breakthrough for me." Another woman acknowledged being more emotionally engaged, stating, "I was a drug addict out there so my feelings were all bottled up. This is opening up pathways for me to tell my family things I couldn't before. I tell them what I'm feeling now."

Most participants reported having increased prosocial interactions with those around them because of their involvement in the program. One woman said she has become "more outgoing. I am less nervous reading out loud in group. I've come out of my shell and can be open with people I don't know." A number of respondents indicated that they have dog-focused interactions with other inmates, facility staff, and administrators with whom they would not have interacted prior to their participation. "Before I stayed to myself," said one, "now I'm more apt to talk to people about the dogs."

The continual effort, and therefore sense of agency, required of their participation was an obvious theme of the interviews. One woman said, "We have to keep personality issues outside the program. We have to work together for the dogs. We have to have common courtesy for each other." Another declared she "wouldn't jeopardize her [dog's] training for anything. You have to set aside your feelings. You have to put you

last and the puppy first." Comments indicated an awareness that their efforts with the program are connected with benefits they will later receive. One woman described the program as "a tremendous life lesson. I'm trusted with something alive. We've lost trust being in here and to get it back we'll do this hard work."

Participants also gained a sense of empowerment. One woman reported knowing, "I can get through anything. As uncomfortable as life can be, it is bearable. I can achieve anything I want to." Another said she learned "I'm not as stupid as I was always told I was. I have a lot to offer, to the community and to other women in the program, and to the dogs too." Another participant said she learned "to voice my opinion and not be a carpet. I say what I want people to know."

Finally, participants claimed that they experienced positive physical changes, as a result of their program involvement. Nearly everyone reported having lost weight since starting the program. A striking account came from a participant who said, "I gained over 100 pounds in county [jail awaiting trial] and I've lost most of it from the walking and exercise I get from the dogs." An additional four participants reported having lost between 34 and 60 pounds each. Most of the women also reported they are more active now and have more energy. "I used to lay around a lot in max. Here you're constantly busy," said one woman. According to another, "My energy is where it used to be. You're with them for 24 hours a day, being active. It's a great feeling." Almost half the group said they sleep better as a result of their participation. One woman extolled, "I sleep great. I'm physically exhausted. I'm healthier. It's a good clean, tired feeling." Another reported, "I have no more sleepless nights." In addition, one woman said she is "off antidepressants" since beginning the program. Another participant reported that she had struggled with diabetes since age 12, but that "within 3 months of being in the program my blood sugar stabilized at 180. I haven't used insulin in 3 months. Medical here and my family can't understand it. My blood pressure is lower too." While not everyone can achieve such results from participation in a PAP, it is worth noting that the potential for such change exists.

Discussion

The data presented above support the idea that a process of identity formation occurs among PAP participants similar to that occurring in the pet owners studied by Sanders (1993) and Alger and Alger (1997). A duality characterizes PAP participants' relationships with their dogs, influencing how participants view themselves and how they are viewed by others. The new self-definition that can result from their participation may promote criminal desistance, which has been theorized to require a transformation or relabeling.

What is it, in particular, about PAPs that might make for this transformation? The nonverbal nature of the social interactions people have with animals is often used to dismiss this type of contact as less valuable and/or less legitimate than interactions between people. However, contemporary evidence establishes an intersubjectivity between animals and people irrespective of language. Specifically, there are a number of human subpopulations that have been previously ostracized or considered deviant by the dominant culture, including people with disabilities and those institutionalized in prisons and hospitals, whose members may be particularly able to benefit from the unique, nonverbal type of interactions that take place with animals. It is this very lack of language that may facilitate the relationships developed through PAPs. In fact, it may be that interactions not reliant on a common language are of particular benefit to prison inmates who often have long histories of people's words being used to reject and punish them. That is, without language to offend or cause harm, interactions between people and animals can feel less judgmental and therefore more therapeutic for incarcerated people. Indeed, prison inmates and animals may even be regarded as sharing a history of being excluded from the category of "human." As Sanders (1993:210) reminds us,

"'primitives,' African Americans, and members of various other human groups routinely have been, and continue to be, denied the status of human . . . and studies of interactions in total institutions . . . are filled with descriptions of the 'dehumanization' of inmates by staff members, principally on the grounds that the inmates do not possess the requisite level of mind."

Further, the human-animal relationship inside prison appears to support a new, noncriminal label, applied by both the individual participants and others. While primary desistance is any cessation in criminal activity, Maruna *et al.* (2004) argue that both reactions from others *and* personal experience are needed for the transformation that occurs with secondary desistance. It is worth noting that because participation is contingent on maintaining a clean institutional record, participants in these programs are actively demonstrating desistance, albeit while still incarcerated. There is evidence here that the changes in self and others' perceptions that are necessary for successful desistance from crime can occur during participation in a PAP.

Of course, PAPs are not without their critics. Some suggest the government is exploiting inmate labor and then refusing to employ the same individuals upon release. While public agencies will work with the dogs trained by prison inmates, a prison record prevents the participants from ever being hired by these agencies when released. Ironically, it is the growing demand for dogs to work with criminal justice agencies that has helped drive some of the growth in the dog-training industry. Other critics suggest that programs involving inmates and animals may send a message to the public that being incarcerated is enjoyable or easy, while others may oppose PAPs on the grounds that it is too rewarding for the participants; incarcerated people should never experience happiness or pleasure according to this line of thinking. However, this outlook is clearly shortsighted if not vengeful and ignores that participation in PAPs may provide some individuals with an opportunity for a unique pathway to change.

Rather than retreating from PAPs, as the critics above suggest, this article indicates that such programs have wide-ranging policy implications. As the ability of animals to influence a person's selfhood has become more widely recognized, animals should increasingly be included in treatment programs aimed at people with a range of psychosocial needs. Beck and Katcher (1996) point out that it is "when people face real adversity, affection from a pet takes on new meaning" (p. 38). Few in our society face the level of hardship experienced by many of the over 2 million people incarcerated in our prisons and jails. While we have only just begun to examine the extent of the effects experienced by PAP participants, we already know that not only do the inmates benefit, but so too do the animals and those they go on to serve in the community as well (e.g., Strom, 2006). It is difficult to identify other programs being administered in prisons today that can claim to create such a win-win-win situation.

References

Alger, J., and S. Alger. (1997). Beyond Mead: Symbolic interaction between humans and felines. *Society & Animals 5*, 65–81.

Alger, J., and S. Alger. (2003). *Cat Culture: The Social World of a Cat Shelter.* Philadelphia: Temple University Press.

Arkow, P. (1998). *Pet Therapy: A Study and Resource Guide for the Use of Companion Animals in Selected Therapies*, 8th ed. Stratford, NJ: Author.

Arluke, A. (2007). Animal-Assisted Activities for At-Risk and Incarcerated Children and Young Adults unpublished paper presented at the National Technology Assessment Workshop on Animal-Assisted Programs for Youth at Risk. Baltimore, MD.

Beck, A., and A. Katcher. (1996). *Between Pets and People: The Importance of Animal Companionship.* W. Lafayette, IN: Purdue University Press.

Becker, M. (2002). *The Healing Power of Pets.* NY: Hyperion.

Bogdan, R., and S. Taylor. (1989). Relationships with severely disabled people: The social construction of humanness. *Social Problems 36*, 135–148.

Fine, A. (ed.) (2000). *Handbook on Animal-Assisted Therapy: Theoretical Foundations and Guidelines for Practice.* San Diego, CA: Academic Press.

Franklin, A., Emmison, M., Haraway, D., and M. Travers. (2007). Investigating the therapeutic benefits of companion animals: Problems and challenges. *Qualitative Sociology Review 3*, 42–58.

Furst, G. (2006). Prison-based animal programs: A national survey. *The Prison Journal 86*, 407–430.

Graham, B. (2000). *Creature Comfort: Animals That Heal.* Amherst, NY: Prometheus Books.

Hines, L. (1997). Overview of animals in correctional facilities. In Delta Society (ed.), *Animals in Institutions* (1998). Renton, WA: Delta Society.

Lai, J. (1998, April). *Pet Facilitated Therapy in Correctional Institutions.* Prepared for Correctional Services of Canada by Office of the Deputy Commissioner for Women. Available at www.csc-scc.gc.ca.

Lee, D. (1987). Companion animals in institutions. In P. Arkow (ed.), *The Loving Bond: Companion Animals in the Helping Professions* (pp. 23–46). Saratoga, CA: R & E Publishers.

Maruna, S. (2001). *Making Good: How Ex-Convicts Reform and Rebuild Their Lives.* Washington, D.C.: American Psychological Association.

Maruna, S., LeBel, T., Mitchell, N., and M. Naples. (2004). Pygmalion in the reintegration process: Desistance from crime through the looking glass. *Psychology, Crime & Law 10*, 271–281.

Moneymaker, J., and E. Strimple. (1991). Animals and inmates: A sharing companionship behind bars. *Journal of Offender Rehabilitation 16*, 133–152.

Quinn, P. (2004). *Paws for Love.* Exeter, NH: Townsend.

Sanders, C. (1993). Understanding dogs: Caregivers' attributions of mindedness in canine-human relationships. *Journal of Contemporary Ethnography 22*, 205–226.

Sanders, C. (2003). Actions speak louder than words: Close relationships between humans and non-human animals. *Symbolic Interaction 26*, 405–426.

Strom, S. (2006, October 27). Trained by inmates, new best friends for disabled veterans. *The New York Times*, A31.

Wilson, C., and D. Turner (eds.). (1998). *Companion Animals in Human Health.* Thousand Oaks, CA: Sage.

Douglas M. Robins
Clinton R. Sanders
Spencer E. Cahill

Pet-Facilitated Interaction in a Public Setting

In public situations, strangers commonly maintain a state of "civil inattention" by visually acknowledging one another's presence and then quickly looking away so as to indicate that no further interaction is desired or welcomed. We seldom converse with those we do not know except perhaps to exchange brief greetings. This widely observed prohibition against talking to unacquainted others makes interaction in public places difficult to initiate, much less sustain. Yet this prohibition is not as commonly or strictly observed when a person is accompanied by a dog. As Messent (1983, 1985) found, individuals in public places with dogs have both more and longer conversation with others than do those without dogs.

Gardner (1980) suggested two possible reasons for this susceptibility of individuals with dogs in public places to conversation. First, civil inattention "may be breached when the citizen is accompanied by a person or animal in an open category, for example, a child or dog" (p. 332). It is as if the interactional openness of pet dogs, as well as of children, is highly contagious, infecting and transforming anyone who accompanies them in public into "open persons" (Goffman 1963, 124–128). Second, according to Gardner (1980), civil inattention is also commonly breached when there is some obvious similarity between individuals.

A pet dog announces that the accompanying person is a dog owner—and probably dog lover—providing a resource for focused interaction and conversation with other owners and lovers.

Thus there are good reasons why dogs facilitate interaction among the unacquainted. However, the *actual processes* through which dogs bring strangers in public places into focused interaction have been inadequately explored.

In the remainder of this article, we examine initial encounters between dog owners and their subsequent interaction in a public place. Our focus is a group of casually acquainted dog owners who gathered regularly in a public park and the typical fate of unfamiliar dog owners who happened upon that group. Focusing on the unfamiliar owners' careers with the group of acquainted owners provides an often overlooked picture of how acquainted persons in public places respond to outsiders.

The Setting and Study

Dog owners came to Westside Park from approximately 6:30 to 8:00 in the morning and between 5:00 and 7:30 in the evening. More were usually there in the evening, and their numbers varied from day to day. They generally arrived alone—except when they met a fellow owner on the way to the park—and stayed for varying lengths of time. Approximately 15 owners were consistently there three times a week or more. These regulars met at the same place each day on the western half of the park's central field. They generally did not go into the other areas of the park except when arriving or departing or to retrieve a wandering dog.

Over 3 months, Robins, the first author and person in the following field-note excerpts, regularly visited Westside Park with Max, his dachshund puppy. So as to observe firsthand how the already aquainted dog owners would react to an unfamiliar owner, Robins simply presented himself as "just another dog owner." This tactic precluded openly taking notes, so Robins continued to write his field notes later in the evening after his visits to the park. He sometimes dictated key incidents and details into a small tape recorder as he and Max walked home and then used the tape to jog his memory when writing the notes. The following description and analysis of patterns of interaction and relationships among dog owners at Westside Park are based on these field notes.

The Dynamics of Inclusion

Like other individuals with dogs in public places, the dog owners who regularly congregated in Westside Park were susceptible to breaches of civil inattention. Individuals who were interested in petting or playing with one or more of the dogs sometimes approached the owners. Although conversation generally ensued, it was brief. The owners graciously acknowledged such implicit compliments to their dogs but seemed uninterested in further interaction with admirers. However, the reception they gave unfamiliar dog owners was quite different.

Recruiting Candidates for Inclusion

The dog owner "regulars" of Westside Park often responded to unfamiliar owners or "outsiders" as potential candidates for inclusion in their gatherings. It was not uncommon for one of their number to engage such an outsider in focused interaction, as Robins learned on his second visit to the park with Max:

Max and I stood about 15 yards from the dogs and their owners. A young woman approached us. She bent down and began petting Max. She spoke to him in the tones a mother uses with her child: "You're so cute! What a good boy. You're so friendly, aren't you? Yes, you are." She then directed a number of questions to me: "What's his name? How old is he? Is he a miniature or standard? How long have you had him?" After I had answered, she said that I should let Max play with the other dogs. When I explained I was afraid he might get hurt, she responded with "My dog did it when he was smaller than Max." I was still hesitant and kept him on the leash.

Another outsider with a much larger dog had a similar experience:

A man appeared leading a large mastiff. When he was about 20 yards from the other owners and dogs, the same woman who had approached me went up to him. She asked if the dog was friendly. The man answered affirmatively. She scratched the dog's head and rubbed its back. The mastiff responded by wagging its tail. She rubbed its ears with both hands and said, "Oh, what a nice dog you are!" She then told the man that if his dog got along with the other dogs he could let it off the leash. He did so, and the mastiff played for over an hour with the others.

These two incidents exemplify initial encounters between the regular dog owners and newcomers at Westside Park. Newcomers precipitated the encounters by entering the area occupied by the owners and dogs. This alone was enough to initiate an "unfocused interaction" (Goffman 1963, 24) in which the other owners could look at the outsider, and he or she could do the same to them. Focused interaction involving verbal communication did not occur unless the newcomer showed an interest in or orientation toward the other owners and dogs by stopping to watch or moving closer to the group. Focused interactions did not take place between regulars and unknown owners who remained in other sections of the park, those who passed by on the outskirts of the area occupied by the regulars, those who entered the area momentarily and quickly left, or any other owners whose actions did not indicate an interest in the regulars and their dogs.

Another feature of this initial "checking out" process was that regulars initiated the verbal interaction. Initiating encounters with strangers entails a threat to the initiator, including potential loss of "face" (Goffman 1982) and embarrassment. As an apparent means of avoiding at least some of these social risks, regulars often initiated the encounter by addressing the newcomer's dog instead of the owner. The dog acted as an accessible "bridging device" to its owner (Goffman 1963, 126 n. 3). When a regular did address the unfamiliar owner directly, the comment was usually about the dog, and the regular typically would look at the dog in the course of the exchange.

A third feature of these initial contacts was that interaction between regulars and unfamiliar owners was brief and limited to dog-related matters. Cavan (1963) observed that "small talk among strangers often revolves around the present scene or current events because these are among the few areas where there is some probability of mutual interest or knowledge" (p. 19). The dogs were something that the owners at Westside Park obviously had in common. They provided a readily available and safe topic of conversation. Like the weather or records on the jukebox for customers in a bar, the dogs were the source of mutual accessibility.

The dogs were participants in the encounters as well as topics of conversation. In the first episode presented earlier, the regular spoke directly to Max while petting him. In the second, after being assured that the mastiff was not a threat, the regular scratched the dog's head and back and spoke to him affectionately. Owners sustained encounters by making the dogs subjects of their conversation and by integrating them into the interaction.

A fourth feature of these encounters was that once the friendliness of the unfamiliar dog had been established, the regular invited the human newcomer to unleash his or her dog. The manner in which this was done evoked the collective nature of the activities in which the dog owners were en-

gaged. In the two encounters described earlier, the woman, in offering an invitation to let Max and the mastiff play with the other dogs, was speaking in the name of the other owners and thus implicitly identifying herself as a regular. This made it clear that the unfamiliar owners had ventured on an area where collective activity was occurring. Those present were more than an unorganized collection of individuals and dogs who just happened to be together at the particular moment. They constituted a social unit with shared interests, activities, and territorial claim to an area of the park.

Not all potential candidates for inclusion in the regulars' activities accepted the invitation to unleash their dogs. Some expressed a desire simply to continue watching, while others declined by saying that they did not have time or because they feared for their dog's safety. Regulars often attempted to convince such reluctant newcomers to let their dogs play with the others but were not always successful.

Although graciously accepting such refusals of their invitations, the regulars apparently had some interest in recruiting new participants for their collective activities.

Regulars' evaluation of candidates for inclusion did not end with the acceptance or rejection of an invitation to join the activities. Once a new dog had been allowed into the group, his or her owner and regulars monitored the dog's behavior to make sure he or she got along with the others. Once free of the leash, the new dog was carefully examined by the other dogs. Most passed the "inspection" and joined in the play. Others were intimidated or reacted aggressively. Both the newcomer and regular owners watched this process carefully and when trouble occurred, a regular and/or newcomer stepped in to separate the dogs. The unfamiliar owner would then put the leash back on his or her dog and take it away.

Once a newcomer and his or her dog had been checked out by a regular, other regulars would similarly evaluate the unfamiliar dog and its human companion.

The sequencing of encounters either could be determined by the dog—as just described—or by the owners. These encounters allowed regulars to meet the new owner. In a relatively short time, regulars could acquire such information about the newcomer as to which dog was his or hers and the animal's name, age, and breed. These encounters also gave the newcomer the opportunity to direct similar questions to the other owners. However, owners "thinned out" these initial encounters by keeping them impersonal and not exchanging identifying names.

By this point, the regulars had begun to transform the newcomer into a potential regular by making contact and inviting her or him to join their collective activities. They used the dogs as "social catalysts," to borrow Messent's (1985, 387) apt phrase, to help initiate and facilitate these interactions. Early interactions usually were brief, consisting of little more than an exchange of questions and answers regarding dogs. For several weeks following the initial encounter, interaction between the newcomer and other owners continued to be limited to these dog-related topics. In order for the newcomer to be successfully accepted as a viable candidate for regular membership, the interactions would have to be expanded.

Probationary Membership

Bounded Interactions During Robins's visits to the park over the next 4 weeks, he had conversations with a number of owners. While the people changed, the topics of conversation did not; they talked of almost nothing but dogs. They commented about the dogs at play, shared information about various physical and behavioral problems and cures, and compared dog food brands. Robins came to realize that the regulars were purposefully directing the conversations away from a broader and more personally revealing range of topics.

Sometimes individuals used the dogs to control the topic of talk. The following is an example of an individual trying unsuccessfully to move a conversation beyond dog-related topics. In this case, rather than redirecting the conversation, the regular broke it off when it started to move to personally revealing topics:

> A man who looked to be in his mid-30s was at the park. He had a black Labrador retriever. He wandered around petting the other dogs for a while and then walked over to Jill and her dog, Ginger. He petted Ginger for a few seconds while speaking to Jill. I moved closer so I could hear what they were saying. He said something about living close by. Then he asked Jill how long she'd been coming to the park. She said about a year, and pulled a tennis ball out of her sweatshirt pocket and began tossing it up and down. Ginger looked excited. The guy said, "So, what do you do?" Jill said she worked downtown. Then she said to the dog, "OK Ginger, do you wanna play?" The dog started jumping all around. She said to the guy, "It's tennis ball time," and then to the dog, "OK Ginger, let's go." They trotted off. The guy watched her for a second, then walked over to where his dog was standing.

The man's questions were attempts to acquire what Gardner (1988) called "access information" —facts about an individual that can be used to gain access to that person in another place or at some later date. In order to deflect this conversational move, the woman used the readily available ploy of precipitating her dog's desire to play and designating it as "tennis ball time."

Another interesting aspect of these early encounters between newcomers and regular owners was the typical way in which greetings and farewells were delivered. In their first few weeks at the park, newcomers rarely were greeted when they arrived. Instead, regulars said hello to newcomers' dogs. Similarly, when newcomers left the park, others would often say good-bye to the dogs but not to the owners themselves. In this way, regulars indirectly acknowledged the arrival and departure of newcomers through their dogs. By addressing the dog instead of the person, regulars avoided greeting and saying good-bye to a person they did not really know or perhaps were not ready to know.

Although regular owners learned a dog's name during the initial "checking out" process, they had not as yet exchanged names or other personal information with the human newcomers. After 2 weeks at the park, Robins introduced himself to two owners with hopes of prompting conversation about other than dog-related matters and of acquiring introductions to other regulars. This failed on both counts, so he decided to wait and see if any of the regular owners would introduce themselves. It took 3 additional weeks for someone to do so.

Negotiating Trouble While both regulars and newcomers had to deal with trouble at the park, the way in which newcomers handled troublesome situations was especially important as it could affect their standing with other owners, the likelihood of their returning to the park, and their consequent chances of acceptance as a regular.

Trouble at the park took many forms. In some cases, unfamiliar dogs were a problem, as when strangers with unfriendly dogs approached the group. At other times, a dog might stray from where it was playing and invade other parts of the park, disturbing joggers, sunbathers, or others. Occasionally, dogs might eat or chew on debris left by picnickers or do the same with other objects that were potentially injurious. After a rain, at least a few would roll in the mud and then shake off, getting owners and other dogs dirty.

When trouble like this did arise at the park, the owners acted to restore both behavioral and moral order. One remedial technique involved the owner of the offending dog taking steps to explain or smooth over the consequences of the canine companion's infractions.

The owner of a dog causing trouble would act to remedy the disruption without prompting from others, typically by recognizing the problem, addressing the dog directly, and removing it from the scene of the trouble. These actions were usually accompanied by explanatory accounts of the dog's behavior and apologies to potentially offended humans.

Troublesome situations at the park made it clear that owners were held responsible for their dogs' behavior. When a dog got into trouble, it

was expected that its owner would take appropriate measures to correct the problem. Additionally, the owner commonly attempted to ritually atone for any moral offense through "remedial exchanges" involving apologies and accounts (Goffman 1971). Owners were clearly concerned that they would be judged by the canine company they kept and with good reason. When their dogs got into trouble, their social standing with the other owners was threatened. In order to redeem themselves in the other owners' eyes, they needed to demonstrate their own commitment to the moral order that their dogs, and by association they themselves, had transgressed.

On some occasions when an owner failed to respond appropriately to trouble, other owners took matters into their own hands. The following excerpt concerns a young woman and her bulldog named Mack who returned to the park a second time after having run into trouble on their first visit 2 days earlier:

> Mack's owner let him off his leash despite the fact that Lori had told her last time that it might be a good idea to keep it on until he got friendlier with the other dogs. Mack started lumbering around, and Carrie said, "Uh, oh, he's back," to no one in particular but loud enough for most everyone to hear. However, things seemed fine until Mack started sniffing Trooper. The two dogs growled at each other, and Nancy said, "Whoa, Trooper. Let's go, let's go," and pushed Trooper away with her hands. She ran a short distance away and called to Trooper, who followed. For the next minute or so, Mack trotted around while the other owners tried to keep their dogs away from him. The owners of some of the smaller dogs picked their pets up and moved a few steps back. Mack's owner caught her dog by the collar and said loudly to the other owners who were a few feet away, "It's weird. He's usually so friendly." A few people were looking at her but didn't say anything. Others were talking among themselves or had wandered off. She put the leash back on her dog. They stayed for a little while longer, but the other owners kept their distance from them.

The withdrawal from an owner and dog usually lasted only until the owner demonstrated that he or she would prevent the trouble from reoccurring or would act quickly if it did. When Mack's owner returned to the park a few days later, she kept the dog on a leash, so he would not cause trouble, and the other owners did not hesitate to talk with her.

The dynamics of inclusion among dog owners at Westside Park was clearly a long and sometimes trying process. After accepting a regular's invitation to participate in group activities and passing their initial inspection, newcomers followed a probationary period of carefully circumscribed interaction. During that time, regulars monitored the behavior of newcomers' dogs and their responses to it. Only those newcomers who withstood that moral scrutiny and were sufficiently patient eventually won the regulars' acceptance as one of their own.

Becoming a Regular

That turning point in Robins's dealings with the other owners came during the fifth week when an older man with a keeshond named Tasha introduced himself. They had spoken several times before but only about dogs. Robins recorded the gist of the conversation in his field notes:

The old guy and I were watching our dogs sniff each other when he said, "You know, I don't even know your name." We introduced ourselves. He said his real name was Jacob, but everyone called him Jack. In the military, they called him Jake, Sergeant Jake. During World War II, he was stationed at an air base in French Guyana. He was there for 9 months and loved it. He was drunk every day and made love all the time. At first, Germans were living there. The Americans wired and gave them 18 hours to depart; they left for Argentina. There wasn't even an airstrip at first, but when ex-football star Tom Harmon crashed his plane nearby, the soldiers were ordered to build an airstrip. Jack said he was in charge. He seemed to remember everything as if it were yesterday.

Beside the fact that Jack initiated the introductions, this encounter was significant in that the conversation had nothing to do with dogs and entailed a fair amount of self-disclosure. While Jack only revealed his first name, the exclusive use of first names was typical among the regular owners and preserved a degree of anonymity.

Following his revealing conversation with Jack, a number of similar changes occurred in Robins's relations with other owners. Although he already knew a few names as a result of overhearing conversations, he felt it was inappropriate to address these individuals by name until they actually had been introduced. Soon after their own introduction, Jack introduced Robins to other owners, and still others introduced themselves. These experiences convinced Robins that it was now appropriate for him to begin to initiate introductions, and over the next 2 weeks he came to know the names of about 10 regulars.

As this important phase of his movement from newcomer to regular proceeded, Robins's conversations with other owners became more varied even though talk about dogs continued to be their most common topic. Robins spoke with Terry, a young man who spent a great deal of his time at the park exercising, about his new job at a movie studio. Jen told about her two unsuccessful attempts to pass the bar exam and about her current efforts to prepare for a third. Kelly spoke of the difference between her new neighborhood and the one from which she had just moved. Fred, the owner of a large German shepherd, and Robins discussed the advantages and disadvantages of living in the city. These more diverse conversations soon began to involve exchanges of access information, such as workplace and residence location.

Another indicator that Robins was being accepted as a regular was that the other owners now expected him to be at the park regularly. They made this clear through their greetings and farewells. Prior to his acceptance as a regular, Robins was rarely greeted when he arrived. Owners would say hello to Max, but Robins's presence was seldom acknowledged directly. In the weeks following his conversation with Jack,

Robins was greeted by a number of owners each time he arrived. On those occasions when he returned to the park after missing 1 or more days, greetings were often followed by a question or comment, such as "Hi, where were you yesterday?" or "Hey, Doug, didn't see you last week." Regulars thereby expressed their acceptance of Robins as one of their own. They now explicitly acknowledged both his presence and absence, requesting explanations of only the latter as if it were more problematic than the former.

Closing salutations also attested to Robins's acceptance as a regular. As he prepared to leave the park, other owners often supplemented standard farewells with statements or questions expressing their expectation of future encounters. Most often this took the form of "Bye, Doug, we'll see you tomorrow" or "See ya later, you gonna be here tomorrow?" At times, a similar farewell was also addressed to Max: "Bye-bye, Max, see you tomorrow, little guy." This type of closing presumed that Robins and Max would return to the park the following day and renew their relationships with other regulars.

Of course, not all newcomers became regulars. Some came to the park and never returned. Others came too infrequently to become regulars. Although these latter owners were not checked out each time they returned, their conversations with other owners never strayed from dog-related subjects. A few owners came to the park frequently and long enough to become regulars but avoided doing so. Sometimes, they engaged in other activities, such as exercising or walking, while their dogs played or they simply remained on the fringes of the area where the regulars gathered. These owners had apparently passed regulars' initial inspection and occasionally talked with them but never became one of them. This was not a consequence of exclusion by the regulars but of self-imposed exclusion.

Inclusion among the regulars also eluded the occasional jogger, bicyclist, or other person without a dog who approached them. The ensuing encounters did have some of the same features of early encounters between dog owners: They were often initiated through the dog; talk was about dogs; the human participants interacted with the dog as well as each other; and the dogs were sometimes addressed in concluding the encounter. These encounters were generally brief. Lacking the necessary companion to join the regulars' activities, the outsider soon resumed his or her own interrupted activity.

Conclusions

Goffman (1971) reminded us that "social settings and social occasions are not organized in terms of individuals but in terms of participation units" (p. 21). That was clearly the case with the social gatherings each weekday morning and evening on the western half of the central field at Westside Park. Those gatherings were organized not in terms of single individuals but in terms of what Goffman (1971, 19) termed "withs"—and "withs" of a particular composition. Participation was limited to parties of a human and at least one dog that were apparently "together," as was membership in the ongoing public collectivity that had developed out of those gatherings. Perhaps to replace defections from their ranks or simply to add new life to their interactions, the regulars of Westside Park actively recruited new members for their group but only humans and dogs in one another's company.

The ease with which the regulars initiated encounters with unfamiliar dog owners exemplifies the interactional vulnerability of humans with dogs in public places. The presumedly more approachable canine end of such a "with" exposes the human end to overtures from other members of his or her own species. Strangers can minimize the risk of being judged overly forward by addressing the dog and using it as a conduit for remarks actually intended for its human companion—a process that Cain (1983) called "triangling." The dog also provides a ready focus of attention and supply of safe conversational topics, thus reducing the chances of offensive glances or words in encounters among previously unacquainted humans. The regulars at Westside

Park clearly took advantage of these interactional conveniences with unfamiliar owners, although perhaps at the convenience of at least some of those newcomers to the park. Rather than simply exposed, some of them may have been exposing themselves to just such treatment. Whatever attracts attention in public places, including the company of a dog, is also a means of attracting the attention of the otherwise civilly inattentive. A dog, then, is not only a bridging device to but also for its human companion. Interactional traffic may move in both directions.

The dynamics of inclusion among dog owners at Westside Park reveal yet another contribution of dogs to relations among unacquainted persons in public places. Unfamiliar owners' progress from candidacy, through probationary participation, to ultimate acceptance as regulars was largely decided by how they dealt with troublesome situations in which their dogs were implicated. Their responses to the immediate trouble and remedial offerings to potentially offended human parties apparently established whether they were responsible dog owners and, therefore, human confidants in the regulars' eyes. The dogs and their unruly behavior provided numerous opportunities for regulars to assess as well as for newcomers to display their reliability. It is doubtful that such symptomatic readings and expressions of the moral character of dogs' human companions are confined to Westside Park.

Having little if any information about one another, unacquainted persons in public places must assess one another's trustworthiness on the basis of immediately apparent expressions but also be aware that such expression may be staged to deceive. However, like young children, dogs are notoriously unreliable members of performance teams. Whether or not that well-earned reputation actually discourages dogs' human companions from fraudulent presentations of self and intentions, it may allay concerns about them doing so. Dogs' penchant for trouble is sure to

test their human companions' moral reliability, providing some assurance that the truth will eventually tell. There is also reassurance in this for sincere human companions of dogs in public places. Every time their canine companion puts them to such a test, they can demonstrate their reliability and win the trust and perhaps the admiration of other members of their species.

Dogs, then, can provide more companionship for humans than merely their own company. They are also an antidote for the human anonymity of the public places of our contemporary society. Dogs facilitate contact, confidence, conversation, and confederation among previously unacquainted persons who might otherwise remain that way. At least that is what the dogs did at Westside Park.

References

Cain, A. 1983. A study of pets in the family system. In *New perspectives on our lives with companion animals,* edited by A. Katcher and A. Beck, 71–81. Philadelphia: University of Pennsylvania Press.

Cavan, S. 1963. Interaction in home territories. *Berkeley Journal of Sociology* 8:17–32.

Gardner, C. 1980. Passing by: Street remarks, address rights, and the urban female. *Sociological Inquiry* 50:328–356.

———. 1988. Access information: Public lies and private peril. *Social Problems* 35:384–397.

Goffman, E. 1963. *Behavior in public places.* New York: Free Press.

———. 1971. *Relations in public.* New York: Basic Books.

———. 1982. *Interaction ritual.* New York: Random House.

Messent, P. 1983. Social facilitation of contact with other people by pet dogs. In *New perspectives on our lives with companion animals*, edited by A. Katcher and A. Beck, 37–46. Philadelphia: University of Pennsylvania Press.

———. 1985. Pets as social facilitators. *Veterinary Clinics of North America: Small Animal Practice* 15:387–393.

PART TEN

Selfhood

Introduction

One of the most exciting recent developments within sociological human-animal studies has been the focus on everyday interactions between people and animals. Much of this work directly confronts the conventional scientific view that, because they are not able to use language, nonhuman animals are "mindless" (unable to think as we do) and do not possess "selves." To a major degree, this commonplace scientific belief about the failings of animals is based on the fifteenth-century French philosopher René Descartes who regarded nonhuman animals essentially as machines made of flesh who could not pass the "conversation test." As he observed (Descartes 1976):

> For it is a very remarkable fact that there are none so depraved and stupid, without even excepting idiots, that they cannot arrange different words together, forming of them a statement by which they make known their thoughts; while, on the other hand, there is no other animal, however perfect and fortunately circumstanced it may be, which can do the same. It is not the want of organs that brings this to pass, for it is evident that magpies and parrots are able to utter words just like ourselves, and yet they cannot speak as we do, that is, so as to give evidence that they think of what they say. (61–62)

This Cartesian perspective came to be reflected in modern-day sociological psychology as it was incorporated into the perspective of the influential early twentieth-century social philosopher George Herbert Mead. Mead maintained that "mind" was a linguistic phenomenon and that actual thinking involved a literal internal conversation as a person "talked" to him or her self. In a well-known passage, Mead (1962) stated:

> We, of course, tend to endow our domestic animals with personality, but as we get insight into their conditions we see there is no place for this sort of importation of the social process into the conduct of the individual. They do not have the mechanism for it—language. So we say that they have no personality; they are not responsible for the social situation in which they find themselves. . . . We put personalities into the animals, but they do not belong to them. . . . And yet the common attitude is that of giving them just such personalities as our own. We talk to them and in our talking to them we act as if they had the sort of inner world that we have. (182–183)

In turn, according to the way Mead and those for whom his theoretical perspective came to be important, the "self" that one talked to or focused on when one was "self conscious" was a social product. As people spoke and interacted with others they used the information they received to build up a "self concept." In everyday life, people presented this self to others (see Goffman 1959) while paying attention to the ways those around them presented who they were (or, at least, how they wanted others to see them). This everyday interplay of socially constructed selves, then, formed the core of interaction. As conventionally seen, it was an activity in which only those who possessed a linguistic mind and related social self could participate. From the conventional perspective, therefore, nonhuman animals were thoughtless, selfless, and emotionless since these attributes required the ability to use language.

A number of the sociologists who have turned to examining people's relationships with animals have devoted themselves to calling this conventional view of mind and the self, and the consequent exclusion of animals, into question. Some recent examples are Leslie Irvine's (2004) observations of an animal shelter, Clinton Sanders' (1999) research with people who live and work with dogs, Gene Myers' (1998) description of the interactions between children and animals in a preschool program, and Janet and Steven Alger's (2003) ethnographic study of a cat shelter. These writers examine the intersubjectivity that emerges when people routinely interact with animals and the process by which people understand the individual tastes, emotions, and behaviors of animal-others.

This sociological work on everyday interactions between people and animals has already had considerable impact on conceptions of mind, as sociologists who share this new perspective have offered research-based information that calls into question the orthodox view that mind is solely a linguistic phenomenon. Instead, they offer an understanding of mind as the outcome of social interaction and social experience. Guided by prior work of researchers who have examined the interactional worlds of people with Alzheimer's disease (e.g., Gubrium 1986), those with severe physical and mental disabilities (e.g., Bogdan and Taylor 1989, Goode 1994), and infants (e.g., Stern 1985), these sociologists have called into question the centrality of language use to mindedness and have emphasized the interactional process of "doing mind" (Dutton and Williams 2004). Mind, from this perspective, arises from shared experience and is central to the way that those who interact with alingual others construct and understand them. Caretakers of animals, like those who routinely interact with the severely disabled, infants, and Alzheimer's patients, put together a "theory of mind" that allows them to understand the thinking, emotions, preferences, desires, and intentions of the animal-other. Typically, writers interested in expanding an understanding of mind and self in this way use their own personal experiences living and working with animals as the basis for their analyses.

One clear indication of the power of the interpersonal connection between people and animals is seen in a common practice engaged in by pet caretakers. People demonstrate their intimate knowledge of their animals' unique ways of thinking and responding—they employ their theory of mind—by "speaking for" them in certain circumstances. In essence, people "give voice" to what, based on their personal relationship with their animals, they know to be in the animals' minds. For example Arluke and Sanders (1996) quote from observations of a client encountered in a veterinary clinic:

A young male shepherd with long hair is brought into the exam room by an older couple. . . . The woman goes on at some length about the dog's long hair and how they hadn't anticipated this when the dog was a puppy. . . . The dog lies down with his head on the woman's feet and she says, "Oh, I'm so tired. I just have to lie down here." Later, as the dog is having his nails trimmed, she (again) speaks for the dog in observing, "Oh, I have such nice nails." During much of the time she holds the dog's head tenderly and stares into his eyes. (69)

Bound up in the work on animal mind, the animal self, and people's relationships with nonhuman animals is the issue of *identity*. Most basically, when sociological psychologists speak of identity they are referring to how one sees one's self ("personal identity" or "self-concept") and how one is seen by others ("social identity"). As illustrated by the above quote, people who live day-to-day with animals construct and routinely use an understanding of their animals' unique identities. This is a key element shaping human-animal interaction.

Another way in which people's relationships with animals relate to identity is that animals affect how the people with them interact with and are seen by others. Numerous observational studies (e.g., Messent 1983, Robins, Sanders, and Cahill 1991) have shown that being with an animal in public increases a person's "social velocity" as strangers are more likely to approach and interact with him or her. On the other hand, when a person's animal "misbehaves"—especially when in a public situation—the social identity of the caretaker commonly is diminished and he or she responds with embarrassment or by making various excuses. Here, for example, is a description of a public encounter in which the owner sees his dogs act up and, fearing the consequences, offers excuses for their violations.

Something happened on the walk today that I realize is typical. As we were going along the trail we encountered a group of four people (an older couple and a young couple about our age) coming toward us. As usual, Emma and Isis were overjoyed to see someone and tore off to greet them tails wagging furiously and bounding in pleasure. Understandably taken aback by the sight of two sizeable dogs running toward them . . . the four of them gather in an uneasy clump with Isis and, especially, Emma leaping happily around them. Not wanting to have trouble and fearing that the dogs could injure the older people, El and I began to shout commands and run toward the group. As we ran up I said, "It's OK. They're just puppies. They won't hurt you." I realize that "they're just puppies" is, along with, "we're still working on this" (i.e., trying to break them of doing whatever it is I am excusing), a kind of ritual incantation I trot out when we meet other people on walks. (Sanders 1999, 35)

Yet another way in which one's animal companion shapes the caretaker's identity is when the attributes of the species or breed are presumed to reflect the owner's personal characteristics. For example, it is common for people with "aggressive" dog breeds to be seen as similarly aggressive or dangerous. On the other hand, people who live with cats, house rabbits, or presumably tractable dogs are not infrequently seen as "weak" or "feminine" (see Nash 1989).

The first selection by Keri Brandt is an excellent example of the use of "autoethnographic" data as the foundation for a serious discussion. Brandt, a committed horse person, uses her own experiences, interviews with other riders, and observations in horse barns to provide a vivid picture of how humans and animals can understand each other and communicate apart from spoken language. In expanding language "beyond the verbal," she presents the tactile interactions between horse and rider as the way in which each party learns about the other. It is out of this shared experience that subtle, sophisticated, and practically useful communication emerges. Knowing the "mind" of the human or nonhuman actor involves each party feeling and responding appropriately to the information physically communicated.

The next selection turns to examine the experience of a very different animal and people's interactions with them. The article by Isabel Bradshaw focuses on the emotional experience of elephants in the wild and in zoos. She maintains that violence by humans disrupts elephant communities and upsets the culture shared by elephants. Mourning the loss of community members is a central cultural ritual and, as human encroachment on elephant habitat and violent human interventions result in death, elephants individually and collectively experience emotional trauma. After presenting moving examples of the effects of this trauma, Bradshaw turns to examine the efforts of the David Sheldrick Wildlife Trust in Kenya. Here shocked, malnourished, injured, and displaced elephants are given sanctuary and their physical and emotional wounds are cared for. Human caretakers in the Sheldrick Trust develop supportive relationships with traumatized animals who have been ripped from their families and communities. Here we see human communication and relationships with animals as the source of healing.

In the final article of this part, Leslie Irvine builds on and extends the focus on animal mind and human-animal interactions by presenting a case for animals possessing a "core self." Following a critique of the conventional discounting of animals' abilities discussed above, Irvine makes the case for the animal self as being constituted, first, by a sense of *agency*. The animal recognizes that he or she has control over his or her action. In turn, the animal experiences *coherence* as he or she understands that his or her physical body both exists and acts. Irvine then maintains that another key component of the animal's core self is a sense of *affectivity* as the animal-actor realizes that certain emotions are associated with certain experiences. Finally, animals possess a basic sense of *self-history*. They remember past events, experiences, people, animals, and places they have encountered. These memories provide a sense of continuity of self and relationships. Irvine concludes, then, that the animal's understanding of self, like that of humans, is stable, emotionally rich, and embedded

in past experiences. The animal's self, like his or her mind, arises out of relationships and its existence is not dependent on the ability to use language.

References

Alger, J., and S. Alger. 2003. *Cat Culture: The Social World of a Cat Shelter*. Philadelphia: Temple University Press.

Arluke, A., and C. Sanders. 1996. *Regarding Animals*. Philadelphia: Temple University Press.

Bogdan, R., and S. Taylor. 1989. "Relationships with Severely Disabled People: The Social Construction of Humanness." *Social Problems* 36(2):135–148.

Descartes, R. 1976. "Animals are Machines." In T. Regan and P. Singer, eds., *Animal Rights and Human Obligations*, 60–66. Englewood Cliffs, NJ: Prentice Hall.

Dutton, D., and C. Williams. 2004. "A View from the Bridge: Subjectivity, Embodiment and Animal Minds." *Anthrozoös* 17(3):210–224.

Goffman, E. 1959. *The Presentation of Self in Everyday Life*. New York: Anchor.

Goode, D. 1994. *A World without Words: The Social Construction of Children Born Deaf and Blind*. Philadelphia: Temple University Press.

Gubrium, J. 1986. "The Social Preservation of Mind: The Alzheimer's Disease Experience." *Symbolic Interaction* 9:37–51.

Irvine, L. 2004. *If You Tame Me: Understanding Our Connections with Animals*. Philadelphia: Temple University Press.

Mead, G. H. 1962. *Mind, Self, and Society*. Chicago: University of Chicago Press.

Messent, P. 1983. "Social Facilitation of Contact with Other People by Pet Dogs." In A. Katcher and A. Beck, eds., *New Perspectives on Our Lives with Companion Animals*, 37–46. Philadelphia: University of Pennsylvania Press.

Myers, G. 1998. *Children and Animals*. Boulder, CO: Westview Press.

Nash, J. 1989. "What's in a Face? The Social Character of the English Bulldog." *Qualitative Sociology* 12:357–370.

Robins, D., Sanders, C., and S. Cahill. 1991. "Dogs and Their People: Pet-Facilitated Interaction in a Public Setting." *Journal of Contemporary Ethnography* 20(1):3–25.

Sanders, C. 1999. *Understanding Dogs: Living and Working with Canine Companions*. Philadelphia: Temple University Press.

Stern, Daniel. 1985. *The Interpersonal World of the Infant*. New York: Basic Books.

Keri Brandt

Human-Horse Communication

Within the social sciences there is scant research about the relationships humans share with their equine companions. Most of the literature available examines cowboys of the Old West and Indian warriors and the purpose horses served in their lives.

Currently, an exciting and growing body of literature on human-nonhuman animal relationships highlights the ability of different species to achieve intersubjectivity and communicate with one another. Much of this research focuses specifically on cats and dogs and employs a symbolic interactionist perspective to investigate how humans and their nonhuman animal companions create shared meanings (Irvine, 2004; Alger and Alger, 1997; Arluke and Sanders, 1993).

Little has been written about how humans and horses build a system of communication that allows the two to experience rewarding interactions and successful partnerships. Using the guiding principles of symbolic interaction to understand the ways in which two different species create a world of shared meaning, I will explore the process by which humans and horses co-create a language system—a language of their own. Of particular interest will be the significance of the body as a vehicle for expression—given that the body as a basis for symbolic interaction has been largely unexplored. I also will explore the various elements and rules of the "grammar" that enables effective human-horse communication and allows the two to engage in a wide range of activities together. The embodied nature of human-horse communication raises two questions: How can the body be a vehicle for symbolic interaction and, more broadly, what is the possibility of symbolic interaction on a non-discursive basis? Finally, and perhaps most important, the application of symbolic interactionist theoretical approaches to the study of non-verbal communication challenges the human/animal binary it originally—and ironically—enforced, rendering all alingual beings—humans and nonhuman alike—inferior.

Unique Relationships

New human-animal research within a symbolic interactionist tradition provides the theoretical and empirical groundings for understanding human-horse relationships. However, human-horse interaction differs greatly from human-dog and human-cat interaction; therefore, the unique quality of human-horse relationships must be noted. The most obvious difference is the large size of horses in comparison to their human partners. This brings an element of danger into the interaction that rarely is present with dogs and cats and makes crucial the establishment of an effective communication system.

Another important distinction is the high level of body-to-body contact between humans and horses when engaged in interaction. Certainly, humans and their dog and cat companions connect their bodies for reasons of affection, play, occasional grooming, and, at times, for obedience training. Nonetheless, humans do not ride their dogs or cats and so do not ask them to do complicated physical and mental tasks while astride their backs.

Because of these unique qualities, an explicit exploration of the role of the body (both human and horse) in human-horse communication is essential. Given this, an understanding of symbolic interaction at the level of embodiment is central to understanding how non-verbal communication facilitates meaning making between the two species.

The language of the horse operates through the body such that horses must use their bodies to communicate their subjective presence. Because humans cannot convey intentions to horses through spoken language, they too must use their bodies to generate a communication style to which the horse can respond. In the human-horse relationship, the body is the basis from which a system of communication can grow. Like Shapiro's (1990) idea of "kinesthetic empathy," communication between humans and horses is an embodied experience. Given that the human ability to verbalize thoughts is seen as the starting point for language, suggesting that the body, too, can be a basis for language, challenges its privileged status.

By reformulating thinking about the role of verbal language, an interactionist approach to human-horse communication can explore how the two species create shared meanings that— even in the absence of shared verbal language— shape the way they interrelate and live together.

In her research on human and animal relationships, Irvine (2004) argues that a de-privileging of spoken language as the form of meaningful communication would create a model of the self that allows animals' subjective presence to become visible through interaction. Irvine writes, "In order for interaction to become a relationship, which is key to selfhood, both parties must sense the subjective presence of the other" (p. 183). Expanding what counts as language beyond the merely verbal further opens the door to a deeper understanding of human-animal interactions and provides a space for the body to be understood as a basis for symbolic interaction. By recognizing non-verbal forms of communication, an exploration and understanding of how humans and their nonhuman animal companions can come to know the "subjective presence of the other" becomes possible.

Methods and Data

Over a 2-year period, I conducted 25 in-depth interviews and observed women and horses work-

ing together in various horse barn settings. I interviewed only women because men's relationships to horses have been amply showcased in the form of the cowboy, the ranch hand, and the Indian warrior. In line with feminist research principles, this research is an effort to bring women's relationships with horses to the center and to take seriously women's ways of thinking about horses as data.

Like many scholars engaged in qualitative research, my current biography and personal history became a meaningful starting point for sociological research. Almost all my life with horses has been in the hunter/jumper community, a subculture of a larger world of show horses. Recently, I became a student of natural horsemanship training methods.[1] In this setting, as both a horse owner and rider. I was a known observer and full participant. I was a complete member and added a research role to my existing membership role. My role as a full participant provided me invaluable insider knowledge and helped grant me entrée to the setting. My life experiences with horses provided me the required familiarity and knowledge of horse behavior and their unique way of relating in the world.

I chose to undertake in-depth interviewing and participant observation for this setting. My sample consisted of 25 in-depth interviews and hundreds of hours of participant observation. I knew several of the participants personally and used "snowball" or chain referral sampling to recruit informants. In addition, I attended various horsemanship clinics in the area, which allowed me to recruit women.

The women willingly granted me interviews. Many wanted to talk at length both about their horses and their ideas about human and horse communication and horsemanship. The interview format generated general descriptions of the women's history with horses, more detailed descriptions of their relationships with particular horses, and the processes by which the two species communicated.

Each interview lasted about $1\frac{1}{2}$ to 3 hours. However, because I most often met with respondents where their horses lived, I regularly spent 1 to 2 hours before the interview—meeting the horses, touring the facility, looking at photographs, and listening to stories of horses now deceased.

While engaged in observation, I took special note of how women—using their bodies and voices to convey their intention—worked with their horses. I also noted carefully how the horses responded to those acts.

Body to Body

Humans cannot "speak" horse, and horses do not use verbal language as a means of communication. This means that together the human and horse must create a system of communication, using a medium they both can understand. For both species, the body is a tool through which they can communicate a wide range of emotions and desires. Both horses and humans can learn a complicated system of body language different from the elements of spoken language, thus enabling each to express a subjective presence to the other and work together in a goal-oriented fashion. In the discussion that follows, I use excerpts from interviews and field observations to illustrate how the body can be a site for symbolic interaction and, more broadly, for exploring the possibility of symbolic interaction on a nondiscursive basis.

Tessa, a young woman in her early twenties, grew up riding horses and works as a large animal veterinarian technician, allowing her to spend most of her days with horses. Tessa explained the need to be "hyperaware" of her body, knowing that her physical movements and expressions always are translating an idea or feeling to the horse. Smiley (2004) writes, "If humans have smarter brains, then horses have smarter bodies" (p. 198).

Horses, in general, have highly sensitive bodies because their bodies are their vehicle for communication. Because horses rely on their bodies to transmit and receive information, they are highly skilled at reading (and using) body language.

Jane, a horse trainer and riding instructor for more than 30 years said, "I'd say probably their most acute sense is their tactile sense." With the understanding that horses send and collect ideas through their bodies, Tessa explained developing a greater "physical awareness" in order to become a more effective communicator with horses. Without this awareness, it would make it difficult, if not impossible, to understand why horses respond to a person the way they do.

Humans who work with horses develop a similar heightened awareness about their body language, rather than spoken words, and are careful to think about the messages they are conveying, or intend to convey, to the horse by way of their bodies. As humans develop a more acute tactile sense, they become more effective with their bodies and better able to "tune in" to the horse's body to understand what is being communicated to them. Doing both simultaneously enables the horse and the human to engage in a two-way conversation.

Co-Creative Language Building Process

It is important to acknowledge that what I am describing is not just a one-way relationship of humans merely imitating "horse language." Horses, too, are thinking, emotional, decision-making beings who, like humans, develop ways to communicate their subjectivity to their human partners. In this way, communication between the two is a cyclical and dynamic process, and both species are full participants in the process.

Sara, who has spent most of her life working with horses, is a well-known teacher of horsemanship clinics who travels around the world teaching humans how better to communicate with and understand their equine companions. Sara explained that it is necessary for humans to learn and refine ways of communicating with horses and, concurrently, it is important to think about the horse as an active member in the communication process:

> There will not be the kind of blending and the kind of naturalness about your interactions

with an animal that you might desire . . . until you adapt your capacity to think and understand through feel what the horse's experience of your decisions and actions are. . . . See, horses are intelligent, decision-making beings that can think and they can decide. They can decide what they want to do and when they want to do with their bodies and at what speeds . . . and in what fashion . . . if they are given credit for having a mind.

Horses use various parts of their bodies with a wide range of movements to communicate a feeling or desire. The ears of a horse are very expressive, and different positions can tell a human whether the horse is relaxed, curious, scared, angry, or listening. When I asked Jane how she could tell the difference between a horse who bucks out of a sense of playfulness from a horse who bucks out of anger, she answered, "I mean, the ears will be different. You know, one good little squeal and a buck, that's exuberance. Ears back and rooting you out of the saddle and bucking, that's pissed off." Tenseness in a horse's body can signal fear and anxiety; a constant swishing or wringing of the tail can indicate emotional agitation or physical discomfort. To assess a horse's emotional state, humans who work with horses need to be acutely aware of these—and many other—signals.

This co-creative process, resulting in a shared language system between humans and horses, is important for several reasons. First, effective communication between horses and humans helps ensure safe and humane interactions for both species. The average horse weighs about 1,200 pounds. The average human's weight is a mere 10 to 15 percent of the horse's weight. Humans need to communicate effectively to the horse and also understand what the horse communicates to them so that no misunderstandings cause one or the other to react in a manner that may be harmful to both. Second, when the horse and human are effectively communicating with each other they can work together in a goal-oriented fashion. Without the establishment of a shared language system, humans and horses

would experience constant conflict at the expense—more often than not—of the horse's well-being. Finally, and more important, creating a system of communication helps horses and humans develop a deeper understanding of each other.

The Grammar of Human-Horse Language

Through this multidimensional system of a shared body language, horses and humans can develop an intersubjective understanding of one another. Undoubtedly, the elements and rules of a body language are different from those of a verbal language. Although body language traditionally is not considered a complicated form of communication, for horses and humans it clearly is a form that enables complex human-horse working and emotional relationships.

Initially, both humans and horses must learn a basic system of communication. This system is taught to almost all young or "green" horses and beginning riders. When horses first begin working with humans, they are taught a basic vocabulary of bodily cues. In general, the cues work within a system of pressure and release. The horse learns that pressure on the right side of the body from a rider's leg or from a person's hand when the person is standing on the ground means, "move left." When the horse moves, pressure is released to communicate to the horse that was the desired outcome. The same basic cues (or signifiers) are taught to a person learning how to work with a horse from the ground or learning how to ride. Putting pressure on the left side of the horse's body tells the horse, "move right." When the horse moves right, the pressure should be released.

The basic cues of pressure and release become the alphabet of body language, the foundation from which a more sophisticated use of the language system can grow. The language becomes more complex and nuanced as the vocabularies of both horse and human expand. Gradually, horse and rider can synchronize various cues at once. The more humans and horses engage with one another, the more refined, clear, and subtle becomes their ability to communicate. Missy described the process of humans learning how to ride horses:

> It's all the subtlety . . . you know, when you start out and you're a beginner . . . you're unsteady . . . I mean you have to develop all that. And a lot of that is . . . your body discipline, too. I mean you have to be disciplined in your body to ride well . . . you need to have a balance . . . you need to maintain a balance on your horse. You know, you can't be flying around and your legs need to be still and your hands need to be still and steady and . . . that's not easy and that takes a lot of years to develop all that and it's very subtle . . . that stuff, that sounds simple and . . . when people wanna ride it's like, "Oh, how hard can this be." People don't understand how difficult riding is and they think, "Oh, there's nothing to it," but you know it's all, what separates all the good riders [from the bad] is all these little tiny nuances.

Horsepeople often say the best riders and horses are the ones who can go around the ring and make it look effortless, as if there are no visual signs of communication taking place. Well-developed riders and horses learn how to communicate and understand each other on such subtle levels that it can look as though no discussion is taking place between the two, just two united bodies moving together seemingly effortlessly and silent. This takes body discipline and a well-developed understanding of one's body as a vehicle for receiving and communicating different signals.

The embodied experience of human-horse communication, in part, relies on what Shapiro (1990) calls "kinesthetic empathy." He writes, "Empathic experience involves appropriating a second body that then becomes my auxiliary focus. Through my lived body, I accompany yours as it intends an object" (p. 192). When horse and rider are moving together, the rider must use his/her own body to make the horse's body the focal point, as literally both accompany the other in a shared embodied experience. Without this empathic basis, horse and rider would be

disjointed and in conflict, unable to have a shared experience of other.

Clearly, it takes a great deal of time and experience for humans to develop their body language skills and, in return, to understand horses' body language. This learning is part of the co-creative process of the human-horse language system that makes communication and emotional relationships between the two species possible. As the two work to develop a deeper understanding of each other and refine the communication process, so too grows the possibility of a shared, embodied subjectivity between horse and rider moving together, body to body, united.

Conclusion

I have tried to explain the process of embodied non-verbal communication between humans and horses, but it must be acknowledged that verbal language always will be limited in its capacity to explain an embodied non-verbal language system. I have argued that humans can understand the meaning of bodily gestures in horses, and horses can understand the meaning of bodily gestures in humans. Together, they co-create a system of language—a language of their own—through the medium of the body. This is not merely a conversation of gestures and, as Mead (1934) would have argued, animals are not simply impulsive beings. It is a mutually created language, a third language that enables the two to create a world of shared meaning and foster a deeper understanding of each other. This research is an effort to continue the challenge to the Cartesian divide begun by new human-animal research. It posits horses as sentient beings who live valuable lives of their own and brings to the center the deep and dynamic relationships women share with horses, not as a replacement of the human form, but as an equally valuable relationship with its own unique qualities, benefits, and complexities.

A de-privileging of Mead's (1934) emphasis on spoken language, as new human-animal research has shown, opens the door for investigation of the ways in which animals and humans alike use a variety of modes of communication to convey subjectivity. In particular, it allows for a deeper investigation into the body as a basis for symbolic interaction. As Shapiro (1990) writes, "We are out there in the world through our bodies. Our bodies do not encase us; rather, we are our bodies" (p. 192).

Research must begin to grapple with questions of how we understand communication with other species or with humans who do not have the capacity for verbal language. Exploration of these questions could generate new possibilities for understanding the subjective and intersubjective lives of those who cannot speak—humans and non-humans alike. The actual constructive process of a non-verbal language between horses and humans, as well as other human and animal pairings, also begs for empirical study. In sum, this article has shown that the study of human-horse communication can offer insights extending far beyond the exclusive world of horses and riders.

With an expansion of language beyond the verbal, there are distinctive advantages to the application of a symbolic interactionist approach to human and animal relationships. Specifically, this approach promises to further our understanding of non-verbal communication, meaning making, and subjectivity.

Notes

1. Natural horsemanship is a style of working with horses that is based on the premise that humans must understand the horse's thought process and way of being in the world and structure their interactions with horses based on this premise. As a training philosophy it endorses humane, non-forceful, and compassionate interactions between humans and horses.

References

Alger, J. M., and S. F. Alger. (1997). Beyond Mead: Symbolic interaction between humans and felines. *Society & Animals*, 5, 65–81.

Arluke, A., and C. Sanders. (1993). If lions could speak: Investigation of animal-human relationships and the perspectives of nonhuman others. *Sociological Quarterly*, 34, 377–390.

Irvine, L. (2004). *If you tame me: Animal identity and the intrinsic value of their lives.* Philadelphia: Temple University Press.

Mead, G. H. (1934). *Mind, self and society.* Chicago: University of Chicago Press.

Shapiro, K. J. (1990). Understanding dogs through kinesthetic empathy, social construction, and history. *Anthrozoös*, 3, 184–195.

Smiley, J. (2004). *A year at the races: Reflections on horses, humans, love, money, and luck.* New York: Alfred A. Knopf.

Isabel Gay A. Bradshaw

Symbolic Loss, Trauma, and Recovery in Elephant Communities

In the West, relationships between human and nonhuman animals have been largely defined by a power differential. This differential has denied non-human animals agency and a psychological life. Increasingly, however, culture and emotions are no longer viewed as exclusive property of humans—evidenced by an accumulation of personal testimony, scientific literature, and emergence of diverse animal rights groups.

The recent epistemological re-orientation and attitude change are related to the development of an environmental ethic that sees nonhuman nature as something more than a commodity. Further, there is a growing realization that European anthropocentrism and the Enlightenment's project of progress have exacted a tragic cost to all beings. A significant number of human and nonhuman animals live in severely degraded physical and psychological landscapes far different from the cultures and places from which they historically derive.

Certainly, neither stress nor trauma are new to human and nonhuman animals. The effects of colonialism, genocide, and the overwhelming capacity for global destruction are, however, unprecedented. Social and ecological violence is increasing, and the cultural mechanisms historically employed for mediation of trauma—mourning, ritual, a sense of community coherence—are no longer vital in many societies.

Impacts of human actions have made deep changes in the way of life of many species, even in areas considered as "wilderness." Death by hunting and traps, injury, maiming, disease, pursuit, habitat degradation, and fragmentation are common conditions.

Sanctuaries and rescue centers continue to be established to address this crisis but are overwhelmed with increasing numbers of injured nonhuman animals. Many of the centers are much more than first-aid stations: They are psychological and cultural rehabilitation facilities.

Here, I describe how trauma has become an increasingly commonplace experience among elephant communities and how sanctuaries such as The David Sheldrick Wildlife Trust, Kenya, are engaged in the rebuilding of these cultures in crisis. Poaching and habitat loss have decimated elephant herds and broken the intricate social structures that govern and guide elephant culture and threaten the future viability of the species. Like many recovering post-colonial human communities, there is an "absence of, or great destruction of, psychological structure" among the traumatized elephants (Homans, 2000, p. 29).

Through individual care of the orphans, the elephant keepers at the Trust play a critical role in helping rebuild elephant communities shattered by violence. By restoring the psychological, emotional, and social well being of young elephants toward their reintroduction to outside herds, the keepers are recreating the bonding needed for reconstituting the elephant's sense of community in the midst of genocide. These rehabilitation processes provide a valuable example of a conceptual framework and practice currently lacking in conservation and in ethology that "incorporates the vital ingredient of compassion and animal welfare" (Sheldrick, 2004).

Elephants: Communities in Trauma

Elephants are the subject of numerous legends and myths. They play a critical role in African communities and ecosystems at large. Among many tribes, the elephant is attributed with "superintelligence and almost human feelings for its companions" (Moss, 1992). Elephants are known for their intimate and intricate social organization, spending much of the time in community where family members act as a coordinated body of a larger, affiliated group. There is a marked lack of territoriality among males, and the elephants alternately move together and apart in aggregate throughout the course of the year. The females move through the bush eating, playing, drinking, and grooming as a structured group of cows and calves led by a senior matriarch who is "responsible for making all the decisions" (Sheldrick, 1992).

Elephants' communication system is well documented. Within sight of each other, two or more elephants can rely on and utilize myriad combinations of trunk waving, positioning of head and bodies, tail and feet, and vocalizations. African elephant researchers now realize that elephants use subsonic patterns to communicate over large distances (Payne, 1998). Elephants can hear and produce frequencies in the region of 14 to 16 Hz, well below the range of the human ear. This mode of communication often is used to broadcast the death of a community member or announce any sudden changes (Payne, 1998). Community coherence is maintained through close physical contact among generations and communication within, and between, elephant social groups.

The importance of visible intimate contact among elephants cannot be overemphasized. Birthing mothers are tended attentively by other females, and calf care is shared by the entire group. Young calves are constantly being touched, guided, snuggled, and provided with reassurance intensively throughout the first years of life. There is always "good enough" mothering for young elephants. "The cow-calf bond is extremely strong and the mother will go to her child's rescue (and to other calves' as well) at any sign of trouble, and she will not abandon her calf under any circumstances" (Moss, 1975, p. 16). Even in the event of a mother's death, there are ample aunts and grandmothers to raise the calf. Female elephants reach menopause only in their early fifties and continue in the role of babysitter and grandparent well beyond their reproductive years. Because of this longevity, elephants' relationships are maintained for decades, and communities generally remain intact for these periods. It has been only since the extensive and intensive killing that has occurred dramatically over recent decades that fragmented groups and dysfunctional behaviors have been observed with increasing frequency (Sheldrick, 1992; Moss, 1992).

Group bonding is engaged in everyday activities of eating, playing, and drinking and demonstrated in times of illness. When any member ails, others gather around and try to rouse the sickened member to health. In the case of a middle-aged female named Polly, a family male, after unsuccessful attempts with other members to raise Polly to her feet after she had collapsed, mounted her in a last effort to revive her (Poole, 1996). When a young elephant, Ely, was born crippled with poorly articulated carpal joints, the herd stayed with him, assisting, prodding, and giving physical therapy by massaging and nursing.

> The threesome [Ely and two herd members] headed toward us through the picturesque palms of Ol Tukai Orok. As the two older elephants walked, they continually turned to look back at the calf that was shuffling along behind. Every few feet they stopped and waited for him to catch up before moving on. Their progress was very slow, but they showed no impatience. It was a poignant sight and highlighted the incredibly caring nature of these nonhuman animals. (Moss, 1992, p. 72)

Eventually, months later, the therapy worked, and Ely became capable of walking unassisted.

Perhaps more than any other quality, the elephant is thought of as having understanding of death. Grieving and mourning rituals are an integral part of elephant culture. Mothers often are observed grieving over their dead child for days after the death, alternately trying to bring the baby back to life and caressing and touching the corpse. Poole (1996) observed a mother grieving over her stillborn child for several days: "As I watched Tonie's vigil over her dead newborn, I got my first very strong feeling that elephants grieve. . . . Every part of her spelled grief" (p. 95).

The death of a matriarch is particularly difficult for the community. The senior females form the pillars of elephant communities; when they die, the entire community is affected. Emily, a matriarch in the "EB" group studied for many years by Cynthia Moss and Harvey Croze, died in 1989: an "event that would have profound repercussions in the family. The deaths of calves are distressing for their mothers but the death of an adult female disrupts the whole family" (Moss, 1992, p. 30). In the case of Emily, the group participated in several, observed mourning rituals with her body and, later, her bones. When Emily was found and examined, it was discovered that her stomach contained massive amounts of bottle caps, glass, batteries, and plastic that had come from the trash of nearby ecotourism resorts. The aftershocks of Emily's passing were observed for months and years later when the group visited Emily's bones.

> The animal[s] stopped and reached their trunks out. They stepped closer and very gently began to touch the remains with the tips of their trunks, first light taps, smelling and feeling, then strokes around and along the larger bones. Eudora and Elspeth, Emily's daughter and granddaughter, pushed through and began to examine the bones. And soon after Echo and her two daughters arrived. All elephants were quiet now and there was a palpable tension among them. Eudora concentrated on Emily's skull caressing the smooth cranium and slipping her trunk into the hollows in the skull. Echo was feeling the lower jaw running her trunk along the teeth—the area used in greeting when elephants place their trunks in each others' mouth. The younger animals were picking

up the smaller bones and placing them in their mouths before dropping them again. . . . Several years before, I had also seen the EBs start to bury the carcass of a young female from another family who had died of natural causes. (Moss, 1992, p. 61)

The combined pressures of encroaching human habitation, land conversion, and genocidal levels of hunting have brought elephants to the edge of extinction (IUCN, 2003). Many of the areas to which elephants are now confined are too small for viable residence, and elephant groups are severely limited in their ability to migrate through the region and continent that are part of their natural heritage.

In these transformed landscapes, the life of an elephant is fraught with violence. Poaching is intensive, and the larger elephants of a group are culled systematically for their ivory. It is increasingly more difficult to maintain elephant community coherence. Orphaned elephants are left to die unless they can be rescued. The marks of trauma are found everywhere. Sheldrick (1992), who has spent more than half a century caring for orphaned elephants in Kenya writes: "[T]he poaching holocaust has disrupted Elephant society and plung[ed] their social structure into chaos. It has left them traumatized, rudderless and even more vulnerable and fragile."

Increasingly, elephants are observed to have "intrusive behaviour" indicative of trauma (Caruth, 1996, p. 5). In each case, some manipulation of the elephant group involving the forcible disruption of social bonds, denied participation in ritual, or an extremely violent experience has occurred. Reintroduction of elephants typically entails bringing in unfamiliar elephants and the fragmenting of existing groups and families. In South Africa, such social shuffling created a culture of young, violent males. Translocated juvenile male elephants rampaged throughout the reserve killing rhinos, charging tourist trucks, and even threatening the older female elephants. With the introduction of senior male elephants the young males desisted, and "the population settled down to, what we describe as, a normal population structure, in terms of the social behavior" (Slotow, 2001). Reflecting on this experience, Slotow, a biologist, notes that "[n]ot only should one consider what the elephants eat, is their food present, etc., but also, what the sociological consequences would be for animals such as elephants."

Many zoos have reported incidents involving similar intrusive behavior. Recently at the Denver Zoo, Hope, an Asian elephant, suddenly became aggressive and injured another elephant. This behavior was ascribed to her reaction to the death of another elephant and repeated disruptions in the group because of transferring of elephants between various zoos (Good, 2001).

Some zoos are becoming more sensitized to nonhuman animal emotions. Several years ago, a zoo called a well-known, nonhuman animal communicator to consult with their elephants because of similar irregular behavior. In conversation with the elephants, the consultant learned that a resident elephant who had died was removed before the remaining elephants could mourn the body of their dead companion of many years. When the skull of the deceased was brought back to the elephant group, the elephants immediately gathered around and began a ritual of touch and caressing much as described by Moss (1992). Thereafter the elephants resumed "normal" behavior.

Violent conditions have become the norm for elephant both in what was called "the wild" and in captivity. The rapid destruction of social structure and ecosystems in which these nonhuman animals have evolved has left a fractured and psychologically damaged community at levels that western culture is only beginning to appreciate. "Considering elephants' ability to communicate over long distances, the tentacles of pain and agony may stretch farther than we know" (Ellis, 2002, p. 135). At the David Sheldrick Wildlife Trust, each rescued orphan elephant has been highly traumatized. This is illustrated by the story of the orphan Dika.

Dika demonstrated despair and heartbreak graphically. Some of his family were gunned down en mass, others fled, wounded amidst gunfire, and Dika had raced through a thorn thicket because when he arrived [at the Preserve] he had hundreds of long acacia thorns protruding from almost every square inch of his body. For four long months we could get no sparkle from him and there were times when we wondered if he was, in fact, mentally normal. Even the other elephants could get no response from him as he stood by refusing to play, reluctant to eat, tears staining his cheeks, unable to sleep—so obviously tragically distraught. (Sheldrick, 1991)

Most orphaned elephants at the Trust have witnessed the slaughter or mutilation of their entire family. As a result of this shocking experience and dis-orientation, the young elephants become lost. When one orphan, Ndume, strayed onto their land, tribesmen beat him unconscious. "When he regained consciousness, he was extremely confused, and spent days searching for his family, rushing around the bush, and crying pathetically" (Sheldrick, 2004). Often in the course of wandering with no elder to guide them, young elephants are caught in deep wells in search of water or are found near starving and dehydrated. Because of land erosion, overuse, and drought, farmers must dig very deep wells that normally exist as shallow ponds in which young elephants can wallow safely. Here, they remain in psychological and physical shock, starving and doomed to a painful death unless they can be rescued.

Such scenarios are by definition traumatic and tragically have become commonplace. Trauma is "an overwhelming experience of sudden or catastrophic events in which the response to the event occurs in the often delayed, uncontrolled, and repetitive appearance of hallucinations and other intrusive phenomena" (Caruth, 1996, p. 11). The magnitude of the trauma is so great that elephant culture is endangered. Not only are the processes that create social bonding broken by the traumatic events but also the capacity to recover and renew these processes is lost or, at best, severely impaired because of the selective killings of elder and matriarch elephants.

Trauma becomes a culture unto itself. "Trauma is not the result of a group experiencing pain. It is the result of this acute discomfort entering into the core of the collectivity's sense of its own identity" (Alexander, 2003, p. 38). In this context, elephant rehabilitation means more than healing an individual: Rehabilitation is faced with the task of renewing a culture as well.

Unfortunately, most ethological and conservation models do not integrate sufficiently the nonhuman psyche at the individual and cultural levels to address these situations adequately. In the tradition of western science, most conservation has focused on the state of the biophysical environment. Ethology, while concerned with nonhuman animal behavior, has, until very recently, labored under a limited interpretation of a nonhuman animal emotion and psychology. Now, however, at places like the David Sheldrick Wildlife Trust, the practice of elephant conservation is attempting to breach traditional barriers of psyche and soma.

Interspecies Witnessing: Alternate Models for Human-Nonhuman Relationships

At the Trust, care of orphaned and injured elephants extends beyond the immediate treatment of shock and nourishment to include the re-building of elephant communities. The rescue center is designed to support recovery processes that aid in the restitching of the emotional and social *aporia*—gaps—created in the elephant psyche by human violence. Immediate, and sometimes chronic, physical injuries are treated, but equal attention is directed toward the healing of the young elephant's emotions and re-socialization. Like humans, child-adult bonding is considered critical for the development of a healthy psyche. At the sanctuary, the elephants live among their family of elephants and keepers:

> During the day, the elephants and their Keepers go as a group free ranging, but at night one keeper will sleep with each elephant in its sta-

ble, rotating. It is important not to allow too strong a bond to develop between individuals, because when the man has time off, or is sick, the elephant will grieve and go into a decline, losing another family member. If they are fond of all the Keepers, they do not miss the presence of any particular one too acutely because there are others of which they are equally fond. (Sheldrick, 2004)

Gradually, as the young elephants revive, they are reintegrated into elephant groups and learn to engage in routine patterns of life while interacting with both humans and other elephants.

The elephant keeper becomes closely tuned to each elephant, such that species differentiation recedes into a secondary feature. "Elephants are 'human' animals, encompassed by an invisible aura that reaches deep into the human soul in a mysterious and mystifying way" (Sheldrick, 2004). This capacity extends beyond the confines of speciesism and, like one of the keepers, Mishak Nzimbi, evokes the "elephant spirit" in each.

> To an elephant youngster, the tight community of matriarchal herd into which it is born represents safety, food, knowledge, and a link to the past. Their reality is shaped by their childhood experiences in the herd. Replicating that reality for the orphans is a formidable task for the keepers. Head keeper Mishak Nzimbis seen by the babies as their surrogate matriarch, and in his gentle confident manner exudes enormous influence over them. (Ellis, 2002, p. 53)

It is important to note the critical role played by the humans in the rehabilitation process at the Trust. Orphan elephants necessarily are adopted, nursed, and re-socialized by humans because of an absence of such capacity within the elephant community. Either the entire family-group has been massacred or dispersed or the orphan elephant has been so badly traumatized that intensive care is necessitated. The human caretaker is an essential facilitator in bringing the orphan to health. Sanctuaries like the David Sheldrick Wildlife Trust are islands of human-mediated healing which, because of their own state of trauma, bridge a deep chasm and fill a role that even other elephants are not always capable of filling.

Keepers at the Trust are in every sense witnesses as defined by Caruth (1996). Many trauma treatment clinicians and theorists today argue that alternate models for the healer-victim relationship are necessary. Using the same structures responsible for creating the violence— power and anthropocentrically based human- nonhuman relationships—merely reinforces the experience of trauma. It is, instead, necessary to go beyond the dichotomous structures that characterize colonial thinking, to go where Oliver (2001) calls "beyond recognition" to a stance of witnessing. To "re-conceive of ourselves, what it means to be a self, a subject, to have subjectivity, to consider oneself an active agent" is prerequisite to working through rather than repetition of violence and trauma" (p. 18). Witnessing is relating to an individual not as the object of a traumatic event nor as an identifiable symptom or problem. As many truth and reconciliation commissions attest, recognition alone is often experienced by victims as yet another replay of the traumatic event (Hayner, 2001; Tutu, 1999). Victims of "oppression, slavery and torture are not merely seeking visibility and recognition, but they are also seeking witness to horrors beyond recognition" (Oliver, 2001, p. 8). It is only in the place of witnessing that deep communication can take place:

> Communication would be impossible if it should have to begin in the ego . . . to whom every other would be a limitation that invited war, domination, precaution and information. To communicate is indeed to open oneself, but the openness is not complete if it is on the watch for recognition. It is complete not in the opening to the spectacle of, or the recognition of, the other, but in becoming a responsibility for him. (Levinas, 1993, p.119)

Dismantling the perceptual mode of differencing to one of subjectivity provides a portal for communication across species' lines and allows a "remapping [of] the borderlands between nature and culture" (Haraway, 1989, p. 15).

Witnessing is an ethical journey to a third space of subjectivity: a deconstruction of the subject-object incarnation that defines most human-nonhuman relationships in the West. In the role of witness, the keepers at the Trust provide the structure and pathway that support the process of bringing back meaning to a disjunct experience and bridging past, present, and future.

These people are motivated by the calling of a heart ethic. "We must liken the emotional trauma of the Elephants to that of humans under similar circumstances of hardship and deprivation. To deny this is simply to display gross ignorance born of human arrogance" (Sheldrick, 1992). This willingness to go beyond species' differences makes elephant rehabilitation possible. To move beyond language and otherness is to walk a different ethos. "[E]thical obligation at the heart of subjectivity is inherent in the process of witnessing. Moving from recognition to witnessing provides other notions of ethical, social, and political responsibility entailed by this conception of subjectivity" (Oliver, 2001, p. 15).

Here, the connection between witnessing and political action becomes evident. As Herman (1997) states: "The systematic study of psychological trauma . . . depends on the support of a political movement" (p. 9). The departure for new meanings of difference beyond the dichotomy of speciesism makes the topic of trauma a political issue of the times because it deconstructs the fundamental assumption of human privilege. In this light, then, interspecies witnessing is neither psychological triage nor a temporary "fix" but a re-creation of elephant-human relationships as partnerships.

Elephant Orphan Sanctuaries: Bridges to Rebuilding Community

The pervasive nature of trauma has sown seeds for a potentially very different notion of culture and social contract among diverse human and non-human cultures. The David Sheldrick Wildlife Trust offers a model for how interspecies community can function where human and nonhuman animals learn new ways to live together in transformed landscapes. However, although clearly the Trust is highly successful—to date, over fifty elephants have been hand-reared and already are, or in the process of, being reintroduced to wild herds—the fact remains that entire sets of cultures have been shattered. A recreation of life before the trauma usually is not possible.

When home, family, and land are shattered and cultural genocide becomes the shocking reality, going back to the "way it was" is not always possible. Survival into a post-trauma world—Lacan's (1973) "trauma of waking"—has changed even the perception of what reality seemed to be. Rehabilitation may help bring elephant communities to health, but it is unclear how this culture will resemble traditional elephant societies.

The experience of the Trust seems to indicate that the process of rehabilitation, while perhaps unable to reconstruct elephant life to pre-genocide conditions, nonetheless engenders the hope of an interspecies culture beyond the confines of orphan care. In some cases, former orphans bring their wild-born young to introduce to their former human families at the sanctuary. Ndume, the orphan who lost his family and very nearly was beaten to death, is now grown and independent of the Sheldrick Trust Keepers, fully integrated into the wild herds. Ndume, nonetheless, returns periodically to keep in touch with his erstwhile human family. The Trust keepers are not only caretakers of elephant young but also guardians of elephant culture. Through their work, they nurture the seeds of elephant culture that allow for continuation of the species.

Conclusions

Trauma theory has brought attention to the severe psychological damage that victims of violence experience. Here, elephant communities have been described through the lens of trauma theory to understand better how they have been affected by systematic violence. By addressing individual and cultural trauma of elephants, The

David Sheldrick Wildlife Trust is taking part in the creation of a new interspecies epistemology and ethic based on partnership. The framing of trauma "[a]llows collectivities to define new forms of moral responsibility" (Alexander, 2003, p. 38). Further, by its "holographic" framing (Grotstein, 1994), trauma theory brings attention to the shared suffering that human and nonhuman animals experience with the widespread social and ecological violence promulgated by colonization. By acknowledging the validity of nonhuman animal subjectivity—their psychological and cultural lives—conservation ecology can become a natural history: the narrative of human and nonhuman nature.

Traditionally, nature has served as a source of healing for humans. Now, humans can participate actively in the healing of both themselves and non-human animals. Although the tragedy of these elephants cannot be erased, places such as the David Sheldrick Wildlife Trust offer a way in which the beginnings of healthy and equitable interspecies communities can develop.

References

Alexander, J. C. (2003). Towards a theory of cultural trauma. In J. C. Alexander (Ed.), *The meaning of social life: A cultural sociology* (pp. 6–27). Oxford University Press: Oxford.

Caruth, C. (1996). *Unclaimed experience: Trauma, narrative, and history.* Johns Hopkins University Press: Baltimore.

Deloria, V., Jr. (1999). *For this land: Writings on religion in America.* Routledge Press: New York.

Ellis, G. (2002). *Wild orphans.* Welcome Books: New York.

Good, O. W. (2001, June 18). Activists give zoo an earful: Protesters demand inquiry into elephants' care, mental health. *Rocky Mountain News.* www.rockymountainnews.com/drmn/local/article/0,1299,DRMN_15_670161,00.html.

Grotstein, J. S. (1994). *Affect regulation and the origin of the self: The neurobiology of emotional development.* Lawrence Erlbaum Associates: Hillsdale, NJ.

Haraway, D. (1989). *Primate visions: Gender, race, nature in the world of modern science.* Routledge Press: New York.

Hayner, P. B. (2001) *Unspeakable truths: Confronting state terror and atrocity.* Routledge: New York.

Herman, J. (1997). *Trauma and recovery.* Basic Books: Boulder, CO.

Homans, P. (2000). *Symbolic loss: The ambiguity of mourning and memory at century s end.* University of Virginia Press: Charlottesville.

IUCN. (2003). African elephant databases. Species Survival Commission. IUCN. www.iucn.org/themes/ssc/sgs/afesg/aed/index.html.

Lacan, J., and J.-A. Miller (Eds.). (1973). *The four fundamental concepts of psychoanalysis.* Norton: New York.

Levinas, E. (1993). *Collected philosophical papers.* Trans. Alphonso Lingis Kiuwer. Academic Publishers: San Diego.

Moss, C. (1975). *Portraits in the wild: Nonhuman animal behaviour in East Africa.* University of Chicago Press: Chicago.

Moss, C. (1992). *Echo of the elephants: The story of an elephant family.* William Morrow, Inc.: New York.

Oliver, K. (2001). *Witnessing: Beyond recognition.* University of Minnesota Press: Minneapolis.

Payne, K. (1998). *Silent thunder: In the presence of elephants.* Penguin Books: London.

Poole, J. (1996). *Coming of age with elephants: A memoir.* Hyperion Press: New York.

Sheldrick, D. (1991). *Elephant emotion,* www.sheldrickwildlifetrust.org/html/elephant_emotion.html.

Sheldrick, D. (1992). *The impact of elephants in Tsavos.* www.Elephant.elehost. com/About_Elephants.

Sheldrick, D. (2004, January 4). Saving Olly-now named Madiba. *The David Sheldrick Trust Newsletter.*

Slotow, R. (2001, December 15). *Delinquent elephants, in interview with Living on Earth.* www.loe.org/archives/001215.html.

Tutu, D. M. (1999). *No future without forgiveness.* Doubleday: New York.

Leslie Irvine

Animal Selfhood

The notion that animals, like people, have selves is controversial for sociology. The field has defined its subject matter as that which is uniquely human. Along with culture, rationality, and language, the self is one of the entities for which animals purportedly lack the tools. The word *tool* is important here, for tool use and, later, tool making long served to distinguish humans from (and portray them as superior to) other animals. When Jane Goodall (1990) observed the chimpanzee David Greybeard not only *using* a tool but also *making* one, her observation called for redefining the existing boundary between humans and animals. If some animals have the ability to make and use various *physical* tools, perhaps they also possess the *conceptual* tools required for selfhood. In other words, if we humans were wrong about tool use among animals, there are likely other things we have underestimated and overlooked, such as their capacity for selfhood. Perhaps the boundary of self-consciousness that has long divided humans from animals is also illusory. If so, then how can sociologists, in particular, interactionists, study animal selfhood? What might we gain from and contribute to the task?

Scholars from a range of disciplines have repeatedly challenged the once-distinct boundary between human and nonhuman animals by showing that the latter can feel emotions and communicate with symbols. In humans, emotions and symbol use indicate the presence of capacities that constitute selfhood. In interactionist sociology, Sanders (1990, 1999) draws on everyday interaction between people and dogs to illustrate the construction of personhood and the sharing of basic emotions and intentions. Likewise, Alger and Alger (1997) examine attributions of selfhood

among cat owners. Following Sanders, they observed cats engaged in taking the role of the others, defining situations, choosing courses of action, and having memories of past events. In addition, Alger and Alger's research in a cat shelter reveals that cats have culture, in that they transmit behaviors socially, as well as instinctually, through symbolic interaction (1999, 2003).

The interactionist paradigm is well suited to the study of animal selfhood, and applying it expands the notion of what it means to be social. Using interactionism in this way requires moving beyond Mead's ([1934] 1962) language-driven model of selfhood. For Mead, spoken language constituted the social psychological barrier between humans and nonhumans because it enables humans to understand and communicate the symbols for self, such as our names and the names of objects. Mead acknowledged that animals have their own social arrangements but claimed that their interaction involves a "conversation of gestures." This term denotes primitive, instinctual acts, such as when a dog growls at another who threatens to steal his bone or a cat hisses at a rival. Mead considered the conversation of gestures insignificant because it allegedly has only one meaning. According to Mead, animals, lacking the capacity to use significant symbols, were incapable of having any meaningful social behavior.

In making spoken language the key to what distinguishes humans from other animals, Mead (and, consequently, social psychology) established two states of consciousness: one for those who could converse about it and another, lesser form for those who could not. Mead thus advanced the anthropocentric, rationalist tradition of Descartes, whose claim *I think, therefore I am* required the ability to *talk* about thinking. My intention here is to offer a model of animal selfhood that expands the possibilities of empirical interactionist research. I examine the capacities that animals must have in order to achieve this shared experience. My conclusions apply only to companion animals, by which I mean the dogs and cats with whom so many of us share our homes and our daily lives. Although some of my arguments might well apply to other animals, I have studied only dogs and cats. I leave it to other researchers to incorporate other species.

Methods

The evidence presented here draws on several sources of data collected and analyzed through continuous, emergent inductive techniques. I conducted more than three hundred hours of research in what Adler and Adler (1987) call a "complete membership role" at a humane society that I refer to as "the Shelter." This private, nonprofit organization offers adoptions, veterinary services, humane education, dog training, and cat behavior consultations and serves as the headquarters for the city's animal control services and welfare investigations. In 1998 I began working as one of the Shelter's volunteers. I have served in many volunteer roles; this article draws chiefly but not exclusively on that of adoption counselor. This position involves introducing people to animals whom they are considering for adoption, providing information about behavior and training, and answering questions. Moreover, it involves determining whether the animal and the person will be a good "match." As an adoption counselor, I became curious about people's interactions with animals in the adoption area and began taking notes. I recorded how long they looked at particular animals, whether they adopted an animal that day or just visited, and what, if anything, they said to the animals or to the people with them.

My volunteer service on what I call the Adoption Mobile, a thirty-foot recreational vehicle that serves as a traveling branch of the Shelter,

produced an additional 150 hours of observation. Five days a week, a volunteer and a staff member take a selection of adoptable cats, rabbits, rodents, and a dog to various sites throughout the county. The locations include shopping centers, libraries, and local festivals. On board, people can adopt animals, make donations, and obtain answers to their questions about animal care and behavior or the Shelter's services. The Adoption Mobile spends 4 hours at a given site, and an average of 100 people visit during this time. The work entails intense interaction with the public.

In spring 1999 I began developing another source of data through autoethnography. Autoethnography offers an "insider's" view that can only come through immersion in and intimate knowledge of the group's interaction. In these works the researcher puts himself or herself into the inquiry, but the result is much more than a report on the ethnographer.

I began the autoethnographic phase of this research by taking notes about my interactions with my own companion cats. I had lived with cats all my adult life, but I stopped taking our lives together for granted and became a participant-observer of our daily routines. Then, in summer 1999, I adopted a dog from the Shelter. As the cats and I adjusted to life with him, I wrote it all down. I examined my autoethnographic notes and those from the Shelter regularly, searching for emergent themes and patterns. Over repeated readings, one idea—the way in which animals communicate their personalities, emotions, preferences, and knowledge to people—came through clearly. I conducted 40 semistructured interviews that focused on how people made decisions to adopt, how they had chosen particular animals, and how everyday life and activities with the animal unfolded after adoption.

Rethinking the Self

Observations of the interactions between people and animals in the adoption areas revealed three themes. The first is seeking relationships with the animals. A steady stream of people, most having no intention to adopt, came to visit the animals. Some even came regularly, to visit long-term Shelter residents. They often came in pairs or groups, making the visit a social event. Their interaction with animals was not limited to looking at them but also involved talking to them and about them. Everyone wanted to touch the animals, know their names and their stories, and, whenever possible, hold and play with them outside of their kennels or cages. Moreover, many people who had browsed the Shelter's Web site wanted to meet the animals whom they had seen in thumbnail photos. In other words, they did not simply want to know that the animals existed; they wanted to interact with them face-to-face. In other words, they wanted relationships with the animals.

The second theme has to do with concern for animals' well-being. Shelter clients wanted to learn the animals' histories and, in the case of adoption, provide what he or she needed. This concern appeared in phrases I heard frequently, such as "I feel so sorry for them" and "I wish I could take them all home." People were genuinely concerned when animals seemed afraid or were obviously recovering from an operation or injury.

The third theme involves increasing complexity of interaction. In the adoption areas, I found that people who had had animals previously, some for most of their lives, interacted with a wider range of animals and did not fuss as much over the puppies and kittens. Moreover, with repeated or sustained interaction, people began to explore more facets of the animal's character and capabilities. For instance, a first visit might involve strolling past the kennels and cages, just looking. Then, when a particular animal captured someone's attention, the person might begin talking to the animal, perhaps squatting down to get closer. When this offered an opportunity for an animal to display some unique trait, such as playfulness or attentiveness, the person then engaged the animal further. This, in turn, revealed additional aspects of the animal's "personality" and continued in a reciprocal process, allowing the person to discover more about the animal as interaction grew more complex, albeit within the confines of the kennels. Moreover, animals served as "social facilitators," sparking conversations among visitors and thus encouraging the use of interactional skills with other people as well.

The interaction in the adoption areas thus suggests that people seek relationships with animals, express concern for their well-being, and engage in increasingly complex behaviors with them. These three themes, I argue, have one thing in common: they point in the direction of the self. More specifically, they are behaviors or activities that manifest goals of the self. For instance, we know from Mead and others that the self emerges through relationships. Once the self has developed, it can exist without relationships, so that the person in solitary confinement continues to have a sense of self. However, relationships allow us to develop a mutual history that is simultaneously a history of the self.

If we can agree that relationships are essential for the self, it would be important to increase the skills that make relationships possible. Maintaining relationships requires the use of the interactional skills that foster relationships in the first place. One of the signs that a relationship is "good for" the self is that it exercises and improves our interactional skills. Good relationships stretch our interactional abilities by requiring us to see things in new ways. Good relationships offer "new information—incongruities, interruptions of expectations, challenges—in the context of familiar otherness" (Myers 1998:78). They challenge our interactional skills *just enough* and consequently increase our abilities to have relationships. As with physical exercise, we build "muscle" that equips us for further challenges. Eventually, the exercise itself becomes intrinsically rewarding. Moreover, concern for the well-being of others, expressed through an interest in their needs, ensures the continuity that provides the relationships on which the self depends.

Sensing Subjectivity

The key, I argue, is the subjective presence of the Other. The interaction must seem to have a source, and we must see the Other as having a mind, beliefs, and desires, just as we do. This not only confirms the Other's sense of self to us; it also confirms our own. How do we sense an Other's subjective presence? With people, we can rely on self-reports. However, these reveal more about the norms of self-reports than about anything else. Self-reports reveal the influence of what people know to be good, desirable, acceptable depictions of the self. They reveal a self digested in consciousness and shaped by language. They indicate how people talk and think about the self, not how they experience it. A stronger objection is that, even with other people, we simply do not rely on language first or foremost for information about selfhood. As Goffman (1959) wrote, only *part* of the self is conveyed through "impressions given." Other aspects appear through "impressions given off."

Relying on language eliminates a considerable amount of interaction as a source of information that contributes to selfhood. Moreover, it restricts the significant interactants to other people. If we can agree that factors beyond spoken language matter for the creation of the self, then animals can participate in the process. In the model of the self that I am using, in order for animals to do so, they must themselves *be* subjective Others. How can we sense their subjective presence? As with other people, we cannot observe subjectivity directly. We perceive it *indirectly*, during interaction. To illustrate how this is so, I turn to a model of self that originates in William James's ([1890] 1950) efforts to gain access to the "I," or the subjective sense of self. Along the way, James distinguished four facets that underlie and make us aware of subjectivity. Others have since refined these into a set of basic self-experiences that manifest themselves in infancy, before the acquisition of language (see Myers 1998; Stern 1985). Therefore, the case can be made for the presence of these experiences among animals, who have the same structures of the brain, nervous system, musculature, and memory. Whereas human development takes us into a stage of language acquisition that adds to

these basic experiences, the experiences themselves are preverbal. The four self-experiences consist of

1. a sense of *agency*, meaning that you are the author of your actions and movements and not the author of the actions and movements of others;
2. a sense of *coherence*, meaning that you understand yourself as a physical whole that is the locus of agency;
3. a sense of *affectivity*, meaning patterned qualities of feelings that are associated with other experiences of the self; and
4. a sense of *self-history*, meaning that you maintain some degree of continuity, even while changing.

Human beings attain these four senses of self through interaction with others, beginning at birth. They not only underlie our *own* senses of subjective experience, but, as we shall see, they also form the basis for distinguishing self from Other. Combined, these four senses compose a "core" self that is considered necessary for normal psychological functioning (Stern 1985:71). The absence of one of them manifests itself in psychosis and other pathologies. Granted, there are additional senses of self, many of which require the acquisition of language, but the four I draw attention to here are prior to and essential for additional senses. Here, I offer illustrative examples of how these aspects of core self are manifested among dogs and cats.

Agency In sociology, the term "agency" is used (and misused) in many ways. I use it to refer to the capacity for self-willed action. Agency implies subjectivity, in that an agentic being, by definition, has desires, wishes, and intentions, along with a sense of having those things. In other words, it is the actor's awareness of having desires or wishes that is an element of selfhood, not simply having them. Agency also implies having control over one's own actions (i.e., I can sit when I decide to, and if you push me into a chair, that is something different) and awareness of the felt consequences of those actions.

Several indicators of a sense of agency appear in the first months of life. Examples include reaching for objects and hand-to-mouth skills. At about 4 months, infants begin to use visual information to shape the fingers to accommodate objects of particular sizes. Since agency does not depend on verbal ability, it is therefore feasible among other species. Some of the best examples of animals' agency come from the arena of dog training, even at the beginner's level. As Sanders (1999) explains, the main thing that trainers teach dogs is to exercise *self-control*—and they use precisely this term. Self-control implies that the dog has a sense that he or she can initiate action, since in order to *control one's self* one must first *have* a sense of will or volition. At the Shelter, I saw frequent examples of this when I worked with staff members to make undersocialized dogs more adoptable. A typical case involved a young, mixed-breed dog who jumped up on the gate of his kennel and barked wildly for attention whenever anyone came near, making most potential adopters think twice. The key to modifying the dog's behavior was to change his understanding of the cause of the rewards he receives. Changing his understanding in this way highlights the nonverbal capacity to distinguish self from Other.

A dog who jumps up on his kennel and barks receives two kinds of rewards. To the extent that the behavior is *self-directed* (i.e., aimed at releasing energy), it is constantly rewarding. However, to the extent that it is *directed at others*, as an attempt to gain their attention, there is only a probabilistic chance that it will be rewarded. Many people will avoid such a dog—as was the case with the dog in this example. As long as the reward of attention depends on others, it will be unpredictable. The dog does not control that reward. The only thing he controls (or should) is his behavior. We had to make the dog aware of this and show him how to increase the probability of rewards from others. To do so, we removed him from the adoption area for a few days to reduce the foot traffic past his kennel. We scheduled regular exercise to reduce

his need for the jumping. Most important, we stopped reinforcing his bad behavior. We paid attention to him only when he was quiet and had all four paws on the floor. If he stood up on his hind legs or barked, we moved away from his kennel. Because he had released some of his pent-up energy through exercise, the reward of attention quickly became a higher priority. Moreover, because attention depended on *others*, he soon learned to control himself to get it. This subtle act of behavior modification helped the dog to distinguish self from Other by distinguishing different reinforcement schedules.

One day, as a staff member and I discussed our work with the above-mentioned dog, she said, "We have to get him to be able to show people that he'll be worth it." It occurred to me that although our explicit task was to help him to learn basic canine manners, our larger, albeit implicit, goal was to enable him to demonstrate to people that he had something *underneath,* or *other than,* the problem behaviors. In other words, we had to help him to develop the control over his own behavior that would show people that he had—or was—a self.

Coherence   If agency provides a sense of self versus Other, then coherence provides the boundaries of the self. We acknowledge coherence when "we say of some others that they seem to 'have their act together,' or of our own Self, that some particular line of endeavor is 'very much part of me'" (Bruner and Kalmar 1998:311). Coherence gives agency somewhere to "live." Several indicators of coherence do not rely on language, making their presence likely in nonhuman animals.

Infancy research indicates that the capacity to recognize distinct others, such as primary caregivers, becomes available as early as 2 or 3 months of age. Animals, too, can recognize distinct others. At the Shelter, volunteers who regularly work with certain animals for weeks or even months find that these animals begin to recognize them. More relevant for the discussion of coherence is how animals are able to understand that parts of people belong together. For example, at the Shelter's veterinary clinic, I had regular contact with a dog who required several surgeries and diagnostic tests. I often held him while a technician drew blood, and I sat with him as he woke up after his first surgery. When he recovered and went into the adoption area, other volunteers spent more time with him, but whenever he saw me, he brightened up. One day, when an E-collar obscured his vision, I approached him from behind as he stood next to another volunteer who was conversing with a third person. As I passed an adjoining hall, I greeted someone in that direction. As I did, the dog's tail wagged and he turned as if to confirm that the physical form matched the voice. Although some might dismiss this as simply a conditioned response (that is, my voice had been programmed into his behavioral repertoire), critical anthropomorphism calls for a more contextualized and sympathetic understanding. Familiarity with dogs' behavior, and with this dog's behavior, leads me "to discount perspectives that rely on instinctual or rigidly behavioristic explanations" (Arluke and Sanders 1996:43).

Animals indicate the capacity for coherence in the act of hiding, which requires a sense of self as an object to conceal from others. According to Sanders (1999:137), hiding "shows an awareness that the 'embodied self' is in danger and that concealment is in order." Cats, having evolved as skilled predators, relied on the ability to hide in order to hunt. Those mechanisms did not disappear with domestication. As one guardian explains: "Anyone who has lived around cats has seen this: they hide, they watch, and they attack. They also have very strong notions of when it's okay for them to be seen and any cat-person knows that cats have got to have hiding places." Alger and Alger (2003:58) found that cats can adapt their hiding into games of peek-a-boo and hide and seek.

Coherence has generated the cultural practice of naming animals, which "underscores the animal's particularity—the sense of uniqueness between subjective self and other" (Myers 1998:71).

One of the things people do on adoption is name—or rename—their animals. Some guardians have a name in mind already; others take some time to decide on one, emphasizing the extent to which the name has to suit the animal. The act of changing an animal's name reflects the degree to which an animal's identity emerges through interaction.

Affectivity Another dimension of the core self that makes animals' subjectivity available to us is their capacity for emotions. In interviews, guardians reported two ways that they read the emotions of their dogs and cats, and these correspond to two dimensions of feeling.

The first dimension encompasses what are called "categorical affects." Most of the time when we think of "emotions," we think of discrete *categories* of feelings, such as sadness, happiness, fear, anger, or shame. Anyone who lives around animals has seen manifestations of various categorical affects. For example, I have seen cats display grief. Two of my cats, a male and a female, formed a very close bond. They slept together, ate and played together, and groomed each other. When the male had to be euthanized, his companion went through a distinct period of grieving. Indeed, her sadness started before her friend died, when he gradually became withdrawn and disinterested. When the male was gone, the female searched their favorite places for him and stopped eating for a few days. She did not become "herself" again until we moved into a new house. Granted, the behaviors I characterize as feline grief may not be the same as human grief; this is irrelevant. However, I do know that she behaved differently after her friend's death than she behaves when she is sunning herself (a state I would call happiness or contentedness) or inspecting my belongings after I return at the end of a day (curiosity). Along the same lines, Alger and Alger (2003) describe displays of happiness, affection, frustration, irritability, depression, empathy, and jealousy among sheltered cats.

A second dimension of emotions comprises "vitality affects." These are *ways* of feeling, rather than discrete emotions, and they give the behavior of human and nonhuman animals much of its texture. Bruner and Kalmar (1998:311) point out that vitality affects "signal the 'feel' of a life—mood, pace, zest, weariness, or whatever." Long before I knew the term "vitality affects," I knew *about* them. This is so for most of us, for the perception of vitality affects occurs early in infancy. When my niece, Amanda, now a teenager, was very young, I entertained her by making my index and middle fingers into the "legs" of a character whose "body" was my hand. This character could make her laugh by walking up her arm, but we both had more fun when it danced the cancan. This little "person"—it did seem to have what it takes for personhood—could act as if exhausted or take a jaunty walk.

Instances such as these work because we can read vitality affects. We know when the character portrayed by fingers "feels" chipper or bedraggled, and it has nothing to do with facial expressions, for there are no faces to do the expressing. This is an important way in which the comparison applies to animals. Animals' limited ability to change their facial expressions (relative to humans) makes their expressions an unreliable means by which we can infer their emotional states. The vitality affects of animals inform us more than their facial expressions do. In our interaction with animals, we read vitality affects and perceive certain individuals as "sweet," "mellow," "hyper," and so on. These are characteristics of *individual* animals, that is, the core self, rather than the expressions of particular emotions. Vitality affects are important vehicles of the core self. A woman who described her dog as "sweet," for example, was referring to the dog's overall calmness and submissive tendencies. Likewise, a couple who called their cat a "character" used the phrase as shorthand for his confidence and curiosity, the combination of which often sent him rushing in where more angelic cats would not dare to tread.

Self-History Self-history, or continuity, makes *interactions* into *relationships*. As Stern (1985:90)

writes, "a sense of a core self would be ephemeral if there were no continuity of experience." The capacity that makes continuity possible is memory. Events, objects, others, and emotions gain their meaning and are preserved in memory, in the context of relationships. There are many different modalities of memory, some of which begin to operate very early. The memory required for self-history is preverbal, and several aspects of it appear in animals.

Anyone who has ever taken a dog or a cat to a veterinarian knows that animals remember places. The cat who loves affection at home now hisses and scratches the vet's offending hand. Skeptics might say that the animal "just smells fear," thereby dismissing the reaction as instinctual. However, even if it were "only" instinct, the consistent ability to register a particular emotion in a particular setting nevertheless implies a sense of continuity. Others have also documented animals' "place memory" (Alger and Alger 2003; Sanders 1999). Indeed, Shapiro (1990, 1997) suggests that the lives of dogs are oriented in terms of place, rather than time, as ours are.

In behaviorist terms, the animal who feels fear at a veterinary clinic or pleasure in another setting merely perceives an impulse associated with previous positive or negative reinforcement. To be sure, in light of Occam's razor, which favors behavioristic accounts, cognitive explanations seem implausible. However, just as it is unwise to attribute simple behaviors to complex mental processes, it is equally unwise to dismiss, ignore, or deny the possibility that some behaviors may be best explained in cognitive terms. The question is *which* behaviors are best explained this way, and the answer is far from clear.

Allen and Bekoff (1997:56–62) make a distinction that is useful in this context. They distinguish between behavior that is "stimulus bound," meaning an invariable (or nearly so) response to external stimulus, and behavior that is "stimulus free," or motivated by internal factors. When external factors are seen to dominate internal factors, behaviorist explanations are preferred. However, in many instances, behaviorist conclusions have been drawn from research that ignores or disregards internal factors. For example, many laboratory studies of allegedly stimulus-bound behaviors must modify conditions so that animals will be sufficiently motivated to perform according to behaviorist expectations. This is especially the case in experiments involving food rewards, in which researchers must keep animals motivated to eat even when internal responses perceive satiation. Laboratory researchers introduce protocols that interfere with metabolism in order for the animals to eat beyond satiety. In such cases, stimulus-bound conclusions are drawn from behaviors that under normal circumstances would be stimulus-free. Drawing on an example closer to home, two of my cats regularly sleep on a fleece blanket. It is not stretching the point to say that they find this blanket comforting. This comfort has been to some degree conditioned. Nevertheless, if I were to produce the same blanket while the cats were being examined at the vet's office, I can confidently say that neither cat would respond with kneading and napping. The behavioral explanation becomes inadequate in contexts that involve various inputs. A more complex explanation is needed, and the possibility of memory seems a reasonable alternative.

Animals may have no sense of today, tomorrow, and next week, but they do remember what happened to them in the past. They do not need the sense of past, present, and future that gives purpose to human lives. Consequently, their memory skills differ from ours, but they differ in degree rather than kind. In interaction with humans, animals' memories give humans a sense of the animal as having a concrete history.

Conclusion

The structure of people's interaction with adoptable animals (seeking relationships with them, demonstrating concern for their well-being, and engaging in increasingly complex interaction with them) suggests that animals contribute something to the experience of human selfhood. Understanding *how* they "mean something" requires examining further interactions, such as those that take place when an animal is part of a human home and family. This type of interaction reveals aspects of the animal's subjective presence. Subjectivity, in turn, accounts for what makes animals different from the other factors that contribute to our sense of self.

Evidence of subjectivity appears in the core dimensions of self. If we think of self as a system of experiences having the features of agency, coherence, affectivity, and history, then our interaction with others will reflect our perception of those features. For example, agency evokes agency. When I perceive it in an animal or another person, doing so confirms my own sense of agency. My interaction with the Other will manifest my expectation and recognition of that agency, along with my response to it. The assumption that the Other can initiate action gives our interaction a particular structure. The Other and I will act toward each other as two beings who are authors of their own conduct. Moreover, when I assume agentic qualities in an Other, I assume the Other's subjectivity. At the same time, I understand myself as agentic, albeit without dwelling on the matter.

In the case of coherence, an Other's recognition of me as an embodied, bounded being confirms my own sense of myself in that way. When I come home, for example, the dogs and cats recognize me and greet me in ways that they would not extend to someone else. Their doing so confirms my sense of myself, although this occurs unconsciously, for I seldom pause to check that I am indeed "me." The animals' (and other people's) consistent recognition of me makes this unnecessary. In the case of affectivity, people who live with animals regularly respond to the qualities and intensity of animals' emotions. Moreover, our recognition of animals' affectivity usually occurs in particular contexts, which provides another avenue to confirming our own experience.

Finally, animals' capacity for memory, which enables self-history, confirms our own sense of history, albeit in a more limited way than the confirmation we experience with other people. With other people, we can create a shared narrative, which is an undeniably more complex account of mutual experience. However, animals use bodies, gestures, preferences, and habits to demonstrate that they share a history with us. For instance, for the past 13 years, I have slept with my grey, female cat, Pusskin, at my side. Regardless of what she is doing when I go to bed, she joins me. She and I nestle close in a way that I share with none of the other cats. After 13 years, this way of sleeping together defines our relationship. I cannot imagine sleeping without the warmth and weight of her beside me, and I dread the time when she will no longer be there. Whatever reasons she has for seeking me out at night, I cannot be certain. What I can say is that she remembers where she likes to sleep, and she and I have built a history because she does so.

In this article, I have worked inductively, moving from observations to a model of selfhood instead of beginning with a particular notion of the self. However, the result is an incomplete picture of selfhood for animals, as it would be for humans. Research by Sanders and Alger and Alger completes the model I offer here. Whereas I have focused on the *subjective* presence of animals, these scholars illuminate *intersubjectivity* by documenting animals' ability to share intentions, feelings, and other mental states with their human companions. By interpreting the content of other minds—whether human or nonhuman—we develop a sense of self-in-relation. The selves of animals, evinced through agency, affectivity, coherence, and history, acquire another dimension through interaction that reveals their capacity to share thoughts and feelings. Although we humans can put our accounts of this experience into words, the capacity for intersubjectivity does not depend on language. Animals and people can share thoughts, intentions, and feelings, albeit at a less complex level than that which occurs between two people.

The point of this article has been to show that there is something to animal selfhood and that this "something" becomes apparent during interaction. Our attributions of animals' selves are not merely wishful anthropomorphic projection. Because animals have agency and the other dimensions of the core self, they can choose courses of action that do not always coincide with our projections of what they "should" be like. Humans and animals *can* share meanings and emotions, but that does not imply that they always *will* share them. Nevertheless, in much of human–animal interaction, the features of agency, coherence, self-history, and affectivity coalesce, with memory helping to integrate them. Together, these give the animal an organizing, subjective perspective, or a core self, and concurrently make core Others available.

References

Adler, Patricia A., and Peter Adler. 1987. *Membership Roles in Field Research.* Newbury Park, CA: Sage.

Alger, Janet M., and Steven F. Alger. 1997. "Beyond Mead: Symbolic Interaction between Humans and Felines." *Society & Animals* 5:65–81.

———. 1999. "Cat Culture, Human Culture: An Ethnographic Study of a Cat Shelter." *Society & Animals* 7:199–218.

———. 2003. *Cat Culture: The Social World of a Cat Shelter.* Philadelphia: Temple University Press.

Allen, Colin, and Marc Bekoff. 1997. *Species of Mind: The Philosophy and Biology of Cognitive Ethology.* Cambridge, MA: MIT Press.

Arluke, Arnold, and Clinton R. Sanders. 1996. *Regarding Animals:* Philadelphia: Temple University Press.

Bruner, Jerome, and David A. Kalmar. 1998. "Narrative and Metanarrative in the Construction of Self." Pp. 308–331 in *Self-Awareness: Its Nature and Development*, edited by M. Ferrari and R. J. Sternberg. New York: Guilford.

Goffman, Erving. 1959. *The Presentation of Self in Everyday Life.* Garden City, NY: Anchor Books.

Goodall, Jane. 1990. *Through a Window: My Thirty Years with Chimpanzees of Gombe.* Boston: Houghton Mifflin.

James, William. [1890] 1950. *The Principles of Psychology*. New York: Dover.

Mead, George Herbert. [1934] 1962. *Mind, Self and Society*. Chicago: University of Chicago Press.

Myers, Gene. 1998. *Children and Animals: Social Development and Our Connections to Other Species*. Boulder, CO: Westview Press.

Sanders, Clinton R. 1990. "Excusing Tactics: Social Responses to the Public Misbehavior of Companion Animals." *Anthrozoös* 4:82–90.

——. 1999. *Understanding Dogs: Living and Working with Canine Companions*. Philadelphia: Temple University Press.

Shapiro, Kenneth J. 1990. "Understanding Dogs through Kinesthetic Empathy, Social Construction, and History." *Anthrozoös* 3:184–195.

——. 1997. "A Phenomenological Approach to the Study of Nonhuman Animals." Pp. 277–295 in *Anthropomorphism, Anecdotes, and Animals*, edited by R. Mitchell, N. Thompson, and H. Miles. Albany: State University of New York Press.

Stern, Daniel N. 1985. *The Interpersonal World of the Infant: A View from Psychoanalysis and Developmental Psychology*. New York: Basic Books.

PART ELEVEN

Rights

Introduction

Since the publication in 1975 of Peter Singer's *Animal Liberation* (and later, in 1984, of Tom Regan's *The Case for Animal Rights*), there has been considerable growth in what has come to be called the animal rights movement (Beers 2006). This is by no means a unified or coherent movement, and the activities in which its constituent groups engage vary from lobbying and protest marches to attacks on laboratories or people or the removal of animals. Needless to say, this growth has been bound up with a proliferation of books and articles deliberating the philosophical pros and cons of animal rights (Sunstein and Nussbaum 2005).

Rather than debating its pros and cons, social scientists have focused on other questions, such as why certain people are drawn to the animal rights movement. Studies have found that grassroots activists and sympathizers are more likely to be women than men, which was also true of the Victorian anti-vivisection movement. Activists are also very likely to be white, middle or upper class, well educated, and politically liberal. And most live in cities or large towns, with companion animals of their own.

Beyond these demographic characteristics, the animal rights movement tends to draw people having a view of human-animal relations that differs from their opponents. Movement supporters tend to see more similarity than difference between humans and animals, while movement opponents see a significant gap between the species. Moreover, the gap acknowledged by supporters is a difference of degree, while the gap for opponents is a difference in kind. The question then becomes, are these differences significant enough to exclude animals' interest and welfare when there is a conflict between their interests and our own? Debate ensues as to whether animals possess intrinsic value regardless of their contribution to human life, or whether their value is primarily instrumental because they are useful to humans.

The movement also appeals to people who share a common ethos. The prevailing ethos of animal rights activists is an opposition to what is perceived as a growing tendency to see nature/the environment only as a means to an end, or what Jasper and Nelkin (1992) call "anti-instrumentalism." In Britain, the rapid growth of "roads protesters" in the 1990s is an example; protesters built houses in trees or tunnels underground in order to make things difficult for road construction companies. These protesters valued the environment for itself, and valued it over the construction of yet more roads, which they saw as embodying destructive, instrumental values. With regard to animal protests, that anti-instrumentalism may be linked to an ever more-apparent public uneasiness about science and technology, and concomitant loss of trust in scientific expertise. Governments in the United States and Europe actively promote "public understanding of science" in the belief that there is insufficient awareness of the benefits of science.

Given this ethos, some might think that the animal rights movement would also appeal to those drawn to the environmental movement, since a similar ethos exists among the latter's supporters too. One might even predict that these movements would provide co-support and resource sharing because they seem to share much in common, having what seem to be compatible aims. Nonhuman animals can be considered one part of the physical environment. They are both used by humans and, in the opinion of some people, are both abused. Yet, not all who are active in one movement are necessarily active, or even supportive, of the other movement.

Finally, the animal rights movement appeals to people who want to participate in a moral crusade—or even one providing a religious cosmology (Sutherland and Nash 1994) or experience (Herzog 1993). Although research on activists suggests that traditional religious beliefs are negatively associated with ideological support for animal rights, supporters sometimes demonstrate intense activism and extraordinary commitment to the cause, akin to the fervor observed among religious zealots. As a secular religion, the animal rights movement can provide its followers with many of the same experiences they would have in conventional religions, such as being part of a community or acquiring a belief system.

A second line of research on the animal rights movement looks at its outcomes and consequences. In the last few decades, activists have influenced how institutions treat animals. For example, the use of laboratory animals by scientists is now far more scrutinized and controlled than it was in the past. Fewer animals are used in experiments and there is more concern to experiment humanely by reducing pain and suffering when possible. Other examples of successful activism include pressuring school systems to provide alternatives to dissection, the fishing industry to use dolphin-safe nets, circuses to eliminate harmful practices, slaughter-houses to use more humane methods, and zoos to improve animal housing, to name just a few. Nevertheless, the movement has had only slight influence on the every-day choices of many Americans. While some people no longer want to wear fur coats, most continue to eat chicken and meat. And of course, many of the movement's gains are incremental; more absolutist-minded activists will only be satisfied if these practices, regard-less of how humane they become, simply end.

Scholars have tried to identify the social factors that impede or facilitate successful animal rights protests. Some researchers take a micro approach to assessing the impact of the animal rights movement by looking at the process by which activists try to change the behavior of their targets. This approach identifies specific, localized factors that influence the ability of activists to achieve their goals. For example, movement success will depend on the specific prac-tices that activists target for change and the reasons why people engage in them. In their protests, animal rights activists target practices they think exploit or are cruel to animals, such as hunting or experimentation. However, not all of these targeted practices will be equally vulnerable to change. The degree to which par-ticular activities are perceived as necessary will influ-ence their susceptibility to change. Practices framed as essential will be less vulnerable to change, while those defined as discretionary will be more vulnerable.

Other researchers take a macro approach to as-sessing movement outcomes by locating the sources of animal oppression in large-scale features of soci-ety, such as its social institutions, traditions, media, legal system, and economic structure (Nibert 2002). These powerful ideological and social forces can nor-malize the exploitation of nonhuman animals, build-ing oppression into our social order. These societal features also create an environment within which the animal rights movement must operate. Depending on the nature of this environment, the movement will be presented with opportunities or constraints for mak-ing change. However, transforming these societal fea-tures will do more than advance animal rights. Changing the structural roots of oppression speaks to ending the oppression of both humans and animals, since the two are interrelated.

Articles in this part speak to both questions about the animal rights movement: namely, who is drawn to it and when is it effective? The first two selections explore the appeal of this movement and what participation provides its supporters. Under-standing the appeal of the animal rights movement is a complex matter. Some factors that draw and main-tain participation may not be directly related to our view of animals and nature. For example, Wesley Jamison and his co-authors examine whether animal rights activism functions like a religious belief for its members. Activists studied in Switzerland and the United States experienced their participation in the movement as though it were a religion. Such func-tional religions have five characteristics. Entry into functional religions, like the animal rights movement, often starts with an intense and memorable conver-sion experience—an emotional epiphany—in which growing uneasiness over not doing more for animals is finally overcome by committing themselves to their new cause. Once recruited to the movement, mem-bers discover a newfound community where they can share their animal concerns and experiences with like-minded people. Along with the sense of fellow-ship, the community provides a normative creed or belief system—comparable to religious doctrine—that goes beyond fighting for the rights of animals to include beliefs about nature, suffering, and death. In addition, the community provides elaborate behav-ioral codes that guide a new way of living with ani-mals. And finally, much like traditional religions, participation in the movement and the expression of its ideology are expressed through symbols and ritu-als. These features of secular religions may partly ex-plain the growth of the animal rights movement.

Barbara Noske asks why the animal rights move-ment has evolved, drawn support, and engaged in protest often without support from the deep green move-ment and its membership. She argues that, while some people participate in both movements, many do not be-cause the movements have very different, if not contra-dictory, views of animals, nature, and our obligation to each. Animal activists tend to focus on the sentience of individual animals—they can feel pain, pleasure, and fear. Concern for animal sentience stems from a recog-nition that human and animal nature are alike in that both are sentient creatures. However, many activists are indifferent to other forms of nature in which there is no evidence of sentience, such as plants and trees. In turn, activists' concentration on sentience allows them to mentally separate animals from the environment within which they live. Alternatively, when deep green followers think about animals, they focus more on wild animals than on domestic or feral ones. Sentience or cruelty, to them, is not the defining factor when considering animals; rather, it is their context in nature. Thus, individual animals are less important than the animal's species and its relationship to the environment. Noske explores whether there is common ground to bridge differences that now separate the two movements. Should this be possible, the animal rights movement could expect to further broaden its base of support.

The selection by Rachel Einwohner takes a more micro approach to assessing the impact of the animal rights movement. To explain their effectiveness, research on social movement outcomes usually focuses on the characteristics of movements and their environments. In other words, it is assumed that protests work or fail because of the particular tactics or resources available to activists or because of events at the state or cultural level. By studying four animal rights campaigns, Einwohner demonstrates another, and perhaps more accurate, way to understand the effectiveness of the animal rights movement—by focusing on the targets of its protest. Two campaigns she studied—those against animal experimentation and hunting—were unsuccessful. Activists could not block several targeted experiments, were denied information on other experiments, and did not convince researchers to stop using animals. On the other hand, two other campaigns she studied—those against the circus and fur salons—were successful. Declines occurred in circus attendance and the number of fur stores. As Einwohner points out, not all political issues are created equally, as evidenced by these campaigns. Animal experimenters and hunters resisted protest because they could define their practices as necessary and central to people's lives, while the more vulnerable circus and fur targets could not say this about their activities. Of course, structural issues play a role in the success or failure of protests, but so too will their target's practices.

The next two selections examine the potential impact of the animal rights movement. Bonnie Berry's article puts the question of movement effectiveness into a larger context—that of progress, or lack thereof, in combating the oppression of animals and humans. Her macro approach helps us understand the social forces behind both kinds of oppression and how they are connected. Tradition is one social force that affects the protection or encroachment of the rights of all animals—certain practices have always been done a certain way, such as hunting, so people assume they are important to continue. Another social force is the corporate and cultural promotion of ideal health and beauty that relies on animal experimentation for product development and safety. Indeed, the pharmaceutical industry is one part of a larger social force—capitalistic enterprises that profit from the exploitation of animals—whether for food, clothing, or entertainment. Although laws may restrict such oppression, thereby specifying what makes for a rights violation, offenses against nonhuman animals are often hard to prosecute, and when prosecuted successfully, rarely involve serious punishment. Indeed, under law, animals are considered a form of property. However, these social forces can change over time; rights often progress as societies become more modern and democratic.

References

Beers, D. 2006. *For the Prevention of Cruelty: The History and Legacy of Animal Rights Activism in the United States.* Athens, OH: Swallow Press.

Herzog, H. 1993. "'The Movement Is My Life': The Psychology of Animal Rights Activism." *The Journal of Social Issues* 49:103–119.

Jasper, J., and D. Nelkin. 1992. *The Animal Rights Crusade.* New York: Free Press.

Nibert, D. 2002. *Animal Rights/Human Rights: Entanglements of Oppression and Liberation.* Lanham, MD: Roman and Littlefield.

Sunstein, C., and M. Nussbaum. 2005. *Animal Rights: Current Debates and New Directions.* Oxford University Press.

Sutherland, K., and W. Nash. 1994. "Animal Rights as New Environmental Cosmology." *Qualitative Sociology* 17:171–186.

Wesley V. Jamison
Caspar Wenk
James V. Parker

Animal Rights Activism as Functional Religion

In politics, intensity matters. Organizations and movements that are able to muster and sustain intense support generally are able to effect change over time; hence, the passionate participation of true believers has always marked the politics of successful mass movements. The animal rights movement exemplifies this political fervor and has met with varying degrees of success. The movement, which traces its contemporary emergence to 1975, combines a critique of scientific empiricism characteristic of the Victorian anti-vivisection movement with the reaction to modernity that has mobilized many modern social movements. Uncommon levels of commitment to the cause and zeal for social redemption characterize its activists. Indeed, the resultant normative goals of animal rights activists often require extraordinary levels of personal commitment and conviction.

What are the sources of this intensity and commitment? Once mobilized, what keeps an animal rights activist motivated toward the transformation of society's relationship with animals? And what course of action will the movement take should it fail to redeem society? A guide for activists who object in conscience to classroom vivisection and dissection advises that their objection is a constitutionally protected exercise of religious belief (Francione and Charlton, 1992). The authors' claim that such activists are acting out of religious belief may surprise many observers. Social science data indicate that most

animal rights activists are not members of traditional churches; indeed, they think of themselves as atheist or agnostic. Nonetheless, social scientists have argued that animal rights may serve as a cosmological buttress against anomie and bewilderment in modern society.

Yinger (1970) articulated the distinction between substantive and functional definitions of religion for social scientists. It is a distinction that allows us to analyze seemingly secular movements as religions because they function as religions; that is, they provide meaning around which individuals coalesce, interpreting life through a system of beliefs, symbols, rituals, and prescriptions for behavior. Indeed, Berger (1992; 1999) has noted the emergence of such functional, secular religiosity as an alternative expression of "repressed transcendence." Berger argues that in response to modernity's cultural delegitimization of traditional religions and objective truth, individuals, rather than ending their quest for religious truth, shift the foci of their quest toward other outlets.

Francione and Charlton (1992) leave it to individuals to determine if their beliefs function as religions. However, their advice opens up an intriguing line of inquiry about the movement itself. If Berger's (1992) hypothesis is correct, and if Sutherland and Nash's (1994) argument is accurate, the contemporary animal rights movement may serve as an outlet for the expression of functional religiosity. Indeed, if the recollections of activists are any indicator, then indeed animal rights ideology may serve as functional religion.

We drew the data for this article from long interviews with informants in both the United States and Switzerland. Although the political manifestations of animal rights ideology are context dependent, social scientists have hypothesized that mass movement activism (e.g., animal rights) may be a reaction to sociological factors that transcend culture and thus share relatively uniform causes. Switzerland and the United States share similar representative, federal political systems that are highly decentralized and shunt many political issues toward the lowest levels of political participation where, over time, intensity in citizen involvement is emphasized. Likewise, democracy in the United States resembles Swiss democracy in that citizens have the opportunity to pass or amend legislation through direct democracy, and this similarly emphasizes political intensity among political participants. The Swiss and U.S. systems are similar in that multiple checks and balances thwart radical political movements and cause incremental change. Hence, success in stifling, incremental systems is achieved not only through the mobilization of enthusiastic belief but also its maintenance.

The animal rights movements in both countries differ in significant ways. The U.S. movement has diverged into a reformist arm that allows for humane use of animals and a radical arm that seeks to protect them from all human use through the extension of inalienable rights. In Switzerland, the *Tierschutz* movement similarly contains reformist and radical branches, but because of political history the Swiss movement tends to shy away from the language of rights. Another difference is that the U.S. system is intentionally confrontational, pitting interest groups against each other in perpetual conflict, whereas the Swiss system is by intent more consensual and cooperative. One manifestation of this difference is that in the United States the animal rights movement has sought confrontation outside the boundaries of political legislation both to shock citizens and to bring about strategic

legislative change, while in Switzerland the animal rights movement has sought redress through primarily political means and has stayed relatively nonconfrontational.

Nevertheless, the movements are very similar in that activists are intensely committed to changing the way people view and interact with nonhuman animals. More important, since Switzerland offers the closest analog to the U.S. political system, it offers an opportunity to test the hypothesis that animal rights functions as a religion in the lives of activists, thereby affording lasting intensity in the face of incremental social change.

Results: The Elements of Functional Religion

Conversion

Morally persuasive religious belief often originates in an experience of conversion. Coming from a biblical expression meaning "to be turned around," conversion can reverse a person's life. Enlightenment may come with the force of epiphanic revelation, stopping converts in their tracks and turning them around so that they see a whole new world. Conversion, according to theologian Lonergan (1972), is the transformation of a person's epistemological horizon. Conversion can include several experiences that, despite differences, bear resemblance. Psychic conversion, such as one often facilitated by a counselor or analyst, happens when one comes to understand and master one's feelings. Intellectual conversion occurs when someone not only knows but also becomes conscious of what counts for knowledge and truth. Moral conversion turns one from acting on previous values toward making decisions on the basis of newly perceived values that often deride and trivialize the previous forms of belief. Living by such newfound values often means giving up immediate and personal gratification as the convert first identifies the creedal norms of the new belief and then begins implementing its behavioral codes. Indeed, religious conversion achieves reconciliation and union with a previously unnoticed, transcendent Truth that may lessen guilt for previous unenlightened action. Its unfathomable mystery relativizes all life's woes, even the problem of innocent suffering.

At its essence, conversion provides a cosmological lens with which believers may interpret reality and an epistemological keel to balance their existence. In some people, these myriad conversions appear as a single experience; in others, they occur separately, one often precipitating the next. Thus, although frequently entailed in religious conversion, moral conversion can occur by itself. When that happens, as it did most often among our informants, the convictions and behaviors it generates may function like traditional religion.

In his study of religious experience, James (1958) defined conversion as "the process, gradual or sudden, by which a self hitherto divided, and consciously wrong, inferior, and unhappy, becomes unified and consciously right, superior, and happy" (p. 157). He draws this definition from several accounts in which converts attribute their pre-conversion uneasiness and aimlessness to wrongdoing and sin. That sense was prevalent among our informants.

Our informants reported having had formative events that sensitized them to movement rhetoric and images and began the process of dissonance. Our informants confirmed Jasper and Poulsen's (1995) hypothesis concerning activist recruitment. For our informants, awareness of incongruence between behavior and feelings remained a vivid but nebulous reality coupled to a vague sense of guilt over not doing more. Their unease grew until it eventually became manifest in a single emotional epiphany. One informant noted:

> I received literature, [that was] doing an exposé on dog-meat markets in Asia; I still remember it vividly. I was reading this mailing postcard while eating a ham sandwich. There was a picture of this dog, his legs tethered, a tin cup over his muzzle; then it hit me! I made the connection between the being in the picture and the being in my mouth. Before, everything seemed

to be OK, but now, I realized that treating animals as objects was bad. It was like someone had opened a door. I felt incredible sadness, and at the same time incredible joy. I knew that I would never be the same again, that I was leaving something behind . . . that I would be a better person, that I had been cleansed . . . I knew that it was now all right to tell others that it's OK to believe. It was as if I was coming out of a closet; there was no more shame or guilt.

The epiphanic event and its place in helping overcome dissonance by consolidating a new belief were central to the stories of our informants. For them, life could not remain as it was. Again and again in the stories of both Swiss and American informants, a persuasive epiphany caused conversion to the cause. Indeed, Jasper and Poulsen (1995) identify moral shocks and epiphanic events as central to recruiting new believers. Among our informants, the epiphany was not uniformly precipitated by morally shocking imagery, but facilitated first by movement arguments, followed by exposure to emotionally charged contact with animals or animal imagery. One informant recounted how he had felt dim misgivings about doing experiments on animals—that is, until one day he looked into the eyes of a rat he was cutting and felt immense conviction. He felt his previously vague misgivings suddenly crystallize into an encompassing moral mandate and knew that his life would never be the same after his conversion. Our informants were conscious of their conversion and aware of its enormity.

Community

Converts create communities. Having foregone the old order, they seek inclusion in the new. They gather together, share their common views, and sustain each other's commitments. Animal rights activists reflect this need for community as they come together on a regular basis to recount their personal tribulations and triumphs. The U.S. organization, Students for the Ethical Treatment of Animals, provides evidence of the centrality of fellowship. Participant observation and our informants confirmed that participants take turns at the meetings, informally relating their experiences to the group. One activist related:

> [As] I tried to relate frustration over my dog's death to friends, they didn't understand. Some of them even laughed. They said, "It's only an animal!" That was really disheartening for me. So I eventually became cautious over telling non-activists about my experience . . . I only told others who were like me.

Another informant experienced separation from her previous relationships: "I had a sense of being 'called out.' I had trouble relating to some people. People would stare when I would order [vegetarian food] in restaurants. It was embarrassing for me, and very uncomfortable." Indeed, some of our informants attributed their divorces to their newfound beliefs. After their conversion, our informants uniformly experienced feelings of social isolation, which in turn led them to seek out others who believed. Our informants often faced ostracism and scorn from family and friends as they tried to relate to their conversion.

Although our informants experienced varying degrees of isolation from individuals who didn't share their beliefs, conversion doesn't necessarily entail separation for those who are converted. Indeed, if converts regard their transformations as complete, they may form a community or sect that cuts it off from the unconverted world (Yinger, 1970). They are more likely to have dysfunctional relationships with their natural families, acquaintances and friends whom they have left behind. They still retain contact with non-believers, but they return to their community of belief for rejuvenation of enthusiasm and reification of their epistemology. Conversely, if converts think of themselves as people undergoing continual transformation, then their resulting community may remain in the world, just as the world remains in the members awaiting transformation. Members maintain positive interactions with family and friends. In this case of inclusive membership, the community is what Yinger calls a church. Nevertheless, our informants exhibited primarily sectarian behavior.

The epiphany and subsequent isolation surfaced in the stories of most informants. Indeed, one informant lost a prestigious job because of his conversion, losing the respect and friendship of colleagues and becoming the object of scorn and the focus of accusations ranging from insanity to irrationality:

> After I thought about it, I couldn't do [research on animals] any more. I was very radical, very confrontational, very "in your face." My boss and colleagues all hated me and thought I was a traitor, like I betrayed them or something. [There were] no more dinner parties for me! So my wife and me only stayed around others who believed in protecting animals. I eventually was able to be around [colleagues] again . . . after I came to see how, why they were the way they were. I could understand them because I used to be like them.

Many of our informants mirrored other religious adherents who encounter contrary secular phenomena; they amalgamated their traditional and new secular beliefs, thus overcoming dissonance and allowing them to interpret the world positively and relate to those in it when necessary.

Creed

Although most animal rights activists do not recite a formal profession of faith, they have beliefs that may be compared to traditional religious doctrines. At first glance, their creed seems obvious and simple: Animals either have the right to live their lives without human interference or have the right to be considered equally with humans in the ethical balance that weighs the right and wrong of any action or policy. Nevertheless, the commitment of our informants to political guarantees of rights for animals is part of a larger system of beliefs about life and the human-non-human animal relationship. That system includes several beliefs about nature, suffering, and death and is typified by creedal doctrinaire beliefs. Our informants agreed that active inclusion in the movement carries with it certain proscribed beliefs such as the assertion of the moral righteousness of the movement and the necessity of spreading that revelation. Believing entails spreading the faith, and animal rights activists are proselytizers. Herzog (1993) has found that the involvement of almost all animal rights activists contains an evangelical component. One informant related that. . . . "Seeing the light come on for somebody is really rewarding!"

Our informants each depicted the world as tainted, where the human-caused suffering of animals is wrong and can be abated. Each placed at least partial blame for this suffering on the shoulders of a blind and unfeeling humanity. One stated, ". . . everywhere I turned I saw suffering permeating the world," while another felt that. . . . "There seems to be so much needless pain caused by people. If people realized the level of suffering that they cause, they would probably do something about it." Central to the creed is an acknowledgement of the distressing totality of suffering in the world, coupled with a paradoxical, ecological perspective that links humanity to the nonhuman world—while placing ethical obligations and failures singularly upon humans. One informant recounted:

> Humans are one species among many. We're not owners of the planet. All life is interconnected. And like us, other animals have a desire to lead their own lives. They want to be left alone. However, unlike animals, we have choices, we can make decisions. This is wonderful! People cause so much suffering for selfish reasons.

In our informants' creed, suffering is evil, and its alleviation is good; humans are at once derived from, and unique in, the natural world. In other words, people are related through evolution to animals but ethically constrained from using them because we, alone, are conscious of the suffering such use causes and can exercise free will to end it. Interestingly, each of the informants had struggled with the problem of how far to extend the moral sphere outward to the nonhuman world. Yet, many employed the same litmus test to mark the separation. They drew a

distinction between animals who possess eyes and those who don't. One activist stated, "I personally draw the line at an animal that can see me and evades humans." Another responded that "there's something about eyes that makes it personal . . . they can see me," while still another believed that "animals see what people will do to them!" Indeed, for our informants, animals' ability to recognize humans as a threat, and thus something to be evaded, accentuates the divide between human and nonhuman nature. Scholars have noted that many activists view humanity as a malignancy upon the natural world, and thus the animal's ability to see people as they really are becomes paramount.

The divergence of these beliefs from Western religious beliefs that influence the cultural milieus in Switzerland and the United States might appear slight, but it is significant. The tradition we know as mainline western Christianity takes its instruction about life from the constant refrain in *Genesis* (New Jerusalem Bible), "And God saw that it was good." The theocentric doctrine posits humans as the pinnacle of creation—often interpreted as, "humans alone really matter." However, our informants spoke of the goodness of nature but not people. To our informants, nature acquires normative value and is the repository of nobility and virtue, while humans acquire negative and even evil attributes. Activists celebrate the heavens and the earth, the sun and the moon, the birds and the beasts, but not humankind. The boundary between good and evil, rather than dividing the human heart and making everything in nature ambiguous as is common with substantive religious beliefs, demarcates nature's goodness on the one hand and human evil on the other. Thus, humans are singularly to blame for animal suffering.

Certainly, animals are part of nature, but to our informants their goodness lies in their perceived moral innocence. The wolf may stalk the lamb and one bird may impale another for its dinner, but these animals are not evil by intention. Our informants echoed an editorial letter to the *New York Newsday* columnist, Colen: "Unlike you, the cockroach has never done anything deliberately malicious in its life—unlike every human that ever lived. I actually have more moral grounds to murder you, than you have to, say, swat a fly" (Colen, 1992). Indeed, for our informants it appeared that people were the problem, that innocence could be found only in animals, and that humans—just by existing—are detrimental to animals. Their comments closely mirrored Ingrid Newkirk, leader of People for the Ethical Treatment of Animals, who expresses it most forcefully:

> I am not a morose person, but I would rather not be here. I don't have any reverence for life, only for the entities themselves. I would rather see a blank space where I am. This will sound like fruitcake stuff again, but at least I wouldn't be harming anything. All I can do—all you can do—while you are alive is try to reduce the amount of damage you do by being alive. (Brown, 1983, p. B9)

The belief that humans could put an end to suffering in nature also served as part of the creedal doctrines for our informants, and its plausibility and attraction may be a derivative of the urbanization of western culture, where most people live far removed from traditional interactions with nonhuman nature and where modern society often portrays animals not as predators but as fluffy and fuzzy friends propped up on the bed. Furthermore, when "nature, red in tooth and claw," manifested itself in our informants' consciousness, the demarcation equating nature with moral good while concurrently equating humanity with moral "bad" allowed at least temporary cognitive resonance, for death in "nature" becomes a natural process, whereas death at the hands of humanity becomes "unnatural" (Dizard, 1994).

Code

Conversion places animal rights partisans under the sway of a new set of values—the newly recognized importance of animals esteemed for their own sake rather than their usefulness to society. No longer do our informants drift in the mainstream of consumer culture, pulled this way and that by what they thought were needs and pleasures. Conversions always entail new ways of living that come to be codified in guidelines and rules. It is not surprising, then, that our informants, whose conversion is primarily moral in nature, had elaborate codes of behavior. They uniformly identified well-defined behavior codes. Furthermore, content analysis revealed similar behavior codes in both countries: their publications were filled with advice for vegetarian and vegan cooking, cruelty-free shopping, cruelty-free entertainment, and cruelty-free giving.

An all-encompassing statement of faith professed by some of our informants demonstrated the codified edicts of animal rights: "Animals are not ours to eat, wear, experiment on, or use in any way!" Finding its ultimate expression in the form of veganism, this lifestyle consciously forgoes the use of materials that have, in any way, caused animal suffering. Our informants defined vegans as "a person who doesn't use, to the greatest extent possible, any products that come from animals . . . it's impossible to get away from animal use . . . but if an alternative is available, they use it."

Unlimited in scope, veganism provides an elaborate superstructure with which activists support their lives. Bordering on asceticism, the constraints placed on personal behavior and the resultant emotional demands of compliance can be extraordinary.

Such legalism confronts activists with a dilemma. Our informants acknowledged the impossibility of keeping the code but, nevertheless, felt compelled to achieve it. The compulsion derived from their conversions, whereby they became individually responsible for animal suffering. Hence, with a normative goal of minimizing pain and suffering, they are driven to attempt reforming themselves through strict codes of conduct.

Cult (Collective Meanings Expressed as Symbols and Rituals)

Substantive religions often organize their worship around the teachings of sacred texts/inspired narrative or the consumption of a holy food. Although nothing so formal as listening to the inspired text or eating a sacred meal characterizes the gatherings of animal rights partisans, elements of those gatherings nevertheless resemble the ritual behavior of traditional religions. An informant reflected this repetitive reification of belief:

> [I] was shy. . . . I don't classify myself as an activist, but I went along with a friend. When we got there, the meeting began with people introducing themselves and talking about the problems [professing the creed and keeping the behavioral code] they had had.

Another informant demonstrated striking similarity to Yinger's (1970) definition of cult in recounting. . . . "Most of the meetings I go to usually follow along some sort of pattern; we usually talk about ourselves, and sometimes people will talk about slipping up, but everyone is really supportive." Animal rights activists often share news clippings, letters, and personal stories that tell of recent conversions and encourage participants in their commitment. The introduction and welcoming of new and potential members often are an integral part of animal rights meetings. Group meetings that we attended followed this pattern, and many of our informants mentioned the centrality of personal profession whereby resolving to amend one's life followed acknowledging discovery of behavior that had infringed upon the well-being of animals.

Less frequently, someone will confess particular and culpable failures in the manner of animal activist and writer Alice Walker: "Since nearly a year ago, I have eaten several large pieces of Georgia ham, several pieces of chicken, three crab dinners and even one of shrimp" (Walker, 1988, p. 172). Like Walker, one infor-

mant confessed to specific sins that were accompanied by a sense of guilt. Asked about eating meat, the person leaned over and quietly whispered, "I eat chicken, but I don't tell anybody." Asked about the role of a personal community of belief, the informant noted it helped as a reminder of reasons for becoming an activist and why the movement would triumph. Indeed, we found that the cult served to resolve dissonance, reinforce "proper" belief, and subtly reemphasize individual culpability for suffering.

It seemed that our informants had only one principal method of assuaging guilt in the face of disconfirmation: They ratcheted up their commitment and resolve. The absence of absolution may serve to fuel the animal rights movement's intensity. Many informants repeatedly acknowledged that early in their conversion they had difficulty with the ascetic behavioral code. In order to avoid personal conviction for causing suffering, they repeatedly ratcheted up their activism. Many informants agreed that the attraction of increased activism as secular penance was indeed strong. Thus, the community of belief serves as a functional cult, reifying activist beliefs, policing dissension, rejuvenating enthusiasm, and encouraging increased proselytizing as a mechanism to assuage dissonance.

New converts, at first tentative in their approach to activism and the vegan ethos, are often drawn into the movement through a highly personal epiphany. After confronting the enormity of societal transformation, they confront their own complicity in animal suffering. Yet, ending animal suffering in their lives proves to be difficult. With no exterior source of atonement, they see increased activism as an act of penance. Likewise, although animal rights activists have no explicitly ritual meals, eating is very much a redemptive act. Through vegetarianism and veganism, they purify themselves while liberating animals. "The more I got involved, the more my diet changed. And the more my diet changed, the more involved I got" (Herzog, 1993, p. 117).

Whereas the shared, ritualized behavior of their fellow believers often reminded our informants of their commitment, they often found their beliefs challenged when they left fellowship and returned to their day-to-day lives. During such moments of epistemological challenge, symbols helped to remind and rejuvenate our informants. Symbols, like rituals, play a large role in religion. Animal symbols such as the dove (the Holy Spirit), the serpent (Satan), the lion (the apostle Mark), the eagle (the apostle John), the ox (the apostle Luke), and the birds that flocked to the sermons of St. Francis, are especially significant in Christianity. Similarly, animistic and pantheistic religions employ animals as symbolic projections of god/human attributes, whereby the crow represents wisdom, the fox represents craftiness, and the jackal represents cunning. Animal rights activists use pictures of monkeys strapped in chairs, cats wearing electrodes and rabbits with eye or flesh ulceration in much the same way: that is, as symbolic representations of human values and the corresponding affronts to those values. Looking on and identifying with those innocent victims, just as Christians look upon and identify a lamb as the propitiatory sacrifice of Jesus, can bring about conversion and redemption. Indeed, most of our informants had such symbols in their social environments.

Hence, the cult as used in a definition of functional religion is defined by symbolic interaction around images that crystallize and manifest the horror of animal suffering. The symbols and rituals reified the separateness of our informants' beliefs; and the pictures reminded and rejuvenated our informants' commitment to the cause.

Analysis and Forecast

We have argued that the animal rights movement may serve as a functional religion in the lives of our informants. This thesis may help to explain its phenomenal growth. In times of rapid social change, people are cut loose from traditional communities of meaning. Indeed, one of the hallmarks of modernity is secularization, or "pluralization." Modernity tends to castigate tradition, and, when coupled with the effects of naturalistic science, traditional transcendent religious beliefs are debunked as "myth" (Berger, 1976; 1990; 1999). Such beliefs then become repressed. In such a milieu, individuals are open to the offer of alternative communities that provide a filigree of meaning through which they can interpret their world. In their search for meaning, they may be attracted to absolutes such as those found in mass movements and functional religion.

A functional definition of religion also aids in understanding the dedication of our informants for the cause, their adherence to abolitionist goals, and their enthusiasm. Their uncommon passion constitutes religious zeal fueled by conversion to a distinctive worldview most often embraced as an alternative to traditional epistemologies about nature.

Finally, the thesis may explain how our informants retain enthusiasm and how the movement retains its cohesion in the face of seemingly insurmountable obstacles posited by the incremental U.S. and Swiss political systems. Central to the stories of our informants was a profound sense of guilt at discovering personal complicity in the suffering of animals. The movement places moral culpability squarely upon their shoulders, and its rhetoric exacerbates this. Then, in the tradition of all purposive mass movements, it offers itself as the ultimate form of absolution. With a creed that presents a disheartening picture of their world and a code of behavior that at once is unattainable and noble, believers are drawn into further activism as a source of penance. The community reinforces belief, and the cult provides symbols around which our informants interacted. Likewise, the same unattainability that thwarts their most virtuous efforts also deflects informant disillusionment away from the movement and turns it toward the corrupt society that shuns them. In other words, the movement's failure is offered as evidence of the omnipotent corruption of society. Ultimately, the total disconfirmation of informant beliefs may serve only to strengthen them. In response, activists often redouble their commitment to the cause. Indeed, our informants related how, upon confronting the enormity of their mission, the only recourse was to ratchet up their activism. The movement offers absolution through increased activism, and the increased activism refuels its zeal.

Predictive Power

Our informants believed that the extension of some degree of rights to animals is inevitable but were disheartened by the pace of change. Like activists of all political persuasions, they believed that they have the moral high ground and that time is on their side. However, what should happen if the movement should fail to achieve its redemptive aim? We can't infer that the movement, foiled or at least stalled in advancing its cause, will pursue the option of acting out rage and despair.

More likely alternatives are what Wilson (1994) calls inward-looking sectarianism/collapse and pragmatism, or what we name sectarian exclusiveness and ecclesial inclusiveness. The movement's leaders face a clearly defined choice that is rare in politics. In an attempt to retain their membership, they can remain doctrinally pure and risk permanent political marginalization (sectarian exclusiveness). Or, in an attempt to move into the cultural mainstream, they may become politically pragmatic and risk alienating their core of zealous activists who were converted to a distinct worldview and whose intensity serves to recruit new members, police behavior, and fulfill the numerous maddening details of politics (ecclesial inclusiveness). The Swiss *Tierschutz* movement has adopted this strategy, but many of our informants expressed exasperation with compromise and waxed for the confrontational tactics of their American counterparts.

Already we are witnessing conflict about a strategy for survival. Regan and Francione (1992) and Francione (1996) have argued that even though the steps taken by the movement may be gradual, they must always be ideologi-

cally pure. Just as American abolitionists could have no truck with those who wanted more humane treatment of slaves, so, according to Regan and Francione, animal rightists cannot work with those who call for a gentle use of animals. Enactment of any welfarist position, they contend, actually impedes the animal rights agenda by distracting people from the real goal. On the other hand, Newkirk (1992) has pleaded for building coalitions and excluding no one from the cause of animals. Achievements of welfarists become the spring-board for further advances by animal rightists. The Swiss movement is facing the same choice, having lost recent ballot initiatives that were conciliatory to their opponents, thus giving lie to the notion of pragmatic progress for the cause. For the animal rights movement, two moral paths have diverged in the political woods: the one less traveled, an elitist purity, and the other, a well-trammeled pragmatism.

Emerging Beliefs

If the movement disintegrates, our data indicate that two distinct sets of belief would emerge: (a) those that are ameliorative and reconciliatory, given to compromise within the political institutions and (b) those that are radical and see conflict and protest as much as social functions as agents of change. On the one hand, the pragmatists would lose their distinctiveness and influence—after all, our informants uniformly attributed their conversion to the evangelical zeal and enthusiasm of the movement. On the other hand, the purists would become "further marginalized and socially isolated, and some indicated that they would turn to direct action out of frustration, while others contemplated leaving the movement.

We might ask how the movement, should it evolve into a mainstream political force, might retain its distinctive redemptive flavor? First, while maintaining its transcendent goal, it could pick and choose its battles, settling for those it can win: not the end of animal use in agriculture, but the end of raising calves for veal; not the end of all animal products, but the end of wearing furs; not the end of using animals in medical research, but the end of research that can be presented as an affront to decency. Second, the movement might develop two distinctive and separable tiers of membership.

An elite would hold out for the original vision of societal transformation, keep themselves from any compromise, and pursue a prophetic course. Others entangled in earning a living, rearing a family, and enjoying friendships do what they can: adopt a dog, write a protest letter to a shampoo manufacturer, or buy synthetic clothes.

Second Generation Leadership

Inevitably, current leadership will pass to a second generation. The outcome of its choice of survival strategy might very well determine the nature of that transition. If it evolves from an exclusive, sect-like phenomenon into the inclusive, church-like organization, more institutional types will replace its charismatic leaders. Sect leaders are self-appointed, relying upon nepotism or divine fiat. Church leaders are selected in some manner by the members. The former rule autocratically while the latter are held accountable through checks and balances. The former gather followers by the strength of their personalities and fecundancy of their doctrine while the latter do so through good organizational management.

Will more organizational types replace charismatic founders? In the early 1990s, editors of *Animals Agenda* magazine had raised questions of organization and accountability (Bartlett, 1991; Clifton, 1991). *Animals Agenda* is widely seen as a principal publication of the animal protection movement and hence is important as a harbinger of change and conflict. Indeed, some observers of the movement saw the replacement of those early *Animals Agenda s* editors with Kim Stallwood as evidence that the movement was heading toward institutionalized accountability. By publishing data on the financial assets, ratio of program to administrative expenses, and compensation and benefits for staff of all animal protection groups, *Animals Agenda* editors as well as

others in the movement have created pressure for a style of leadership that, though more responsible, will likely dissipate some of the movement's energy.

Conclusion

We have argued that animal rights activism fulfills Yinger's (1970) typology of functional religion. Our informants were socialized in doctrinal creeds and behavioral codes. Our informants experienced conversions to a distinctive epistemology, realigned themselves with new communities of belief, and relied upon cult symbols and rituals to manifest latent beliefs and reinforce their commitment. Indeed, uniform throughout the stories of both Swiss and American informants were the elements of Yinger's functional religiosity.

We believe that Yinger's (1970) typology is accurate; in applying it, we may obtain a unique perspective on the politics of the animal rights movement. This is not to say that animal rights activism or the legitimate concerns it raises regarding the status of nonhuman animal in industrialized countries are contrived or marginal. Rather, we believe that—as the nineteenth century French political commentator Proudhon declared about all politics—the animal rights controversy, if pursued far enough, turns out to be religious in nature. In so acknowledging, we can begin to strip away the polemic and gain valuable insight into the epistemology of a significant and growing number of citizens. We likewise can understand how a redemptive mass movement may be able, over time, to muster the intensity that is required to reform societies with incremental political systems. It is no mistake that the movement has had success—although each of the informants was disheartened by the glacial rate of change. The modern movement to protect animals, whether it be in Switzerland or the United States, has, at the least, sensitized non-believers to the plight of animals and perhaps even continued to sow the seeds of epistemological discontent that led our informants to convert to the cause.

References

Bartlett, K. (1991). Reform or revolution? *Animals' Agenda, xi* (3), 2.

Berger, P. (1976). *Precarious vision: A sociologist looks at social fictions and Christian faith.* New York: Greenwood Publishing.

Berger, P. (1990). *A rumor of angels: Modern society and the rediscovery of the supernatural.* New York: Anchor.

Berger, P. (1992). *A far glory: The quest for faith in an age of credulity.* New York: Basic.

Berger, P. (1999). *The desecularization of the world: Resurgent religion and world politics.* New York: Eerdmans Publishing Company.

Brown, C. (1983, November 13). She's a portrait of zealotry in plastic shoes. *The Washington Post,* B8–B10.

Clifton, M. (1991). Who gets the money? *Animals Agenda, xi* (3), 33–35.

Colen, B. D. (1992, June 23). Of fanged bunny huggers. *New York Newsday.*

Dizard, J. (1994). *Going wild: Hunting, animal rights, and the contested meaning of nature.* Amherst: University of Massachusetts Press.

Francione, G. (1996). *Rain without thunder: The ideology of the animal rights movement.* Philadelphia: Temple University Press.

Francione, G., and A. Charlton. (1992). *Vivisection and dissection in the classroom: A guide to conscientious objection.* Jenkintown: The American Anti-Vivisection Society.

Herzog, H. (1993). "The movement is my life": The psychology of animal rights activism. *The Journal of Social Issues, 49,* 103–119.

James, W. (1958). *The varieties of religious experience.* New York: Mentor.

Jasper, J., and J. Poulsen. (1995). Recruiting strangers and friends: Moral shocks and social networks in animal rights and anti-nuclear protests. *Social Problems, 42,* 493–512.

Lonergan, B. (1972). *Method in theology.* New York: Herder and Herder.

Newkirk, I. (1992). Total victory, like checkmate, cannot be achieved in one move. *Animals Agenda, xii* (1), 43–45.

Regan, T., and G. Francione. (1992). A movement's means create its ends. *Animals Agenda, xii* (1), 40–43.

Sutherland, K., and W. Nash. (1994). Animal rights as new environment cosmology. *Qualitative Sociology, 17,* 171–186.

Walker, A. (1988). *Living by the word: Selected writings 1973–1987.* San Diego: Harcourt Brace Jovanovich.

Wilson, J. (1994). *Political organizations.* New York: Basic Books.

Yinger, M. (1970). *The scientific study of religion.* New York: Macmillan Publishing Company.

Barbara Noske

Two Movements and Human-Animal Continuity

Introduction

This article is about the images, representations, and treatment of animals in two movements: the animal welfare/rights/liberation movement—the animal movement for short—and the deep green/deep ecology movement. More specifically it looks at the way each of these movements comes to terms with—or fails to come to terms with—the natural continuity existing between animals and humans.

No matter how each movement is typified, any definition will contain some form of generalization. This is inevitable since there are people, among them ecofeminists (Warren 1994), who would define themselves as animal advocates as well as deep green.

Individualistic Reductionism

Members of the animal movement tend to focus on animal individuals as sentient beings and on our ethics vis-à-vis these beings. The domain for animal defenders is *that* nature which has evolved individual and sentient, and *that* nature which can feel pain, pleasure, and fear (Singer 1990).

Because many animal advocates (short for the members of the animal movement) live in urban areas and are city dwellers, the animals they encounter tend to be those we have incorporated into our work and living places such as production animals in factory farms, animals used as organic instruments in laboratories, and companion animals. That is, urban individuals encounter animals that are either domesticated or have been made to live (and die) in human-manufactured habitats. Having said this, animal advocates also focus on hunted animals and this concerns wild rather than domesticated animals. Recreational hunting has a long history, especially in North America.

The animal movement's focus on *sentience* stems from the understanding that there is continuity between the human and animal condition. Human sentience has ethical significance. It is at the root of the condemnation of oppression, torture, and genocide. Human-animal continuity implies the acknowledgment that many animals have bodies and nervous systems that resemble ours. If well-being is important to humans, it cannot but be important to animals also. Not only do many animals have bodies like ours, their subjectivity—their mind and their emotional life—bears resemblance to us. Like us, animals are, in Tom Regan's terms, "subject-of-a-life" (Regan 1983). Human-animal continuity in body and mind calls for parallel continuity in ethics, such that ethical obligations vis-á-vis animals cannot be radically different from those vis-á-vis humans.

Many people in the animal movement tend to be almost indifferent to all nature other than animal nature. Supposedly, nonsentient living nature, such as plants and trees, is generally not taken into consideration. Neither are nonliving, inorganic natural entities such as rocks, rivers, or even ecosystems. In themselves, these parts of nature are not sentient and individually they cannot suffer, so the animal movement often overlooks or dismisses them.

The animal movement is highly critical of the traditional Cartesian notion of "animal-machine" and constitutes the most important group world-wide to condemn factory farming. But it seems to have no objection against similar things done to plants. A concept such as "plant-machine" and the intensive vegetable and plant farming that is currently taking place do not raise the same eyebrows. The movement's critique of objectification and exploitation seems to rest solely on the aforementioned notion of sentience. The objectification—including things like genetic manipulation—of the rest of nature goes largely unnoticed or is dismissed.

By concentrating on sentient beings, animal advocates abstract from the environmental context of animal existence. Many animal activists have no conception of how animals, even as individuals, are integrated into other nature. One sometimes encounters a certain uneasiness among members of this movement about nature's meat eaters—as though the eating of animals by other animals were something that ideally should not exist. Some animal rightists and liberationists tell me that, were it possible, they would like to "phase out" predator-prey relationships or at least liberate (save) the prey animal from the equation (pers. comm. in several countries).

Another example of refusing to accept animal meat eating as a zoological necessity is the tendency among vegetarian/vegan animal advocates to turn their carnivorous companion animals into vegetarians as well by feeding them plant-derived food often accompanied by special dietary supplements. Admittedly in North America standard pet food is hardly ever fresh and tends to come out of a packet or tin, unlike Europe where one can get fresh and increasingly organic free-range meat for one's companion animals at the local butcher. While many of these people do acknowledge that their animal's body may not "be built" for vegetarian or vegan food, it is apparently no problem for them that the necessary daily intake of supplements will make that animal totally dependent on the health industry. Inadvertently these people are turning animals into duplicates of themselves: modern consumers of the manufactured products of an industrial age.

The animals' lives are humanized and *colonized*—their alienation taken to another extreme. Is this about protecting companion animals from nonethical food or about imposing human ethics on the animal other? Incidentally, much plant-based and processed food happens to be the end-product of unsustainable monocultures—to which many animal habitats have had to give way—and has been put on the market by the same globalized and diversified agro-industrial complex that also produces standard pet foods.

Many animal advocates thus seem to have trouble accepting nature as an interdependent system where everything has its place, function, and appropriate physical organization. Organic beings took a long time evolving in relation to each other and to nonliving inorganic nature. Nature is a community where every living thing lives off everything else (food, even vegan food, is living nature in a killed state), and in the zoological realm this means that both plant eating and meat eating have their respective *raisons d'être*. Predation is neither a negligible anomaly nor an ethical deficiency in the ecosystem (Plumwood 1999).

At the risk of generalizing too much, I see a lack of environmental awareness and environmental critique among many animal advocates. Urbanization, technological optimism, the modern urbanocentric mindset are often taken for granted. I have met animal rightists, themselves living in high rise blocks in a North American city, who feel they should persuade Inuit people in the continent's north to move down south. The argument offered is that by abandoning the frozen lands their ancestors lived on for so many generations these Inuit could take up a more moral lifestyle vis-á-vis animals and become vegetarians (which at present they cannot be for the simple reason that where they are living hardly anything grows).

I also have come across animal shelters whose managers on principle do not give companion animals to people with a garden, for fear that by going outdoors such animals could escape and come to harm. Accidental death in traffic was seen as infinitely more horrific than a lifelong existence indoors.

Many members of the animal movement seem to move surrounded by machines in an entirely humanized, electronic technoworld and tend to treat this circumstance simply as a given. The hegemony of the car in modern society, for example, hardly seems cause for concern to them. However, even apart from everything else that the car represents, this type of private transport does result in numerous animal deaths. According to Wildcare, a wildlife rehabilitation center in Toronto, most injured and orphaned animals brought in are victims of auto transport and to a lesser extent cat attacks. While cars are causing direct death or injury, habitat destruction connected with automobility and road building causes extensive indirect death and even extinction. Members of the animal movement often show no awareness of the violence involved in bulldozing an acre of land or building a road. One doesn't see much blood but it causes whole communities of animals and plants to perish.

In sum: the animal movement tends to portray animals as though they were isolated, city-dwelling consumer-citizens, living entirely outside of any ecological context. Such a view amounts to a form of reductionism: *individualistic reductionism.*

Ecosystemic Reductionism

Animals for people in the deep green/deep ecology movement are first and foremost wild animals, that is, fauna living in the wild. It is not sentience or cruelty issues that are central here; it is nature, naturalness, and environment. Incidentally, the word *environment* itself is a very problematic term: it literally means that which surrounds us. By definition it is not "us ourselves." In the term environment the separation between ourselves and nature is already final (Noske 1997).

Deep greens tend to come down hard on anything that is no longer considered "environment," no longer pristine or positively contributing to the ecosystem. Feral animals and domesticated animals are not popular in these circles. Central concepts are nature, species, and biodiversity. Only those animals that are still part of a given ecosystem really count for this movement. Animals are approached as representatives of their species. They are almost equated with their species or with the ecosystem of which they are part. The animal as individual is often downplayed.

Feral animals seem to be getting the worst of both worlds: they are neither an interesting species, nor individuals worthy of somebody's moral concern (Reads 2003). If anything, they are seen as vermin. It goes without saying that as species they do pose a threat to the natural ecosystems. Rats, cats, rabbits, dogs, foxes, horses, donkeys, pigs, goats, water buffaloes—animals intentionally or unintentionally brought into the continent (by humans)—threaten local biodiversity. These feral animals can and do destroy the balance in naturally evolved communities. The predators among them sometimes totally wipe out indigenous species whose members have no natural defense against these "foreigners." Herbivorous feral animals can totally devastate habitats that native animals are dependent upon (Reads 2003). (Unfortunately, such ecological hazards are sometimes belittled or downplayed by the animal movement.)

Deep green–leaning people perceive feral animals as members of unwanted species and advocate their destruction, often by very inhumane means. Until recently the National Parks and Wildlife Service in Australia was in the habit of shooting brumbies (feral horses) from the air, thereby indiscriminately massacring herds and disrupting whole horse societies and families. In the north of the continent, water buffaloes are being run down by four-wheel drives equipped with huge "roo bars." Rabbits are purposely being targeted with introduced deadly diseases, often by means of specially infected fleas which are then released into their burrows (Reads 2003). Foxes and feral cats and dogs are being killed by means of poison baits. From the literature on human poisoning (Bell 2001) and from quite recent cases of food poisoning in China (newspaper reports September 2002) we know what horrendous suffering is involved in death by poisoning. It can't be all that different for animals. Among deep greens, however, the suffering of feral and farm animals hardly counts.

Sentience in the deep ecology/deep green discourse is often treated as some sort of byproduct of animal life. So is individuality. The natural capacity of sentience is never included in any notion of environment, ecology, or nature.

Some deep greens/deep ecologists such as Aldo Leopold, Gary Snyder, and Paul Shepard (cf. Leopold 1949, Shepard 1996) endorse modern recreational hunting as a way to be at one with nature. Not many deep greens are taking a critical position on hunting except when it involves endangered species. The issue tends to revolve around numbers rather than the preciousness of individual lives. Neither do deep greens tend to take a critical stance on animal experimentation. After all, professional ecologists and conservation biologists often conduct experiments themselves.

Mostly, experimenters are using individuals of numerically strong species or species especially bred for the purpose such as white mice and rats. In the eyes of deep greens and deep ecologists these are no longer "nature" and so their well-being is low on their priority list.

Deep greens/deep ecologists have been known to argue that hunting is part of human nature when it was still in tune with other nature. They usually point toward hunter/gatherer societies. Hunting is natural, they say. In deep green circles, the hunting of animals is felt to be more natural than having animals for companions, which is often seen as degenerate. However, the roots of the phenomenon of companion animals go as far back as hunting. All societies from Paleolithic times onwards have been known to keep animals as pets or companions. It occurs in all societies, in all periods of history and in all economic classes. It may not exactly be "human nature," but apparently many people have felt the need for a face-to-face or touch-to-touch relation-

ship with individuals of another species. So much for the "unnaturalness" of companion animals.

Because deep greens do not have much time for domesticated animal nature they tend to be rather uninformed and unconcerned about what happens to animals in factory farms and laboratories. During various ecotours in the Australian outback it strikes me time and again how no effort whatsoever is made to avoid serving factory-farmed meat to the participants of such a tour. When queried on the issue, the often ecologically astute tour guides tend to demonstrate an entirely value-free and neutral attitude to where the tour food was coming from. Deep greens/deep ecologists might disapprove of factory farming because of its unsustainability and its polluting effect on the nature outside, but not because of the things done to natural beings inside. Production and companion animals simply do not figure as "green."

In sum: the deep green/deep ecology movement tends to equate animals with their species. Equating animals with their species or with their ecosystem amounts to another form of reductionism: *ecosystemic reductionism.*

Disembodied Empathy versus Embodied Antipathy

Both movements are potentially united in their struggle against anthropocentrism—the idea of humanity as the measure of all things. But apart from this there seem to be few platforms where the two groups actually meet: only during some international campaigns such as the ones against seal-hunting and whaling. The first time a group like Greenpeace showed any concern for individual animal welfare was when many years ago in Canada three whales got stuck in the ice. The International Fund for Animal Welfare, though essentially an animal welfare organization, does from time to time put forward arguments to do with habitat destruction and extinction of endangered species.

Strangely enough—because one would expect it the other way round—it is the animal movement rather than the deep ecology movement that invokes animal-human continuity as a line of reasoning for considering animals as individuals. On the other hand, many animal advocates are themselves almost the embodiment of human-animal *discontinuity*. As mentioned before, in this movement there hardly exists any critique of the way present-day technology is alienating humans from their "animalness." This issue is tackled by the deep green/deep ecology movement rather than by the animal lobby.

Again consider the car issue. For all other species, bodily movement is first and foremost organic movement: it involves muscle power, fatigue, or sweat. But for modern humans, bodily movement is more and more being replaced by mechanization and computerizing. They let machines do the moving for them and as a result they are becoming more and more *unanimal-like*. Hardly anybody in animal advocacy circles looks upon this as something problematic that could stand in the way of the natural human condition, that is, our physical animalness. For them this issue appears to have nothing to do with human-animal continuity. But continuity is not just about the "humanlike-ness" of animals but also about the "animallike-ness" of humans. There is an existential and crucial connectedness between the two. In circles of the animal lobby, however, human-animal continuity remains largely an abstract moral principle which is hardly "lived" in reality. One could perhaps say that this attitude is characterized by *disembodied empathy*: the empathy is real but its material basis forgotten.

The deep green/deep ecology movement, by contrast, does appreciate the wonders of nature, is conscious of animal-human continuity, and denounces various technologies (including the car) as alienating and harmful to nature. But there exists a strange contradiction here too. Though in deep green circles it is acknowledged that modern human practices have been extremely exploitative of nature and the wild, this does not seem to have induced much sympathy for exploited animals. Animal victims, be they domesticated or feral, are blamed for their own predicament and

in some cases for posing an active threat to what is perceived as real nature.

Although the deep greens, in contrast to their city-based counterparts in the animal movement, are more likely to opt for a natural lifestyle and to be more mindful of a shared animal-human past, this doesn't translate into sympathy with animals that have fallen by the wayside. This attitude could be characterized as *embodied antipathy*. Human-animal continuity is lived and "realized," but instead of empathy is often accompanied by a disdain for those beings that no longer lead natural lives in the appropriate ecosystem. Denatured though such beings may be, they nevertheless are still close enough to nature to possess the *natural* capacity for suffering whether it be pain, boredom, listlessness, social and ecological deprivation, or agonizing death.

Another contradiction is apparent here as well. In regions like North America and Australia, the ecosystemic focus is strong and as mentioned before is often expressed by advocating harsh measures against the exotic and the feral (Reads 2003). One wonders what self-image underlies such attitudes. Is this a curious case of human foreigners (in the ecological sense) condemning animal foreigners? Would such people advocate the eradication of themselves, members of a group of exotic white invaders whose adverse impact on the local ecosystem has been well documented? Would they be in favor of curbing all—non-aboriginal—human lives and births, not to mention more drastic measures? If the answer is negative, how can such measures be justified with regard to animals? Downplaying animal sentience and animal cruelty issues while at the same time upholding human sentience arguments endorses ethical discontinuity between humans and animals, albeit perhaps unintentionally.

The recent developments in animal biotechnology are going to be a test case for both movements. Some animal welfarists have claimed that genetic engineering may enable us to design animal species that are fully adapted to factory farming conditions (Rollin 1995). Others, among them veterinarians, are toying with possibilities of cloning and engineering "more suitable" and "made-to-measure" transgenic companion animals (Quain 2002). For deep greens, the issue of genetic engineering highlights pressing dilemmas with regard to species integrity (Birke and Michael 1998).

How will the animal movement react? And will the deep ecology movement tackle the issue at all? Admittedly, the deep green/deep ecology movement concerns itself with species but only with species in the wild. Deep greens may be worried about what will happen if transgenic populations come into contact with naturally evolved wild ones. How will that affect the community of species? Most genetic engineering is done to already domesticated species, the ones the green movement isn't interested in. But recently there have been calls by green-leaning scientists to bring back extinct wild species such as the Tasmanian tiger (*thylacine*) by way of genetic engineering.

Common ground?

How are we to navigate between individualized ethics and ecosystemic reductionism? The animal lobby bestows on the sentient in nature a status of individual humanness: it asks how animals are part of human society and ethics. The movement could perhaps bridge the gap which separates it from deep ecology by overcoming its exclusive focus on sentience. It could extend its compassionate ethics so as to include the nonsentient and even the inorganic. The tricky part would be how to include the whole earth without simultaneously humanizing and colonizing it. Moreover, there always will be clashes of interest between animals and animals, animals and plants, individuals and species, the organic and inorganic.

If compassionate society is about extending ethics as far as we can, deep ecology is not. It is about compliance with and obedience to nature's measure, nature's rhythm, and nature's limitations. It concerns compliance with a nature that includes things like mortality, predator-prey

relationships, the "previousness" of species, imperfect bodies, and our own finiteness. Instead of asking how animals are part of ethics, deep ecology asks how animals *and* humans are part of nature.

Consider Val Plumwood's musings about "Being Prey." In 1985, this vegetarian ecophilosopher barely survived a crocodile attack in Kakadu National Park, in Australia's Northern Territory. Thereby she came face to face with her own *edibility*. It made her realize that not only had she a body, like all animals she *was* a body: she was (potential) meat for another animal to devour. The experience has forced her to rethink the ethics/ecology dualism. It is good to focus on large predators such as crocodiles, bears, sharks—those that can take a human life—Plumwood states, because these animals present a test for us (also for the two movements, I would add). Are we prepared to share and co-exist with the free, wild, and mortally dangerous otherness of the earth, without colonizing it into a form that eliminates all friction, challenge, or consequence? Predator populations test our recognition of our human existence in mutual, ecological terms, seeing ourselves as part of the food chain: eaten as well as eater (Plumwood 1999).

The two viewpoints—compliance with nature and societal ethics—at times seem incompatible. It is a difficult dilemma. Midgley (1983) and Baird Callicott (1992) tried to solve it by arguing that wild animals deserve our protection as part of the ecosystem and that domesticated animals are entitled to our care, because they are part of a mixed human-animal community and we have ethical obligations to *all* the individuals of such a community. The problem is: this arrangement would not cover all animals. Feral animals and exotics belong to neither the first group (the original ecosystem) nor to the second (the mixed domestic community). The reason commonly given for persecuting and eradicating these animals is precisely that they do *not* seem to belong to any community. "Pests" are interesting neither as species nor as individuals, it is felt, and this turns them into outlaws.

Nevertheless all of us, animals as well as humans, somehow exist in nature and also in society (or at least in a human-defined nation-state). Each and everyone of us is a sentient individual, a species-member as well as a "place" in the world. In this world, nature and society intersect. It is all there is, nobody and nothing exist outside either.

The animal lobby needs to realize the importance of wildness, the relative "otherness" of nonhumans, and what Livingston has called the "previousness" of species. It should guard against an ethical colonization and humanization of nature. The deep ecology movement will need to pay more heed to matters of sentience, cruelty, and suffering in the way it conceives of and treats individual animal beings, including those that objectively do damage to other nature. Many feral species did not choose to live where they are now living. Humanity took them there.

To really do justice to animal-human continuity we must ask ourselves what it is we (should) do with nature but also how we ourselves are "of nature." According to Plumwood (1999) we cannot in a neo-Cartesian way divide the world into two separate domains: an ethical, human realm and an animal, ecological realm. Everyone and everything exist in both. All food is souls, she says—and ultimately all souls are food.

References

Baird Callicott, J. (1992). Animal liberation and environmental ethics: Back together again. In E. C. Hargrove, ed., *The animal rights/environmental ethics debate: The environmental perspective.* Albany: State University of New York Press. 249–261.

Bell, G. (2001). *The poison principle.* Sydney: Picador Pan MacMillan Australia.

Birke, L., and M. Michael. (1998). The heart of the matter: Animal bodies, ethics and species boundaries. *Society & Animals* 6(3):245–262.

Leopold, A. (1949). *A sand county almanac.* New York: Oxford University Press.

Midgley, M. (1983). *Animals and why they matter.* Harmondsworth: Penguin Books.

Noske, B. (1997). *Beyond boundaries: Humans and animals.* Montreal: Black Rose Books.

Plumwood, V. (1999). Being prey. In D. Rothenberg and M. Ulvaeus, eds., *The new earth reader. The best of Terra Nova.* Cambridge: MIT Press. 76–92.

Quain, A. (2002). Improving their bodies, improving our bodies. *Artlink, Contemporary Art Quarterly* 22 (1):33–37.

Reads, J. L. (2003). *Red sand, green heart: Ecological adventures in the outback.* South Melbourne: Lothian Books.

Regan, T. (1983). *The case for animal rights.* Berkeley: University of California Press.

Rollin, B. (1995). *The Frankenstein syndrome: Ethical and social issues in the genetic engineering of animals.* Cambridge: Cambridge University Press.

Shepard, P. (1996). *The others: How animals made us human.* Washington, DC: Island Press.

Singer, P. (1990). *Animal liberation.* 2nd ed. London: Jonathan Cape.

Warren, K., ed. (1994). *Ecological feminism.* London and New York: Routledge.

Rachel L. Einwohner

The Protest Effectiveness of Four Animal Rights Campaigns

Protest is an attempt by members of one group to convince or coerce others to take sort of action. One area of research within the field of social movements attempts to understand the conditions under which these efforts bear fruit. A great deal of work has focused on the usefulness of specific protest tactics, such as the use of violence, or of non-violent "constraints" in bringing about change. Yet, action alone does not necessarily bring about a desired outcome: an *opporunity* for change is also required. Consequently, the notion of opportunity has become central to many explanations of collective action—both the conditions under which it emerges and the outcomes it produces.

Despite its wide usage, however, the concept of opportunity is problematic. As movement scholars use the term, it refers to those features of the environments in which social movements operate that make it possible—or impossible—for protest to emerge and suceed. Most studies of opportunity take place at the national level, focusing on aspects of the national state or culture that either create or constrain opportunity for protest. Yet such analyses can obscure more localized factors that also shape opportunity.

I argue that the opportunities and constraints that shape protest—and, in particular, protest outcomes—may be found not only in elements of the broader culture and national political system in which protest takes place, but also in more localized opportunity structures that either motivate or discourage individuals from engaging in particular practices. Using the animal rights movement as an illustrative case, I focus on the practices—in this case, animal experimentation, hunting, circus attendance, and the fur retail trade—that protesters target for change. Rather than taking the perspective of the movements or of protesters themselves, however, my analysis centers on those individuals and groups who engage in the challenged practices or are targeted by protest efforts—here, biomedical researchers, hunters, circus patrons, and furriers. I examine opportunity by focusing on the targets' understanding of their practices and their reasons for engaging in them. Practices that are defined by targets as central and necessary are difficult for protesters to work against, whereas more peripheral practices create a certain target "vulnerability" (Jasper and Poulsen 1993) that aids protest efforts.

Practices Targeted by Four Animal Rights Campaigns

In the following sections, I illustrate this argument with data from a study of four campaigns waged by members of a nonviolent animal rights organization in the Seattle area, between 1990 and 1994. These included campaigns against animal experimentation at the University of Washington, hunting in Western Washington, attendance at circus performances in the Seattle area, and the fur retail business in downtown Seattle. The activists achieved the most success against the fur trade and circus attendance, as there was a decline in those practices. In contrast, their efforts against hunting and experimentation were less successful; hunting activity remained steady in the area throughout the period of study, and various protest efforts directed toward University administrators and researchers regarding the treatment of animals did not have their intended results. I argue that part of the reason for the differential outcomes across the campaigns lies in the opportunity structure presented by the practices targeted by each campaign—specifically, the centrality and necessity (or lack thereof) of each practice.

I illustrate the opportunities and constraints presented by each of these practices with representative quotes from semi-structured interviews with 31 respondents, each of whom was targeted by the activists' protest activity. These individuals were members of four different groups: biomedical researchers at the University of Washington; hunters living in Western Washington state; circus patrons who attended circus performances picketed by the activists; and downtown Seattle furriers. I use pseudonyns when referring to respondents in the text of this article.

Animal Experimentation

Animal rights activists hope to reduce and, ultimately, eliminate the use of animals in scientific experimentation. Yet the possibility that they will succeed depends in part on the use of animals in experimentation itself, and on the centrality of this practice to biomedical research. From the perspective of researchers, the use of animals is fundamental to the work that they do. Biomedicine "refers to all those activities that play a role in finding out how living things work and interact and how best to protect humans and our dependent charges from harm" (Rowan 1984:10). Thus, every biomedical research question focuses on or has some application to living organisms. It follows that the use of biological organisms is seen as necessary for such inquiries. As Henry, a biomedical researcher at the University of Washington, explained,

> There is information gained by some non-animal research, there's no question about it. But ultimately I cannot see a situation where significant advances can be made in treating humans without the use of other biological systems.

Indeed, researchers see few feasible alternatives to the use of animals in biomedical research. Although most advocate the "three R's"—reduction of the number of animals used, replacement of animals where possible (i.e., replacing higher-order mammals with lower organisms, such as rats and mice), and refinement of techniques so as to minimize animal suffering (Rowan 1984:59)—in practice, animals are difficult to replace. When asked about the future of animals in experimentation, Will, another researcher, responded,

> I have a hard time believing that it won't continue. It has to continue, as long as society wants to understand physiology and behavior and wants to come up with therapies, for animal and human problems. I cannot envision in vitro models or models based on computer simulation or anything like that doing that. I mean, it would be a joke to think that a computer could simulate behavior of an animal in a complex situation.

These comments illustrate a *structural commitment* to the use of animals in biomedical research, a practice for which researchers cannot imagine widespread, viable alternatives. This lack of alternatives commits researchers to the practice, regardless of their personal desires to either continue or discontinue it. In fact, many of the respondents made a point of saying that they do not necessarily want to perform or support experiments on animals, yet do so because such experiments are necessary. As Carl explained,

> Animals are expensive. Animals are tough to work with . . . so you've got an automatic incentive not to use animals. But if you sit down with any researcher that—in fact, you can find some that just really are uncomfortable with using animals, just because of their own personal beliefs—they'll quickly tell you, "No, I could not have done this without an animal, I could not have got this work done."

An additional source of researchers' structural commitment to the use of animals is the fact that the practice is mandated by some institutions. Here, it is not so much that researchers cannot imagine alternatives, but that institutions require the use of animals in experimentation. Structural requirements of this sort are more in keeping with the focus of traditional research on political opportunity structures; that is, some element of the broader political system, such as a national policy regarding the testing of drugs and chemicals, requires certain individuals to engage in certain practices, and therefore constrains protest efforts against those practices. As Barry, another researcher, said, "Everything in biomedicine has to be done in an animal at some point. In fact, there's nothing that you can get approved by the FDA that hasn't been done on animals." Will also had experience with institutional mandates for animal experimentation:

> I couldn't do my research without animals. In fact, I've tried to do it with humans, and the Human Subjects Committee won't let me. In fact, they explicitly told myself and my colleagues that before we ever moved to humans we had to do more animal work.

From the perspective of those who perform and oversee biomedical research, then, the use of animals in such research is a requirement, a product of researchers' questions and study designs as well as mandates from the institutions that fund, house, and regulate their research. As the above quotes indicate, biomedical researchers can seldom avoid using animals, even if they wish to do so. Both structural requirements (e.g., institutional policies) and individual perceptions of available alternatives foster a commitment to the practice; this commitment constrains opportunities for effective social protest against animal experimentation.

Hunting

Like the use of animals in biomedical research, hunting is also a practice that is seen as necessary by those who do it. The necessity of hunting is encapsulated by the concept of "wildlife management." Hunters "manage" wildlife populations by killing a limited number of members of certain species, thereby limiting those species to numbers that can be supported by the available habitat. Hunters believe that this management helps wild species, because when populations are controlled through hunting, fewer animals die from other causes such as starvation and disease. As Ann, who hunts with her husband, argued, "If the question is, is hunting a necessity, the answer is a definitive yes. I mean, it's just a necessary thing. It's got to be. I don't see any way that you could never kill animals. They would just multiply until, eventually you'd have to kill some, anyway." Jim, another hunter, made a similar point. When asked if there was any argument that would be compelling enough to convince him not to hunt, he replied,

> My immediate answer is no. . . . I believe in wildlife management, and I believe that people have to be involved in that. We have altered the systems out there to the point that it's become a necessary part of keeping it alive and keeping it vital, in my opinion.

According to hunters, then, hunting *must* be performed. The above quotes illustrate hunters' structural commitment to hunting, in the sense that they believe it to be necessary, with no viable alternatives.

In addition to their structural commitment to hunting, hunters show a *personal commitment* to the practice as well. For many hunters, hunting is central to their sense of self. As one hunter, Chuck, said, "It's that thing inside me that says I need to do it." Similarly, Earl described hunting as an "instinct," saying, "I think a lot of it is inborn." And as Jim put it, "[Hunting] heightens my awareness, it makes me much more aware of everything about me when I'm out there. . . . It keeps me grounded and connected to all the things that I think I am." The language that these individuals use when describing hunting—words and phrases like "inside me," "inborn," and "connected"—illustrate the centrality of this practice to their self-definition. This connection between a practice and some aspect of an individual's identity is a source of personal commitment. As Ulmer writes, "Commitment to an identity implies commitment to lines of action (or roles) mobilized by that identity, and these lines of action vary in importance to actors in defining themselves. Thus, people become personally committed to the extent that they define themselves in terms of the identities which are activated in everyday transactions" (1994:147).

In addition to describing hunting as a part of themselves, most hunters discussed hunting in the context of social networks, namely of friends and family. Many remembered learning to hunt from family members, usually older males, and continue to hunt with family and friends. As George, another hunter, explained,

> If I was going to describe the average hunter, I would say that . . . he's probably a family-oriented person that is using hunting season as a means of recreation. A camp out, something like that. It's a hell of a bonding deal with your kids. I mean, it's incredible what it does with your kids when you get out there. . . . You can really build values on a thing like that. Memories. I guess just a bonding deal. I remember walking through the woods with my dad and having things pointed out to me.

Of course, this is not to say that hunting is the only activity that hunters share with loved ones. Nonetheless, this practice is enjoyable, in part, because it is enjoyed in the company of friends and family. This connection to loved ones is an additional source of personal commitment, and serves as another reason for hunters' commitment to hunting.

From the perspective of hunters, then, hunting is a practice that is both necessary and enjoyable. As Chuck said, "It's a well-rooted, fundamental part of my life. If it tears out, it would be really—it would be hard." His use of language—referring to hunting as something that, if discontinued, would be like something "tearing out" of him—illustrates the depth of his commitment to the practice and the role that it plays in his life. Similarly, George summed up his commitment to hunting by equating it to his love for his family. When asked if animal rights activists can convince hunters to stop hunting, he replied, "Is anybody ever going to be able to convince me not to love my wife and kids? It [hunting] is part of me. It's in me. It has been in me forever, as long as I

have lived." Something this important, something that is this central to these individuals, is difficult to change. The meanings hunters associate with hunting therefore constrain the possibilities for effective anti-hunting protest.

Circus Attendance

Just as the perceived centrality and necessity of certain practices can limit the opportunity for protest efforts against those practices, the meanings associated with more peripheral practices can create opportunity for change. Circus attendance, a third practice targeted by the activists, is an example of an activity that is neither an institutional requirement nor a central component of circus patrons' identity. The meanings associated with this practice therefore create an opportunity for animal rights activists to achieve their primary goal of convincing patrons to boycott circus performances.

Why go to the circus? Most of the circus patrons I interviewed said that they decided to go to the circus because it was something that they thought their children would enjoy. As Marsha, who took her young godchildren to the show, noted, "A circus is somehow a child thing. It's— I wouldn't think about bringing my grown-up friends. Circuses I specifically associate with children and sharing with children." Supporting this link between circuses and children, many schools and children's groups plan annual outings to circuses. Circus acts and practices are also commonly featured in children's literature, and circus-related instructional material is promoted by large circuses such as Ringling Brothers.

Despite this association with children, however, circus attendance is defined as neither necessary nor central to circus patrons' lives and identities. In fact, several patrons admitted that they really did not like circuses at all, and only went because they felt it was something that they should do with their children. Jenny actually described circuses as "tacky" and "sleazy," and said that throughout the performance she attended, she and her husband "kept turning to each other and cringing." And Greg, another patron, explained,

Circuses don't play a high point in my life, and if I hadn't gotten these tickets I can probably say it's almost a certainty I probably would have never gone to a circus. . . . We did it mainly because they [the tickets] were free and the kids, we thought it would be something entertaining for them.

Unlike hunting and the use of animals in biomedical research, then, this practice neither defines one's identity and meaningful group memberships, nor is it fundamental to one's daily work. Instead, going to the circus is a form of entertainment; although it may be enjoyable, it does not foster the kind of commitment expressed by hunters.

Another notable difference between circus attendance and the other two practices is the frequency with which each is performed. Since each practice is affected by certain institutional constraints (i.e., patrons can attend performances only when circuses are in town, hunting can take place legally only during hunting season, and researchers can conduct animal experiments only after receiving institutional approval), there are structural impediments that limit individuals' abilities to engage in them. Still, circus attendance is relatively infrequent compared to the other practices. At most, circus patrons have the opportunity to attend performances several times a year, and it is not uncommon to attend only a few performances over the course of a lifetime. Biomedical researchers, in contrast, are often involved with animal research on a daily basis, including actual work with animals as well as the time devoted to the background work required for such experiments to take place (e.g., writing grant proposals and reading research literature). Hunting-related activities are also a frequent practice in hunters' lives. In addition to the time actually spent hunting, hunters spend time in the off-season preparing to hunt (e.g., by taking target practice, training hunting dogs, or simply observing animals in the wild). Mack, for instance, referred to hunting as a "lifestyle":

See, what I consider hunting, I hunt year round, in that I go out, and I look for them, and I watch them. . . . It's just two or three weeks during the year that I get to actually go out and shoot something . . . but I spend the whole year watching them.

Partly because they are performed much more frequently, hunting and the use of animals in biomedical research are more central to their practitioners' lives. Yet it is the meanings that these practices hold, and not just their relative frequency, that shows their importance to those who perform them. Because going to the circus is defined by circus patrons as a fun event, but not necessary or central to patrons' lives, animal rights activists have an opportunity to convince at least some people to boycott circuses.

Fur

Similarly, the meanings associated with fur garments create opportunities for effective protest activity directed against the fur retail trade. A fur coat is seen as a luxury item rather than something that is defined as crucial to some aspect of an individual or group's life. As Dennis, a Seattle furrier, said, "It's like people buying a Rolls Royce instead of buying a Volkswagen. If you want something nice you will buy something nice, if you can afford it." Certainly, "something nice" has a value; however, it is not essential. Given adequate resources, one can also find many substitutes for luxury items such as furs: jewelry, homes, and automobiles can also be used to display wealth or social standing. In addition, synthetic alternatives exist for those who wear fur garments more purely for fashion reasons. Of course, synthetic furs are not real furs, and therefore do not appeal to all consumers. As Dennis noted, "People that would buy furs would not be caught dead in one of those things [synthetic furs], because it has nothing to do with the fur! Even if it may look like it. I mean, people that knew a little bit about furs could spot one ten miles away." Nonetheless, well-known designers such as Karl Lagerfeld and Calvin Klein have used synthetic fur in their designs, and consumers have responded positively: the fashion industry publication *Women's Wear*

Daily (1994) reported that synthetic furs were very popular on the West Coast at the time this research was conducted. The available alternatives, coupled with the fact that luxury items are, by definition, unnecessary, means that people are unlikely to be as committed to buying and wearing furs as are biomedical researchers and hunters who see their practices as necessary.

Fur does not carry the same meaning everywhere, however. Climate also helps to determine the meanings associated with wearing fur: fur can be defined as functional, even necessary, in cold climates, whereas other garments can provide sufficient warmth for warmer climates. In a relatively mild climate such as Seattle's, fur garments are worn more to display wealth than to provide warmth. As Andy, another furrier, explained: "[Seattle doesn't have] cold weather. I mean, it [fur] is stylish. The only time people wear furs is when they go downtown or . . . go to the opera or go to theaters and stuff like that."

Yet there are standards for the appropriateness of such displays, standards that also vary by region. In Seattle, wearing fur is frequently seen as inappropriate. As Ellie, who runs a fur cleaning and storage business in downtown Seattle, noted, "I have seen a drop off in clientele in the last couple of years. And I feel one of the reasons is that we're in Seattle—Seattle is so environmental and green, in our standards." Again, this is in contrast with other cities. When asked how often she saw people wearing fur in Seattle, Ellie replied, "Not too often. We don't see that too often. Operas, and different events around town. If you lived in Colorado or New York and went skiing in Aspen, I mean, that's a different story. But not here. You don't really see them too often around here."

Ellie's comments illustrate the combined effect of climate and regional styles in creating the demand for fur. In places such as Aspen and New York, not only may there be a greater justification for fur because of the colder weather, but fur is also considered appropriate apparel for those wishing to display wealth and status. Not surprisingly, Aspen voters defeated a referendum in 1990

that would have banned fur sales in that city. In contrast, for even the wealthiest Seattle citizens, wearing fur is thought to be "politically incorrect." It is notable that when Microsoft founder and Seattle area resident Bill Gates, one of the world's wealthiest individuals, married Melinda French in January 1994, the fact that the bride as well as many guests wore fur garments to the wedding reception was front page news. These regional variations in cultural meanings are an important component of the possibilities that exist for effective protest against fur, yet differences such as these can be missed if opportunity structures are examined only at the level of national culture.

Multiple Targets and Audiences

The preceding discussion has shown that not all political issues are created equally. Because they are defined as necessary and central to the lives and daily work of those who perform them, practices like hunting and the use of animals in biomedical research are difficult for animal rights activists to curtail. In contrast, circus attendance and wearing fur garments are not defined as necessary or central to people's lives, particularly in the Seattle area; hence, the meanings associated with those practices create opportunity for effective protest against circuses and the fur retail trade. The different sets of requirements and understandings that shape peoples' motivations for engaging in practices either solidify individuals' commitment to the practices or render them vulnerable to change. These localized variations create opportunity structures that are obscured by more traditional examinations of political and cultural opportunity.

The views held by biomedical researchers, hunters, circus patrons, and furriers are important in the case of these four campaigns, because these four groups were explicitly identified by activists as the primary targets of their protest activity. Nonetheless, activists surely hoped to influence other audiences as well. For example, one activist told me that she hoped that her anti-hunting activities would have an effect on hunters' children: "For the hunters, it's sort of a lost cause, as far as I'm concerned. . . . [But] I hope that some of their kids just realize that there is another way of life, there's another—you don't have to follow the tradition of going off and murdering."

As this quote illustrates, protest activity can target multiple audiences, each of which may react to it differently. The opportunities that exist for effective social protest are therefore a function of multiple, and at times competing, institutional constraints and sets of meanings. It is likely, for instance, that circus owners and workers define circuses as more central to their lives than do most circus patrons; clearly, circus workers cannot boycott circuses as easily as patrons can.

Implications for Protest Strategy

Careful consideration of the perspectives of different audiences can encourage activists to avoid confrontations with audiences that are deeply committed to the targeted practices and to focus on other, less committed audiences who might then themselves be motivated to target the practitioners. This suggests, for example, that activists should direct their efforts not against individual hunters who are unlikely to give up the practice, but toward less invested targets who have the power to change hunters' behavior. In many situations, the state would be an appropriate target, as lawmakers can be targeted and encouraged to enact policies that limit or eliminate the practice in question. Similarly, other third parties and even the public at large can be targeted (as voters, letter writers, or consumers) in an attempt to change the behavior of certain parties; as Turner (1969) argues, third parties are more likely to see protest as legitimate than are those who are targeted by the protest activities. In fact, Seattle animal rights activists appear to have followed this strategy in the case of the circus campaign, as they targeted circus patrons rather than circus owners or workers.

A similar strategy has been employed in a current campaign on an issue that has attracted a great deal of press coverage. Seattle animal rights activists have opposed the gray whale hunt planned by the Makah, a Native American tribe living in northwestern Washington state. The Makah have treaty rights to hunt the gray whale, an animal that was removed from the Endangered Species list in 1994, and hope to resurrect their traditional whale hunt as a way of promoting and maintaining cultural identity; one tribal member was quoted in a newspaper article as saying, "It's [the hunt] a link to the past, and it validates us, who we are as a people and a culture" (*Los Angeles Times* 1998). Seattle animal rights activists have joined other animal rights and environmental groups in efforts against the hunt; however, rather than focusing their efforts primarily against the Makah people, many of whom define the gray whale hunt as central to their cultural identity, Seattle activists have mostly targeted state officials and the public at large, asking the latter to write protest letters to both government and tribal leaders.

The relative power of each protest audience is another important consideration when planning protest strategy. Powerful groups have more resources to promote their framing of a particular issue or practice, and their views are more likely to enjoy support from potential audiences. Protest directed against practices that are defined as necessary or central to a dominant group is therefore likely to face more difficulties than similar efforts against practices that are seen as central to subordinate groups. Similarly, practices defined as central or necessary by powerless groups are more easily dismissed by the public at large, and therefore can be more susceptible to change.

That said, though, it is not necessarily always the case that a greater opportunity exists for effective protest against practices performed by relatively powerless groups. Again, religious practices are a good example in this regard; for instance, some Jews continued to practice their religion secretly during the Spanish Inquisition despite prohibitions against doing so. The broader point is that if a practice is defined as necessary or central to the life of an individual or community, and people are committed to it, they can be motivated to find a way to continue to observe it, even if more powerful groups and institutions declare such activity illegal or inappropriate.

Indeed, many of the hunters I interviewed admitted that if hunting were banned in the state of Washington, they would probably move to another state so that they could continue to hunt; some even said that they would continue to hunt in Washington even if it meant breaking the law. As one hunter, Todd, said,

> [If hunting were outlawed] I think I would probably join the thousands or millions of other people and hunt any damn way. This is supposed to be a free country. I went and fought in a damn war for this country. And if I come back here and they tell me that I can't go harvest an animal, kill an animal, and put it in my freezer if I want, that's going to make me real angry. And I'm going to do it anyway.

As Todd's quote suggests, even if activists succeed in convincing lawmakers to ban or place restrictions on a targeted behavior, that behavior might not necessarily change. Furthermore, even if behavior should change, it might not reflect a change in the targeted audience's belief system; for instance, Harding (1984) argues that the successes of the civil rights movement against Jim Crow laws and segregationist practices entailed a shift in power relations rather than a replacement of the Southern worldview. Greater monitoring efforts are therefore needed in such situations if protesters are to succeed in achieving their goals.

Note, though, that this sort of staying power is not characteristic of all practices defined by their adherents as necessary or central; for instance, it is hard to imagine biomedical researchers engaging in animal experimentation even if such practices were made illegal. This point recalls the distinction between structural and personal commitment. Personal commitment stems from the practice's strong association with the individual's identity and community; structural commitment, on the other hand, derives from factors such as a lack of alternatives to the practice in question. When circumstances

change such that alternatives are made available, structural commitment may dissipate or disappear altogether. Presumably, animal experimentation would only be outlawed if widespread and acceptable alternatives existed.

This last point suggests that activists can actually create their own opportunities for effective social protest. Some animal rights groups have been actively involved in supporting and promoting non-animal alternatives to experimentation, for example. More broadly, activists can create their own opportunities by shaping the meanings that people attach to various practices. Many scholars have argued that social movements have the ability to bring about such shifts in cultural meanings, either by creating oppositional subcultures or by challenging dominant codes. By the same token, activists may also unwittingly create their own constraints if protest activity inspires countermobilization or if it causes some targets to "dig in" by increasing their commitment to the targeted practice. This enhanced commitment may take two different forms: the threat presented by protest activity may cause some targets to value their practice even more, thereby increasing their personal commitment; or it may increase targets' desire to persist in their practice, which would increase moral commitment. In this sense, opportunity and strategy are intertwined: by choosing to target a certain practice or group of practitioners, activists can set in motion a process which can either create or constrain opportunity for protest success. It is important to note that the identities and meanings illustrated in the interview quotes were made salient in part because the individuals quoted were the targets of protest activity. Protest strategy must therefore take these dynamics into account as well.

Conclusion

As many scholars have noted, the context in which protest takes place can either create or constrain opportunity for protest effectiveness. My examination of protest opportunity and constraint has focused not at the level of the state or broad cultural patterns, as other scholars have, but on the specific practices that protesters target for change. In particular, I have focused on the centrality and necessity of the practices, as defined by those who engage in them.

I have drawn on data from four animal rights protest campaigns. All of these campaigns were waged by one organization, and campaign activities took place in one region, under one set of national, state, and local laws. By following traditional approaches to the study of political opportunity, one would have to conclude that the four campaigns operated under a single political opportunity structure, and therefore that each campaign had the same possibilities for success. Yet differential outcomes across the campaigns point to the need for a different means of assessing political opportunity. As the preceding discussion shows, those who were targeted by the campaigns define their respective practices in certain ways. Hunters, for instance, define hunting as something that is fundamental to their identities as well as their sense of how the natural world works, whereas circus patrons define going to the circus as a fun family event but not something that is necessary or central to their lives. The meanings associated with these practices shape individuals' commitment to the practices and their abilities and willingness to change them. These meanings are, therefore, components of the "openness" or "closeness" of the environment in which protest operates, which is the focus of research on political and cultural opportunity. Focusing on practices, and on those who engage in them, identifies target vulnerabilities and strengths that create or constrain opportunity for effective social protest, and therefore illustrates elements of opportunity structures that would otherwise be hidden from view.

That is not to say that the structural forces that are generally the focus of research on political opportunity can play no role in shaping the opportunity for protest effectiveness in these four campaigns. In the case of hunting, for instance, patterns of immigration caused by economic changes that take people away from rural areas can make this practice less central to the lives of some individuals and communities. Similarly, unforeseen technological advances might make the use of animals in biomedical research obsolete. Note, however, that these structural factors can shape the meanings that people attach to things—when alternatives exist, practices are less likely to be defined as necessary.

References

Harding, Susan. 1984. "Reconstructing order through action: Jim Crow and the southern civil rights movement." In *Statemaking and Social Movements: Essays in History and Theory*, eds. Charles Bright and Susan Harding, 378–402. Ann Arbor: University of Michigan Press.

Jasper, James M., and Jane D. Poulsen. 1993. "Fighting back: Vulnerabilities, blunders, and countermobilization by the targets in three animal rights campaigns." *Sociological Forum* 8:639–657.

Los Angeles Times. 1998. "Clashes feared over whale hunt to trigger conflict." August 28.

Rowan, Andrew N. 1984. *Of Mice, Models, and Men: A Critical Evaluation of Animal Research*. Albany: State University of New York Press.

Turner, Ralph. 1969. "The public perception of protest." *American Sociological Review* 34: 815–831.

Ulmer, Jeffery T. 1994. "Revisiting Stebbins: Social reaction and commitment to deviance." *The Sociological Quarterly* 35:135–157.

Women's Wear Daily. 1994. "From runway to retail: What they're buying, what they're avoiding." (October 26):1–3.

A R T I C L E   3 5

Bonnie Berry

International Progress and Regress on Animal Rights

Introduction

The term "animals" covers human and nonhuman species; in this context, then, the term "animal oppression" refers to the oppression of human and nonhuman animals. When examining oppression across time and culture, as we will see, the link between nonhuman and human oppression is a close one. This analysis addresses general trends in animal oppression and rights across cultures, explains the social forces that allow for animal oppression as well as the more progressive forces that encourage equal treatment across species, describes the present-day United States as a rights-regressive society, and concludes with a prediction for reversal of animal oppression.

Worldwide Forces on Human and Nonhuman Rights

No society is free of animal (nonhuman or human) oppression. All societies oppress human and nonhumans historically and to date, as demonstrated by ethnic cleansing in the Balkans, the United States' refusal to fund women's health care in other countries if "choice" is involved, Africa's mass murder of primates, fox hunting in England, whaling in Iceland, etc. Some societies do better than others on the whole, with individual societies fluctuating over time on the protection of rights, and generally it can be said that human and nonhuman rights expand as societies progress toward democracy. There are no known quantitative measures of how societies rank on oppression. One could count the number of rights

organizations set up to protect against oppression, laws enacted, number of known abuses, and so on; but thus far, such cross-cultural comparisons are absent and may not be all that helpful in any case in terms of eliminating rights abuses.

The social forces affecting nonhuman rights (NHR) and human rights (HR) are numerous, with some forces (such as economics), even within an individual society, affecting rights more at some times than at other times. These forces affecting rights can be broad, longstanding forces, such as religion—with religion, for instance, viewing nonhuman animals variously as sacrifices or as objects of reverence and religion providing "divine" justification for homophobia, sexism, and other human oppressions. Social forces can also be more temporally and culturally limited, specific to time and conditions, such as SARS and Mad Cow diseases, both having turned out to increase nonhuman oppression. Social forces, as a rule, are interactive; they affect each other directly and indirectly, and these interactions influence social outcomes. For example, a poor economy can reduce educational opportunities that can affect rights activism.

There are many social forces determining how a society protects or impinges on rights but I will not wander too far afield and will, regrettably, give only brief mention to a very few of the many important rights-related forces.

Traditions

Tradition has long been an explanation (a "reconstruction," in sociological terms) for nonhuman abuse. Because "things have always been this way," some would say they should remain so. The fact that some practices are traditions is taken to mean that they are intrinsically good and serve important social functions; thus, they must be allowed to continue. Nonhuman-abusing traditions common to the United States include hunting, cockfighting, and coyote killing. Other countries practice their own brands of traditional non-human abuse, as illustrated by fox hunting in England and camel-fighting in Turkey. The same rationales, resting on prejudicial attitudes taken as fact, operate in traditional human abuse as well. Once upon a time, in the United States and elsewhere, it was tradition to deny women all manner of rights and for husbands to beat them if they disobeyed. It was the United States tradition during and after slavery to deny African Americans rights and to abuse them in unthinkable ways. In short, species-ism, sexism, racism, homophobia, and many forms of bigotry have all fallen under the protection of "tradition." Where matters get a little sticky is when human rights and nonhuman rights come into conflict. For example, the Makah Indians in Neah Bay, Washington, have been hoping to resurrect a long-forgotten tradition of whaling, which was once a means of sustenance as well as cultural transfer (involving artistry, preparation of food and other products). The desire for carrying on tradition was questioned when the Makahs failed to use traditional whaling methods and, instead, gunned down the whales from motorized craft and were reluctant to prepare and use the whale products. A federal court order later prohibited the practice. Similarly, Emberley (1997) rationalizes, against NHR logic, the continuing murder of fur-bearing nonhumans by First Nation people in Alaska and Canada because the killing, processing of fur, and sale of fur is economically necessary and ensuring of tradition.

The Search for Health, Beauty, and Virility

In the United States, Great Britain, and elsewhere, corporate structures continue to test health, hygiene, and beauty products on nonhuman animals, although laboratory testing is increasingly recognized as cruel and unnecessary. Non-human animals are subjected to large-scale and hideously painful tests to ensure that humans can safely use shave creams, deodorants, cosmetics, and all manner of products. In the medical field, surgeries are tested on nonhumans and some medicines are derived from nonhumans, such as Premarin, a treatment for menopausal symptoms painfully extracted from mares' bladders. Less-formalized enterprises, often in the form of street vendors and commonly found in Asia (Thailand, China, Taiwan), abuse nonhuman animals in the name of increasing male virility; witness, men drink snake venom and eat tiger penises in hopes of enhancing their strength and sexual prowess.

Economic Structures

Nonhuman oppression is frequently an outcome of capitalist venture. The pharmaceutical industry, meat industry (particularly factory farming), hunting ("canned," fox, etc.), the fur industry, entertainment (circuses, zoos, dog and horse races), and the like are evidence of capitalist-level abuse of nonhuman animals that ordinarily proliferate in "advanced" societies. These industries have paid off immeasurably, in monetary terms, at the expense of nonhuman well-being. This is true, of course, for human exploitation as well. Indeed, interlocking oppression of nonhumans and minority (women, nonwhites, children, the aged, and other disenfranchised) humans speaks to power—specifically the power to exploit, the power to profit from oppression—derived from a myriad of motives, from culinary to scientific to sexual access to cheap labor and beyond.

The effects of money on nonhuman oppression are rife with market-value considerations, with the less monetarily valuable being more vulnerable to destruction. Spotted owls are deprived of habitat because they get in the way of timber industry profits. Wolves are murdered because they harm livestock; the livestock are also assuredly oppressed, but wolves are killed because they threaten a more economically viable product.

The environmental assault in search of oil and mineral wealth, as in the case of proposed destruction of national parks and wildlife preserves, is clearly an affront on nonhuman life and is explained by capitalism. In similar fashion, the allowance, under the Bush administration, for snowmobiling in national parks makes snowmobile manufacturers (who lobby and financially support the Bush administration) profitable and happy. Abuse at the corporate, military, and governmental level is more deadly, unnecessary, and devastating than individual-level abuse; it is simply more covert. And when environmental damage is (falsely) couched in national-interest terms, the destruction can seem "legitimate." The Bush administration's plan to destroy the Alaska National Wildlife Refuge and nonhuman habitat and thereby destroy nonhuman lives has been justified as keeping us safe from terrorist countries and our reliance on their oil reserves. In fact, the administration's desire to drill in a fragile environment has to do with energy profits. Moreover, if the administration were truly interested in making the United States less dependent on foreign oil, it would seriously suggest that United States auto manufacturers make energy-efficient cars; political leaders do not do this because they do not want to disrupt auto manufacturers' huge profits from the sale of SUVs.

With power and money being inseparable, both permit access to the political and legislative wherewithal to win favorable governmental and legal decisions. That is, decisions by the powerful are often ruled in favor of the powerful, permitting them to (in the case of a profit-motivated, environmentally unfriendly government) destroy environments and wildlife, and to support animal-oppressive pharmaceutical companies, factory farms, and the like. The United States is not alone in the search for profit at the expense of nonhumans, obviously. If seal fur were not profitable, Canada would not murder seals. If whaling were not profitable, Japan, Norway, and Iceland would halt whaling operations. In sum, "The oppression

of humans and other animals is entangled and . . . exploitation is motivated primarily by economic interests" (Nibert, 2002: 15). This oppression is more rampant, Nibert finds, in affluent cultures like the United States, with a disproportionate number of powerful and privileged members.

Laws

Advanced and complex cultures, such as European societies and the United States, are more likely than simpler cultures to have elaborate legal definitions of animal abuse, delineating what constitutes human and nonhuman animal rights violations and the resultant penalties. Changes in law are always under consideration, as demonstrated by England's proposed ban on fox hunting, a long and dearly held tradition of the elite, with fox hunting successfully coming under legal fire and a hunting ban in sight by 2005 (Reuters, 2003; Tempest, 2003). The United States has recently made some headway on declaring some nonhuman abuses as criminal and on setting harsher punishments, such as prison sentences for these offenses.

As has been argued elsewhere, victimization (criminal victimization, all victimization) itself brings about power loss and this is especially true for oppressed human minorities and nonhuman animals. Human minorities and nonhuman animals are more likely to find themselves in the victim role because they already occupy a minority status. The minority status itself is replete with indicators of powerlessness, such as unsafe living environments, few economic resources, and little influence with protective social agencies. That is, minorities and nonhumans start out with a massive disadvantage, as they have few (in the case of minority humans) or no (in the case of nonhumans) rights, with disproportionately little legal recourse.

Analysis of crime definitions applied to nonhumans delivers the unsurprising finding that offenses against nonhumans are not viewed in the same light as offenses against humans. The United States has advanced, slowly and minimally, against criminal offenses as perpetrated against nonhumans, yet crime definitions and penalties remain starkly unequal across species. Indeed, comparing criminal penalties for the same offenses (murder, assault, sexual abuse, etc.) committed against nonhuman and human animals shows vast inequities. Not only are there disparities in penalties exacted for human and nonhuman violations, but also disparities exist depending on the identity (specifically socioeconomic status) of the perpetrators. People who abuse their nonhuman companions, or who run small-scale but heinous cockfighting operations, are more likely than large-scale corporate violators to be arrested and face criminal penalties. The penalties are not onerous, usually fines and community service, but, when applied, are applied to individual-level and small-scale abusers, rather than large-scale abusers—slaughterhouses, testing corporations, fur producers, factory farms, and so on.

Civil sanctions have, compared to criminal ones, different rules for determining fault and different punishment outcomes. The Animal Legal Defense Fund champions the use of civil remedies for nonhuman abuse. The ALDF strategy couches civil law definitions in objectifying terms, referring to nonhuman animals as property and the harm done to them as property loss to the human "owner." Civil definitions depicting nonhumans as property may not sit well with staunchly egalitarian-minded NHR activists, but this same curious remedy is used when we set an economic value for violating human rights. Witness the Southern Poverty Law Center's successes at bankrupting the White Aryan Resistance, the Aryan Nation, and various Ku Klux Klan organizations via criminal and civil routes. Likewise, NHR advocacy groups, such as People for the Ethical Treatment of Animals, Humane Society of the United States, and (especially pertinent to this article) the International Fund for Animal Welfare, press civil and criminal cases against nonhuman oppression.

The Invisible Nature of Animal Oppression

Worldwide, oppression is made possible, according to Wolch and Emel (1998), by hidden and unacknowledged desires of humans. In their book, *Animal Geographies*, Wolch and Emel describe the unintentional, invisible, almost unknown oppression of nonhumans as depicted in various cultures around the globe. The reality of animal oppression, they write, "is mostly obscured by the progressive elimination of animals from everyday human experience, and by the creation of a thin veneer of civility surrounding human-animal relations, embodied largely by language tricks, isolation of death camps, and food preparation routines that artfully disguise the true origins of flesh-food" (p. xi). Nonhumans have become indispensable to humans, they write, becoming "tied up with our visions of progress and the good life," and thus we have become unwilling to view them as viable, worthy beings. Unfortunately, animal-oppressive practices "now threaten the animal world and the entire global environment as never before" (p. xi).

Dwelling on the suffering of nonhumans is inconvenient and uncomfortable and thus not an activity that all humans would want to pursue. Oppressive practices (abuse, homelessness, neglect, starvation, humiliation, etc.) against nonhumans are easier if one can be convinced that nonhumans do not feel or think as humans do. Evidence has mounted over many years of research that they indeed do feel and think, as humans do. But even if it were allowed that nonhuman animals feel and think, they may still be subject to exploitation because, as Singer (1990) asserts, species-ists believe that their most trivial interests outweigh the vital interests of other (nonhuman) species. Humans are superior, according to the homocentric view, thus condemning nonhumans to be sacrificed for human needs and desires. Likewise, Stephen Jay Gould (1999) wrote of the human refusal to see ourselves as other than "separate and superior" to nonhuman animals. Homocentric humans have an unfortunate tendency to dichotomize, to divide human and nonhuman animals as good versus bad, higher versus lower, and (I would add) powerful exploiters versus powerless exploitees. These dichotomies, with nonhumans being far less equal and less deserving, justify oppression.

Interlocking Oppression

Human and nonhuman oppression so overlap that the concept is expressed by Adams and Donovan (1995) as "interlocking oppression," referring to the relative powerlessness experienced by both nonhumans and human minorities. Carol Adams (1995) has focused specifically on the interlocking oppression of female humans and animals, and I would add that, in an international context, we might consider shared oppression across rights-less humans and nonhumans in rights-repressive cultures such as China, Thailand, and temporarily but increasingly the United States.

Shared oppression can provide the catalyst for sympathy as well as activism on the part of unlike victims of oppression, as has been observed on international, national, and local levels. This has been true for human-human rights activism (with unlike humans, such as whites and blacks, aiding each other in rights causes) and it is true for human activism on the part of nonhumans. As the world has become more of a global community, the actions of one culture are deeply felt by other cultures. When one culture engages in animal (human and nonhuman) oppression, there is a strong, disapproving reaction from rights advocates in other cultures, which takes the forms of boycotting, petitioning, and other strategies. Globally, human cooperative efforts, such as the world panel created to conserve the whale population, move NHR forward (Pohl, 2003).

This brings us to a discussion of societies and their varying states of "advancement." Let us consider societal descriptors, such as "advanced," "primitive," "modern," "progressive," and so on, in a new light. Occasionally, a society can be technically and materially "advanced" without being progressive on rights, the topic to which I now turn.

The United States as a Devolving Society

Nonhuman rights and human rights, generally, evolve over time in a linear fashion, such that as time passes toward "modernity," rights increase. Terms such as "modern," "primitive," and "advanced" have value-laden qualities, probably wrongly so, with advanced and modern seeming good and primitive seeming bad. More objectively, these terms describe a society's place on a continuum of progress toward technological advancement and other material changes but also (and significantly for this analysis) toward equal rights and democracy. This evolution, the continuum of progress, and the terms that define it are complicated. Not only can a society be modern on some dimensions (say, technology) and primitive on others (such as rights), individual societies can fluctuate over time between progress and regress. As to the former, Japan, Iceland, and Norway are considered modern societies, yet they engage in nonhuman rights–violating whaling. As to the latter, the best example, presently, of a society regressing away from modernity, specifically away from rights, is the United States.

Some societies progress faster than others on NHR as well as HR; for example, England, Germany, Netherlands, and France have progressed more rapidly than other societies in the latter half of the twentieth century and beginning of the twenty-first century. In "primitive" cultures, such as Afghanistan where time seems to stagnate in the eighth century, oppression is obvious and rampant, notably but not exclusively in the treatment of women. In parts of the Middle East and Africa, women continue to be denied rights to education, continue to be stoned to death for adultery, and continue to be subject to genital mutilation. On nonhuman oppression, it is true that all societies oppress nonhumans, and even though some societies have moved forward in reducing this form of oppression, some societies progress very little on that score, to remain quite static on nonhuman oppression. For example, above-mentioned Asian cultures traditionally are exploitative and cruel to nonhuman animals. In the Western hemisphere, small tribal cultures culturally isolated from more "advanced" cultures, such as First Nation societies in Alaska and the Pacific Northwest, stubbornly adhere to exploitative practices, as illustrated by fur trading and whaling. All this is not to say that these non-modern societies are necessarily more animal oppressive than the modern ones. For example, the United States, a modern if momentarily a rights-repressive society, participates in enormous amounts of nonhuman oppression, as illustrated by factory farming and environmental destruction.

Modernity is dependent upon, if not defined by, social forces (politics, education, the economy, rights movements). In modern societies, we find that HR are highly interactive such that as one category of humans gains rights, other categories are increasingly likely to gain rights, evidenced by conjoined involvement of minorities in civil rights, women's rights, gay rights, immigrants' rights, and so on. Human rights are also a strong correlate of progress on nonhuman rights, with humans providing the voice for nonhumans, and succeeding in abolishing a number of oppressive practices (leghold traps and bear baiting, product testing, etc.).

The reverse is also true, that setbacks to human and nonhuman rights vary depending upon the social, economic, and political occurrences ongoing in their respective cultures, such that if HR are infringed upon so is the advancement of NHR. For example, a reduction in human rights to assemble, to lawfully belong to civic and activist organizations, to be gainfully employed, and to participate in higher education leads to a reduced ability to improve the lot not only of humans but also of nonhuman animals. Likewise, when humans are free to be employed, to be educated, to assemble lawfully and to serve activist causes, HR and NHR will be facilitated. We already know that HR advocates, who are more likely to be middle class and educated, are not uncommonly NHR advocates; they possess the social power to be so (Pluhar, 1995). An infringement on their social power is

an infringement on nonhuman power for self-determination.

The willingness of the public, and NHR advocates specifically, to challenge NHR violations varies by international scope, with this willingness dependent upon how "open" the society is to public protest. England and Western European countries (France, Belgium, Germany) are relatively tolerant of social activism, and more open to allowing public voice challenging human and nonhuman oppression, compared with the present-day United States.

The United States as a Case of Rights-Regression

The United States is usually considered a modern society—along material indices as technology, education, and medical science and along more humanist indices as human rights and democratic governing styles. At this very specific and probably temporary point in time, however, the United States has regressed in guaranteeing rights.

A regression on HR causes a regression in NHR. Under the Bush administration, humans are threatened with losing their rights and their civil liberties, most notably via the USA Patriot Act. Rights-respecting humans are also losing their influence because of much poorer educational opportunities (with education being strongly related to rights awareness), because of economic ruin inhibiting contributions to NHR charities, because United States citizens have less voice in environmentally disastrous events like the feared destruction of Alaska National Wildlife Reserve, and because NHR civic organizations are being redefined as terrorist organizations (Barcott, 2002).

The USA Patriot Act can be "used against domestic political protestors, such as environmentalists . . . with no link to international terrorism" (*New York Times*, 2003: 20). The Act, enacted after 9/11, gives the government unprecedented powers to monitor citizens. The Act allows libraries to track who borrows what books, allows bookstores to track who buys what books, asks businesses to "hand over electronic records on finances, telephone calls, e-mails and other personal data," and permits investigators to "subpoena private books, records, papers, documents, and other items" . . . all in the name of anti-terrorism (Nieves, 2003). None of this plays any effective role in preventing terrorism. It merely allows monitoring, with threatened punishment, of civil rights groups, antiwar groups, and other "dissident" organizations that do not support a neoconservative agenda (Cole, 2002).

Members of the public are increasingly reluctant to apply the "terrorist" label to progressive activists, including NHR advocates, even when the public disagrees with NHR. Two letters to the editor of the *Seattle Times* (2003) say as much, referring to a recent Animal Liberation Front (ALF) release of minks from a mink ranch, with one letter-writer calling the activists "knuckleheads" but retaining the opinion that these activists are by no means terrorists. The second letter finds that the word "terror" applies to states of intense fear and violence, not to trespassing and vandalism, as was the case in the mink release by ALF.

Summary and Conclusion

No society is free from human and nonhuman animal oppression, although some societies do better than others on ensuring rights. There are paradoxes within societies, with contradictory patterns on rights, as illustrated by Canada's 2003 decision to permit gay marriages while continuing to murder seals for their fur. And societies may fluctuate in their rights protection depending upon the social (economic, political, etc.) conditions they are operating under at any given time.

The United States and many other societies, especially European societies, were moving toward greater equality between human and nonhuman animals, but since 2001, in the United States several factors have slowed this forward, rights-propelled movement. Among the oppressive economic conditions set in motion were the immense tax cut for the wealthy and tax breaks for corporations, coinciding with the general lack of concern

for laborers. The consequential poor economic state for the majority has reduced educational opportunities as well as funds available for rights-protecting organizations. Furthermore, civic protest has been limited by the USA Patriot Act.

On a brighter note, the J-curve theory of revolution suggests that movement activity is more likely to occur when progress, as we saw in the 1970s through 2000 on animal and environmental rights, is suddenly threatened. When hopes of movement forward are dashed, when the movement suffers a political reversal, social movement activity may become more radical (Davies, 1962; Garner, 1996). With the approval of snowmobiles in national parks, proposals to drill for oil in national parks, relaxation of rules on air and water pollution, and refusals to consider the scientific validity of global warming and to do anything about it, we might anticipate a backlash by the proponents of nonhuman rights and environmental protection. As Goldstone and Tilly (2001) point out in their discussion of threats and opportunities in social movement activity, social movement organizations may "decide to risk protest, even if opportunities seem absent, if the costs of not acting seem too great" (p. 183). True, the costs that an activist group incurs from protest are significant, particularly now when progressive activists are labeled "terrorists." Yet the dangers of engaging in activism may predictably take a backseat to the damage from inaction and the further decay of rights (Goldstone and Tilly). In other words, activists will engage in progressive action toward NHR and HR perhaps especially under such repressive circumstances.

References

Adams, Carol. J. 1995. *Neither Man nor Beast: Feminism and the Defense of Animals.* New York, NY: Continuum.

Adams, Carol J., and Josephine Donovan. 1995. *Animals and Women: Feminist Theoretical Perspectives.* Durham, NC: Duke University.

Barcott, Bruce. 2002. "From Tree-Hugger to Terrorist." *New York Times Magazine,* April 7, pp. 56–59, 81.

Cole, David. 2002. "Misdirected Snooping Doesn't Stop Terror." *New York Times*, June 4, p. A23.

Davies, James. 1962. "Toward a Theory of Revolution." *American Sociological Review* 27:5–19.

Emberley, Julia V. 1997. *The Cultural Politics of Fur.* Ithaca, NY: Cornell University.

Garner, Roberta. 1996. *Contemporary Movements and Ideologies.* New York. McGraw-Hill.

Goldstone, Jack A., and Charles Tilly. 2001. "Threat (and Opportunity): Popular Action and State Response in the Dynamics of Contentious Action." Pp. 179–194 in *Silence and Voice in the Study of Contentious Politics*, edited by R.R. Aminzade, J.A. Goldstone, D. McAdam, E.J. Perry, W.H. Sewell, Jr., S. Tarrow, and C. Tilly. Cambridge, UK: Cambridge University.

Gould, Stephen Jay. 1999. "The Human Difference." *New York Times*, July 2, p. A19.

New York Times. 2003. "An Unpatriotic Act." *New York Times*, August 25, p. A20.

Nibert, David. 2002. *Animal Rights/Human Rights: Entanglements of Oppression and Liberation.* Lanham, MD: Rowman and Littlefield.

Nieves, Evelyn. 2003. "Local Officials Defy the Patriot Act." *Washington Post* (http://msnbc.com), April 21.

Pluhar, Evelyn B. 1995. *Beyond Prejudice: The Moral Significance of Human and Nonhuman Animals.* Durham, NC: Duke University.

Pohl, Otto. 2003. "World Panel Will Now Act to Conserve the Whale Population." *New York Times,* June 17, p. All.

Reuters. 2003. "U.K. Moves Closer to Fox-Hunting Ban." Reuters (http://msnbc.com), July 1.

Seattle Times. 2003. "Let's Apply Label of Ecoterrorists to Those Who Have Earned It" and "Crime, Not Terrorism." *Seattle Times* (http://seattletimes.com), August 28.

Singer, Peter. 1990. *Animal Liberation.* New York: Random House.

Tempest, Matthew. 2003. "Hunting Ban in Sight for 2005." *The Guardian* (http://politics.guardian.co.uk).

Wolch, Jennifer, and Jody Emel (eds.). 1998. *Animal Geographies: Place, Politics, and Identity in the Nature-Culture Borderlands.* New York: Verso.

CREDITS

Article Credits

1. "The How and Why of Thinking with Animals," Lorraine Daston and Gregg Mitman, in *Thinking with Animals*, edited by L. Daston and G. Mitman, New York: Columbia University Press, 2005, pp. 1–14.
2. "Dirty Birds, Filthy Immigrants, and the English Sparrow War," Gary Alan Fine and Lazaros Christoforides, *Symbolic Interaction* 14(4): 375–393, 1991.
3. "Race, Place, and the Human-Animal Divide," Glen Elder et al, in *Animal Geographies*, edited by J. Wolch and J. Emel, New York and London: Verso, 1998, pp. 72–90.
4. "Creating and Representing Foxhounds," Gary Marvin, *Society & Animals* 9:273–292, 2001.
5. "Close Relationships between Humans and Nonhuman Animals," Clinton R. Sanders, *Symbolic Interaction* 26(3): 405–426, 2003.
6. "Dog Ownership as a Gender Display," Michael Ramirez, *Symbolic Interaction* 29:373–391, 2006.
7. "Women of Color and Animal-Human Connections," Christina Risley-Curtiss, Lynn C. Holley, Tracy Cruickschank, Jull Porcelli, Clare Rhoads, Denise N. A. Bacchus, Soma Nyakoe, and Sharon Murphy, *Affilia: Journal of Women and Social Word* 21(4): 433–447, 2006.
8. "The Causes of Animal Abuse," Robert Agnew, *Theoretical Criminology* 2:177–209, 1998.
9. "The Relationship of Animal Abuse to Violence and Other Forms of Antisocial Behavior," Arnold Arluke, Jack Levin, Carter Luke, and Frank Ascione, *Journal of Interpersonal Violence* 14:963–975, 1999.
10. "Battered Women and Their Animal Companions," Clifton P. Flynn, *Society & Animals* 8:99–127, 1999.
11. "Swimming with Dolphins," Susanna Curtin, *International Journal of Tourism Research* 8:301–315, 2006.
12. "Zoopolis," Jennifer Wolch, in *Animal Geographies* edited by J. Wolch and J. Emel, New York and London: Verso, 1998, pp. 119–137.
13. "The Transformation of Wildlife Law in the Vanishing Wilderness," Robert Granfield and Paul Colomy, in *Mad about Wildlife* edited by A./T. Herda-Rapp and Goedeke, Leiden and Boston: Brill Academic Publishers, 2005, pp. 147–169.
14. "The Researcher's Perception of Pain," Mary Phillips, *Society & Animals* 1:61–82, 1993.
15. "Human Morality and Animal Research," Harold Herzog *American Scholar*, 62 (Summer):337–349, 1993.
16. "Cloning Mutts, Saving Tigers," Donna Haraway, in *Remaking Life and Death: Toward an Anthropology of the Biosciences* edited by S. Franklin and M. Lock, Santa Fe, NM: SAR Press, 2003, pp. 292–328.
17. "Expanding Meat Consumption and Animal Oppression," Bill Winders and David Nibert, *International Journal of Sociology and Social Policy* 24: 76–96, 2004.
18. "The Feminist Traffic in Animals," Carol J. Adams, in *Ecofeminism Women, Animals, Nature* edited by Greta Gaard, Philadelphia: Temple University Press, 1993, pp. 195–218.
19. "Becoming Vegan," Barbara McDonald, *Society & Animals* 8:1–23, 2000.
20. "Greyhound Racing and Sports-Related Violence," Michael Atkinson and Kevin Young, *International Review for the Sociology of Sport* 40(3): 335–356, 2005.

21. "The Disneyization of Zoos," Alan Beardsworth and Alan Bryman, *Tourist Studies* 1(1): 83–104, 2001.
22. "Representations of the Animal World on the Discovery Channel," David P. Pierson, *Journal of Popular Culture* 38(4): 698–712, 2005.
23. "Veterinary Dilemmas," Joanna Swabe, in *Companion Animals & Us* edited by Anthony Podberscek, Elizabeth Paul, James Serpell, Cambridge University Press, 2000, pp. 292–312.
24. "How Shelters 'Think' about Clients' Needs and Unwanted Pets," Leslie Irvine, *Social Problems* 50:550–566, 2003.
25. "Hope and Conflict in the Social World of Animal Sheltering,' Arnold Arluke, in *Animal Sheltering*, Jan-Feb:31–39, 2007 (permission granted to reprint revisions, without cost).
26. "Domestic Dogs and Human Health," Deborah L. Wells, *British Journal of Health Psychology* 12:145–156, 2007.
27. "How Prison-Based Animal Programs Help Inmates," Gennifer Furst, (permission from author for use of unpublished paper).
28. "Pet-Facilitated Interaction in a Public Setting," Douglas Robbins, Clinton Sanders, and Spencer Cahill, *Journal of Contemporary Ethnography* 20:3–25, 1991.
29. "Human-Horse Communications," Keri Brandt, *Society & Animals* 12(4): 299–316, 2004.
30. "Symbolic Loss, Trauma, and Recovery in Elephant Communities," Isabel Bradshaw, *Society and Animals* 12:143–158, 2004.
31. "Animal Selfhood," Leslie Irvine, *Symbolic Interaction* 27:3–21, 2004.
32. "Animal Rights Activism as Functional Religion," Wesley Jamison, Caspar Wenk, and James Parker, *Society and Animals* 8:305–330, 2000.
33. "Two Movements and Human-Animal Continuity," Barbara Noske, *Animal Liberation Philosophy and Policy Journal* 2(1): 1–12, 2004.
34. "The Protest Effectiveness of Four Animal Rights Campaigns," R. Einwohner, *Social Problems* 46: 169–186, 1999.
35. "Interactional Progress and Repress on Animal Rights," Bonnie Berry, *International Journal of Sociology and Social Policy* 24:58–75, 2004.

Photo Credits